British Society of Gastroenterology
Diamond Jubilee
1937–1997

A Collection of Scientific Papers 1988–1997

Editor
Roy Pounder

Editorial Committee
Robert Allen, Andrew Burroughs, George Misiewicz,
Robert Walt, Robin Williamson, Nick Wright

Preface by
Hermon Dowling
President,
British Society of Gastroenterology 1996–1997

Introduction by
John Lennard-Jones
President,
British Digestive Foundation

The publication of this Diamond Jubilee Collection has been made possible by financial contributions from Blackwell Science Ltd and GlaxoWellcome

b
Blackwell
Science

Sponsored by
GlaxoWellcome

Preface

This selection of papers, published by members of the British Society of Gastroenterology over the past 10 years, was commissioned as part of the Society's Diamond Jubilee celebrations. The Society is grateful to Professor Roy Pounder and the members of his Editorial team—the 'hanging committee'—for their efforts, and to Glaxo Wellcome and Blackwell Science for their generous sponsorship of this volume.

This publication is the sequel to a similar book published in 1987 to mark the Society's Golden Jubilee. In his introduction to the 1987 volume, Sir Francis Avery Jones provided a broad historical perspective on the BSG itself, and the scientific contributions of its members during the first 50 years of the Society's life.

In the present volume, a similar overview is given by Professor John Lennard-Jones—a former President of the Society and currently President of the British Digestive Foundation. As noted in his *Introduction*, this selection of scientific papers contains a broad range of contributions dealing with all aspects of gastroenterology and hepatology. Although there is a generous sprinkling of basic science, immunogenetics, cell and molecular biology, undoubtedly Britain's greatest contribution is in the clinical arena.

The BSG has come a long way since November 1937 when its forerunner, 'the Gastro Enterological Club', first met at the Royal Society of Medicine in London. This meeting was attended by 36 members and seven guests under the Presidency of the late Sir Arthur Hurst, a distinguished physician at Guy's Hospital.

Sixty years on, 1997 is also an exciting year for the Society. Not only is the BSG celebrating its Diamond Jubilee; it is also hosting the 6th United European Gastroenterology Week (UEGW). This will take place in Birmingham on 18–23 October 1997. It will be the first major Gastroenterology Congress to be organized in the UK since the International Congress was held in London more than 40 years ago, under the Presidency of the late Dr Thomas Hunt in 1956.

The theme of the Society's Diamond Jubilee meeting in March 1997 will be 'Looking back, looking forward'. In gastroenterology, as in other specialties, today's fashions include audit and evidence-based medicine. As we approach the Millennium and plan our future research, therefore, what better way to take stock of our efforts than to look back at some of the best of our scientific contributions over the past 10 years? It is an excellent record of achievement and, on occasions such as this, the Society can feel justifiably proud. However, if Britain is to maintain this enviable reputation, we must compete on the International scene, ensuring an equally impressive compilation for our Centenary celebrations on the Internet in 2037.

Hermon Dowling
President,
British Society of Gastroenterology
1996–1997

Introduction

The papers reproduced in this volume are selected to give a representative impression of British gastroenterology during the decade since a similar volume was published in 1987. Approximately 1800 papers on gastroenterological topics emanate from Britain each year* so this collection represents only a tiny proportion of the total. Many important papers are absent because of the need to maintain balance between different aspects of the subject.

What has characterized British Gastroenterology during the last 10 years? Molecular genetics has made its mark. The molecular basis of some single-gene disorders is now understood, genetic variation among hepatitis viruses has been recognized and a start has been made on defining the genetic heterogeneity of disease (Satsangi *et al.*, 1996; p 210). Immunology has made great progress, as for example the characterization of the mitochondrial antigen in primary biliary cirrhosis (Yeaman *et al.*, 1988; p 6). Hepatitis C and *Helicobacter pylori* have burst upon the scene. It is now possible to cure peptic ulcers using a short course of drug treatment. Laparoscopic and minimal access surgery have had particular impact on the treatment of biliary disease. New imaging techniques have refined soft-tissue diagnosis, for instance anal ultrasound has enabled structural damage of the anal sphincter muscles to be distinguished from muscle weakness due to denervation (Sultan *et al.*, 1993; p 150). There has been increased awareness of nutritional depletion as a complication of illness and gastroenterologists have contributed to long-term enteral tube feeding by endoscopic placement of a gastrostomy tube (Norton *et al.*, 1996; p 206). Alteration of the colonic bacterial flora by adding particular carbohydrate supplements to the diet has marked progress towards pre-biotic treatment (Gibson *et al.*, 1995; p 194).

Hepatologists have responded to the clinical problems posed by the hepatitis viruses. At St Mary's Hospital, London, sequencing of hepatitis B DNA has shown that the HBe antigen may be absent in some patients with active infection due to one or two nucleotide substitutions in the pre-core region of the genome, such is the sophistication of current molecular analysis (Carman *et al.*, 1989; p 16). Infection with different genotypes of hepatitis C have been correlated with geographic source, investigations and clinical outcome (Dusheiko *et al.*, 1994; p 180). End-stage cirrhosis related to hepatitis C is a common reason for transplantation but the virus often persists. It was encouraging to find at 5 years that the rates of graft and overall survival among 149 such patients were similar to those given a transplant for other reasons. However, the most recent biopsy showed evidence of chronic hepatitis in the majority of patients transplanted for hepatitis C (Gane *et al.*, 1996; p 235).

The Liver Unit at King's College Hospital, London, has built up great experience of treating fulminant hepatic failure. In a large series prognostic variables suggesting the need for urgent transplantation have been defined (O'Grady *et al.*, 1989; p 26). Their experience also enabled them to show that acetyl cysteine given 10 or more hours after ingestion of a toxic dose of paracetamol is still beneficial (Harrison *et al.*, 1990; p 38).

Research into the genesis of gall stones at Guy's Hospital, London, continues; composition and physical chemistry of bile, nucleation of cholesterol crystals, mucus secretion by the gall bladder and its muscular activity are all important factors (Hussaini *et al.*, 1994; p 193). Surgery for chronic pancreatitis has developed at the Royal Postgraduate Medical School and a review of their results has shown that deterioration of endocrine or endocrine function is not invariable after partial pancreatectomy (Jalleh *et al.*, 1992; p 94).

Healing and proliferative mechanisms in the liver and gut are basic reparative phenomena. In the liver there is a rapid surge of hepatocyte DNA synthesis after partial hepatectomy or acute chemical damage that ceases after one or two cell divisions. Why does division stop so soon? A team at the Royal Postgraduate Medical School has shown that non-parenchymal cells in the regenerating liver liberate a powerful but unidentified inhibitor of hepatocyte proliferation during the period 24–48 hours after operation (Woodman *et al.*, 1992; p 87). Perhaps this basic research provides a clue to a future treatment for acute hepatic failure.

In the gut healing of ulceration is a key feature of repair. The identification of a previously unrecognized cell lineage that develops in glands around an ulcer, and that secretes epidermal growth factor (EGF) was important enough to be published in *Nature* (Wright *et al.*, 1990; p 33). EGF is concerned in the proliferation of small intestinal epithelium. Other workers hypothesized that the atrophy of the gut that occurs when no food, or aminoacids without protein, is present in the lumen might be due to digestion of EGF and transforming growth factor (TGF-α) by pancreatic enzymes. They found that fasting jejunal juice does destroy these growth factors but EGF was preserved in the presence of casein or an enzyme inhibitor (Playford

* *Report of Unit for Policy Research in Science and Medicine, The Wellcome Trust, 1996.*

et al., 1993; p 117), providing yet more evidence that polymeric enteral feeds should be used in preference to elemental or parenteral feeding whenever possible.

In his introduction to the 1987 collection of papers Sir Francis Avery Jones encouraged gastroenterologists to take a greater interest in nutrition. This has happened, but slowly. One of the papers from the Central Middlesex Hospital, London, shows that fluid secretion in the ascending colon during an intragastric enteral tube feed is possibly important in the troublesome side-effect of diarrhoea (Bowling *et al.*, 1993; p 114). Malnutrition is a common feature in the later stages of severe liver disease and correlates with a poor outcome of surgery. Investigators at St James's Hospital, Leeds, have shown that one factor contributing to loss of body tissue in severe primary biliary cirrhosis is a raised basal metabolic rate and an increased energy output after food (Green *et al.*, 1991; p 64).

Coeliac disease remains a tantalizing enigma. The team at St Thomas's Hospital, London, has narrowed the damaging fraction of gluten to a synthetic peptide of 18 amino acids (Sturgess *et al.*, 1994; p 189). Although the response to gluten is greatest in the jejunum, rectal challenge with a peptic digest of gluten increases the number of rectal intra-epithelial lymphocytes (Loft *et al.*, 1990; p 49) so the whole intestine shows an abnormal response.

Intestinal absorption and secretion offer much scope to basic scientists. One example is the elegant demonstration of a single amino-acid substitution involving the aldolase-B enzyme in the rare condition of hereditary fructose intolerance (Cross *et al.*, 1988; p 1). Utilizing a functionally intact colonic cell line, inhibition of chloride secretion by somatostatin and an α-adrenergic agonist can be analysed (Warhurst *et al.*, 1993; p 110). From the same group at Hope Hospital, Salford, comes a detailed analysis of the effects of inflammatory mediators generated by colitic mucosa on the secretory response of colonic epithelium (Wardle *et al.*, 1993; p 104).

The recognition in the early 1980s that *H. pylori* infection of the stomach is associated with chronic gastritis and peptic ulcer has stimulated a burst of research effort involving many groups throughout the country. How do we acquire infection? Is it passed from member to member within a family? In a family with a high incidence of duodenal ulcer over three generations, DNA testing of pure bacterial isolates showed that clustering over three successive generations did occur but some other members harboured different strains (Nwokolo *et al.*, 1992; p 82). Are some strains more virulent than others? Some strains of the organism express a 120 kDa surface protein and workers from St James's Hospital, Leeds, showed that when gastric mucosal biopsies or mononuclear cells secreted IgA which reacts with this protein there is a strong association with peptic ulcer and vice versa (Crabtree *et al.*, 1991; p 60). Can infection lead to gastric hypersecretion of acid so explaining this known association with duodenal ulcer? Representative papers show that infection is associated with raised levels of circulating gastrin which are abolished by eradication of the infection (Prewett *et al.*, 1991; p 52: El-Omar *et al.*, 1993; p 123). *H. pylori* colonizes the duodenal bulb within areas of gastric metaplasia, why do these occur? Significant correlations were observed between maximal acid output and extent of gastric metaplasia, but its prevalence or extent was not affected by the presence or absence of the organism (Harris *et al.*, 1996; p 246).

The presence of *H. pylori* can be detected by serology or by a non-invasive breath test. Can younger patients with a negative test be treated expectantly, so reducing the number of endoscopies and increasing the cost-effectiveness of the procedure (Sobola *et al.*, 1991; p 65)? Should younger patients with a positive test be treated to eradicate the organism without endoscopy? The argument for and against these policies is not resolved. There is no representative paper illustrating the intensive effort to devise a simple, short, cheap regimen of eradication treatment.

Elimination of *H. pylori* can also lead to regression and cure of primary low-grade B-cell gastric lymphoma (Wotherspoon *et al.*, 1993; p 111). This achievement in a rare tumour, rightly but over-enthusiastically hailed by the media, is presumed to follow withdrawal of immune stimulation from the mucosa-associated lymphoid tissue (MALT). But what of the common type of gastric adenocarcinoma? An epidemiological study from 13 European countries (Eurogast Study Group, 1993; p 140) is one of several papers suggesting that cancer is associated with previous infection. These cancers tend to be situated in the distal stomach. For this reason there is concern that short-term treatment of infected patients with a proton pump inhibitor resulted in decreased histological density of the organism in the antrum and body of the stomach, but an increased density in the fundus (Logan *et al.*, 1995; p 196). Could such treatment increase the risk of proximal tumours?

The other major cause of peptic ulcer is ingestion of non-steroidal anti-inflammatory drugs (NSAIDs). The previous volume began in 1938 and ended in 1987 with papers on this topic. The saga rumbles on. A team in Glasgow undertook a large post-mortem study that showed there was a significantly increased risk not only of peptic, but also of small intestinal ulcers among those who had been prescribed NSAIDs during the previous 6 months; three of the latter died from perforated ulcer of the small bowel (Allison *et al.*, 1992; p 88). A collaborative case control study involving six centres showed that peptic ulcer bleeding was associated with the use of non-aspirin NSAIDs of any type during the previous 3 months and it proved possible to rank different drugs according to their propensity to cause haemorrhage (Langman *et al.*, 1994; p 171). Given these results, it is important to know if the risk of ulcer among those who need to take an NSAID for arthritis can be reduced. A controlled trial of high doses of an H_2-receptor antagonist given over 6 months has shown that it can (Taha *et al.*, 1996; p 241).

In collaboration with the Royal Colleges of Surgeons of England and Physicians of London, the Society first produced guidelines for the management of upper gastrointestinal haemorrhage and then set up a National audit of outcome in four NHS regions. Multiple logistic regression analysis showed that age, shock, co-morbidity, diagnosis, endoscopic stigmata of recent bleeding, and re-bleeding were all independent predictors of mortality. A simple numerical score was derived which reproducibly predicted risk of death in a subsequent series (Rockall *et al.*, 1996; p 216). This score can be used to determine case mix and thus allows comparisons of mortality in different reports. A practical use of the score allows approximately a quarter of patients to be discharged early from hospital after endoscopy because they have a low risk of re-bleeding and negligible risk of dying from the bleed. For those with endoscopic stigmata of recent haemorrhage, controlled comparisons of different techniques for reducing the rate of re-bleeding have been undertaken. One such paper showed that use of the NdYAG laser for coagulation halved the rate compared with controls; the heater probe showed an intermediate but not statistically significant reduction (Matthewson *et al.*, 1990; p 43).

For initial treatment of bleeding oesophageal varices, a trial of octreotide infusion has shown benefit (Burroughs *et al.*, 1990; p 37). Sclerotherapy is well established but not always successful. Prospective random allocation of patients to sclerotherapy or stapled transection of the oesophagus at the Royal Free Hospital, London, resulted in similar mortality and complication rates. Re-bleeding was significantly less frequent after transection compared with the first injections of sclerosant but similar to that after three sessions of sclerotherapy. Staple transection is therefore a reasonable treatment if initial injections fail (Burroughs *et al.*, 1989; p 10).

Cumulation of genetic and somatic mutations as a cause of cancer have been the subject of intense study. The finding that the familial adenomatous polyposis (APC) gene is also important in sporadic colorectal cancer gives possible wider significance to the genetic investigation of rare hereditary cancer syndromes. Genetic linkage analysis of a large family with one such syndrome permitted localization of the gene and exemplifies such work (Thomas *et al.*, 1996; p 222).

Large controlled population studies of methods for the detection of pre-cancerous colonic polyps and early colorectal carcinoma were undertaken during the decade. The British study of occult blood detection in stools among symptomless subjects has concluded that colorectal cancer mortality can be reduced by about 15% using this method. Screening studies in high-risk families are also in progress. None of these papers is included here, though their results will influence gastroenterological practice in years to come. However, studies on the cancer risk in colitis and Crohn's disease are included.

Investigators in Liverpool have put forward the interesting hypothesis that binding of a food lectin to a particular mucosal blood group antigen could be a possible factor in development of cancer in ulcerative colitis. Peanut agglutinin increases the crypt cell proliferation rate when it binds to the antigen which is normally hidden but is exposed in colitic epithelium (Ryder *et al.*, 1994; p 170). Regular colonoscopy for patients with long-standing extensive ulcerative colitis with the aim of detecting dysplastic change or carcinoma at an early curable stage has proved controversial. A paper from the General Infirmary at Leeds (Lynch *et al.*, 1993; p 144) entitled 'Failure of Colonoscopic Surveillance in Ulcerative Colitis' based its conclusion on a low yield of carcinoma, the occurrence of several cancers outside the surveillance programme and the finding that low-grade dysplasia proved to be an unreliable indicator of pre-cancer. Another paper from St Mark's Hospital, London, reported operation for a reasonable proportion of patients with high-grade dysplasia or symptomless curable carcinoma, and showed that the predictive value of low-grade dysplasia depends on the criteria for its diagnosis (Connell *et al.*, 1994; p 175). Taken together, the two studies illustrate the limitations of dysplasia, the practical impossibility of including every patient at risk, and the dependence of results on the referral pattern to the hospital. For the future, a case-controlled study of regular flexible sigmoidoscopy with biopsies is needed combined with assessment of genetic markers. And what about Crohn's disease? A careful study based on the large series of cases in Birmingham has shown that the cumulative cancer risk in both extensive Crohn's and ulcerative colitis is the same (Gillen *et al.*, 1994, p 186).

One-fifth of the papers in this collection relate to inflammatory bowel disease. The genetic studies of the Oxford group have been referred to (Satsangi *et al.*, 1996; p 210) and whole genome searches are now in progress there and at Guy's Hospital in London. Taking a different line, the team at the Royal Free Hospital, London, have prepared operation specimens removed for Crohn's disease by arterial perfusion with histological fixative and applied sophisticated techniques for demonstration of micro-anatomy. The arresting illustrations in their papers (Wakefield *et al.*, 1989; p 20) show marked vascular injury, with occlusion of small vessels often at the level of the muscularis propria and new vessel formation. Since granulomata were shown by this technique frequently to be within the walls of blood vessels, they coined the term 'granulomatous vasculitis' (Wakefield *et al.*, 1991; p 68). Their research has since been directed to finding the reason for this vascular injury.

During treatment of a severe acute attack of ulcerative colitis it is often difficult to know when medical treatment has failed, or is likely to fail, and surgery should be advised. A prospective study in Oxford showed that bowel frequency on the third or seventh day after starting treatment was the most predictive marker when combined with blood levels of C-reactive protein (Travis *et al.*, 1996; p 229). The original observations on the dearth of tobacco smoking among patients with ulcerative colitis came from Cardiff and so it is appropriate that they should now have tested nicotine skin patches as a treatment for mild or moderate acute colitis. The treatment did reduce symptoms but there were side-effects; it seems unlikely that it will prove to be more than an adjunctive measure (Pullan *et al.*, 1994; p 165). A multicentre controlled trial has shown benefit from azathioprine in cases of ulcerative colitis stabilized on it and in remission (Hawthorne *et al.*, 1992; p 101). Sufficient experience of the drug has now accumulated over the past 30 years to show that the neoplastic risk of using it for inflammatory bowel disease over a median period of 1 year is, at most, slight (Connell *et al.*, 1994; p 176). Whether longer treatment duration will alter this view deserves further study. Dietary treatment of Crohn's disease remains controversial. An elemental feed appears beneficial in the acute stage as long as a patient can tolerate it, and there is now evidence that a polymeric diet can give similar results. The subsequent use of an individualized diet selected by exclusion of foods that appear to aggravate symptoms did not give a clear-cut result at 2 years in a multicentre controlled trial (Riordan *et al.*, 1993; p 129).

Surgery is the mainstay of treatment for gastro-intestinal cancer. A large-scale European trial of two surgical techniques for gastric cancer has shown that the possible benefits of extended lymph node resection are offset by greater postoperative mortality and morbidity (Cuschieri *et al.*, 1996; p 201). In contrast, the value of careful dissection and wide excision of rectal cancer is validated by a correlation of tumour involvement of the circumferential excision margin with outcome (Adam *et al.*, 1994; p 157). The team from Basingstoke, well known for advocacy of mesorectal excision, have shown that the distal excision margin during anterior resection of the rectum can be less than 1cm without detriment. These tumours were situated at a mean of 4.7cm from the anal verge with the result that only approximately 10% of their total series required abdomino-perineal excision with a permanent colostomy (Karanjia *et al.*, 1990; p 40).

The commonest conditions seen in a gastroentero-logical clinic are symptomatic disorders of function. It is remarkable that the only paper on motility among this collection is one showing that the colonic muscle contracts expectantly when food is discussed or smelt (Rogers *et al.*, 1993; p 133). Research in functional bowel disease is difficult because it so often depends on analysis of symptoms—but these are what trouble patients. Good work has been done in this field during the last 10 years, including observational surveys, measurements of gut muscle function, studies of visceral sensation, and psychological assessments and treatment.

I have alluded to the promising results showing that dietary manipulation can favour the proliferation of 'good' bifidobacteria in the large bowel (Gibson *et al.*, 1995; p 194). 'Bad' bacteria cause many of the episodes of acute diarrhoea so familiar to all travellers. A trial organized from St Bartholomew's Hospital, London, in collaboration with army personnel in Belize, has shown that a single dose of ciprofloxacin markedly shortens symptoms (Salem *et al.*, 1994; p 162). Such an episode of diarrhoea is probably the only occasion when most of us fear faecal incontinence. Not so for the many women who date this devastating disability to a difficult childbirth. A collaborative study with obstetricians has shown that occult anal sphincter defects are common after childbirth, especially after forceps delivery (Sultan *et al.*, 1993; p 150). The findings of this and related research are likely to have a marked effect on international obstetric practice.

Gastroenterology thrives on collaboration of different disciplines within the specialty, including basic science, and also with nurses, dietitians, and other specialties. The past decade shows much evidence of collaborative studies of all kinds: by such sharing of expertise the specialty will continue to advance.

John Lennard-Jones
President,
British Digestive Foundation

Contents

129 Riordan AM, Hunter JO, Cowan RE, Crampton JR, Davidson AR, Dickinson RJ, Dronfield MW, Fellows IW, Hishon S, Kerrigan GNW, Kennedy HJ, McGouran RCM, Neale G, Saunders JHB. Treatment of active Crohn's disease by exclusion diet: East Anglian multicentre controlled trial. Lancet 1993; 342: 1131–1134.

133 Rogers J, Raimundo AH, Misiewicz JJ. Cephalic phase of colonic pressure response to food. Gut 1993; 34: 537–543.

140 The Eurogast Study Group. An international association between *Helicobacter pylori* infection and gastric cancer. Lancet 1993; 341: 1359–1362.

144 Lynch DAF, Lobo AJ, Sobala GM, Dixon MF, Axon ATR. Failure of colonoscopic surveillance in ulcerative colitis. Gut 1993; 34: 1075–1080.

150 Sultan AH, Kamm MA, Hudson CN, Thomas JM, Bartram CI. Anal-sphincter disruption during vaginal delivery. New England Journal of Medicine 1993; 329: 1905–1911.

157 Adam IJ, Mohamdee MO, Martin IG, Scott N, Finan PJ, Johnston D, Dixon MF, Quirke P. Role of circumferential margin involvement in the local recurrence of rectal cancer. Lancet 1994; 344: 707–711.

162 Salam I, Katelaris P, Leigh-Smith S, Farthing MJG. Randomised trial of single-dose ciprofloxacin for travellers' diarrhoea. Lancet 1994; 344: 1537–1539.

165 Pullan RD, Rhodes J, Ganesh S, Mani V, Morris JS, Williams GT, Newcombe RG, Russell MAH, Feyerabend C, Thomas GAO, Säwe U. Transdermal nicotine for active ulcerative colitis. New England Journal of Medicine 1994; 330: 811–815.

170 Ryder SD, Parker N, Ecclestone D, Haqqani MT, Rhodes JM. Peanut lectin stimulates proliferation in colonic explants from patients with inflammatory bowel disease and colon polyps. Gastroenterology 1994; 106: 117–124.

171 Langman MJS, Weil J, Wainwright P, Lawson DH, Rawlins MD, Logan RFA, Murphy M, Vessey MP, Colin-Jones DG. Risks of bleeding peptic ulcer associated with individual non-steroidal anti-inflammatory drugs. Lancet 1994; 343: 1075–1078.

175 Connell WR, Lennard-Jones JE, Williams CB, Talbot IC, Price AB, Wilkinson KH. Factors affecting the outcome of endoscopic surveillance for cancer in ulcerative colitis. Gastroenterology 1994; 107: 934–944.

176 Connell WR, Kamm MA, Dickson M, Balkwill AM, Ritchie JK, Lennard-Jones JE. Long-term neoplasia risk after azathioprine treatment in inflammatory bowel disease. Lancet 1994; 343: 1249–1252.

180 Dusheiko G, Schmilovitz-Weiss H, Brown D, McOmish F, Yap P-L, Sherlock S, McIntyre N, Simmonds P. Hepatitis C virus genotypes: an investigation of type-specific differences in geographic origin and disease. Hepatology 1994; 19: 13–18.

186 Gillen CD, Walmsley RS, Prior P, Andrews HA, Allan RN. Ulcerative colitis and Crohn's disease: a comparison of the colorectal cancer risk in extensive colitis. Gut 1994; 35: 1590–1592.

189 Sturgess R, Day P, Ellis HJ, Lundin KEA, Gjertsen HA, Kontakou M, Ciclitira PJ. Wheat peptide challenge in coeliac disease. Lancet 1994; 343: 758–761.

193 Hussaini SH, Murphy GM, Kennedy C, Besser GM, Wass JAH, Dowling RH. The role of bile composition and physical chemistry in the pathogenesis of octreotide-associated gallbladder stones. Gastroenterology 1994; 107: 1503–1513.

194 Gibson GR, Beatty ER, Wang X, Cummings JH. Selective stimulation of bifidobacteria in the human colon by oligofructose and inulin. Gastroenterology 1995; 1978: 975–982.

195 Gupta SD, Hudson M, Burroughs AK, Morris R, Rolles K, Amlot P, Scheuer PJ, Dhillon AP. Grading of cellular rejection after orthotopic liver transplantation. Hepatology 1995; 21: 46–57.

196 Logan RPH, Walker MM, Misiewicz JJ, Gummett PA, Karim QN, Baron JH. Changes in the intragastric distribution of *Helicobacter pylori* during treatment with omeprazole. Gut 1995; 36: 12–16.

201 Cuschieri A, Fayers P, Fielding J, Craven J, Bancewicz J, Joypaul V, Cook P, for the Surgical Cooperative Group. Postoperative morbidity and mortality after D_1 and D_2 resections for gastric cancer: preliminary results of the MRCP randomised controlled surgical trial. Lancet 1996; 347: 995–999.

206 Norton B, Homer-Ward M, Donnelly MT, Long RG, Holmes GKT. A randomised prospective comparison of percutaneous endoscopic gastrostomy and nasogastric tube feeding after acute dysphagic stroke. British Medical Journal 1996; 312: 13–16.

210 Satsangi J, Welsh KI, Bunce M, Julier C, Farrant JM, Bell JI, Jewell DP. Contribution of genes of the major histocompatibility complex to susceptibility and disease phenotype in inflammatory bowel disease. Lancet 1996; 347: 1212–1217.

216 Rockall TA, Logan RFA, Devlin HB, Northfield TC, and the steering committee and members of the National Audit of Acute Upper Gastrointestinal Haemorrhage. Risk assessment after acute upper gastrointestinal haemorrhage. Gut 1996; 38: 316–321.

222 Thomas HJW, Whitelaw SC, Cottrell SE, Murday VA, Tomlinson IPM, Markie D, Jones T, Bishop DT, Hodgson SV, Sheer D, Northover JMA, Talbot IC, Solomon E, Bodmer WF. Genetic mapping of the hereditary mixed polyposis syndrome to chromosome 6q. American Journal of Human Genetics 1996; 58: 770–776.

229 Travis SPL, Farrant JM, Ricketts C, Nolan DJ, Mortensen NM, Kettlewell MGW, Jewell DP. Predicting outcome in severe ulcerative colitis. Gut 1996; 38: 905–910.

235 Gane EJ, Portmann BC, Naoumov NV, Smith HM, Underhill JA, Donaldson PT, Maertens G, Williams R. Long-term outcome of hepatitis C infection after liver transplantation. New England Journal of Medicine 1996; 334: 815–820.

241 Taha AS, Hudson N, Hawkey CJ, Swannell AJ, Trye PN, Cottrell J, Mann SG, Simon TJ, Sturrock RD, Russell RI. Famotidine for the prevention of gastric and duodenal ulcers caused by non-steroidal anti-inflammatory drugs. New England Journal of Medicine 1996; 334: 1435–1439.

246 Harris AW, Gummett PA, Walker MM, Misiewicz JJ, Baron JH. Relation between gastric acid output, *Helicobacter pylori*, and gastric metaplasia in the duodenal bulb. Gut 1996; 39: 513–520.

© *Cell* 1988; 53: 881–885

Catalytic Deficiency of Human Aldolase B in Hereditary Fructose Intolerance Caused by a Common Missense Mutation

Nicholas C. P. Cross,* Dean R. Tolan,† and Timothy M. Cox*
* Royal Postgraduate Medical School
London, W12 ONN
England
† Biological Science Center
2 Cummington Street
Boston, Massachusetts 02215

Summary

Hereditary fructose intolerance (HFI) is a human autosomal recessive disease caused by a deficiency of aldolase B that results in an inability to metabolize fructose and related sugars. We report here the first identification of a molecular lesion in the aldolase B gene of an affected individual whose defective protein has previously been characterized. The mutation is a G→C transversion in exon 5 that creates a new recognition site for the restriction enzyme AhaII and results in an amino acid substitution (Ala→Pro) at position 149 of the protein within a region critical for substrate binding. Utilizing this novel restriction site and the polymerase chain reaction, the patient was shown to be homozygous for the mutation. Three other HFI patients from pedigrees unrelated to this individual were found to have the same mutation: two were homozygous and one was heterozygous. We suggest that this genetic lesion is a prevailing cause of hereditary fructose intolerance.

Introduction

Hereditary fructose intolerance (HFI) is an autosomal recessive disease that is characterized by abdominal pain, vomiting, and hypoglycaemia following the ingestion of fructose or related sugars (Chambers and Pratt, 1956; Gitzelmann et al., 1983). In infants at weaning, the condition may be severe and cause fatal liver dysfunction (Odievre et al., 1978), but it responds dramatically to dietary exclusion. Although the incidence of the disease in different populations is unknown, a survey in Switzerland estimated a frequency of 1 in 20,000, and therefore a carrier frequency of 1% (Gitzelmann and Baerlocher, 1973). The association of a catalytic defect in aldolase B with HFI has been well documented (Hers and Joassin, 1961).

Aldolase B (EC.4.1.2.13) catalyzes the cleavage of fructose-1-phosphate to form dihydroxyacetone phosphate and D-glyceraldehyde (Hers and Kusaka, 1953). The enzyme is expressed exclusively in the liver, kidney, and intestine—tissues that actively assimilate fructose. Aldolase B is thus functionally distinct from the homologous isozymes, aldolases A and C, which are abundant in muscle and nervous tissue, respectively, and which have a greater activity with respect to fructose 1,6-diphosphate (Penhoet and Rutter, 1971).

Hereditary fructose intolerance is genetically heterogeneous (Gitzelmann et al., 1974; Gregori et al., 1982; Cox et al., 1983a), but immunologically detectable aldolase B has been found in biopsy samples of all affected tissues examined thus far (Nordmann et al., 1968; Grégori et al., 1982). In several studies, the apparent concentration of cross-reacting material (crm^+) was markedly reduced, and a regulatory defect of tissue-specific expression has been proposed (Grégori et al., 1982). However, immunotitration studies in patients with diminished apparent crm^+ in liver and intestine demonstrated the presence of abundant tissue aldolase B with reduced specific activity and impaired recognition by polyclonal antibodies (Cox et al., 1983b). Thus naturally occurring mutations in crm^+ patients alter regions of the aldolase B protein that are critical for functional activity, but they may also induce major structural changes that lead to impaired antibody recognition. Precise characterization of such genetic defects should help to define critical regions of the enzyme and clarify the relationship between aldolase structure and its function.

The aldolase B gene has been mapped to human chromosome 9 and sequenced (Tolan and Penhoet, 1986). It consists of nine exons, the first of which is untranslated. The cognate mRNA encodes 364 amino acids and there are three independent reports of its sequence (Rottman et al., 1984; Sakakibara et al., 1985; Paolella et al., 1984). Previously, molecular defects of aldolase B in hereditary fructose intolerance have not been identified. Here, we report the sequence analysis of the aldolase B genes of a patient in whom the mutant protein has been characterized with respect to enzymatic activity, immunological reactivity, and subunit structure (Cox et al., 1982; Cox et al., 1983b).

Results and Discussion

Cloning and Sequencing of a Mutant Aldolase B Gene

A genomic library was constructed from leucocyte DNA prepared from an HFI patient who has been described previously and studied (Cox et al., 1982; Cox et al., 1983b). Six clones, containing exons 3–9 on a 9 kb BamHI fragment, were recovered. The complete sequence of the coding regions from one of these clones was determined and a single base pair change was found—a G→C transversion at codon 149 (Figure 1). The mutation causes a proline residue to be substituted for an alanine at this position and hence is designated A149P. Exon 2 from the same patient was cloned directly into a plasmid after specific amplification of that exon by the polymerase chain reaction (PCR) (Saiki et al., 1985). Five independent clones were sequenced and found to be normal.

The splicing signals for all the introns, comprising the 5′GT/3′AG splice sites and the intron sequences containing the lariat branch point signal within 50 bp of the 3′ splice site, were determined. These sequences were identical to the wild type with the exception of a deleted C resi-

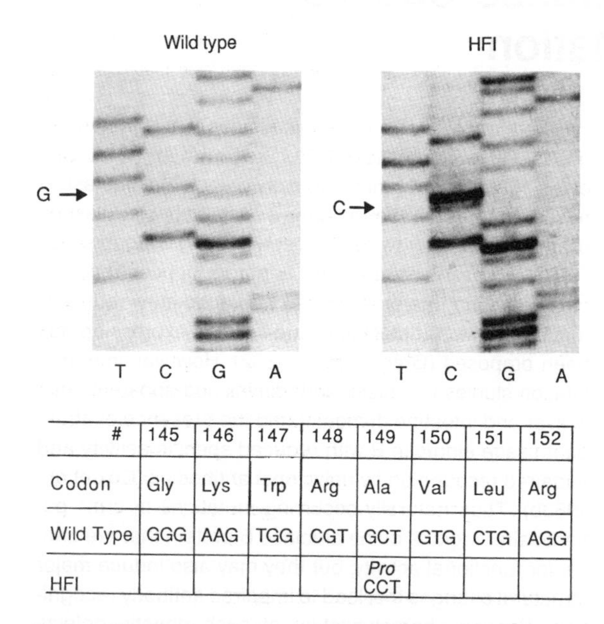

#	145	146	147	148	149	150	151	152
Codon	Gly	Lys	Trp	Arg	Ala	Val	Leu	Arg
Wild Type	GGG	AAG	TGG	CGT	GCT	GTG	CTG	AGG
HFI					*Pro* CCT			

Figure 1. Identification of a Missense Mutation in the Human Aldolase B Gene

The gene sequence was obtained from an individual affected by HFI. A single discrepancy was found between the mutant and wild-type coding sequences: a G→C transversion resulting in the replacement of an alanine by proline at position 149, thus designated A149P. The lesion generates a new recognition site for the restriction enzyme AhaII.

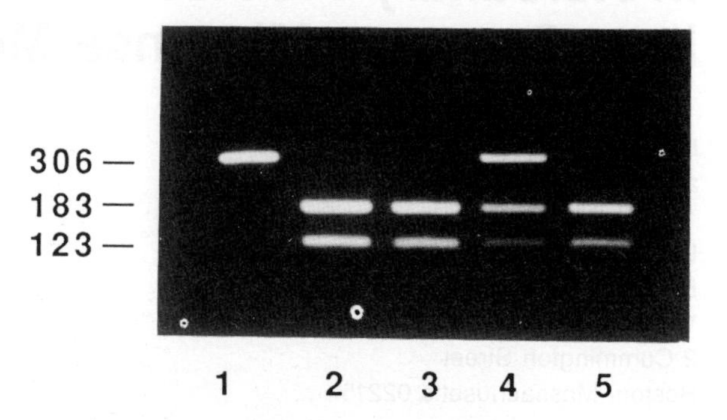

Figure 2. Genotype Analysis of Patients with HFI

Lane 1: healthy individual; lanes 2–5: HFI patients.

Lane 5 represents the individual from whom the genomic library was constructed and the A149P mutation characterized. Aldolase B exon 5 was selectively amplified from genomic DNA by the PCR to give a 306 bp fragment. This was then digested with AhaII; the A149P is cleaved to give bands of 183 bp and 123 bp, while alleles without this mutation remain uncut. Lanes 2, 3, and 5 therefore represent individuals who are homozygous for A149P, while lane 4 represents an individual who is heterozygous for A149P.

due 16 bp upstream of the start of exon 8. This is the first base of the polypyrimidine tract that precedes the 3′ splice site and is too far downstream to disrupt the lariat branch point signal found between −37 and −18 (Reed and Maniatis, 1985). Indeed, the only candidate sequence (GACTAAT, see consensus PyXPyTPuAPy) lies between positions −35 and −29 in this intron. The deleted C cannot cause activation of a cryptic 3′ splice site since the use of alternative AG sites within the intron would generate a truncated product due to stop codons in the retained intron sequence. Activation of the first in frame AG within exon 8 would produce a protein 11 amino acids shorter, with altered charge and incompatible with the mutant aldolase B in this patient, which has a slightly increased apparent subunit size without a change in charge (Cox et al., 1983b).

Detection of the A149P Mutation by Direct Analysis of Amplified Genomic DNA

The A149P mutation creates a new recognition site for the restriction enzyme AhaII (GPuCGPyC). However, this enzyme and its isoschizomers were found to cut leucocyte DNA very poorly even when used in large excess, and detection of the mutation by Southern blotting of genomic DNA was not undertaken. This may be due to methylation of genes not actively expressed in white cells. Cloned DNA was efficiently cleaved by AhaII, and all six HFI clones were found to contain the A149P mutation (data not shown), suggesting that the individual was homozygous. To confirm this, exon 5 sequences were specifically amplified from genomic DNA of this patient by the PCR and digested with AhaII. The amplified 306 bp fragment was cleaved completely by the restriction enzyme to give products of 183 bp and 123 bp, thus demonstrating the presence of the mutation in both alleles of the gene (Figure 2, lane 5). As expected, exons 5 from normal individuals were not digested by AhaII (Figure 2, lane 1). An identical analysis was carried out on three HFI individuals unrelated to the patient above. Two of them, a brother and sister, were also found to be homozygous for the A149P mutation (Figure 2, lanes 2 and 3). The third patient was heterozygous (Figure 2, lane 4). This latter patient is therefore a compound heterozygote, and the amplified exon 5 fragment that was not cut by AhaII represents and originated from a different mutant allele. This corroborates the previous study of the mutant enzyme in this patient in which the aldolase differed structurally from that of the HFI individual first shown to be homozygous for the A149P mutation. Nonetheless, the phenotypic manifestations of disease in these two patients are clinically indistinguishable (Cox et al., 1982; Cox et al., 1983a).

Segregation of the A149 Allele in an Affected Pedigree

To demonstrate segregation of the A149P alleles, genomic DNA was isolated from five members of a pedigree affected by HFI and was analyzed by digestion with AhaII after PCR amplification. The family includes the two affected individuals shown to be homozygous for the A149P allele (Figure 2, lanes 2 and 3; Figure 3, lanes 3 and 4). As predicted by the autosomal recessive transmission of the disorder, both unaffected parents carry one wild-type and one mutant allele (Figure 3, lanes 1 and 2). Their asymptomatic daughter was found to be a heterozygous carrier of the disease (Figure 3, lane 5). These data show that inheritance of two alleles bearing this mutation is associated with expression of the disease in this kindred.

Our findings indicate that homozygosity for the A149P allele is directly responsible for the HFI phenotype in several apparently unrelated patients. Aldolase B was cloned

© *Cell* 1988; 53: 881–885

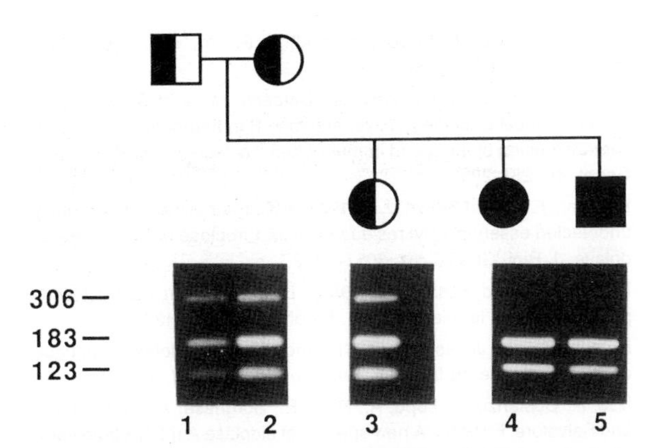

Figure 3. Genotype Analysis of Family Affected by HFI

Lane 1: father, lane 2: mother, lane 3: unaffected daughter, lanes 4 and 5: affected children. The parents are distant cousins. Open symbols represent the normal haplotype and solid symbols the mutant haplotype. Exon 5 was specifically amplified by the PCR and cut with AhaII as described in the text.

from an affected homozygote whose defect is known to reduce specific activity rather than levels of expression of the enzyme, i.e., catalytic rather than regulatory (Cox et al., 1983b). The mutant gene was sequenced and found to contain a single base pair change with respect to the wild type, resulting in a missense mutation in the protein. In addition, this lesion was found in other unrelated individuals with HFI and segregated with the disease in an affected pedigree as a recessive Mendelian character.

Implications of the A149P Mutation for Catalytic Function

Aldolase isozyme cDNA clones have been sequenced from diverse species and show considerable homology. It is notable that the amino acid residue at position 149 (the site of the mutation shown here) is specific for aldolase B (Figure 4). In the human, rat, and chicken enzyme this is

	146	147	148	149 ↓	150	151
Human B	Lys	Trp	Arg	Ala	Val	Leu
Rat B	Lys	Trp	Arg	Ala	Val	Leu
Chicken B	Lys	Trp	Arg	Ala	Val	Leu
Human A	Lys	Trp	Arg	Cys	Val	Leu
Rabbit A	Lys	Trp	Arg	Cys	Val	Leu
Human C	Lys	Trp	Arg	Cys	Val	Leu
Mouse C	Lys	Trp	Arg	Cys	Val	Leu

Figure 4. Comparison of Aldolase Protein Sequences Surrounding the Site of the Mutation Described Here (position 149 marked by an arrow)

This residue is an alanine in aldolase B but cysteine in aldolases A and C and thus may be involved in aldolase B–specific catalysis. The sequences were obtained from the following publications: human B (Rottmann et al., 1984); rat B (Tsutsumi et al., 1985); chicken B (Burgess and Penhoet, 1985); human A (Izzo et al., 1987); rabbit A (Tolan et al., 1984); human C (Rottmann et al., 1987); mouse C (Paolella et al., 1986).

an alanine, but aldolases A and C possess a cysteine at this position. The residue may therefore be involved in aldolase B-specific catalysis. The insertion of a proline residue, an imino acid in which peptide bond formation involves the rigid pyrollidone ring, is known to alter protein secondary structure. Moreover, vicinal residues (Lys 146 and Arg 148) are implicated in the binding of substrate (Hartman and Brown, 1976; Patthy et al., 1979) and have been shown by X-ray crystallography of muscle aldolase to be located on the β strand of a binding pocket (Sygusch et al., 1987). Thus mutation resulting in the change of Ala 149 to proline is likely to disrupt the spatial configuration of juxtaposed residues in aldolase B and adversely affect its catalytic properties. That this mutation drastically modifies enzyme structure is shown by the markedly reduced immunoreactivity of the protein and by its altered electrophoretic mobility without change in charge (Cox et al., 1983b).

Carrier Detection and Diagnosis of Fructose Intolerance

The A149P mutation has been found in five out of the six HFI alleles studied. This implies that the methods employed here may facilitate carrier detection and diagnosis in families affected by the disease. Further work is needed to ascertain the true prevalence of this mutation. We suggest that the selection pressure against HFI was probably minimal before sugars became widely available with the advent of the industrial revolution. Mutations in aldolase B may have been able to accumulate by genetic drift and it is therefore possible that a limited number of mutant alleles may account for the great majority of individuals affected by fructose intolerance.

Experimental Procedures

Cloning of a Mutant Aldolase B Gene

Genomic DNA obtained from peripheral leucocytes of an HFI patient was digested to completion with BamHI and size-fractionated on an agarose gel. An aldolase B-enriched fraction of approximately 9 kb (Tolan and Penhoet, 1986) was recovered by the freeze-squeeze technique (Tautz and Renz, 1983) and ligated to λL47 arms (Loenen and Brammar, 1980). Packaging extracts were prepared and the reactions performed as described (Scherer et al., 1981). A sequence in intron 6 of aldolase B has previously been found to be unclonable in rec A strains of E. coli (Tolan and Penhoet, 1986), presumably because it contains a long palindrome or homopolymer tract (Leach and Stahl, 1983; Nader et al., 1986). This problem was obviated by plating the library on a rec BC sbcB host (Leach and Stahl, 1983). Six aldolase B clones, containing exons 3–9 on a 9 kb BamHI fragment, were retrieved by probing with the cDNA clone pHL413 (Rottmann et al., 1984). Exon 2 was cloned directly from genomic DNA after specific amplification of that exon by the polymerase chain reaction (PCR; see below).

DNA Sequence Analysis

Fragments of one phage clone, designated λEE13, were subcloned into pEMBL 18 or 19 (Dente et al., 1983) and sequenced by the chain terminator method (Sanger et al., 1977) using either the M13 universal primer (New England Biolabs) or specific oligonucleotide primers derived from the genomic sequence (Tolan and Penhoet, 1986) and synthesized on a Cyclone DNA synthesizer (Biosearch, Inc.).

DNA Amplification

The polymerase chain reaction was performed as follows: 1 μg genomic DNA was dispersed in 100 μl PCR reaction buffer (50 mM

KCl, 2 mM $MgCl_2$, 10 mM Tris (pH 8.3), 0.1% gelatin, 0.2 mM each PCR primers, 0.2 mM dATP, 0.2 mM dTTP, 0.2 mM dCTP, 0.2 mM dGTP) in 0.5 ml microfuge tubes. The DNA was denatured by heating to 95°C for 7 min. The samples were transferred to a water bath (45°C) for 5 min to allow annealing of the primers. One unit of Taq polymerase (Anglian Biotechnology Ltd.) was added, and the reaction mixes were overlaid with 50 μl mineral oil (Sigma). The tubes were transferred to a 70°C water bath for 3 min to allow primer extension, denatured to 91°C for 2 min, and reannealed at 45°C for 2 min. This cycle was repeated 30 times with the addition of a further unit of Taq polymerase after every 10 cycles. Aliquots of the reactions were analyzed on 2% minigels: usually 200 ng–1 μg of the desired fragment was produced. Occasionally, however, additional spurious bands were also found, usually of very small size. In these cases the correct fragment was excised from the gel and recovered. The primers used for amplification were: 5′GTTGTTATATGATGAGACTG3′ and 5′GAGCCACCCATGGTTCTGTG3′ for exon 2, which produced a 201 bp fragment, and 5′CCATGGATCAGGTACAAAGG3′ and 5′GGTCCATTTGTAGTTATAGT3′ for exon 5, which produced a 306 bp fragment.

Detection of A149P Allele

Aldolase B exon 5 was specifically amplified by the PCR from genomic DNA obtained from HFI patients and normal controls. The 306 bp fragment was digested with AhaII (New England Biolabs) according to the manufacturer's recommendations. The mutant A149P allele is cleaved to produce bands of 183 bp and 123 bp.

Acknowledgments

We thank Professor W. J. Brammar for supplying the vector λL47, Dr. D. Leach for supplying E. coli strain CES200, and Drs. J. and D. Harding for providing family blood samples. Dr. F. E. Baralle and Professor L. Luzzatto gave generous advice and Dr. W. J. Marshall kindly referred two patients for study. This work was supported by the Medical Research Council.

The costs of publication of this article were defrayed in part by the payment of page charges. This article must therefore be hereby marked *"advertisement"* in accordance with 18 U.S.C. Section 1734 solely to indicate this fact.

Received January 25, 1988; revised April 1, 1988.

References

Burgess, D. G., and Penhoet, E. E. (1985). Characterization of the chicken aldolase B gene. J. Biol. Chem. *260*, 4604–4614.

Chambers, R., and Pratt, R. T. C. (1956). Idiosyncrasy to fructose. Lancet *II*, 340.

Cox, T. M., Camilleri, M., O'Donnell, M. W., and Chadwick, V. S. (1982). Pseudodominant transmission of fructose intolerance in an adult and three offspring. Heterozygote detection by intestinal biopsy. N. Engl. J. Med. *307*, 537–540.

Cox, T. M., O'Donnell, M. W., and Camilleri, M. (1983a). Allelic heterogeneity in adult hereditary fructose intolerance. Detection of structural mutations in the aldolase B molecule. Mol. Biol. Med. *1*, 393–400.

Cox, T. M., O'Donnell, M. W., Camilleri, M., and Burghes, A. H. (1983b). Isolation and characterization of a mutant liver aldolase in adult hereditary fructose intolerance. Identification of the enzyme variant by radioassay in tissue biopsy specimens. J. Clin. Invest. *72*, 201–213.

Dente, L., Cesareri, G., and Portesi, R. (1983). pEMBL, a new family of single stranded plasmids. Nucl. Acids Res. *11*, 1645–1655.

Gitzelmann, R., and Baerlocher, K. (1973). Vorteile und nachteile der fructose in der nahrung. Pädiat. Fortbildiung Praxis. *37*, 40–55.

Gitzelmann, R., Steinmann, B., Bally, C., and Lebherz, H. G. (1974). Antibody activation of mutant fructosediphosphate aldolase B in liver extracts of patients with hereditary fructose intolerance. Biochem. Biophys. Res. Commun. *59*, 1270–1277.

Gitzelmann, R., Steinmann, B., and Van den Berghe, G. (1983). Hereditary fructose intolerance. In The Metabolic Basis of Inherited Disease, Fifth Edition, J. B. Stanbury, J. B. Wyngaarden, D. S. Fredrickson, J. L. Goldstein, and M. S. Brown, eds. (New York: McGraw-Hill), pp. 118-132.

Gregori, C., Shapira, F., Kahn, A., Delpech, M., and Dreyfus, J. C. (1982). Molecular studies of liver aldolase B in hereditary fructose intolerance using blotting and immunochemical techniques. Ann. Hum. Genet. *46*, 281–292.

Hartman, F. C., and Brown, J. B. (1976). Affinity labelling of a previously undetected essential lysyl residue in class 1 fructose bisphosphate aldolase. J. Biol. Chem. *251*, 3057–3062.

Hers, H.-G., and Kusaka, T. (1953). Le metabolism du fructose-1-phosphate dans le foie. Biochim. Biophys. Acta *11*, 427–430.

Hers, H.-G., and Joassin, G. (1961). Anomalie de l'aldolase hepatique dans l'intolerance au fructose. Enzymol. Biol. Clin. *1*, 4–14.

Izzo, P., Costanzo, P., Lupo, A., Ripa, E., Borghese, A., Paolella, G., and Salvatore, F. (1987). A new species of aldolase A mRNA from fibroblasts. Eur. J. Biochem. *164*, 9–13.

Leach, D. R. F., and Stahl, F. (1983). Viability of λ phages carrying a perfect palindrome in absence of recombination nucleases. Nature *305*, 448–451.

Loenen, W. M., and Brammar, W. J. (1980). A bacteriophage λ vector for cloning large DNA fragments made with several restriction enzymes. Gene *10*, 249–259.

Morris, R. C., Ueki, I., Loh, D., Eanes, R. Z., and McLin, P. (1967). Absence of renal fructose-1-phosphate aldolase activity in hereditary fructose intolerance. Nature *214*, 920–921.

Nader, W. F., Isenberg, G., and Sauer, H. W. (1986). Structure of physarum actin gene locus ard A: a non-palindromic sequence causes inviability of phage lambda and rec A-independent deletions. Gene *48*, 133–144.

Nordmann, Y., Schapira, F., and Dreyfus, J.-C. (1968). A structurally modified liver aldolase in fructose intolerance: immunological and chemical evidence. Biochem. Biophys. Res. Commun. *31*, 884–889.

Odievre, M., Gentil, C., Gautier, M., and Alagille, D. (1978). Hereditary fructose intolerance in childhood. Am. J. Dis. Child. *132*, 605–608.

Patthy, C., Varadi, A., Thesz, J., and Kovacs, K. (1979). Identification of the C-1-phosphate binding arginine residue of rabbit muscle aldolase. Eur. J. Biochem. *99*, 309–313.

Paolella, G., Santamaria, R., Izzo, P., Constanzo, P., and Salvatore, F. (1984). Isolation and nucleotide sequence of a full length cDNA coding for aldolase B from human liver. Nucl. Acids Res. *12*, 7401–7409.

Paolella, G., Buono, P., Mancini, F. P., Izzo, P., and Salvatore, F. (1986). Structure and expression of mouse aldolase genes. Eur. J. Biochem. *256*, 229–235.

Penhoet, E. E., and Rutter, W. J. (1971). Catalytic and immunochemical properties of homomeric and heteromeric combinations of aldolase subunits. J. Biol. Chem. *246*, 318–323.

Reed, R., and Maniatis, T. (1985). Intron sequences involved in lariat formation during pre mRNA splicing. Cell *41*, 95–105.

Rottmann, W. H., Tolan, D. R., and Penhoet, E. E. (1984). Complete amino acid sequence for human aldolase B derived from cDNA and genomic clones. Proc. Natl. Acad. Sci. USA *81*, 2738–2742.

Rottmann, W. H., De Selms, K. R., Niclas, J., Camerato, T., Holman, P. S., Green, C. J., and Tolan, D. R. (1987). The complete amino acid sequence of human aldolase C isozyme derived from genomic clones. Biochimie *69*, 137–145.

Saiki, R. K., Scharf, S., Faloona, F., Mullis, K. B., Horn, G., Erlich, H., and Arnheim, N. (1985). Enzymatic amplification of β-globin sequences and restriction site analysis for diagnosis of sickle cell anaemia. Science *230*, 1350–1354.

Sakakibara, M., Mukai, T., Yatsuki, H., and Hori, K. (1985). Human aldolase isozyme gene: the structure of multispecies aldolase B mRNAs. Nucl. Acids Res. *13*, 5055–5069.

Sanger, F., Nicklen, S., and Coulsen, A. (1977). DNA sequencing with chain terminating inhibitors. Proc. Natl. Acad. Sci. USA *74*, 5463–5467.

Scherer, G., Telford, J., Baldari, C., and Pirrotta, V. (1981). Isolation of cloned genes differentially expressed at early and late stages of Drosophila embryonic development. Dev. Biol. *86*, 438–447.

Sygusch, J., Beaudry, D., and Allaire, M. (1987). Molecular resolution of rabbit skeletal muscle aldolase at 2.7 A resolution. Proc. Natl. Acad. Sci. USA *84*, 7846–7850.

Tautz, D., and Renz, M. (1983). An optimized freeze-squeeze method for the recovery of DNA fragments from agarose gels. Anal. Biochem. *132*, 14–19.

Tolan, D. R., and Penhoet, E. E. (1986). Characterization of the human aldolase B gene. Mol. Biol. Med. *3*, 245–264.

Tolan, D. R., Amsden, B., Putney, S. D., Urdea, M. S., and Penhoet, E. E. (1984). The complete nucleotide sequence for rabbit muscle aldolase A messenger RNA. J. Biol. Chem. *259*, 1127–1131.

Tsutsumi, K., Mukai, T., Tsutsumi, R., Hidaka, S., Arai, Y., Hori, K., and Ishikawa, K. (1985). Structure and genomic organisation of the rat aldolase B gene. J. Mol. Biol. *181*, 153–160.

© *Lancet* 1988, i: 1067–1070

PRIMARY BILIARY CIRRHOSIS: IDENTIFICATION OF TWO MAJOR M2 MITOCHONDRIAL AUTOANTIGENS

S. J. YEAMAN[1] S. P. M. FUSSEY[1]
D. J. DANNER[2] O. F. W. JAMES[3]
D. J. MUTIMER[3] M. F. BASSENDINE[3]

Departments of Biochemistry[1] and Medicine[3], The Medical School, University of Newcastle upon Tyne, Newcastle upon Tyne, UK; and Division of Medical Genetics, Emory University, Atlanta, USA[2]

Summary Primary biliary cirrhosis (PBC) is characterised by the presence of antimitochondrial antibodies. The PBC-specific, immunoreactive, trypsin-sensitive antigens on the inner mitochondrial membrane (M2) have hitherto not been identified. A major 70 kD M2 autoantigen is the E2 component (lipoate acetyltransferase) of the pyruvate dehydrogenase enzyme complex located within mitochondria. This has been confirmed by immunoblotting of PBC patients' sera against purified E2 protein: sera from 38/40 (95%) patients with established clinical, biochemical, and histological features of PBC (18 stage II/III, 22 stage IV) reacted positively with E2; whilst no sera from 39 controls (27 non-PBC chronic liver disease, 12 healthy normal women) gave a positive response. Immunoblotting showed that a second subunit of the pyruvate dehydrogenase complex, a 50 kD polypeptide of unknown function (component X), is also an M2 autoantigen. Identification of these M2 mitochondrial antigens should facilitate the development of a specific serological test for PBC and the study of autoimmunising epitopes.

Introduction

PRIMARY biliary cirrhosis (PBC) is a chronic cholestatic liver disease most common in middle-aged women, and is characterised by inflammatory obliteration of intrahepatic bileducts, progressing to fibrosis and liver cell damage beyond the portal tracts, and ultimately to cirrhosis with complications of liver failure or portal hypertension.[1] The cause is unknown, but evidence supports an autoimmune process[2]—notably an autoantibody response to an antigen or antigens associated closely with mitochondria.[3] These antimitochondrial antibodies in serum are demonstrated by indirect immunofluorescence in which they display a typical pattern on unfixed cryostat sections of human thyroid gland and rat stomach and kidney.[4]

Berg and colleagues have shown that the antimitochondrial antibodies in PBC fix complement with a trypsin-sensitive antigen on the inner mitochondrial membrane.[5] This non-organ-specific antigen, defined as M2, is a specific marker for the serological diagnosis of PBC. Sera from patients with other disorders in which antimitochondrial antibodies are found (eg, syphilis, pseudolupus syndrome, and myocarditis) do not react with M2.[6] The use of immunoblotting has shown that the PBC-specific M2 mitochondrial antigen consists of at least 3 polypeptides of molecular weight approximately 70, 45, and 39 kilodaltons (kD).[7]

The 70 kD polypeptide reacts with sera from approximately 95% of patients with PBC, and is present in mammals, yeast, and bacteria.[8] Gershwin and co-workers have recently reported the molecular cloning and sequencing of a cDNA encoding at least part of this major

© Lancet 1988, i: 1067–1070

TABLE I—CLINICAL AND LABORATORY DATA ON PBC PATIENTS AND CONTROLS

Diagnosis	No (sex)	Immunoblot	AMA (IFL titre)	Other autoantibodies (no in which present)
PBC: histological stage II/III	18 (17 F, 1 M)	17 pos	All pos	Tmic (4), Tglob (1), ANA (2), Rhf (3), SMA (2)
		1 neg	Pos (1/80)	Tmic, SMA
PBC: histological stage IV	22 (21 F, 1 M)	21 pos	All pos	Tmic (8), Tglob (2), ANA (5), Rhf (6)
		1 neg	Pos (1/320)	None
Other liver diseases				
Chronic active hepatitis	10			
Alcoholic liver disease	10			
Sclerosing cholangitis	2			
Cryptogenic cirrhosis	2 } 27 (12 F, 15 M)	All neg	All neg	ANA (5), SMA (7), LKM (1), Tmic (5), Tglob (2), Rhf (4), GPC (2)
Secondary biliary cirrhosis	1			
Idiopathic cholestasis	1			
Idiopathic steatosis	1			
Healthy volunteers	12 (all F)	All neg	All neg	Tmic (2), ANA (1), SMA (1)

F = female; M = male; Pos = positive; Neg = negative; AMA = antimitochondrial antibody; Tmic = antithyroid microsomal antibody; Tglob = antithyroglobulin antibody; ANA = antinuclear antibody; SMA = anti smooth muscle antibody; LKM = anti liver kidney microsomal antibody; Rhf = rheumatoid factor; GPC = anti gastric parietal cell antibody.

70 kD M2 antigen,[9] but the data obtained did not lead to identification of the M2 protein. They concluded that the nucleotide and deduced aminoacid sequence of the recombinant protein showed no significant homologies with known proteins. We, however, found that detailed inspection of the predicted protein sequence of this M2 antigen strongly suggested its identity as being the E2 component of the mammalian pyruvate dehydrogenase complex, and carried out a study to examine this hypothesis. The pyruvate dehydrogenase complex—a large multi-enzyme complex catalysing the oxidative decarboxylation of pyruvate to acetyl coenzyme A—is located within the mitochondrial matrix, loosely associated with the inner face of the inner mitochondrial membrane. The complex consists of multiple copies of three different catalytic components termed E1, E2, and E3: E2 forms a symmetrical core around which are arranged the E1 and E3 components. E2 is an acetyl transferase which utilises the covalently-bound lipoic acid as an essential co-factor.[10]

Patients and Methods

Pyruvate dehydrogenase complex was purified from bovine heart as previously described,[11] and the E2 component was obtained by resolution with gel filtration chromatography on 'Superose 6' (Pharmacia). The final material contained only two polypeptides, corresponding to E2 and the recently described component X,[12] as judged by polyacrylamide gel electrophoresis in 10% gels, in the presence of sodium dodecyl sulphate, by the method described by Laemmli and Favre.[13]

The E2 component (0·5 μg per gel lane) of the pyruvate dehydrogenase complex was subjected to polyacrylamide gel electrophoresis in the presence of sodium dodecyl sulphate, and then transferred electrophoretically to nitrocellulose.[14] After blocking and washing, individual lanes were incubated for 2 h with human sera at a dilution of between 1:100 and 1:10 000. Detection of human antibodies was by use of secondary goat anti-human IgG (γ-chain specific) peroxidase-conjugated antibodies (Sigma), with 4-chloro-l-naphthol as substrate.

Sera were obtained (and stored at −20°C) from 40 patients (38 female, 2 male) known to have PBC, according to the usual clinical, biochemical, and histological criteria (18 histological stage II/III, 22 stage IV).[15] Sera were also taken from 39 control subjects: 12 of these were "normal controls" (healthy hospital staff with normal conventional liver blood tests and negative for antimitochondrial antibodies on immunofluoresence), and 27 were patients with other chronic liver diseases (diagnosis confirmed by conventional clinical, serological, and radiological criteria including liver biopsy in every case—see table I). Immunofluorescence tests for serum autoantibodies were performed routinely in the regional immunology laboratory. Antimitochondrial antibody was detected on a composite block of mouse kidney and stomach, rat liver, and human thyrotoxic thyroid, and was assayed by indirect immunofluorescence on cryostat sections of mouse stomach and kidney with a fluorescein-conjugated anti-human IgG (Tago Inc, California). A positive reading for antimitochondrial antibodies was defined as showing staining of all renal tubules, but preferentially the distal tubular cells, as well as thyroid epithelium and gastric parietal cell granular staining: all PBC patients had a positive titre of 1:40 or greater.

Results

Structural Identification of M2 Mitochondrial Autoantigen

The primary structure around the lipoate attachment site on the E2 component of bovine heart pyruvate dehydrogenase complex has been determined.[11] This 10-residue aminoacid sequence corresponds exactly to a region in the deduced aminoacid sequence of the cloned 70 kD mitochondrial antigen described by Gershwin et al[9] (table II). Comparison of the predicted protein sequence of the 70 kD mitochondrial antigen with the previously determined sequence of the E2 component of the pyruvate dehydrogenase complex from *E coli*[16] indicates an overall homology of 48%. This homology is even higher in certain key regions of the polypeptide, including the binding site for E3 and in the catalytic domain where, in one stretch of 60 aminoacids, 23 of these are identical in the two proteins and 45 are conserved residues (a detailed comparison will be presented elsewhere). Several other known features of the E2 component of mammalian pyruvate dehydrogenase

TABLE II—STRUCTURE OF THE LIPOIC ACID CONTAINING REGION OF E2 OF MAMMALIAN PYRUVATE DEHYDROGENASE COMPLEX COMPARED WITH A REGION OF THE 70 kD M2 MITOCHONDRIAL ANTIGEN

Protein	Source	Aminoacid sequence
E2 component	Bovine heart	1 2 3 4 5 6 7 8 9 10 Val—Glu—Thr—Asp—Lys—Ala—Thr—Val—Gly—Phe Ile (1); * (5); Ile (8)
70 kD antigen	Rat liver (cDNA library)	Ile— Glu—Thr—Asp—Lys—Ala—Thr— Ile—Gly—Phe

*Denotes the position of attachment of the lipoic acid residue. Both valine and isoleucine have been detected at positions 1 and 8 in the E2 protein ([11] and Bradford, Yeaman, and Aitken, unpublished). The 70 kD sequence corresponds to bases 247–276 in the cDNA sequence.[9]

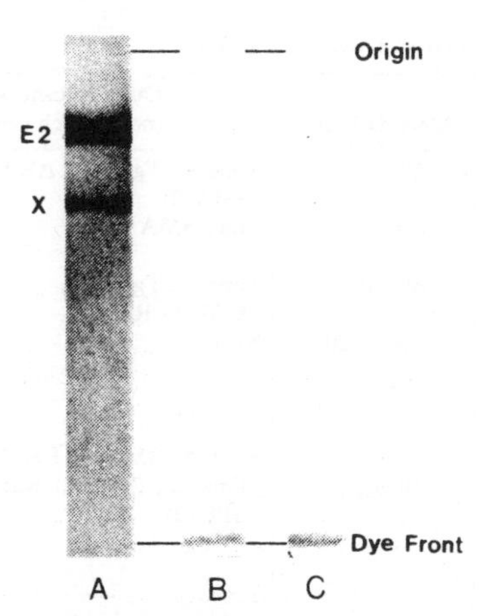

Reactivity of PBC sera with E2 and X components.

A: E2 and X components from purified bovine pyruvate dehydrogenase complex. Gel (15 µg protein) stained with Coomassie brilliant blue R.
B: PBC serum (dilution 1:1000). Nitrocellulose (0·5 µg protein).
C: Control serum (dilution 1:100). Nitrocellulose (0·5 µg protein).

complex are also consistent with the reported properties of the M2 PBC antigen, summarised in table III.

Verification of Identity of M2 Antigens by Immunoblotting

38 of 40 sera from PBC patients reacted strongly with the E2 polypeptide at a dilution of 1:1000 or greater (table I). All 38 sera reacting with the E2 polypeptide also recognised the additional component X present in the purified E2 preparation (figure). None of the sera either from the 27 patients with non-PBC chronic liver disease or 12 normal controls reacted with E2 or X, even at a dilution of only 1:100. The two PBC patients whose sera gave a negative response to E2 by immunoblotting were indistinguishable by clinical, biochemical, or histological criteria from the other patients with PBC.

Discussion

Immunoblotting has previously been used to show that the PBC-specific M2 mitochondrial antigen consists of several polypeptides, which have been characterised according to their molecular weight.[5-8,18] Serum autoantibodies to one of these polypeptides, the 70 kD protein, have been found in between 85–95% of patients with PBC. Our finding that sera from 95% of patients with established clinical, biochemical, and histological features of PBC react with the E2 component of the mammalian pyruvate dehydrogenase complex is thus consistent with previous data obtained with the "unknown" M2 antigen. We have identified this 70 kD M2 antigen as the E2 component of the pyruvate dehydrogenase complex: this enzyme complex has been isolated from bacteria, yeast, and mammalian cells, and thus explains the cross-reactivity of PBC sera with bacterial and yeast antigens.[8] Identification of this major M2 mitochondrial protein should facilitate the development of a sensitive and specific serological test for the diagnosis of PBC. A different aetiological factor may be implicated in the two PBC patients whose sera did not react with the E2 component of the pyruvate dehydrogenase complex, as the clinical spectrum of PBC is broad.[19,20]

TABLE III—PROPERTIES COMMON TO THE 70 kD M2 MITOCHONDRIAL ANTIGEN AND THE E2 COMPONENT OF THE PYRUVATE DEHYDROGENASE COMPLEX

Property	Reference
Non-organ-specific	5–8, 10
Present in mammals, yeast, and bacteria	7, 8, 10
Nuclear encoded	9, 10
Localised in inner mitochondrial membranes	5, 6, 10
70 kD on SDS polyacrylamide gel electrophoresis	7, 10
Trypsin-sensitive	5, 6, 8–10
Contains region rich in alanine and proline	9, 16

(The pyruvate dehydrogenase complex is located on the inner face of the inner mitochondrial membranes).[10,17]

The reaction of PBC sera with the additional protein, component X, present in the E2 preparation may help to determine the pathogenesis of the disease. Component X was originally thought to be a proteolytic fragment of E2, but immunological and structural data show that it is a distinct polypeptide.[12] All PBC sera that reacted with E2 also reacted with component X and, therefore, this polypeptide is another constituent of the "M2" antigen, with an apparent molecular weight of approximately 50 kD.[6,12,21]

The structure of the pyruvate dehydrogenase multi-enzyme complex has been extensively studied.[17] It is large, with a molecular weight of about $8{\cdot}5 \times 10^6$ kD. The E2 core has a molecular weight of greater than 3×10^6 kD, consisting of 60 copies of the E2 polypeptide arranged in icosahedral symmetry. The complex is arranged about this E2 core with multiple copies of the E1 and E3 components bound by non-covalent forces. E2 has a large central cavity in its structure and consists of two distinct domains; a compact central domain containing the active site, and a highly flexible domain bearing the lipoic acid co-factor.[17]

The generation of an autoantibody response requires cooperation between B and T lymphocytes. The symmetry and size of the E2 core may be relevant to the production of autoantibodies, but T cell recognition sites have not yet been found within the E2 polypeptides. Rothbard has proposed that immunogens that are aggregates (such as viruses) may be treated by the immune system as single molecules.[22] Milich and colleagues have shown that, for hepatitis B virus, priming of the immune system with an internal core antigen recognised by T cells (in association with MHC molecules) can result in the primed T cells helping B cells to react with a second protein on the viral surface.[23]

The role of non-organ-specific, non-species-specific autoantibodies to the M2 mitochondrial antigens in the pathogenesis of PBC is unclear.[24] There is some evidence that the primary mechanism of bileduct injury is T cell mediated cytotoxicity.[25] However, all histological stages of PBC are marked by an autoantibody response to M2 antigen(s) and the antimitochondrial antibody titre by immunofluorescence bears some correlation to disease progression.[26] This would suggest that identification of the major M2 mitochondrial autoantigen as the E2 component of the pyruvate dehydrogenase complex will lead to clarification of the immunopathogenesis of primary biliary cirrhosis.

S. J. Y. is a Lister Institute research fellow; S. P. M. F. holds a research studentship from the Science and Engineering Research Council; D. J. M. is supported by the British Digestive Foundation.

We thank Dr I. M. Shepherd (University of Newcastle upon Tyne) for advice on immunoblotting, Dr G. Bird (Regional Immunology Laboratory) for indirect immunofluorescence data, and Prof J. R. Guest, FRS, and Miss Sally Woods (University of Sheffield) for assistance with computer analysis of the sequence data.

Correspondence should be addressed to M. F. B., Department of Medicine, The Medical School, Framlington Place, Newcastle upon Tyne NE2 4HH.

REFERENCES

1. Kaplan MM. Primary biliary cirrhosis. *N Engl J Med* 1987; **316:** 521–28.
2. James SP, Hoofnagle JH, Strober W, Jones EA. Primary biliary cirrhosis: a model autoimmune disease. *Ann Intern Med* 1983; **99:** 500–12.

References continued at foot of next page

S. J. YEAMAN AND OTHERS: REFERENCES—*continued*

3. Munoz LE, Thomas HC, Scheuer PJ, Doniach D, Sherlock S. Is mitochondrial antibody diagnostic of primary biliary cirrhosis? *Gut* 1981; **22:** 136–40.
4. Walker JG, Doniach D, Roitt IM, Sherlock S. Serological tests in diagnosis of primary biliary cirrhosis. *Lancet* 1965; i: 827–31.
5. Berg PA, Klein R, Lindenborn-Fotinos J. Antimitochondrial antibodies in primary biliary cirrhosis. *J Hepatol* 1986; **2:** 123–31.
6. Berg PA, Klein R. Immunology of primary biliary cirrhosis. *Ballière's Clin Gastroenterol* 1987; **1:** 675–706.
7. Frazer IH, Mackay IR, Jordan S, Whittingham S, Marzuki S. Reactivity of anti-mitochondrial autoantibodies in primary biliary cirrhosis: definition of two novel mitochondrial polypeptide autoantigens. *J Immunol* 1985; **135:** 1739–45.
8. Baum H, Palmer C. The PBC-specific antigens. *Molec Aspects Med* 1985; **8:** 201–36.
9. Gershwin ME, Mackay IR, Sturgess A, Coppel RL. Identification and specificity of a cDNA encoding the 70kD mitochondrial antigen recognised in primary biliary cirrhosis. *J Immunol* 1987; **138:** 3525-31.
10. Yeaman SJ. The mammalian 2-oxo-acid dehydrogenases: a complex family. *Trends Biochem Sci* 1986; **11:** 293–96.
11. Bradford AP, Howell S, Aitken A, James LA, Yeaman SJ. Primary structure around the lipoate attachment site on the E2 component of bovine heart pyruvate dehydrogenase complex. *Biochem J* 1987; **245:** 919–22.
12. De Marcucci O, Lindsay JG. Component X—an immunologically distinct polypeptide associated with mammalian pyruvate dehydrogenase multi-enzyme complex. *Eur J Biochem* 1985; **149:** 641–48.
13. Laemmli UK, Favre M. Maturation of the head of bacteriophage T4. *J Mol Biol* 1973; **80:** 575–99.
14. Towbin H, Staehelin T, Gordon J. Electrophoretic transfer of proteins from polyacrylamide gels to nitrocellulose sheets: procedure and some applications. *Proc Natl Acad Sci USA* 1979; **76:** 4350–54.
15. Scheuer P. Primary biliary cirrhosis. *Proc R Soc Med* 1967; **60:** 1257–60.
16. Stephens PE, Darlison MG, Lewis HM, Guest JR. The pyruvate dehydrogenase complex of *Escherichia coli* K12. Nucleotide sequence encoding the dihydrolipoamide acetyltransferase component. *Eur J Biochem* 1983; **133:** 481–89.
17. Reed LJ, Yeaman SJ. Pyruvate dehydrogenase. The Enzymes, vol 18. New York: Academic Press, 1987: 77–95.
18. Mendel-Hartvig I, Nelson BD, Loof L. Totterman TH. Primary biliary cirrhosis: further biochemical and immunological characterisation of mitochondrial antigens. *Chi Exp Immunol* 1985; **62:** 371–79.
19. James OFW, Macklon AF, Watson AJ. Primary biliary cirrhosis—a revised clinical spectrum. *Lancet* 1981; i: 1278–81.
20. Roll J, Boyer JL, Barry D, Klatskin G. The prognostic importance of clinical and histological features in asymptomatic and symptomatic primary biliary cirrhosis. *N Engl J Med* 1983; **308:** 1–7.
21. Jilka JM, Rahmatullah M, Kazemi M, Roche TE. Properties of a newly characterised protein of the bovine kidney pyruvate dehydrogenase complex. *J Biol Chem* 1986; **261:** 1858–67.
22. Rothbard J. Synthetic peptides as vaccines. *Nature* 1987; **330:** 106–07.
23. Milich DR, McLachlan A, Thornton GB, Hughes JL. Antibody production to the nucleocapsid and envelope of the hepatitis B virus primed by a single synthetic T cell site. *Nature* 1987; **329:** 547–49.
24. Gershwin ME, Coppel RL, MacKay IR. Primary biliary cirrhosis and mitochondrial autoantigens—insights from molecular biology. *Hepatology* 1988; **8:** 147–51.
25. Yamada G, Hyodo I, Tobe K, et al. Ultrastructural immunocytochemical analysis of lymphocytes infiltrating bile duct epithelium in primary biliary cirrhosis. *Hepatology* 1986; **6:** 385–91.
26. Christensen E, Crowe J, Doniach D, et al. Clinical pattern and course of disease in primary biliary cirrhosis. *Gastroenterology* 1980; **78:** 236–46.

© N Eng J Med 1989; 321: 857–862

A COMPARISON OF SCLEROTHERAPY WITH STAPLE TRANSECTION OF THE ESOPHAGUS FOR THE EMERGENCY CONTROL OF BLEEDING FROM ESOPHAGEAL VARICES

Andrew K. Burroughs, M.R.C.P., George Hamilton, F.R.C.S., Andrew Phillips, Ph.D., Guerrino Mezzanotte, Ph.D., Neil McIntyre, F.R.C.P., and Kenneth E.F. Hobbs, F.R.C.S.

Abstract We compared two procedures for the emergency treatment of bleeding esophageal varices in patients who did not respond to blood transfusion and vasoactive drugs. We randomly assigned 101 patients with cirrhosis of the liver and bleeding esophageal varices to undergo either emergency sclerotherapy (n = 50) or staple transection of the esophagus (n = 51). Four patients assigned to sclerotherapy and 12 assigned to staple transection did not actually undergo those procedures, but all analyses were made on an intention-to-treat basis.

Total mortality did not differ significantly between the two groups; the relative risk of death for staple transection as compared with sclerotherapy was 0.88 (95 percent confidence interval, 0.51 to 1.54). Mortality at six weeks was 44 percent among those assigned to sclerotherapy and 35 percent among those assigned to staple transection. Complication rates were similar for the two groups. An interval of five days without bleeding was achieved in 88 percent of those assigned to staple transection and in 62 percent of those assigned to sclerotherapy after a single injection ($P<0.01$) and 82 percent after three injections. In only 2 of the 11 patients who received a third sclerotherapy injection was bleeding controlled for more than five days, and 9 died.

We conclude that staple transection of the esophagus is as safe as sclerotherapy for the emergency treatment of bleeding esophageal varices and that it is more effective than a single sclerotherapy procedure. We currently recommend surgery after two injection treatments have failed. (N Engl J Med 1989; 321:857-62.)

EMERGENCY sclerotherapy of esophageal varices, with or without an earlier balloon tamponade, is more effective than balloon tamponade alone for the control of acute variceal bleeding.[1-3] In many medical centers, sclerotherapy is the procedure of choice and surgery is a second-line treatment. However, emergency sclerotherapy often requires more than one injection session to stop the bleeding[1-7]; in some patients the varices bleed again within a few hours of injection. The efficacy of emergency sclerotherapy is difficult to assess, because definitions of success differ and the injection is performed at various times — at the time of diagnostic endoscopy,[1,5,6] when other measures have already controlled bleeding,[3,4] or when they have failed.[3,4,7]

Hoffmann[8] reviewed the results of emergency esophageal transection with a staple gun for variceal bleeding, and included our early experience.[9] The procedure controlled bleeding in nearly all patients, and the mortality was similar to that with emergency sclerotherapy.

The aim of this prospective, randomized study was to compare endoscopic sclerotherapy with staple transection of the esophagus in the emergency management of variceal bleeding in patients with hepatic cirrhosis, with regard to short-term efficacy in controlling bleeding and mortality. We studied only patients who had failed to stop bleeding after transfusion and the administration of vasoactive drugs. We selected this group because we agree with Fleischer[10] that invasive therapy should be evaluated to treat any form of upper gastrointestinal bleeding in those who do not respond to simple noninvasive measures.

From the Hepato-biliary and Liver Transplantation Unit (A.K.B., G.H., N.M., K.E.F.H.) and the Department of Clinical Epidemiology and General Practice (A.P., G.M.), Royal Free Hospital and School of Medicine, London; and the Istituto de Biometria e Statistica Medica, University of Milan, Milan, Italy (G.M.). Address reprint requests to Dr. Burroughs at the Academic Department of Medicine, Royal Free Hospital, Pond St., London NW3 2QG, United Kingdom.

Methods

Selection of Patients

All patients admitted to the Royal Free Hospital between January 1984 and July 1987 with hematemesis or melena were included in the study if they met these conditions: an endoscopic examination showed spurting or oozing varices, the presence of a white nipple or clot on the varices, or the presence of varices without other lesions in the stomach or duodenum; there was a failure to control variceal bleeding as defined below; noncirrhotic portal hypertension had not been diagnosed; esophageal transection had not been performed previously; and no decision had been made to avoid invasive treatment for bleeding (e.g., in patients who had already reached a terminal phase of liver disease or cancer). All patients were 16 years of age or older. The study was approved by the ethics committee of the Royal Free Hospital. Written consent was obtained from the patients or from their next of kin if they had severe encephalopathy.

Failure to control acute variceal bleeding was defined as variceal bleeding that could not be controlled with the transfusion of blood or another colloid, with or without the concomitant use of drugs, within five days of time zero — defined as the time of admission to the first hospital after hematemesis or melena developed, or (for already hospitalized patients) the time when hematemesis or me-

© N Eng J Med 1989; 321: 857–862

lena occurred — according to the following criteria: if in the first 24 hours six or more units of blood or plasma were transfused within a six-hour period (in which case a balloon tamponade was used immediately); if between 18 and 24 hours there was either hematemesis or melena associated with a change in vital signs (a decline in the systolic blood pressure of 20 mm Hg or more, an increase in the pulse of at least 20 beats per minute, or both) or the need to transfuse two units of blood or plasma to maintain stable vital signs; and if between 24 hours and five days there was either hematemesis or melena associated with a change in vital signs or a decline in hemoglobin concentration of 2 g per deciliter. These criteria were used whether patients were admitted directly to the Royal Free Hospital or referred from another hospital. When the patients arrived at our hospital, their medical and nursing charts were immediately reviewed. If the eligibility criteria, including those of failure to control bleeding, were met, the patients underwent an immediate endoscopic examination and were randomly assigned to a treatment group.

Assignment to Treatment Groups

Patients were randomly assigned to treatment groups at the time of failure to control variceal bleeding. To ensure similarity in the prognostic variables, we stratified the patients into four groups, using Pugh et al.'s modification of Child's grading system[11]: grades A and B alcoholic, grades A and B nonalcoholic, grade C alcoholic, and grade C nonalcoholic. The grading is based on a numerical score derived from bilirubin and albumin levels, prothrombin time values, and measures of the severity of ascites and encephalopathy. Grade A represents well-compensated cirrhosis, grade B moderately well compensated cirrhosis, and grade C decompensated cirrhosis. For each group, a series of consecutively numbered, opaque sealed envelopes contained the assigned treatments as derived from a table of random numbers.

Treatment Protocols

Sclerotherapy

If a balloon tamponade had been used, the tube was removed in the endoscopy room. Sclerotherapy was performed with an oblique forward-viewing endoscope (Olympus GIF K_2 or K_{10}) and a 23-gauge, 4-mm or 5-mm needle (Teflon Injector, Hospital Medical Supplies; or Olympus NM3). Five percent ethanolamine oleate was injected into varices seen in the lower 2 to 3 cm of the esophagus above the esophagogastric junction. Repeated washing was used to obtain the best possible view. All variceal columns were injected, with no more than 5 ml of fluid per column. No external sheath was used.

If there was continued bleeding or a further episode of bleeding (according to the criteria above) within five days of the first injection, the patient underwent another endoscopic examination. If this confirmed further bleeding, a second injection was performed. When bleeding occurred a third time, a third endoscopic examination was performed and a final injection was administered. Variceal columns with visible ulceration were not reinjected. If bleeding — whatever its source — did not stop or if it recurred within five days of the third injection, sclerotherapy was classified as a failure, and an alternative therapy was used.

Staple Transection of the Esophagus

If a balloon tamponade had been used, the tube was removed in the operating room. Staple transection of the esophagus (EEA, Auto Suture UK) was performed through a left subcostal incision as described previously.[9] The lower esophagus was mobilized, and the staple gun was then inserted into the esophagus through a small gastrotomy. A ligature was tied around the esophagus, trapping it between the cartridge and the anvil of the gun, which was then fired, automatically transecting the esophagus and reconnecting the two ends between two rows of staples, leaving a doughnut-shaped portion of transected esophagus behind.

The successful control of bleeding was defined as a five-day interval without bleeding after the procedure. If further bleeding occurred, an endoscopic examination was performed. Alternative therapy was used only if the bleeding met any of our criteria and was considered to be major.

Patients who could not receive the assigned trial treatment were given the alternative trial treatment if possible. The criteria defining failed therapy remained the same.

All patients alive on the sixth day after the last procedure were randomly assigned to groups in a separate trial designed to compare two treatments for the prevention of variceal rebleeding (weekly elective injection of the varices vs. sucralfate). The interim analysis of that study has been reported in abstract form.[12]

Patient Outcomes

During the trial period, 192 patients were admitted with bleeding esophageal varices. In 113 of them, noninvasive measures did not control the bleeding during the first or a subsequent hospital admission; 12 of these patients were ineligible for random assignment (Table 1). Hence, 101 patients were randomly assigned to treatment groups. Among the 192 patients, there were 336 separate episodes of bleeding esophageal varices, of which 193 responded to conservative measures (severity of disease according to Pugh's grade: A, 56; B, 87; and C, 50). Only six deaths occurred within six weeks of admission, all in patients with grade C disease. Bleeding did not respond to treatment in 143 episodes (Pugh's grade: A, 17; B, 55; and C, 71).

The patients' characteristics are shown in Table 2. Clinical and laboratory variables were recorded at time zero and at the time of the procedure. The presence and cause of cirrhosis were diagnosed by liver biopsy, autopsy, or a combination of clinical and biochemical findings. Only one patient in each group had idiopathic portal hypertension.

Statistical Analysis

Our estimation of sample size was based on the expected efficacy in achieving a five-day interval without bleeding of 70 percent with a single session of sclerotherapy and 95 percent with esophageal transection. With a two-tailed test, 85 patients with 15 treatment failures were required.[13] Only one interim analysis was performed.[14]

The trial ran from time zero until either death or our last follow-up. Noncensored variables were compared by standard nonparametric methods. Analyses were carried out according to the intention-to-treat principle. Kaplan–Meier analyses were used to trace survival curves, and possible differences were tested by log-rank analysis. Survival was evaluated at six weeks and at our last follow-up. Control of bleeding was evaluated for the initial five-day interval, and rates of rebleeding after five days were also analyzed. Certain variables were evaluated as potential prognostic factors for short-term survival with the use of a Cox proportional-hazards model. Differences in survival between patients assigned to sclerotherapy and those assigned to staple transection were adjusted according to the variables found to have independent prognostic significance in the proportional-hazards model.

Results

The interval between time zero and the failure of conservative measures as assessed by a Kaplan–Meier analysis did not differ significantly between treatment groups, irrespective of the pattern of referral. There was also no significant difference between the groups in the time between the failure of conservative measures and the assigned intervention.

Four patients assigned to sclerotherapy did not receive it: one had a massive cerebral hemorrhage, one had a fatal cardiac arrest, in one the therapeutic endoscopic examination revealed bleeding from fundal varices, and in one there was a technical failure due to poor visibility, because bleeding began as soon as the

© N Eng J Med 1989; 321: 857–862

Table 1. Distribution of Pugh–Child's Grades among Patients with Cirrhosis and Bleeding Esophageal Varices during the Trial Period.

Patients	Total	Grades at Time Zero A	B	C
		number of patients		
Observed during study period	192	32	66	94
Responding to transfusion and vasoactive drugs	79*	21	27	31
Not responding to transfusion and vasoactive drugs	113	11	39	63
Ineligible for trial	12	1†	4‡	7§
Eligible for trial	101	10	35	56

*Only three (all with grade C disease) died within six weeks of time zero.

†The patient was under age 16 and was alive six weeks after time zero.

‡The patients were ineligible because of a previous transection; one died within six weeks.

§The patients were ineligible because of terminal liver disease; six died within five days (including two from known hepatocellular carcinomas).

balloon tamponade was removed. Esophageal staple transection was performed in the last two patients, and the fundal varices were oversewn in one of them.

Twelve patients assigned to staple transection did not have surgery for the following reasons: revocation of consent (one patient); uncertainty over whether the coma was due solely to hepatic encephalopathy (one); technical failure due to intraabdominal adhesions with no history of previous abdominal sepsis or surgery (one); a concomitant decision to undertake liver transplantation, which might have been jeopardized by recent upper-abdominal surgery (two); and the surgeon's refusal to operate because of hepatic deterioration with major complications, such as acute renal failure, cardiorespiratory failure, and septicemia (seven). Three of these 12 patients died within a short time; in the remaining 9, emergency sclerotherapy was performed.

Analysis of Survival

There was no significant difference in six-week survival after time zero between patients assigned to sclerotherapy (22 deaths; 44 percent) and those assigned to transection (19 deaths; 35 percent). Nor was there a significant difference in the proportion discharged from the hospital or in the length of the hospital stay (Table 3). The proportional-hazards model showed that the factors independently associated with death within six weeks were the severity of ascites and encephalopathy, the prolongation of prothrombin time, and the use of a balloon tamponade. After adjustment for these prognostic factors, there was still no significant difference in survival between the two groups.

Long-term survival (Fig. 1) was not significantly different. At 12 months, 42 percent and 45 percent of the sclerotherapy and transection groups, respectively, were still alive. The relative risk of death with transection as compared with sclerotherapy was 0.88 (95 percent confidence interval, 0.51 to 1.54). The elective treatment — either sclerotherapy or oral sucralfate — to which patients from both trial groups were randomly assigned did not influence the comparison of survival.

Efficacy of Controlling Bleeding

The efficacy of controlling bleeding was evaluated according to the intention-to-treat principle (Table 3). There was an interval of five days without bleeding in 45 of the 51 patients (88 percent) assigned to transection (5 of whom actually received sclerotherapy as the primary procedure), as compared with 31 of the 50 (62 percent) assigned to sclerotherapy who had five days without bleeding after a single injection (2 of whom actually had transection as the primary procedure) ($P<0.01$). Of the 50 patients assigned to sclero-

Table 2. Characteristics of Treatment Groups.

Characteristic	Sclerotherapy Group (N = 50)	Transection Group (N = 51)
Age (yr) — median (range)*	55 (17–77)	53 (22–83)
Male/female (no.)*	36/14	27/24
Cause of cirrhosis (no.)*		
Alcoholic	24	27
Cryptogenic	10	10
Biliary	8	9
Other	8	5
Pugh's grade at time zero (no.)		
A	5	5
B	17	18
C	28	28
Ascites at time zero (no.)*		
None	20	29
Minimal	12	15
Moderate or severe	18	17
Encephalopathy at time zero (%)*		
None	24	31
Minimal	14	14
Moderate or severe	11	6
Bilirubin at time zero (μmol/liter) — median (range)*	53 (6–600)	64 (15–630)
Albumin at time zero (g/liter) — median (range)*	30 (15–40)	30 (16–42)
Prothrombin time at time zero (sec) — median (range)*	19 (12–34)	18 (13–47)
Previous variceal bleeding (no.)	23	26
Previous elective sclerotherapy (no.)	5	9
Previous nonvariceal bleeding (no.)	8	7
Started bleeding as inpatient (no.)*	19	17
Referred patients/referred patients in whom conservative measures had failed before referral	35/18	30/13
Hours between start of bleeding and admission to hospital — median (range)*	4 (1–58)	5 (1–132)
Vasoactive drugs (no.)*		
None	8	6
Vasopressin or terlipressin (Glypressin)	27	22
Somatostatin	15	23
Balloon tamponade (no.)*	31	24
Hours from time zero to failure of conservative management — median (range)*	24 (3–129)	35 (5–119)
Hours from time zero to procedure — median (range)*	46 (6–140)	53 (9–153)
Units of blood and plasma used before procedure — median (range)*	13 (5–34)	14 (5–49)

*Variable analyzed in Cox's proportional-hazards model as a potential prognostic factor for short-term survival.

therapy, 41 (82 percent) had bleeding controlled with up to three injection sessions. Excluding the 4 who did not receive sclerotherapy, the efficacy of a single injection session was similar in those originally assigned to this treatment (29 of 46 [63 percent]) and those who crossed over from the group assigned to transection (5 of 9 [55 percent]). Success with up to three sessions was also of the same magnitude: 37 of 46 (80 percent) and 9 of 9, respectively.

Sources of further bleeding within five days of the procedures were very different (Table 3). Three sessions of sclerotherapy failed to control bleeding in nine patients, in six of whom the sources were esophageal (one ulcer and five varices). Further procedures were required in seven: five had esophageal transection (although bleeding was controlled in all of them, only one survived), and two had transhepatic percutaneous sclerosis of varicies (both died after bleeding had been controlled only temporarily).

Of the 51 patients assigned to transection, 39 underwent the procedure. None of them had further bleeding from varices, and none required further procedures. Nine patients who were assigned to transection in fact received sclerotherapy as the primary procedure; four of them had further bleeding from varices within five days and required a second injection session, which was successful in all. The number of units of blood and plasma used during the procedures and

Table 3. Efficacy of Emergency Sclerotherapy and Staple Transection in Achieving Hemostasis in Patients with Cirrhosis and Bleeding Esophageal Varices Who Did Not Respond to Conservative Measures.

Measure	Sclerotherapy Group (N = 50)*	Transection Group (N = 51)†
	number of patients	
Bleeding controlled after		
One session	31 (62%)‡	45 (88%)§
Two sessions	39 (78%)	49 (96%)¶
Three sessions	41 (82%)	0
Failed procedures	9	2
Cause of rebleeding		
Esophageal varices	5	0
Esophageal ulcer	1	0
Gastric varices	2	0
Peptic ulcer	1	1
Gastrostomy site	0	1
Further procedures	7	0
Blood and plasma units used during procedures and for next five days	380	291
Death within six weeks	22 (44%)	18 (35%)
Discharged from hospital	28 (56%)	31 (61%)
Hospital stay (days) — median (range)	15 (1–48)	19 (1–96)

*Includes two patients who did not receive treatment because of rapidly fatal complications (intracerebral bleeding and cardiac arrest).

†Includes three patients who did not receive treatment because of rapidly fatal complications (septicemia with renal and cardiopulmonary failure).

‡Includes both of the patients who received a transection as the primary procedure.

§Includes five of the nine patients who received sclerotherapy as the primary procedure. P<0.01 for the comparison with the sclerotherapy group.

¶Includes four of the nine patients who received sclerotherapy as the primary procedure and required two sessions to achieve hemostasis. P<0.05 for the comparison with the sclerotherapy group.

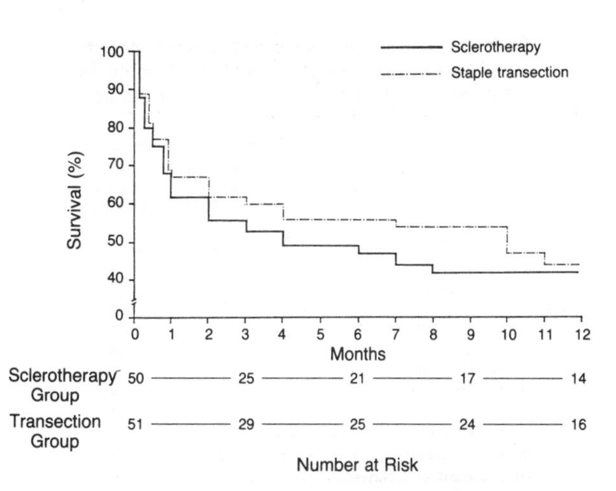

Figure 1. Long-Term Survival from Time Zero in 101 Patients in Whom Conservative Measures Failed in the First Five Days.
P = 0.45 by the log-rank test for the comparison between the transection and the sclerotherapy groups.

in the next five days was substantially lower in the group assigned to transection: 291 units, as compared with 380 units in the sclerotherapy group.

An evaluation of episodes of rebleeding during the first 42 days according to the treatment received rather than the treatment assigned (regardless of severity and source) showed rebleeding in 23 of the 55 patients (42 percent) who received a single injection, as compared with 3 of the 41 patients (7 percent) who received staple transection (P<0.001). The magnitude of these differences was comparable to that of the differences between patients assigned to long-term sclerotherapy and sucralfate in the separate trial for the prevention of rebleeding.[12]

Complications

Complications were assessed between admission to the hospital and discharge or death, according to the intention-to-treat principle (Table 4). Their incidence was similar in both groups, with the exception of ascitic infections and dysphagia lasting more than four days, which were more frequent in the transection group, and bleeding sclerotherapy ulcers, which were more common in the sclerotherapy group. Complications were thought to have contributed directly to death in about 10 percent of the patients in each group.

Discussion

This randomized, controlled trial compared esophageal staple transection with endoscopic sclerotherapy as emergency procedures in 101 patients with hepatic cirrhosis whose variceal bleeding had failed to respond to blood transfusion and vasoactive drugs. We found no significant difference in either short-term or long-term survival between patients in the two groups. In more than half the patients, conservative measures to control variceal bleeding had failed within 35 hours; over half the patients underwent a procedure within 53 hours of the onset of bleeding. As a single measure,

© N Eng J Med 1989; 321: 857–862

Table 4. Complications Recorded between Hospital Admission and Discharge or Death in Patients Assigned to Emergency Sclerotherapy or Staple Transection.

Complication	Sclerotherapy Group (N = 50)	Transection Group (N = 51)
	no. of patients	
Renal failure	18	17
Bronchopneumonia	16	19
Ascitic infection	10	16
Septicemia	15	14
Pleural effusion	11	8
Wound infection	2	4
Other infection	2	1
Pulmonary embolism	3	1
Incisional hernia	0	1
Gastric stasis or recurrent vomiting	0	1
Portal-vein thrombosis	2	0
Splenic and bowel infarct	1*	0
Dysphagia (of 4 days' duration)	0	7
Bleeding sclerotherapy ulcer	7	1
Bleeding staple line	1†	7
Esophageal perforation	0	1‡
Esophageal dehiscence	1†	0
Dilated esophageal stricture	0	1
Complications considered related to death	5	5

*Associated with portal-vein thrombosis.

†In one of the five patients who had transection after the failure of three sessions of sclerotherapy; in the other four the anastomosis was intact.

‡In one patient who was referred with a Sengstaken-Blakemore tube that had been in situ for 72 hours, with pressure ulceration and necrosis at the mouth due to traction of the tube. At autopsy a perforation 3 cm above the transection line was seen.

staple transection was more effective than sclerotherapy and was followed by a lower incidence of rebleeding in the long term. Two similar studies have been published since the start of our trial. Among 66 patients in one study,[15] staple transection was superior in controlling bleeding and preventing further bleeding (despite repeated injection in the sclerotherapy group) and had a similar mortality rate. In the other,[16] only 26 of the 32 patients randomly assigned were analyzed; only 1 was included because of continued bleeding close to the time of admission (within 60 hours). Despite a comparatively low success rate with transection (71 percent),[8] the mortality and late rebleeding rates among patients who underwent that procedure were not significantly different from those among the patients who received sclerotherapy. The results of these studies are difficult to compare with ours because of different times of entry into the trials.[17,18]

In an earlier randomized study with only 13 patients, Cello et al.[19] concluded in a retrospective analysis that emergency sclerotherapy was better than staple transection and that patients who underwent staple transection did worse than those who received shunts. In their subsequent trial of emergency sclerotherapy as compared with portacaval shunts,[20] the shunts resulted in better control of early (19 vs. 50 percent) and late (0 vs. 75 percent) rebleeding and had a similar mortality. The characteristics of our patients and the timing of our procedures were similar to those of Cello et al. According to Cello's method of classification,[20] the severity of disease in 80 percent of the patients in our sclerotherapy group and 75 percent of those in our transection group was Child's grade C at the time of the procedures.

The high rebleeding rate (50 percent or more) after emergency sclerotherapy with repeated injections that was found in all the randomized studies, including this one, is probably related to the severity of the underlying liver disease. In all these studies at least 80 percent of the patients had grade B or C disease. In a prospective evaluation of sclerotherapy in 175 patients, Sauerbruch et al.[21] found a rebleeding rate of 68 percent in patients with grade C disease, 47 percent in those with grade B, and only 13 percent in those with grade A; only half the patients received sclerotherapy as an emergency procedure. Prindiville et al.[22] found a more frequent incidence of rebleeding after sclerotherapy when the procedure was performed during the episode of acute variceal bleeding (50 percent) rather than as an elective treatment (30 percent). The combined influences of the timing of the injection and the severity of the liver disease make detailed comparisons between randomized trials difficult. The severity of the liver disease also affects rates of rebleeding after staple transection.[16] Our incidence of early rebleeding (within 30 days after transection) was 3 of 41 (7 percent); in none of these cases was the source of bleeding the varices. This is comparable to the incidence reported after emergency or urgent shunts: 37 of 180 (21 percent) among unselected patients[23] (only 4 from varices); 6 of 32 (19 percent) among patients with decompensated cirrhosis[20]; and only 1 of 36 (3 percent) among well-compensated patients with hepatic cirrhosis.[24]

In only 2 of the 11 patients in our study who had another episode of bleeding after the second emergency injection was their bleeding controlled for at least five days after the third session, and only 2 survived. All of them had been assigned to sclerotherapy. Five of the nine patients in whom sclerotherapy failed subsequently underwent esophageal transection. All stopped bleeding, but only one survived. The other four died of hepatic failure and sepsis, suggesting that their surgery was too late. This emphasizes the fact that a decision about whether sclerotherapy has failed must be made early, because treating these patients successfully becomes increasingly difficult. Thus, we currently perform surgery after two injections have failed to control bleeding. Bornman et al. use a similar schedule.[25]

Our rate of success with emergency sclerotherapy may appear lower than that reported in other series. However, it is important to emphasize that unlike some others,[1,5,6] we performed emergency sclerotherapy only in patients who failed to stop bleeding or had a further episode of bleeding within five days of their admission to the hospital. If emergency sclerotherapy had been performed for all 336 admissions during the trial period — and assuming that the 193 cases of bleeding that were arrested with conservative measures would have stopped equally quickly with emergency injections — a five-day interval without bleeding would have followed in 87 percent of the cases treated with one injection and in 92 percent of those treated with three.

The reported efficacy of emergency sclerotherapy (performed without awaiting the results of conservative measures) in unselected patients with cirrhosis and bleeding esophageal varices is quite variable. Paquet et al.[1] achieved immediate hemostasis in 95 percent (22) of their patients; Soderlund and Ihre.[3] controlled bleeding for 48 hours in 95 percent (57) of theirs; Larson et al.[2] achieved five days without bleeding in 81 percent (44, at least a third of whom received a second injection within four days); and Terblanche et al.[4] achieved control in 75 percent after one injection and 92 percent after multiple injections (35 cases with active variceal bleeding at diagnostic endoscopic examination). Crotty et al.[5] reported that 65 percent of their 56 patients went 48 hours without bleeding, and 50 percent went five days. Westaby et al.[26] had an 82 percent success rate after 12 hours (33 cases) with a single injection for active variceal bleeding when endoscopic examination was performed within 4 hours of admission. Further bleeding after admission occurred in 31 percent of the patients. Thus, our success rates with sclerotherapy are comparable to these, even disregarding our rigid selection procedure. Recent claims of improved efficacy with new techniques in consecutive series of patients should be examined in randomized studies.[27,28]

Staple transection has a role as a first-line treatment in the emergency management of bleeding esophageal varices. If emergency sclerotherapy is used, no more than two injection sessions should be attempted. The hospital costs of the two treatments are similar in our institution.[29]

We are indebted to the following consultant physicians and surgeons for referring the patients enrolled in this trial: Drs. Armstrong and Storing (Barking Hospital); Drs. Apthorpe, Spence, and Williams and Mr. Sagor (St. Alban's City Hospital); Drs. Borthwick and Willoughby (Lister Hospital); Drs. Barnes, Gray, and Pearson (Barnet General Hospital); Dr. Bevan (Edgware General Hospital); Drs. Freedman, Kinlock, and Peters and Mr. Bolton (Chase Farm Hospital); Drs. Diggle and Fairman (Pilgrim Hospital); Dr. Farrow (Watford General Hospital); Dr. Govan (Hillingdon Hospital); Drs. Glick and Wright (Whipps Cross Hospital); Dr. Hodgson (Royal Postgraduate Medical School–Hammersmith Hospital); Drs. Jain and Nicoll and Mr. Rothwell-Jackson (Luton and Dunstable Hospital); Dr. Keir (Queen Elizabeth Hospital, Welwyn Garden City); Dr. McMichael (Ealing General Hospital); Mr. Noon (King George's Hospital, Ilford); Drs. Pringle, Ramsay, and Woolf (North Middlesex Hospital); Dr. Room (Bromley Hospital); Dr. Saunders (Bedford General Hospital); and Dr. Souhami (University College Hospital). We are also indebted to the following medical and surgical junior staff members who contributed to the smooth running of the trial: Drs. Jeffrey, Kibbler, Thomas, Kaye, Sawyerr, and McCormick and Messrs. Evans, Li, and Shaw.

References

1. Paquet KJ, Feussner H. Endoscopic sclerosis and esophageal balloon tamponade in acute hemorrhage from esophagogastric varices: a prospective controlled randomized trial. Hepatology 1985; 5:580-3.
2. Larson AW, Cohen H, Zweiban B, et al. Acute esophageal variceal sclerotherapy: results of a prospective randomized controlled trial. JAMA 1986; 255:497-500.
3. Soderlund C, Ihre T. Endoscopic sclerotherapy v. conservative management of bleeding oesophageal varices: a 5-year prospective controlled trial of emergency and long-term treatment. Acta Chir Scand 1985; 151:449-56.
4. Terblanche J, Northover JM, Bornman P, et al. A prospective evaluation of injection sclerotherapy in the treatment of acute bleeding from esophageal varices. Surgery 1979; 85:239-45.
5. Crotty B, Wood LJ, Willett IR, Colman J, McCarthy P, Dudley FJ. The management of acutely bleeding varices by injection sclerotherapy. Med J Aust 1986; 145:130-3.
6. Sarin SK, Nanda R, Kumar N, Vij JC, Anand BS. Repeated endoscopic sclerotherapy for active variceal bleeding. Ann Surg 1985; 202:708-11.
7. Fleig WE, Stange EF, Ruettenauer K, Ditschuneit H. Emergency endoscopic sclerotherapy for bleeding esophageal varices: a prospective study in patients not responding to balloon tamponade. Gastrointest Endosc 1983; 29:8-14.
8. Hoffmann J. Stapler transection of the oesophagus for bleeding oesophageal varices. Scand J Gastroenterol 1983; 18:707-11.
9. Osborne DR, Hobbs KE. The acute treatment of haemorrhage from oesophageal varices: a comparison of oesophageal transection and staple gun anastomosis with mesocaval shunt. Br J Surg 1981; 68:734-7.
10. Fleischer D. Etiology and prevalence of severe persistent upper gastrointestinal bleeding. Gastroenterology 1983; 84:538-43.
11. Pugh RN, Murray-Lyon IM, Dawson JL, Pietroni MC, Williams R. Transection of the oesophagus for bleeding oesophageal varices. Br J Surg 1973; 60:646-9.
12. Burroughs AK, D'Heygere F, Phillips A, Dooley J, Epstein O, McIntyre N. Prospective randomised trial of chronic sclerotherapy for prevention of variceal rebleeding using the same protocol to treat bleeding: interim analysis. J Hepatol 1986; 3:Suppl 2:S55. abstract.
13. Freedman LS. Tables of the number of patients required in clinical trials using the logrank test. Stat Med 1982; 1:121-9.
14. Burroughs AK, D'Heygere F, Phillips A, Hobbs KEF, McIntyre N. Prospective, randomised trial of endoscopic sclerotherapy versus esophageal staple transection for acute variceal bleeding: single interim analysis. J Hepatol 1986; 3:Suppl 2:S25. abstract.
15. Huizinga WK, Angorn IB, Baker LW. Esophageal transection versus injection sclerotherapy in the management of bleeding esophageal varices in patients at high risk. Surg Gynecol Obstet 1985; 160:539-46.
16. Teres J, Baroni R, Bordas JM, Visa J, Pera C, Rodes J. Randomized trial of portacaval shunt, stapling transection and endoscopic sclerotherapy in uncontrolled variceal bleeding. J Hepatol 1987; 4:159-67.
17. Smith JL, Graham DY. Variceal hemorrhage: a critical evaluation of survival analysis. Gastroenterology 1982; 82:968-73.
18. Burroughs AK, Mezzanotte G, Phillips A, McCormick PA, McIntyre N. Cirrhotics with variceal hemorrhage: the importance of the time interval between admission and the start of analysis for survival and rebleeding rates. Hepatology 1989; 9:801-7.
19. Cello JP, Crass R, Trunkey DD. Endoscopic sclerotherapy versus esophageal transection in Child's class C patients with variceal hemorrhage: comparison with results of portacaval shunt: preliminary report. Surgery 1982; 91:333-8.
20. Cello JP, Grendell JH, Crass RA, Weber TE, Trunkey DD. Endoscopic sclerotherapy versus portacaval shunt in patients with severe cirrhosis and acute variceal hemorrhage: long-term follow-up. N Engl J Med 1987; 316:11-5.
21. Sauerbruch T, Weinzierl M, Ansari H, Paumgartner G. Injection sclerotherapy of oesophageal variceal haemorrhage: a prospective long-term follow-up study. Endoscopy 1987; 19:181-4.
22. Prindiville T, Miller M, Trudeau W. Prognostic indicators in acute variceal hemorrhage after treatment by sclerotherapy. Am J Gastroenterol 1987; 82:655-9.
23. Orloff MJ, Bell RH Jr, Hyde PV, Skivolocki WP. Long-term results of emergency portacaval shunt for bleeding esophageal varices in unselected patients with alcoholic cirrhosis. Ann Surg 1980; 192:325-40.
24. Villeneuve J-P, Pomier-Layrargues G, Duguay L, et al. Emergency portacaval shunt for variceal hemorrhage: a prospective study. Ann Surg 1987; 206:48-52.
25. Bornman PC, Terblanche J, Kahn D, Jonker MA, Kirsch RE. Limitations of multiple injection sclerotherapy sessions for acute variceal bleeding. S Afr Med J 1986; 70:34-6.
26. Westaby D, Hayes PC, Gimson AE, Polson RJ, Williams R. Controlled clinical trial of injection sclerotherapy for active variceal bleeding. Hepatology 1989; 9:274-7.
27. Soehendra N, Grimm H, Nam VC, Berger B. N-butyl-2-cyanoacrylate: a supplement to endoscopic sclerotherapy. Endoscopy 1987; 19:221-4.
28. Kitano S, Koyanagi N, Iso Y, Higashi H, Sugimachi K. Prevention of recurrence of esophageal varices after endoscopic injection sclerotherapy with ethanolamine oleate. Hepatology 1987; 7:810-5.
29. Burroughs AK, Qadiri M, D'Heygere F, et al. Hospital costs of upper gastrointestinal bleeding in cirrhotics. Gut 1986; 27:A596. abstract.

© *Lancet* 1989; ii: 588–591

MUTATION PREVENTING FORMATION OF HEPATITIS B e ANTIGEN IN PATIENTS WITH CHRONIC HEPATITIS B INFECTION

W. F. CARMAN
M. R. JACYNA
S. HADZIYANNIS
P. KARAYIANNIS
M. J. MCGARVEY
A. MAKRIS
H. C. THOMAS

Departments of Medicine, St Mary's Hospital Medical School, London, and Hippocration Hospital, Athens, Greece

Summary Some patients with chronic hepatitis B virus (HBV) infection are HB e antigen (HBeAg) negative, have circulating HBV particles, and often have especially severe chronic hepatitis. To test the hypothesis that the absence of HBeAg production may be due to a change in the nucleotide sequence of the pre-core region of the genome, 18 Greek and 3 non-Greek patients positive for HB surface antigen underwent direct sequencing of HBV-DNA amplified from sera. In 7 out of 8 HBeAg negative patients, two mutations (guanosine to adenosine) were found in the terminal two codons of the pre-core region, giving the sequence TAGGACATG. The remaining patient had the first mutation only. The sequence TGGGGCATG was found in 4 of 5 of the HBeAg positive patients. The first mutation results in a translational stop codon that is predicted to result in failure to produce HBeAg. The rest of the pre-core region in the HBeAg negative patiénts was otherwise homologous to that of the HBeAg positive patients and to known sequences.

Introduction

PATIENTS who are chronically positive for hepatitis B surface antigen (HBsAg) in serum can be divided into three groups: (A) HB e antigen (HBeAg) positive, viraemic, and with chronic liver disease;[1] (B) HBeAg negative and anti-HBe positive, yet viraemic and frequently with more severe and rapidly progressive liver disease;[2,3] and (C) anti-HBe positive without viraemia or liver disease. The third group are either from group A and have seroconverted or have gone from acute hepatitis into a simple carrier state without chronic hepatitis developing. From the second group the possibility arises that HBeAg may modify the course of the disease.

© *Lancet* 1989; ii: 588–591

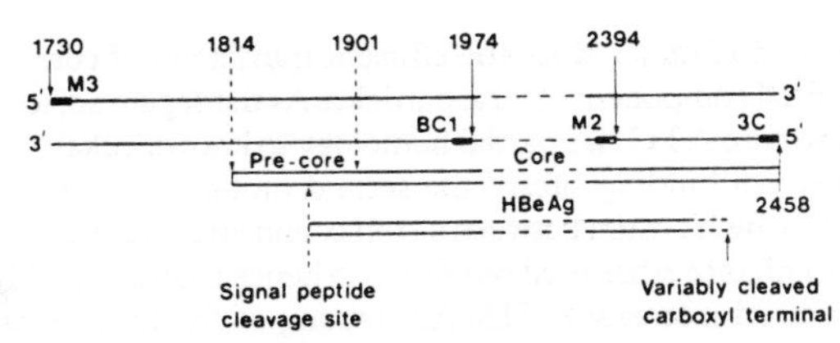

Fig 1—Target sequence for DNA amplification.

Upper strand has positive polarity. In-vivo derivation of translated peptides is shown. Nucleotide numbering is taken from Ono et al.[4] Precore ATG begins at position 1814, and that of core at 1901. Positions of DNA amplification primers M3 (5'CTGGGAGGAGTTGGGGGAGGA-GATT), 3C (5'CTAACATTGAGATTCCCGAGA), and M2 (5'GGCGAGGGAGTTCTTCTTCTAGGGG), and sequencing primer BC1 (5'GGAAAGAAGTCAGAAGGCAA) are shown.

HBeAg is derived by proteolysis of the translation product of the entire pre-core/core open reading frame (ORF) (fig 1). The pre-core region consists of 87 base pairs (encoding 29 aminoacids) immediately upstream of the core gene, which codes for nucleocapsid protein. Both regions are in the same reading frame, but have separate start codons. The pre-core region is not necessary for production of viral particles,[5] yet is highly conserved in all of the hepadna viruses.[4,6] The aminoterminus of the pre-core region encodes a 19-aminoacid signal peptide,[5] which facilitates the secretion of HBeAg via the intracellular membrane system. After cleavage of the signal peptide, HBeAg consists of the remaining 10 aminoacids and most of the core protein (fig 1).

We have sequenced HBV-DNA enzymatically amplified from the sera of patients in groups A–C. We detected mutations that are likely to account for the lack of HBeAg secretion in patients from group B.

Patients and Methods

Patients.—Sera were taken from 21 HBsAg positive Greek patients. 6 were HBeAg positive and HBV-DNA positive by dot-blot hybridisation (group A); 8 were positive for anti-HBe and HBV-DNA (group B); and 7 were anti-HBe positive but HBV-DNA negative (group C). All isolates were subtype ayw. Sera were also taken from 3 non-Greek patients. Details of the 18 Greek patients who had a positive result on DNA amplification and whose DNA was sequenced are shown in the table. During the period of known HBsAg positivity, which dates from the time of first presentation with chronic hepatitis, only patients 6 and 12 in group B were HBeAg positive at any stage.

HBV markers.—Serum HBV markers were assayed with Abbott kits. HBV-DNA was detected by dot-blot hybridisation.[7] HBcAg was detected in liver biopsy specimens by immunofluorescence with polyclonal antisera.[8]

DNA amplification.—100 µl serum was digested with 1 mg/ml proteinase K (Boehringer-Mannheim) in 25 mmol/l sodium acetate and 2·5 mmol/l edetic acid buffer pH 8 containing 0·6% sodium dodecyl sulphate for 2 h at 56°C. After phenol/chloroform extraction and ethanol precipitation, the viral nucleic acid was resuspended in water. The pre-core/core gene was amplified.[9] Fig 1 shows the target sequence and the positions and sequences of the oligonucleotide primers. Forty cycles were done (95°C 1 min, 55°C 1 min, and 72°C 2 min) in the presence of 2·5 units of *Taq* polymerase (Anglian Biotec). Controls included two sera taken from staff with no HBV markers and the substitution of water for DNA template.

Sequencing.—The amplified products were made up to 200 µl with 10 mmol/l "tris" and 1 mmol/l edetic acid buffer pH 8·0 and spun through a 'Sephadex G-50' column (Pharmacia). The void volume was ethanol-precipitated, dried, and resuspended in 20 µl water. Depending upon concentration (agarose gel electrophoresis), 1–3 µl DNA was used for sequencing. 10 pmol primer BC1 was end-labelled with 20 µCi γ-^{32}P-ATP (Amersham) with 10 units polynucleotide kinase (Boehringer-Mannheim). Unincorporated label was separated on a G-50 column. Labelled primer was precipitated and resuspended in 20 µl water; 5 µl was adequate for each sequencing reaction. The protocol recommended for use with 'Sequenase 2·0' (United States Biochemicals) was used for sequencing. DNA and labelled BC1 were heated to 95°C for 2 min, held at 55°C for 10 min, then allowed to cool to room temperature. No labelling step was done. Primed-DNA/enzyme mixtures were added directly to termination mixes which had been diluted with an equal volume of water. The reaction proceeded for 5 min at 37°C. 2 µl sequence mixture was electrophoresed on 6% and 5% 'Sequagel' (National Diagnostics). Autoradiography was done with and without intensifying screens.

CLINICAL AND LABORATORY DETAILS OF 18 GREEK PATIENTS WITH SEQUENCED ISOLATES

Patient (Age [yr]/sex)	ALT (IU/l)	Liver histology	HBcAg* (%)	Period of HBsAg positivity (yr)
Group A (HBeAG+, HBV-DNA+)				
1 (21/M)	108	CPH + lob	50	1·3
2 (50/F)	285	CAH	50	5·0
3 (66/F)	120	CAH	80	1·0
4 (30/M)	232	CAH	30	1·2
5 (36/M)	180	CAH	15	1·7
Group B (anti-HBe+, HBV-DNA+)				
6 (40/F)	197	CPH + lob	< 5	1·8
7 (54/M)	149	CAH	15	1·3
8 (41/M)	141	CAH	10	4·0
9 (33/M)	198	CAH + cirr	20	5·0
10 (65/M)	488	CAH + cirr	50	11·0
11 (32/M)	255	CAH	55	1·2
12 (57/M)	128	CAH	ND	13·0
13 (43/M)	180	CAH	10	13·0
Group C (anti-HBe+, HBV-DNA−)				
14 (58/M)	26	Normal	0	10·0
15 (59/M)	19	Fibrosis	0	17·0
16 (44/M)	27	CPH	<5	15·0
17 (44/M)	17	Normal	0	2·2
18 (31/M)	60	Normal	0	1·3

*Percentage of hepatocytes positive by immunofluorescence.
ALT = alanine aminotransferase, CPH = chronic persistent hepatitis, CAH = chronic active hepatitis, lob = lobular hepatitis, and cirr = cirrhosis.

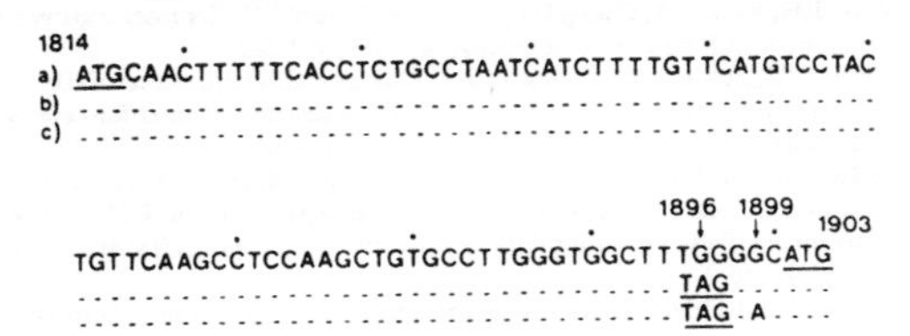

Fig 2—Sequences a, b, and c of pre-core genes of HBV.

Translational start (ATG) and stop (TAG) codons underlined. Mutations are at positions 1896 and 1899.

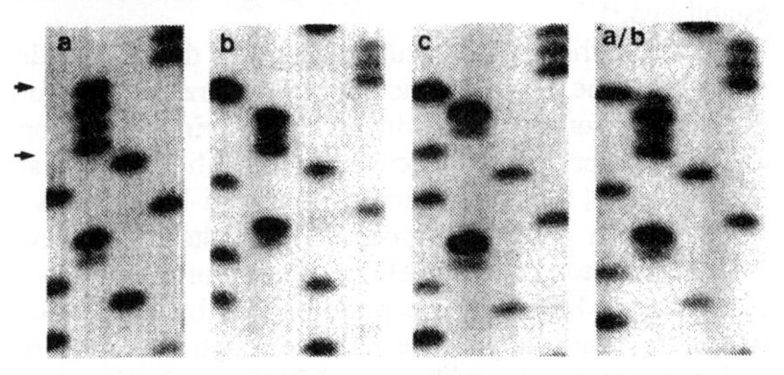

Fig 3— Sequencing gel of negative strand of four isolates (patients 3, 6, 9, and 14; left to right) showing point mutations.

Order of lanes is TCGA. Mutations (C to T) arrowed (upper = 1896, lower = 1899). Isolate from patient 14 shows mixture of strains (sequences a and b) at 1896.

Results

DNA was successfully amplified from 5 out of 6 patients in group A, 8 out of 8 in group B, and 5 out of 7 in group C, and from the 3 non-Greek sera. All controls were negative.

4 patients in group A had sequence a (figs 2 and 3), which is homologous to known HBV sequences.[6] The 3 non-Greek HBeAg positive patients also had sequence a. 7 out of 8 group B patients had sequence c, resulting from the substitution of an adenosine for guanosine at positions 1896 and 1899. Patient 6 (in group B) had a single mutation at position 1896 (sequence b). Patients 14–18 (group C) seemed to have a mixture of strains, as shown by bands at the same position in two lanes on the sequencing gel (fig 3). This occurred only in sera from this group of patients. In these 5 cases, adenosine was present at position 1896 (sequence b), either as the stronger band (compared with the expected guanosine) in 3 patients, or the fainter band in 2 cases. The second mutation occurred in 3 of these 5 patients, but only as a faint band.

Patient 5, in group A, had sequence b. This is difficult to explain, since a translational stop codon (TAG) should result in an inability to secrete HBeAg. However, this patient is unusual in that he is known to have been anti-HBe positive 1 year previously. The sequence of the pre-core gene from all patients was otherwise homologous to the published sequence. Patient 5 (group A) and patient 6 (group B) had less HBcAg staining than the other patients in their respective groups (table); both these patients had sequence b.

Discussion

Point mutations in viral sequences have important effects on pathogenicity. For example, in poliovirus type 3, a single base change results in loss of neurovirulence.[10] Enzymatic DNA amplification and sequencing[11,12] allows the rapid comparison of sequences of multiple viral isolates without the need for cloning. For example, before our study, the pre-core sequences of 11 HBV isolates only had been described.[5] With our additional sequences, the conservation of this region in HBV isolates has been confirmed.

Seroconversion from HBeAg to anti-HBe was thought to imply loss of viraemia, but the new molecular techniques have revealed HBV-DNA in some anti-HBe positive patients (5–60%, depending on racial origins).[13] However, as we found, even patients who are anti-HBe positive and HBV-DNA negative by dot-blot hybridisation had HBV-DNA detectable by enzymatic amplification. Less than 1 pg of nucleic acid is being detected by this method, but whether this represents intact virions or free viral DNA released from leucocytes or necrotic hepatocytes has not been established.[14,15]

We tested the hypothesis that changes in the nucleotide sequence of the pre-core region of HBV are responsible for the failure of some patients with continuing viral replication and severe liver disease to secrete HBeAg. The mutation at position 1896, which was found in all anti-HBe positive patients with viraemia (group B), results in a new translational stop codon (TAG) at the end of the pre-core region. Since HBeAg is a peptide derived by continuous translation from the pre-core region through into the core region, this stop codon will prevent HBeAg production. In 7 of these patients, a second mutation at position 1899 was also found. Since translation of the core ORF is thought to occur by ribosome binding to the 5′ end of the pre-core/core mRNA followed by initiation at the core ATG,[16] the new stop codon may reduce the efficient translation of core, an essential component of viral particles. As the region adjacent to the core ATG has partial homology to known eukaryotic ribosomal binding sites,[17] the second mutation at position 1899, which occurs between a stop codon and a start codon, may enhance ribosomal binding and hence translation. The decreased intensity of HBcAg staining of the liver biopsy specimens from both patients with a stop codon alone (no 5 and 6) is evidence to support this hypothesis, which we are now testing. Patient 6 did not have the additional mutation at position 1899 and had milder histological disease. She was known to have been HBeAg positive previously.

Patients in group C had little replicating virus, as shown by the lack of HBcAg in liver tissue and the inability to detect HBV-DNA in serum by dot-blot hybridisation. Sequence analysis of amplified DNA showed a heterogeneous population of viral genomes. The significance of this is unclear and studies on viral DNA obtained from liver are required.

No patient in this study gave a history of acute hepatitis, so we do not know if the patients in group B were ever HBeAg positive. Thus whether these mutations are present in the infecting virus or whether they occur in response to pressure in the infected host is not resolved. Whether these mutations influence the severity of the liver disease is also not known. Both HBcAg and HBeAg have been suggested as targets for cytotoxic T cells[18,19] and circulating HBeAg may modulate the attack. If HBe epitopes are presented on the hepatocyte surface, then the absence of circulating HBeAg may allow more aggressive cell-mediated immune lysis of infected hepatocytes and, therefore, more severe disease. A second possibility is that a truncated pre-core peptide is produced, terminating at the stop codon produced by the mutation. This peptide may be transported to the cell membrane in association with major histocompatibility complex glycoprotein, where it could become a new target for cytotoxic T cells. A third possibility is that the peptide is directly cytopathic to the hepatocyte.

We thank Helen Alsop for preparation of the typescript and Sheila Jones for the line drawings. W. F. C. receives a James Gear Fellowship of the Poliomyelitis Research Foundation. M. J. M. is supported by the Wellcome Trust.

Correspondence should be addressed to W. F. C., Department of Medicine, St Mary's Hospital, Paddington, London W2 1NY.

REFERENCES

1. Chu CM, Karayiannis P, Fowler MJF, Monyardino J, Liaw YF, Thomas HC. Natural history of chronic hepatitis B virus infection in Taiwan: studies of hepatitis B virus DNA in serum. *Hepatology* 1985; 5: 431–34.
2. Bonino F, Rosina F, Rizzetto M, et al. Chronic hepatitis in HBsAg carriers with serum HBV-DNA and anti-HBe. *Gastroenterology* 1986; 90: 1268–73.
3. Wu J-C, Lee S-D, Tsay S-H, et al. Symptomatic anti-HBe positive chronic hepatitis B in Taiwan with special reference to persistent HBV replication and HDV superinfection. *J Med Virol* 1988; 25: 141–48.
4. Ono Y, Onda H, Sasada R, Igarashi K, Sugino Y, Nishioka K. The complete nucleotide sequences of the cloned hepatitis B virus DNA; subtype adr and adw. *Nucl Acid Res* 1983; 11: 1747–57.
5. Schlicht HJ, Salfedt J, Schaller H. The duck hepatitis B virus pre-c region encodes a signal sequence which is essential for synthesis and secretion of processed core proteins but not for virus formation. *J Virol* 1987; 61: 3701–09.
6. Miller RH, Kaneko S, Chung CT, Girones R, Purcell RH. Compact organisation of the hepatitis B virus genome. *Hepatology* 1989; 9: 322–27.
7. Weller IVD, Fowler MJF, Monjardino J, Thomas HC. The detection of HBV-DNA in serum by molecular hybridisation: a more sensitive method for detection of complete HBV particles. *J Med Virol* 1982; 9: 273–80.
8. Hadziyannis SJ, Lieberman HM, Karvountzes GG, Shafritz DA. Analysis of liver disease, nuclear HBcAg, viral replication, and hepatitis B virus DNA in liver and serum of HBeAg versus anti-HBe positive carriers of hepatitis B virus. *Hepatology* 1983; 2: 656–62.
9. Carman WF, Kidd AH. An assessment of optimal conditions for amplification of HIV cDNA using *Thermus aquaticus* polymerase. *J Virol Methods* 1989; 23: 277–90.
10. Evans DMA, Dunn G, Minor PD, et al. A single nucleotide change in the 5′ non-coding region of the genome of the Sabin type 3 poliovaccine is associated with increased neurovirulence. *Nature* 1985; 314: 548–50.

References continued at foot of next page

W. F. CARMAN AND OTHERS: REFERENCES—*continued*

11. Stoflet ES, Koeberl DD, Sarkar G, Sommer SS. Genomic amplification with transcript sequencing. *Science* 1988; **239:** 491–94.
12. Innis MA, Myambo KB, Gelfand DH, Brow MAD. DNA sequencing with *Thermus aquaticus* DNA polymerase and direct sequencing of polymerase chain reaction-amplified DNA. *Proc Natl Acad Sci USA* 1988; **85:** 9436–40.
13. Karayiannis P, Fowler MJF, Lok ASF, Greenfield C, Monjardino J, Thomas HC. Detection of serum HBV-DNA by molecular hybridisation: correlation with HBeAg/anti-HBe status, racial origin, liver histology and hepatocellular carcinoma. *J Hepatol* 1985; **1:** 99–106.
14. Kaneko S, Miller RH, Feinstone SM, et al. Detection of serum hepatitis B virus DNA in patients with chronic hepatitis using the polymerase chain reaction assay. *Proc Natl Acad Sci USA* 1989; **86:** 312–16.
15. Sumazaki R, Motz M, Wolf H, Heinig J, Gilg W, Deinhardt F. Detection of hepatitis B virus in serum using amplification of viral DNA by means of the polymerase chain reaction. *J Med Virol* 1989; **27:** 304–08.
16. Ganem D, Varmus HE. The molecular biology of the hepatitis viruses. *Annu Rev Biochem* 1989; **56:** 651–93.
17. Kozak M. At least six nucleotides preceding the AUG initiator codon enhance translation in mammalian cells. *J Mol Biol* 1987; **196:** 947–50.
18. Eddleston AWLF, Mondelli M, Mieli-Vergani G, Williams R. Lymphocyte cytotoxicity to autologous hepatocyte in chronic hepatitis B virus infection. *Hepatology* 1982; **2:** 122S–27S.
19. Pignatelli M, Waters J, Lever AML, et al. Cytotoxic T cell responses to the nucleocapsid proteins of HBV in chronic hepatitis B. *J Hepatol* 1987; **4:** 15–21.

PATHOGENESIS OF CROHN'S DISEASE: MULTIFOCAL GASTROINTESTINAL INFARCTION

A. J. WAKEFIELD[1] A. M. SAWYERR[1]
A. P. DHILLON[1] R. M. PITTILO[2]
P. M. ROWLES[2] A. A. M. LEWIS[1]
R. E. POUNDER[1]

Academic Departments of Medicine, Histopathology, and Surgery, Royal Free Hospital School of Medicine;[1] and Bland-Sutton Institute of Histopathology, University College and Middlesex Hospital Schools of Medicine,[2] London

Summary In a prospective study, specimens of resected small and large intestine from fifteen patients with Crohn's disease were prepared by heparin-saline vascular perfusion, followed by either resin casting of the mesenteric vascular supply and tissue maceration or glutaraldehyde perfusion-fixation, resin casting, and tissue clearance. The specimens were examined by macrophotography, histopathology, and either scanning or transmission electronmicroscopy. A pathogenetic sequence of events in Crohn's disease was seen—vascular injury, focal arteritis, fibrin deposition, arterial occlusion mainly at the level of the muscularis propria, followed by tissue infarction or neovascularisation. These features were confined to segments of intestine affected by Crohn's disease and did not occur in normal bowel. The findings suggest that Crohn's disease is mediated by multifocal gastrointestinal infarction. This pathogenetic process is compatible with many of the clinical features of Crohn's disease, and its recognition has important implications for the identification of the primary cause of the illness and advances in clinical management.

Introduction

Crohn's disease is a chronic inflammatory process of unknown pathogenesis. Cutaneous,[1] ocular,[2] systemic,[3] and mesenteric vasculitis[4,5] have been described in patients with the disorder. Spontaneous thrombosis at unusual sites occurs in young Crohn's disease patients and in association with exacerbations of the illness.[6-8] These features suggest the possibility of an underlying vascular inflammatory process, but only a few reports have identified primary vascular lesions of the mesenteric vessels in a minority of Crohn's disease patients.[4,5,9] In two of those studies vessels in areas of pronounced inflammation and those showing chronic obliterative changes were excluded,[4,5] but these changes could represent important extremes in the spectrum of vascular injury.

The cellular procoagulant pathway, a facet of the cell-mediated immune response that initiates fibrin formation in delayed-type hypersensitivity reactions, is active in Crohn's disease; studies of this pathway[10-12] have suggested a possible vascular pathogenesis of the disorder. We believe that the result of intravascular fibrin deposition brought about by this pathway is the simultaneous disruption not only of microvascular haemodynamics but also of the physiological interface of the vascular endothelium.[13,14]

We propose that Crohn's disease is characterised by multifocal gastrointestinal infarction mediated by a chronic mesenteric vasculitis—a pathogenetic mechanism that is compatible with many of the clinical features. Substantiation of the hypothesis would require the definition of a consistent vascular lesion in segments of intestine affected by Crohn's disease, that is very mild or not present in intestine spared from disease, and absent from normal intestine. The purpose of this paper is to describe the morphology of the vascular lesion in Crohn's disease and its evolution, and to present evidence for the role of mononuclear cell/endothelial cell interaction that culminates in intravascular focal fibrin deposition and multifocal gastrointestinal infarction.

Patients and Methods

Resected intestine from fifteen patients with Crohn's disease was examined: six patients had isolated ileocaecal disease, three had colonic involvement only, five had recurrence at a previous ileocolonic anastomosis, and one had both ileal and diffuse colonic disease. Before their operations ten patients had received corticosteroids and nine sulphasalazine. The diagnosis of Crohn's disease was made clinically, radiologically, and on histopathology of the resected specimens.

To prevent blood clotting within the resected specimens, the standard resection technique was modified to preserve the main vascular pedicle of the affected intestinal segment, which was divided as the last step before removal. An arterial clamp was placed on the proximal side of the pedicle only, to avoid damage to the vessels in the specimen and to facilitate their identification. The artery supplying the specimen was immediately cannulated and perfused with heparinised saline. Part of the specimen was removed and placed in formol-saline for histopathology.

Control specimens of normal small intestine were collected by the same method from one organ donor and two patients undergoing right hemicolectomy for carcinoma of the caecum.

For microcorrosion casting of the specimens a low-viscosity casting compound (Batson's Number 17 Plastic, Polysciences, Northampton) was injected manually by way of the arterial cannula. This compound has been used extensively for vascular casting, with excellent resolution of the vascular ultrastructure.[15,16] The main vein and artery were then ligated. The specimen was left undisturbed overnight in a water-bath at room temperature, to dissipate heat from the exothermic polymerisation of the compound. The specimen was then digested in 35% hydrochloric acid for 3–4 days, washed, photographed, and cut into sections and dried. Individual sections were mounted on scanning electronmicroscopy (SEM) stubs and sputter-coated with gold/palladium (Polaron Ltd). The casts were examined with a Jeol JSM35 scanning electronmicroscope.

Specimens for freeze-fracture and SEM were perfusion-fixed with glutaraldehyde, and resin cast as above. Specimens were cut into 1 cm transverse sections, snap-frozen in liquid nitrogen, and fractured. Individual fragments were dehydrated through an ethanol series and transferred to trichlorotrifluoroethane, from which they were critically point-dried with carbon dioxide as the drying fluid. The specimens were prepared and examined by SEM as above.

For transmission electronmicroscopy (TEM) specimens were perfusion-fixed immediately with 2·5% glutaraldehyde in 0·1% sodium cacodylate buffer. The vasculature was subsequently cast as described, but the specimens were left overnight in 2·5% glutaraldehyde as the resin polymerised. To define specific areas of vascular abnormality, the intestine was sliced into longitudinal sections and cleared in methyl salicylate. Samples of tissue (1 mm^3) were cut from areas of macroscopic vascular abnormality observed in all specimens of Crohn's disease prepared by this method, and also from areas of the intestinal wall adjacent to these lesions. The samples were dehydrated through graded concentrations of alcohol to acetone and embedded in 'Araldite' after treatment with propylene oxide. Thin sections were cut on a Reichart OM U4 ultramicrotome, mounted on copper grids, stained with uranyl acetate and lead citrate, and examined on a Jeol 100S or Phillips 301 transmission electronmicroscope.

The in-vitro analysis of resected tissue was approved by the ethics committee of the Royal Free Hospital.

Results

Normal intestinal morphology of control specimens was confirmed by histology. Vessels were patent and regular with normal mural architecture. In all patients with Crohn's disease there was irregular and patchy ulceration, with transmural chronic inflammation and fibrosis. Most cases showed fissures, but granulomas were seen in four cases only. In all patients with Crohn's disease there were changes in small blood vessels adjacent to inflamed and ulcerated areas, consisting of endothelial prominence and variable intimal thickening. Away from ulcers and fissures, chronic inflammatory foci (lymphoid and macrophage aggregates) were found close to small and medium, in many cases thin-walled, submucosal and subserosal blood vessels. In two cases there was apparent destruction of vessel wall by a lymphoplasmacytic granulomatous and eosinophilic inflammatory infiltrate with the deposition of intravascular fibrin (confirmed immunohistochemically; fig 1a) in these areas. Mural fibrinoid necrosis was not seen. In one case of Crohn's ulceration of the colon, the terminal ileum was macroscopically normal; on microscopy there was no mucosal ulceration, but there was transmural chronic inflammation with granulomatous inflammation of subserosal and submucosal blood vessels in the terminal ileum (fig 1b).

Visual and macrophotographic examination of the vascular casts of normal intestine showed regular, well-filled subserosal vessels coursing the circumference of the intestinal wall and anastomosing with corresponding vessels from the opposite side; these larger vessels were linked by a rich submucosal plexus of small vessels and the plexus was more abundant on the mesenteric border than on the antimesenteric border (fig 2a).

On SEM of normal casts the subserosal vessels were smooth and regular, tapering towards the antimesenteric border and overlying the submucosal plexus (fig 3a). At higher power, endothelial cells were arranged in regular ridges oriented according to the prevailing contraction of vascular smooth muscle (fig 3b).

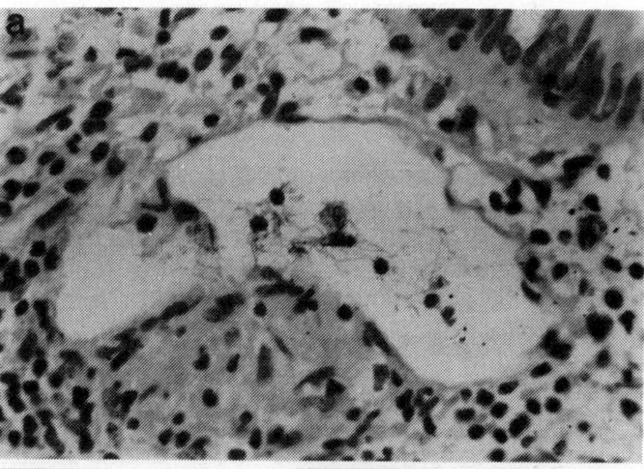

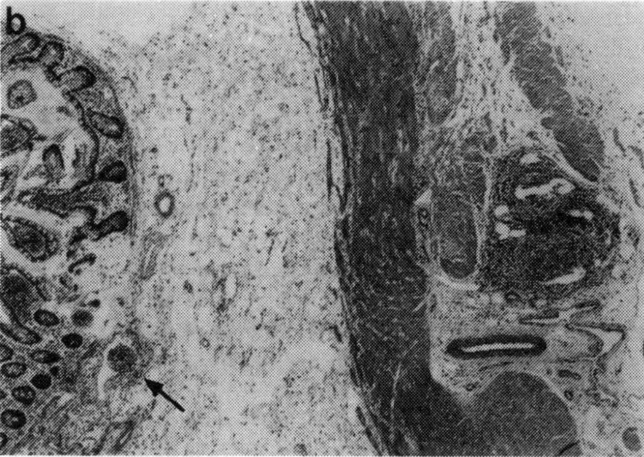

Fig 1—Glutaraldehyde-perfused specimens of ileal Crohn's disease (reduced by 50% from magnifications given).

a: small group of inflammatory cells (lymphocytes and macrophages) is entangled in fibrinous mesh. Some cells are adherent to vessel wall, and lower part of fig shows a granuloma involving vessel wall. Upper right of vessel wall shows permeation by lymphocytes. Immunoperoxidase for fibrinogen/haematoxylin (× 660).

b: no macroscopic abnormality and no microscopic mucosal ulceration. Granulomatous vasculitis within muscularis propria, and a small blood vessel contains polypoid nodule of inflammatory material (arrow). Haematoxylin and eosin (× 40).

© *Lancet* 1989; ii: 1057–1062

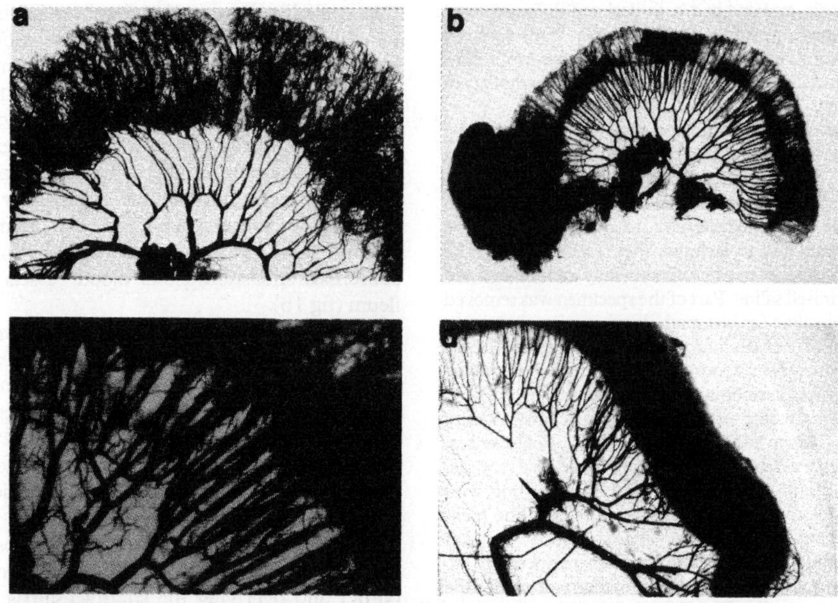

Fig 2—Resin casts of normal and Crohn's disease intestine.

a: normal ileum.

b: Crohn's disease ileum. Macroscopic lesions were apparent at proximal and distal limits (proximal lesion removed for histology). Skip lesions, characterised by intense vascular proliferation, occur in intervening macroscopically normal intestine.

c: isolated lesion in area of macroscopically normal intestine from (b), in which vessels subjacent to the Crohn's lesion in bottom right are stenosed or occluded, in contrast to normal vessels seen in centre which pass around lesions.

d: severe case of Crohn's colitis; antimesenteric border of sigmoid colon completely devoid of subserosal vasculature.

On visual and macrophotographic examination of casts of Crohn's disease, areas of intestine identified as being macroscopically diseased at operation were characterised by intense neovascularisation. However, areas considered macroscopically normal at operation (resected in continuity with macroscopic lesions) showed "skip" lesions characterised by a similar pattern of vascular proliferation (fig 2b). Intervening "spared" segments showed a vascular pattern similar to that of normal intestine.

Macrophotography of casts from disease-affected segments of intestine showed that all vessels subjacent to inflammatory lesions were grossly stenosed or completely occluded immediately proximal to the level of vascular proliferation (fig 2c). These changes were patchy, with normal vascularity between diseased areas.

Fig 2d shows an example of severe Crohn's disease of the sigmoid colon, in which the antimesenteric border is devoid of all normal subserosal vasculature, and represented only by a bed of neovascularisation penetrated by holes. In later specimens these holes were found to correspond to fissures, suggesting a direct association between the degree of ischaemia and the extent of intestinal mural injury.

SEM of resin casts of Crohn's disease intestine and freeze-fractured Crohn's disease tissue showed a spectrum of vascular injury in the area of abnormality in the arterial tree identified by macrophotography. Early lesions were focal, occurring in continuity with and next to morphologically normal vessels (fig 3b), and were characterised by irregular pitting of the resin cast (fig 3c). This pitting was caused by monocytes, adherent to the vascular endothelium, that were the focus of fibrin formation (fig 3d). Stenotic occlusions of vessels were seen in more developed lesions (fig 3e), progressing to complete thrombotic occlusion (fig 3f) in which fibrin was a prominent feature (fig 3g, h). Subserosal neovascularisation seemed to occur early in the evolution of Crohn's disease, since it was seen in macroscopically normal intestine. There was apparently a further vascular proliferative response, seen around vessels that had undergone complete thrombotic occlusion (fig 3f).

To define areas of vascular abnormality, tissues were perfusion-fixed with glutaraldehyde, resin cast, cut in longitudinal section, and clarified. This technique identified the location of arterial lesions as the muscularis propria. Specimens for TEM were taken from this area of vascular abnormality and from areas on both sides of each lesion.

The presence of mononuclear cell infiltration in one or more layers of the blood vessel wall was used as evidence of vasculitis, as previously.[4,5] We also required the presence of vessel wall necrosis to confirm vasculitis.[17]

Although vessels of normal morphology could be observed within the tissues, there were widespread vascular abnormalities in all specimens. Within the lumen of blood vessels, both in the muscularis propria and submucosa, large numbers of inflammatory cells were seen in contact with the endothelium (fig 4a); these inflammatory cells migrated into the subendothelial space. There was an electronlucent substance, consistent in morphology with fibrin, within the lumen of many vessels in both the muscularis propria and submucosa (fig 4b).

Generally the endothelium appeared morphologically normal, though many cells were lipid-laden. Where there had been migration of inflammatory cells into the subendothelial space, the vessel wall architecture was destroyed and we could not identify the intima, media, or adventitia even in some quite large vessels (fig 4a). Within the submucosa, there was evidence of the formation of large numbers of new capillary vessels.

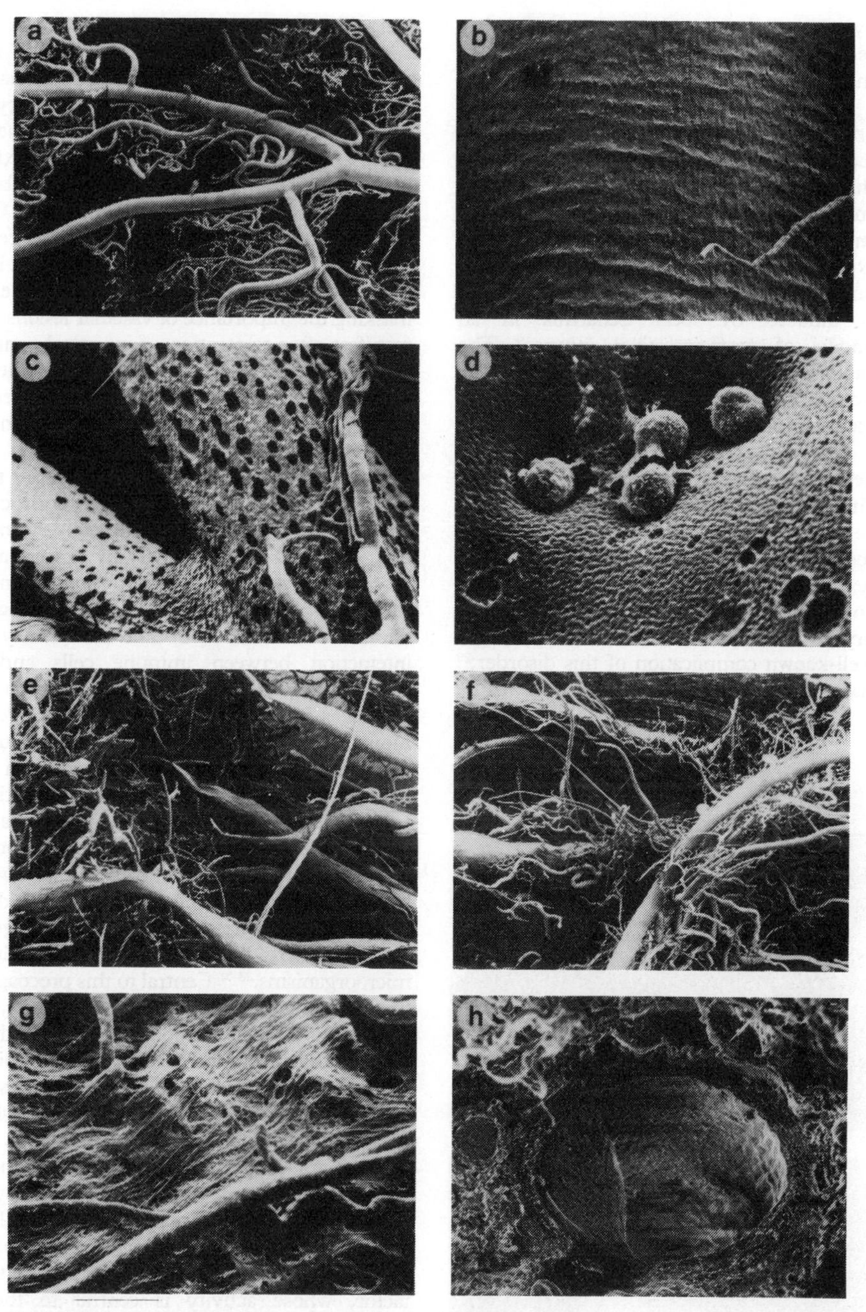

Fig 3—SEM of resin casts of normal intestine, and sequence of vascular changes in Crohn's disease (reduced by 40% from magnifications given).

a: subserosal vessels overlying submucous plexus in normal bowel (× 10·6).
b: normal vessel at high power (× 127).
c: Crohn's disease showing focal arterial injury characterised by irregular pitting (× 95).
d: a freeze-fracture-prepared specimen of Crohn's disease showing adherent monocytes and associated fibrin deposition (× 1950).
e: Crohn's disease showing pronounced stenosis of all vessels subjacent to area of vascular proliferation (× 12·5).
f: Crohn's disease with completely occluded arteries proximal to region of vascular proliferation. A more normal vessel in the centre courses round affected area. Lumen of intestine appears at bottom right (× 10·6).
g: high power view of occluded vessel in centre of (f), showing fibrin matrix of occlusive thrombus (× 5700).
h: Crohn's disease freeze-fractured through muscularis propria, showing partial thrombotic occlusion of artery (× 249).

Discussion

Our morphological studies have shown an occlusive fibrinoid lesion of arteries supplying areas of intestine affected by Crohn's disease. Vessels did not show such changes in spared segments of intestine or in normal intestine. The vascular damage seems to occur early in the evolution of Crohn's disease lesions and it precedes mucosal ulceration—a feature previously thought to be the initial lesion.[18] The early lesions were focal, occurring in continuity with and adjacent to normal vessels. This combination of

© *Lancet* 1989; ii: 1057–1062

features strongly suggests that the observed vasculitis is a primary process rather than one occurring in response to general inflammation. The severity of this vascular injury seemed directly related to the extent of intestinal damage. The occlusive arterial injury was focal and occurred mainly within the muscularis propria; thus random histological sections of Crohn's disease tissue[4,5] would probably reveal vasculitis only in a minority of samples.

Can the clinical and histological features of Crohn's disease be explained by multifocal gastrointestinal infarction—a chronic intestinal ischaemic insult? Mucosal ulceration was induced by local ischaemia in an experimental model of gastrointestinal injury.[19] The location of the vascular lesion within the muscularis propria, causing localised infarction, would explain the frequent submucosal penetration of fissures and would resolve the observation of Knutson and Lunderquist[4] of relative ischaemia of the thickened submucosa in fully developed lesions of Crohn's disease.[4] Giant cell and granuloma formation were described in experimental models of inflammatory bowel disease in which vasculitis was a principal feature.[20,21] Healing by fibrous stricture formation, a characteristic of Crohn's disease, is a feature of ischaemic intestinal injury.[22] Perianastomotic recurrence after resection is a well-known complication of this disorder;[23] creation of an anastomosis, causing what would otherwise be insignificant vascular disruption, at an area of microscopic vascular disease due to Crohn's disease might produce sufficient ischaemia to induce local intestinal infarction and macroscopic disease. The higher frequency of colocolonic anastomotic recurrence[23] of Crohn's disease may be due to the lesser vascularity of the colon compared with the small intestine, superimposed on primary vascular disease at the anastomosis. Faecal diversion in colonic Crohn's disease induces remission, with reactivation after restoration of the faecal stream;[24,25] these observations might be explained by the reduced blood requirement of the excluded colon, masking the importance of vascular lesions which becomes manifest after restoration of intestinal continuity, when a greater oxygen demand is placed on the colon.[26] This phenomenon may explain the beneficial effect of bowel rest, by means of either an elemental diet or parenteral feeding, in the treatment of Crohn's disease.

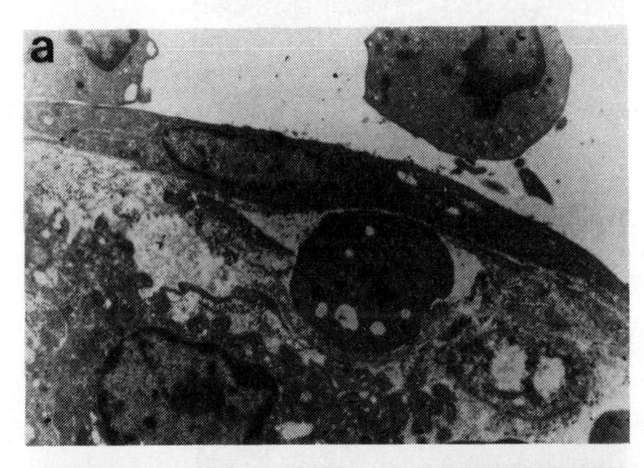

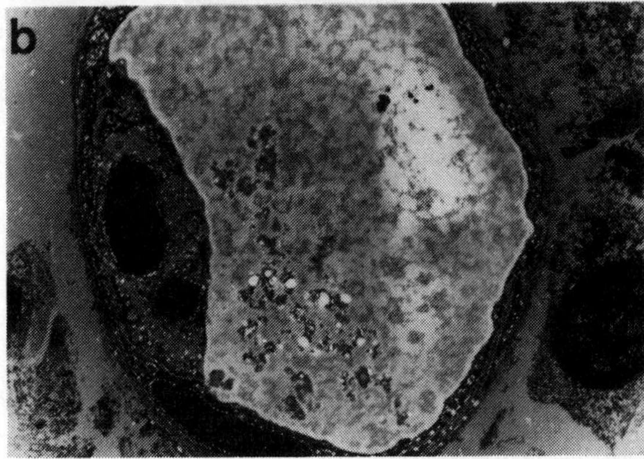

Fig 4—TEM (reduced by 33% from magnifications given).

a: section through muscularis propria of colonic Crohn's disease showing two inflammatory cells adhering to luminal surface of vascular endothelium. Endothelium is morphologically normal, but subendothelium is severely disrupted by inflammatory infiltrate (× 9000).

b: amorphous material (fibrin deposition, confirmed by immunoperoxidase in [a]) within a vessel from junction of muscularis propria and submucosa of colonic Crohn's disese. Endothelial cells contain large quantities of lipid (× 7500).

Epidemiological evidence suggests that the oral contraceptive pill and smoking may be associated with more severe disease.[27] These two potentially thrombogenic agents may augment disease activity by exacerbating underlying vascular injury and tendency to focal thrombosis.

By what mechanism is the thrombogenic injury of Crohn's disease induced? The answer may come from the interaction between immune cells and the vascular endothelium, and the role these cells have in controlling the balance of intravascular haemostasis. Peripheral blood monocytes, macrophages (their tissue counterparts), and vascular endothelial cells can express a continuum of haemostatic properties, whose anticoagulant or procoagulant bias depends on their state of activation.[10,11] In the quiescent state these cells exert a predominance of anticoagulant activity, compatible with optimum haemodynamics. This highly integrated anticoagulant status may be displaced in favour of procoagulant activity by a range of biological stimuli, including various microorganisms.[28-31] Central to this procoagulant activity is the synthesis, and cell surface expression, of initiators of coagulation, which include tissue factor (thromboplastin), factor VII activity, and a direct prothrombinase.[12]

The cellular procoagulant pathway is an important effector arm of cell-mediated immunity, which is active in delayed-type hypersensitivity reactions. In outline, it involves a T-helper-cell-stimulated, lymphokine-mediated monocyte activation, with the subsequent synthesis and cell surface expression of monocyte procoagulant activity. In addition, activated monocytes secrete inflammatory cytokines which include interleukin-1 and tumour necrosis factor, whose activity is central to the simultaneous inhibition of anticoagulant activity and augmentation of procoagulant activity in both monocytes and endothelial cells.[32-36] The ability of the endothelial cells to synthesise and express inflammatory cytokines[37] implies a degree of autoregulation of procoagulant activity at the level of the endothelium.[37] The culmination of these cooperative cellular interactions is the intravascular and perivascular precipitation of fibrin, which may cause an ischaemic insult to dependent tissues.

Various haemostatic abnormalities have been described in patients with Crohn's disease. There are reports of low anticoagulant activities of antithrombin III,[38] protein S (a cofactor for protein C activation),[39] and tissue plasminogen activator.[40] In addition, enhanced procoagulant activities have been reported, including thrombocytosis, raised fibrinogen and factor VIII levels,[7] and an enhanced monocyte procoagulant activity.[12] Monocyte procoagulant activity is higher in patients with active Crohn's disease than in patients with inactive disease or normal controls.[12] We have noted greatly enhanced macrophage procoagulant activity in cells derived from mesenteric lymph nodes, adjacent to foci of active Crohn's disease (unpublished).

More direct evidence for the ongoing formation of fibrin in Crohn's disease has been provided by the consistent demonstration of high concentrations of fibrinopeptide-A in the plasma of patients with active disease.[12,41] Fibrinopeptide-A is a 16-aminoacid peptide cleaved from the A-chain of fibrinogen by thrombin. Since its plasma half-life is less than 4 min, the plasma concentration of fibrinopeptide-A is a sensitive indicator of ongoing fibrin formation, which is strongly correlated with disease activity in patients with Crohn's disease.[12] In addition, immunocytochemical studies have shown fibrin deposition in Crohn's tissue.[42]

High concentrations of inflammatory cytokines have been reported in Crohn's disease,[43,44] a finding which may explain the activation of coagulation within the inflammatory focus of the disease. Corticosteroids inhibit both interleukin-1 synthesis[45] and the generation of monocyte procoagulant activity,[46] which may explain the efficacy of these drugs in Crohn's disease.

Two further effects of interleukin-1 and tumour necrosis factor may relate to the pathogenesis of Crohn's disease. These peptide regulatory factors induce an endothelial-cell-derived adhesion molecule (ELAM), which binds inflammatory cells[11,37] and stimulates new vessel formation.[47,48] Two characteristic features of early Crohn's disease lesions in our studies were the adherence of leucocytes to endothelial cells and intense neovascularisation.

The cellular procoagulant pathway requires specific biological stimuli for its induction. We believe that the discrete thrombotic vascular lesion that we have defined in these studies represents the local activation of this pathway and thus the possible focus of activity for the biological stimulus that causes Crohn's disease. We hope that by concentrating our future studies on this lesion we may be able to identify a primary causative agent in Crohn's disease.

We thank the following surgeons for their help in these studies—Mr J. P. Bolton, Mr M. W. N. Ward (Chase Farm Hospital, Enfield), Mr N. Menzies-Gow (Central Middlesex Hospital, London), and Mr R. C. Springall (North Middlesex Hospital, London), Miss Doris Elliott for help in preparing the paper; and Dinesh Dasandi, Alan Sneddon, and Ian Harrigan for help and technical expertise.

A. J. W. is a Wellcome Research Fellow and A. M. S. is supported by a grant from the Crohn's in Childhood Research Appeal.

Correspondence should be addressed to R. E. P., Academic Department of Medicine, Royal Free Hospital, Pond Street, London NW3 2QG.

REFERENCES

1. Mayer L, Janowitz H. Extraintestinal manifestations of inflammatory bowel disease. In: Kirsner JB, Shorter RG, eds. Inflammatory bowel disease. New York: Lea and Febiger, 1988: 299–317.
2. Knox RL, Schachat AP, Mustonsen E. Primary secondary and coincidental ocular complications of Crohn's disease. *Ophthalmology* 1984; **91:** 163–73.
3. Yassinger S. Association of inflammatory bowel disease and large vascular lesions. *Gastronenterology* 1979; **71:** 844A.
4. Knutson H, Lunderquist A. Vascular changes in Crohn's disease. *Am J Roentgenol* 1968; **103:** 380–85.
5. Geller SA, Cohen A. Arterial inflammatory infiltration in Crohn's disease. *Arch Pathol Lab Med* 1983; **107:** 473.
6. Sisbigee B, Rottenberg DA. Saggital sinus thrombosis as a complication of regional enteritis. *Ann Neurol* 1978; **3:** 450–75.
7. Koenigs KP, McPhedran P, Spiro HM. Thrombosis in inflammatory bowel disease. *J Clin Gastroenterol* 1987; **9:** 627–31.
8. Talbot RW, Heppell J, Dozois RR, Beart RW. Vascular complications of inflammatory bowel disease. *Mayo Clin Proc* 1986; **61:** 140–45.
9. Antonius JI, Gump FE, Lattes R, Lepore M. Study of certain microscopic features in regional enteritis, and their possible prognostic significance. *Gastronenterology* 1960; **28:** 889–905.
10. Edwards RL, Rickles FR. Macrophage procoagulants. Progress in thrombosis and haemostasis. New York: Grune & Stratton, 1984: 183–209.
11. Pober JS. Cytokine-mediated activation of the vascular endothelium. *Am J Pathol* 1988; **133:** 426–33.
12. Edwards RL, Levine JB, Green R, et al. Activation of blood coagulation in Crohn's disease. *Gastroenterology* 1987; **92:** 329–37.
13. Wakefield AJ, Cohen Z, Levy GA. Procoagulant activity in gastroneterology. *Gut* (in press).
14. Petty R, Pearson JD. Endothelium—the axis of vascular health and disease. *J Royal Coll Phys* 1989; **23:** 92–102.
15. Nopanitaya W, Aghajanian JG, Gray LD. An improved plastic mixture for corrosion casting of the gastrointestinal microvascular system. Scanning Electron Microscopy III. Illinois: O'Hare, 1979: 751–55.
16. MacPhee PJ, Schmidt EE, Keown PA, Groom AC. Microcirculatory changes in the livers of mice infected with murine hepatitis virus. Evidence from microcorrosion casts and measurements of red cell velocity. *Microvasc Res* 1988; **36:** 140–49.
17. Bariety J, Jacquot C. The vasculitis syndromes in small and medium-sized vessels. In: Camilleri J-P, ed. Diseases of the arterial wall. New York, Berlin: Springer-Verlag, 1989: 423–546.
18. Kelly JK, Sutherland LR. The chronological sequence in the pathway of Crohn's disease. *J Clin Gastroenterol* 1988; **10:** 28–33.
19. Piaseki C. Role of ischaemia in the initiation of peptic ulcer. *Ann R Coll Surg Engl* 1977; **59:** 476–78.
20. Goldberger MB, Kirsner JB. The arthus phenomenon in the colon of rabbits: a serial histological study. *Arch Pathol* 1959; **67:** 566–71.
21. Goldberger MB, Kirsner JB. The Schwartzman phenomenon in the colon of rabbits: serial histological study. *Arch Pathol* 1963; **68:** 539–52.
22. Marston A. Ischaemia of the gut. In: Misiewicz JJ, Pounder RE, Venables CW, eds. Diseases of the gut and pancreas. Oxford: Blackwell Scientific Publications, 1987: 1029–43.
23. Block GE, Schraut W. Complications of the surgical treatment of ulcerative colitis and Crohn's disease. In: Kirsner JB, Shorter RG, eds. Inflammatory bowel disease, 3rd ed. New York: Lea & Febiger, 1988: 685–713.
24. McIlrath DC. Diverting ileostomy or colostomy in the management of Crohn's disease of the colon. *Arch Surg* 1971; **103:** 308–10.
25. Harper PH. Split ileostomy and ileocolostomy for Crohn's disease of the colon and ulcerative colitis. A 20 year survey. *Gut* 1983; **24:** 106–13.
26. Kvietys PR, Granger DN. Physiology and pathophysiology of the colonic circulation. *Clin Gastroenterol* 1986; **15:** 967–83.
27. Mendelhoff AI, Calkins BM. The epidemiology of idiopathic inflammatory bowel disease. In: Kirsner JB, Shorter R, eds. Inflammatory bowel disease, 3rd ed. New York: Lea and Febriger, 1988: 3–34.
28. Visser MR, Tracey PB, Vercellotti GM, Goodman JL, White JG, Jacob HS. Enhanced thrombin generation and platelet binding on *Herpes simplex* virus-induced endothelium. *Proc Natl Acad Sci USA* 1988; **85:** 8227–30.
29. Osterud B, Flaegsted T. Increased tissue thromboplastin activity in monocytes of patients with meningococcal infection. Related to unfavourable prognosis. *Thromb Haemost* 1983; **49:** 5–7.
30. Rossi BC, Dean R, Roland JT. T-lymphocyte requirement activity by *Trypanosoma brucei*. *Parasite Immunol* 1987; **9:** 697–704.
31. Dindzans VJ, MacPhee PJ, Fung LS, Leibowitz JL, Levy GA. The immune response to mouse hepatitis virus: expression of monocyte procoagulant activity and plasminogen activator during infection in vivo. *J Immunol* 1985; **135:** 4189–97.
32. Narworth PP, Stern DM. Modulation of endothelial haemostatic properties by tumour necrosis factor. *J Exp Med* 1986; **163:** 740–45.
33. Narworth PP, Handley CT, Esmon C, Stern D. Interleukin-1 induces endothelial procoagulant activity while suppressing cell surface anticoagulant activity. *Proc Natl Acad Sci USA* 1986; **83:** 3460–64.
34. Emeis JJ, Kooistra T. Interleukin-1 and lipopolysaccharide induce an inhibitor of tissue-type plasminogen activator in vivo and in cultured endothelial cells. *J Exp Med* 1986; **163:** 1260–65.
35. Nachamn RL, Hajjar KA, Silverstein RL, Dinarello CA. Interleukin-1 induces endothelial synthesis of plasminogen activator inhibitor. *J Exp Med* 1986; **163:** 1595–604.
36. Conkling PR, Greenberg CS, Weinberg JB. Tumor necrosis factor induces tissue factor-like activity in human leukaemia cell line U937 and peripheral blood monocytes. *Blood* 1988; **72:** 128–33.
37. Cotran RS. New roles for the endothelium in inflammation and immunity. *Am J Pathol* 1987; **129:** 407–13.
38. Ghosh S, Mackie MJ, McVerry BA, Galloway M, Ellis A, McKay K. Chronic inflammatory bowel disease, deep venous thrombosis and antithrombin activity. *Acta Haematol* 1983; **70:** 50–53.
39. Wyshock E, Caldwell M, Crowley JP. Deep venous thrombosis, inflammatory bowel disease and protein S deficiency. *Am J Clin Pathol* 1988; **90:** 633–35.
40. Bruin PAF, Crama-Bohbouth G, Verspaget HW, et al. Plasminogen activators in the intestine of patients with inflammatory bowel disease. *Thromb Haemost* 1988; **60:** 262–66.
41. Wisen O, Garlund B. Haemostasis in Crohn's disease: low factor XIII levels in active disease. *Scand J Gastroenterol* 1988; **23:** 961–66.
42. Koffler D, Minkowitz S, Rothamn W, Garlock J. Immunocytochemical studies in ulcerative colitis and regional ileitis. *Am J Pathol* 1962; **41:** 733–45.
43. Suzuki Y, Tobin A, Quinn D, Whelan D, O'Morian C. Interleukin-1 in inflammatory bowel disease. *Gastroenterology* 1989; **96:** A498.
44. Satsangi J, Walstencroft JC, Cason J, Ainley CC, Dumonde DC, Thompson RPH. Interleukin-1 in Crohn's disease. *Clin Exp Immunol* 1987; **67:** 594–605.
45. Kern JA, Lamb RJ, Reed JC, Dariek RP, Nowell DC. Dexamethasone inhibition of interleukin-1 beta production by human monocytes. *J Clin Invest* 1988; **81:** 237–44.
46. Murfelder TW, Niemetz J, Kang S. Glucocorticoids inhibit the generation of leukocyte procoagulant (tissue factor) activity. *Blood* 1982; **60:** 1169–72.
47. Tracey KJ, Vlassara H, Cerami A. Peptide regulatory factors: cachectin/tumour necrosis factor. *Lancet* 1989; i: 1122–25.
48. Nathan C. Secretory products of macrophages. *J Clin Invest* 1987; **79:** 319–26.

© Gastroenterology 1989; 97: 439–445

Early Indicators of Prognosis in Fulminant Hepatic Failure

JOHN G. O'GRADY, GRAEME J. M. ALEXANDER,
KAREN M. HAYLLAR, and ROGER WILLIAMS
Liver Unit, King's College School of Medicine and Dentistry, Denmark Hill, London, United Kingdom

The successful use of orthotopic liver transplantation in fulminant hepatic failure has created a need for early prognostic indicators to select the patients most likely to benefit at a time when liver transplantation is still feasible. Univariate and multivariate analysis was performed on 588 patients with acute liver failure managed medically during 1973–1985, to identify the factors most likely to indicate a poor prognosis. In acetaminophen-induced fulminant hepatic failure, survival correlated with arterial blood pH, peak prothrombin time, and serum creatinine—a pH <7.30, prothrombin time >100 s, and creatinine >300 μmol/L indicating a poor prognosis. In patients with viral hepatitis and drug reactions three static variables [etiology (non A, non B hepatitis or drug reactions), age <11 and >40 yr, duration of jaundice before the onset of encephalopathy >7 days] and two dynamic variables (serum bilirubin >300 μmol/L and prothrombin time >50 s) indicated a poor prognosis. The value of these indicators in determining outcome was tested retrospectively in a further 175 patients admitted during 1986–1987, leading to the construction of models for the selection of patients for liver transplantation.

The use of orthotopic liver transplantation (OLT) in the management of fulminant hepatic failure (FHF) (1–11) has highlighted the urgent need for "better prognostic indicators . . . to indicate who will benefit from transplantation and (determine) when the procedure should be carried out" (12). Orthotopic liver transplantation has been proposed as the optimal treatment for "all-comers" with FHF (10), this philosophy being based on the assumption that survival rates are homogeneously <20%, whereas survival rates of 54%–74% are being currently achieved with OLT (2,3,11). This approach appears justified when the underlying etiology is non A, non B hepatitis, halothane hepatitis, idiosyncratic drug reactions, or acute Wilson's disease (13–16), and with the variant of FHF known as late-onset hepatic failure (17). However, in our unit survival rates as high as 67% for hepatitis A, 53% for acetaminophen-induced FHF, and 39% for hepatitis B have been attained with intensive care directed toward the condition of the liver (13). Nevertheless, even within the latter groups there are undoubtedly patients whose chances of survival would be enhanced by early OLT, indicating a need for a more accurate method of assessing prognosis in individual patients.

At present there is no consensus on the prediction of outcome in FHF. One study of 33 patients described a complex discriminant score that utilized 10 variables—etiology, blood glucose, duration of history, leukocyte count, age, prothrombin time, sex, serum potassium, serum albumin, and blood group—to predict outcome (18). Other factors appearing to carry prognostic value were recently reviewed and those identified in at least one cited study included the duration of jaundice, serum bilirubin, α_1-fetoprotein, factor V level, bile acid conjugation, galactose and antipyrine clearance, and hepatocyte volume (19). In fulminant hepatitis B, factor V level, age, hepatitis B surface antigen status, and serum α-fetoprotein concentration were found to be independent predictors of survival (20). Clinical complications like cerebral edema, renal failure, hypotension, and hemorrhage undoubtedly influence outcome (13,19), but they develop too late in the clinical course to be useful in planning management strategies in individual patients.

Tygstrup and Ranek, in the review of prognostic factors in FHF referred to above (19), concluded that there was a need for a study using multivariate

Abbreviations used in this paper: **FHF, fulminant hepatic failure; OLT, orthotopic liver transplantation.**

0016-5085/89/$3.50

analysis in a relatively large group of patients as a learning set and subsequent validation in a separate group of patients. In the present study, based on 588 patients with FHF and grade III–IV encephalopathy admitted to our unit during 1973–1985, we have attempted to define prognosis by deliberately using standard and easily obtainable parameters, including static variables definable on admission and dynamic laboratory variables that could be followed sequentially thereafter. The prognostic indicators so identified were then examined retrospectively in a second group of 175 patients with FHF admitted during 1986–1987 to determine their sensitivity and specificity in prediction of a fatal outcome.

Patients and Methods

The underlying diagnoses in the 588 patients (1973–1985) were acetaminophen overdose (310 patients), viral hepatitis A (37 patients), viral hepatitis B (79 patients), non A, non B hepatitis (79 patients), presumed viral hepatitis with incomplete serology (38 patients), halothane hepatitis (34 patients), and idiosyncratic drug reactions (11 patients). The diagnoses were made on the basis of criteria previously outlined (13). In each instance encephalopathy had developed within 8 wk of the onset of symptoms, thus fulfilling the criteria for FHF as defined by Trey and Davidson (21). These 588 patients represent 96.7% of 608 consecutive admissions to the Liver Failure Unit, the 20 exclusions being patients who had evidence of irreversible brainstem coning on arrival and died shortly afterwards. Of these, 570 developed grade IV encephalopathy (only responding to painful stimuli or unresponsive), and 18 cases did not progress beyond grade III encephalopathy (responding to simple commands).

The second group of 175 patients used for the validation study represented consecutive admissions to the Liver Failure Unit in 1986–1987, and the underlying etiologies were acetaminophen overdose (121 patients; all had prothrombin times >32 s, 94 developed encephalopathy, progressing to grade III or IV in 68 patients), hepatitis A (5 patients), hepatitis B (10 patients), non A, non B hepatitis (30 patients), Epstein–Barr virus (1 patient), halothane hepatitis (3 patients), and idiosyncratic drug reaction (5 patients). All but 3 of the nonacetaminophen cases progressed to grade III or IV encephalopathy.

Statistical Methods

Stepwise logistic regression was performed using BMDP software (University of California). The static and therapeutic variables studied in 588 patients were age, sex, etiology, year of admission, grade of encephalopathy on admission, and the major interventions in therapy—charcoal hemoperfusion, resin hemoperfusion, hemodialysis—in addition to the duration of symptoms and jaundice before the onset of encephalopathy in nonacetaminophen patients. The dynamic variables studied were prothrombin time, serum bilirubin, aspartate aminotransferase, alkaline phosphatase, arterial pH, urea, serum creatinine, serum sodium, total white cell count, and platelet count. Two values were analyzed for each parameter—the value obtained at the time of admission and that which represented the greatest deviation from normal thereafter (peak or nadir). Separate analyses were performed for acetaminophen and nonacetaminophen cases because of the previously demonstrated higher incidence of renal failure and metabolic acidosis in the former group (13). To minimize the impact of missing values, only those parameters that differed between survivors and nonsurvivors on univariate analysis using the Mann–Whitney U test were entered into the stepwise logistic regression analysis. Variables with skewed distributions were normalized using log transformation prior to multivariate analysis. Significant variables identified by multivariate analysis were analyzed in the total population for whom that variable was known, using cross-tabulations and the Pearson χ^2 test. Although up to eight subdivisions were examined for each variable, the cutoff points yielding the greatest discriminant value with regard to survival are reported. Each analysis was repeated in two cohorts to determine possible differences between the findings in the time periods 1973–1980 and 1981–1985, the dividing year 1981 marking the introduction of mannitol in the management of cerebral edema, thus allowing assessment of the impact of this therapy on the results obtained. The Spearman rank correlation test was used when correlating nonparametric variables.

Results

Static Variables

Etiology was the most important variable in predicting outcome ($p < 0.001$). Survival rates were 44.7% for hepatitis A, 34.4% for acetaminophen, 23.3% for hepatitis B, 13.6% for drug reactions (including halothane hepatitis), and 9.0% for non A, non B hepatitis. The second most important variable was age ($p < 0.02$). In the acetaminophen overdose group, 36.8% of 163 patients aged 15–30 yr, 32.2% of 118 aged 31–50 yr, and 24.1% of 29 aged >50 yr survived. In viral hepatitis and drug-induced FHF, the survival rate was 32.6% of 147 patients aged 11–40 yr, as compared with 10.3% of 29 and 7.8% of 104 patients aged <11 and >40 yr, respectively. The final variable found to be independently significant in the overall analysis was the grade of encephalopathy on admission ($p < 0.05$). In acetaminophen patients survival fell steadily from 50% in those admitted before the onset of encephalopathy to 24% in those admitted in established grade IV encephalopathy. Conversely, in the nonacetaminophen patients only 12.1% of patients with grade 0–II encephalopathy on admission survived, as compared with 28.4% and 20.0% of patients with grade III and IV encephalopathy, respectively. When the time periods were examined separately, multivariate analysis

© Gastroenterology 1989; 97: 439–445

Table 1. Univariate Analysis of Dynamic Factors in Fulminant Hepatic Failure

Factor	Acetaminophen		Viral/drugs	
	Survivors	Nonsurvivors	Survivors	Nonsurvivors
PT–OA (s)	72 (35)	93 (51)[a]	51 (31)	81 (57)[a]
PT–P (s)	73 (36)	104 (58)[b]	52 (32)	96 (67)[b]
Bilirubin–OA (μmol/L)	162 (85)	133 (84)[c]	299 (205)	404 (188)[b]
Bilirubin–P (μmol/L)	317 (194)	185 (140)[b]	373 (230)	460 (222)[a]
AST–OA (IU/L)	2600 (3108)	3019 (3479)	948 (1181)	1409 (2291)[c]
AST–peak (IU/L)	2489 (3119)	2957 (3470)	1134 (1757)	1329 (1957)
AP–OA (IU/L)	178 (65)	184 (98)	189 (66)	235 (125)
AP–P (IU/L)	247 (122)	208 (110)	240 (166)	253 (133)
pH–OA	7.41 (0.1)	7.31 (0.15)[b]	7.43 (0.09)	7.39 (0.1)[c]
Sodium–OA (μmol/L)	131 (6.4)	129 (8.3)	131 (5.4)	132 (7.8)
Sodium–N (μmol/L)	128 (7.7)	125 (10.5)	125 (18.3)	129 (10.0)
Urea–OA (μmol/L)	9.8 (6.8)	9.7 (7.2)	8.9 (11.9)	7.1 (9.2)
Urea–P (μmol/L)	17.9 (18.6)	14.1 (18.6)	13.6 (14.3)	8.7 (10.3)[c]
Creatinine–OA (μmol/L)	241 (180)	351 (234)[a]	254 (411)	211 (253)
Creatinine–P (μmol/L)	374 (286)	439 (262)[a]	322 (442)	279 (268)[c]
WCC–OA (× 109/L)	12.5 (9.2)	14.6 (8.5)[c]	11.4 (5.6)	13.6 (6.3)[c]
WCC–P (× 109/L)	15.6 (8.3)	16.1 (10.7)	16.0 (8.1)	15.6 (8.6)
Platelets–OA (× 109/L)	164 (105)	148 (91)	228 (109)	196 (119)
Platelets–N (× 109/L)	93 (75)	112 (89)[c]	138 (87)	159 (112)

AP, alkaline phosphatase; AST, aspartate aminotransferase; N, nadir; OA, on admission; P, peak; PT, prothrombin time; WCC, white cell count. Values are mean (±SD). [a] $p < 0.01$. [b] $p < 0.001$. [c] $p < 0.05$.

identified etiology and age as the most important factors in 1973–1980 and 1981–1985, respectively, with grade of encephalopathy on admission no longer achieving significance in these smaller cohorts. In this analysis, the therapeutic modalities were not identifiable as independent factors influencing outcome.

A second stepwise logistic regression analysis was performed in 215 patients with either viral hepatitis or drug reactions to assess the importance of the duration of symptoms and jaundice before the onset of encephalopathy (these factors show little variation in acetaminophen-induced FHF). Following etiology ($p < 0.001$) as the most important variable were the interval between the onset of jaundice and encephalopathy ($p < 0.005$) and age ($p < 0.05$). The survival rate in 103 patients developing encephalopathy within 7 days of the onset of jaundice was 34.0%, as compared with 6.7% of 119 patients in whom the interval was ≥8 days (6.5% of 46 patients at 8–14 days, 5.5% of 55 patients at 15–28 days, 11.1% of 18 patients at >28 days). The interval between the onset of symptoms and encephalopathy was not found to be a significant independent variable. In the more recent 1981–1985 cohort, the duration of jaundice before the onset of encephalopathy and age were more important.

Dynamic Variables

The results of univariate analysis for each parameter in acetaminophen and nonacetaminophen patients are given in Table 1. Logistic stepwise regression for all significant variables in 146 acetaminophen patients identified pH of arterial blood at the time of admission as the best indicator of outcome ($p < 0.001$). This parameter was known in 214 patients and the survival rates were 56.9% in 51 cases with pH >7.45, 41.7% in 48 with pH 7.38–7.45, 21.4% in 42 with pH 7.30–7.37, and 15.1% in 73 with pH <7.30. The peak bilirubin was the second strongest predictor of outcome ($p < 0.001$), and correlated directly with survival; 25.4% of 134 patients with levels <200 μmol/L, 44.2% of 43 patients in the 200–300 μmol/L range, and 74.1% of 58 patients with a peak bilirubin >300 μmol/L survived. The peak prothrombin time was the next most important variable ($p < 0.001$), and in 299 patients the survival rates were 73.7% of 19 cases with prothrombin times <30 s, 38.9% of 175 in the 30–100-s range, and 19.0% of 105 cases with prothrombin times >100 s. The final significant variable was serum creatinine level on admission ($p < 0.005$), the survival rates falling from 64.9% in 37 cases with creatinine <100 μmol/L to 40.4% of 104 cases with values in the 100–300 μmol/L range and 23.2% of 125 cases with creatinine levels >300 μmol/L. Significance levels were similar in the 1981–1985 cohort as in the overall analysis, but in the earlier 1973–1980 subgroup arterial pH was not identified as a prognostic indicator.

When stepwise logistic regression analysis was applied to the significant variables in 125 patients with viral hepatitis or drug reactions, the two param-

© Gastroenterology 1989; 97: 439–445

Table 2. Assessment of Prognostic Indicators in 121 Patients With Acetaminophen-Induced Fulminant Hepatic Failure

Prognostic indicator	n	Died	Positive predictive value	Specificity	Sensitivity	Predictive accuracy
pH <7.30	22	21	0.95	0.99	0.49	0.81
Prothrombin time >100 s	60	34	0.72	0.67	0.79	0.71
Serum creatinine >300 μmol/L	54	30	0.56	0.69	0.70	0.69
Nonacidotic patients (n = 99)						
Prothrombin time >100 s	39	17	0.44	0.71	0.77	0.73
Serum creatinine >300 μmol/L	49	17	0.35	0.58	0.77	0.63
Prothrombin time >100 s and serum creatinine >300 μmol/L						
All	22	12	0.55	0.87	0.55	0.80
Grade III-IV encephalopathy	15	10	0.67	0.94	0.45	0.83

eters that correlated strongly with survival were serum bilirubin ($p < 0.001$) and prothrombin time ($p < 0.001$), both the admission and peak values. The peak bilirubin level and survival were inversely correlated, with survival rates of 41.5% in 65 cases with levels <300 μmol/L and 14.3% of 161 cases with levels >300 μmol/L. The Spearman correlation coefficient for the peak bilirubin and the duration of jaundice before the onset of encephalopathy was 0.48, indicating a trend but not a strong correlation between these two parameters. The survival rate in 38 patients with a peak prothrombin time of ≤30 s was 44.7%, compared with 29.4% in 51 cases between 31–50 s, 20.0% of 104 between 51–100 s, and only 3.8% of 78 cases with prothrombin times >100 s. Arterial pH was a much less powerful indicator of outcome than in acetaminophen patients ($p < 0.05$), and similarly was identified only in the later cohort. The peak prothrombin time and peak serum bilirubin were the more important variables in the 1973–1980 and 1981–1985 cohorts, respectively. None of the therapeutic variables correlated with outcome.

Application of Prognostic Indicators

Arterial pH, peak prothrombin time, and serum creatinine level were assessed retrospectively as predictors of outcome in 121 patients admitted after an acetaminophen overdose in 1986–1987. The peak serum bilirubin was not included for reasons outlined in Discussion. The positive predictive value, specificity, sensitivity, and predictive accuracy of each poor prognostic indicator, taking cutoff values associated with survival rates <20%, was calculated for this group, which had a mortality rate of 35.5% (Table 2). Although the presence of a metabolic acidosis (pH <7.30) was highly predictive of a fatal outcome—95% of these patients died—it was found in just under half of the fatal cases. Sixty of the cases had peak prothrombin times >100 s and 72% of these died, accounting for 79% of the 43 deaths. Serum creatinine was the least discriminating of the variables. After exclusion of the patients with a metabolic acidosis, the best predictor of death was a prothrombin time >100 s combined with a serum creatinine >300 μmol/L in patients who developed at least grade III encephalopathy—67% died accounting for 67% of the remaining fatal cases. The presence of the latter set of indicators or a metabolic acidosis predicted 77% of the total deaths.

Three static and two dynamic variables identified by multivariate analysis were assessed in the 54 patients with non-acetaminophen-induced FHF admitted during 1986–1987, again using cutoff points giving survival rates <20% for each variable. Ten of these patients survived with medical management, and 12 underwent OLT but are considered "nonsurvivors" in the context of this analysis. All 15 patients with a prothrombin time >100 s died, but this was found in only 33% of fatal cases. When the cutoff point for prothrombin time was lowered to 50 s (including those >100 s), it and each of the other four poor prognostic indicators had positive predictive values for a fatal outcome ranging from 0.90–0.97, but their predictive accuracy ranged from 0.57–0.83 (Table 3). The most powerful discriminatory function in patients with a prothrombin time <100 s was found to be the presence of any three of these factors (96.4% died), whereas 8 of 10 patients with only one indicator, and 1 of 2 with two indicators survived.

Discussion

This analysis is based on the largest number of patients with FHF treated in a single unit yet reported, and it would appear to provide the learning set advocated by Tygstrup and Ranek (19). However,

© Gastroenterology 1989; 97: 439–445

Table 3. Assessment of Prognostic Indicators in 54 Patients With Non-Acetaminophen-Related Fulminant Hepatic Failure

Indicator	n	Died	Positive predictive value	Specificity	Sensitivity	Predictive accuracy
Age <10 or >40 yr	23	22	0.96	0.90	0.50	0.57
Unfavorable etiology	39	35	0.90	0.60	0.80	0.76
Jaundice for >7 days before encephalopathy	37	36	0.97	0.90	0.82	0.83
Prothrombin time >50 s	34	33	0.97	0.90	0.75	0.78
Prothrombin time >100 s	15	15	1.0	1.0	0.34	0.46
Serum bilirubin >300 μmol/L	40	37	0.93	0.70	0.84	0.81
Patients with prothrombin time <100 s (n = 39)						
Any 2 indicators	30	28	0.93	0.80	0.97	0.92
Any 3 indicators	28	27	0.96	0.90	0.93	0.92
Any 4 indicators	17	17	1.0	1.0	0.59	0.67
All patients not treated by liver transplantation (n = 42)						
Any 1 indicator	40	32	0.80	0.20	1.0	0.81
Any 2 indicators	32	30	0.94	0.80	0.94	0.90
Any 3 indicators	30	29	0.97	0.90	0.91	0.90
Any 4 indicators	19	19	1.0	1.0	0.59	0.69

there are limitations imposed on the study by the period of time over which the patients were collected. Referral patterns to the Liver Failure Unit may have changed, but we attempted to standardize for disease severity by only including patients with grade III–IV encephalopathy in the initial study, and the etiologic breakdown of the patients did not alter with time. The 13-yr period during which the 588 patients were gathered undoubtedly saw many changes in the management of this condition, leading to improved survival rates in some etiologic subgroups (13). However, no prognostic significance was identified for the treatments included in the study, and the stronger prognostic indicators identified by the overall analysis were confirmed on further analysis of the 1981–1985 cohort. This indicates that these prognostic indicators are currently relevant, a conclusion endorsed by their favorable performance when applied retrospectively to the test populations admitted in 1986–1987. While some of the parameters identified might be considered to be components of normal intuitive clinical practice, this study assigns to them discriminatory values, both alone and in combination with other variables, some of which have not been previously recognized as carrying prognostic import.

In acetaminophen patients the serum bilirubin on admission did not correlate with survival, in contrast to the strong direct correlation found for the peak value, suggesting that the latter is a function of the duration of survival after drug ingestion (i.e., the patients with the highest bilirubin levels are those who survive the hazards of the first week, especially cerebral edema and hypotension), and consequently this variable was not applied in the retrospective testing of the indicators in the 121 patients admitted during 1986–1987. The inverse correlation between the grade of encephalopathy on admission and survival is of considerable interest as it highlights the benefits of early referral, but it is of limited prognostic value in individual patients. The presence of a metabolic acidosis carries a 95% mortality, irrespective of the grade of encephalopathy present. In the remaining cases, the best predictor of a fatal outcome was the development of grade III encephalopathy in patients with prothrombin times >100 s and serum creatinine >300 μmol/L. This is the only circumstance in which the prognostic indicators identified in this study are dependent on the coexistence of advanced encephalopathy. Taking these two sets of prognostic indicators would have identified 77% of the deaths in the acetaminophen group, whereas the mortality in the remaining cases was only 11.4%. It is of note that once liver failure develops, neither blood paracetamol levels nor the previous administration of *n*-acetylcysteine or methionine are of prognostic significance.

Although etiology was shown to be of major importance in determining prognosis in the nonacetaminophen group, the use of the other prognostic indicators allows for the identification of individual patients defying the general trend associated with their underlying etiology, e.g., patients with hepatitis A more likely to have a poor prognosis or the cases of non A, non B hepatitis falling within the 10%–20% who recover with medical management. Although age has been identified as a prognostic indicator in FHF in a number of series (20,21), the poorer prognosis found in children aged <10 yr has not previously been reported. The latter finding is not due to the predominance of etiologic subgroups associated with a poor prognosis, but may reflect the belief that the development of encephalopathy in children indicates more advanced liver disease than in adults. The somewhat surprising impact of the tempo of progression in FHF on prognosis is manifested by the inverse correlation between survival and the duration of jaundice before the onset of encephalopathy (the sharp cutoff point at 7 days has not previously been reported). The higher mortality found in patients with less severe grades of encephalopathy at the time of admission is probably also a reflection of this relationship. The serum bilirubin level correlated inversely with survival in one previous study with a discrimination limit of 384 μmol/L (18), supporting the findings of this study. The correlation coefficient of 0.48 for peak serum bilirubin and the duration of jaundice before the onset of encephalopathy suggests that the former parameter reflects both the tempo of disease progression and the severity of hepatocellular dysfunction. The contrasting pattern of serum bilirubin levels in acetaminophen and nonacetaminophen patients is probably due to differences in the rapidity and duration of hepatocyte injury, together with variations in achieving net hepatic regeneration. The severity of the disturbance in coagulation is probably the best recognized prognostic indicator in FHF, and a prothrombin time >100 s carried a very high mortality. The latter or the presence of any three poor prognostic indicators (taking prothrombin time >50 s) predicted 95.5% of fatal cases, whereas 81.8% of the remaining cases survived.

Guidelines for selection of patients with FHF for OLT are needed, not only to minimize unnecessary transplantation, but also to maximize the period of time available to find a suitable donor organ by identifying suitable candidates at the earliest possible stage. In acetaminophen patients, the arterial pH and serum creatinine values relevant to prognosis are definable on the second and third days, respectively, after drug ingestion, and the prothrombin time usually peaks on the third or fourth day. Thus, in most cases prognosis can be evaluated before the onset of grade IV encephalopathy and cerebral edema. In nonacetaminophen patients, the initial prognostic evaluation should be reviewed daily on the basis of changes in the dynamic variables, with the patients being referred for OLT once the appropriate score is attained. As these criteria are independent of the grade of encephalopathy, with the exception of nonacidotic acetaminophen patients, they should have an impact on survival by generating greater confidence in proceeding with OLT before the onset of grade IV encephalopathy. While the latter is currently considered to be a prerequisite for OLT in some centers (8), it is often associated with cerebral edema, which almost certainly increases the attendant risks. Based on the findings in this study we have now adopted criteria for referring patients with FHF for liver transplantation (Table 4), and it is anticipated that these will improve the speed and accuracy of the selection of appropriate candidates.

Table 4. Criteria Adopted in King's College Hospital for Liver Transplantation in Fulminant Hepatic Failure

Acetaminophen
- pH <7.30 (irrespective of grade of encephalopathy)
- or
- Prothrombin time >100 s and serum creatinine >300 μmol/L in patients with grade III or IV encephalopathy.

Nonacetaminophen patients
- Prothrombin time >100 s (irrespective of grade of encephalopathy)
- or
- Any 3 of the following variables (irrespective of grade of encephalopathy):
  - Age <10 or >40 yr
  - Etiology—non A, non B hepatitis, halothane hepatitis, idiosyncratic drug reactions
  - Duration of jaundice before onset of encephalopathy >7 days
  - Prothrombin time >50 s
  - Serum bilirubin >300 μmol/L

References

1. Bismuth H, Castaing D, Ericzon BG, et al. Hepatic transplantation in Europe: first report of the European liver transplant registry. Lancet 1987;ii:674–6.
2. Peleman RR, Gavaler JS, Van Thiel D, et al. Orthotopic liver transplantation for acute and subacute hepatic failure in adults. Hepatology 1987;7:484–9.
3. Bismuth H, Samuel D, Gugenheim J, et al. Emergency liver transplantation for fulminant hepatitis. Ann Intern Med 1987; 107:337–41.
4. Wall WJ, Duff JH, Ghent CN, Stiller CR, Keown PA, Kutt JL. Liver transplantation: the initial experience in a Canadian centre. Can J Surg 1985;28:286–9.
5. Ringe B, Pichlmayr R, Lauchart W, Muller R. Indications and results of liver transplantation in acute hepatic failure. Transplant Proc 1986;18:86–8.
6. Sokol RJ, Francis PD, Gold SH, Ford DM, Lum DM, Ambruso DR. Orthotopic liver transplantation for acute fulminant Wilson's disease. J Pediatr 1985;107:549–52.
7. Woodle ES, Moody PR, Cox KL, Cannon RA, Ward RE. Orthotopic liver transplantation in a patient with *Amanita* poisoning. JAMA 1985;253:69–70.
8. Vickers C, Neuberger J, Buckels J, McMaster P, Elias E. Liver transplantation for fulminant hepatic failure (abstr). Gut 1987;28:A1345.
9. Rakela J, Kurtz SB, McCarthy JT, et al. Fulminant Wilson's disease treated with postdilutional hemofiltration and orthotopic liver transplantation. Gastroenterology 1986;90:2004–7.
10. Brems JJ, Hiatt JR, Ramming KP, Quinones-Baldrich WJ,

Busuttil RW. Fulminant hepatic failure: the role of liver transplantation as primary therapy. Am J Surg 1987;154: 137–41.
11. Edmond J, Aran P, Thistlethwaite J, et al. Liver transplantation and the management of fulminant hepatic failure (abstr). Gastroenterology 1988;94:A537.
12. Anonymous. Transplantation for acute liver failure (editorial). Lancet 1988;ii:1248–9.
13. O'Grady JG, Gimson AES, O'Brien CJ, Pucknell A, Hughes RD, Williams R. Controlled trials of charcoal hemoperfusion and prognostic factors in fulminant hepatic failure. Gastroenterology 1988;94:1186–92.
14. Rakela J. Etiology and prognosis in fulminant hepatitis: acute hepatic failure study group (abstr). Gastroenterology 1979; 77:A33.
15. Papaevangelou G, Tassopoulos N, Roumeliotou-Karayannis A, Richardson C. Etiology of fulminant viral hepatitis in Greece. Hepatology 1984;4:369–72.
16. Sternlieb I. Wilson's disease: indications for liver transplants. Hepatology 1984;4:15S–7S.
17. Gimson AES, O'Grady J, Ede R, Portmann B, Williams R. Late-onset hepatic failure: clinical, serological and histological features. Hepatology 1986;6:288–94.
18. Christensen E, Bremmelgaard A, Bahnsen M, et al. Prediction of fatality in fulminant hepatic failure. Scand J Gastroenterol 1984;19:90–6.
19. Tygstrup N, Ranek L. Assessment of prognosis in fulminant hepatic failure. Semin Liver Dis 1986;6:129–37.
20. Bernuau J, Goudeau A, Poynard T, et al. Multivariate analysis of prognostic factors in fulminant hepatitis B. Hepatology 1986;6:648–51.
21. Trey C, Davidson CS. The management of fulminant hepatic failure. In: Popper H, Schaffner F, eds. Progress in liver disease. Volume 3. New York: Grune & Stratton, 1970:282–98.

Received February 16, 1988. Accepted March 3, 1989.

Address requests for reprints to: Dr. Roger Williams, Liver Unit, King's College Hospital, Denmark Hill, London SE5 8RX, United Kingdom.

This work was presented to the European Association for the Study of the Liver in August 1988.

© *Nature* 1990; 343: 82–85

Induction of a novel epidermal growth factor-secreting cell lineage by mucosal ulceration in human gastrointestinal stem cells

Nicholas A. Wright, Christine Pike & George Elia

ICRF Laboratories, Lincoln's Inn Fields, London WC2 3PN, UK

EPIDERMAL growth factor, and its human homologue urogastrone (EGF/URO)[1], are secreted by the gut-associated salivary and Brunner's glands[2,3]. Recombinant EGF/URO is a powerful stimulator of cell proliferation and differentiation in the rodent[4–7] and neonatal human[8] intestine. But EGF/URO is not absorbed from the adult gut[9,10] and has no action when given through the gut lumen[6]; thus the role of secreted EGF/URO is unknown. We now report that ulceration of the epithelium anywhere in the human gastrointestinal tract induces the development of a novel cell lineage from gastrointestinal stem cells. This lineage initially appears as a bud from the base of intestinal crypts, adjacent to the ulcer, and grows locally as a tubule, ramifying to form a new small gland, and ultimately emerges onto the mucosal surface. The lineage produces neutral mucin, shows a unique lectin-binding profile and immunophenotype, is nonproliferative, and contains and secretes abundant immunoreactive EGF/URO. We propose that all gastrointestinal stem cells can produce this cell lineage after mucosal ulceration, secreting EGF/URO to stimulate cell proliferation, regeneration and ulcer healing. This cell lineage is very commonly associated with gastrointestinal mucosal ulceration, and we conclude that a principal *in vivo* role for EGF/URO is to stimulate ulcer healing throughout the gut through induction of this cell lineage in the adjacent mucosa.

Chronic ulceration of the gastrointestinal mucosa is frequent in man, occurring particularly in Crohn's disease and peptic ulcer disease. We have studied freshly-frozen and formalin-fixed tissue from 56 patients with Crohn's disease[11] (multiple sites were analysed in ulcerated small intestine (45 cases) and colon (21 cases)), and also from 66 patients with chronic gastric and duodenal peptic ulcers[12]. In the mucosa adjacent to ulcers, small buds appear at the bottom of the intestinal crypts (Fig. 1*a*). These buds are composed of columnar cells with basal nuclei; the cytoplasm contains large amounts of neutral mucin, unlike the intestinal mucous cells (goblet cells), which contain mainly acid sialomucin. The buds develop into a new small gland, still maintaining its connection with the parent crypt (Fig. 1*b*). Having reached a certain size, the new gland develops a tubule which, in the small intestine, grows as a duct up the connective tissue core of an adjacent villus (Fig. 1*c–f*), and emerges onto the villus surface through a stoma (Fig. 1*f*) providing access to the intestinal lumen for the secretion of the new gland. Additionally, the cells from the duct migrate directly onto the villus surface, often covering it (Fig. 1*g*). On the villus, these cells maintain their singular morphology, and are quite different from adjacent enterocytes and goblet cells (Fig. 1*g*). These morphogenetic events are summarized diagrammatically in Fig. 2.

The phenotype of the cells was investigated by orthodox histochemistry, lectin-binding characteristics and immunocytochemistry using antibodies against several differentiation antigens. The cell lineage is phenotypically different from other small intestinal lineages. Thus only cells on the villus surface stain with antibody 3B10, which recognizes a glycoprotein of relative molecular mass 150,000 that is related to carcinoembryonic antigen[13] (Fig. 3); cells in the gland area are negative for staining, as are enterocytes and goblet cells. Most cells in the lineage are positive for staining with SM3, an antibody raised against the mucin core protein[14], whereas HMFG1 and HMFG2 antibodies, which recognize overlapping sequences in the mucin core protein[15], show an interesting pattern: the cells lining the gland are HMFG1 positive and HMFG2 negative, whereas the cells on the villus surface are HMFG2 positive and HMFG1 negative, that is, they show complementary staining. Again, indigenous intestinal cell lineages are negative for staining with these monoclonal antibodies. Moreover, *Lens culinaris* (LCA), a lectin which identifies binding sites for α-mannose, α-galactose and *N*-acetylgalactosamine (in that order of preference), binds to the cell membranes of the surface cell but not cells in the gland area. These observations indicate that the lineage

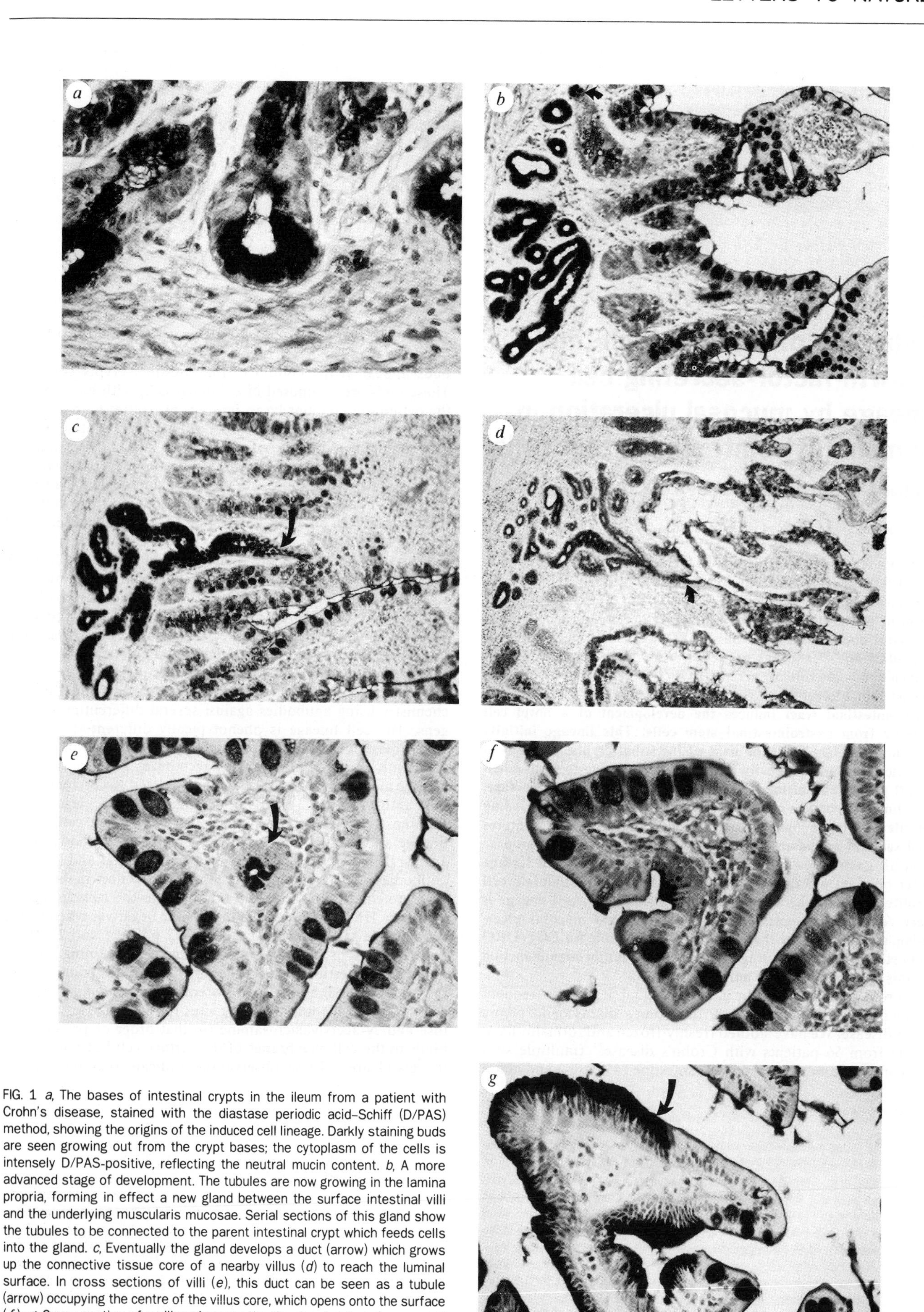

FIG. 1 *a*, The bases of intestinal crypts in the ileum from a patient with Crohn's disease, stained with the diastase periodic acid–Schiff (D/PAS) method, showing the origins of the induced cell lineage. Darkly staining buds are seen growing out from the crypt bases; the cytoplasm of the cells is intensely D/PAS-positive, reflecting the neutral mucin content. *b*, A more advanced stage of development. The tubules are now growing in the lamina propria, forming in effect a new gland between the surface intestinal villi and the underlying muscularis mucosae. Serial sections of this gland show the tubules to be connected to the parent intestinal crypt which feeds cells into the gland. *c*, Eventually the gland develops a duct (arrow) which grows up the connective tissue core of a nearby villus (*d*) to reach the luminal surface. In cross sections of villi (*e*), this duct can be seen as a tubule (arrow) occupying the centre of the villus core, which opens onto the surface (*f*). *g*, Cross-section of a villus closer to the tip, showing that the new cell lineage also migrates onto the villus surface (arrow). The distinct morphological difference between the surface enterocytes and goblet cells can be seen.

acquires new antigens as it migrates, and also changes the nature of its secretory glycoconjugates by adding new carbohydrate groups to the core protein. This suggests that the cells differentiate as they pass through the tubules onto the surface.

Both rabbit and sheep anti-human EGF/URO antibody shows abundant immunoreactive EGF/URO in cells in the gland area and in the secretion (Fig. 4); the staining appears granular, as seen in other EGF/URO-secreting glands[3]. Some acini are only faintly positive, especially in the more superficial areas, as is expected when staining for a secreted molecule, and surface cells are usually negative. The cells in basal crypt buds and small glands are faintly stained or negative for staining, indicating that the ability to secrete EGF/URO is acquired later in the lineage.

It is singular that mitotic activity in this lineage is conspicuous by its absence, even in the early basal buds (Fig. 1*a*), in sharp contrast to the parent crypt and adjacent crypts. Moreover the

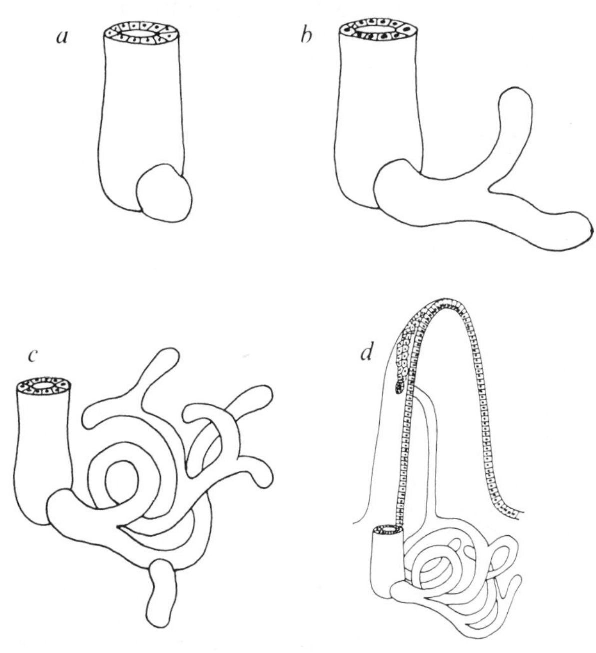

FIG. 2 A diagrammatic representation of the morphogenesis of the cell lineage: a bud appears in the base of the crypt, within the stem cell zone (*a*); the resulting tubules then grow in the lamina propria (*b*) to form a new gland (*c*), which eventually communicates with the surface by a duct, which pours secretion into the intestinal lumen and feeds cells onto the surface (*d*). For three-dimensional analysis, serial sections were prepared of the earliest stages and of glands of various sizes. These were traced onto paper using a drawing tube, the drawings stuck onto polystyrene tiles, cut out with a hot wire, and glued together. Several examples of each stage (*a*–*d*) were studied.

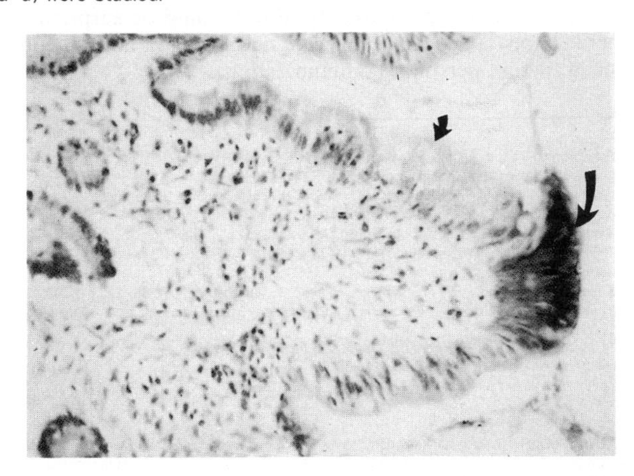

FIG. 3 The tip of an ileal villus showing a group of the cells occupying the very tip, expressing the 3B10 antigen, an M_r 150K glycoprotein related to carcinoembryonic antigen (large arrow). The surrounding villous enterocytes and goblet cells are negative (small arrow), as are the glandular portions of the cell lineage in the lamina propria. Paraffin-embedded sections were de-waxed and taken down to 100% alcohol, and endogenous peroxidase was blocked with 30% hydrogen peroxide for 15 min. Sections were incubated for 35 min with 3B10, an IgG mouse monoclonal antibody raised against normal human colon[13], washed, and incubated with biotinylated rabbit anti-mouse antibody. After 35-min incubation in avidin-biotin complex, the sections were incubated for 2 min in peroxidase substrate (diaminobenzidine, PBS, in addition to 30% hydrogen peroxidase) and counterstained with haematoxylin.

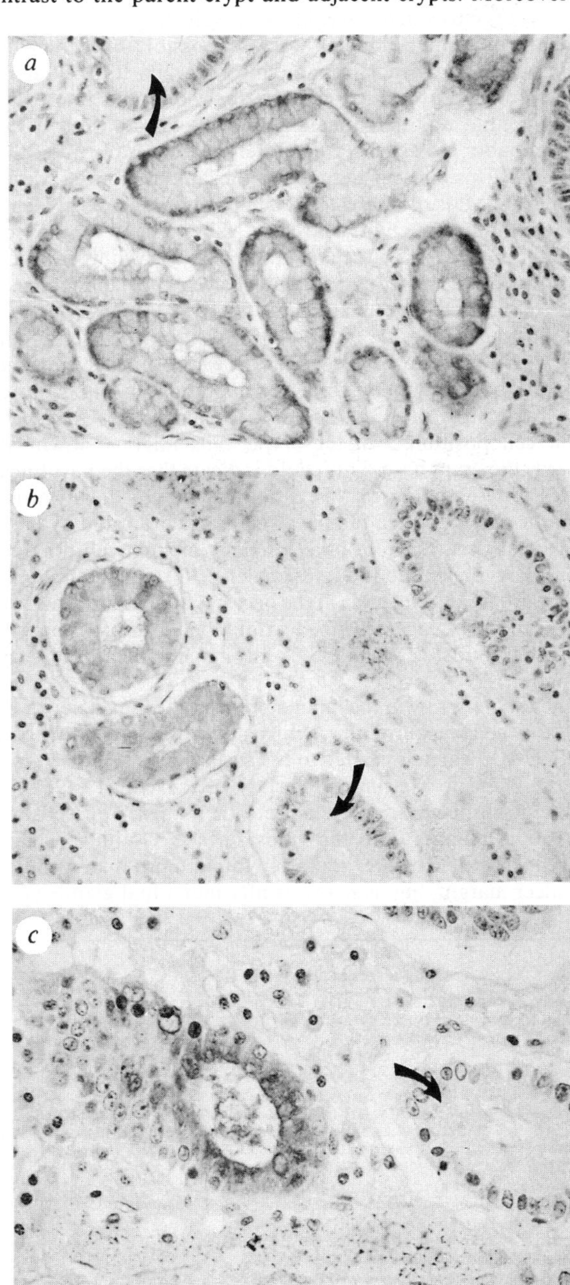

FIG. 4 The cell lineage in ileum (*a*, *b*) and colon (*c*) showing immunoreactive cytoplasmic and luminal EGF/URO. *a*, *b*, *c*, The normal crypt (arrow) shows negatively stained columnar cells and goblet cells. The staining is granular and varies considerably between individual cells in the lineage (*a*). The primary antibody was a polyclonal antibody against recombinant EGF/URO[27] raised in rabbits. The method was similar to that given in the legend to Fig. 3, apart from incubation in swine anti-rabbit antibody. Controls (absorption controls, absorbing the primary antibody with recombinant EGF/URO, and controls omitting the primary antibody) showed abolition of staining. Positive staining is also seen with a polyclonal antibody against recombinant human EGF/URO raised in sheep.

cell lineage stains uniformly negative with the monoclonal antibody Ki67, which recognizes a proliferation-dependent nuclear antigen in human cells[16].

A search for other defined lineages of small intestinal origin in the newly formed glands reveals occasional Paneth cells (lysozyme-positive), a few chromogranin A and Grimelius-positive neuroendocrine cells and very infrequent but typical goblet cells, containing acid sialomucin.

These observations lead us to propose that mucosal ulceration is the signal for the development of this cell lineage. Development occurs close to the ulcer margin, indicating a concentration gradient of some inducing factor (possibly mesenchymal-derived[13]) with distance from the ulcer margin. It is initiated as a bud growing from the crypt base, where the intercalated multipotential undifferentiated stem cells are housed[17,18], and thus probably represents direct differentiation progeny of these stem cells. This bud pushes out into the lamina propria, forming a new gland. It is of interest that cell proliferation, as evidenced by lack of mitotic activity and Ki67 staining, is not involved in this morphogenesis; but the usually slowly cycling stem cells are fully capable of reducing their cell cycle time and increasing their cell production rate at times of need[18]. Moreover, because cells appear to migrate along the tubule, the local crypt stem cells would seem to be providing the entire lineage (although probably not the motive force for migration[19]). The stem cell zone hypothesis of Bjerkness and Cheng[20] states that below about cell position 5 in the crypt, cells migrate downwards towards the crypt base. This could indicate that the new lineage begins differentiation in this zone, and moves downwards to enter the newly formed tubule, as is further indicated by (1) the occasional occurrence of other progeny of stem cell differentiation (Paneth, endocrine and goblet cells) caught up in the downward migration, and (2) the occasional observation of cells similar to the lineage described within the bases of crypts without basal buds (presumably seen immediately before bud formation).

The tubules grow in the lamina propria, forming a new gland, and the cells acquire the ability to synthesize and secrete EGF/URO, which is carried to the surface by a tubule connecting the gland to the luminal surface of the villus. EGF/URO and neutral mucin are secreted into the lumen, and cells from the tubule migrate onto the villus surface, clothing its upper portion. The new glands are rarely found more than 1 cm from the ulcer margin, but as many as fifty individual glands can be found around small (5 mm) ileal ulcers; in larger ulcers, many more glands are found, and they can reach appreciable size (>5 mm diameter). They are commonest in the small intestine in Crohn's disease, present in all ulcers examined in 39 out of 45 cases, and although rarer, the same lineage is induced in the colon in Crohn's disease (5 out of 21 cases; Fig. 4). It is a constant finding in duodenal ulcer disease and duodenitis (36 out of 36 cases), and fairly common in gastric ulcer disease (15 out of 30 cases). Thus chronic mucosal ulceration anywhere in the gastrointestinal tract can induce this cell lineage from multipotential stem cells in intestinal crypts or gastric glands; the new glands so formed secrete EGF/URO.

EGF/URO, although an extremely potent stimulator of cell proliferation in the intestine when given parenterally[7,8] is not absorbed and has no effect when administered lumenally when the mucosa is intact[6,9,10], even though there are now numerous reports of epidermal growth factor receptors on small intestinal and colonic epithelial cells[21]. It has instead been proposed that transforming growth factor alpha (TGF-α) could be the main ligand for EGF receptors in the gut[22]. But EGF/URO heals and prevents experimentally induced ulceration in the rat[23,24], and is absorbed through damaged mucosa[25]; thus the EGF/URO produced locally by the new glands is available to regenerating epithelial and connective tissue cells in and around the ulcer. We therefore propose that a principal *in vivo* role of EGF/URO is to assist in the healing of ulceration in the gastrointestinal mucosa through induction of this lineage.

What is the nature of this cell lineage? Similar proliferations have usually previously been regarded as metaplasias, called 'pyloric' or 'gastric' because of morphological resemblance to gastric epithelial cells, or even as Brunner's gland metaplasia on similar grounds[26]. The latter could seem most reasonable because of the common EGF/URO production, but the lectin-binding profile and immunophenotype are different from those of both gastric and Brunner's gland epithelium, and seems unique among gastrointestinal epithelial cells. The term metaplasia implies a change from one defined differentiated cell type to another, but if, as these results indicate, this is a novel cell lineage, then it cannot strictly be regarded as a metaplasia. It could be that abnormal conditions induce novel cell lineages in epithelial stem cells, until now regarded as metaplasias, but only defined by detailed phenotyping. But it would be surprising if, generally speaking, such cells were never seen in normal conditions (J. Slack, personal communication). □

Received 3 October; accepted 7 November 1989.

1. Gregory, H. *Nature* **257,** 325-327 (1975).
2. Cohen, S. & Carpenter, G. *Proc. natn. Acad. Sci. U.S.A.* **72,** 1317-1321 (1975).
3. Heitz, P., Kasper, M., Van Noorden, S., Polak, J. M., Gregory, H. & Pearse, A. G. E. *Gut* **19,** 408-413 (1978).
4. Al-Nafussi, A. & Wright, N. *Virchows Arch. Cell Path.* **40,** 63-70 (1982).
5. Malo, C. & Menard, D. *Gastroenterology* **83,** 28-35 (1982).
6. Goodlad, R., Wilson, G., Lenton, W., Gregory, H., MacCullagh, K. & Wright, N. *Gut* **28,** 573-582 (1987).
7. Thompson, T. S., Sharp, J. G., Saxena, S. K. & MacCullagh, K. *J. surg. Res.* **42,** 402-410 (1987).
8. Walker-Smith, J. *et al. Lancet* **ii,** 1239-1240 (1985).
9. Olsen, P. *et al. Gut* **25,** 1234-1240 (1984).
10. Skov-Olsen, P., Poulsen, S. S., Kierkegaard, P. & Nexo, E. *Dig. Dis. Sci.* **29,** 615-622 (1984).
11. Morson, B. & Dawson, I. *Gastrointestinal Pathology*, 293-312 (Blackwell, Oxford, 1979).
12. Magnus, H. *Postgrad. Med. J.* **30,** 131-146 (1954).
13. Richman, P. & Bodmer, W. *Int. J. Cancer* **39,** 317-328 (1987).
14. Burchell, J. *et al. Cancer Res.* **47,** 5476-5482 (1987).
15. Gendler, S., Taylor-Papadimitriou, J., Duhig, T., Rothbard, J. & Burchell, J. *J. biol. Chem.* **263,** 12820-12823 (1988).
16. Schwarting, R. *et al. J. immunol. Meth.* **90,** 365-371 (1986).
17. Cheng, H. & Leblond, C. P. *Am. J. Anat.* **141,** 537-562 (1974).
18. Wright, N. & Alison, M. R. *The Biology of Epithelial Cell Populations Vol. 2* (Clarendon, Oxford, 1984).
19. Kaur, P. & Potten, C. S. *Cell Tissue Kinet.* **19,** 601-610 (1986).
20. Bjerknes, R. & Cheng, H. *Am. J. Anat.* **160,** 76-92 (1981).
21. Thompson, J. *Am. J. Physiol.* **264,** G429-G435 (1988).
22. Barnard, J. *et al. Gastroenterology* **96,** A27 (1989).
23. Kirkegaard, P., Olsen, P. S., Poulsen, S. S. & Nexo, E. *Gastroenterology* **85,** 1277-1283 (1983).
24. Konturek, S., Dembinski, A., Warzecha, A., Brzozowski, T. & Gregory, H. *Gastroenterology* **94,** 1300-1307 (1988).
25. Poulsen, S. *Scand. J. Gastroenterd.* (Suppl. 22) **128,** 20-21 (1987).
26. Lee, F. *J. pathol. Bact.* **87,** 267-277 (1964).
27. Smith, J. *et al. Nucleic Acids Res.* **10,** 4467-4482 (1982).

ACKNOWLEDGEMENTS. We thank Gordon Stamp, Paul Richman and Jonathan Slack for discussions, Harry Gregory for the gift of the anti-human EGF/URO antibodies, Joyce Taylor-Papadimitrou for SM3 and HMFG-1 and -2 antibodies, Paul Richman for the 3B10 antibody, and Chris Foster for lectins.

© *Gastroenterology* 1990; 99: 1388–1395

LIVER, PANCREAS, AND BILIARY TRACT

Randomized, Double-Blind, Placebo-Controlled Trial of Somatostatin for Variceal Bleeding

Emergency Control and Prevention of Early Variceal Rebleeding

ANDREW K. BURROUGHS, P. AIDEN McCORMICK, MICHAEL D. HUGHES, DIRK SPRENGERS, FRANCOIS D'HEYGERE, and NEIL McINTYRE

Hepato-biliary and Liver Transplantation Unit and Department of Clinical Epidemiology and General Practice, Royal Free Hospital and School of Medicine, Hampstead, London, England

A randomized, double-blind, placebo-controlled trial of somatostatin was conducted among 120 patients admitted for bleeding esophageal varices (59 placebo, 61 somatostatin). An initial 250-μg bolus of somatostatin followed by a 5-day continuous infusion of 250 μg/h and an identical administration of placebo were evaluated for both the control of bleeding and prevention of early rebleeding from varices. Failure to control bleeding occurred in 22 (36%) somatostatin patients vs. 35 (59%) placebo patients, with time to failure occurring earlier with placebo ($P = 0.036$). Blood and plasma transfused per hour during drug infusion of trial drug was reduced in the somatostatin group: median 0.033 vs. 0.105 unit/h ($P = 0.025$). Use of balloon tamponade was halved in somatostatin-treated patients. The average effect of somatostatin was a 41% reduction in the hazard of failure (95% confidence interval, −1% to 65%, $P = 0.0545$) after adjustment for the severity of liver disease, which was the only other variable having a significant influence on time to failure. There was no difference in 30-day mortality per admission (7 placebo, 9 somatostatin) or complications. It is concluded that somatostatin is safe and more effective than placebo for the control of variceal bleeding.

0016-5085/90/$3.00

© *Lancet* 1990; 335: 1572–1573

Improved outcome of paracetamol-induced fulminant hepatic failure by late administration of acetylcysteine

P. M. HARRISON R. KEAYS G. P. BRAY G. J. M. ALEXANDER
ROGER WILLIAMS

The influence of acetylcysteine, administered at presentation to hospital, on the subsequent clinical course of 100 patients who developed paracetamol-induced fulminant hepatic failure was analysed retrospectively. Mortality was 37% in patients who received acetylcysteine 10–36 h after the overdose, compared with 58% in patients not given the antidote. In patients given acetylcysteine, progression to grade III/IV coma was significantly less common than in those who did not receive the antidote (51% *vs* 75%), although the median peak prothrombin time was similar for both groups. Whether the beneficial effect is related to replenishment of glutathione stores or a consequence of another hepatic protective mechanism of acetylcysteine requires further study.

Lancet 1990; **335**: 1572–73.

Introduction

Acetylcysteine (N-acetylcysteine) administered within 10 h of a paracetamol (acetaminophen) overdose is accepted to be a highly effective treatment to prevent massive hepatic necrosis,[1-3] but it is less effective when given after 10 h,[1,2] and the efficacy of acetylcysteine when a patient attends hospital more than 15 h after an overdose is controversial. Prescott and colleagues[1,4] concluded that intravenous therapy after 15 h had elapsed was of no benefit because it failed to prevent hepatotoxicity, defined by a rise in the aspartate transaminase above 1000 IU/l, in 9 of 11 patients. However, in a retrospective review of oral acetylcysteine treatment, Smilkstein et al[3] found that therapy up to 24 h after ingestion was associated with a lower incidence of hepatotoxicity compared with historical controls. As far as we are aware, the efficacy of acetylcysteine has been assessed by its ability to prevent hepatic necrosis; if a patient developed fulminant hepatic failure the antidote was assumed to have failed and its administration thought to have had no influence on the subsequent clinical course. Is such an assumption valid? We reviewed a series of 100 patients consecutively admitted to this hospital with evidence of severe hepatic necrosis after paracetamol overdose to determine whether acetylcysteine administered at presentation had had any effect on the subsequent clinical course and outcome of the fulminant hepatic failure.

Patients and methods

The patients were treated in the Liver Failure Unit between October, 1986, and April, 1988. All 100 had a serum aspartate transaminase concentration above 1000 IU/l and met the criteria of Trey and Davidson[5] for diagnosis of fulminant hepatic failure. Most patients were referred from other hospitals on the second or third day after a paracetamol overdose because of early encephalopathy or other features to indicate a poor prognosis (eg, a rapidly rising prothrombin time, renal failure, or early acidosis[6]).

In the retrospective analysis, patients were assigned to 1 of 3 groups according to the time that had elapsed between the overdose and administration of acetylcysteine: 2 patients had been treated within 10 h; 41 had received acetylcysteine 10 h or more after overdose; and 57 had not been given the antidote. When given, acetylcysteine had always been administered by intravenous infusion according to a standard regimen.[1] In our assessment of the course of the fulminant hepatic failure after admission to the Liver Failure Unit, we took account of known indicators of poor prognosis and two others we recently identified,[7] namely a peak prothrombin time of 180 s or longer, and a continued rise in prothrombin time on the fourth day compared with the third day after overdose. The χ^2, Mann Whitney U, or Student's *t* tests were used as appropriate for statistical analysis.

Results

The late and no antidote groups were similar with regard to age (mean 28·6 years [SD 10·7] and 33·4 years [13·5], respectively), sex (female/male ratio 1·7/1 in both groups), and quantity of paracetamol taken (mean 38 g [SD 39·9] and 35·8 g [13·5], respectively). There was no significant difference in the time between overdose and first presentation to hospital: median 17 h (interquartile range 13·25–24 h) for those who had late antidote and median 16 h (interquartile range 14–36) for those who did not receive antidote.

Significantly fewer patients with hepatic failure who received acetylcysteine 10 h or more after overdose progressed to grade III/IV coma compared with those who received none (51% *vs* 75%, respectively; $p<0·05$). In patients who received acetylcysteine the maximum grade of encephalopathy recorded did not correlate with the time between overdose and administration of antidote (median 15·5 h [interquartile range 14–24 h] for patients with maximum grade I encephalopathy, 20 h [12–22] for those with grade II, 24 h [18–30] with grade III, and 19 h [14–24] for those with grade IV coma).

Mortality was significantly lower in patients given acetylcysteine 10 h or more after overdose (15 of 41, 37%) compared with those who did not receive antidote (33 of 57, 58%; $p<0·05$). In those who received late acetylcysteine, the time of administration after the overdose was similar for survivors (median 15·5 h [interquartile range 12–24 h] and for those who died (median 18 h [14–24]. Both patients who received the antidote within 10 h of the overdose survived.

The overall reduction in mortality with late administration of acetylcysteine was also shown when outcome was considered in relation to previously described prognostic criteria. Of 17 patients who did not receive antidote and who had either a peak prothrombin time of or above 180 s, or a prothrombin time that rose between days 3

ADDRESS: **Liver Unit, King's College Hospital and School of Medicine and Dentistry, London SE5 9RS, UK** (P. M. Harrison, MRCP, R. Keays, MRCP, G. P. Bray, MRCP, G. J. M. Alexander, MRCP, R. Williams, MD). Correspondence to Dr R. Williams.

© Lancet 1990; 335: 1572–1573

OUTCOME OF PARACETAMOL-INDUCED FULMINANT HEPATIC FAILURE IN RELATION TO ACETYLCYSTEINE ADMINISTRATION

Treatment	n	Survivors	Deaths	Progress to grade III/IV coma	Dialysis required†
No antidote	57	24 *(42%)**	33 *(58%)**	43 *(75%)**	38 *(67%)*
Early <10 h	2	2 *(100%)*	0	0	0
Late ≥10 h	41	26 *(63%)**	15 *(37%)**	21 *(51%)**	21 *(51%)*

*p<0·05 between no-antidote and late-antidote groups.
†Anuria or oliguria with creatinine above 400 μmol/l.

and 4, all died, compared with 11 of 16 similar patients who received late acetylcysteine ($p < 0{\cdot}05$). For patients with less severe hepatic disturbance, late administration of acetylcysteine was associated with a 16% mortality (4 of 25), significantly less than the 40% mortality (16 of 40) for patients not given the antidote.

Peak prothrombin times were similar in patients who received late acetylcysteine (median 130 s [interquartile range 88·5–180 s]; control 15 s) and those who did not receive antidote (122 s [85·5–165]), and there was no correlation between peak prothrombin time and time between overdose and administration of antidote. There was also no statistical difference in the number of patients who required dialysis for renal failure (anuria or oliguria with serum creatinine above 400 μmol/l) between patients who received late antidote or none (21 of 41 [51%] and 38 of 57 [67%], respectively).

Careful review of all notes revealed no record of side-effects associated with late administration of acetylcysteine.

Discussion

The main protective actions of acetylcysteine after paracetamol overdose are replenishment of intracellular reduced glutathione[8,9] and detoxification of the arylating metabolite of paracetamol, N-acetyl-p-benzoquinonimine,[10] which is produced by direct 2-electron oxidation through the cytochrome P450 system.[11] However, there are several other possible mechanisms by which acetylcysteine given late after paracetamol ingestion could be of benefit. In isolated hepatocytes, acetylcysteine can restore the capacity of the intracellular proteolytic system to degrade toxic arylated proteins;[12] thus, if this mechanism is active in vivo, poisoned cells may remain viable. Alternatively, neutrophil accumulation within the liver exacerbates paracetamol-induced damage,[13] and the potent antioxidant properties of acetylcysteine could prevent this. Although the improved outcome with the antidote was not associated with a reduction in the severity of liver damage as measured by median peak prothrombin time, this is only one indicator of liver injury and a different result may have been obtained if overall liver function had been assessed by galactose elimination. Late acetylcysteine treatment reduced progression to grade III or grade IV encephalopathy, which would be consistent with reduced liver damage, and the beneficial effect on survival was shown even in patients with poor prognostic criteria.

In the UK about 150 people annually die after paracetamol overdose;[14] as shown in an earlier study,[15] these represent patients who do not seek medical attention until late after the overdose. The results of this retrospective study strongly indicate that standard intravenous administration of acetylcysteine significantly improves survival in patients who develop paracetamol-induced fulminant hepatic failure, even when the antidote is given late after the overdose. Potential side-effects such as hypersensitivity reactions did not occur after late administration of acetylcysteine, and fewer patients who received late treatment progressed to deep coma—which refutes the fear that late therapy would lead to an increased incidence of encephalopathy.

It is of interest that 2 patients developed fulminant hepatic failure despite administration of antidote within 10 h of the overdose, both of whom survived. Both were young women with no known history of chronic alcohol abuse or use of drugs that may induce liver enzymes.

Whenever possible, acetylcysteine should be given early after the overdose, but we found a benefit of treatment in patients given acetylcysteine with a median delay of 17 h and a range of 10 to 36 h after the overdose. There were no other discernible differences between patients who received late or no antidote treatment to account for the better outcome in the former group; in particular, the delay between overdose and presentation to hospital was similar for both groups. The findings of this retrospective study strongly indicate that acetylcysteine treatment should be considered in patients who present to hospital more than 15 h after a paracetamol overdose. These results, and the longest delay for a benefit to be observed (perhaps up to 36 h), need to be confirmed in a prospective, randomised, placebo-controlled trial.

We thank Dr John Spooner (Sterling Research Laboratories) for generous support of studies into paracetamol hepatotoxicity.

REFERENCES

1. Prescott LF, Illingworth RN, Critchley JAJH, Stewart MJ, Adam RD, Proudfoot AT. Intravenous N-acetylcysteine: the treatment of choice for paracetamol poisoning. *Br Med J* 1979; ii: 1097–1100.
2. Rumack BH, Peterson RC, Koch GC, Amara IA. Acetaminophen overdose: 662 cases with evaluation of oral acetylcysteine treatment. *Arch Intern Med* 1981; **141:** 380–85.
3. Smilkstein MJ, Knapp GL, Kulig KW, Rumack BH. Efficacy of oral N-acetylcysteine in the treatment of acetaminophen overdose. *N Engl J Med* 1988; **319:** 1557–62.
4. Prescott LF. Paracetamol overdosage: pharmacological considerations and clinical management. *Drugs* 1983; **25:** 290–314.
5. Trey C, Davidson CS. The management of fulminant hepatic failure. New York: Grune & Stratton, 1970: 282–98.
6. O'Grady J, Alexander GJM, Hayllar KM, Williams R. Early indicators of prognosis in fulminant hepatic failure. *Gastroenterology* 1989; **97:** 439–45.
7. Harrison PM, O'Grady JG, Alexander GJM, Williams R. Serial prothrombin ratios: a prognostic indicator in paracetamol induced acute liver failure. *Gut* 1988; **29:** A1462.
8. Miners JO, Drew R, Birkett DJ. Mechanism of action of paracetamol protective agents in mice in vivo. *Biochem Pharmacol* 1984; **33:** 2995–3000.
9. Slattery JT, Wilson JM, Kalhorn TF, Nelson SD. Dose dependent pharmacokinetics of acetaminophen: evidence of glutathione depletion in humans. *Clin Pharmacol Ther* 1987; **41:** 413–18.
10. Corcoran GB, Mitchell JR, Vaishnav YN, Horning EC. Evidence that acetaminophen and N-hydroxyacetaminophen form a common arylating intermediate, N-acetyl-p-benzoquinoneimine. *Mol Pharmacol* 1980; **18:** 536–42.
11. van de Straat R, Vromans RM, Bosman P, de Vries J, Vermeulen NP. Cytochrome P-450-mediated oxidation of substrates by electron-transfer; role of oxygen radicals and of 1- and 2-electron oxidation of paracetamol. *Chem Biol Interact* 1988; **64:** 267–80.
12. Bruno MK, Cohen SD, Khairallah EA. Antidotal effectiveness of N-acetylcysteine in reversing acetaminophen-induced hepatotoxicity. Enhancement of the proteolysis of arylated proteins. *Biochem Pharmacol* 1988; **37:** 4319–25.
13. Jaeschke H, Mitchell JR. Neutrophil accumulation exacerbates acetaminophen-induced liver injury. *FASEB J* 1989; **3:** A920.
14. Meredith TJ, Prescott LF, Vale JA. Why do patients still die from paracetamol poisoning? *Br Med J* 1986; **293:** 345–46.
15. Read RB, Tredger JM, Williams R. Analysis of factors responsible for continuing mortality after paracetamol overdose. *Hum Toxicol* 1986; **5:** 201-06.

Br. J. Surg. 1990, Vol. 77, May, 510–512

'Close shave' in anterior resection

N. D. Karanjia, D. J. Schache, W. R. S. North* and R. J. Heald

*Basingstoke District Hospital, Hampshire and *Imperial Cancer Research Fund Clinical Oncology Unit, Guy's Hospital, London, UK*

Correspondence to:
Mr R. J. Heald, Basingstoke District Hospital, Basingstoke, Hampshire RG24 9NA, UK

Of 192 anterior resections for rectal cancer performed over 10 years by one author (R.J.H.), 169 (88 per cent) included total mesorectal excision and all included lavage of the clamped distal rectum. Of this series, 152 (79 per cent) were classed as curative, 110 with a resection margin >1 cm and 42 with a resection margin ⩽1 cm. The group with a >1 cm margin had a significantly lower Dukes' A to B ratio than the group with a margin ⩽1 cm, although the proportion with Dukes' C lesions was similar in both groups ($\chi^2=6{\cdot}712$; P=0·035). There were no local recurrences in the latter group (95 per cent confidence interval (CI) is 0–5·9 per cent) while there were four (3·6 per cent) in the former group (95 per cent CI is 0·8–7·4 per cent). There were no significant differences in recurrence rates, local and distant, between the two groups (Fisher's exact test, P=0·2). Reduction of resection margin, provided total mesorectal excision and washout is properly performed, does not increase local recurrence or compromise survival.

Keywords: Carcinoma of the rectum, total mesorectal excision, resection margin, anterior resection

Recent critical appraisal of the 5 cm rule[1,2] has led to the suggestion that the distal resection margin in anterior resection for rectal cancer may be reduced and the number of abdominoperineal excisions kept to a minimum.

Patients and methods

From 1978 prospective records were kept on computer of all anterior resections performed by one author (R.J.H.) at Basingstoke. All rectal cancer specimens fixed unpinned in theatre were later opened, pinned and photographed by a consultant pathologist who accurately measured the distal resection margins. The relevant stapler 'doughnut' was separately examined and represented approximately an extra 0.5 cm. Regular follow-up included rectal examination and endoscopy by a consultant oncologist and surgeon with data recording by a full-time research assistant with close personal knowledge of all patients. An independent statistician (W.R.S.N.) analysed the relationship between distal resection margin and local recurrence.

Results

The series consists of 192 anterior resections, 152 (79 per cent) of which were classed as curative and 40 (21 per cent) of which were classified as non-curative because of metastases in 23 (12 per cent) or failed local clearance in 17 (8·8 per cent). During the same period 21 abdominoperineal excisions were undertaken, representing 9·8 per cent of all rectal cancers. Analysis of the anterior resections by resection margin size showed that 55 (29 per cent) margins were ⩽1 cm and 26 of these were ⩽0·5 cm. The ⩽1 cm and >1 cm margins were evenly distributed throughout the 10-year period. Total mesorectal excision was performed in 88 per cent of the patients and all had water lavage of the rectum distal to the clamp. This paper considers specifically those patients whose surgery was completed with a hope of 'cure'.

Curative anterior resections

The analysis of 152 curative anterior resections is summarized in *Table 1*; of these, 42 cases (28 per cent) had a resection margin <1 cm and 110 cases (72 per cent) had a resection margin >1 cm.

The <1 cm group had a higher Dukes' A to B ratio but the proportion of Dukes' C tumours was similar in the two groups ($\chi^2=6{\cdot}712$; $P=0{\cdot}035$). There was no significant difference with regard to tumour differentiation. The <1 cm group contained significantly lower tumours, at a mean of 4·7 cm from the anal verge at sigmoidoscopy compared with 9·5 cm for the other group ($t=8{\cdot}84$; $P<0{\cdot}001$). There were no local recurrences in the 42 curative anterior resection patients with a margin <1 cm. The 95 per cent confidence interval (CI) for this was 0–5·9 per cent. Three (7·1 per cent) patients have developed distant metastases with a mean time to presentation of 1·9 years.

Of 110 patients with curative resection with a margin >1 cm, four (3·6 per cent) have developed local recurrence. The 95 per cent CI for this is 0·8–7·4 per cent. The mean time to presentation with local recurrence was 1 year. Analysis of these four local recurrences suggested a potentially preventable surgical cause for each (*Table 2*). In this group a further 11 (10 per cent) patients developed distant metastases with a mean time to presentation of 1·8 years.

Statistical analysis showed no significant difference in either local recurrence rates or distant metastases in the two groups (Fisher's exact test).

Non-curative anterior resections

The classification of 40 non-curative anterior resections is complex. Thirteen had a resection margin ⩽1 cm and 27 had a margin >1 cm. There was no significant difference with regard to tumour staging or differentiation, and the ⩽1 cm group contained significantly lower tumours at a mean of 5·1 cm from the anal verge at sigmoidoscopy compared with 9·5 cm for the other group ($t=3{\cdot}99$; $P<0{\cdot}01$).

In the ⩽1 cm group seven patients had no metastases but doubtful local clearance; only one of these developed local recurrence. In four of the remainder, complete local clearance was achieved despite distant metastases; none of these developed local recurrence. The last two patients were known to have distant metastases and incomplete local clearance; both developed early local recurrence.

In the >1 cm group ten patients had no metastases but doubtful local clearance; only one of these developed local recurrence. In 12 of the remaining 17, local clearance was achieved despite the presence of distant metastases; none of these developed local recurrence. The last five patients were known to have distant metastases and incomplete local clearance; these patients all developed local recurrence.

Comparing the ⩽1 cm with the >1 cm group as a whole revealed no significant difference in local recurrence rates and the same conclusion was reached after analysis of the minor subgroups.

0007–1323/90/050510–03

Table 1 *Clinical details of 152 curative anterior resections comparing patients with ⩽1 cm margin of tumour clearance with those with >1 cm margin*

	Tumour clearance			
	⩽1 cm margin	>1 cm margin	Statistical test	Probability
Number of resections	42	110	–	–
Dukes' classification A	15	19		
B	13	53	$\chi^2=6{\cdot}712$	$P=0{\cdot}035$
C	14	38		
Differentiation Well	13	27		
Moderate	21	64	$\chi^2=0{\cdot}892$	$P=0{\cdot}64$
Poor	8	19		
Tumour distance from anal verge in cm*	4·7(1·4)	9·5(2·9)	$t=8{\cdot}84$	$P<0{\cdot}001$
Anastomotic distance from anal verge in cm*	3·4(0·9)	5·8(2·0)	$t=7{\cdot}33$	$P<0{\cdot}001$
Tumour clearance in cm*	0·7(0·4)	3·3(1·6)	–	–
Number of anastomotic leaks	8	12	$\chi^2=1{\cdot}122$	$P=0{\cdot}29$
Number of local recurrences	0	4	FET	$P=0{\cdot}27$
Time to local recurrence in years*	–	1(1·24)	–	–
Number of distant recurrences	3	11	FET	$P=0{\cdot}424$
Time to distant recurrence in years*	1·9(1·2)	1·8(1·2)	–	–
Deaths	10	39	$\chi^2=1{\cdot}391$	$P=0{\cdot}238$

FET, Fisher's exact test; * values are mean(s.d.)

Table 2 *Details of four local recurrences in the group of 110 curative resections with a resection margin >1 cm*

Sex	Age at operation (years)	Dukes' classification	Tumour differentiation	Height above anal verge (cm)	Clearance (cm)	Time to recurrence (years)	Type of recurrence	Course	Cause of local recurrence	Comment
Male	77	A	Moderate	7	2·5	2·75	Pararectal nodule. Biopsy suggestive of tumour	Radioactive gold. Recurrence cleared completely. Well 8 years after surgery	Clamp slipped at operation. Presumed implantation	Technical error. Recurrence never proven histologically
Male	76	B	Well	11	2·5	0·67	Staple line, pelvic and disseminated peritoneal metastases	Died 1·33 years after surgery	Second adenocarcinoma below main primary tumour cut through. This may have seeded to anastomotic leakage cavity	Technical error. Defunctioned throughout
Female	61	B	Poor	5	3·0	0·5	Local and metastatic	Died 0·6 years after surgery	Large primary tumour ulcerating anteriorly into the Pouch of Douglas. Cleared with a disc of vagina	Aggressive disseminating tumour
Female	81	C	Poor	6	2·0	0·8	Pelvic and hepatic	Died 1·5 years after surgery	Distal mesorectum full of tumour 2 cm below carcinoma	Local recurrence asymptomatic. Death metastatic

Discussion

The absence of local recurrence in the group with a margin ⩽1 cm is presumed to be due to chance (CI is 0–5·9 per cent compared with 0·8–7·4 per cent in the >1 cm group). The Fisher exact test showed no statistically significant difference in local recurrence rates between these groups.

That those with a margin of >1 cm had significantly less Dukes' A tumours probably results from a technical factor. In low rectal cancer total mesorectal excision and tumour mobilization eventually require that the fingers and thumb compress normal rectum around the tumour and below its palpable lower edge. The clamp is then applied below the fingers. Thus a more solid and bulky tumour tends to result in a larger resection margin.

It may be argued that measurement of the resection margin after fixation of the specimen detracts from these results. Williams *et al.*[1]. looked critically at operative specimens and concluded that the effect of fixation was minimal when the resection margins were small. Furthermore, it is the view of the authors that pinning out when the specimen is soft and flexible produces a variable degree of stretching of the tissues.

The idea that a wide margin of normal bowel should be resected distal to a rectal cancer originated from reports by Handley[3] and Cole[4] in 1913 of extensive intramural spread. Grinnell[5] later found distal intramural spread in 12 per cent of his 76 curative anterior resections and became an advocate of the 5 cm rule. Penfold[6] found a downward spread in 8·8 per cent of 546 abdominoperineal excision specimens and reported no 5-year survivors in the group with more than 1 cm spread, despite the maximal distal clearance obtained by abdominoperineal excision. However, Quer *et al.*[7] found distal spread of more than 1·5 cm in only one of 89 curative anterior resections and recommended varying the resection margin with tumour differentiation. Black and Waugh[8] stated that only 2 cm of bowel need be removed distal to the tumour and other authors[9–12] have found no correlation between a smaller distal clearance and local recurrence.

In our experience distal intramural spread below the palpable edge of a rectal cancer is unusual and a sign of very advanced or highly malignant disease. It has not been identified as a cause for local recurrence amongst any patient considered to have undergone a curative operation. Our results[11] strongly suggest that total mesorectal excision combined with routine lavage below a clamp can minimize local recurrence rates to well below 5 per cent, despite drastic reduction of mural margins. Thus a low sphincter-saving anterior resection with a limited resection margin is a viable option which does not compromise the patient's survival prospects.

References

1. Williams NS, Dixon MF, Johnston D. Reappraisal of the 5 centimetre rule of distal excision for carcinoma of the rectum: a study of distal intramural spread and of patients' survival. *Br J Surg* 1983; **70**: 150–4.
2. Kirwan WO, Drumm J, Hogan JM, Keohane C. Determining safe margin of resection in low anterior resection for rectal cancer (short note). *Br J Surg* 1988; **75**: 120.
3. Handley WS. The surgery of the lymphatic system. *Br Med J* 1910; **i**: 922–8.
4. Cole PP. The intramural spread of rectal carcinoma. *Br Med J* 1913; **i**: 431–3.
5. Grinnell RS. Distal intramural spread of carcinoma of the rectum and rectosigmoid. *Surg Gynecol Obstet* 1954; **99**: 421–30.
6. Penfold JB. A comparison of restorative resections for carcinoma of the middle third of the rectum with abdomino-perineal excision. *Aust NZ J Surg* 1974; **44**: 354–6.
7. Quer EA, Dahlin DC, Mayo CW. Retrograde intramural spread of carcinoma of the rectum and rectosigmoid. *Surg Gynecol Obstet* 1953; **96**: 24–30.
8. Black WA, Waugh JM. The intramural extension of carcinoma of the descending colon, sigmoid and rectosigmoid: a pathological study. *Surg Gynecol Obstet* 1948; **87**: 457–64.
9. Deddish MR, Sterns MW. Anterior resection for carcinoma of the rectum and rectosigmoid area. *Ann Surg* 1961; **154**: 961–6.
10. Heald RJ, Ryall RDH. Recurrence and survival after total mesorectal excision for rectal cancer. *Lancet* 1986; **ii**: 1479–82.
11. Wilson SM, Beahrs OH. The curative treatment of carcinoma of the sigmoid, rectosigmoid and rectum. *Ann Surg* 1976; **183**: 556–65.
12. Pollett WJ, Nicholls RJ. Does the extent of distal clearance affect survival after radical anterior resection for carcinoma of the rectum? *Gut* 1981; **22**: 872.

Paper accepted 25 November 1989

© Gastroenterology 1990; 98: 1239–1244

Randomized Comparison of Nd YAG Laser, Heater Probe, and No Endoscopic Therapy for Bleeding Peptic Ulcers

KENNETH MATTHEWSON, C. PAUL SWAIN, MARTIN BLAND, J. SQUIRE KIRKHAM, STEPHEN G. BOWN, and TIMOTHY C. NORTHFIELD

Norman Tanner Gastroenterology Unit, St. James' Hospital; Gastroenterology Unit, University College Hospital; and Department of Epidemiology and Social Medicine, St. George's Hospital Medical School, London, England

Of 550 patients admitted with acute upper gastrointestinal hemorrhage, 143 with peptic ulcers containing stigmata of recent hemorrhage accessible to endoscopic therapy were included in a randomized comparison of neodymium yttrium aluminum garnet laser, heater probe, and no endoscopic therapy. The rebleeding rate in laser-treated patients (20%) was significantly less than in controls (42%; $p < 0.05$), but in heater probe–treated patients (28%) it was not significantly different from either of the other two groups. The mortality rate in the laser group (2%) was not significantly different from either the heater probe (10%) or the control (9%) group. This trial has confirmed the efficacy of the Nd YAG laser but not that of the heater probe in the prevention of rebleeding from recently bleeding peptic ulcers.

In patients with acute upper gastrointestinal bleeding, the single most important prognostic factor is that of continued or recurrent hemorrhage following hospital admission (1), which confers a tenfold increase in mortality rate. This finding has led to policies of emergency surgery either before or after rebleeding has occurred, but deaths still occur from the cardiorespiratory complications of emergency surgery. The endoscopic finding of a visible vessel in a peptic ulcer indicates a relatively high rebleeding risk of approximately 50% (2) and is the essential target for endoscopic therapy. The rationale behind endoscopic therapy is that by preventing rebleeding in high-risk patients without the need for a general anaesthetic or emergency surgery, the risk of death may be decreased.

The most extensively studied form of endoscopic therapy for bleeding peptic ulcers is laser photocoagulation. The argon ion laser emits visible blue green light which causes relatively superficial photocoagulation (3,4), whereas the neodymium yttrium aluminium garnet (Nd YAG) laser emits near infrared light which is more penetrating and has a deeper tissue effect (4–7). Our randomized controlled trial of argon ion laser photocoagulation (8) showed a significant reduction in the rebleeding rate in patients with visible vessels who were treated with lasers, as well as a significant reduction in the overall mortality rate. A subsequent randomized controlled trial of Nd YAG laser photocoagulation (9) using an identical trial design also showed significant decreases in rebleeding and mortality rates in treated patients, and comparison of the trials supports the hypothesis that the more deeply penetrating Nd YAG beam has superior efficacy in preventing rebleeding.

Lasers are expensive and are unlikely to become available at every hospital. A number of cheaper alternatives collectively known as "electrodes" are available. These include dry and liquid monopolar electrodes, multipolar electrodes, and the heater probe. In a comparative experimental study of these electrode systems in canine bleeding gastric ulcers (10), the heater probe had the best combination of efficacy and safety. We report here a randomized comparison of Nd YAG laser, heater probe, and no endoscopic therapy in human bleeding peptic ulcers using a trial protocol identical to that used in our two previous trials to facilitate comparison.

Abbreviations used in this paper: **Nd YAG, neodymium yttrium aluminum garnet; SRH, stigmata of recent hemorrhage.**

0016-5085/90/$3.00

© Gastroenterology 1990; 98: 1239–1244

Materials and Methods

Patients

All patients admitted to St. James' Hospital, London, and University College Hospital, London, with hematemesis or melena or both between June 16, 1984, and December 31, 1986, were considered for inclusion in the trial, and their consent was requested. Endoscopies were performed within 12 h of admission to the hospital, and usually when the patients left the casualty department after initial resuscitation. To maintain consistent standards of diagnostic and therapeutic endoscopy, all endoscopic examinations were performed by one of three experienced endoscopists, and more than 90% were attended by a single operator (K.M.) who was continually available for this purpose.

Patients were included in the trial if they were found to have gastric, stomal, or duodenal ulceration containing stigmata of recent hemorrhage (SRH) (8) accessible to both laser and heater probe therapy. Assessment of the presence of SRH was made after adherent debris on the ulcer base had been washed away. Patients were stratified prospectively into 6 different groups, depending on whether there was a raised red or black spot (a visible vessel), nonraised red or black spots, or overlying clot, and on whether there was active bleeding. Patients with multiple ulcers or superficial lesions <5 mm in diameter were excluded unless one ulcer could be clearly identified as the source of bleeding. Accessibility of the bleeding site was assessed by pointing the aiming beam of the laser and by lightly touching with the heater probe.

Randomization

Randomization was performed during endoscopy. The different stratification groups were separately randomized to receive either laser, heater probe, or no endoscopic therapy. Randomization was achieved by opening sealed envelopes numbered according to stratification class. From June 16, 1984, to April 30, 1986, equal numbers of patients were randomized to the three treatment groups, but from May 1, 1986, to December 31, 1986, following a preliminary examination of the results, randomization was in the proportions of 3 heater probe, 1 laser, and 1 no endoscopic therapy.

Laser Treatment

The Nd YAG laser (Fiberlase 100, Living Technology, Clydebank, England) emits continuous-wave infrared light of wavelength 1064 nm with a power of up to 100 W. This is delivered via a 600-μm glass fiber within a 2.5-mm Teflon catheter passed down the endoscope biopsy channel. Carbon dioxide gas was passed coaxially along the Teflon catheter to blow away blood from the bleeding site and to keep the fiber tip cool and free from debris. A filter was fitted to the endoscope eyepiece to prevent reflected laser light from entering the operator's eye. The tip of the laser fiber was held approximately 1 cm above the ulcer base and multiple 0.5-s, 80-W pulses of laser light were aimed to produce approximately 8 blanched spots in a tight ring around the bleeding point.

Heater Probe Treatment

The heater probes used (12) were custom built for this study, although they have since been manufactured by Olympus (Tokyo, Japan). The probe consists of a 2.4- or 3.2-mm-diameter brass cylinder with a rounded end. It contains an avalanche diode which under the influence of a small solid-state control unit is heated to 250°C when the foot switch is depressed. This temperature is maintained until a preset amount of energy, between 5 and 30 J, is delivered. When the probe is immersed in water, 30 J is delivered in 3–5 s, but in air it takes 8–10 s. Heat passes into the tissue with which it is in contact entirely by thermal conduction. A nonstick coating on the probe is intended to reduce adherence during coagulation. For treatment, the probe was firmly pressed against the ulcer bed adjacent to the bleeding point at 4 different sites to form a ring around it. With the control unit preset at 30 J, the footswitch was depressed on 2 or 3 occasions for each positioning of the probe. Finally the probe was positioned directly over the bleeding site and 2 or 3 further 30-J pulses were delivered. Whenever possible, the 3.2-mm-diameter probe was used rather than the 2.4-mm device.

Monitoring

Laser, heater probe, and control treated ulcers were observed for 5 min after treatment for evidence of further bleeding. The diagnosis of rebleeding and all further management decisions were made by a team unaware of the treatment group to which the patient had been randomized. The endoscopy report was limited to describing the diagnostic findings, whether the patient had been entered into the trial, and whether there was any active bleeding at the end of the proceedure. Each patient was treated with cimetidine, 1 g/day, and blood transfusions as indicated by assessment of central venous pressure (13) and the patient's clinical state. Emergency surgery was considered at the earliest evidence of persisting or recurrent bleeding. Rebleeding was considered definite if there was a subsequent fresh hematemesis or if fresh melena was accompanied by a decrease in blood pressure. An increase in pulse rate or decrease in blood pressure, central venous pressure, or hemoglobin concentration was regarded as an indication of possible rebleeding, but required confirmation by repeat endoscopy. Each patient was treated by endoscopic therapy on only one occasion during the trial. Patient involvement in the trial continued until the time of death or discharge from the hospital.

Statistical Methods

The significance of differences was assessed by χ^2 analysis with Yates' continuity correction in proportions and by the Wilcoxon rank sum test in continuous variables. Adjustment for data were adjusted for third factors by

© Gastroenterology 1990; 98: 1239–1244

testing across several 2 ×2 tables. Ninety-five percent confidence intervals for the principal findings were also calculated.

The project was approved by the local hospital ethical committees.

Results

During the trial period, 550 patients were admitted to the two hospitals with hematemesis or melena or both; peptic ulcers were identified in 273. Ninety-two of these ulcers contained no SRH, and none of these patients rebled. Of the 181 cases involving SRH, 36 were not randomized for the reasons listed in Table 1. Two of the 145 patients who were randomized were later withdrawn because their gastric ulcers proved to be malignant. The three treatment groups were well matched for factors known to affect prognosis (Table 2). In patients randomized to heater probe therapy, the 3.2-mm-diameter probe was used in 42 patients and the 2.4-mm-diameter probe in 15 in whom a large biopsy channel endoscope was not available.

The overall rebleeding, emergency surgery, and mortality rates for the three treatment groups are shown in Figure 1. The rebleeding rate for laser-treated patients (20%) was significantly lower than for controls (42%; $\chi^2 = 4.0$, df = 1, $p < 0.05$), but the rebleeding rate of patients treated with the heater probe (28%) was not significantly different from either of the other two groups. The rebleeding rate in patients treated with the 3.2-mm heater probe (24%) was not significantly different from those treated with the 2.4-mm heater probe (40%), nor was it significantly different from the controls. There was no significant difference in rebleeding rate between any of the treatment groups within any of the individual stratification groups (Table 3). As in our previous trials, the majority of the rebleeding episodes occurred in patients with visible vessels. There was a significantly higher rebleeding rate in the patients recruited in first 6 mo of the trial compared with the remainder in the laser group (57% vs. 14%; $\chi^2 = 4.3$, df = 1, $p < 0.05$) but not in the heater probe (40% vs. 26%; $\chi^2 = 0.3$, df = 1, NS) or control groups (44% vs. 42%; $\chi^2 = 0.1$, df = 1, NS). Excluding this first 6-mo period, the rebleeding rates in the laser (14%) and control (42%) groups were very similar to the rates of 10% and 40%, respectively, obtained in our previous randomized Nd YAG laser trial. There was no significant change in rebleeding rates in any of the treatment groups following the biasing of randomization in favor of the heater probe (Table 4). When the groups were compared after adjusting for the allocation period, the heater probe was not significantly different from the controls ($\chi^2 = 2.5$, df = 1, p = 0.1) or the laser group ($\chi^2 = 1.0$, df = 1, p = 0.3). Table 5 shows 95% confidence intervals for the differences in rebleeding rates.

One patient in the control group who was thought to be rebleeding was found to have a spurting vessel on

Table 1. Details of Patients Admitted Consecutively With Gastrointestinal Bleeding Who Were Included in and Excluded From the Trial

550 consecutive patients admitted with hematemesis or melena
- 277 no peptic ulcer
- 273 peptic ulcers
  - 92 no SRH
  - 181 peptic ulcer contained SRH
    - 36 excluded
      - 16 inaccessible
        - 13 duodenal
        - 2 gastric
        - 1 stomal
      - 3 uncooperative
      - 2 refused to consent
      - 3 laser not working
      - 1 heater probe not working
      - 3 overwhelming bleeding, immediate surgery
      - 8 operator unavailable
    - 145 randomized
      - 2 withdrawn, ulcer malignant on biopsy
      - 143 in trial
        - 44 laser
        - 57 heater probe
        - 42 control

Table 2. Matching of Treatment Groups

	Laser (n = 44)	Heater probe (n = 57)	Control (n = 42)
Median age (yr)	69	66	68
Median initial hemaglobin (g/dl)	9.2	9.7	9.3
Systolic blood pressure <100 mmHg (%)	29	29	23
Gastric ulcers (%)	30	36	38

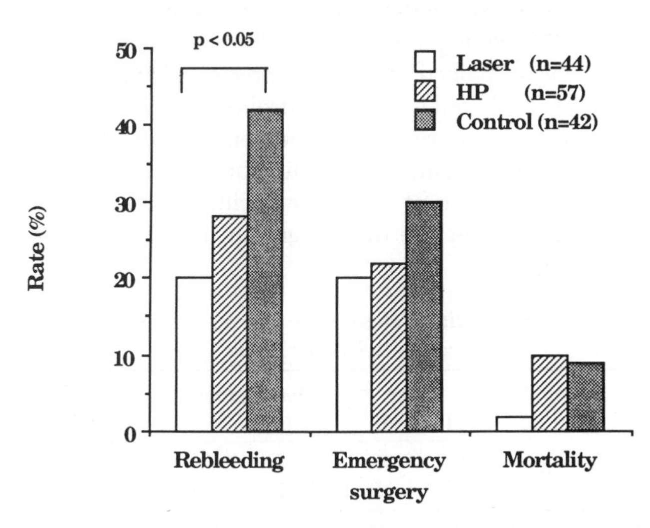

Figure 1. Rebleeding, emergency surgery, and mortality rates in laser-treated, heater probe-treated, and control patients.

© Gastroenterology 1990; 98: 1239–1244

Table 3. Rebleeding by Stratification Group

		Laser (n = 44)		Heater probe (n = 57)		Control (n = 42)	
	Total	Rebleed	No rebleed	Rebleed	No rebleed	Rebleed	No rebleed
Group 1 (visible vessel, bleeding)	15	3	2	2	4	1	3
Group 2 (visible vessel, nonbleeding)	90	5	21	12	24	14	14
Group 3 (red or black spots, bleeding)	6	0	3	0	2	0	1
Group 4 (red or black spots, nonbleeding)	21	1	6	1	8	0	5
Group 5 (overlying clot, bleeding)	5	0	2	1	1	0	1
Group 6 (overlying clot, nonbleeding)	6	0	1	0	2	3	0
Total	143	9	35	16	41	18	24

check endoscopy. He would not consent to surgery and therefore underwent laser therapy following which he had no further hemorrhage. Two patients in the heater probe group rebled after discharge from the hospital, 10 and 12 days after their initial endoscopic therapy. They were both readmitted and required emergency surgery.

Median blood transfusion requirements were significantly lower ($p < 0.05$) in laser-treated (4 units) and heater probe–treated (3 units) groups than in the control group (6 units). There were no significant differences in emergency surgery rates among the three groups. The mortality rate in the laser-treated group (2%) was not significantly different from the heater probe–treated group (10%; $\chi^2 = 1.49$) or the control group (9%; $\chi^2 = 0.95$). Furthermore, there was no significant difference between the heater probe–treated and control patients (10% vs. 9%; $\chi^2 = 0.04$). During a 6-wk follow-up period after discharge from the hospital, there was one additional death in the laser-treated group and two in the control group.

Bleeding was provoked by laser treatment in 9 patients, but this was always controlled by further pulses of laser coagulation or stopped within a few minutes of observation. None of these patients were actively bleeding at the end of the procedure. Bleeding was provoked by heater probe treatment in 3 patients and could not be controlled by further therapy in 1, who required emergency surgery. In 1 additional patient, the heater probe disappeared through the base of the ulcer during treatment. Gas was seen under the diaphragm on a postendoscopy chest x-ray, and he later came to laparotomy when a sealed perforation was found with no evidence of free peritonitis.

Table 4. Rebleeding Rates Before and After Biasing of Radomization to Heater Probe

	Laser (n = 44)		Heater probe (n = 57)		Control (n = 42)	
	Rebleed	No rebleed	Rebleed	No rebleed	Rebleed	No rebleed
Before biasing	7	30	12	28	13	22
After biasing	2	7	4	13	5	2

Combined $\chi^2 = 0.42$, df = 1, p = 0.5.

Discussion

The results of this trial confirm that the Nd YAG laser can significantly reduce the rebleeding rate in treated compared with untreated patients. The rebleeding rate in the laser-treated group was significantly higher than during the first 6 mo than during the remainder of the trial. This was not found in the heater probe–treated and control groups, and is attributed to a particularly long learning period with the laser compared with the heater probe. Other controlled trials of Nd YAG laser photocoagulation for bleeding peptic ulcers have shown significant decreases in rebleeding rates when adequate numbers of patients with a high rebleeding risk are randomized and when an adequate power setting is used (14,15). Absence of significant benefit from Nd YAG laser treatment of bleeding peptic ulcers in a controlled trial has recently been reported by an American group (16). This trial appears to have been limited by failure to identify high-risk patients, as untreated visible vessel patients had a rebleeding rate of only 13%. This study was further disadvantaged by the exclusion of 571 of the 1062 patients considered, including 122 who failed to consent and 221 who were considered "too unstable" to be moved to the laser facility for treatment. There were 5 operators in this study in which a total of 85 patients were laser treated, approximately 17 per operator. Therefore, a high proportion of patients may have been treated by operators during their learning

Table 5. 95% Confidence Intervals for Differences in Rebleeding Rates

	Difference	Confidence interval
Laser vs. control	−22%	−41% to −3%
Laser vs. heater probe	−7%	−24% to 9%
Heater probe vs. control	−15%	−34% to 4%

period. Finally, the mean age of the patients was 49 yr, compared with 68 yr in our study. This is the probable explanation of the higher mortality rate in our control group.

The unusual step of altering the randomization to 3 heater probe, 1 laser, and 1 control was taken to increase the power of the most important comparisons, namely those between heater probe treatment and control treatment and between heater probe and laser treatment. The superiority of laser to control treatment had been convincingly demonstrated in a previous trial (9). In this previous trial, the rebleeding rates were 10% in laser-treated and 40% in the control patients. To have a 90% chance of obtaining a significant difference at the 5% level between two sample proportions when the true population proportions are are 10% and 40%, the sample size required is about 40 in each group. Therefore, the present trial was designed to have 50 patients in each group, which would be adequate to demonstrate that the laser was superior to the heater probe if the heater probe was ineffective, or to show that the heater probe was superior to control if the heater probe was as efficacious as the laser. If the heater probe was inferior to the laser but superior to control treatment, it would be quite possible for no statistical difference to emerge when compared with either laser or control treatment. An interim analysis of the results suggested that this was the case. At the time of this analysis, excluding the 6-mo learning period, the laser and control rebleeding rates were 10% and 40%, respectively, which were identical to those from the previous trial. The heater probe rebleeding rate of 25% was midway between the rates for laser and control. The biasing of randomization toward the heater probe was intended to increase the data regarding the efficacy of the device with which we had least experience and to increase the chance of demonstrating a significant difference between it and either laser or control treatment. Patients with minor stigmata of recent hemorrhage (red or black macules) were included in this trial to facilitate comparison with our previous trials. The results confirm that patients with this finding have a low rebleeding risk, and we no longer consider that endoscopic therapy is needed for such patients, they should no longer be included in randomized trials of therapy for bleeding peptic ulcers.

The results have failed to show any significant difference in rebleeding rates between heater probe-treated and control groups. There was a trend toward a lower rebleeding rate with the 3.2-mm-diameter heater probe than with the 2.4-mm probe, but even excluding the minority of patients in whom the small probe was used there was no significant improvement over the control rebleeding rate. There is some evidence from the data that the heater probe did influence the natural history of these bleeding peptic ulcers as the transfusion requirement in heater probe-treated patients was significantly less than in controls. It is possible that the absence of a significant difference in the heater probe and control rebleeding data represents a type 2 error, and it is possible that a significant difference might have been demonstrated in a larger study using only the 3.2-mm probe. Our results are at variance with those of Johnston et al. (17), who reported "ultimate haemostatic success" in 19 of 20 patients with major peptic ulcer bleeding treated by heater probe compared with 24 of 35 treated by Nd YAG laser. There are important differences between our trial and theirs: the trial by Johnston et al. was a retrospective comparison of two separate series of patients, whereas ours was prospective, randomized, and controlled; and in the trial by Johnston et al., heater probe-treated patients were allowed treatment on a second occasion if rebleeding occurred, whereas fewer Nd YAG laser-treated patients were retreated because of concern regarding tissue damage and perforation.

There are now a number of published controlled trials of other electrodes for bleeding peptic ulcers. The simplest device is the dry monopolar electrode. A small controlled trial (18) has reported significantly reduced rebleeding rates in patients with visible vessels treated by this technique. Liquid monopolar electrocoagulation is a modification of the above technique in which a film of liquid between the electrode and tissue provides a good electrical contact and helps reduce adherence when the electrode is withdrawn. Two controlled trials of its use have been reported (19,20), and both claim to demonstrate significantly lower rebleeding rates in treated patients. Both trials were small, and the latter included patients with gastric ulceration only. These findings require confirmation in larger clinical trials.

The most widely studied electrode has been the "bicap" (ACMI), a form of multipolar electrode. A small, early controlled trial (21) failed to show any significant benefit, and there was even a trend in favor of the control group in terms of rebleeding. More recently, two larger controlled trials have been published (22,23); both showed significant reductions in the rebleeding rate in treated patients. O'Brien et al. (22) also noted a learning curve for this form of therapy, and this could explain the disappointing results in the earlier, small trial. In a recently reported uncontrolled randomized comparison of Nd YAG laser photocoagulation and multipolar electrocoagulation for severely bleeding peptic ulcers, no significant difference between the two forms of therapy emerged (24).

In conclusion, a randomized comparison of Nd YAG laser, heater probe, and no endo copic therapy for bleeding peptic ulcer has confirmed the efficacy of the laser in reducing the rebleeding rate but failed to show heater probe efficacy. Both hospitals involved in this trial now use the Nd YAG laser, despite its greater cost, in preference to the unproven heater probe.

References

1. Avery-Jones F. Haematemesis and melaena with special reference to causation and the factors influencing mortality from bleeding peptic ulcer. Gastroenterology 1956;30:166–190.
2. Swain CP, Storey DW, Bown SG, Heath J, Mills TN, Salmon PR, Northfield TC, Kirkham JS, O'Sullivan JP. Nature of the bleeding vessel in recurrently bleeding gastric ulcers. Gastroenterology 1986;90:595–608.
3. Bown SG, Salmon PR, Kelly DF, Calder BM, Pearson H, Weaver BMQ, Read AE. Argon laser photocoagulation in the dog stomach. Gut 1979;20:680–687.
4. Silverstein FE, Protell RL, Gilbert DA, Gulacsik C, Auth DC, Dennis MB, Rubin CE. Argon vs neodymium YAG laser photocoagulation of experimental canine gastric ulcers. Gastroenterology 1979;77:491–496.
5. Dixon JA, Berenson MM, McCloskey DW. Neodymium YAG laser treatment of experimental canine gastric bleeding. Acute and chronic studies of photocoagulation, penetration and perforation. Gastroenterology 1979;77:647–651.
6. Johnston JH, Jensen DM, Mautner W, Elashoff J. YAG laser treatment of experimental bleeding canine gastric ulcers. Gastroenterology 1980;79:1252–1261.
7. Bown SG, Salmon PR, Storey DW, Calder BM, Kelly DF, Adams N, Pearson H, Weaver BMQ. Nd YAG laser photocoagulation in the dog stomach. Gut 1980;21:818–825.
8. Swain CP, Bown SG, Storey DW, Kirkham JS, Northfield TC, Salmon PR. Controlled trial of argon laser photocoagulation in bleeding peptic ulcers. Lancet 1981;2:1313–1316.
9. Swain CP, Kirkham JS, Salmon PR, Bown SG, Northfield TC. Controlled trial of Nd YAG laser photocoagulation in bleeding peptic ulcers. Lancet 1986;1:1113–1116.
10. Swain CP, Mills TN, Shemesh E, Dark JM, Lewin MR, Clifton JS, Northfield TC, Cotton PB, Salmon PR. Which electrode? A comparison of four endoscopic methods of electrocoagulation in experimental bleeding ulcers. Gut 1984;25:1424–1431.
11. Storey DW, Bown SG, Swain CP, Salmon PR, Kirkham JS, Northfield TC. Endoscopic prediction of recurrent bleeding in peptic ulcers. N Engl J Med 1981;305:915–916.
12. Protell RL, Rubin CE, Auth DC, Silverstein FE, Terou F, Dennis M, Piercey JRA. The heater probe: a new endoscopic device for stopping massive gastrointestinal bleeding. Gastroenterology 1978;74:257–262.
13. Northfield TC, Smith T. Central venous pressure in clinical management of acute gastrointestinal bleeding. Lancet 1970;2: 584–586.
14. MacLeod IA, Mills PR, MacKenzie JF, Joffe SN, Russell RI, Carter DC. Neodymium yttrium aluminium garnet laser photocoagulation for major haemorrhage form peptic ulcers: a single blind controlled study. Br Med J 1983;286:345–348.
15. Rutgeerts P, Vantrappen G, Broeckert L, Janssens J, Coremans G, Geboes K, Schurmans P. Controlled trial of YAG laser treatment of upper digestive haemorrhage. Gastroenterology 1982;83:410–416.
16. Krejs GJ, Little KH, Westergaard H, Hamilton JK, Polter DE. Laser photocoagulation for the treatment of acute peptic ulcer bleeding: a randomized controlled clinical trial. N Engl J Med 1987;316:1618–1621.
17. Johnston JH, Sones JQ, Long BW, Posey EL. Comparison of heater probe and YAG laser in treatment of major bleeding from peptic ulcers. Gastrointest Endosc 1985;31:175–180.
18. Papp JP. Endoscopic electrocoagulation in the management of upper gastrointestinal tract bleeding. Surg Clin North Am 1982; 62:797–806.
19. Freitas D, Donato A, Monteiro JG. Controlled trial of liquid monopolar electrocoagulation in bleeding peptic ulcers. Am J Gastroenterol 1985;80:853–857.
20. Moreto M, Zaballa M, Ibanez S, Setien F, Figa M. Efficacy of monopolar electrocoagulation in the treatment of bleeding gastric ulcer: a controlled trial. Endoscopy 1987;19:54–56.
21. Kernohan RM, Anderson JR, McKelvy STD, Kennedy TL. A controlled trial of bipolar electrocoagulation in patients with upper gastrointestinal bleeding. Br J Surg 1984;71:889–891.
22. O'Brien JD, Day SJ, Burnham WR. Controlled trial of small bipolar probe in bleeding peptic ulcers. Lancet 1986;1:464–466.
23. Laine L. Multipolar electrocoagulation in the treatment of active upper gastrointestinal tract haemorrhage. A prospective controlled trial. N Engl J Med 1987;316:1613–1617.
24. Rutgeerts P, Vantrappen G, Vanhootgern PH, Broesckehart L, Jansens J, Coremans G, Geboes K. Nd YAG laser photocoagulation vs multipolar electrocoagulation for the treatment of severely bleeding peptic ulcers. Gastrointest Endosc 1987;33:199–201.

Received November 30, 1988. Accepted November 9, 1989.

Address requests for reprints to: Kenneth Matthewson, M.R.C.P. (U.K.), Hexham General Hospital, Hexham, Northumberland NE46 1QJ, England.

This work was supported by a grant from the office of the Chief Scientist of the Department of Health and Social Security.

© *Lancet* 1990; 335: 1293–1295

MEDICAL SCIENCE

Rectal gluten challenge and diagnosis of coeliac disease

DUNCAN E. LOFT MICHAEL N. MARSH PETER T. CROWE

44 patients referred consecutively for jejunal biopsy underwent rectal gluten challenge with 2 g peptic-tryptic digest (Frazer's fraction III; FF3). Rectal biopsy was done before the challenge and 6 h afterwards. Total intraepithelial lymphocytes (IEL) overlying a 10^4 μm² test area of muscularis mucosae were quantified by computerised image analysis. The subjects comprised 21 controls with disorders other than coeliac disease and 23 patients (14 treated, 9 untreated) with coeliac disease diagnosed by strict jejunal biopsy gold standard criteria. There was no difference between the groups in IEL numbers before challenge. Coeliac disease patients but not controls responded to FF3 with a rise in mucosal IEL (median 60·5% rise for treated, 63·0% for untreated). There was no response to challenge with β-lactoglobulin in coeliac disease or control subjects. When a predefined, post-challenge IEL "predictive index" of more than 10% above baseline was used to indicate a diagnosis of coeliac disease, it gave a sensitivity of 90% and specificity of 91% (95% confidence intervals 78–93%). Rectal gluten challenge is a simple, safe, and reliable test of gluten sensitivity, both as a screening test for untreated coeliac disease and as a confirmatory test in patients with treated coeliac disease.

Lancet 1990; **335**: 1293–95.

Introduction

Frazer's fraction III (FF3) is a peptic-tryptic digest of gluten that damages the mucosa of the small intestine in gluten-sensitive subjects.[1] The inflammatory response to rectal instillation of FF3 can be measured by the rise in intraepithelial lymphocytes (IEL) which is greatest 6 h after the challenge.[2] From retrospective analysis of our previous data[2] we calculated that an IEL response 6 h after challenge (expressed as a percentage of the prechallenge value) of 10% or more would have a predictive value of 100% for coeliac disease.

We have now studied the rectal response to FF3 challenge in patients with untreated coeliac disease and prospectively assessed the value of the predictive index in the diagnosis of coeliac disease and as a confirmatory test for treated coeliac disease.

Subjects and methods

We studied 44 patients (20 male, 24 female) referred consecutively for jejunal biopsy. Indications for biopsy were diarrhoea, anaemia, and suspected malabsorption and assessment of the effect of gluten restriction in patients thought to have coeliac disease. There were no exclusion criteria. All patients gave written informed consent. The study was approved by the ethical committee of Salford District, North-Western Regional Health Authority.

Jejunal biopsy samples were taken from about 20 cm beyond the ligament of treitz with a Watson/Crosby capsule. On the same day, rectal biopsy samples were taken before and 6 h after FF3 challenge. With the patient in the left lateral position, 2 g FF3 suspended in 10 ml water was instilled into the rectum with a 20 ml syringe and quill. To test the specificity of the response, 12 subjects (6 patients with treated coeliac disease and 6 controls with other disorders) underwent rectal instillation of 0·5 g β-lactoglobulin.

Samples of jejunal and rectal mucosa were quickly oriented on card, fixed for 3 h at room temperature in 0·1 mol/l cacodylate-buffered 2·5% ultrapure glutaraldehyde, and cured in resin ('Araldite'; Ciba, Cambridge, UK). Plastic sections, 1 μm thick, were stained with 1% aqueous toluidine-blue. By means of

ADDRESSES: **University Department of Medicine, Hope Hospital (University of Manchester School of Medicine), Salford, UK** (D. E. Loft, MRCP, M. N. Marsh, DM, P. T. Crowe, BSc). Correspondence to Dr D. E. Loft, Department of Gastroenterology and Nutrition, Central Middlesex Hospital, London NW10 7NS, UK.

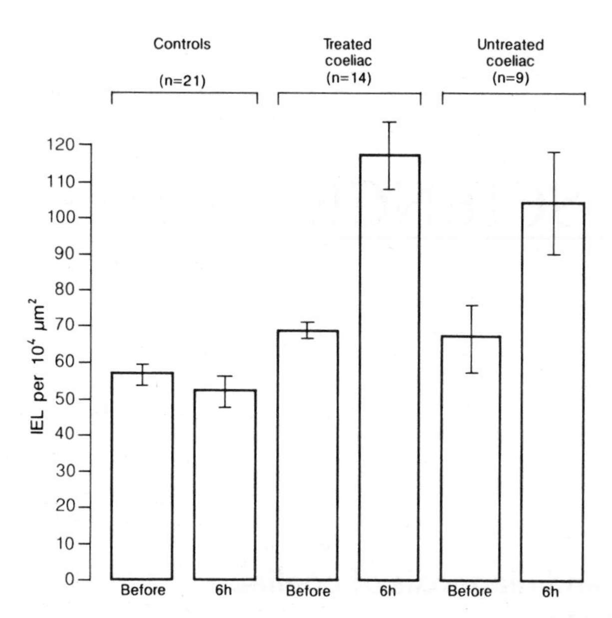

Fig 1—Mean (SEM) total IEL per 10^4 μm² muscularis mucosae before and 6 h after rectal gluten challenge.

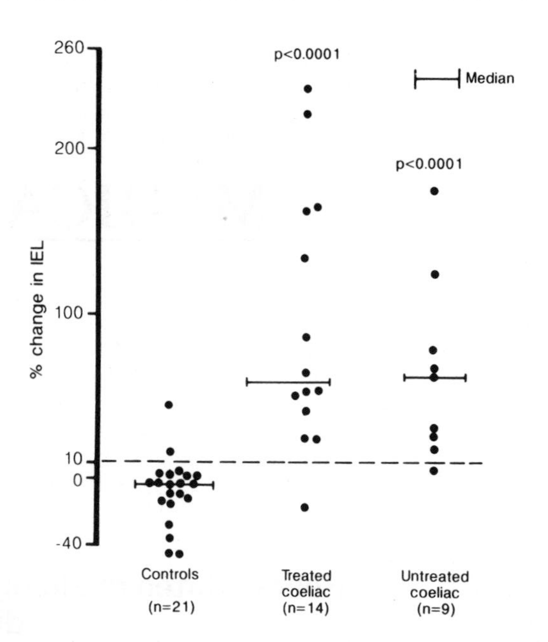

Fig 2—Percentage change in IEL after challenge and predictive index.

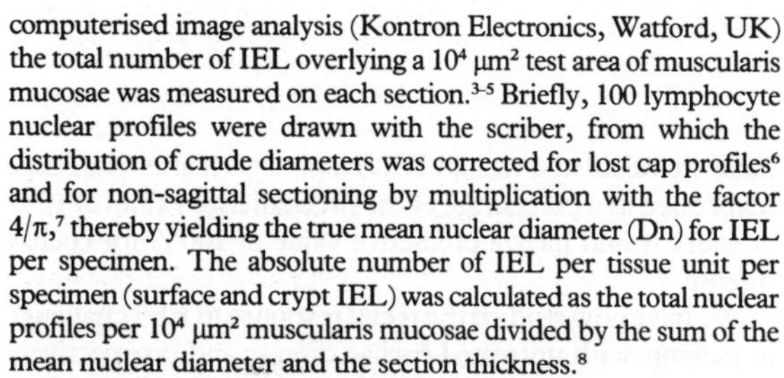

computerised image analysis (Kontron Electronics, Watford, UK) the total number of IEL overlying a 10^4 μm² test area of muscularis mucosae was measured on each section.[3-5] Briefly, 100 lymphocyte nuclear profiles were drawn with the scriber, from which the distribution of crude diameters was corrected for lost cap profiles[6] and for non-sagittal sectioning by multiplication with the factor $4/\pi$,[7] thereby yielding the true mean nuclear diameter (Dn) for IEL per specimen. The absolute number of IEL per tissue unit per specimen (surface and crypt IEL) was calculated as the total nuclear profiles per 10^4 μm² muscularis mucosae divided by the sum of the mean nuclear diameter and the section thickness.[8]

An IEL response after challenge of more than 10% above the prechallenge value was taken to indicate coeliac disease. The true diagnosis was established by jejunal biopsy gold standard criteria.[9]

Because many of the data were not normally distributed, medians were used in non-parametric tests of significance—the two-tailed Mann-Whitney U test for unpaired data and the two-tailed Wilcoxon signed rank test for paired data. Probability values below 0·05 were taken as significant. Where data approached a normal distribution mean and standard error are reported.

Results

No patient presenting for jejunal biopsy was excluded from the study. There were 21 patients with disorders other than coeliac disease (5 microscopic colitis, 3 irritable-bowel syndrome, 3 small-intestinal bacterial overgrowth, 2 oral aphthous ulceration, 2 scleroderma, 2 ileal Crohn disease, 2 intestinal pseudo-obstruction, 1 CREST syndrome, and 1 hepatic secondary carcinoma). We studied 14 patients with treated coeliac disease and 9 with untreated coeliac disease whose diagnoses were established by gold standard jejunal biopsy criteria.[9] The median ages were 40 years for the controls, 47 years for the treated patients, and 52 years for the untreated patients. The patients with treated coeliac disease had been on a gluten-free diet for a median of 3·6 (range 0·25–42) years.

Total IEL per sample rose significantly after FF3 challenge in both untreated ($p=0{\cdot}0039$) and treated ($p=0{\cdot}00036$) coeliac patients but not in the controls (fig 1). Furthermore, since there was no lymphocytic response to rectal challenge with β-lactoglobulin in either coeliac patients (before 68 [13], 6 h 59 [8]) or controls (61 [10], *vs* 48 [5]), the effect of rectal gluten challenge in coeliac patients was a specific response to gluten.

Use of an IEL response 6 h after challenge of 10% or more above the pre-challenge value to predict coeliac disease gave 2 false-positive and 2 false-negative results (fig 2). The false-negatives were 1 treated and 1 untreated patient. The false-positives were controls with normal jejunal biopsy samples—a 71-year-old woman with diarrhoea and microscopic colitis and a 34-year-old man with a 10-year history of recurrent aphthous ulcers and no other gastrointestinal complaints.

Thus, the index identified the majority of gluten-sensitive subjects with a sensitivity of 90% and specificities of 92% for treated, 89% for untreated, and 91% for all coeliac disease patients (95% confidence intervals 78–93%).

Discussion

In this prospective study of rectal gluten challenge, we have confirmed our previous findings[2] and have also shown that a response to gluten challenge occurs in untreated coeliac patients. For convenience, we have expressed our results as total IEL per specimen, although in counting we artificially segregated the IEL into surface and crypt lymphocytes. It is not surprising that both populations responded to challenge in the coeliac disease patients, since they are presumably from the same, predominantly CD8$^+$ suppressor/cytolytic, subset. The specificity of the IEL response for gluten in subjects with coeliac disease was shown by the lack of response to β-lactoglobulin in both patients and controls with other disorders.

We used strictly controlled morphometric techniques for the measurement of absolute IEL populations.[3-5] Few centres are likely to have access to computerised image analysis and we have not tried to find out whether simpler graticule measurements would have adequate sensitivity. However, a study with standard graticule methods would be justified: mean nuclear IEL diameters did not change after challenge, so for semiquantitative analysis of ratios of values before and after challenge, calculations of effective section thickness[8] and true mean nuclear diameter[6,7] would not be necessary; and most coeliac patients showed a much greater than 10% rise in IEL, which suggests that they would be identified even by a less sensitive method.

Over the past 30 years, various tests to identify coeliac disease patients have been advocated. Early tests, such as faecal fat excretion,[10] serum[11,12] and red cell folate[13,14] levels, and d-xylose excretion,[15-19] lacked diagnostic accuracy, and attention has lately swung toward specific immunological tests, such as antibodies against reticulin and gliadin. Fairly good results have been reported with IgG antibodies to gliadin and though sensitivities of around 90%[20] have been reported, this test gives many false-positive results[21] and no single antibody test has proved to be sufficiently discriminating.[22-25] Hallstrom[26] has reported sensitivity of more than 90% with IgA class reticulin and endomysial antibodies; although such assays are difficult to undertake in routine practice, they may prove valuable in the future.

Rectal gluten challenge is a simple, safe, and reliable test for gluten sensitivity. The prospective evaluation of a predetermined, predictive index derived from retrospective analysis of a previous study[2] adds further weight to the findings. This test should also be valuable in screening for gluten sensitivity when jejunal biopsy is difficult or hazardous, as in the very young, the elderly, or in pregnancy when X-rays are contraindicated. It is also useful as a rapid confirmatory test of gluten sensitivity in patients already taking a gluten-free diet, since results of rectal challenge may be available within 24–48 h. It provides a welcome alternative to the longer oral gluten challenge, for which neither the ideal dose of gluten nor the optimum duration of challenge have been satisfactorily defined. Furthermore, some patients, especially adolescents, may refuse oral gluten challenge followed by repeat jejunal biopsy; their compliance is important since many have been treated since childhood with a gluten-free diet, without substantiated evidence of coeliac disease.

We thank the Medical Research Council for financial support.

REFERENCES

1. Frazer AC, Fletcher RF, Ross CA, Shaw B, Sammons HC. Gluten-induced enteropathy: the effect of partially digested gluten. *Lancet* 1959; ii: 252–55.
2. Loft DE, Marsh MN, Sandle GI, et al. Studies of intestinal lymphoid tissue. XII Epithelial lymphocyte and mucosal responses to rectal gluten challenge in celiac sprue. *Gastroenterology* 1989; **97:** 29–37.
3. Niazi NM, Leigh R, Crowe P, Marsh MN. Morphometric analysis of small intestinal mucosa. I-Methodology, epithelial volume compartments and enumeration of inter-epithelial space lymphocytes. *Virchow Arch [A]* 1984; **404:** 49–60.
4. Dhesi I, Marsh MN, Kelly C, Crowe P. Morphometric analysis of small intestinal mucosa. II-Determination of lamina propria volumes: plasma cell and neutrophil populations within control and coeliac disease mucosae. *Virchow Arch [A]* 1984; **403:** 173–80.
5. Marsh MN, Hinde J. Morphometric analysis of small intestinal mucosa. III-The quantification of crypt epithelial volumes and lymphoid cell infiltration with reference to celiac sprue mucosa. *Virchow Arch [A]* 1986; **409:** 11–22.
6. Giger H, Riedwyl H. Bestimmung der grobenverteilung von kugeln aus schnittkreisadien. *Biometr Zeitschr* 1970; **12:** 156–65.
7. Weibel ER. Stereological methods, vol 1. New York: Academic Press, 1979.
8. Marsh MN, Mathan M, Mathan VI. Studies of intestinal lymphoid tissue. VII- The secondary nature of lymphoid cell "activation" in the jejunal lesion of tropical sprue. *Am J Pathol* 1983; **112:** 302–12.
9. Rubin CE, Brandborg LL, Phelps PC, Taylor HC. Studies of celiac disease. I- The apparent, identical and specific nature of the duodenal and proximal jejunal lesion in celiac disease and idiopathic steatorrhoea. *Gastroenterology* 1960; **38:** 28–49.
10. Mann JG, Brown WR, Kern F. The subtle and varied clinical expressions of gluten induced enteropathy (adult coeliac disease, non-tropical sprue). *Am J Med* 1970; **48:** 357–66.
11. Dormandy KM, Waters AH, Mollin DL. Folic acid deficiency in coeliac disease. *Lancet* 1963; i: 632–35.
12. Hallert C, Tobiasson P, Walan A. Serum folate determinations in tracing adult coeliacs. *Scand J Gastroenterol* 1981; **16:** 263–67.
13. Cooke WT. Adult coeliac disease. In: Jerzy Glass GB, ed. Progress in gastroenterology. New York: Grune and Stratton, 1968: 299–338.
14. Hoffbrand AV. Anaemia in adult coeliac disease. *Clin Gastroenterol* 1974; **3:** 71–89.
15. Benson JA, Culver PJ, Ragland S, Jones CM, Drummey GD, Bougas E. The D-xylose absorption test in malabsorption syndromes. *N Engl J Med* 1957; **256:** 335–39.
16. Finlay JM, Wightman KJR. The xylose tolerance test as a measure of intestinal absorption of carbohydrate in sprue. *Ann Intern Med* 1958; **49:** 1332–46.
17. Sladen GE, Kumar PJ. Is the xylose test still a worthwhile investigation? *Br Med J* 1973; iii: 223–26.
18. Shmerling DH. Screening tests in coeliac disease. In: Hekkens WTJM, Pena AS, eds. Coeliac disease. Leiden: Stenfert Kroese, 1974: 339–45.
19. Krawitt EL, Beeken WL. Limitations of usefulness of d-xylose absorption test. *Am J Clin Pathol* 1975; **63:** 261–63.
20. Friis SU, Gudmand-Hoyer E. Screening for adult coeliac disease in adults by simultaneous determination of IgA and IgA gliadin antibodies. *Scand J Gastroenterol* 1986; **21:** 1058–62.
21. Kelly J, O'Farrelly C, Rees JPR, Feighery C, Weir DG. Humoral response to α gliadin as serological screening test for coeliac disease. *Arch Dis Child* 1987; **62:** 469–73.
22. Labrooy JT, Hohmann AW, Davidson GP, Hetzel PAS, Johnson RB, Shearman DJC. Intestinal and serum antibody in coeliac disease: a comparison using ELISA. *Clin Exp Immunol* 1986; **66:** 661–68.
23. Arranz E, Blanco A, Alonso M, et al. IgA-1 antigliadin antibodies are the most specific in children with coeliac disease. *J Clin Nutr Gastroenterol* 1986; **1:** 291–95.
24. Stahlberg MR, Savilahti E, Viander M. Antibodies to gliadin by ELISA as a sctreening test for childhood celiac disease. *J Pediatr Gastroenterol Nutr* 1986; **5:** 726–29.
25. Kumar V, Jain N, Lerner A, Beutner EH, Chorzelski TP, Lebenthal E. Comparative studies of different gliadin preparations in detecting antigliadin antibodies. *J Pediatr Gastroenterol Nutr* 1986; **5:** 730–34.
26. Hallstrom O. Comparison of IgA-class reticulin and endomysium antibodies in coeliac disease and dermatitis herpetiformis. *Gut* 1989; **30:** 1225–32.

© *Aliment Pharmacol Ther* 1991; 5: 283–290

Eradication of Helicobacter pylori *abolishes 24-hour hypergastrinaemia: a prospective study in healthy subjects*

E. J. PREWETT, J. T. L. SMITH, C. U. NWOKOLO, M. HUDSON, A. M. SAWYERR & R. E. POUNDER

University Department of Medicine, Royal Free Hospital School of Medicine, London, UK

Accepted for publication 18 February 1991

SUMMARY

In a prospective study, eight young healthy subjects (five with an active *H. pylori* infection in the antral mucosa) were treated with a course of tripotassium dicitrato bismuthate, amoxycillin and metronidazole. The triple therapy eradicated infection when assessed 20–24 weeks later by antral biopsy (urease, histology, and ^{13}C urea breath test [4 out of 5 subjects]). Twenty-four hour intragastric acidity and plasma gastrin concentration were measured before treatment, and 4–6 weeks and 20–24 weeks post-treatment. Treatment did not affect acidity in either the *H. pylori*-positive or *H. pylori*-negative groups, nor did it affect the plasma gastrin profile in the *H. pylori*-negative group. Eradication of *H. pylori* infection in five subjects caused a drop of the median integrated 24-hour plasma gastrin concentration from 558 pmol.h/L before treatment to 307 and 289 pmol.h/L at 4–6 and 20–24 weeks post-treatment, respectively. It is concluded that *H. pylori* infection is associated with 24-hour hypergastrinaemia, and that in apparently healthy subjects normal gastric physiology can be restored by eradication of the infection.

Correspondence to: Dr R. E. Pounder, University Department of Medicine, Royal Free Hospital School of Medicine, London NW3 2QG.

INTRODUCTION

Infection with *Helicobacter pylori* is associated with gastritis and duodenal ulceration, but the precise mechanism by which this organism might cause duodenal ulcers has not been established.[1–3]

Duodenal ulcer patients with evidence of *H. pylori* infection have elevated basal and meal-stimulated plasma gastrin concentrations.[4,5] It has been demonstrated on retrospective analysis that asymptomatic individuals with serological evidence of *H. pylori* infection, but no evidence of duodenal ulcer disease, have an elevated 24-h plasma gastrin profile but normal intragastric acidity, compared with uninfected subjects.[6] It has been postulated that hypergastrinaemia induced by *H. pylori* infection could in due course result in the parietal cell hyperplasia and increased intragastric acidity which are characteristic of duodenal ulceration.[6]

The aim of the study was to observe the effect of eradication of *H. pylori* on 24-h intragastric acidity and 24-h plasma gastrin concentration in a group of healthy subjects with serological evidence of *H. pylori* infection.

SUBJECTS AND METHODS

Eight subjects were identified as being potentially infected with *H. pylori* on the basis of serology using an ELISA test (Professor D. Y. Graham's Laboratory, Houston, United States).[7] Seven were male; they had a median age of 23.5 years (range 21–25 years); two were smokers. None had a previous history of gastro-intestinal disease; all were normal on physical examination and all had normal haematological and biochemical profiles. All the subjects gave written informed consent prior to entry to the study, which was approved by the Ethics Committee of Hampstead Health Authority.

Endoscopy and biopsies

Each subject had an initial upper gastrointestinal endoscopy performed with intravenous sedation (10 mg diazepam emulsion). Antral biopsies were taken and assessed for urease activity using the CLOtest (Delta West Ltd, Bently, Australia),[8] or by histology. The latter specimens were fixed in formalin and paraffin-processed; sections were stained with haematoxylin and eosin for assessment of gastritis and using the Warthin-Starry method for the detection of *H. pylori*. The subjects were endoscoped before entry to the study, and 20–24 weeks after a course of treatment to eradicate *H. pylori*.

Twenty-four-hour acidity and gastrin studies

Each subject was studied on three occasions using the Royal Free Hospital (London) protocol for measurement of simultaneous 24-h intragastric acidity and plasma gastrin concentration.[9] After an overnight fast, a 10F Salem Sump nasogastric tube (Argyle Medical, Crawley) was positioned in the stomach. Aliquots (5–10 ml) of

© Aliment Pharmacol Ther 1991; 5: 283–290

intragastric contents were aspirated at hourly intervals throughout the study, and the pH of each aliquot was measured immediately to the nearest 0.01 pH unit using a glass electrode and digital pH meter (Radiometer, Copenhagen, Denmark). The aliquots were discarded after measurement, and scrupulous care was maintained to prevent cross-infection between subjects. The electrode was calibrated with standard buffers (pH 7.00, 4.01, and 1.09; Radiometer, Copenhagen) before each hourly batch of samples. Intragastric acidity (hydrogen ion acidity) was calculated using the formula: pH = $-\log_{10}$ (hydrogen ion activity).

Every hour from 08.00 to 24.00 hours, and 2-h thereafter, blood was taken via a venous cannula for assay of plasma gastrin concentration. The blood was collected in lithium heparin tubes which contained 0.2 ml aprotinin (Trasylol; Bayer, Newbury). The tubes were centrifuged immediately, and the plasma transferred to plastic tubes and frozen to -20 °C. A radioimmunoassay for gastrin using antibody GAS 179 was performed in Professor Bloom's laboratory at the Royal Postgraduate Medical School, London; this antibody reacts equally with the 17- and 34-peptide forms of gastrin.[10] During the studies the subjects were fully ambulant around the research ward. The food and environmental conditions were identical on each study day; breakfast, coffee, lunch, tea, dinner and a bedtime snack were served at 08.15, 10.45, 13.15, 15.45, 18.15 and 22.45 hours, respectively.

^{13}C-urea breath tests

A ^{13}C-urea breath test was performed at the end of each 24-h study.[11,12] Gastric emptying was delayed by drinking 250 ml of Ensure (Abbott, Maidenhead) and then 250 mg ^{13}C-urea was swallowed (Sigma, Poole). End-expiratory breath samples were collected in 20 mol Vacutainers (Becton Dickinson, Rutherford, New Jersey, US) before dosing, and at 10-min intervals from 20 to 50 minutes after ingestion of the ^{13}C-urea. The assays were performed at the Bureau of Stable Isotope Analysis (Brentford, UK) and the test was considered to be positive when the $^{13}CO_2$ abundance rose by greater than 6 parts per million.

A 24-hour study with a breath test was performed three times in each subject: before treatment, and 4–6 weeks and 20–24 weeks after treatment.

Treatment regimen

With the aim of eradicating the *H pylori* infection in the gastric mucosa, each subject took a 6-week course of DeNoltab i q.d.s. (tripotassium dicitrato bismuthate; Gist-Brocades, Weybridge) together with 250 mg amoxycillin t.d.s. and 400 mg metronidazole t.d.s. for the first week. Symptoms during this treatment period were diarrhoea (2 subjects), dyspepsia (2), and pruritis ani (1). All of the subjects completed their course of treatment.

Mathematical analysis

Twenty-four-hour profiles of intragastric acidity and plasma gastrin concentration were obtained for every study. The area under the time-concentration curve for each profile was calculated by the trapezoid rule, with integrated 24-h acidity expressed as mmol.h/L and integrated 24-h plasma gastrin concentration expressed as pmol./L.

RESULTS

The first endoscopy, at entry to the study, revealed no evidence of past or present peptic ulceration in any of the eight volunteers. Of the eight subjects identified by serology, five had triple confirmatory evidence of active *H. pylori* infection: a positive urease test (CLOtest), *Helicobacter*-like organisms seen on Warthin–Starry staining of the antral biopsies, and a positive ^{13}C-urea breath test. The other three subjects had negative biopsies, urease tests and ^{13}C breath tests. The three subjects

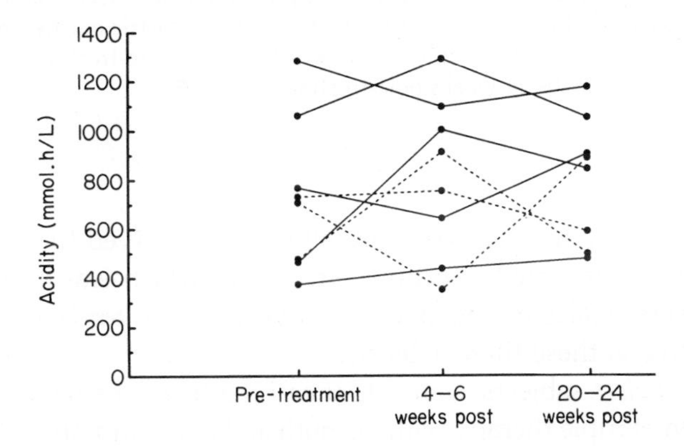

Figure 1. Twenty-four-hour integrated intragastric acidity before treatment, and 4–6 weeks and 20–24 weeks post-treatment in eight healthy subjects: *H. pylori* positive (—●—), *H. pylori* negative (--●--).

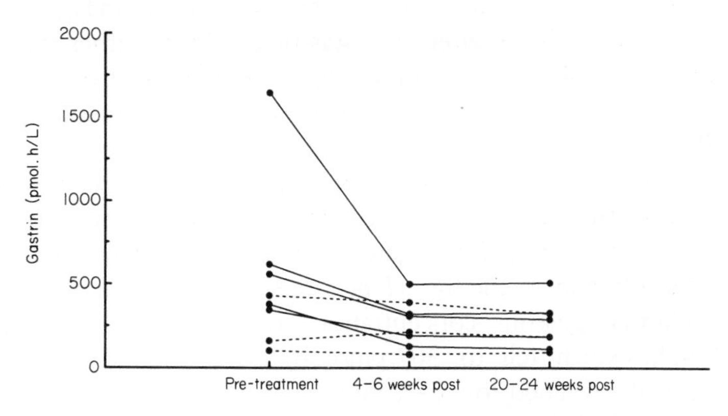

Figure 2. Twenty-four-hour integrated plasma gastrin concentration before treatment, 4–6 weeks and 20–24 weeks post-treatment in eight healthy subjects: *H. pylori* positive (—●—), *H. pylori* negative (--●--).

© *Aliment Pharmacol Ther* 1991; 5: 283–290

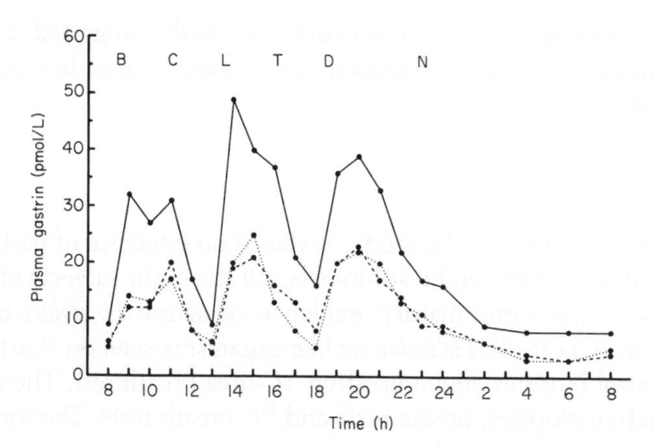

Figure 3. Median plasma gastrin concentration before treatment, and 4–6 weeks and 20–24 weeks post-treatment in five healthy subjects with *H. pylori* infection in the gastric mucosa. B = Breakfast, C = Coffee, L = Lunch, T = Tea, D = Dinner and N = Nightcap. Pre-treatment (—●—), 4–6 weeks post-treatment (---●---), 20–24 weeks post-treatment (· · · · ● · · · ·).

continued in the study as negative controls, all having received the full course of treatment to eliminate presumed infection—treatment which was initiated before the above results were available. The follow-up investigations for *H. pylori* infection were always negative in these three subjects.

All the five *H. pylori* subjects were ^{13}C-urea breath test negative 4–6 weeks after the completion of triple therapy with bismuth and two antibiotics. After 20–24 weeks there was no evidence of recrudescence of *H. pylori* infection in four of these five subjects. However, one subject's breath test had become positive, but she had a negative urease test and no organisms were seen in her antral biopsies.

The 24-h integrated intragastric acidity results are shown in Figure 1. Treatment to eradicate *H. pylori* did not affect intragastric acidity in either the five subjects who were *H. pylori* positive or the three subjects who were *H. pylori* negative. The values of median 24-h integrated intragastric acidity before and after treatment (4–6 and 20–24 weeks) to eradicate *H. pylori* were 768, 1004 and 905 mmol.h/L and 708, 755, and 497 mmol.h/L in the two groups of subjects, respectively.

The 24-h integrated plasma gastrin concentration results are shown in Figure 2. The values for the three *H. pylori* negative subjects were unchanged by treatment. However, before treatment the five *H. pylori* positive subjects had a median 24-h integrated plasma gastrin concentration of 558 pmol.h/L (range 345–1644 pmol.h/L) which fell to 307 pmol.h/L (127–499 pmol.h/L) 1 month after treatment. It remained low 5–6 months after the completion of treatment: median 289 pmol.h/L (113–507 pmol.h/L). Figure 3 demonstrates the 24-hour profiles of median plasma gastrin concentration in the five *H. pylori* positive subjects before and after eradication of the organism: eradication resulted in a decrease of the plasma gastrin concentration throughout the 24 h—a change which persisted for 4–5 months following cessation of treatment.

DISCUSSION

The results of studies measuring 24-h intragastric acidity and 24-h plasma gastrin concentration simultaneously have provided an additional insight into the relationship between these two variables in health and disease. Compared with healthy subjects, duodenal ulcer patients were found to have a higher acidity but a similar plasma gastrin concentration which was considered to be 'inappropriately high'—that is, high acidity might have been expected to be associated with a decreased plasma gastrin concentration.[9] Similar studies reported that healthy subjects with positive serology for *H. pylori* had an integrated 24-h plasma gastrin concentration that was exactly twice that of a group with negative serology, with a similar integrated 24-h acidity in both groups—providing a second example of 'inappropriately high' plasma gastrin concentration.[6] 'Appropriate' elevation of plasma gastrin concentration occurring at the time of decreased intragastric acidity, has been seen in pernicious anaemia patients,[9] women,[13] and patients taking most gastric antisecretory drugs.[14]

The results of the present prospective study indicate that eradication of *H. pylori* results in a decrease of 24-h plasma gastrin concentration. Three subjects had false positive serology for *H. pylori* when recruited for the study; they provided an unplanned control group which demonstrated that the triple therapy does not have a direct effect on acidity or plasma gastrin concentration. It appears that the hypergastrinaemia associated with *H. pylori* infection persists throughout the 24 h, but it is accentuated in the three post-prandial periods. Eradication of *H. pylori* resulted in a 50% decrease of integrated 24-h plasma gastrin concentration, a result that is almost identical to the difference observed in the retrospective analysis of the two larger groups of sero-positive and sero-negative healthy subjects.[6] In the present prospective study eradication of *H. pylori* was not associated with any change of intragastric acidity—which is again a similar finding to the earlier retrospective study in healthy subjects.[6]

Six other papers have also investigated the relationship between *H. pylori*, intragastric acidity and plasma gastrin concentration. Brady *et al.* suggested that *H. pylori* infection does not affect gastrin release.[15] Levi *et al.* showed that *H. pylori*-infected duodenal ulcer patients, compared with non-infected patients have elevated mean basal, pentagastrin-stimulated, and meal-stimulated plasma gastrin concentrations.[4] In a later report, Levi *et al.* treated 10 of their patients with tripotassium dicitrato bismuthate and metronidazole; when assessed 2 days after completing this therapy (that is, with no evidence that *H. pylori* was eradicated), it was found that the integrated post-prandial gastrin response had fallen significantly, but there was no change in peak gastric acid output.[16] In another group of nine duodenal ulcer patients, the elevated basal and peptide-meal stimulated gastrin release fell following eradication of *H. pylori* infection, at a time when there was no change of intragastric acidity.[17] Meal-stimulated plasma gastrin release was measured in a group of eight duodenal ulcer patients and one normal subject, before and after eradication of infection with *H. pylori*; it fell from 141 pg.h/μl before to 98 pg.h/μl after treatment.[5] Finally, in a group of 32 children, the fasting plasma gastrin concentration fell by 32% following eradication of *H. pylori* infection.[18]

The cause of the hypergastrinaemia associated with *H. pylori* infection remains uncertain. It has been shown that *H. pylori* infection is associated with an increase in the intensity of immunostaining for gastrin within G-cells, without an apparent rise of the number of G-cells in the antral mucosa.[19] In-vitro experiments have demonstrated that a toxin from *H. pylori* can result in decreased gastric acid secretion by the parietal cell.[20] Hence, it is possible that the observed hypergastrinaemia in *H. pylori*-infected individuals is necessary to drive gastric acid secretion at a normal level. Alternatively, the local release of ammonia in the antral mucosa may produce an alkaline signal in the mucus, which in turn stimulates gastrin release.[4] The inflammation associated with *H. pylori* infection (gastritis)[21] may have a direct effect on gastrin release, in the same way that oral indomethacin augments post-prandial gastrin release,[22] perhaps by a direct irritation of the gastric mucosa.

Eradication of *H. pylori*, has eliminated 24-hour hypergastrinaemia and 'normalized' gastric physiology in five *H. pylori*-infected apparently healthy individuals. Will this treatment decrease their risk of future peptic ulceration?[23–25] Will this treatment prevent long-term gastrin-induced changes in their gastric mucosa? Should otherwise healthy subjects, found by chance to be infected with *H. pylori*, be offered treatment to eradicate infection with the organism? Further prospective studies will be required to answer these questions.

ACKNOWLEDGEMENTS

This study was supported by a grant from Glaxo Group Research Ltd. Technical assistance was provided by Nurse Judith Sercombe. The manuscript was prepared by Miss Doris Elliott.

REFERENCES

1 Marshall B J, Warren J R. Unidentified curved bacilli in the stomachs of patients with gastritis and peptic ulceration. Lancet 1984; i: 1311–5.

2 Dooley C P, Cohen H. The clinical significance of *Campylobacter pylori*. Ann Intern Med 1988; 94: 229–38.

3 Graham D Y. *Campylobacter pylori* and peptide ulcer disease. Gastroenterology 1989; 96: 614–25.

4 Levi S, Beardshall K, Haddad G, Playford R, Ghosh P, Calam J. *Campylobacter pylori* and duodenal ulcers: the gastrin link. Lancet 1989; i: 1167–8.

5 Graham D Y, Opekun A, Ginger M L, Evans D J, Klein P D, Evans D G. Ablation of exaggerated meal-stimulated gastrin release in duodenal ulcer patients after clearance of *Helicobacter* (*Campylobacter*) *pylori* infection. Am J Gastroenterol 1990; 85: 394–8.

6 Smith J T L, Pounder R E, Nwokolo C U, *et al.* Inappropriate hypergastrinaemia in asymptomatic healthy subjects infected with *Helicobacter pylori*. Gut 1990; 31: 522–5.

7 Evans D J, Evans D G, Graham D Y, Klein P D. A sensitive and specific serological test for detection of *Campylobacter pylori* infection. Gastroenterology 1989; 96: 1004–8.
8 Szeto M-L, Pounder R E, Hamilton-Dutoit S J, Dhillon A P. Rapid urease test provides specific identification on *Campylobacter pylori* in antral mucosa biopsies. Postgrad Med J 1988; 64: 935–6.
9 Lanzon-Miller S, Pounder R E, Hamilton M R, *et al.* Twenty-four hour intragastric acidity and plasma gastrin concentration in healthy subjects and patients with duodenal or gastric ulcer or pernicious anaemia. Aliment Pharmacol Therap 1987; 1: 225–37.
10 Bryant M G, Adrian T E. Gastrin. In: Bloom S R, Long R G, eds. Radioimmunoassay of gut regulatory peptides. London: Saunders, 1982: 51–9.
11 Graham D Y, Klein P D, Evans D J, *et al.* *Campylobacter pyloridis* detected non-invasively by the ^{13}C-urea breath test. Lancet 1987; i: 1174–7.
12 Klein P D, Graham D Y. Detecting *Campylobacter pylori* by the ^{13}C-urea breath test. In: Rathbone B J, Heatley R V, eds. Campylobacter pylori and gastro-duodenal disease. Oxford, Blackwell 1989: 94–105.
13 Prewett E J, Smith J T L, Nwokolo C U, Sawyerr A M, Pounder R E. 24-hour intragastric acidity and plasma gastrin concentration in female and male subject. Clinical Science 1991; in press.
14 Pounder R E, Smith J T L. Drug-induced changes of plasma gastrin. Gastroenterology Clinics of North America 1990; 19: 141–54.
15 Bray C E III, Hadfield T L, Hyatt J R, Utts S J. Acid secretion and serum gastrin levels in individuals with *Campylobacter pylori*. Gastroenterology 1988; 94: 923–7.
16 Levi S, Beardshall K, Swift I, *et al.* *Helicobacter pylori*, hypergastrinaemia, and duodenal ulcers: effect of eradicating the organism. Br Med J 1989; 299: 1504–5.
17 McColl K E L, Fullarton G M, El Nujumi A M, MacDonald A M I, Dahil S, Hilditch T E. Serum gastrin and gastric acid status one and seven months after eradication of *Helicobacter pylori* in duodenal ulcer patients. Gut 1990; 31: A601 (Abstract.)
18 Oderda G, Holton J, Altare F, Vaira D, Ainley C, Ansaldi N. Amoxycillin plus tinidazole for *Campylobacter pylori* gastritis in children: assessment by serum IgG antibody, pepsinogen I, and gastrin levels. Lancet 1989; i: 690–2.
19 Sankey E A, Helliwell P A, Dhillon A P. Immunostaining of antral gastrin cells is quantitatively increased in *Helicobacter pylori* gastritis. Histopathology 1990; 16: 151–5.
20 Cave D R, Vargas M. Effect of a *Campylobacter pylori* protein on acid secretion by parietal cells. Lancet 1989; ii: 187–9.
21 Misiewicz J J, Tytgat G N J, Goodwin C S, *et al.* The Sydney System: a classification of gastritis. Working Party Reports, World Congress of Gastroenterology 1990; 1–10.
22 Lanzon-Miller S, Allison M C, Pounder R E, Ball S, Hamilton M R, Chronos N A F. Enprostil inhibits post-prandial gastrin release: a dose-response study. Aliment Pharmacol Therap 1988; 2: 317–23.
23 Coghlan J G, Gilligan D, Humphries H, *et al.* *Campylobacter pylori* and recurrence of duodenal ulcers. A twelve month follow-up study. Lancet 1987; ii: 1109–11.
24 Marshall B J, Goodwin C S, Warren J R, *et al.* Prospective double-blind trial of duodenal ulcer relapse after eradication of *Campylobacter pylori*. Lancet 1988; ii: 1437–41.
25 Rauws E A, Tytgat G N J. Cure of duodenal ulcer associated with eradiation of *Helicobacter pylori*. Lancet 1990; i: 1233–5.

© Lancet 1991; 338: 332–335

Mucosal IgA recognition of *Helicobacter pylori* 120 kDa protein, peptic ulceration, and gastric pathology

J. E. CRABTREE J. D. TAYLOR J. I. WYATT R. V. HEATLEY
T. M. SHALLCROSS D. S. TOMPKINS B. J. RATHBONE

The gastric IgA response to *Helicobacter pylori* was examined in 100 dyspeptic patients by means of immunoblotting of supernatants from antral biopsy and gastric mononuclear cell cultures. 76 of 78 patients with chronic gastritis, 2 of 8 with reactive gastritis, and 1 of 14 subjects with normal mucosa showed positive responses. Of patients with chronic gastritis, 75%, 83%, 97%, and 76%, respectively, showed responses to the 120 kDa, 90 kDa, 61 kDa, and 31 kDa proteins. None of the 19 patients with chronic gastritis who did not recognise the 120 kDa protein had peptic ulcers, whereas 25 of 57 with positive recognition had peptic ulcers ($p<0{\cdot}001$). Mucosal recognition of the *H pylori* 120 kDa protein was also positively associated with the activity of gastritis (polymorph infiltration) ($p<0{\cdot}002$) and with the extent of surface degeneration ($p<0{\cdot}01$). These findings suggest that 120-kDa-positive strains of *H pylori* have pathogenic features associated with active gastritis and peptic ulceration. Infection with 120-kDa-negative strains may explain why peptic ulceration develops in only a proportion of subjects infected with *H pylori*.

Lancet 1991; **338**: 332–35.

Introduction

The strong association between colonisation of the gastric mucosa by *Helicobacter pylori* and chronic gastritis has been firmly established.[1,2] In addition, many studies have shown that 70–100% of patients with duodenal ulcers have gastric *H pylori* infection, and the relation with gastric ulceration (56–96% of patients) is also strong.[2-4] Nevertheless, it remains unclear why peptic ulcers develop in only some individuals infected with *H pylori*, since 50–60% of the general population are infected with this organism.[5] Several pathogenetic mechanisms of mucosal damage have been proposed.[6] One possibility is that some strains of *H pylori* are more pathogenic or ulcerogenic. Bacterial cytotoxin production does, however, seem to vary in different isolates[7,8] and infection with cytotoxin-producing strains is more frequent in subjects with peptic ulceration.[7]

Western blotting analysis of systemic IgG responses to *H pylori* has shown the antigenicity of 110–120 kDa, 89 kDa, 61 kDa, 54 kDa, and 31 kDa proteins, although there is substantial variability among subjects.[9-12] The 120 kDa protein, which is recognised systemically in 83% of *H pylori* positive subjects, is a surface protein not expressed in some *H pylori* strains.[11] We have studied the mucosal IgA response to *H pylori* by western blotting of supernatants of cultured antral mononuclear cells and biopsy samples. The relation between the mucosal IgA recognition of *H pylori* proteins and gastroduodenal disease was investigated.

Patients and methods

We studied 100 randomly selected dyspeptic patients attending an outpatient dyspepsia clinic (mean age 51·7 [SD 16·5], range 20–88 years), who were undergoing routine upper gastrointestinal endoscopy. No patient was taking non-steroidal anti-inflammatory drugs. The study was approved by the Research Committee (Ethics) of the Leeds Eastern Health Authority. Antral biopsy samples were taken at endoscopy for histopathology and organ culture (n = 81) or cell culture (n = 19). The presence or absence of active gastric or duodenal ulceration was recorded. Gastritis was classified by one histopathologist unaware of the clinical details, according to the Sydney System,[13] which includes assessment of the degree of atrophy, chronicity, activity, and intestinal metaplasia on a scale of 0 to 3. *H pylori* was detected by means of modified Giemsa stain. Biopsy samples were also scored histologically for the presence and degree of degeneration of surface epithelial cells[14] (0 to 3).

Samples for culture were immediately placed into RPMI 1640 medium (Flow Laboratories, Rickmansworth, UK) containing 10% fetal calf serum and 40 μg/ml gentamicin. They were cultured[15] in 1 ml medium at 37°C in a humidified 5% carbon dioxide, 95% air, incubator for 72 h. Medium was changed daily and supernatants stored at − 70°C until assay. Gastric mononuclear cells were isolated from the antral biopsy samples of 19 subjects as previously described.[16] Purified cells were cultured at 5×10^5/ml in duplicate or triplicate in 96-well round-bottomed microtitre plates (Flow Laboratories). After 6 days, supernatants were removed, centrifuged, and stored at − 70°C.

H pylori strain NCTC 11637 was used as a standard antigen preparation. Bacteria were grown microaerobically on Columbia agar (Oxoid, Basingstoke, UK) with 7% defibrinated horse blood for 72 h. Bacteria were harvested from agar plates, washed in 10 mmol/l "tris"-buffered saline, pH 7·4, and whole cell sonicates were prepared for sodium dodecyl sulphate polyacrylamide gel electrophoresis.[12,17] Samples containing 300 μg protein were separated by means of a 5% stacking gel and 12·5% separation gel. Separated proteins were transferred to nitrocellulose paper (Schleicher & Schuell) by semi-dry blotting for 80 min at 145 mA in an LKB 'NovaBlotter'. After blocking of non-specific binding by overnight incubation at 4°C in tris-buffered saline containing 0·25% 'Tween 20', nitrocellulose sheets were incubated with biopsy culture supernatants (1 in 10 dilution in tris-buffered saline/tween containing 20% fetal calf serum) and cell culture supernatants (1 in 4 dilution) in a miniblotter apparatus. Bound IgA was detected by sequential incubation with alkaline-phosphatase-conjugated goat antibody to human IgA (1 in 500 dilution) and 5-bromo-4-chloro-3-indolyl phosphate and nitroblue tetrazolium.[17] Immunoblots were scored for IgA recognition of *H pylori* proteins by observers unaware of the endoscopic or histological diagnoses.

Statistical analyses of 2 × 2 tables were done with Yates' corrected chi-square and Fisher's exact tests, as appropriate,[18] with a

ADDRESSES: **Department of Medicine** (J. E. Crabtree, DPhil, J. D. Taylor, PhD, R. V. Heatley, MD, T. M. Shallcross, MRCP, B. J. Rathbone, MD) **and Pathology** (J. I. Wyatt, MRCPath), **St James's University Hospital, Leeds, and Department of Microbiology, Bradford Royal Infirmary, Bradford, UK** (D. S. Tompkins, MRCPath). Correspondence to Dr J. E. Crabtree, Department of Medicine, St James's University Hospital, Leeds LS9 7TF, UK.

TABLE I—RELATION BETWEEN GASTRIC AND DUODENAL PATHOLOGY, H PYLORI HISTOLOGICAL STATUS, AND MUCOSAL IgA IMMUNOBLOT RESULTS

Histology	n	No *(%)* Positive for *H pylori*	Positive by IgA immunoblot	With ulcers: Gastric	Duodenal
Normal	14	0	1 *(7)*	0	0
Chronic gastritis	78	69 *(88)*	76 *(97)*	9 *(12)**	16 *(21)*
Reactive gastritis	8	0	2 *(25)*	0	0

*1 also had a duodenal ulcer.

Bonferroni correction to take account of multiple tests on four antigens.[19] Data on histological features and antigen recognition were analysed by a chi-square test for trend.

Results

78 of the patients investigated had chronic gastritis, 14 normal antral mucosa, and 8 reactive gastritis (one of the special forms of gastritis recognised in the Sydney System). All peptic ulcers occurred in the group with chronic gastritis (table I). Immunoblotting of both biopsy culture supernatants and cell supernatants from patients with chronic gastritis showed a strong mucosal IgA response against *H pylori* (fig 1). 76 of the 78 patients with chronic gastritis had a positive local IgA response to *H pylori* (table I). *H pylori* was not identified histologically in 7 of these positive subjects and in 2 subjects with no evidence of a local IgA response to *H pylori*. 2 patients with reactive gastritis and 1 subject with a normal mucosa had local IgA responses to *H pylori* (table I); all 3 were negative for *H pylori* on histology.

There was substantial variation in the recognition of *H pylori* proteins among patients. 74 (97%) of the 76 positive subjects with chronic gastritis had a positive IgA response to the 61 kDa urease protein: 57 (75%) recognised the 120 kDa protein, 63 (83%) the 90 kDa protein, and 58 (76%) the 31 kDa protein.

The association between mucosal IgA recognition of these antigens and peptic ulcers is shown in table II. All subjects with peptic ulcers had a positive IgA response to the 120 kDa protein, whereas none of the 19 120-kDa-negative chronic gastritis subjects had peptic ulcers ($p<0{\cdot}001$). There was no significant association between peptic ulcers and recognition of the other proteins (table II).

Among the patients with chronic gastritis, those with positive responses to the 120 kDa protein had a significantly greater density of mucosal neutrophil infiltration than those without such responses (fig 2A; $\chi^2=9{\cdot}646$, $p<0{\cdot}002$, for trend). Although ulceration is associated with higher polymorph scores in the antral mucosa,[20] even the subgroup of patients without ulcers (n = 32) positive for the 120 kDa protein had significantly higher polymorph scores than 120-kDa-negative patients ($\chi^2=4{\cdot}117$, $p<0{\cdot}05$). Subjects

TABLE II—MUCOSAL IgA RECOGNITION OF H PYLORI ANTIGENS AND PEPTIC ULCERS IN PATIENTS WITH CHRONIC GASTRITIS

Antigen	No *(%)* of patients (with chronic gastritis) positive: No ulcer (n = 51)	Peptic ulcer (n = 25)
31 kDa	38 *(75)*	20 *(80)*
61 kDa	50 *(98)*	24 *(96)*
90 kDa	41 *(80)*	22 *(88)*
120 kDa	32 *(63)*	25 *(100)**

*p<0·001 Fisher's exact test with Bonferroni correction for multiple tests.

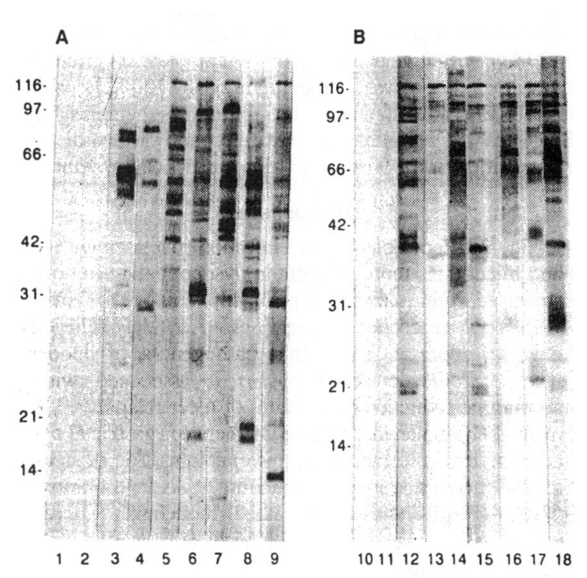

Fig 1—*H pylori* IgA immunoblots.

A = antral biopsy culture supernatants; B = cell culture supernatants. Lanes 1, 2, 10, and 11 = controls with normal gastric mucosa; lanes 3–9 and 12–18 = patients with chronic gastritis. Patients in lanes 3 and 4 have no recognition of 120 kDa protein. Protein molecular weight standards in kDa.

responding to the 120 kDa protein also had significantly greater evidence of surface degeneration than 120-kDa-negative subjects (fig 2B; $\chi^2=7{\cdot}414$, $p<0{\cdot}01$). Again, even the 120-kDa-positive subjects without ulcers had

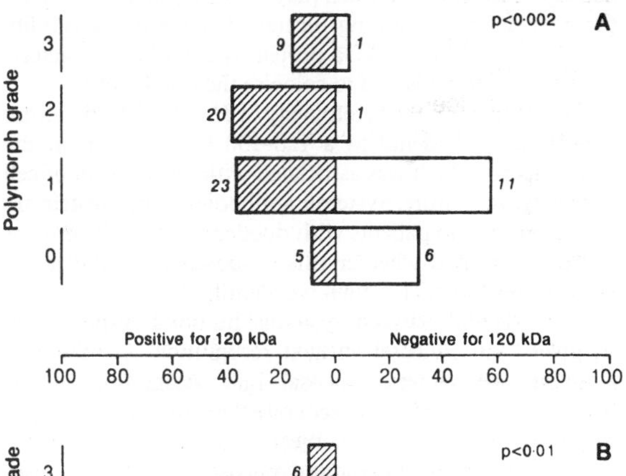

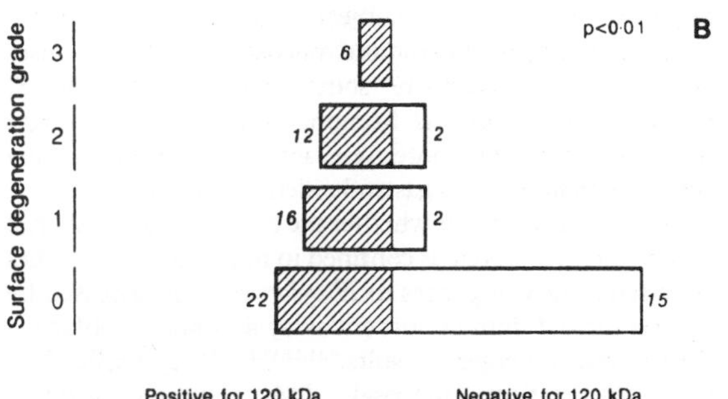

Fig 2—Relations between polymorph density (A: n = 76) and epithelial surface degeneration (B: n = 75) and mucosal IgA recognition of *H pylori* 120 kDa protein in patients with chronic gastritis.

Numbers of patients given beside blocks. 1 biopsy sample was inadequate for assessment of surface degeneration.

significantly higher surface degeneration scores than the 120-kDa-negative patients ($\chi^2 = 5{\cdot}83$, $p < 0{\cdot}02$). There was no association between recognition of the 120 kDa protein and the grade of atrophy or intestinal metaplasia nor between any histological feature and mucosal IgA recognition of the 90 kDa, 61 kDa, or 31 kDa proteins.

Discussion

The incidence of *H pylori* infection increases with age, and infection is more frequent in dyspeptic than in normal subjects.[5] Peptic ulcers develop in only a minority of patients with *H pylori* infection, and yet *H pylori* is widely believed to have an important role in the pathogenesis of duodenal ulcers. Eradication of *H pylori* is associated with a substantial reduction in the rates of ulcer relapse.[21,22] The most likely explanation for the link between gastric *H pylori* and duodenal ulceration is *H pylori* colonisation of areas of gastric metaplasia in the duodenum.[23] As in the antrum, when *H pylori* colonises the duodenum, there is inflammation (duodenitis), which is considered a preulcerative state.

In this study the mucosal IgA recognition of the *H pylori* 120 kDa protein was specifically associated with peptic ulceration. Since this antigen is not expressed by all *H pylori* strains,[11] this observation suggests virulence differences between isolates of *H pylori*. The finding that a positive local immune response to the 120 kDa protein was associated with increased mucosal polymorph infiltration and ephithelial surface degeneration suggests that this enhanced inflammatory damage may be the means by which these strains induce ulceration, providing more aggressive damage to the mucosa which may intermittently overwhelm the host defences, causing ulceration. Another possibility would be that the 120 kDa protein is a marker of bacteria which are better adapted to colonise the duodenum.

Two studies on the cytotoxicity of *H pylori* broth culture supernatants[8,24] identified a 128–130 kDa protein in the supernatants which was associated with vacuolation of cell lines in tissue culture. Systemic antibodies to this protein are more common in patients with duodenal ulcers. It remains to be determined whether this proposed cytotoxin is the same as the 120 kDa protein we identified.

The relation between systemic humoral responses to *H pylori* and mucosal antigen recognition is unknown, although we showed mucosal IgA recognition of the major *H pylori* antigens recognised by the systemic IgG response[9-12] in 97% of subjects with chronic gastritis. Disparity between systemic and mucosal humoral responses is known to occur in some intestinal disorders.[25] Examination of mucosal humoral responses to *H pylori* could therefore be more relevant in determining any potential relations with gastroduodenal pathology.

It is similarly unclear whether the observed IgA response to the 120 kDa protein is confined to mucosal sites. Studies of systemic IgA responses to *H pylori* proteins assessed by enzyme-linked immunosorbent assay and immunoblotting have given divergent results.[9,11,12,17,26] If systemic IgG responses reflect mucosal IgA immunoreactivity, assessment of seropositivity to the 120 kDa protein may help in identification of dyspeptic individuals who need endoscopic investigation.[27] In our study 44% of patients with chronic gastritis who recognised the 120 kDa *H pylori* protein had active peptic ulceration.

In conclusion, our findings show that peptic ulceration is specifically associated with mucosal recognition of a 120 kDa *H pylori* protein in patients with chronic gastritis. Mucosal responses to this antigen are likely to reflect the bacterial strains colonising the patient. Infection with *H pylori* strains that do not express the 120 kDa protein may partly account for the absence of peptic ulceration in a proportion of infected subjects.

This study was supported by Glaxo plc and the Yorkshire Regional Health Authority. We thank the staff of the Gastroenterology Department of St James's University Hospital for their cooperation and Dr G. M. Sobala for valuable discussion.

REFERENCES

1. Marshall BJ, Warren JR. Unidentified curved bacilli in the stomach of patients with gastritis and peptic ulceration. *Lancet* 1984; i: 1311–14.
2. Rauws EAJ, Langenberg W, Houthoff HJ, Zanen HC, Tytgat GNJ. *Campylobacter pyloridis*-associated chronic active antral gastritis. *Gastroenterology* 1988; **94:** 33–40.
3. Kalogeropoulos NK, Whitehead R. *Campylobacter*-like organisms and *Candida* in peptic ulcers and similar lesions of the upper gastrointestinal tract: a study of 247 cases. *J Clin Pathol* 1988; **41:** 1093–98.
4. Raskov H, Lanng K, Gaarslev B, et al. Screening for *Campylobacter pyloridis* in patients with upper dyspepsia and the relation to inflammation of the human gastric antrum. *Scand J Gastroenterol* 1987; **22:** 568–72.
5. Shallcross TM, Rathbone BJ, Heatley RV. *Campylobacter pylori* and non-ulcer dyspepsia. In: Rathbone BJ, Heatley RV, eds. *Campylobacter pylori* and gastroduodenal disease. Oxford: Blackwell Scientific Publications, 1989: 155–66.
6. Morgan DR, Leunk RD. Pathogenesis of infection by *H pylori*. In: Blaser MJ, ed. *Campylobacter pylori* in gastritis and peptic ulcer disease. New York: Igaku-Shoiu, 1989: 115–33.
7. Figura N, Guglielmetti A, Rossolini A, et al. Cytotoxin production by *Campylobacter pylori* strains isolated from patients with peptic ulcers and from patients with chronic gastritis only. *J Clin Microbiol* 1989; **27:** 225–26.
8. Cover TL, Dooley CP, Blaser MJ. Characterisation of and human serological response to proteins in *Helicobacter pylori* broth culture supernatants with vacuolising cytotoxin activity. *Infect Immun* 1990; **58:** 603–10.
9. von Wulffen H, Grote HJ, Gatermann S, Loning T, Berger B, Buhl C. Immunoblot analysis of immune response to *Campylobacter pylori* and its clinical associates. *J Clin Pathol* 1988; **41:** 653–59.
10. Newell DG. Identification of the outer membrane proteins of *Campylobacter pyloridis* and antigenic cross reactivity between *C pyloridis* and *C jejuni*. *J Clin Microbiol* 1987; **133:** 163–70.
11. Apel I, Jacobs E, Kist M, Bredt W. Antibody response of patients against a 120 kDa surface protein of *Campylobacter pylori*. *Zbl Bakt Hyg A* 1988; **268:** 271–76.
12. Crabtree JE, Mahony MJ, Taylor JD, Heatley RV, Littlewood JM, Tompkins DS. Immune responses to *Helicobacter pylori* in children with recurrent abdominal pain. *J Clin Pathol* 1991; **44:** 768–71.
13. Misiewicz JJ, Tytgat GNJ, Goodwin CS, et al. The Sydney System: a new classification of gastritis. Working Party Reports of the World Congresses of Gastroenterology. Oxford: Blackwell Scientific Publications, 1990: 1–10.
14. Hessey SJ, Spencer J, Wyatt JI, et al. Bacterial adhesion and disease activity in *Helicobacter* associated chronic gastritis. *Gut* 1990; 31: 134–38.
15. Crabtree JE, Shallcross TM, Heatley RV, Wyatt JI. Mucosal tumour necrosis factor alpha and interleukin-6 in patients with *Helicobacter pylori*-associated gastritis. *Gut* 1991; **44:** 768–71.
16. Crabtree JE, Heatley RV, Losowsky MS. Immunoglobulin secretion by isolated intestinal lymphocytes: spontaneous production and T-cell regulation in normal small intestine and in patients with coeliac disease. *Gut* 1989; **30:** 347–54.
17. Crabtree JE, Shallcross TM, Wyatt JI, et al. Mucosal humoral immune response to *Helicobacter pylori* in patients with duodenitis. *Dig Dis Sci* 1991; **44:** 768–71.
18. Armitage P, Berry G. Statistical methods in medical research, 2nd ed. Oxford: Blackwell Scientific Publications, 1987.
19. Emery AEH. Methodology in medical genetics. An introduction to statistical methods. Edinburgh: Churchill Livingstone, 1976: 98–106.
20. Eidt S, Stolte M. Differences between *Helicobacter pylori* associated gastritis in patients with duodenal ulcer, pyloric ulcer, other gastric ulcer, and gastritis without ulcer. In: Malfertheiner P, Ditschuneit H, eds. *Helicobacter pylori*, gastritis and peptic ulcer. Berlin: Springer-Verlag, 1990: 228–36.
21. Coghlan JG, Gilligan D, Humphreys H, et al. *Campylobacter pylori* and recurrence of duodenal ulcers: 12 months follow-up study. *Lancet* 1987; ii: 1109–11.

© *Lancet* 1991; 338: 332–335

22. Rauws EAJ, Tytgat GNJ. Cure of duodenal ulcer associated with eradication of *Helicobacter pylori*. *Lancet* 1990; **335:** 1233–35.

23. Wyatt JI, Rathbone BJ, Dixon MF, Heatley RV. *Campylobacter pyloridis* and acid-induced gastric metaplasia in the pathogenesis of duodenitis. *J Clin Pathol* 1987; **40:** 841–48.

24. Figura N, Bugnoli M, Guglielmetti P, Musmanno RA, Russi M, Quaranta S. Antibodies to vacuolating toxin of *Helicobacter pylori* in dyspeptic patients. *Rev Esp Enf Digest* 1990; **78** (suppl 1): 7.

25. O'Mahony S, Arranz E, Barton JR, Ferguson A. Dissociation between systemic and mucosal humoral responses in coeliac disease. *Gut* 1991; **32:** 29–35.

26. Goodwin CS, Blincow E, Peterson G, et al. Enzyme-linked immunosorbent assay for *Campylobacter pyloridis:* correlation with presence of *C pyloridis* in the gastric mucosa. *J Infect Dis* 1987; **155:** 488–94.

27. Sobala GM, Crabtree JE, Pentith JA, et al. Screening dyspepsia by serology to *Helicobacter pylori*. *Lancet* 1991; **338:** 94–96.

Are Patients with Primary Biliary Cirrhosis Hypermetabolic? A Comparison between Patients before and after Liver Transplantation and Controls

J. Hilary Green, Peter N. Bramley and Monty S. Losowsky

Department of Medicine, St. James's University Hospital, Leeds LS9 7TF, United Kingdom

Wasting is common in end-stage primary biliary cirrhosis and causes concern in patients facing liver transplantation. We have quantified resting metabolic rate and diet-induced thermogenesis in seven patients with primary biliary cirrhosis, in seven patients after liver transplantation who had previously been diagnosed as having primary biliary cirrhosis and in seven controls.

Resting metabolic rate was elevated in the primary biliary cirrhosis group (4.44 ± 0.81 kJ/hr/kg body wt; mean ± S.D.) compared with the post-liver-transplantation group (3.39 ± 0.40 kJ/hr/kg body wt) ($p < 0.005$) and compared with control subjects (3.65 ± 0.23 kJ/hr/kg body wt) ($p < 0.01$). A highly significant relationship was found between the severity of liver disease in the primary biliary cirrhosis group, as assessed by Child-Pugh score, and the resting metabolic rate group ($r = 0.93$; $p < 0.005$).

After a liquid meal (41 kJ/kg body wt), the metabolic rate increased, with similar peak changes from baseline occurring in all three groups. However, the rise persisted significantly longer in the primary biliary cirrhosis patients, and thus the integrated mean postprandial energy expenditure over the 4-hr postprandial observation period was greater in the primary biliary cirrhosis group than in the other two groups ($p < 0.001$).

Fasting glucose and protein oxidation rates were similar between groups, but fasting fat oxidation rate was higher in the primary biliary cirrhosis group (3.90 ± 0.83 kJ/hr/kg body wt) than in the post-liver-transplantation group (2.11 ± 0.90 kJ/hr/kg body wt) ($p < 0.025$) and than in the control group (2.49 ± 1.19 kJ/hr/kg body wt) ($p < 0.05$). Postprandial glucose oxidation rates were similar in all groups, but the protein oxidation rate was lower in the primary biliary cirrhosis group than in the other two groups ($p < 0.01$). The fat oxidation rate remained higher after food intake in the primary biliary cirrhosis group than in the post-liver-transplantation group ($p < 0.05$), but no significant differences were found between the primary biliary cirrhosis and control groups or between the post-liver-transplantation and control groups. No differences in total fasting plasma free fatty acids were seen between groups, but the level of stearic acid was higher in the control group (41.3 ± 10.3 μmol/L) than in the primary biliary cirrhosis group (27.5 ± 9.2 μmol/L) ($p < 0.05$) or than the post-liver-transplantation group (26.9 ± 6.6 μmol/L) ($p < 0.05$).

These data suggest that, as liver disease progresses, resting metabolic rate increases. This, together with the greater overall diet-induced thermogenesis in these patients, could make a significant contribution to increased energy expenditure and thereby exacerbate malnutrition. (Hepatology 1991;14:464-472.)

Received July 3, 1990; accepted April 23, 1991.

The Boots Co., Nottingham, UK, provided the Vita Food for these studies.

This study was supported by the Medical Research Council.

Address reprint requests to: Dr. J. Hilary Green, Department of Medicine, St. James's University Hospital, Leeds, LS9 7TF, United Kingdom.

31/1/31241

© *Lancet* 1991; 338: 94–96

CLINICAL PRACTICE

Screening dyspepsia by serology to *Helicobacter pylori*

G. M. SOBALA J. E. CRABTREE J. A. PENTITH
B. J. RATHBONE T. M. SHALLCROSS J. I. WYATT M. F. DIXON
R. V. HEATLEY A. T. R. AXON

Owing to limited endoscopy resources, various screening strategies for endoscopy have been proposed. *Helicobacter pylori* can be detected with high sensitivity and specificity by serology, and therefore we assessed the effects on diagnostic accuracy and endoscopic workload of a policy of screening clinic patients with dyspepsia before endoscopy by a strategy based on age, *Helicobacter pylori* serology, and use of non-steroidal anti-inflammatory drugs. 1153 patients were studied, of whom 842 were of known histological *H pylori* status (histology group) and 293 had serum assessed prospectively by in-house and commercial ELISAs for detection of IgG antibodies to *H pylori*. Overall, the screening strategy would have reduced endoscopy workload by 23·3% (95% confidence interval 20·9–25·8%) and would have had a sensitivity for detection of peptic ulcer of 97·4% (94·5–99·1%). No peptic ulcer or malignant disease was missed in the patients studied prospectively, but 6 of 192 peptic ulcers in the histology group would have been missed. A policy of screening young dyspeptic patients for *H pylori* by serology is more sensitive than symptom-based screening strategies, and may have an important role in reducing endoscopy workload.

Lancet 1991; **338**: 94–96

Introduction

The extent to which dyspepsia should be investigated is controversial, especially in younger patients.[1,2] Only a few patients have peptic ulcer disease and even fewer have cancer; nonetheless, in most centres in the UK demand for endoscopy exceeds the resources available. That eradiation of *Helicobacter pylori* may lead to longlasting remission of duodenal ulcer disease[3-6] strengthens the case for accurate endoscopic diagnosis of dyspepsia. Limited endoscopy resources must therefore be allocated effectively. Various screening policies for endoscopy have been proposed—ie, use of simple age restrictions,[2,7] strategies that attempt to identify patients at high risk of ulcer disease and cancer on the basis of their symptoms,[8-10] suggestions that all patients should initially be treated empirically.[11]

The close association between *H pylori* and the chronic gastritis that accompanies both peptic ulcer disease and gastric cancer offers a new approach for screening that is based on pathogenesis. *H pylori* can be detected with high sensitivity and specificity by non-invasive techniques such as serology[12] and carbon-labelled urea breath testing. Therefore, we decided to assess the likely effect of screening dyspeptic patients for *H pylori* infection by serology on both endoscopic workload and diagnostic accuracy for peptic ulcer disease.

Patients and methods

Screening strategy

Our hypothetical screening strategy was defined as follows:[13] all patients aged 45 years or more would undergo endoscopy without further screening, as would all patients under 45 taking non-steroidal anti-inflammatory drugs (NSAIDs). Other patients under 45 would first have blood taken for *H pylori* serology, and seropositive patients only would then need endoscopy. The age cut-off of 45 was taken to minimise the risk of missing cases of upper gastrointestinal malignant disease since gastric cancer below this age is rare.[2]

Patients

Histology group—First, we assessed the screening policy in 842 patients who had been selected either randomly or consecutively into three studies from three dyspepsia clinics in Leeds during the previous 5 years.[14-16] We considered age, presence of peptic ulcer disease on endoscopy, and *H pylori* status as judged by Giemsa staining of two or more antral biopsy samples. In 696 patients, NSAID use had also been recorded. This series excluded patients with upper gastrointestinal malignant disease. Because there were no serology results for this group, we assumed that the sensitivity and specificity of serology for *H pylori* were similar to those of histology.

Serology group—We then assessed the screening strategy prospectively in 293 consecutive patients referred to a dyspepsia clinic that offers local general practitioners open access to diagnostic endoscopy. Pre-treatment with H_2-receptor antagonists is discouraged in patients referred to this clinic, with a resulting high detection rate for peptic ulcer disease and cancer.[17] All patients gave written informed consent, and details of their drug history and symptoms were recorded by the examining physician with a structured questionnaire. Blood was then taken into a plain container and serum was separated and stored at −20°C for subsequent analysis. All patients underwent endoscopy and the findings were recorded on the questionnaire. The study was approved by the local research ethics committee.

Serology

Sera were assayed without knowledge of the patients' diagnoses for *H pylori* IgG antibodies by an in-house enzyme-linked immunosorbent assay (ELISA) as previously described.[18] A standard curve of positive control sera in addition to negative controls were included in each assay. The threshold of positivity was calculated by analysis of sera from 116 patients of known

ADDRESSES: **Gastroenterology Unit** (G. M. Sobala, MRCP, J. A. Pentith, A. T. R. Axon, FRCP), **and University Department of Pathology** (M. F. Dixon, MD), **The General Infirmary, Leeds; and Departments of Medicine** (J. E. Crabtree, DPhil, B. J. Rathbone, MD, T. M. Shallcross, MRCP, R. V. Heatley, FRCP), **and Pathology** (J. I. Wyatt, MRCPath), **St James' University Hospital, Leeds UK.** Correspondence to Dr G. M. Sobala, Gastroenterology Unit, The General Infirmary, Great George Street, Leeds LS1 3EX, UK.

© Lancet 1991; 338: 94–96

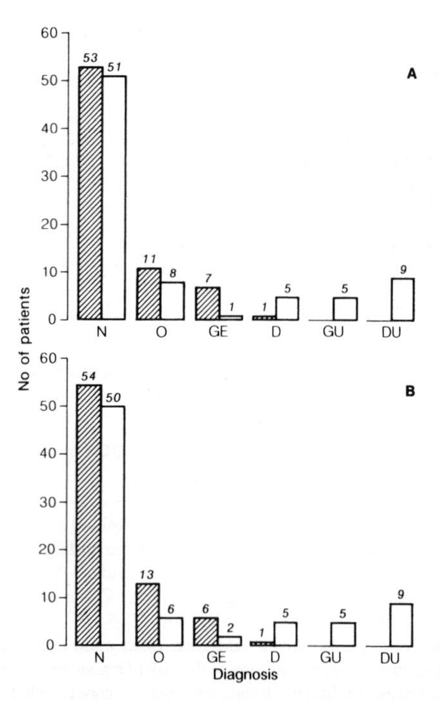

(A) In-house ELISA and (B) commercial ELISA.

Endoscopic diagnoses in patients aged under 45 who would (open columns) and would not (closed columns) have undergone endoscopy if the screening strategy had been followed.

histological *H pylori* status, giving an assay sensitivity of 97% and specificity of 95%.

All sera were than retested with a commercial ELISA ("Helico-G", Porton Cambridge Ltd, UK). This ELISA was first evaluated locally, and, to improve the sensitivity, the threshold for positivity was lowered below that of the reference serum supplied by the manufacturers (10 antibody units/ml) to 7·7 antibody units/ml. This cut-off value gave a sensitivity of 97% and a specificity of 87% when tested on 143 sera from patients not taking part in the study.

Results

Histology group

If the screening policy had been applied to the 842 patients in whom *H pylori* status was determined by histology there would have been 193 fewer endoscopies; 6 of 192 peptic ulcers would have been missed.

Serology group

Of the 293 patients assessed prospectively by serology, 169 were men and 124 women (mean age 44·1 years, range 18–71). 151 patients were younger than 45. 31 (10·6%) were taking H_2-receptor antagonists or other ulcer-healing agents before endoscopy, and 15 (5·1%) were taking NSAIDs.

In-house ELISA—72 patients were under the age of 45, seronegative for *H pylori* by in-house ELISA, and not

TABLE I—ENDOSCOPIC DIAGNOSES ACCORDING TO SEROLOGY

Diagnosis	Total no of patients	No of patients seropositive by ELISA	
		In-house	Commercial
Normal	169	87 *(51%)*	84 *(50%)*
Oesophagitis	44	19 *(43%)*	14 *(32%)*
Gastric erosion	16	6 *(37%)*	7 *(44%)*
Duodenitis	17	15 *(88%)*	14 *(82%)*
Gastric ulcer	17	15 *(88%)*	15 *(88%)*
Duodenal ulcer	25	24 *(96%)*	23 *(92%)*
Malignant disease	5	5 *(100%)*	5 *(100%)*

TABLE II—COMPARISON OF *H PYLORI*-BASED SCREENING POLICY WITH 3 SYMPTOM-BASED SCREENING STRATEGIES

Strategy	No of patients		% saving* (95% CI)	% sensitivity† (95% CI)
	Assessed	With peptic ulcer		
H pylori strategy, combined data	1135	234	23·3 (20·9–25·8)	97·4 (94·5–99·1)
Davenport et al[9]	1041	248	28·9 (26·2–31·7)	87·5 (83·3–91·6)
Mann et al[8] according to Davenport et al[9]	397	92	33·2 (28·6–37·9)	85·9 (77·0–92·2)
Holdstock et al[10]	1279	246	22·8 (20·5–25·0)	95·9 (92·7–98·0)

*% reduction in endoscopies achievable by use of screening strategy.
†Sensitivity of screening strategy for peptic ulcer disease.
CI = confidence interval.

taking NSAIDs and would thus not have had endoscopy if the screening policy had been applied. The endoscopic diagnoses in these patients are shown in the figure (A) together with those of the other 79 patients aged under 45 for comparison. Thus, the screening strategy would have led to a reduction of 24·5% in the total number of endoscopies, and would not have led to any missed diagnoses of peptic ulcer disease. 5 patients had upper gastrointestinal malignant disease (2 adenocarcinoma of the stomach, 3 adenocarcinoma of the cardia or oesophagus) but they were all seropositive and over 45. Seropositivity for *H pylori* in relation to each endoscopic diagnosis is shown in table I.

Commercial ELISA—Results with the commercial ELISA were broadly similar to those obtained with the in-house ELISA. 74 patients under 45 were seronegative and not taking NSAIDs; diagnoses are shown in the figure (B). No patient with peptic ulcer disease would have been missed with the screening policy, and all patients with malignant disease were seropositive. There was some discrepancy between the two ELISAs (14·6% of all results); of the 131 patients who were seronegative by commercial ELISA, 105 were seronegative and 26 were seropositive by in-house ELISA. Of the 162 patients who were seropositive by commercial ELISA, 17 were seronegative and 145 were seropositive by in-house ELISA. 1 patient with gastric ulcer and 1 with duodenal ulcer were positive by the in-house ELISA but negative by the commercial ELISA, and 1 patient with gastric ulcer was negative by in-house ELISA but positive by commercial ELISA; these 3 patients were over the age of 45. Nearly all discordant results were close to the cut-off points of the ELISAs.

Combined analysis

265 (23·3%; 95% confidence interval [CI] 20·9–25·8) of the total 1135 patients studied were under the age of 45, *H pylori* negative by the in-house ELISA, and not known to be taking NSAIDs, and thus would not have required endoscopy according to the screening strategy. Since only 6 of the 234 patients with peptic ulceration were in this group, this strategy had a sensitivity for peptic ulcer disease of 97·4% (95% CI 94·5–99·1).

Discussion

Our findings support the validity of a screening strategy based on *H pylori* serological status, age, and use of NSAIDs. Individuals who are seronegative for *H pylori* and who are not taking NSAIDs can be reassured that they do not have peptic ulcer disease. Appropriate management can then be instituted for non-ulcer dyspepsia or gastro-oesophageal reflux according to the nature of the symptoms. The gastric erosions found in a few young seronegative patients were small and of doubtful clinical significance.

This screening policy cannot yet be extended to all age groups because adequate data on the association between *H pylori* serology and gastric cancer (and especially early gastric cancer) are not yet available. Such data can only realistically be gathered in a multicentre study. Since gastric cancer inevitably develops on a background of chronic gastritis, many cases are likely to be seropositive for *H pylori*, but this cannot be taken for granted[19] and we accept that in the older age groups one of the principal aims of endoscopy is to detect malignant disease at an early and treatable stage.[2,7] We believe that any savings in endoscopic workload achieved by a screening policy in the younger patients could be used to improve the service for older patients. Additionally, the screening strategy based on *H pylori* serology compares favourably with policies based on symptoms (table II). A symptom-based screening strategy would have done poorly in our study population. For example, 6 of the 42 patients with peptic ulcer disease in the prospective part of our study would have been missed by the strategy proposed by Holdstock et al.[10]

We believe that a policy of screening young dyspeptic patients for *H pylori* by serology can have an important role in reducing endoscopy workload.

This study was supported from the Yorkshire Regional Health Authority. We thank Dr D. Tomkins for providing the *H pylori* strain used in the in-house ELISA, Mr Ian Hosie for valuable technical assistance, and Porton Cambridge Ltd for providing the Helico-G kit for assessment.

REFERENCES

1. Heatley RV, Rathbone BJ. Dyspepsia: a dilemma for doctors? *Lancet* 1987; ii: 779–82.
2. Williams B, Luckas M, Ellingham JHM, Dain A, Wicks ACB. Do young patients with dyspepsia need investigation? *Lancet* 1988; ii: 1349–51.
3. Coghlan JG, Gilligan D, Humphreys H, et al. *Campylobacter pylori* and recurrence of duodenal ulcers: 12 months follow-up study. *Lancet* 1987; ii: 1109–11.
4. Marshall BJ, Goodwin CS, Warren JR, et al. Prospective double-blind trial of duodenal ulcer relapse after eradication of *Campylobacter pylori*. *Lancet* 1988; ii: 1439–42.
5. Rauws EA, Tytgat GN. Cure of duodenal ulcer associated with eradication of *Helicobacter pylori*. *Lancet* 1990; **335:** 1233–35.
6. Tytgat GNJ, Axon ATR, Dixon MF, Graham DY, Lee A, Marshall BJ. *Helicobacter pylori*: causal agent in peptic ulcer disease? In: Working Party Reports. World Congress of Gastroenterology, August 26–31, 1990. Oxford: Blackwell Scientific Publications, 1990.
7. Hallissey MT, Allum WH, Jewkes AJ, Ellis DJ, Fielding JWL. Early detection of gastric cancer. *Br Med J* 1990; **301:** 513–15.
8. Mann J, Holdstock G, Harman M, Machin D, Lohry CA. Scoring system to improve effectiveness of open access endoscopy. *Br Med J* 1983; **287:** 937–40.
9. Davenport PM, Morgan AG, Darnborough A, De Dombal FT. Can preliminary screening of dyspeptic patients allow more effective use of investigational techniques? *Br Med J* 1985; **290:** 217–19.
10. Holdstock G, Harman M, Machin D, Patel C, Lloyd RS. Prospective testing of a scoring system designed to improve case selection for upper gastrointestinal investigation. *Gastroenterology* 1986; **90:** 1164–69.
11. Brown C, Rees WDW. Dyspepsia in general practice. *Br Med J* 1990; **300:** 829–30.
12. Newell DG, Rathbone BJ. The serodiagnosis of *Campylobacter pylori* infection. *Serodiag Immunother Infect Dis* 1989; **3:** 1–6.
13. Sobala GM, Rathbone BJ, Wyatt JI, Dixon MF, Heatley RV, Axon ATR. Investigating young patients with dyspepsia. *Lancet* 1989; i: 50–51.
14. Sobala GM, Schorah CJ, Sabnderson M, et al. Ascorbic acid in the human stomach. *Gastroenterology* 1989; **97:** 357–63.
15. Sobala GM, Dixon MF, Axon ATR. Symptomatology of *Helicobacter pylori* associated dyspepsia. *Eur J Gastroenterol Hepatol* 1990; **2:** 445–49.
16. Shallcross TM, Rathbone BJ, Wyatt JI, Heatley RV. *Helicobacter pylori* associated chronic gastritis and peptic ulceration in patients taking non-steroidal anti-inflammatory drugs. *Aliment Pharmacol Ther* 1990; **4:** 515–22.
17. Sobala GM, Axon ATR. High diagnostic yield of a dyspepsia clinic. *Gut* 1989; **30:** 1514 (abstr).
18. Crabtree JE, Shallcross TM, Wyatt JI, et al. Mucosal humoral immune response to *Helicobacter pylori* in patients with duodenitis. *Dig Dis Sci* (in press).
19. Loffeld RJLF, Willems I, Flendrig JA, Arends JW. *Helicobacter pylori* and gastric carcinoma. *Histopathology* 1990; **17:** 537–41.

© Gastroenterology 1991; 100: 1279–1287

Granulomatous Vasculitis in Crohn's Disease

ANDREW J. WAKEFIELD, ELIZABETH A. SANKEY, AMAR P. DHILLON, AF M. SAWYERR, LINDA MORE, ROSALIND SIM, ROBERT M. PITTILO, PETER M. ROWLES, MARK HUDSON, ADAM A. M. LEWIS, and RON E. POUNDER

The Inflammatory Bowel Disease Study Group, Royal Free Hospital School of Medicine, and the Bland-Sutton Institute of Histopathology, University College and Middlesex Hospital Schools of Medicine, London, England

This study investigated a possible vascular origin for granulomas in Crohn's disease. Twenty-four consecutive resected specimens of small and large intestinal Crohn's disease were preserved by arterial perfusion-fixation with 10% formol saline, at mean arterial pressure (100 mm Hg). Fifteen specimens contained granulomas on routine examination of H&E-stained sections. These 15 specimens were examined in detail using a range of immunohistochemical staining techniques to identify vascular structures and granulomas. A total of 485 granulomas were found, 85% of which were identified as being directly involved in vascular injury. The majority (77%) of granulomas were deep to the mucosa; they were found most frequently in the submucosa (42%). The techniques used in this study enhanced the recognition of granulomatous vasculitis. The results suggest that the majority of granulomas in Crohn's disease form within walls of blood vessels. Vascular localization of granulomatous inflammation suggests that the intestinal microvasculature contains an early element in the pathogenesis of Crohn's disease.

A possible pathogenic mechanism in Crohn's disease has recently been described: inflammatory microvascular occlusion, which appears to be mediated by a mesenteric vasculitis (1). The microvascular injury occurs principally within the deeper layers of the bowel wall, although mucosal vessels may also be involved. This injury is focal and it may occur in the absence of either macroscopic disease or microscopic mucosal ulceration—features suggesting that vasculitis may be a primary process in Crohn's disease.

A chronic microvascular injury mediated from within the deeper layers of the bowel wall may explain many of the pathological and clinical features of Crohn's disease. However, the origin and pathogenetic significance of granulomas, which are frequent and early features in the evolution of Crohn's disease (2), have yet to be clarified despite the prominent position of this type of inflammation in diagnosis.

Granulomatous vasculitis has been reported as an occasional feature in Crohn's disease. Knutson et al. observed the presence of focal granulomatous vasculitis in 5 of 11 cases (3); others have seen it less frequently (4). Our perspective of this proble.n has been different for two reasons: first, the discrete foci of inflammatory vascular lesions in the wall of intestine affected by Crohn's disease means that they will be identified in only a minority of routine histological sections. Our observations have indicated that these foci are consistently present in arteries that subtend lesions of Crohn's disease (1). In addition, we have observed that aggregates of chronic inflammatory cells, including granulomas, arise within the walls of blood vessels (1). More advanced granulomas could be expected to destroy the vessel and to occlude the lumen of the affected vessels, obscuring the apparent vascular origin of these lesions. Extensive vascular disruption within the fully developed granulomas of other "primary" granulomatous vasculitides can make it difficult to identify the vessel of origin (5). These features suggest the possibility that granulomas in Crohn's disease could have a vascular origin, and that a granulomatous vasculitis may be an integral part of the spectrum of vascular inflammation that appears to be central to the pathogenesis of this condition (1).

The purpose of this study was to investigate the

0016-5085/91/$3.00

© Gastroenterology 1991; 100: 1279–1287

relationship between blood vessels and granulomas in Crohn's disease.

Patients, Materials, and Methods

For this study, 24 consecutive resected specimens of small and large intestinal Crohn's disease were examined. The diagnosis of Crohn's disease was made clinically, radiologically, and on histopathological examination of the resected specimens.

To prevent blood clotting within the resected specimens, the standard resection technique was modified to preserve the main vascular pedicle to the affected segment, which was divided as a last step before removal. An arterial clamp was placed only on the proximal side of the pedicle to avoid damage to the vessels in the specimen and to facilitate their identification. The artery supplying the resected specimen was cannulated and perfused immediately with heparinized saline. To preserve a normal vascular shape, tissues were perfusion-fixed through the arterial cannula with 10% formol saline at 100 mm Hg for 20 minutes and subsequently placed in 10% formol saline. Between 2 and 28 blocks (mean = 11) were studied from each resected specimen, depending on the volume of tissue available for examination.

On histopathological examination of H&E-stained sections taken from these blocks, granulomas were identified in 15 of the 24 resected specimens, a rate that is comparable with other studies (6). Serial sections cut from each block taken from the 15 specimens that contained granulomas were deparaffinized, rehydrated, and treated with hydrogen peroxide to block endogenous peroxidase activity; all sections were trypsinized at 37°C to produce optimal staining results. Sections were then stained immunohistochemically using polyclonal antibodies against fibrinogen (Dako, High Wycombe, England) at a dilution of 1:900 and against macrophages (lysozyme; Dako) at a dilution of 1:50; sections were also stained using monoclonal antibodies against collagen type IV (a constituent of vascular basal lamina (7), Dako) at a dilution of 1:50 and QB-end-10 (Quantum Biosystems, Cambridge, England) at a dilution of 1:2000. QB-end-10 is a recently characterized monoclonal antibody that binds to the CD34 antigen expressed specifically by vascular endothelial cells; QB-end-10 does not stain intestinal lymphatic endothelium in paraffin-processed formalin-fixed tissue (8). Horseradish peroxidase was used as the label, and hydrogen peroxide and diaminobenzidine were used as the colorization step. Sections were counterstained in Mayer's hematoxylin.

To compare the features of granulomas of Crohn's disease with those of a well-characterized "primary" granulomatous vasculitis, serial sections from two cases of nasopharangeal Wegener's granulomatosis were stained immunohistochemically for collagen type IV, lysozyme, and fibrinogen as shown above.

To undertake a three-dimensional reconstruction of vasculitis in Crohn's disease, a pair of consecutive 3-μm sections were cut every 30 μm through selected blocks, obtained from three specimens of Crohn's disease in which granulomas had been identified. Of these serial sets of paired sections, the first was immunostained for collagen type IV (blood vessels) and the second was immunostained for lysozyme (granulomas). Three-dimensional reconstruction of these sections was performed using the SSPROF/SSRCON computer software program (Medical Research Council, Clinical Research Centre, Harrow, England). For each reconstruction, between 10 and 20 pairs of sections were studied.

Ethical approval for these studies was obtained from the Ethics Committee of the Royal Free Hospital.

Table 1. Number and Distribution of Granulomas and Granulomatous Vasculitis in 15 Resected Specimens of Crohn's Disease

Patient	Specimen	No. of blocks	Total no. of granulomas counted	% of granulomas involved in vasculitis	Level as % of total granulomas			
					Mucosa	Submucosa	Muscularis	Serosa
1	Colon	16	8	88	12.5	25	—	62.5
2	Colon	12	25	76	—	100	—	—
3	Ileocolonic recurrence	12	20	85	20	70	—	10
4	Ileum	2	31	100	—	6.5	—	93.5
5	Ileum	28	121	89	20.5	71	—	8.5
6	Ileum	17	28	100	7	64	—	29
7	Ileum	17	37	89	14	62	—	24
8	Ileum	8	28	100	—	14	14	72
9	Colon	4	16	63	19	50	31	—
10	Colon	4	10	60	70	30	—	—
11	Ileocolonic recurrence	10	94	78	48	44	1	7
12	Ileocolonic recurrence	10	24	96	4	75	—	21
13	Anorectum	5	19	84	—	11	89	—
14	Ileum	5	15	73	70	20	—	10
15	Colon	15	9	56	56	—	11	33

© Gastroenterology 1991; 100: 1279–1287

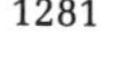

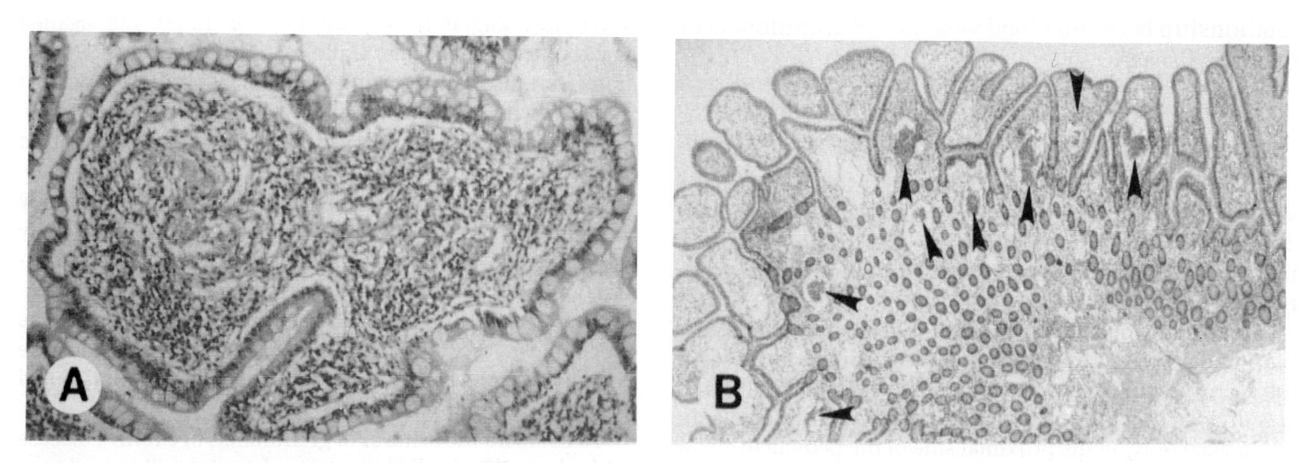

Figure 1. *A.* High-power view of a mucosal granuloma in Crohn's disease from a routinely fixed H&E-stained section (original magnification ×40). The granuloma shows no evidence of vascular involvement.

B. Low-power view of perfusion-fixed specimen of Crohn's disease showing eight granulomas, all arising within and producing apparent obstruction of some small mucosal blood vessels (original magnification ×10).

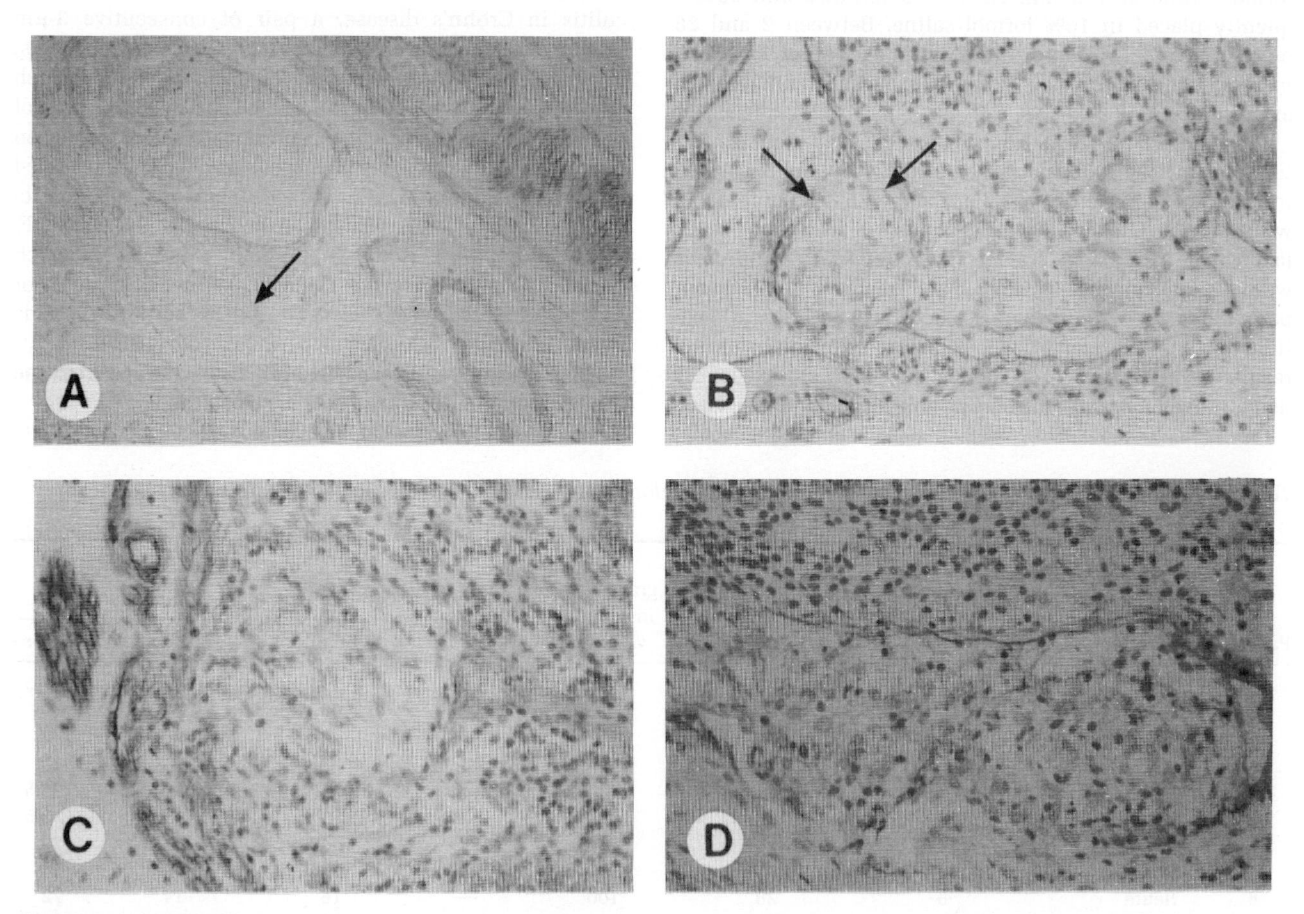

Figure 2. *A.* Routinely fixed normal human intestine. Arteries and veins stain positively for type-IV collagen, but lymphatics (*arrow*) do not stain (original magnification ×40).

B. Perfusion-fixed specimen of Crohn's disease showing granulomatous vasculitis in a small submucosal vessel stained for collagen type IV, with disruption of the vascular basal lamina (*arrow*) around the granuloma (original magnification ×100).

C. Routinely fixed specimen of Crohn's disease showing a granuloma, which bears no obvious relationship to collapsed vessels (immunoperoxidase collagen type IV; original magnification ×100).

D. Perfusion-fixed specimen of Crohn's disease. Early granulomatous vasculitis in a small submucosal vessel (immunoperoxidase for QB-end-10; original magnification ×100).

Results

Fifteen of the 24 resected specimens of Crohn's disease contained granulomas when examined in a conventional manner by light microscopy using routine H&E staining. In these 15 cases, a total of 485 granulomas were identified; of these granulomas, 23% were mucosal, 42% were submucosal, 10% were located in the muscularis propria, and 25% were serosal (Table 1).

Using a combination of perfusion-fixation and immunostaining for vascular structures, granulomatous vasculitis was observed in all of the 15 cases. Of the 485 granulomas seen in these cases, the majority (median, 85%; range, 56%–100%; Table 1) directly involved damaged blood vessels, the vessel wall being the apparent focus of the inflammatory response. Damage was defined as disintegration or reduplication of the vascular basal lamina, infiltration of the vessel wall by chronic inflammatory cells, and intravascular or perivascular fibrin deposition with or without an associated disruption of the vascular endothelium. A minority of granulomas (15%) were seen in close proximity to apparently normal vessels and did not involve damage to the vessel wall. The vascular relationship of the granuloma was not influenced either by its depth within the bowel wall or by whether the mucosa overlying the granuloma was ulcerated or intact.

Perfusion-Fixation

Perfusion-fixation was particularly useful in defining the relationship of granulomas to small mucosal and submucosal vessels. Figure 1*A* demonstrates a mucosal granuloma in a routinely fixed, H&E-stained section; even at high power there is no evident relationship of this granuloma to a blood vessel. The effect of perfusion-fixation is to keep open small mucosal and submucosal vessels that are the site of granuloma formation (Figure 1*B*). In many cases, the granuloma appears to arise from within the blood vessels, lying in intimate contact with the blood vessel wall.

Immunohistochemistry

Positive immunostaining for collagen type IV distinguished blood vessels from lymphatics in paraffin-processed, formalin-fixed tissue from histologically normal human intestine. Identifiable lymphatics did not stain (Figure 2*A*) with collagen IV in this study.

Both arteries and veins that had been perfusion-fixed dilated to become thin-walled structures, in contrast to the collapsed thick-walled arterioles and arteries seen in routinely fixed specimens. This feature was made more obvious by immunostaining for collagen type IV (Figure 2*B* and *C*). Immunostaining for vessels with QB-end-10 identified small mucosal and submucosal vessels, but it was much less effective in staining larger vessels in the muscularis propria and serosa. QB-end-10 confirmed the vascular origin of mucosal and submucosal granulomas. Figure 2*D* shows a small mucosal vessel stained with QB-end-10 that is the site of granulomatous vasculitis.

For the purposes of this study, early granulomatous vasculitis was defined as granulomatous inflammation arising within the wall of a blood vessel producing focal disruption of the mural architecture, which was defined as disintegration or reduplication of the vascular basal lamina on collagen type IV immunostaining that did not include the whole circumference of the vessel such that the vessel of origin was still evident. Advanced granulomatous vasculitis consisted of large granulomas containing no identifiable vascular structures on H&E-stained sections, in which vascular involvement could be identified using immunostaining for vascular elements.

Figure 3 compares the features of early granulomatous vasculitis in Crohn's disease with those of Wegener's granulomatosis. Serial sections from these two

Figure 3. Early granulomatous vasculitis in Crohn's disease and Wegener's granulomatosis (all original magnifications ×100).

A. Perfusion-fixed specimen of Crohn's disease showing early granulomatous vasculitis in a serosal vessel (H&E).

B. Routinely fixed specimen of Wegener's granulomatosis showing granulomatous vasculitis (H&E).

C. Serial section of the vessel shown in 2*A*, immunostained for type-IV collagen showing disruption of the vascular basal lamina by granulomatous inflammation (*arrow*).

D. Serial section of vessel shown in 2*B*, immunostained for collagen type IV showing focal disruption of vascular basal lamina by granulomatous inflammation. The endothelium appears to have been breached in both 2*C* and *D*.

E and *F.* Serial sections of vessels in 2*A* and *B* showing macrophage infiltrate characteristic of granulomatous vasculitis, at the focus of vascular mural injury in both Crohn's disease (2*E*) and Wegener's granulomatosis (2*F*) (immunoperoxidase for lysozome).

G and *H.* Serial sections of vessels in 2*A* and *B* showing intravascular and perivascular fibrin deposition in association with the granulomatous inflammation (immunoperoxidase for fibrinogen).

© *Gastroenterology* 1991; 100: 1279–1287

diseases show identical staining patterns for H&E (Figure 3*A* and *B*), collagen type IV (Figure 3*C* and *D*), macrophages (Figure 3*E* and *F*), and fibrinogen (Figure 3*G* and *H*). Granulomatous vascular injury in both diseases was characterized by focal disruption of the basal lamina of the vessel wall, adherence of circulating macrophages and lymphocyte cells to the damaged endothelium adjacent to the granuloma, and

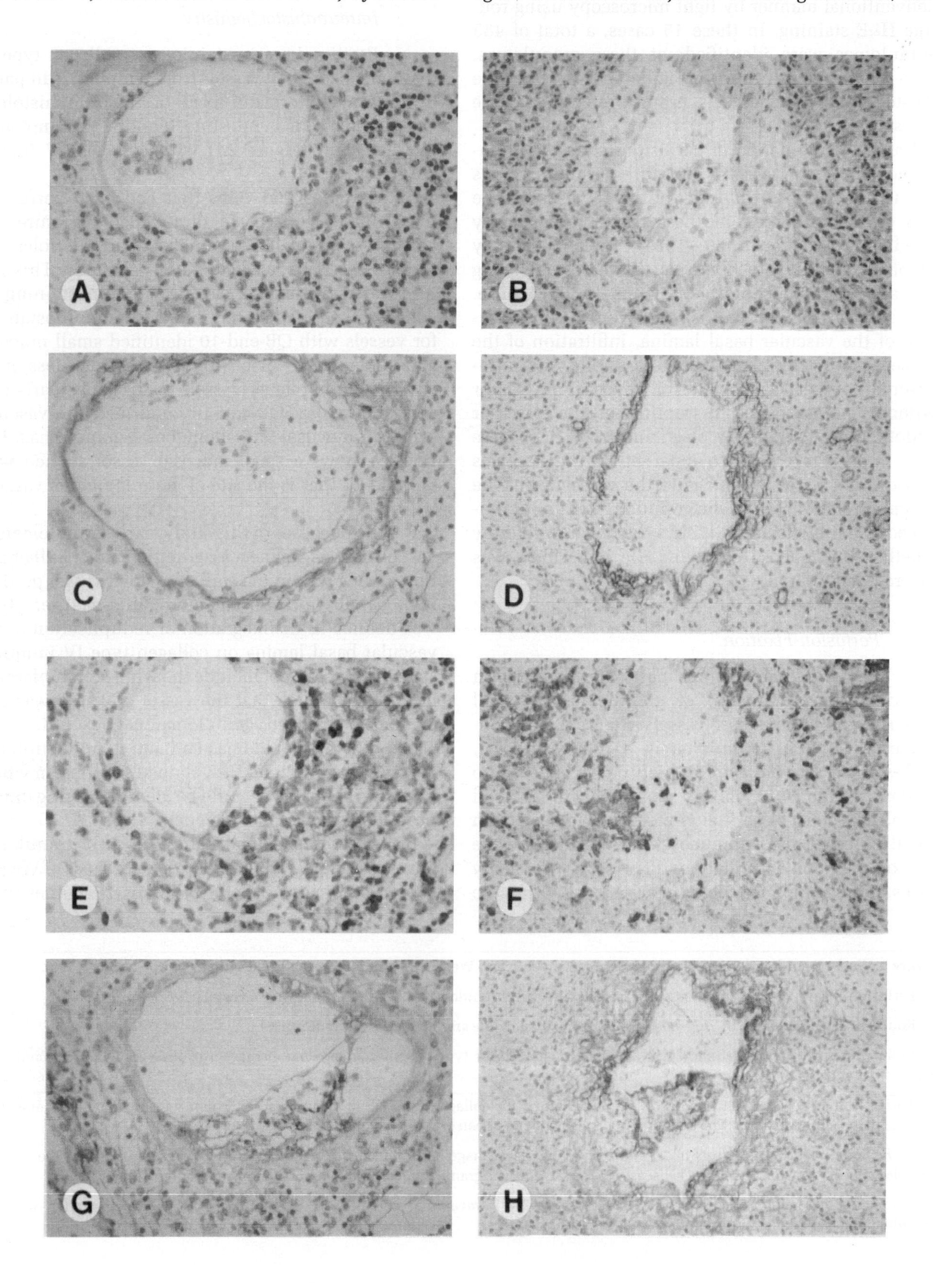

intravascular and perivascular fibrin deposition at the focus of this injury.

Advanced granulomas in both Crohn's disease and Wegener's granulomatosis show no obvious evidence of vascular involvement when examined on H&E-stained sections. Figure 4 shows a typical, advanced serosal granuloma of Crohn's disease stained with H&E (Figure 4*A*) and immunostained for macrophages (Figure 4*B*). The vascular origin of this granuloma is not evident using these stains, but is clearly demonstrated by immunostaining for collagen type IV (Figure 4*C*). A serial section that has been immunostained for fibrinogen shows fibrin deposition within the granuloma (Figure 4*D*). Subsequent serial H&E-stained sections showed that this affected vessel was continuous with both the subserosal vessel seen above and the vessel penetrating the muscularis propria seen in the right of the figure. The features illustrated in Figure 4 were typical of advanced granulomas in both Crohn's disease and Wegener's granulomatosis, that is, granulomatous vasculitis was identified in areas of granulomatous inflammation in which no evidence of vascular involvement in H&E-stained sections was observed.

Computerized three-dimensional reconstruction of blood vessels and granulomas, performed on the paired sections that were stained consecutively for vessels (type IV collagen) and macrophages (lysozyme), showed that these two structures preserved an intimate relationship, the granuloma following the course of the affected vessel (Figure 5).

Discussion

This study has demonstrated a spectrum of granulomatous vascular injury to vessels that supply segments of intestine affected by Crohn's disease. The data suggest that the majority of granulomas in Crohn's

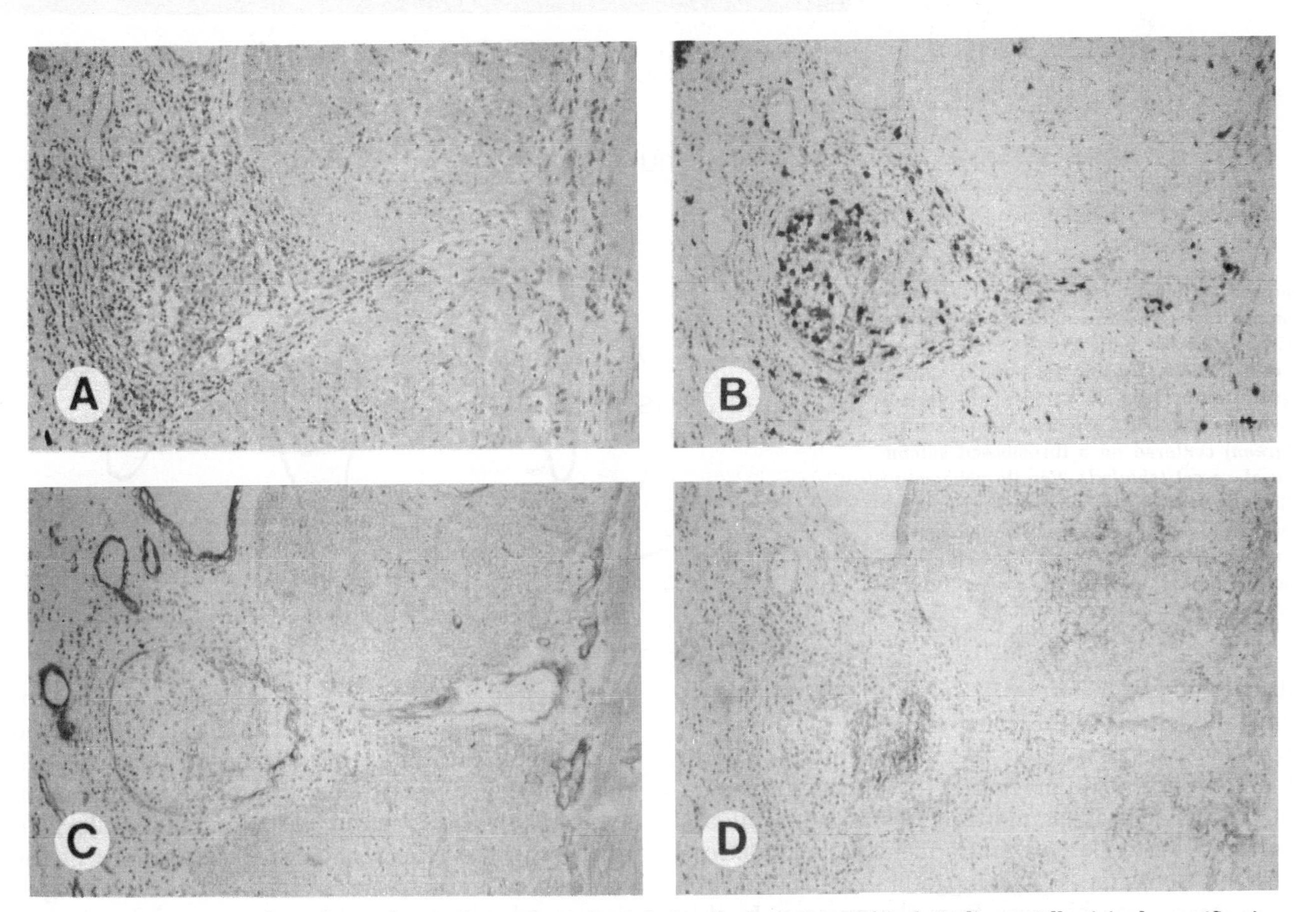

Figure 4. Serial sections of an advanced serosal granuloma in perfusion-fixed specimen of Crohn's disease (all original magnifications ×40).

A. H&E showing granuloma with no evident relationship in blood vessel.

B. Immunoperoxidase for lysozyme showing macrophage infiltrate.

C. Immunoperoxidase for collagen type IV showing outline of vessel involved in granulomatous inflammation.

D. Immunoperoxidase for fibrinogen showing fibrin deposition within the granuloma.

© Gastroenterology 1991; 100: 1279–1287

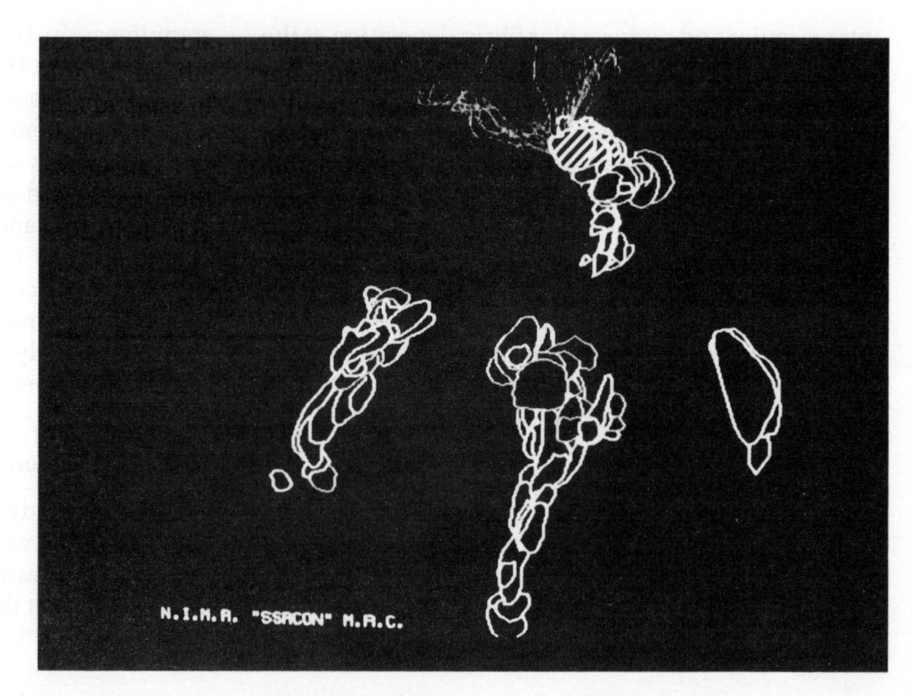

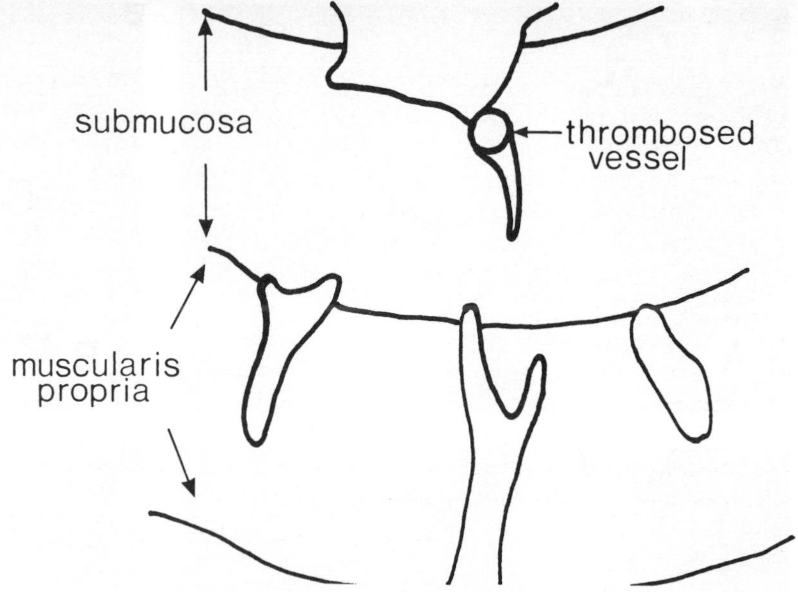

Figure 5. Computer-generated three-dimensional reconstruction of serial sections of Crohn's disease using SSPROF/SSRCON program (MRC), showing the relationship of granulomas (*purple*) to blood vessels (*white*), with the base of a fissuring ulcer (*green*) centered on a thrombosed submucosal vessel (*shaded*). Vessels penetrating the muscularis propria are not occluded but branch to form the submucosal plexus. The majority of these submucosal vessels are too small to reconstruct (original magnification ×10).

disease appear to form within walls of blood vessels and apparently within the lumen of some vessels when viewed in a single plane of section, a feature that has been noted previously (9). The identification of the majority of granulomas deep to the mucosa corroborates the findings of Hadfield (10) and McGovern and Goulston (9) and suggests that the "seat" of the disease may be away from the mucosa. In this study, this impression has been reinforced by the identification of granulomatous vasculitis in areas of intestine that are without mucosal ulceration and remote from macroscopically diseased segments.

Granulomatous inflammation is associated with focal disruption of the blood vessel wall (that may include the endothelium), adherence of chronic inflammatory cells (lymphocytes and macrophages) to the luminal surface of the lesion, and fibrin deposition. Collagen type IV immunostaining clearly demonstrates both the focus of vascular mural injury in relation to the relatively normal appearance of the adjacent vascular-basal lamina, and the disintegration or reduplication of this layer around the chronic inflammatory cell infiltrate in areas of vasculitis.

In addition to destroying the vascular architecture, progressively larger granulomas appear to occlude blood vessels, such that the vascular origin of advanced granulomas may no longer be apparent on H&E-stained sections. In routinely fixed histological

© Gastroenterology 1991; 100: 1279–1287

specimens, this effacement of vessels is compounded by the collapse of small unperfused vessels around the granulomas, a phenomenon that is particularly relevant to small mucosal and submucosal vessels. The combination of perfusion-fixation at a mean arterial pressure of 100 mm Hg and immunostaining for vascular structures has helped to demonstrate the relationship of granulomas to blood vessels. The intimate association between granuloma and blood vessel along the course of the affected vessel has been demonstrated by three-dimensional reconstruction of sections of Crohn's disease tissue. Granulomas are not found coincidently adjacent to blood vessels in a single plane of section but follow the course of the affected vessels in these cases.

We have previously demonstrated focal arterial inflammation in Crohn's disease (1). From the appearance of the vessels involved in granulomatous inflammation in the present study, both arteries and veins seem to be affected. It is notable that arteries distend to become relatively thin-walled vessels when the technique of arterial perfusion-fixation at pressure is used, making it difficult to distinguish medium-sized and small arteries from veins. The vessels involved in granulomatous vasculitis in this study were probably mainly arteries or veins, rather than lymphatics, based on the immunostaining for collagen type IV, fibrinogen, and QB-end-10. However, it is likely that lymphatics may also undergo a primary granulomatous change in Crohn's disease. The difficulty of histologically distinguishing small arteries, veins, and lymphatics is acknowledged. There is no reason to suppose that vessels of all types cannot be involved in this vasculitis. It is also recognized that granulomas may occur in mesenteric lymph nodes that drain segments of intestine affected by Crohn's disease. The tissue relationships of these and other extraintestinal foci of granulomatous inflammation are currently under investigation.

The minority (15%) of granulomas did not appear to involve damaged blood vessels. These may represent true parenchymal granulomas, or alternatively, they may have arisen from small vessels that had been obliterated by the granulomatous inflammation. It is noted that some granulomas in Wegener's granulomatosis did not stain positively for vascular elements, suggesting that the latter had been destroyed by the inflammatory process.

Granulomas are not a universal finding in Crohn's disease. We have observed a spectrum of vascular inflammation in Crohn's disease ranging from a lymphocyte-predominant pattern to granulomatous vasculitis with giant cell formation (1). Patients with nongranulomatous Crohn's disease, including the nine patients in this study that did not have granulomas, show a lymphocyte-predominant pattern of vasculitis. It is notable that this same spectrum of vascular inflammation is seen in Wegener's granulomatosis (11). Devaney et al. recently identified granulomatous vasculitis in only 6% of 126 biopsies of nasopharangeal Wegener's granulomatosis, with lymphocytic vasculitis seen in 22% of these biopsy specimens (11). The presence of lymphocytic and granulomatous vasculitis in 3%–20% of cases of Crohn's disease examined using traditional histological techniques (3,4) compares favorably with the findings reported by Devaney et al. (11). Not until the complex mechanisms of granuloma formation are better understood, and possibly not until the causative agent has been identified in Crohn's disease, will we understand why different patients show varying patterns of vascular inflammation.

These studies have shown the frequent vascular origin of granulomas in Crohn's disease. Though the findings suggest that granulomatous vasculitis is an integral part of the pattern of vascular inflammation seen in this condition, they do not provide conclusive evidence that vasculitis is essential to the development of Crohn's disease. We have shown that granulomatous destruction of the blood vessel acts as a focus for the adherence of inflammatory cells and fibrin deposition, findings that corroborate our previous description of mesenteric vasculitis in Crohn's disease (1) and support the role for this process in the pathogenesis of the disease.

References

1. Wakefield AJ, Sawyerr AM, Dhillon AP, Pittilo RM, Rowles PM, Lewis AAM, Pounder RE. Pathogenesis of Crohn's disease: multifocal gastrointestinal infarction. Lancet 1989;2:1057–1062.
2. Kelly JK, Sutherland LR. The chronological sequence in the pathology of Crohn's disease. J Clin Gastroenterol 1988;10:28–33.
3. Knutson H, Lunderquist A, Lunderquist A. Vascular changes in Crohn's disease. AJR 1968;103:380–385.
4. Geller SA, Cohen A. Arterial inflammatory infiltration in Crohn's disease. Arch Pathol Lab Med 1983;107:473–475.
5. Bariety J, Jacquot C. The vasculitis syndromes in small and medium sized vessels. In: Camilleri JP, ed. Diseases of the arterial wall. Berlin: Springer-Verlag, 1989;27:424–427.
6. Riddell RH. Pathology of inflammatory bowel disease. In: Kirsner JB, Shorter RG, eds. Inflammatory bowel disease. Philadelphia: Lea & Febiger, 1988;329–350.
7. Odermaff BF, Lang AB, Ruttner JR, Winterhalter KH, Trueb B. Monoclonal antibodies to human type IV collagen: useful reagents to demonstrate the heterotrimeric nature of the molecule. Proc Natl Acad Sci 1984;81:7343–7347.
8. Sankey EA, More L, Dhillon AP. QB-end-10: a novel endothelial cell marker in the diagnosis of Kaposi's sarcoma. J Pathol 1990;161:267–271.
9. McGovern VJ, Goulston SJM. Crohn's disease of the colon. Gut 1968;9:164–176.

10. Hadfield G. The primary histological lesion of regional ileitis. Lancet 1939;2:773–775.
11. Devaney KO, Travis WD, Hoffman G, Leariff R, Lebovis R, Franci AS. Interpretation of head and neck biopsies in Wegener's granulomatosis. Am J Surg Pathol 1990;14:555–564.

Received April 29, 1990. Accepted October 16, 1990.

Address requests for reprints to: A. J. Wakefield, F.R.C.S., Academic Department of Medicine, Royal Free Hospital School of Medicine, Pond Street, London NW3 2QG, England.

A. J. Wakefield is a Wellcome Research Fellow.

The authors are greatly indebted to surgeons J. P. Bolton and M. W. N. Ward, Chase Farm Hospital, Enfield; and R. C. Springall, North Middlesex Hospital, London, for their help in these studies. The authors also thank Doris Elliott for her expert help in preparation of this manuscript, the Wellcome Trust for their continued support, the Crohn's in Childhood Research Appeal, Medical Research Council, and G. D. Searle and Co., Ltd.

© Hepatology 1992; 15: 567–571

Original Articles

The Pathology of Hepatitis C

PETER J. SCHEUER,[1] PARVIN ASHRAFZADEH,[1] SHEILA SHERLOCK,[2] DAVID BROWN[3] AND GEOFFREY M. DUSHEIKO[3]

Departments of Histopathology,[1] Surgery[2] and Medicine,[3] Royal Free Hospital and School of Medicine, London NW3 2QG, United Kingdom

To determine the histologic pattern of hepatitis C, 54 liver biopsy specimens from 45 patients with a clinicopathological diagnosis of hepatitis C were studied. All patients were seropositive for antibody to hepatitis C virus by second-generation testing. Both transfusion-related and sporadic cases were included. More than half the samples showed chronic hepatitis without cirrhosis, whereas 44% showed developing or fully established cirrhosis. A histological pattern of mild chronic hepatitis with portal lymphoid follicles and varying degrees of lobular activity was found in many of the patients. Lymphoid aggregates or follicles were seen in 78% of biopsy specimens, but aggregates, less prominent than in hepatitis C, were also seen in 14 of 27 samples (52%) from patients with hepatitis B. We conclude that a characteristic histological pattern exists in chronic hepatitis C, that this pattern is not always found and that prominent lymphoid follicles, though not unique to hepatitis C, provide a useful diagnostic clue. (HEPATOLOGY 1992;15:567-571.)

The histopathological changes in non-A, non-B (NANB) hepatitis have been described in several papers over the past decade (1-5). However, accurate assessment of these changes has been hampered by lack of specific serological tests to support the diagnosis, and it is possible that in some instances the changes have resulted from infection with a number of different hepatitis viruses. Occasionally, epidemiological evidence has suggested that the disease studied was caused by a single agent; examples are the enterically transmitted form of NANB hepatitis now often referred to as hepatitis E (6, 7), and a group of patients with coagulation disorders who contracted a short-incubation hepatitis after administration of factor VIII (1). In most studies, however, evidence of infection with a single virus could not be conclusively established.

The development of a serological test for antibody to a nonstructural antigen (C100-3) of a parenterally-transmitted NANB hepatitis agent, hepatitis C virus (HCV) (8), provided the opportunity to study the pathology of at least one form of this disease. However, first-generation tests gave both false-positive and false-negative results (9-11). Second-generation tests detect antibodies to both structural and nonstructural components of the virus, and they have demonstrated that most patients with parenterally transmitted NANB hepatitis are infected with HCV (12). A substantial proportion of patients with sporadic NANB hepatitis can also be shown to be infected with this virus.

PATIENTS AND METHODS

Fifty-four liver biopsy specimens from 45 patients with hepatitis C were studied. All patients were HBsAg seronegative and were considered to have NANB hepatitis on the basis of exclusion of other causes of hepatitis by clinical, serological, immunological and biochemical criteria. All were positive for antibody to hepatitis C (anti-HCV) by second-generation testing. Thirty-three were men. The mean age of the cohort was 47 yr (range = 25 to 74 yr). In addition to patients from Britain and southern Europe, a substantial number originated from the Middle East or the Indian subcontinent. In 26 patients, onset of hepatitis was related to definite parenteral exposure by blood transfusion, intravenous drug abuse, occupational needle-stick or human bite (13). The interval from exposure to biopsy in these patients averaged 13 yr (range, <1 yr to 46 yr). In one multiple-transfusion patient with thalassemia, the date of onset could not be accurately ascertained. The patient who contracted hepatitis C after sustaining a human bite underwent liver biopsy 6 mo after presumed infection. The mean interval from first clinical diagnosis of chronic hepatitis or cirrhosis to the diagnostic liver biopsy was 2.9 yr (range = 6 mo to 10 yr). Several patients had had cirrhosis established clinically at the time of presentation with symptoms or abnormal liver function test scores, suggesting that the disease, although only recently diagnosed, was in fact long-standing.

Selected patients had been enrolled in a controlled therapeutic trial of interferon-α_{2b} treatment of NANB hepatitis. This trial was approved by the ethical committee of the Royal Free Hospital. Liver biopsy samples were taken with patients' informed consent before treatment began (in some cases during or after treatment). All specimens were obtained by the percutaneous or transjugular route.

Hepatitis C markers were measured by second-generation ELISA (Abbott Laboratories, North Chicago, IL; and Ortho Laboratories, Raritan, NJ). Both assays used detect antibody to nonstructural (NS3 and NS4) regions and to the structural core of the HCV. Test specimens were diluted in microtiter wells to form antigen-antibody complexes to bound antigens.

Received February 22, 1991; accepted November 18, 1991.

Address reprint requests to: Professor P.J. Scheuer, Department of Histopathology, Royal Free Hospital, Pond Street, London NW3 2QG, UK.

31/1/35182

TABLE 1. Overall histological diagnoses and portal-tract features in hepatitis C

Diagnosis	n	Lymphoid aggregates and follicles[a] 0	1	2	3	Bile duct damage[a] 0	1	2
Acute hepatitis	1	1	0	0	0	0	0	1
Mild/moderate chronic hepatitis (CPH, CLH, CAH)	29	4	5	15	5	23	6	0
Severe CAH and/or developing cirrhosis	5	0	2	3	0	3	0	2
Established cirrhosis	19	7	7	4	1	16	3	0
TOTAL biopsy specimens	54	12	14	22	6	42	9	3

CLH = Chronic lobular hepatitis.
[a]For explanation of scoring system, see text.

TABLE 2. Pathological features in acini in hepatitis C

Diagnosis	n	Acidophil bodies[a] 0	1	2	Lymphocytic infiltration of sinusoids[a] 0	1	2	Fatty change[a] 0	1	2
Acute hepatitis	1	0	1	0	1	0	0	0	1	0
Mild/moderate chronic hepatitis (CPH, CAH, CLH)	29	23	6	0	16	10	3	15	11	3
Severe CAH and/or developing cirrhosis	5	3	2	0	4	1	0	1	2	2
Established cirrhosis	19	17	2	0	19	0	0	9	7	3
TOTAL biopsy specimens	54	43	11	0	40	11	3	25	21	8

CLH = Chronic lobular hepatitis.
[a]For explanation of scoring system, see text.

TABLE 3. Overall histological diagnoses and lymphoid aggregates or follicles in hepatitis B

Diagnosis	n	Lymphoid aggregates and follicles[a] 0	1	2	3
Mild/moderate chronic hepatitis (CPH, CAH, CLH)	19	10	6	3	0
Severe CAH and/or developing cirrhosis	1	1	0	0	0
Established cirrhosis	7	2	3	2	0
TOTAL biopsy specimens	27	13	9	5	0

CLH = Chronic lobular hepatitis.
[a]For explanation of scoring system, see text.

Murine monoclonal antibody conjugate was then added. In the final stage, o-phenylenediamine · 2 hydrochloric acid and hydrogen peroxide was added, and the optical density of the end product was measured.

All anti-HCV–positive specimens were tested by second-generation recombinant immunoblot assay (RIBA) (Chiron Corp., Emeryville, CA). In this procedure, four HCV antigens (5-1-1,C100-3,C33c,C22-3) and a control, superoxide dismutase are immobilized as individual bands on nitrocellulose strips. The strips are incubated with serum specimens. Antibodies in serum, if present, bind to the antigens. After washing, the strips are incubated with goat antibody to human IgG conjugated with horseradish peroxidase. After incubation, hydrogen peroxide and 4-chloro-1-naphthol are added to develop the band patterns. If antibodies to two HCV antigens are detected, the test is scored as positive; if antibody to one antigen is present, the test is scored as indeterminate. If no bands are present, the test is scored as nonreactive. For this study, ELISA-positive but RIBA-indeterminate samples were also considered positive because the RIBA test appears more specific but less sensitive (14). Only RIBA-reactive or RIBA-indeterminate patients were included.

Liver biopsy specimens were fixed in buffered formalin, processed to paraffin and routinely stained by the following methods: hematoxylin and eosin, diastase/periodic acid–Schiff, Perls' stain for iron and Gordon and Sweets' method for reticulin. Overall histologic diagnoses were made using standard criteria (15). Semiquantitative assessment of histologic features was carried out by one author (PA), with independent assessment of a proportion of the biopsies by another (PJS). The following features were chosen for this assessment on the basis that they had been previously considered characteristic of or common in NANB hepatitis (1-5): lymphoid aggregates or follicles in portal tracts, infiltration of small bile ducts by inflammatory cells or damaged duct epithelium, acidophil body formation, steatosis and infiltration of sinusoids by lymphoid cells.

Lymphoid aggregates and follicles were scored 0 to 3: 1 represented ill-defined condensations of lymphoid infiltrates, 2 represented definite aggregations or follicles without identifiable germinal centers and 3 represented lymphoid follicles with germinal centers. Other features were graded 0 to 2: 1 represented mild to moderate changes and 2 represented severe changes.

A control group of 27 biopsy specimens from 24 patients with chronic hepatitis B was studied to compare the prevalence

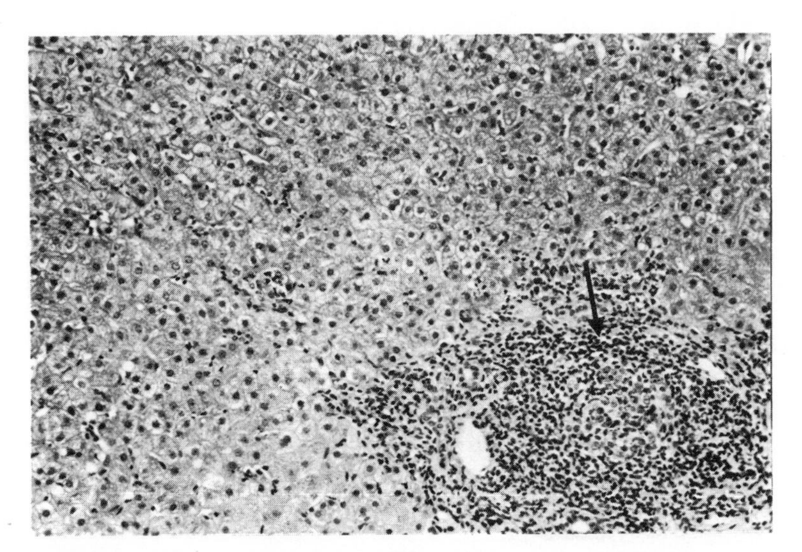

FIG. 1. Photomicrograph of part of a liver biopsy specimen from a patient seropositive for anti-HCV showing a commonly found histological pattern. The chronic hepatitis is characterized by mild piecemeal necrosis, a lymphoid follicle with germinal center in a portal tract *(arrow)* and focal inflammatory infiltration in the acinus (H & E; original magnification ×175).

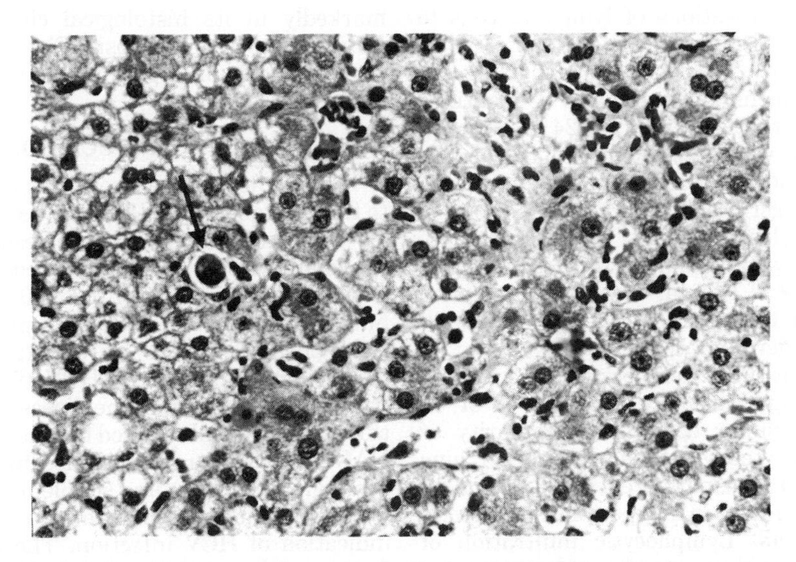

FIG. 2. High-power view of part of a liver biopsy sample from patient with chronic NANB hepatitis who was seropositive for anti-HCV showing lobular activity. Many lymphocytes are seen, and an acidophil body is present *(arrow)*. Some hepatocytes contain fat vacuoles (H & E; original magnification ×440).

of lymphoid aggregates and follicles with that in hepatitis C. All patients were seronegative for anti-HCV by second-generation testing as described above.

RESULTS

Overall diagnoses are given in Table 1. One patient had histological features of acute hepatitis. Twenty-nine had mild or occasionally moderately severe chronic hepatitis without severe disturbance of liver architecture. The pattern included all the described histological categories of chronic hepatitis: chronic persistent hepatitis (CPH), CAH and chronic lobular hepatitis. In five patients, cirrhosis appeared to be developing or nearly developed. Necroinflammatory activity in these patients varied from mild to severe. Nineteen patients had established cirrhosis. No HCCs were seen in any of the biopsy specimens.

Nine of the 45 patients underwent more than one biopsy. The interval between first and last biopsy ranged from 1 to 6 yr. In no patient did the diagnosis change substantially from one biopsy to the next, although there were minor differences in the pattern and extent of histological activity.

The frequency of individually assessed histological features is shown in Tables 1 and 2. The most striking feature was the presence of lymphoid aggregates or follicles in portal tracts, either alone or part of a general inflammatory infiltration of the tracts. The structures

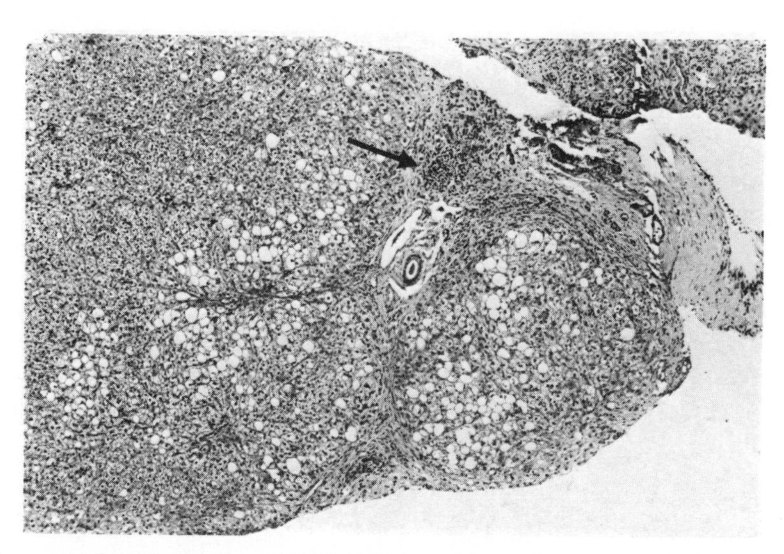

FIG. 3. Fatty cirrhosis in a patient seropositive for anti-HCV. Note the small lymphocytic aggregate in a septum *(arrow)* (H & E; original magnification ×70).

varied from simple aggregations of lymphoid cells to well-formed follicles with germinal centers (Fig. 1). They were more easily seen in specimens not showing cirrhosis (25 of 30 specimens) but could also be identified in cirrhotic or near-cirrhotic livers (17 of 24 specimens). Overall, these features were detected in 42 of 54 samples (78%), usually in the form of easily recognizable aggregates or follicles with germinal centers. In the group of 27 biopsy specimens from patients with hepatitis B, lymphoid aggregates were found in 14 of 27 samples (52%) (Table 3). In 9 of the 14, the aggregates were poorly defined (score 1), and in no patient were well-defined follicles with germinal centers seen.

Other histological features were less striking. Significant bile duct damage was only found in 3 of 54 specimens, although minor epithelial irregularity or infiltration of lymphocytes was found in another nine samples (Table 1). In the acinar parenchyma (Table 2), acidophil bodies were found in 11 specimens, but were relatively scanty in all. Lymphocytic infiltration of sinusoids was striking in three samples and present to a moderate degree in another 11. Fatty change was mild to moderate in 21 and severe in eight specimens.

The presence of lymphoid aggregates or follicles, together with an overall diagnosis of mild CAH or CPH, fatty change and/or lobular activity, gave many of the biopsy specimens a very characteristic and easily recognizable appearance (Fig. 1). However, all four features were found together in only a small minority of specimens. Lobular activity took the form of diffuse or focal infiltration by lymphocytes with or without liver cell dropout, acidophilic change in hepatocytes and acidophil bodies (Fig. 2). The latter were more often seen than acidophilic change in intact liver-cell plates.

Cirrhosis was seen in a high proportion of patients and was present in 15 at first biopsy. Apart from the common finding of lymphoid follicles with fatty change—the latter usually not severe—the cirrhosis did not differ markedly in its histological characteristics from so-called cryptogenic cirrhosis (Fig. 3). Minimal hepatocellular dysplasia of large-cell type was seen in a minority of samples.

DISCUSSION

The histological features observed correspond closely to those given for NANB hepatitis in the literature (1-5). They are consistent with the results of a semiquantitative analysis of liver biopsy specimens from patients with or without antibody to C100-3 in their serum (16), but no histological details were provided in that study. False-positive results were obtained with the first-generation tests for anti-HCV (9, 10), particularly in patients with autoimmune diseases, but the patients in this study were all selected because they had established NANB hepatitis as determined by clinical criteria and serologic tests, including supplemental assays, so that it was likely that the positive serum results were a true indication of HCV infection. The histological features found in our patients were therefore considered to reflect accurately the pathology of hepatitis C.

A common histological pattern has emerged from this study of a mild chronic hepatitis on the borderline of CPH and CAH, with lymphoid aggregates or follicles in portal tracts, lobular activity including acidophil body formation, and fatty change. The most characteristic single feature of this picture is the lymphoid follicle. The lymphoid lesions seen ranged from loose aggregates of lymphocytes to well-defined structures with germinal centers. They were usually recognized easily in reticulin preparations. Clearly follicles are not restricted to hepatitis C; they are seen, for example, in PBC, and may be found in biopsy specimens from patients with chronic HBV infection, as confirmed in our control group. However, in this study, aggregates were found less frequently in hepatitis B than hepatitis C and were generally less well formed. Follicles with germinal centers were seen in six samples from patients with hepatitis C and in none with hepatitis B. The reason for the formation of lymphoid follicles remains obscure and deserves further study. Their presence supports the participation of the patient's immune system in the pathogenesis of the liver lesion.

Many of the patients in this series exhibited cirrhosis; in some it had developed over a period of many years or even decades. The pathology of the cirrhosis is often not characteristic, but lymphoid aggregates and follicles—together with fatty change—were seen in some of the patients. As in the case of the noncirrhotic livers, the presence of lymphoid follicles in cirrhosis should alert the pathologist to the possibility of HCV infection.

REFERENCES

1. Bamber M, Murray A, Arborgh BAM, Scheuer PJ, Kernoff PBA, Thomas HC, Sherlock S. Short incubation non-A, non-B hepatitis transmitted by factor VIII concentrates in patients with congenital coagulation disorders. Gut 1981;22:854-859.
2. Dienes HP, Popper H, Arnold W, Lobeck H. Histologic observations in human hepatitis non-A, non-B. HEPATOLOGY 1982;2: 562-571.
3. Schmid M, Pirovino M, Altorfer J, Gudat F, Bianchi L. Acute hepatitis non-A, non-B: are there any specific light microscopic features? Liver 1982;2:61-67.
4. Kryger P, Christoffersen P. Liver histopathology of the hepatitis A virus infection: a comparison with hepatitis B and non-A, non-B. J Clin Pathol 1983;36:650-654.
5. Rugge M, Vanstapel M-J, Ninfo V, Realdi G, Tremolada F, Montanari PG, van Damme B, et al. Comparative histology of acute hepatitis B and non-A, non-B in Leuven and Padova. Virchows Arch [A] 1983;401:275-288.
6. Khuroo MS. Study of an epidemic of non-A, non-B hepatitis: possibility of another human hepatitis virus distinct from post-transfusion non-A, non-B type. Am J Med 1980;68:818-824.
7. Dienes HP, Hütteroth T, Bianchi L, Grün M, Thoenes W. Hepatitis A-like non-A, non-B hepatitis: light and electron microscopic observations of three cases. Virchows Arch [A] 1986;409: 657-667.
8. Kuo G, Choo Q-L, Alter HJ, Gitnick GL, Redeker AG, Purcell RH, Miyamura T, et al. An assay for circulating antibodies to a major etiologic virus of human non-A, non-B hepatitis. Science 1989; 244:362-364.
9. Gray JJ, Wreghitt TG, Friend PJ, Wight DGD, Sundaresan V, Calne RY. Differentiation between specific and non-specific hepatitis C antibodies in chronic liver disease. Lancet 1990;335: 609-610.
10. McFarlane IG, Smith HM, Johnson PJ, Bray GP, Vergani D, Williams R. Hepatitis C virus antibodies in chronic active hepatitis: pathogenetic factor or false-positive result? Lancet 1990;335:754-757.
11. Weiner AJ, Kuo G, Bradley DW, Bonino F, Saracco G, Lee C, Rosenblatt J, et al. Detection of hepatitis C viral sequences in non-A, non-B hepatitis. Lancet 1990;335:1-3.
12. Brown D, Powell L, Chrispeels J, Morris A, Rassam S, Sherlock S, McIntyre N, et al. Improved diagnosis of chronic HCV infection by antibody to core epitopes [Abstract]. HEPATOLOGY 1991;14:69A.
13. Dusheiko GM, Smith M, Scheuer PJ. Hepatitis C virus transmitted by human bite. Lancet 1990;336:503-504.
14. Van der Poel CL, Reesing HW, Schaasberg W, Leentvaar-Kuypes A, Bakker E, Exel-Oehlers PJ, Lelie PN. Infectivity of blood seropositive for hepatitis C virus antibodies. Lancet 1990;335: 558-560.
15. International Group. Acute and chronic hepatitis revisited. Lancet 1977;2:914-919.
16. Mattsson L, Weiland O, Glaumann H. Application of a numerical scoring system for assessment of histological outcome in patients with chronic post-transfusion non-A, non-B hepatitis with or without antibodies to hepatitis C. Liver 1990;10:257-263.

© Gut 1992; 33: 1323–1327

Evidence of clonal variants of *Helicobacter pylori* in three generations of a duodenal ulcer disease family

C U Nwokolo, J Bickley, A R Attard, R J Owen, M Costas, I A Fraser

Departments of Gastroenterology and Surgery, Walsgrave Hospital, Coventry
C U Nwokolo
A R Attard
I A Fraser

National Collection of Type Cultures, Central Public Health Laboratory, Colindale, London
J Bickley
R J Owen
M Costas

Correspondence to:
Dr C U Nwokolo MRCP, Gastroenterology Unit, Walsgrave Hospital, Clifford Bridge Road, Coventry CV2 2DX.

Accepted for publication
2 March 1992

Abstract

Nine members of a family with a high incidence of duodenal ulcer disease were studied by interview, examination of hospital records, endoscopy, and antral biopsy. *Helicobacter pylori* was confirmed by CLO test, histology and culture. DNA extraction from pure isolates of *H pylori* was possible in six family members and strain typing was performed by restriction fragment length polymorphism. DNA restriction digestion was followed by vacublotting and then DNA hybridisation, using a cDNA probe complimentary to *H pylori* rRNA cistrons. Eight of the nine family members were *H pylori* positive by CLO test and histology. Five had duodenal ulcer disease. Three family members (one from each generation) harboured clonal variants of a single parent strain of *H pylori* but only two had duodenal disease. The other three members harboured different strains. Intrafamilial clustering of clonal variants of *H pylori* occurs in some duodenal ulcer disease families. Family members however, may develop duodenal disease irrespecitve of the colonising strain.

(*Gut* 1992; **33:** 1323–1327)

The microaerobic bacterium *Helicobacter pylori*, is widely accepted as an important cause of gastritis[1] and infections are strongly associated with peptic ulcer disease[2] and gastric cancer.[3] 'The gastrin link'[4 5] and the 'leaking roof'[6] are some of the hypotheses proposed to explain the pathogenic link between *H pylori* and duodenal ulcer disease. Pathogenicity mechanisms of *H pylori* are poorly understood, but the existence of ulcerogenic strains of this bacterium may explain why only a minority of patients harbouring the organism develop duodenal ulcer disease. Certain virulence factors produced by *H pylori* have been identified and include a vacuolating, cytopathic agent[7] and a protein that inhibits rabbit parietal cell acid secretion in vitro.[8] *H pylori* strains positive for a 120-KDa protein have recently been described in duodenal ulcer patients.[9]

Evidence is accumulating from DNA fingerprinting that each infected individual harbours a unique strain of *H pylori*[10] although the reason for this diversity is unknown. As 20–50% of duodenal ulcer patients have a positive family history,[11] it would be of interest to explore the hypothesis that familial peptic ulcer disease is the cluster effect of a virulent, ulcerogenic strain of *H pylori* transfecting family members.

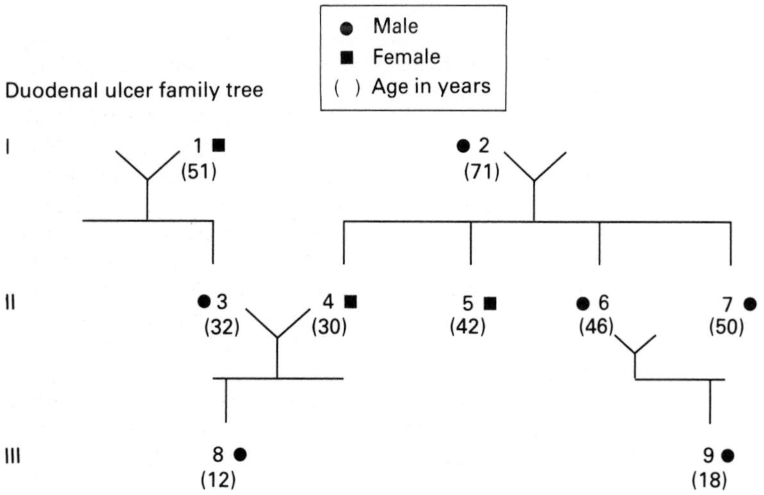

Duodenal ulcer family tree

● Male
■ Female
( ) Age in years

I: 1 ■ (51); ● 2 (71)

II: ● 3 (32); 4 ■ (30); 5 ■ (42); ● 6 (46); 7 ● (50)

III: 8 ● (12); 9 ● (18)

Figure 1: Familial relationships among nine members of three generations (I, II, III) of a duodenal ulcer disease family, with age and sex.

TABLE

Subjects	*Clo test*	*Histology*	*Duodenal ulcer*	*Plasma gastrin (ng/litre)*	H pylori *isolation*	Bam*HI Total digest pattern*	Bam*HI ribopattern*
Generation I							
1	+	+	−	34	+	1	CO-1
2	+	+	+	181	+	2a	CO-2
Generation II							
3	+	+	+	35	+	3	CO-3
4	−	−	−	39	−	na	na
5	+	+	−	114	−	na	na
6	+	+	+	177	+	4	CO-4
7	+	+	−	71	+	2b	nt
Generation III							
8	+	+	+	131	−	na	na
9	+	+	+	199	+	2c	CO-2

CO refers to Coventry strain ribopattern; na=not available; nt=not typable.

Methods

PATIENTS

The extended family studied has been recognised in the Coventry area for up to 20 years. Scrutiny of hospital records revealed that during that period, the majority of family members had presented to the Walsgrave Hospital with duodenal ulceration or its complications.

The matriachial head of the family (Fig 1, subject 1) provided a comprehensive family history. There were 25 family members aged over 10 years. Fourteen members lived in the Coventry area, the remainder living in Scotland or Australia. The 14 members living in the area were invited for interview and subsequent endo-

© Gut 1992; 33: 1323–1327

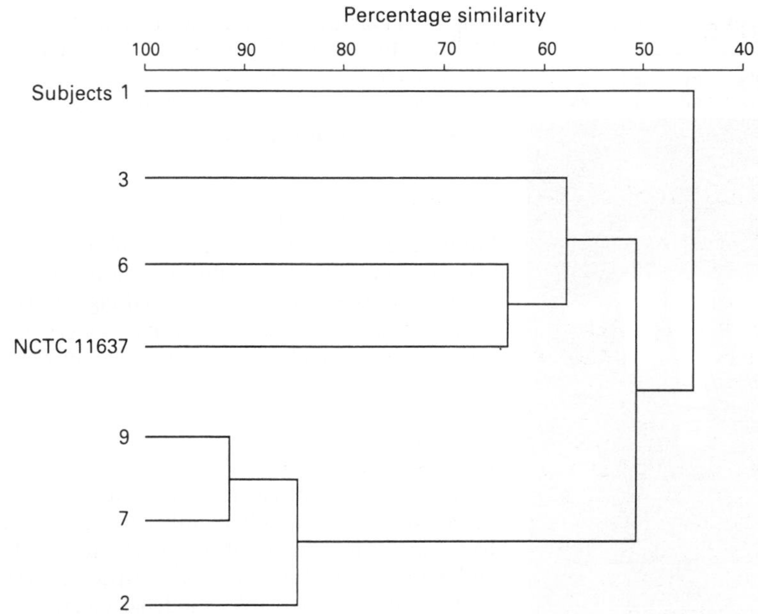

Figure 2: Dendrogram of the cluster analysis to show similarities based on the total DNA digest patterns of Helicobacter pylori *isolates from subjects 1, 2, 3, 6, 7, and 9, and the type strain NCTC 11637. The numbers on the horizontal axis indicate the percentage similarities as determined by the Dice correlation coefficient.*

scopy. Only nine members eventually participated in the study. The other five either declined to participate or had other commitments. Of the 11 family members living outside the Coventry area, only two could be contacted. Both declined to participate in the study.

FAMILY HISTORY

A family history was obtained by direct interview of the patients and examination of their hospital record (Table, Fig 1). The following were recorded: (a) Date and method of diagnosis of duodenal ulcer disease. (b) Complications (gastrointestinal bleed, perforations, pyloric stenosis). (c) Indications for and nature of gastric surgery (undersewing of ulcer, vagotomy and drainage). (d) Drugs within the preceding six months (H2 blockers, antibiotics, bismuth, non-steroidal antiinflammatory drugs). (e) Concurrent illnesses (other inherited disease). (f) Patients' date of birth and body weight. (g) Smoking.

PLASMA GASTRIN, ELECTROLYTES AND CALCIUM

Before endoscopy, blood (10 ml) was taken from an antecubital vein, transferred into a lithium heparin tube and centrifuged. Plasma was decanted into a 10 mm diameter plastic tube and immediately frozen to −20°C. Plasma gastrin was measured by radioimmunassay at the Department of Biochemistry, East Birmingham General Hospital. A further blood sample was taken for routine biochemistry and calcium.

UPPER GASTROINTESTINAL ENDOSCOPY

Endoscopy was performed after an overnight fast. Before each examination, endoscopes were thoroughly cleaned mechanically with detergent as recommended by the British Society of Gastroenterology.[12] Endoscope channels were filled with 2% gluteraldehyde and then immersed in the same disinfectant for a minimum of 20 minutes. Thorough rinsing was then performed. A single biopsy forcep was used for each patient to prevent transfer of *H pylori* between patients. Duodenal ulceration was recorded only when an ulcer crater of at least 5 mm diameter was observed. Pyloroduodenal scarring, antritis, duodenitis and gastric anatomical abnormalities from previous surgery were also recorded.

BIOPSY

Four antral biopsies were taken from each patient. One was used for a CLO test (Delta West limited, Bentley, Western Australia) and one was transferred into 10% w/v formaldehyde for histology. The other two were transferred separately into two bijoux containing *H pylori* selective enrichment (SE) medium[13] and were number coded randomly to ensure that culture and DNA analysis were performed blind.

CULTURE

Antral biopsy specimens were placed in 5 ml of selective enrichment medium and incubated at 37°C on a gyratory platform (150 rpm) in a Variable Atmosphere Incubator (Don Whitley Scientific Ltd, Shipley, Yorks, UK) under microaerobic conditions (5% oxygen, 5% carbon dioxide, 2% hydrogen, 88% nitrogen). A sample from each flask was subcultured onto Oxoid brain heart infusion agar, supplemented with 5% horse blood and 1% Isovitalex after 48 hours. Positive growth was identified by Gram stain and production of urease, and cultures were preserved at −196°C on glass beads in Oxoid nutrient Broth No. 2 containing (v/v) glycerol.

DNA DIGESTION AND ELECTROPHORESIS

H pylori chromosomal DNA was isolated using the guanidium thiocyanate reagent method.[14] The purified DNA was incubated with 11 endonucleases (*Hae*III, *Hind*III, *Eco*RI, *Pvu*II, *Pst*I, *Bam*III, *Sac*I, *Apa*I, *Stu*I, *Hpa*II, *Msp*I) according to the conditions recommended by the manufacturer (Northumbria Biologicals Limited, UK). DNA samples (5 μg) were digested for four hours at 37°C. The digested DNA was electrophoresed at 30 V or 16 hours in a horizontal 0·8% (w/v) agarose gel in a buffer containing 89 mM Tris hydrochloride, 89 mM boric acid, and 2 mM disodium ethylenediaminetetra-acetic acid (EDTA) (pH 8·3). After electrophoresis, the gels were stained with ethidium bromide and photographed.

COMPARISON OF DIGEST PATTERNS BY DENSITOMETRY

Patterns were scanned and analysed with a laser densitometer interfaced to a Compaq Deskpro 386 microcomputer. Profiles were compared by band matching, using the Dice correlation coefficient.[15] Strains were then clustered and a dendrogram plotted (Fig 2).

VACUBLOTTING AND HYBRIDISATION

A biotinylated cDNA probe was prepared from *H pylori* NCTC (National Collection of Type

© Gut 1992; 33: 1323–1327

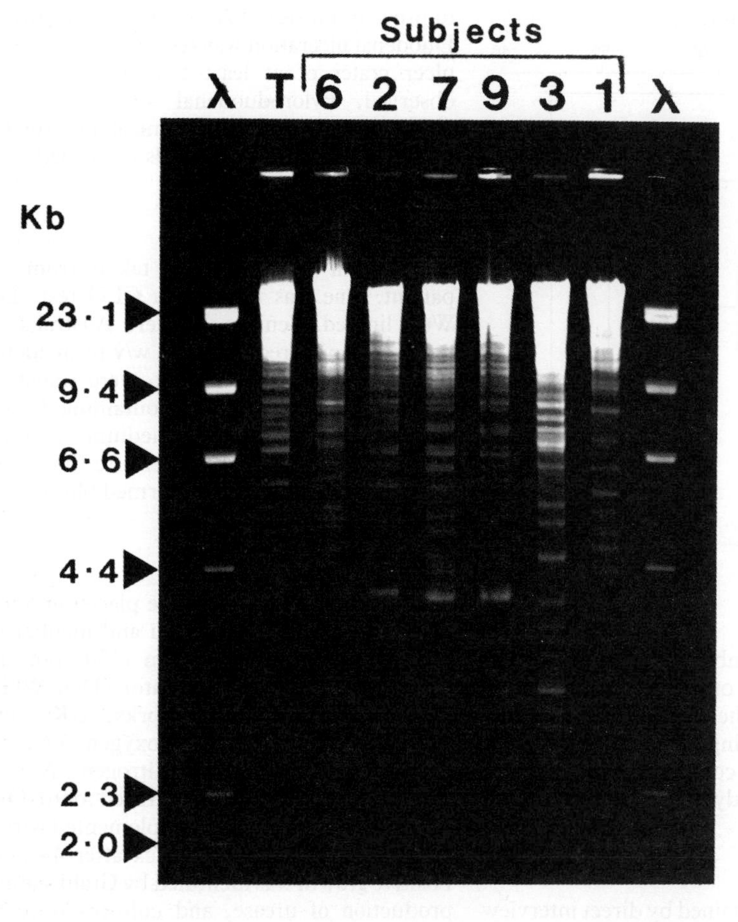

Figure 3: Agarose gel electrophoresis of Bam*HI digest fragments of chromosomal DNA from* Helicobacter pylori. *Sizes indicated are for bacteriophage λ* Hind*III digest (λ). Subjects are numbered according to text and* H pylori *NCTC 11637 (type strain) was included as a reference.*

Cultures) 11638 16S and 23S rRNA using Moloney mouse leukaemia virus reverse transcriptase (Gibco-BRL). Biotinylation was achieved by the incorporation of biotin-16-dUTP.[16] After electrophoresis and photography, the gels were transferred to nylon membranes (Hybond-N, Amersham International) by means of vacublotting (Vacu-Gene XL, Pharmacia LKB Biotechnology). The membranes were then hybridised by standard procedures for 16 hours at 42°C using the hybridised probe detected colorimetrically using a nonradioactive detection kit – BluGENE (Gibco-BRL).

ETHICS

Ethical approval was obtained from the Coventry and Warwickshire Postgraduate Medical Ethics Committee as part of a larger epidemiological study. Informed consent was obtained from all family members except for the 12 year old. In his case an endoscopy was indicated for the investigation of abdominal pain. His mother provided consent.

Results

Nine family members representing three generations (I, II, III) participated in the study (Fig 1). Their median age was 42 years (range 12–71). There were three females and six males. All the males (except for the 12 and 18 year olds in generation III) had smoked, but none had smoked in the year preceding the study.

PLASMA GASTRIN, ELECTROLYTES AND CALCIUM

Mildly raised plasma gastrin were observed in five subjects (Table). Subject 9 was taking omeprazole and subject 8 was taking an H_2 blocker. Two subjects (2 and 6) had undergone vagotomy. Serum electrolytes and calcium were normal.

DUODENAL ULCER DISEASE

A diagnosis of duodenal ulcer disease was accepted only if a family member was found to have an acute duodenal ulcer at the study endoscopy or had a history of gastric surgery performed for intractable duodenal ulceration. Duodenal ulcer disease was confirmed in five subjects (2, 3, 6, 8 and 9). Several other family members had a history of duodenal ulceration but were not available for inclusion in the study. All the subjects with duodenal ulcer disease had become symptomatic in the first or second decade of life. In all cases confirmatory evidence of active duodenal ulceration had been obtained by the end of the third decade, except for the 71 year old man (subject 2), in whom confirmation was obtained in the fifth decade.

H PYLORI STATUS

Eight of the nine (90%) family members were positive for *H pylori* by CLO test and histology (Table). The one negative subject (subject 4) was a woman (age 30) in the second generation. Although she was endoscopically normal, her 12 year old son (subject 8) had confirmed duodenal ulcer disease from the age of eight, requiring maintenance treatment with an H_2 blocker.

ISOLATION AND DNA FINGERPRINTING OF *H PYLORI*

Successful isolation of pure cultures of *H pylori* was possible in six of the nine subjects studied. One family member (subject 4) was negative for *H pylori* (confirmed by CLO test and histology). In one member (subject 5) unsuccessful isolation was caused by non-*H pylori* contaminants. Two biopsies were obtained from subject 8 (12 years old) for histology and CLO test before endoscopy was abandoned for technical reasons, and ethical considerations precluded a second endoscopy.

Subjects 2, 7, and 9, from whom *H pylori* had been successfully isolated, harboured strains with similar but not completely identical DNA fingerprints (Figs 3, 4). The *Bam*HI restriction digest patterns of these three strains differed only in one or two minor bands, whereas all the other strains in the study were very different (Fig 3). All isolates were designated a DNA type based of their *Bam*HI total digest patterns. Subjects 2, 7, and 9 were designated as subtypess 2a, 2b, and 2c respectively, as their digest

© Gut 1992; 33: 1323–1327

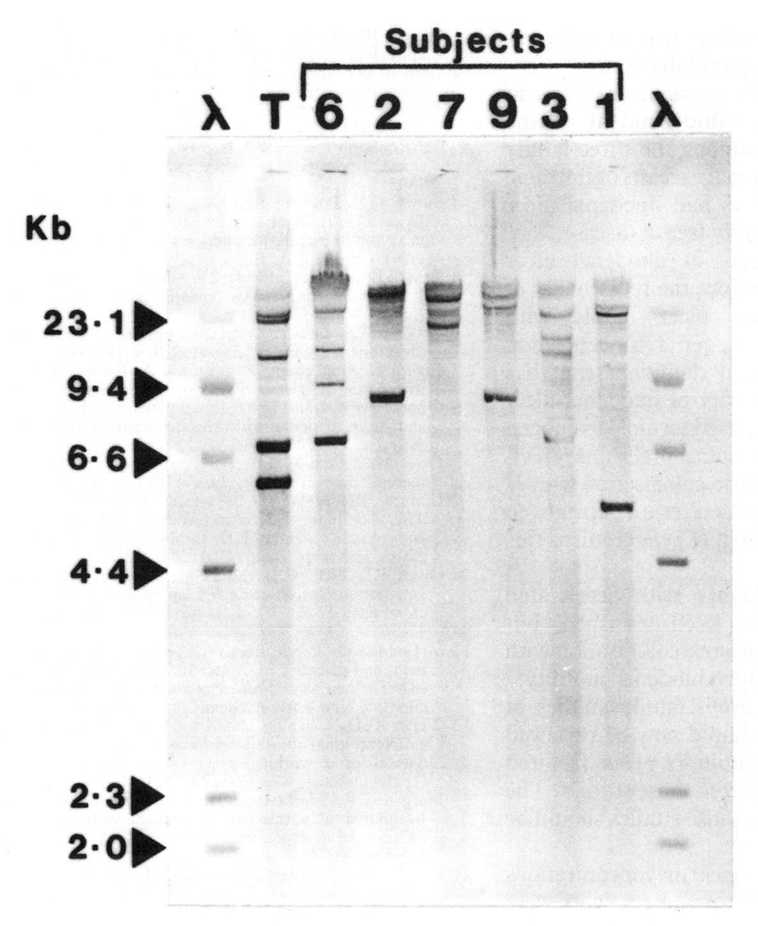

Figure 4: The rRNA gene patterns (ribopatterns) for Bam*HI digests of chromosomal DNA probed with biotinylated cDNA from* Helicobacter pylori *NCTC 11638. Sizes indicated are for bacteriophage λ*Hind*III digest(λ). Subjects are numbered according to text and* H pylori *NCTC 11637 (type strain) was included as a reference.*

patterns were very similar (Table, Fig 3). The dendrogram in Figure 2 illustrates the similarities between the *Bam*HI digest patterns obtained for all subjects. Similarities were obtained using band matching and calculation of the Dice coefficient. Isolates from subjects 2, 7, and 9 clustered at a similarity of 85%, with isolates from subjects 7 and 9 being most closely related at a similarity of 92%. All other subjects (1, 3, 6) clustered at similarities of less than 60%.

Less information was available from the *Bam*HI ribopatterns obtained after hybridisation with the cDNA probe, because few bands were present. Different ribopatterns were obtained for subjects 1, 3, and 6, however, (Fig 4). Subjects 2 and 9 had the same ribopattern (Table, Fig 4), with a common band of molecular weight 8·8 kb. Subject 7 did not, however, have this band.

Results with other endonucleases showed that DNA from *H pylori* isolates from subjects 2, 7, and 9 shared the unusual characteristic of being undigested by enzymes which commonly digest DNA from *H pylori* strains, namely *Hae*III and *Hind*III.

Subjects 2 and 9 had duodenal ulcer disease; one had a vagotomy and drainage procedure, the other had persistent duodenal ulceration despite continuous omeprazole treatment. Subject 7 did not have duodenal ulcer disease according to our stringent criteria, but was a life long dyspeptic and was found to have significant antritis and duodenitis at endoscopy. Subject 6 had a completely different DNA fingerprint. This subject had undergone a vagotomy and pyloroplasty at age 26 years after many years of severe duodenal ulceration. Subjects 1 and 3 also had different strains of *H pylori* and these strains were different from the strains isolated from all other subjects. Subject 3 had a duodenal ulcer at endoscopy and subject 1 was endoscopically normal.

Discussion

The diversity of the strains found in this duodenal ulcer family suggests that cluster infection by a single putative ulcerogenic strain of *H pylori* does not completely explain familial peptic ulcer disease. Clonal variants however, – that is, isolates with a high level of genomic relatedness, of the same strain of *H pylori* colonised three members of the family (subjects 2, 7, and 9). It is of interest that family members (subjects 7 and 9) who harboured the clonal variants with the highest similarity (92%) were only one generation apart. This adds to the evidence supporting a person to person mode of transmission. Alternatively, family members may become infected from a common source.

The reason for the minor genetic differences between these clonal variants is unknown. It may represent a tendency to spontaneous genomic rearrangement which may be in the nature of *H pylori*. Marked genomic heterogeneity is already a recognised characteristic of this bacterium. From our experience, in applying the technique of DNA fingerprinting to strain typing of over 500 isolates of *H pylori*,[15 17] no two patients were found to harbour *H pylori* strains with such marked similarity as observed in subjects 2, 7, and 9. Indeed, the small amount of variation between the digest patterns of these three subjects was consistent with the observed variation within multiple isolates from single patients.[17]

Further evidence for the general similarities of these three isolates was obtained from results with other restriction enzymes. DNA from *H pylori* isolated from subjects 2, 7, and 9 were unusual in not being digested by *Hae*III or *Hind*III. These enzymes would normally digest DNA obtained from the majority of *H pylori* isolates.

Clustering of *H pylori* among relatives of infected individuals has been widely reported.[18] Graham *et al* recently described the influence of age, sex, social class, and race on the prevalence of *H pylori* in a western population.[19] One preliminary report has found a single strain of *H pylori* clustering in a duodenal ulcer family of eight members.[20] This report was, however, based solely on total digest patterns obtained with a single restriction enzyme. Another report has described identical strains of *H pylori* colonising two pairs of mentally subnormal children living in close proximity.[21]

In this study we found eight of nine family members colonised by *H pylori*. Because the colonising strains were not all identical, this

© Gut 1992; 33: 1323–1327

suggests that family members may be independently susceptible to *H pylori* infection.

The development of duodenal ulcer disease in family members seemed independent of the colonising strain. Even among the three family members colonised by clonal variants of the same strain, only two members had duodenal ulcer disease. One was apparently free of disease.

Some genetic subtypes of duodenal ulcer disease were proposed before the rediscovery of *H pylori*.[1] A duodenal ulcer family with raised serum hyperpepsinogen 1 concentration inherited as an autosomal dominant trait has been described.[22] A majority of duodenal ulcer patients, however, have raised serum pepsinogen 1.[23] In addition there is some preliminary evidence to suggest that gastric colonisation with *H pylori* is associated with raised serum pepsinogen 1 and that the eradication of *H pylori* returns this towards normal.[24]

A duodenal ulcer family with accelerated gastric emptying has also been described[25] but recent data suggest that gastric colonisation with *H pylori* may modify antroduodenal motility.[26] Data from the pre *H pylori* family studies of duodenal ulcer disease should now be reviewed and recent knowledge about *H pylori* factored into conclusions derived from those studies. The hypotheses derived from those studies should be reassessed.

Mildly raised fasting gastrin concentrations were observed in family members who were taking antisecretory drugs or who had had a vagotomy. There was no clinical or biochemical evidence to suggest that this family had multiple endocrine adenomatosis or other hypergastrinaemic state.

In general, only limited conclusions may be derived from single family studies. Reports of family studies in which *H pylori* strains have been characterised by molecular biology techniques, however, are infrequent in the medical literature. This study supports the observations of Drumm *et al*[18] that *H pylori* clusters in some duodenal ulcer families. If gastric colonisation with *H pylori* precedes duodenal ulceration in all cases, then it may be that duodenal ulcer family members are simply more prone to *H pylori* infection than members of the general population. The colonising strain of *H pylori* did not seem to influence the development of duodenal ulcer disease in family members. Intrafamilial clustering of clonal variants arising from a common parent strain of *H pylori* may occur. An undefined tendency to duodenal ulceration may be inherited in some duodenal ulcer families. Subsequent colonisation with most strains of *H pylori* promotes this tendency, resulting in active duodenal ulceration.

Sister De Souza and the staff of the Walsgrave Hospital endoscopy unit assisted in the endoscopic procedures. JB is indebted to the Procter and Gamble Company (Cincinnati, Ohio, USA) for financial support.

1 Warren JR, Marshall B. Unidentified curved bacilli on gastric epithelium in active chronic gastritis. *Lancet* 1983 i: 1273–5.
2 Graham DY. *Campylobacter pylori* and peptic ulcer disease. *Gastroenterology* 1989; **96:** 614–25.
3 Forman D, Newell DG, Fullerton F, Yarnell JWG, Stacey, AR, Wald N, *et al.* Association between infection with *Helicobacter pylori* and risk of gastric cancer: evidence from a prospective investigation. *BMJ* 1991; **302:** 1302–5.
4 Smith JTL, Pounder RE, Nwokolo CU, Lanzon-Miller S, Evans DG, Graham DY. Inappropriate hypergastrinaemia in asymptomatic healthy subjects infected with *Helicobacter pylori*. *Gut* 1990; **31:** 522–5.
5 Levi S, Beardshall K, Playford R, Ghosh P, Haddad G, Calam J. *Campylobacter pylori* and duodenal ulcers: the gastrin link. *Lancet* 1989; i: 1167–8.
6 Goodwin CS. Duodenal ulcer, *Campylobacter pylori* and the "leaking roof" concept. *Lancet* 1989; ii: 1467–9.
7 Figura N, Gugliemetti P, Rossolini A, Barberi A, Cusi G, Musmanno RA, *et al.* Cytotoxin production by *Campylobacter pylori* strains isolated from patients with peptic ulcers and from patients with chronic gastritis only. *J Clin Microbiol* 1989; **27:** 225–6.
8 Cave DR, Varges M. Effect of *Campylobacter* protein on acid secretion by parietal cells. *Lancet* 1989; ii: 187–9.
9 Crabtree JE, Taylor JD, Wyatt JI, Heatley RV, Shallcross TM, Tompkins DS, *et al.* Mucosal IgA recognition of *Helicobacter pylori* 120 KDa protein, peptic ulceration and gastric pathology. *Lancet* 1991; **338:** 332–5.
10 Owen RJ, Bickley J, Costas M, Morgan DR. Genomic variation in *Helicobacter pylori*: application to identification of strains. *Scand J Gastroenterol* 1991; **26** (suppl 181): 43–50.
11 McConnell RB. Peptic ulcer: early genetic evidence – families, twins and markers. In: Rotter JI, Samloff IM, Rimoin DL, eds. *The genetics and heterogeneity of common gastrointestinal disorders.* New York: Academic Press, 1989; 31.
12 Weller IVD. Cleaning and disinfection of equipment for gastrointestinal flexible endoscopy: interim recommendations of a working party of the British Society of Gastroenterology. *Gut* 1988; **29:** 1134–51.
13 Morgan DR, Mathewson JJ, Freedman R, Kraft WG. Evaluation of a selective enrichment technique for the isolation of *Campylobacter pylori*. *FEMS Microbiol Lett* 1990; **66:** 303–6.
14 Pitcher DG, Saunders NA, Owen RJ. Rapid extraction of bacterial genomic DNA with Guanidium thiocyanate. *Lett Appl Microbiol* 1989; **8:** 151–6.
15 Costas M, Owen RJ, Bickley J, Morgan DR. Molecular techniques for studying and epidemiology of infection by *Helicobacter pylori*. *Scand J Gastroenterol* 1991; **26** (suppl 181): 20–32.
16 Pitcher DG, Owen RJ, Dyal P, Beck A. Synthesis of a biotinylated probe to detect ribosomal cistrons in *Providencia stuartii*. *FEMS Microbiol Lett* 1987; **48:** 283–7.
17 Owen RJ, Fraser J, Costas M, Morgan DD, Morgan DR. Signature patterns of DNA restriction fragements of *Helicobacter pylori* before and after treatment. *J Clin Pathol* 1990; **43:** 646–9.
18 Drumm B, Perez-Perez GI, Blaser MJ, Sherman P. Intrafamilial clustering of *Campylobacter pylori* infection. *N Engl J Med* 1990; **322:** 359–63.
19 Graham DY, Malaty HM, Evans DG, Evans DJ (junior), Klein PD, Adam E. Epidemiology of *Helicobacter pylori* in an asymptomatic population in the United States. *Gastroenterology* 1991; **100:** 1495–501.
20 Rauws EAJ, Langenberg W, Oudbier J, Mulder CJJ, Tytgat GNJ. Familial clustering of peptic ulcer disease colonised with *C pylori* of the same DNA composition. *Gastroenterology* 1989; **96:** A409.
21 Vincent P, Pernes P, Beju A, Gottrand F, Husson MA, Leclerc H, *et al. Helicobacter pylori* in cohabiting children. *Lancet* 1991; **337:** 848.
22 Rotter JI, Stones JQ, Samloff IM, Richardson CJ, Gurskey JM, Walsh JH, *et al.* Duodenal ulcer disease associated with elevated pepsinogen 1. An inherited autosomal dominant disorder. *N Engl J Med* 1979; **300:** 53–5.
23 Tanaka Y, Mine K, Nakai Y, Mishima N, Nakagawa T. Serum pepsinogen 1 concentrations in peptic ulcer patients in relation to ulcer location and stage. *Gut* 1991; **32:** 849–52.
24 Chittajalu RS, Dorian CA, McColl KEL. Serum pepsinogen 1 in duodenal ulcer – the effect of eradication of *H pylori* and correlation with serum gastrin and antral gastritis. *Gut* 1990; **31:** A1199.
25 Rotter JI, Rubin R, Meyer JH, Samloff MI, Rimoin D. Rapid gastric emptying – an inherited pathophysiologic defect in duodenal ulcer. *Gastroenterology* 1979; **76:** 1229.
26 Testoni RA, Bagnolo F, Passeratti S, Fanti L, Sorghi M, Masci E, *et al. Campylobacter pylori* infection correlates with more severe interdigestive antro-duodenal motor impairment in subjects with chronic gastritis. *Gastroenterology* 1990; **98:** A137.

© *Journal of Cellular Physiology* 1992; 151: 405–414

Partial Purification and Characterisation of an Inhibitor of Hepatocyte Proliferation Derived From Nonparenchymal Cells After Partial Hepatectomy

ANTHONY C. WOODMAN, CLARE A. SELDEN, AND HUMPHREY J.F. HODGSON*
Gastroenterology Unit, Department of Medicine, Royal Postgraduate Medical School, London, W12 0NN, U.K.

We have investigated the influences that nonparenchymal cells from regenerating rat liver exert on hepatocyte proliferation. When primary adult rat hepatocytes isolated from resting liver were co-cultured with nonparenchymal cells (NPCs) from resting liver of a different syngeneic animal, the proliferative response of hepatocytes to epidermal growth factor (EGF) was unaffected by the presence of NPCs. In the presence of NPCs taken from livers that had undergone partial hepatectomy 24 hours before (regen-NPCs), the response of hepatocytes from resting liver to EGF, TGF-α, and hepatocyte growth factor (HGF) was markedly inhibited. Inhibitory activity was not dependent on cell-to-cell contact, and conditioned-medium from regen-NPCs, but not normal NPCs, inhibited EGF-induced hepatocyte DNA synthesis by approximately 50%. After concentration by gel chromatography and lyophilisation, inhibition was 98%. The inhibitory activity migrated on SDS-PAGE gel electrophoresis with an apparent molecular weight of 14 to 17 kDa and was trypsin-sensitive but relatively heat-stable. The effects of blocking antibodies established that it was not TGF-β_1, IL1-β, or IL6. Investigations of regen-NPCs taken at different time points demonstrated that inhibitory activity was released into conditioned medium of cells harvested at 24 and 48 hours after partial hepatectomy, but not 10 or 72 hours. This powerful inhibitor of hepatocyte response to proliferogens is released by cultures of NPCs with a time course suggesting that it may be involved in terminating the surge of hepatocyte replication induced by partial hepatectomy.

Hepatocytes in adult liver are normally predominantly in G_0, with fewer than 0.1% engaged in DNA synthesis (Fabrikant, 1968; Alison, 1986). Following partial hepatectomy or chemically induced hepatic damage, there is a rapid surge of hepatocyte DNA synthesis, which leads to restoration of the normal liver. The experimental model of 70% partial hepatectomy has been extensively studied in the rat to elucidate the underlying processes. A combination of in vivo and in vitro studies has implicated a number of growth factors as initiators of hepatocyte DNA synthesis—particularly hepatocyte growth factor (HGF) (Nakamura et al., 1984, 1989; Gohda et al., 1988; Zarnegar and Michalopoulos, 1989; Selden et al., 1990) and the two ligands of the EGF receptor, TGF-α (Mead and Fausto, 1989) and EGF (Earp and O'Keefe, 1981). In addition, acidic fibroblast growth factor (Kan et al., 1989) and number of other factors may act as mitogens or co-mitogens (see Michalopoulos, 1990).

The process of hepatocyte proliferation in vivo ceases after most hepatocytes remaining after partial hepatectomy have undergone one or two cycles of cell division. The mechanisms controlling the cessation of hepatocyte proliferation have recently been explored. Possibilities include the initial programming of the replicative process to cease after one or two cell cycles have been completed (Michalopoulos, 1990), or that a set of processes similar but opposite to those that initiate DNA synthesis occur, with generation of inhibitors of cell proliferation within or without the liver. Recent work has implicated TGF-β1 (Roberts et al., 1981) as one such potential hepatocyte growth inhibitor (Carr et al., 1986; Strain et al., 1987; Russell, 1988). TGF-β1 is generated in the liver after partial hepatectomy, predominantly within non-parenchymal cells (both sinusoidal endothelial cells and Kupffer cells) (Braun et al., 1988). When administered in vivo, TGF-β1 can delay hepatic regeneration (Russell et al., 1988), and in vitro has been demonstrated to be a powerful inhibitor of the stimulatory effects of TGF-α, EGF, and HGF on hepatocyte proliferation (Carr et al., 1986; Russell et al., 1988; Micholopoulos, 1990). However, a number of other potential growth inhibitors are described, such as Kupffer cell-derived IL-1β (Nakamura et al., 1988) and IL-6 (Huggett et al., 1989), and liver-derived growth inhibi-

Received September 16, 1991; accepted December 16, 1991.

*To whom reprint requests/correspondence should be addressed.

© N Engl J Med 1992; 327: 749–754

GASTROINTESTINAL DAMAGE ASSOCIATED WITH THE USE OF NONSTEROIDAL ANTIINFLAMMATORY DRUGS

MILES C. ALLISON, M.D., ALLAN G. HOWATSON, M.B., CAROLINE J. TORRANCE, M.B.,
FREDERICK D. LEE, M.D., AND ROBIN I. RUSSELL, M.D., PH.D.

Abstract *Background.* Long-term use of nonsteroidal antiinflammatory drugs (NSAIDs) may lead to inflammation of the small intestine associated with occult blood and protein loss. The aim of this study was to investigate the prevalence and structural correlates of this enteropathy.

Methods. We examined the stomach, duodenum, and small intestine of 713 patients post mortem. Of these patients, 249 had had NSAIDs prescribed during the six months before death and 464 patients had not. All visible small intestinal lesions were removed for histologic examination, and specific etiologic factors were sought. The prevalence of nonspecific small-intestinal ulcers and ulcers of the stomach and duodenum was compared in the two groups of patients.

Results. Nonspecific small-intestinal ulceration was found in 21 (8.4 percent) of the users of NSAIDs and 3 (0.6 percent) of the nonusers (difference, 7.8 percent; 95 percent confidence interval, 5.0 to 10.6 percent; P<0.001). Three patients who were long-term users of NSAIDs were found to have died of perforated nonspecific small-intestinal ulcers. Ulcers of the stomach or duodenum were found in 54 (21.7 percent) of the patients who used these drugs and 57 (12.3 percent) of those who had not (difference, 9.4 percent; 95 percent confidence interval, 3.9 to 15.1 percent; P<0.001).

Conclusions. Patients who take NSAIDs have an increased risk of nonspecific ulceration of the small-intestinal mucosa. These ulcers are less common than ulcers of the stomach or duodenum, but can lead to life-threatening complications. (N Engl J Med 1992;327:749-54.)

PATIENTS who take nonsteroidal antiinflammatory drugs (NSAIDs) have an increased risk of mucosal damage in the upper gastrointestinal tract.[1] The development of new lesions weeks after the initiation of treatment with NSAIDs has been confirmed in a prospective study,[2] and the risk of gastric and duodenal ulcers increases with the dose of NSAID.[3] Other epidemiologic studies have shown a link between the use of NSAIDs and serious complications of peptic ulcer disease.[4-7] Evidence that NSAIDs may cause perforation and hemorrhage of the small intestine comes from a case–control study[8] and several case reports.[9-12] These drugs also have been implicated in the development of intestinal strictures[13-15] and narrow-based ileal stenoses.[16,17]

Several indirect approaches have been used to investigate the frequency and nature of NSAID-associated damage to the small intestine. Drug-induced increases in mucosal permeability have been demonstrated in normal subjects and in patients with rheumatic diseases.[18-20] Bjarnason et al. identified inflammation of the small intestine by showing the accumulation of intravenously administered radiolabeled leukocytes in the ileum and their subsequent excretion in feces by two thirds of patients receiving long-term NSAID therapy.[21] They proposed that NSAID enteropathy is a common and underdiagnosed cause of weight loss and occult gastrointestinal bleeding in patients with rheumatic diseases.[22] Fiberoptic enteroscopy has been used to identify mucosal lesions in selected hospitalized patients with iron deficiency anemia who are receiving NSAIDs,[23] but there is little information on the structural correlates and clinical importance of NSAID-associated damage to the small intestine in the wider population.

This study was done to determine the prevalence and morphology of jejunal and ileal mucosal lesions at autopsy in consecutive patients with and without a history of having had an NSAID prescribed for them. In addition, we studied the prevalence of gastric and duodenal ulcers in these groups of patients and investigated whether the presence of ulcers in these two regions was a predictive marker for the occurrence of lesions of the jejunum and ileum in the patients receiving NSAIDs.

METHODS

Patients Who Died in the Hospital

All patients who died at the hospitals involved in the study and were autopsied between January 1990 and October 1991 were eligible for inclusion in the study. The main investigator was told about imminent autopsies on patients thought to have been taking NSAIDs. Consecutive patients were studied unless the main investigator was absent or there were exclusion criteria (Table 1). Control

From the Gastroenterology Unit (M.C.A., C.J.T., R.I.R.) and the Department of Pathology (A.G.H., F.D.L.), Royal Infirmary, Glasgow, Scotland. Address reprint requests to Dr. Allison at Royal Gwent Hospital, Newport, Gwent, NP9 2UB, United Kingdom.

Supported by grants from Searle UK and the Greater Glasgow Health Board.

Table 1. Reasons for Exclusions from the Study.

Reason for Exclusion	No. Excluded
Before autopsy	
Premorbid diagnosis of Crohn's disease	4
Death >48 hr before arrival at morgue	4
Serious risk of infection	3
Presence of ileal conduit or previous radiotherapy	1
Not registered with family physician	1
At time of autopsy	
Small-bowel infarction	14
Dense intraabdominal adhesions	10
Intraabdominal carcinomatosis	4
Gross fecal peritonitis	1

patients were chosen consecutively in a similar manner from two large hospitals. The recruitment policy was designed to include the maximal available number of autopsy results for patients with a history of NSAID use before death. It is important to emphasize, however, that decisions to request autopsies were made on clinical grounds by attending medical staff who were unaware of the purpose of this investigation. No autopsies were done specifically for this study, and small-bowel diseases had not been suspected clinically in any of the patients.

Patients Who Died outside the Hospital

We also studied a consecutive group of patients for whom NSAIDs had been prescribed and who had died outside the hospital, in order to reduce potential bias arising from studying only patients who died in the hospital. All these autopsies were conducted at the Glasgow City Mortuary at the instigation of the local Procurator Fiscal's office. This legal body orders autopsy examinations in cases in which the patient's family physician is uncertain about the cause of death or, rarely, if suicide or foul play cannot be ruled out. Medications in possession of the deceased are routinely recorded in the police report. The Procurator Fiscal's office informed us whenever NSAIDs were included in this report.

Drug Histories

The drug history of each patient was corroborated by the hospital records, the patient's family physician, or both. Patients were classified in four categories: those for whom NSAIDs had not been prescribed during the six months before death (control group); those for whom aspirin had been prescribed for any length of time (aspirin group); those for whom NSAIDs other than aspirin had been prescribed daily for at least six months up to the month before death (long-term NSAID group); and those for whom NSAIDs other than aspirin had been prescribed during the six months before death but who did not fulfill the criteria for inclusion in the long-term NSAID group — that is, NSAIDs had been prescribed daily for less than six months or discontinuous courses of NSAIDs had been prescribed for six months or more (short-term NSAID group). We refer to the three NSAID subgroups as users of NSAIDs, although the extent of compliance with the drug regimen outside the hospital was not known.

Exclusion Criteria

Cadavers considered to present a serious risk of infection (e.g., carriers of the human immunodeficiency virus) were excluded. Other exclusion criteria were a premorbid diagnosis of inflammatory bowel disease, death more than 48 hours before arrival at the morgue, the administration of radiotherapy to the abdomen within the preceding year, and an inability to corroborate the drug history with hospital records or the family physician.

Examination of Viscera

The entire jejunum and ileum were opened along the antimesenteric border, and the mucosal surface was washed with tap water. All visibly abnormal areas were removed for histologic examination by a single study pathologist who was unaware of the individual clinical or drug history. Histologic sections were stained with hematoxylin and eosin, Sirrius red, and methyl scarlet blue.

The stomach and duodenum were opened, washed, and examined for ulcers. Only ulcers exceeding 3 mm in diameter were included in the analysis. Histologic examination of gastric and duodenal ulcers was not carried out routinely but instead at the discretion of the hospital or forensic pathologist. These sections were not analyzed as part of this study, but the results of the local pathologist's interpretation were collected subsequently. All ulcers subsequently found to be malignant were excluded from the analysis.

Definitions

The following definitions of terms were used to describe pathologic processes in the small intestine: abnormality, an abnormal finding on gross inspection that was confirmed histologically; erosion, a breach of epithelial surface not extending beyond the muscularis mucosae; ulcer, a breach of epithelial surface and lamina propria extending beyond the muscularis mucosae into the submucosa; inflammation, an abnormal area of mucosa with histologic evidence of acute or chronic inflammatory-cell infiltration but no mucosal breach; specific mucosal lesion, an abnormality for which a specific cause was identified by histologic or microbiologic investigation (ulcers overlying nodules or metastases were excluded); and nonspecific ulcer, an ulcer without an underlying cause identified by these methods.

Microbiologic Studies

Microbiologic studies were done whenever inflammation or ulceration of the small-bowel mucosa was seen. Cecal contents were cultured and examined for the presence of *Clostridium difficile* toxin. Serum samples were tested for the presence of agglutinating antibodies to *Yersinia enterocolitica* and *Y. pseudotuberculosis* at the public health reference laboratory.

Statistical Analysis

Most of the results are expressed as prevalences, both absolute values and percentages, together with differences in the prevalence between groups (and 95 percent confidence intervals). The differences in the proportions of patients with and those without lesions or complications were compared with chi-square tests. Yates' correction was incorporated whenever the number of patients in one cell of a fourfold table was less than 10.

Results

Postmortem results were available for 755 patients. Thirteen were excluded before autopsy, and 29 were excluded because examination of the small bowel would have been technically difficult or the results uninterpretable for the purposes of this study (Table 1). Thus, the results of autopsy examinations on 713 patients (including 49 who died outside the hospital) are included. Of these, 249 had had some form of NSAID prescribed during the six months before death and 464 had not (Table 2). There were 74 patients in the long-term NSAID group; these included 25 patients with osteoarthritis, 20 with rheumatoid arthritis, 8 with other forms of arthritis, and 2 with bone metastases; the reason for the regular prescription of NSAIDs was not clear in 19 patients. The aspirin group comprised 63 patients, for 61 of whom no more than 300 mg of aspirin daily had been prescribed for cardiovascular or cerebrovascular indications. The short-term NSAID group comprised 112 patients, of whom 34 were receiving analgesia for disseminated cancer, 18 for osteoarthritis, 11 for unclassified low back or sciatic-root pain, 7 for traumatic musculoskel-

© N Engl J Med 1992; 327: 749–754

etal injury, and 16 for a variety of other indications. We were unable to determine why NSAIDs had been prescribed for 26 of the patients in the short-term NSAID group. There were no significant differences in age or the length of time from death to postmortem examination between the four groups. The proportion of women in the long-term NSAID group was higher than in the other three groups. Men predominated in the short-term NSAID and aspirin groups (Table 2). The major causes of death in the NSAID and control groups did not differ significantly (Table 3).

Abnormalities of the Small Intestine

Specific mucosal lesions were identified in the small intestine in 4 of the 249 patients in the NSAID group (1.6 percent) and 7 of the 464 patients in the control group (1.5 percent) (Table 4). Nonspecific erosions or areas of inflammation were found in four patients (1.6 percent) in the NSAID group. In the control group, two patients had acute jejunal erosions, both of whom had received slow-release oral potassium supplements. Two other control patients had areas of unexplained mucosal erosion or inflammation.

Table 2. Demographic Characteristics of the NSAID and Control Groups.*

Group	No. of Patients	Age	Male:Female Ratio	Time between Death and Autopsy
		yr		hr
Long-term NSAID use	74	68±11	0.6	34±23
Short-term NSAID use	112	67±14	1.3	35±24
Aspirin use only	63	70±12	1.4	32±27
Total	249	68±13	1.1	34±24
Control	464	69±15	1.0	34±22

*Plus–minus values are means ±SD. The NSAID group was subdivided according to the length of drug use: daily use for at least six months (long-term use) and intermittent or daily use for less than six months (short-term use).

Nonspecific ulcers were found in 21 patients (8.4 percent) in the NSAID group and 3 patients (0.6 percent) in the control group (Table 4). Possible confounding etiologic factors were identified in four patients with nonspecific ulceration in the NSAID group (recent anticancer chemotherapy or oral potassium supplementation). The difference between the two groups was also significant if these four patients were excluded from the calculation (difference, 6.2 percent; 95 percent confidence interval, 2.9 to 10.5 percent; $P<0.001$). The prevalence of nonspecific ulceration was slightly higher in the long-term NSAID group (10 patients, 13.5 percent) than in the short-term NSAID and aspirin groups combined (11 patients, 6.3 percent) (difference, 7.2 percent; 95 percent confidence interval, −1.3 to +15.5 percent; $0.05<P<0.1$). The lesions in the patients in the long-term NSAID group were single or multiple and ranged from tiny punched-out ulcers on the tips of valvulae conniventes (Fig. 1A) to confluent areas of deep ulceration and stricture formation (Fig. 1B). Three patients (4.1 percent) in the long-term NSAID group died as a direct consequence of peritonitis from perforated, nonspecific small intestinal ulcers; no patient in any other group had such

Table 3. Causes of Death in the NSAID and Control Groups.*

Cause of Death	NSAID Group (N = 249)	Control Group (N = 464)
	no. (%)	
Cardiac infarction or failure	79 (31.7)	131 (28.2)
Pneumonia	23 (9.2)	57 (12.3)
Pulmonary embolism	14 (5.6)	35 (7.5)
Stroke	11 (4.4)	30 (6.5)
Bronchial carcinoma	21 (8.4)	27 (5.8)
Gastrointestinal cancer	14 (5.6)	24 (5.2)
Other types of cancer	25 (10.0)	33 (7.1)
Hepatic failure	2 (0.8)	17 (3.7)
Kidney failure	7 (2.8)	8 (1.7)
Suicide, trauma, or burns	7 (2.8)	10 (2.2)
Bleeding or perforated peptic ulcer	14 (5.6)	12 (2.6)
Small-bowel perforation	3 (1.2)	0
Large-bowel perforation	3 (1.2)	2 (0.4)
Miscellaneous or unknown	26 (10.4)	78 (16.8)

*Percentages do not total 100 percent because of rounding.

Table 4. Small-Intestinal Abnormalities Identified at Autopsy in the NSAID and Control Groups.

Abnormality	NSAID Group (N = 249)	Control Group (N = 464)
	no. (%)	
Specific mucosal lesions		
Vasculitis	0	2
Crohn's disease	0	2
Lymphoma	0	1
Amyloidosis	1	1
Tuberculosis	1	1
Yersiniosis	1	0
Pseudomembranous enterocolitis	1	0
Subtotal	4 (1.6)	7 (1.5)
Nonspecific erosion or inflammation		
Acute erosion of the jejunum	1	2*
Acute erosion of the ileum	2	1
Mucosal inflammation (no erosion or ulcer)	1	1
Subtotal	4 (1.6)	4 (0.9)
Nonspecific ulceration		
Jejunal ulceration	5	0
Ileal ulceration	12	3
Perforated nonspecific ulcer	2	0
Ulcers in jejunum and ileum	4	0
Perforated nonspecific ulcer	1	0
Subtotal	21 (8.4)†	3 (0.6)‡
Total	29 (11.6)	14 (3.0)§

*Both patients were taking slow-release potassium.

†Four patients had recently received chemotherapy or potassium supplements.

‡The difference between groups was 7.8 percent (95 percent confidence interval, 5.0 to 10.6 percent; $P<0.001$).

§The difference between groups was 8.6 percent (95 percent confidence interval, 4.9 to 12.3 percent; $P<0.001$).

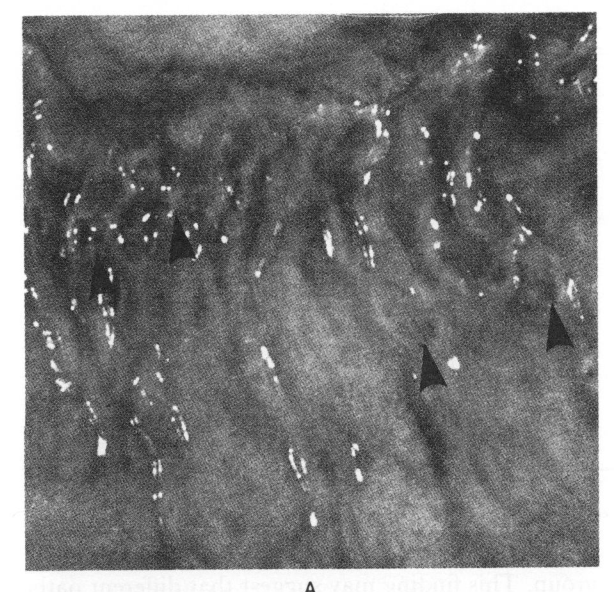
A

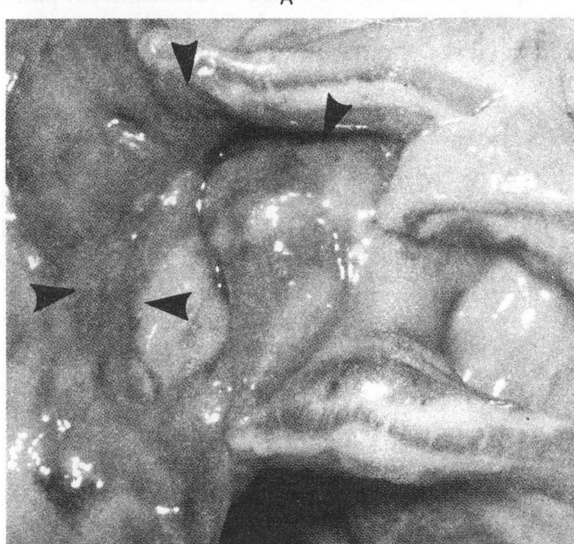
B

C

Figure 1. Pathologic Findings at Autopsy of Three Patients Who Used NSAIDs.

Panel A shows ulcers (arrowheads) on the mucosal surface of the jejunum in an 81-year-old man who had received NSAIDs for cervical spondylosis for seven months. Panel B shows deep ulceration (arrowheads) and stricture of the distal ileum in a 66-year-old woman with rheumatoid arthritis. The mucosa at the bottom left and extreme right of the field is normal. Panel C shows perforation of the proximal jejunum in an 82-year-old woman. Superficial ulcers radiate from the perforation (arrowheads). This patient also had multiple ileal ulcers.

lesions. All three of these patients had widespread ileal ulceration, and one also had a solitary jejunal perforation (Fig. 1C). Small-bowel disease had not been suspected clinically in these patients, and no specific or confounding etiologic factors could be identified. There were no other serious complications or deaths from small-intestinal disease in this series (those with bowel infarction had already been excluded).

Gastric and Duodenal Ulcers

There were 54 patients with gastric or duodenal ulcers in the NSAID group (21.7 percent) as compared with 57 in the control group (12.3 percent) (Table 5). This difference was explained by a significantly greater number of patients with gastric ulcers in the NSAID group (35 as compared with 27 patients in the control group). Gastric ulcers were slightly more prevalent in short-term NSAID users (19 patients, 17.0 percent) than in long-term users (9 patients, 12.2 percent) or those in the aspirin group (7 patients, 11.1 percent). In contrast, duodenal ulcers were more equally distributed between patients with and those without a history of the use of NSAIDs. There were 34 control patients (7.3 percent) and 26 NSAID users (10.4 percent) with duodenal ulcers.

More NSAID users had two or more ulcers of the stomach and duodenum than control patients (21 vs. 14 patients, 8.4 percent vs. 3.0 percent; difference, 5.4 percent; 95 percent confidence interval, 2.1 to 8.7 percent; $P<0.001$). Death from perforation or hemorrhage was more frequent in the NSAID group (14 patients, 5.6 percent) than in the control group (12 patients, 2.6 percent).

Relation between Small-Bowel and Upper Gastrointestinal Lesions in the NSAID Group

There was no demonstrable association between NSAID-associated gastric and duodenal ulcers and lesions of the small intestine. Five of the 54 patients (9.3 percent) who used NSAIDs and had ulcers of the stomach or duodenum had nonspecific ulcers of the small intestine. The latter were present in 16 of 195 patients (8.2 percent) without ulcers of the stomach or duodenum.

Discussion

We studied the prevalence of gastrointestinal ulcers and their complications in a large number of patients at autopsy. The main limitation of the study was the inability to obtain information from the patients

Table 5. Gastric Ulcers, Duodenal Ulcers, and Their Complications at Autopsy in the NSAID and Control Groups.*

Variable	Control Group (N = 464)	Short-Term NSAID Group (N = 112)	Long-Term NSAID Group (N = 74)	Aspirin Group (N = 63)	NSAID Group (N = 249)	Prevalence Difference†	
						% (95% CI)	P value
	number (percent)						
Single gastric ulcer	13	7	5	2	—	—	—
Multiple gastric ulcers	10	9	1	4	—	—	—
Gastric and duodenal ulcers	4	3	3	1	—	—	—
Duodenal ulcer alone	30	11	6	2	—	—	—
Total with gastric ulcer	27 (5.8)	19 (17.0)	9 (12.2)	7 (11.1)	35 (14.0)	8.2 (3.9 to 12.5)	<0.001
Total with duodenal ulcer	34 (7.3)	14 (12.5)	9 (12.2)	3 (4.8)	26 (10.4)	3.1 (−1.2 to 7.4)	NS
Total with gastric ulcer, duodenal ulcer, or both	57 (12.3)	30 (26.8)	15 (20.3)	9 (14.3)	54 (21.7)	9.4 (3.9 to 15.1)	<0.001
Death from bleeding or perforated peptic ulcer	12 (2.5)	6 (5.3)	5 (6.8)	1 (1.6)	14 (5.6)	3.1 (0.2 to 6.0)	<0.05

*CI denotes confidence interval, and NS not significant.

†The differences are those between the control group and the NSAID groups combined.

themselves about compliance and the use of drugs obtained without prescription (aspirin and ibuprofen can be purchased without a prescription in the United Kingdom). It could be argued, however, that the influences of the use of nonprescription drugs and noncompliance led to an underestimation of the risks of ulceration of the stomach and small intestine in patients taking NSAIDs. This argument is based on the belief that more patients in the NSAID population would have had ulcers if all had adhered to their prescribed drug regimens and that nonprescription NSAIDs might have caused some of the lesions in the control group.

Numerous epidemiologic and endoscopic studies have documented the risks of gastric and duodenal ulcers in patients taking NSAIDs.[1] Gastric ulcers are more common than duodenal ulcers in such patients.[2,24] We found that there was also an association between NSAID use and gastric ulcers in older patients with terminal illnesses. Although the prevalence of duodenal ulcers in the NSAID and control groups did not differ, the higher death rate from gastric and duodenal ulcers combined in the NSAID group was accounted for by a higher rate of complications due to duodenal ulcers. These findings, which are in agreement with those from a large case–control study,[25] lend support to the view that NSAIDs increase the risk of complications from preexisting duodenal ulcers.

The main finding in this study was the higher prevalence of nonspecific ulcers of the small intestine in the NSAID group than in the control group. By convention the term "nonspecific ulcer" does not apply to patients with identifiable etiologic factors such as Crohn's disease, vasculitis, or infection.[26] Focal ischemia[27] and the use of slow-release potassium chloride tablets[28] have been implicated in the development of nonspecific ulcers, but one large retrospective study failed to identify any predisposing factors in the great majority of cases.[26] The higher prevalence of ulceration and perforation of the small intestine in our long-term NSAID group contrasted with the more frequent gastric ulceration in the short-term NSAID group. This finding may suggest that different pathophysiologic mechanisms underlie the development of gastric ulcers and ulcers of the small intestine in patients taking NSAIDs.

Techniques involving radionuclides and sugar permeability probes have been used to examine the integrity of the small-intestinal mucosa in patients taking NSAIDs.[18-22] Bjarnason interpreted the results of his work and that of others as indicating that NSAID enteropathy occurs in approximately two thirds of patients taking NSAIDs regularly for at least six months.[29] This enteropathy is thought to be characterized by intestinal inflammation, occult blood loss, and protein-losing enteropathy. Iron-deficiency anemia and occult blood loss in the feces are common clinical problems in patients with rheumatic diseases taking NSAIDs, and upper gastrointestinal endoscopy identifies a possible cause in only half these patients.[30,31] The results of a recent enteroscopic study suggested that 66 percent of such patients have "red spots" or ulcers of the small intestine.[23] Thus, the small intestine is a likely site of occult inflammation and blood loss in long-term users of NSAIDs. Our results support the view that long-term users of NSAIDs are at greater risk of damaging the small intestine than short-term users.[29] The 14 percent prevalence of nonspecific ulcers in long-term users contrasts with the reported 70 percent prevalence of NSAID enteropathy in previous studies.[20,21,29] This difference could be explained by the wider selection criteria used in this study. Alternatively, technical factors, such as mucosal autolysis, could have limited our ability to detect minor erosions in the small intestine.

In conclusion, we found an association between the use of NSAIDs and nonspecific ulceration of the small intestine. The majority of the lesions were subclinical, but some patients had serious complications due to their ulcers. Our findings, taken together with those of the case–control study of Langman et al.[8] and the numerous reports of small-bowel complications in patients taking NSAIDs,[9-15] lead us to propose that these drugs may be responsible for a large proportion of hitherto unexplained ulcers of the small intestine.

We are indebted to the medical and technical staff of the Departments of Pathology at the Western Infirmary and Gartnavel General Hospital, Glasgow, especially Professor R.N.M. MacSween, Dr. A. Mowat, and Dr. B. Michie; to Ms. E. Munro, Glasgow Procurator Fiscal Depute, and her staff; and to the Department of Forensic Medicine, University of Glasgow.

References

1. Soll AH, moderator. Nonsteroidal anti-inflammatory drugs and peptic ulcer disease. Ann Intern Med 1991;114:307-19.
2. Graham DY, Agrawal NM, Roth SH. Prevention of NSAID-induced gastric ulcer with misoprostol: multicentre, double-blind, placebo-controlled trial. Lancet 1988;2:1277-80.
3. Griffin MR, Piper JM, Daugherty JR, Snowden M, Ray WA. Nonsteroidal anti-inflammatory drug use and increased risk for peptic ulcer disease in elderly persons. Ann Intern Med 1991;114:257-63.
4. Somerville K, Faulkner G, Langman MS. Non-steroidal anti-inflammatory drugs and bleeding peptic ulcer. Lancet 1986;1:462-4.
5. Armstrong CP, Blower AL. Non-steroidal anti-inflammatory drugs and life-threatening complications of peptic ulceration. Gut 1987;28:527-32.
6. Holvoet J, Terriere L, Van Hee W, Verbist L, Fierens E, Hautekeete ML. Relation of upper gastrointestinal bleeding to non-steroidal anti-inflammatory drugs and aspirin: a case-control study. Gut 1991;32:730-4.
7. Beardon PHG, Brown SV, McDevitt DG. Gastrointestinal events in patients prescribed non-steroidal anti-inflammatory drugs: a controlled study using record linkage in Tayside. Q J Med 1989;71:497-505.
8. Langman MJS, Morgan L, Worrall A. Use of anti-inflammatory drugs by patients admitted with small or large bowel perforations and haemorrhage. BMJ 1985;290:347-9.
9. Day TK. Intestinal perforation associated with osmotic slow release indomethacin capsules. BMJ 1983;287:1671-2.
10. Deakin M. Small bowel perforation associated with an excessive dose of slow release diclofenac sodium. BMJ 1988;297:488-9.
11. Madhok R, MacKenzie JA, Lee FD, Bruckner FE, Terry TR, Sturrock RD. Small bowel ulceration in patients receiving non-steroidal anti-inflammatory drugs for rheumatoid arthritis. Q J Med 1986;58:53-8.
12. Saw KC, Quick CRG, Higgins AF. Ileocaecal perforation and bleeding — are non-steroidal anti-inflammatory drugs (NSAIDs) responsible? J R Soc Med 1990;83:114-5.
13. Sturges HF, Krone CL. Ulceration and stricture of the jejunum in a patient on long-term indomethacin therapy. Am J Gastroenterol 1973;59:162-9.
14. Neoptolemos JP, Locke TJ. Recurrent small bowel obstruction associated with phenylbutazone. Br J Surg 1983;70:244-5.
15. Saverymuttu SH, Thomas A, Grundy A, Maxwell JD. Ileal stricturing after long-term indomethacin treatment. Postgrad Med J 1986;62:967-8.
16. Bjarnason I, Price AB, Zanelli G, et al. Clinicopathological features of nonsteroidal antiinflammatory drug-induced small intestinal strictures. Gastroenterology 1988;94:1070-4.
17. Lang J, Price AB, Levi AJ, Burke M, Gumpel JM, Bjarnason I. Diaphragm disease: pathology of disease of the small intestine induced by non-steroidal anti-inflammatory drugs. J Clin Pathol 1988;41:516-26.
18. Bjarnason I, Williams P, So A, et al. Intestinal permeability and inflammation in rheumatoid arthritis: effects of non-steroidal anti-inflammatory drugs. Lancet 1984;2:1171-4.
19. Bjarnason I, Williams P, Smethurst P, Peters TJ, Levi AJ. Effect of non-steroidal anti-inflammatory drugs and prostaglandins on the permeability of the human small intestine. Gut 1986;27:1292-7.
20. Jenkins RT, Rooney PJ, Jones DB, Bienenstock J, Goodacre RL. Increased intestinal permeability in patients with rheumatoid arthritis: a side-effect of oral nonsteroidal anti-inflammatory drug therapy? Br J Rheumatol 1987;26:103-7.
21. Bjarnason I, Zanelli G, Smith T, et al. Nonsteroidal antiinflammatory drug-induced intestinal inflammation in humans. Gastroenterology 1987;93:480-9.
22. Bjarnason I, Zanelli G, Prouse P, et al. Blood and protein loss via small-intestinal inflammation induced by non-steroidal anti-inflammatory drugs. Lancet 1987;2:711-4.
23. Morris AJ, Madhok R, Sturrock RD, Capell HA, MacKenzie JF. Enteroscopic diagnosis of small bowel ulceration in patients receiving non-steroidal anti-inflammatory drugs. Lancet 1991;337:520.
24. Silvoso GR, Ivey KJ, Butt JH, et al. Incidence of gastric lesions in patients with rheumatic disease on chronic aspirin therapy. Ann Intern Med 1979;91:517-20.
25. Griffin MR, Ray WA, Schaffner W. Nonsteroidal anti-inflammatory drug use and death from peptic ulcer in elderly persons. Ann Intern Med 1988;109:359-63.
26. Boydstun JS Jr, Gaffey TA, Bartholomew LG. Clinicopathologic study of nonspecific ulcers of the small intestine. Dig Dis Sci 1981;26:911-6.
27. Wayte DM, Helwig EB. Small-bowel ulceration — iatrogenic or multifactorial origin? Am J Clin Pathol 1968;49:26-40.
28. Leijonmarck CE, Raf L. Ulceration of the small intestine due to slow-release potassium chloride tablets. Acta Chir Scand 1985;151:273-8.
29. Bjarnason I. Non-steroidal anti-inflammatory drug-induced small intestinal inflammation in man. In: Pounder RE, ed. Recent advances in gastroenterology. Vol. 7. Edinburgh, Scotland: Churchill Livingstone, 1988:23-46.
30. Collins AJ, Du Toit JA. Upper gastrointestinal findings and faecal occult blood in patients with rheumatic diseases taking nonsteroidal anti-inflammatory drugs. Br J Rheumatol 1987;26:295-8.
31. Upadhyay R, Torley HI, McKinlay AW, Sturrock RD, Russell RI. Iron deficiency anaemia in patients with rheumatic disease receiving non-steroidal anti-inflammatory drugs: the role of upper gastrointestinal lesions. Ann Rheum Dis 1990;49:359-62.

© Ann Surg 1992; 216: 656–662

Pancreatic Exocrine and Endocrine Function After Operations for Chronic Pancreatitis

ROBERT P. JALLEH, F.R.C.S., and ROBIN C. N. WILLIAMSON, M.D., F.R.C.S.

From the Department of Surgery, Royal Postgraduate Medical School, Hammersmith Hospital, London, United Kingdom

Exocrine and endocrine function of the pancreas was assessed in the early postoperative period (≤2 months) and subsequently (mean, 25 months; range, 3 to 120) in 103 patients (69 men, 34 women; mean age, 42.4 ± 11.6 years) undergoing operation for chronic pancreatitis. Alcohol was the main causative agent (69%) and pain the most frequent indication (87%) for operation. Drainage procedures (n = 23) did not alter pancreatic function either initially or on long-term follow-up. In the early postoperative period, distal pancreatectomy (n = 42) often impaired endocrine function without affecting exocrine function; seven patients (17%) became diabetic, and results of oral glucose tolerance test showed deterioration in 23 of 28 patients (82%, $p < 0.05$). On subsequent follow-up, 11 patients developed exocrine failure ($p < 0.01$) and 10 patients endocrine ($p < 0.01$) failure. Proximal pancreatectomy (n = 38) precipitated clinical exocrine failure in 14 patients (37%, $p < 0.01$), yet pancreolauryl tests in 18 patients showed little objective change in exocrine status ($0.50 > p > 0.10$). Endocrine function was initially spared after proximal pancreatectomy, but six additional patients (16%, $p < 0.05$) required treatment for diabetes at a mean of 19 months (range, 3 to 34). Deterioration in pancreatic function is thus not an invariable immediate consequence of pancreatic drainage procedures or partial pancreatectomy for chronic pancreatitis. Progression of disease must account, in part, for failure of both exocrine and endocrine function on long-term follow-up. Drainage operations appear to delay this progressive decline in pancreatic function.

OPERATIONS FOR CHRONIC pancreatitis are performed to relieve severe intractable pain and to deal with complications such as pseudocyst, biliary obstruction, and bleeding. Although success is generally judged on the extent of pain relief, the choice of operative procedure is influenced by consideration of pancreatic exocrine and endocrine function. In patients with pancreatic duct dilatation or pseudocyst, for example, a decompressive (drainage) operation can relieve pain without sacrificing function.[1] Preservation of endocrine function is also the object of newer operations such as pancreatic autotransplantation (segmental or islet cell) after massive pancreatic resection.[2,3]

Preoperative tests of pancreatic function help to assess the severity of disease[4] and to guide perioperative metabolic requirements. After operation, impaired exocrine and endocrine function can lead to malnutrition and other risks, including death.[5] Pancreatic function testing is thus important for proper patient management. Although most surgical series include some description of pancreatic function, full analysis and comparison between different reports is a difficult exercise. Often, only a single type of operation is performed in a particular series, yet considerable variation exists in surgical procedures recommended for chronic pancreatitis.[6,7] Compounding factors include unspecified definitions of normal and abnormal pancreatic function and differences in investigations employed, data interpretation, and duration of follow-up. To our knowledge, no report has yet focused solely on the effect of operations on pancreatic exocrine and endocrine function in chronic pancreatitis. Changes in the immediate postoperative period are especially neglected.

We present a survey of pancreatic function in a personal series of 103 patients undergoing operation for severe chronic pancreatitis. This report is aimed at providing a descriptive analysis of both the early and long-term metabolic sequelae of partial pancreatectomy and drainage procedures, together with implications for patient management. It is based on clinical review and the use of simple but informative investigations that are easily performed in most hospitals.

Address reprint requests to Robin C. N. Williamson, M.D., F.R.C.S., Department of Surgery, Royal Postgraduate Medical School, Hammersmith Hospital, DuCane Road, London W12 ONN, United Kingdom.

Accepted for publication February 4, 1992.

© Ann Surg 1992; 216: 656–662

Materials and Methods

Patients

A personal series was reviewed of 119 patients undergoing partial pancreatectomy or drainage procedures for chronic pancreatitis between February 1978 and September 1991 at Bristol Royal Infirmary or the Hammersmith Hospital, London. The diagnosis was confirmed histologically or on radiologic and operative findings. Our policy throughout this period was to evaluate both exocrine and endocrine function before and after operation, although in some cases emergency presentation or early discharge precluded full documentation. We found sufficient information to allow analysis of pancreatic function in 103 patients, who form the basis of this study. Patient characteristics are outlined in Table 1. There were 69 men and boys and 34 women and girls (male:female = 2:1), with a mean age of 42.4 years (range, 7 to 70 years). Seventy-two patients (69%) gave a strong history of alcohol abuse (estimated consumption = 202 ± 212 g/day, mean ± standard deviation) over an estimated 13.8 ± 9.3 years. Severe abdominal pain, either of a constant or recurrent, episodic nature, was a feature in 90 (87%) patients. At least 60 of these had a history of opiate intake, and eight had failed fluoroscopy-guided percutaneous celiac plexus blocks.

Operations

Operative procedures were classified into three groups: pancreatic drainage, distal pancreatectomy, and proximal pancreatectomy. Twenty-three patients underwent drainage operations. These consisted of longitudinal pancreaticojejunostomy, with at least an 8- to 10-cm pancreaticoenteric anastomosis, in 11 patients and a pseudocyst-jejunostomy Roux-en-Y in eight patients.[8] Four patients had combined pseudocyst and pancreatic duct drainage, and six had concomitant biliary drainage procedures. Distal pancreatectomy involved a 40% to 70% resection, and in 13 of 42 patients the spleen was conserved.[9] Definitions of the estimated amount of pancreatic tissue excised are detailed elsewhere.[10] Pylorus-preserving pancreatoduodenectomy was performed in 33 of the 38 patients undergoing proximal pancreatic resection and involved loss of approximately half the gland.[5] In our current practice, a conventional Whipple's operation is performed only in cases with duodenal scarring or where invasive carcinoma is suspected.

Assessment of Pancreatic Function

Pancreatic function was assessed shortly before and after operation. Assessment was based on clinical criteria and on exocrine and endocrine function tests undertaken in the early postoperative period (defined as within 2 months of operation). Only clinical information was used for long-term assessment, because most of these patients were not readmitted for investigations unless symptomatically indicated. Duration of follow-up was taken as the interval between operation and the last verified record of the patient's condition. In nine patients, six undergoing distal and three proximal pancreatectomy, the duration of follow-up for purposes of this study was limited by completion total pancreatectomy.

Exocrine function. Diarrhea, steatorrhea, and the need for enzyme replacement therapy were clinical criteria for abnormal exocrine function. Objectively, this was measured using one of the following: 3-day collection of feces for estimation of fat content (normal < 7, intermediate 7 to 15, abnormal > 15 mmol/day), duodenal intubation

TABLE 1. *Patient Characteristics*

	Drainage Procedures n = 23	Distal Pancreatectomy n = 42	Proximal Pancreatectomy n = 38	Total n = 103
Sex				
M	13	27	29	69
F	10	15	9	34
Age				
Mean (yr)	43.9	40.5	44.4	42.4
Range (yr)	7–68	20–67	25–70	7–70
Etiology				
Alcohol	15	28	28	71
PAP	1	3	3	7
Congenital	—	—	1	1
Gallstones	1	—	—	1
Idiopathic	6	11	6	23
Duration of follow-up				
Mean (mo)	38	20	24	25
Range (mo)	5–77	3–120	3–120	3–120

PAP, previous attacks of idiopathic acute pancreatitis.

TABLE 2. *Diagnostic Venous Blood Glucose Values for Oral Glucose Tolerance Test*

	Fasting (mmol/L)		2 hr After Glucose (mmol/L)
Diabetes mellitus	≥6.7	and/or	≥10.0
Impaired glucose tolerance	<6.7	and	≥6.7–<10.0
Normal	<6.7	and	<6.7

Adapted from the Report of the WHO Study Group on Diabetes Mellitus 1985.

studies with pancreatic stimulation, and the Pancreolauryl test[11] (normal > 30%, intermediate 20% to 30%, abnormal < 20%). The first two methods were employed in a few patients during the early years of this study and have since been discontinued. Although semiquantitative and an indirect measure of exocrine function, the convenience of the Pancreolauryl test (Charwell Pharmaceuticals, Ltd., Alton, Hampshire, UK) makes this our current investigation of choice.

Endocrine function. Clinically, a diagnosis of abnormal endocrine function was made based on the need to treat diabetes mellitus with diet modification, oral hypoglycemic agents, or insulin. Oral glucose tolerance test (GTT), measuring venous whole blood glucose levels, was used for objective assessment. Blood samples were taken before a 75-g glucose loading dose, and at 30-minute intervals thereafter up to 120 minutes. Patients were classified into diabetes mellitus, impaired GTT, or normal groups according to criteria set by the 1985 WHO Study Group on diabetes mellitus (Table 2).[12]

Statistical Analysis

Chi square and two-tailed paired t tests were used.

Results

Exocrine Function

Drainage operations (n = 23). Using clinical criteria, drainage procedures did not affect pancreatic exocrine function in the early postoperative period (Fig. 1). In six patients in whom data from exocrine function tests were available, three showed worsening of function, and three showed some improvement. These changes were minimal and confined to the intermediate and abnormal ranges. There was also no alteration in exocrine function profile of these patients during long-term follow-up.

Distal pancreatectomy (n = 42). Exocrine function was not altered in the early postoperative period after distal pancreatic resection. Of 11 patients (27%) who had evidence of exocrine insufficiency before operation, nine continued to require enzyme replacement after resection. Treatment was stopped in two patients without side effects, whereas another two needed enzymes for steatorrhea developing after operation. Our clinical assessment was supported by analysis of the pancreolauryl ratio in 17 patients (Fig. 2). A 31-year-old man, who had pancreatic and biliary sphincteroplasty in addition to 50% distal pancreatectomy, showed a marked improvement of pancreolauryl ratio from 11% to 81% after operation. In this particular instance, histologically proven papillary fibrosis probably contributed to the gross preoperative exocrine dysfunction. On long-term follow-up, 11 additional patients developed symptoms of malabsorption and were placed on enzyme replacement at a mean of 13 (range, 3 to 38) months after operation. One patient had apparent improvement in exocrine function and was able to discontinue enzyme therapy without developing symptoms.

Proximal pancreatectomy (n = 38). In contrast to drainage procedures and distal resections, there was substantial deterioration in exocrine function in patients un-

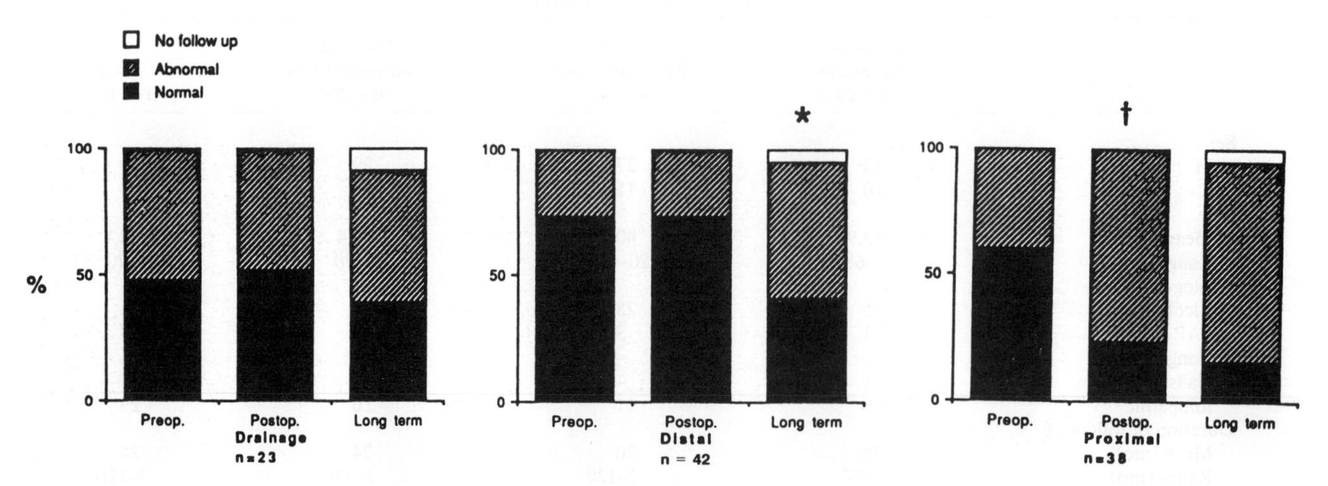

FIG. 1. Clinical assessment of exocrine function. Statistical significance (chi square test): *p < 0.01 *versus* postoperative value, †p < 0.01 *versus* preoperative value.

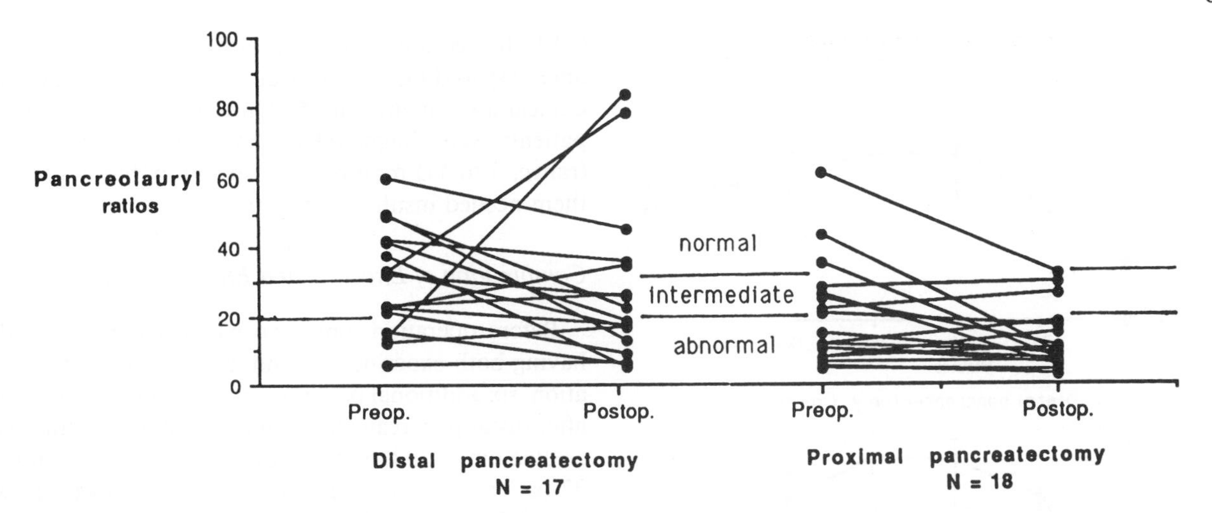

FIG. 2. Pancreolauryl ratios in patients undergoing partial pancreatectomy. There was no significant difference between preoperative and postoperative profiles in either group.

dergoing proximal pancreatectomy. No patient showed an improvement in function. Fourteen patients (37%) were started on enzyme replacement as a direct consequence of operation. Pancreolauryl ratios before and after operation in 18 patients, however, did not reflect our clinical findings (Fig. 2). Long-term follow-up showed that only one further patient went into exocrine failure, 51 months after resection. No difference in exocrine function profiles was observed between those undergoing pylorus-preserving pancreatoduodenectomy and Whipple's operation ($0.50 > p > 0.10$).

Endocrine Function

Drainage operations. There was no change in the incidence of diabetes mellitus during the postoperative period (Fig. 3), and GTT was likewise unaltered (Fig 4). On subsequent follow-up, only two patients required insulin therapy, at 54 and 77 months after operation.

Distal pancreatectomy. Only one of 42 patients was on insulin at presentation. Seven patients were rendered diabetic after operation, all but one of whom had at least a 60% distal resection. Five of these were treated with insulin, with a mean dose of 24 (range, 12 to 56) U/day. One patient was started on glibenclamide, and the other was advised on diet modification. Figure 4 highlights the significant impairment of postoperative GTT profiles in 28 patients, compared with preoperative data. On subsequent follow-up, a further 10 patients were diagnosed as diabetics at a mean of 14 (range, 5 to 24) months after operation. Eight of these, plus the patient initially on glibenclamide, required insulin at a mean daily dose of 25 (range, 6 to 28) units for adequate control of blood sugar levels. Two other patients were treated with oral hypo-

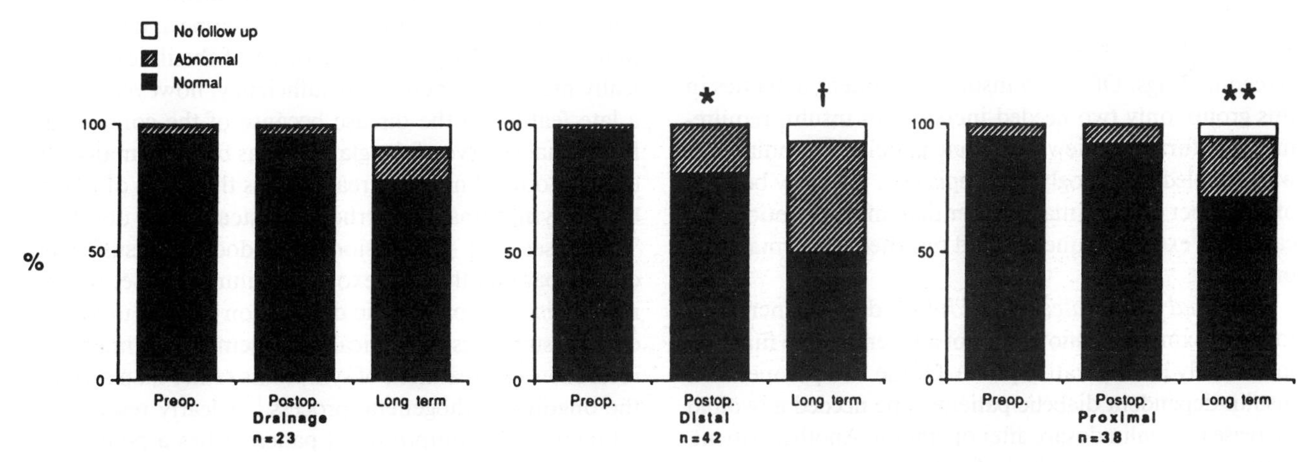

FIG. 3. Clinical assessment of endocrine function. Statistical significance (chi square test): *$p < 0.02$ *versus* preoperative value; †$p < 0.01$, **$p < 0.05$ *versus* postoperative value.

© Ann Surg 1992; 216: 656–662

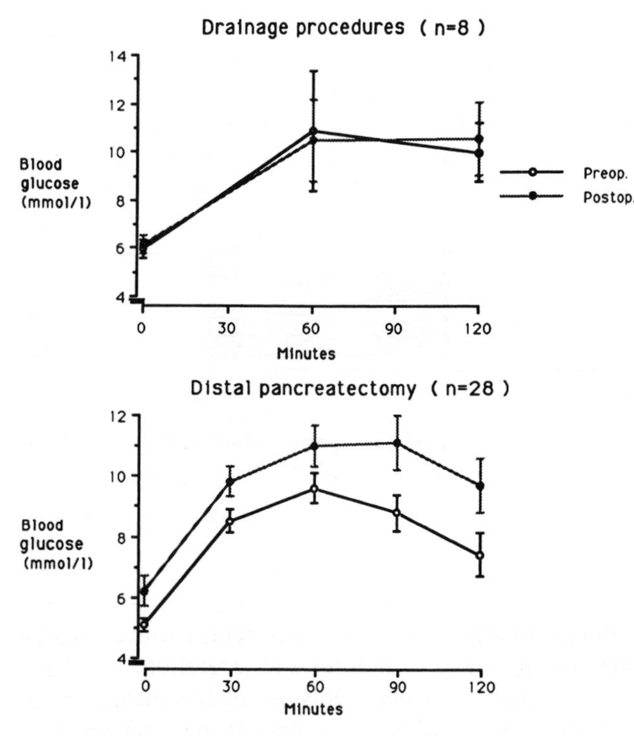

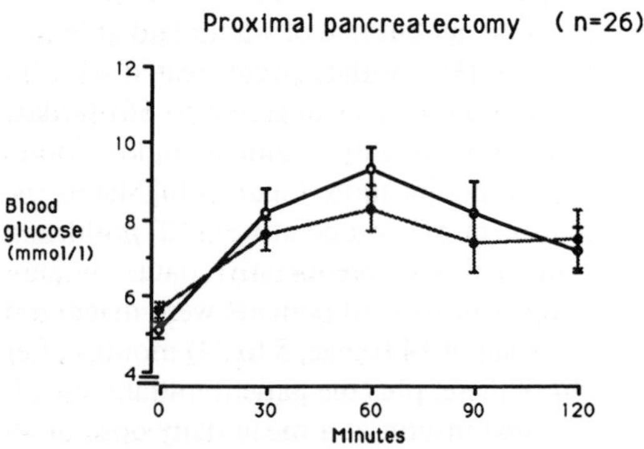

FIG. 4. Results of oral glucose tolerance tests before and after operation. Values represent mean ± SEM. In the distal pancreatectomy group (only), differences between pre- and postoperative mean values were significant at every point except at 30 minutes ($p < 0.05$).

glycemic drugs. Of the 15 insulin-dependent diabetics in this group, only two needed increases in insulin requirement on further review. Only one patient, a nondiabetic, was troubled by hypoglycemic episodes, probably because of improper dietary intake rather than malabsorption, because her exocrine function had returned to normal after operation.

Proximal pancreatectomy. Unlike distal pancreatectomy, proximal resections did not alter endocrine function in the early postoperative phase. Of the two preoperative insulin-dependent diabetic patients, one needed a twofold increase in insulin dosage after operation. Another patient, with a preoperative diabetic GTT but not on any treatment, was started on insulin (24 units) after postoperative GTT showed a deterioration of function. Glucose tolerance test findings in 26 of our 38 patients support this clinical assessment (Fig. 4). On long-term follow-up, six patients were diagnosed as diabetics at a mean of 19 (range, 3 to 41) months after operation, but only two of them needed insulin treatment.

Combination of Exocrine and Endocrine Function

Before operation, only two patients were assessed as having both exocrine and endocrine failure. After operation, six additional patients were diagnosed as such, four after distal pancreatectomy and two after proximal pancreatectomy. On long-term follow-up, however, a total of 22 patients (21%) needed treatment for diabetes as well as malabsorption. Although five late deaths were recorded in these 103 patients, none were related to pancreatic insufficiency or complications of chronic pancreatitis.

Discussion

This study indicates that an appropriate operation does not affect pancreatic function in many patients with chronic pancreatitis, even if half the gland is resected and even though most patients were left with residual disease. Drainage procedures do not alter pancreatic function either in the immediate postoperative period or on subsequent follow-up. Distal pancreatectomy compromises endocrine function without affecting exocrine function at an early stage, and proximal pancreatectomy precipitates exocrine but not endocrine insufficiency. The difference is attributable in part to the relative preponderance of islet cells in the body and tail of the pancreas.[13]

The natural history of chronic pancreatitis involves progressive deterioration of both exocrine and endocrine function, presumably related to progressive destruction of the gland. Ammann et al.[14] have shown that even without an operation, all patients with alcoholic (calcific) chronic pancreatitis develop both exocrine and endocrine failure within 14 years of the onset of the illness.[14] Clinically manifest pancreatic insufficiency, however, is often a late feature of the disease because of the considerable functional reserve of the gland. It has been estimated that enzyme output must decrease to less than 10% of normal before symptoms of diarrhea and steatorrhea develop.[15] The onset and progression of endocrine insufficiency closely parallel those of exocrine failure.[14,16] Because the mechanisms of pancreatic destruction remain unknown, current strategies in surgical management are mainly directed toward treatment of symptoms rather than arresting the ongoing pathogenetic process.[17] Clearly resection of a functionally compromised pancreas has a potential to adversely affect pancreatic function. The finding that it often does not do so presumably reflects the fact that in many cases the resected tissue has already been functionally destroyed.

Various investigations are currently employed to estimate pancreatic function. Tests of exocrine function may be classified into two groups, those quantifying pancreatic enzyme secretion after pancreatic stimulation and indirect measures of the digestive action of enzymes such as fecal fat estimation and various tubeless chemical tests.[18] Developed more than 20 years ago,[19] the Pancreolauryl test has now been shown to have a specificity of up to 97% and a sensitivity of up to 93%.[18] Further, Lankisch and co-workers[20] have shown that, as an indicator of pancreatic steatorrhea, the test has a positive predictive value of 76%.[20] Investigations of endocrine function involve identification of impaired insulin secretion and glucose metabolism. These include measurements of serum insulin and C peptide levels and 24-hour urinary C peptide estimation.[21] Abnormal intravenous and oral GTTs are indicators of impaired glucose metabolism. In this study, we have employed investigations that were noninvasive, inexpensive, and convenient to perform. We found that these tests adequately reflected the clinical status of our patients.

The theoretical advantage of a drainage operation is that it preserves remaining functional pancreatic tissue. Initial optimism, based on an experimental dog model,[22] that such operations may improve pancreatic function has not been supported by long-term clinical results despite radiologic evidence of anastomotic patency.[1,23] Reflecting our earlier experience,[8] both exocrine and endocrine function remained unchanged by drainage procedures, there being neither improvement nor deterioration. These observations suggest that pathologic changes in the diseased pancreatic parenchyma play a more important role in exocrine insufficiency than ductal strictures preventing flow of pancreatic enzymes to the duodenum. In line with findings from some earlier series[1,24] (but not others[23]), the long-term stability in both exocrine and endocrine function in our patients may indicate a beneficial effect of drainage procedures on the progression of pancreatitis. It is conceivable that this stabilization of disease is related to a reduction in the high parenchymal pressure that we and others have found in chronic pancreatitis[25,26] as a consequence of "filleting" the gland.

There was no appreciable change in exocrine function immediately after distal pancreatectomy. On long-term follow-up, however, 28% of patients developed symptoms of malabsorption. This deterioration in function was most likely due to continuing pancreatitis in the remaining proximal pancreas. The incidence of long-term exocrine failure in this study (56%) was comparable to that of earlier reports.[2,27] In the absence of data from the immediate postoperative period, it is impossible to determine whether exocrine failure in these series developed early or late. By contrast, distal pancreatectomy directly precipitated the need for insulin in 17% of patients, and this was accompanied by a significant deterioration in measured glucose tolerance. On long-term follow-up, the percentage of patients with diabetes increased to 46%, a figure similar to that previously reported for a 40% to 80% distal resection.[2,27,28] Although almost all our diabetic patients needed insulin, control was not difficult. It has been shown that the incidence of diabetes is directly related to the extent of resection.[27] In support, 75% of patients who developed postoperative diabetes underwent a 60% or greater distal resection.

The situation with proximal pancreatectomy is quite the reverse. The immediate effect of operation is a sharp decline in clinical exocrine function. Although 39% of patients were in exocrine failure before operation, 76% needed enzyme replacement after operation ($p < 0.01$). Clearly, in most patients, enzyme production in the remaining distal pancreas was unable to meet requirements for normal digestion. In addition, edema of the end-to-end pancreaticojejunostomy anastomosis could have caused temporary obstruction to the flow of pancreatic juice into the gut. The adverse effect of this "nondelivery" of pancreatic juice is highlighted by the Erlangen/Nurnberg experience, in which there was a distinct decline in exocrine function after use of an occlusive gel to obstruct the pancreatic duct after proximal pancreatectomy.[7] Pancreolauryl values remained unchanged after operation, however. It may be that as patients began to eat better with pain relief, pre-existing enzyme insufficiency (hidden by poor food intake) was unmasked. This probably accounts, in part, for the discrepancy between preoperative clinical and biochemical assessment of exocrine status. Exocrine function remained poor on long-term follow-up. Although generally not tested in our patients, anastomotic stricture and occlusion has been observed at autopsy after pancreatoduodenectomy.[29] Unlike exocrine function, endocrine function was preserved after proximal resection both clinically and on testing. Our experience parallels that of Beger et al.,[6] who studied endocrine function in patients 10 days after a modified operation to excise the diseased pancreatic head. Deterioration of glucose homeostasis in the long term is probably related to disease progression. Observed in 25% of patients, this prevalence is in keeping with more favorable reports in the literature.[6,30]

Assessment of exocrine and endocrine function has obvious therapeutic implications. In the immediate postoperative period, these data are used to identify early changes in function so as to either initiate new or modify existing treatment regimens. It also provides baseline values enabling subsequent comparison. Close scrutiny on continued follow-up of all patients forms an essential part in the total management of this disease.

References

1. Prinz RA, Greenlee HB. Pancreatic duct drainage in chronic pancreatitis. Hepatogastroenterology 1990; 37:295–300.
2. Morrow CE, Cohen J, Sutherland DER, Najarian JS. Chronic pancreatitis: long-term surgical results of pancreatic duct drainage, pancreatic resection and near-total pancreatic and islet autotransplantation. Surgery 1984; 96:608–615.
3. Rossi RL, Soeldner JS, Braasch JW, et al. Long-term results of pancreatic resection and segmental pancreatic autotransplantation for chronic pancreatitis. Am J Surg 1990; 159:51–58.
4. Latifi R, McIntosh JK, Dudrick SJ. Nutritional management of acute and chronic pancreatitis. Surg Clin North Am 1991; 71:579–595.
5. Williamson RCN, Cooper MJ. Resection in chronic pancreatitis. Br J Surg 1987; 74:807–812.
6. Beger HG, Buchler M, Bittner R. The duodenum preserving resection of the head of the pancreas (DPRHP) in patients with chronic pancreatitis and an inflammatory mass in the head. Acta Chir Scand 1990; 156:309–315.
7. Gebhardt C. Surgical treatment of pain in chronic pancreatitis. Acta Chir Scand 1990; 156:303–307.
8. Cooper MJ, Williamson RCN. Drainage operations in chronic pancreatitis. Br J Surg 1984; 71:761–766.
9. Aldridge MC, Williamson RCN. Distal pancreatectomy with and without splenectomy. Br J Surg 1991; 78:976–979.
10. Aldridge MC, Williamson RCN. Distal pancreatectomy in chronic pancreatitis. *In* Johnson CD, Imrie CW, eds. Pancreatic Disease: Progress and Prospects. London: Springer-Verlag, 1991, pp 127–135.
11. Barry RE, Barry R, Ene MD, Parker G. Fluorescein dilaurate—tubeless test for pancreatic exocrine failure. Lancet 1982; ii:742–744.
12. Alberti KGMM, Hockaday TAR. Diabetes mellitus. *In* Weatherall DJ, Ledingham JGG, Warrell DA, eds. Oxford Textbook of Medicine, 2nd Edition. New York: Oxford Medical Publications, 1987, pp 9.51–9.101.
13. Wittingen J, Frey CF. Islet concentration in the head, body, tail and uncinate process of the pancreas. Ann Surg 1974; 179:412–414.
14. Ammann RW, Akovbiantz A, Largiadier F, Schueler G. Course and outcome of chronic pancreatitis: longitudinal study of a mixed medical-surgical series of 245 patients. Gastroenterology 1984; 86:820–828.
15. DiMagno EP, Go VLW, Summerskill WHJ. Relations between pancreatic enzyme outputs and malabsorption in severe pancreatic insufficiency. N Engl J Med 1973; 288:813–815.
16. Doty JE, Fink AS, Meyer JH. Alterations in digestive function caused by pancreatic disease. Surg Clin North Am 1989; 69:447–465.
17. Rossi RL. Pancreatic resections for chronic pancreatitis. Hepatogastroenterology 1990; 37:277–282.
18. Li Y, Chiverton SG, Hunt RH. Exocrine pancreatic function tests. J Clin Gastroenterol 1989; 11:376–378.
19. Kaffarnik H, Meyer-Bertenrath JG. Zur Methodik und Klinischen Bedeutung eines neuen Pankreas-lipase-Tests mit Fluoresceindilaurinsaureester. Klin Wochenschr 1969; 47:221–223.
20. Lankisch PG, Otto J, Brauneis J, et al. Detection of pancreatic steatorrhea by oral pancreatic function tests. Dig Dis Sci 1988; 33: 1233–1236.
21. Kendall DM, Sutherland DER, Najarian JS, et al. Effects of hemipancreactomy on insulin secretion and glucose tolerance in healthy humans. N Engl J Med 1990; 322:898–903.
22. Carnevali JF, ReMine WH, Dockerty MB, et al. An experimental study of side-to-side pancreaticojejunostomy after ductal obstruction. Arch Surg 1960; 80:774–787.
23. Warshaw AL, Popp JW Jr, Schapiro RH. Long-term patency, pancreatic function and pain relief after lateral pancreaticojejunostomy for chronic pancreatitis. Gastroenterology 1980; 79:287–293.
24. Nealon WH, Townsend CM, Thompson JC. Operative drainage of the pancreatic duct delays functional impairment in patients with chronic pancreatitis. Ann Surg 1988; 208:321–329.
25. Jalleh RP, Aslam M, Williamson RCN. Pancreatic tissue and ductal pressures in chronic pancreatitis. Br J Surg 1991; 78:1235–1237.
26. Ebbehoj N, Borly L, Madsen, Svendsen LB. Pancreatic tissue pressure and pain in chronic pancreatitis. Pancreas 1986; 1:556–558.
27. Frey CF, Child CG III, Fry W. Pancreatectomy for chronic pancreatitis. Ann Surg 1976; 184:403–414.
28. Warshaw AL. Conservation of pancreatic tissue by combined gastric, biliary and pancreatic duct drainage for pain in chronic pancreatitis. Am J Surg 1985; 149:563–569.
29. Tashio S, Murata E, Hiraoka T, et al. New technique for pancreaticojejunostomy using a biological adhesive. Br J Surg 1987; 74: 292–294.
30. Rossi RL, Rothschild J, Braasch JW, et al. Pancreatoduodenectomy in the management of chronic pancreatitis. Arch Surg 1987; 122: 416–420.

Randomised controlled trial of azathioprine withdrawal in ulcerative colitis

A B Hawthorne, R F A Logan, C J Hawkey, P N Foster, A T R Axon, E T Swarbrick, B B Scott, J E Lennard-Jones

Abstract

***Objective*—To determine whether azathioprine can prevent relapse in ulcerative colitis.**

***Design*—One year placebo controlled double blind trial of withdrawal or continuation of azathioprine.**

***Setting*—Outpatient clinics of five hospitals.**

***Subjects*—79 patients with ulcerative colitis who had been taking azathioprine for six months or more. Patients in full remission for two months or more (67), and patients with chronic low grade or corticosteroid dependent disease (12) were randomised separately. 33 patients in remission received azathioprine and 34 placebo; five patients with chronic stable disease received azathioprine and seven placebo.**

***Main outcome measure*—Rate of relapse. Relapse was defined as worsening of symptoms or sigmoidoscopic appearance.**

***Results*—For the remission group the one year rate of relapse was 36% (12/33) for patients continuing azathioprine and 59% (20/34) for those taking placebo (hazard rate ratio 0·5, 95% confidence interval 0·25 to 1·0). For the subgroup of 54 patients in long term remission (greater than six months before entry to trial) benefit was still evident, with a 31% (8/26) rate of relapse with azathioprine and 61% (17/28) with placebo ($p<0·01$). For the small group of patients with chronic stable colitis (six were corticosteroid dependent and six had low grade symptoms) no benefit was found from continued azathioprine therapy. Adverse events were minimal.**

***Conclusions*—Azathioprine maintenance treatment in ulcerative colitis is beneficial for at least two years if patients have achieved remission while taking the drug. Demonstration of the relapse preventing properties of azathioprine has implications for a large number of patients with troublesome ulcerative colitis, who may benefit from treatment with azathioprine.**

Department of Therapeutics, Public Health Medicine, and Epidemiology, University Hospital, Nottingham NG7 2UH
A B Hawthorne, *research fellow*
R F A Logan, *senior lecturer in clinical epidemiology*
C J Hawkey, *professor of gastroenterology*

Leeds General Infirmary, Leeds LS1 3EX
P N Foster, *senior registrar*
A T R Axon, *consultant physician*

New Cross Hospital, Wolverhampton WV10 0QP
E T Swarbrick, *consultant physician*

Lincoln County Hospital, Lincoln
B B Scott, *consultant physician*

St Mark's Hospital, London EC1V
J E Lennard-Jones, *professor of gastroenterology*

Correspondence to: Dr Logan.

BMJ 1992;**305**:20-2

Introduction

Since the first reports of the use of azathioprine and mercaptopurine in ulcerative colitis,[1] there have been several uncontrolled studies reporting benefit but few placebo controlled trials. Two trials have shown evidence of a significant corticosteroid sparing effect in chronic active ulcerative colitis.[2,3] However, in acute relapse Jewell and Truelove found no significant benefit from adding azathioprine to a standard regimen of corticosteroids.[4] Some patients with chronic active or frequency relapsing disease are treated with azathioprine, and many of these achieve complete remission and can stop taking corticosteroids.[5] The further management of these patients is unclear. In Jewell and Truelove's study the benefit of azathioprine maintenance treatment was equivocal,[4] and many doctors are reluctant to continue prescribing the drug in view of the potential side effects of azathioprine, particularly bone marrow suppression. We designed a study to investigate whether continuing azathioprine treatment in these patients is beneficial.

Subjects and methods

We conducted a one year double blind withdrawal study in which patients who were already established on azathioprine were randomised to either continue the drug at the same dose or switch to an identical placebo. Approval from ethics committees in the participating hospitals was obtained, and all patients gave written informed consent. To be eligible for the study patients had to have had ulcerative colitis diagnosed on the basis of rectal biopsy and barium enema or colonoscopy and to have been taking azathioprine for a minimum of six months. Patients were categorised as being in remission or having chronic stable disease. Remission was defined as absence of symptoms of active disease in patients not taking corticosteroids and with a sigmoidoscopic appearance of grade 0 or 1 (as described by Baron *et al*[6]: 0=normal mucosa; 1=granular or oedematous mucosa with loss of vascular pattern; 2=bleeding to light touch; 3=spontaneous bleeding ahead of the instrument). Chronic stable disease was defined as low grade symptoms or symptom control with low doses of corticosteroids (10 mg prednisolone or less) with a sigmoidoscopic appearance of grade 0 or 1. Patients had to have been in remission or in a stable state with no change in dose of prednisolone if taking corticosteroids for a minimum of two months before entering the trial. For both groups the study end point was relapse, defined as worsening symptoms recognised by the patient as active disease (such as rectal bleeding, loose motions, or bowel frequency) with a sigmoidoscopic appearance of grade 1 or above or grade 2 or 3 appearance at routine sigmoidoscopy regardless of symptoms.

Patients were seen at entry to the trial, after one and two months, and then two monthly through the trial or earlier in the event of relapse. At each visit blood was taken for full blood count, liver function tests, and determination of erythrocyte sedimentation rate and α 1 acid glycoprotein concentration. If the platelet count fell below $120\times10^9/l$ or total white cell count below $3\times10^9/l$ the trial drug was stopped temporarily and reintroduced at a lower dose as indicated. Sigmoidoscopy and rectal biopsy were performed at entry and at two, six, and 12 months or at time of relapse. Patients kept a daily symptom diary, which was reviewed at clinic visits and included a record of tablet consumption. Compliance was monitored by a record of tablet consumption in the diary cards. Relapse was dated from the onset of worsening symptoms as recorded in the diaries.

Trial treatment was either the same dose of azathioprine as previously taken or an equivalent number of placebo tablets of identical appearance. Randomisation was performed in hospital pharmacies in blocks of four. Trial drugs or placebo were dispensed by the hospital pharmacies using separate randomisation schedules for the patients in remission and with chronic stable disease. Treatment with drugs containing 5-aminosalicylic acid was continued during the trial at the dose taken before entry.

We analysed the data initially by the Kaplan-Meier survival method using the generalised Wilcoxon test and the program KMSURV (Kaplan-Meier product limit estimates of S(t), Ludwig Institute for Cancer Research, release Nov 1988). A Cox's proportional hazards survival analysis was also done with the program EGRET. Our previous survey had shown a probability of relapse of about one third for patients in established remission who continued to take azathioprine.[5] To show an increase in relapse from 35% to 70% in those who stop taking azathioprine with a power of 0·8 (two tailed α=0·05) 70 patients would be required.

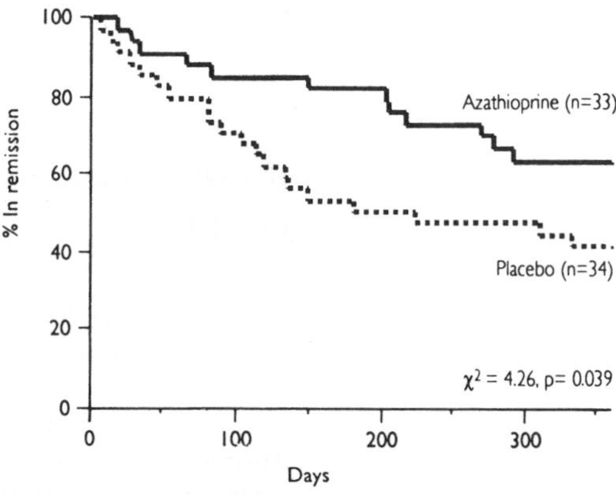

Kaplan-Meier survival plot of the rate of relapse over one year for 67 patients with ulcerative colitis in remission after taking azathioprine

Results

Patients were enrolled at five hospitals, with numbers from each hospital ranging from six to 39. Sixty seven patients with ulcerative colitis in remission were enrolled; 34 were randomised to receive placebo and 33 to continue azathioprine. Twelve patients with chronic stable disease were randomised separately; five received placebo and seven continued azathioprine. The characteristics of patients were generally similar in all trial groups (table), although there was a greater number of men randomised to placebo in the remission group. Overall, half of the patients had total colitis, the median azathioprine dose was 100 mg, and 67 of the 79 patients were taking aminosalicylates.

REMISSION GROUP

One patient defaulted from follow up at eight months and another stopped trial treatment at 11 months because of a misunderstanding (both were taking azathioprine). These patients' data were censored at the time of protocol violation. Two patients in the remission group were found, after completing the trial, to have Crohn's disease rather than ulcerative colitis. These patients were included in the primary analysis, but a secondary analysis was performed which excluded them.

Twelve (36%) of the 33 patients taking azathioprine relapsed compared with 20 (59%) of the 34 patients taking placebo (fig; Wilcoxon χ^2 statistic 4.26, p=0·039). Overall the relapse rate of those who continued taking azathioprine was half that of the patients who switched to placebo (hazard rate ratio 0·5, 95% confidence interval 0·25 to 1·0). All of the patients who relapsed had symptoms and in none was relapse diagnosed on abnormal sigmoidoscopic appearance alone. A secondary analysis excluding the two patients shown subsequently to have Crohn's disease (both were taking azathioprine and one relapsed) gave a relapse rate of 35% (11/31) for the azathioprine group compared with 59% for the placebo group (p=0·04). To investigate whether maintenance treatment was effective in patients with more prolonged remission or was restricted to those patients with a recent relapse a subgroup of 54 patients was identified who had been in remission for more than six months at entry to the trial. The one year relapse rate was 31% (8/26) for the patients taking azathioprine, and 61% (17/28) for those taking placebo (p=0·01).

In view of the modest trial size and the sex imbalance in the two treatment groups (table) the data were also analysed with Cox's proportional hazards model. The effects of sex, age, duration of remission before trial entry, and treatment were analysed independently and in combination. The relapse rate for women was similar to that for men (hazard rate ratio 1·03, p=0·93. There was a highly significant fall in relapse rate with increasing age (hazard rate ratio for one year older 0·95, 95% confidence interval 0·93 to 0·98; p<0·001). Longer duration of remission before trial entry was inversely related to relapse rate (hazard rate ratio 0·97, 0·93 to 1·01; p=0·10). In the model containing all four variables continued azathioprine treatment remained beneficial (hazard rate ratio 0·43, 0·20 to 0·93; p=0·03); the strong association between relapse rate and age was unchanged.

CHRONIC STABLE DISEASE GROUP

In the chronic stable group one patient stopped taking sulphasalazine (4 g daily) at entry to the trial and subsequently stopped trial treatment because of ongoing chronic active symptoms (he was taking azathioprine) and changed to unblinded azathioprine at eight months. Two other patients in the chronic active

Characteristics of patients with ulcerative colitis in remission or with chronic stable disease randomised to receive placebo or azathioprine

	Remission		Chronic stable disease	
	Placebo (n=34)	Azathioprine (n=33)	Placebo (n=5)	Azathioprine (n=7)
Mean (range) age (years)	44 (19-82)	44 (23-73)	37 (24-57)	56 (31-75)
Sex (M/F)	22/12	12/21	4/1	3/4
Colitis extent:				
Total	19	18		1
Left sided	8	5	1	1
Sigmoid	7	8	2	4
Proctitis		2	2	1
Mean (range) azathioprine dose (mg)	100 (50-150)	100 (50-200)	150 (100-150)	100 (50-150)
Sulphasalazine:				
Mean (range) dose (g)	2 (1-4)	2 (1-4)	2 (2-3)	2 (2-4)
No of patients	22	17	4	4
Mesalazine:				
Mean (range) dose (g)	1·2 (1·2-2·4)	1·2 (0·8-3·2)		1·2 (0·8-1·6)
No or patients	13	15		3
No of patients not taking aminosalicylates	4	8	1	0
Mean (range) duration of disease before trial (years)	7 (1-28)	9 (2-30)	3 (3-6)	9 (3-32)
Mean (range) duration of azathioprine treatment before trial (months)	21 (7-93)	19 (7-96)	20 (16-21)	26 (14-37)
Mean (range) duration of remission before entry (months)	11 (4-45)	12 (2-48)		

group stopped trial treatment at four and 10 months because of disillusionment with the trial (both taking placebo). These patients' data were censored at the time of protocol violation.

Of the 12 patients in the chronic stable group, two were receiving corticosteroid enemas at entry, four were taking oral prednisolone (2·5-10 mg), and six had low grade symptoms but were not taking prednisolone. Five of the seven patients taking azathioprine relapsed, two at one month, two at two months, and one at five and a half months. Of the five patients taking placebo, two relapsed (at one and nine months). One relapse was diagnosed on the basis of a grade 3 sigmoidoscopic appearance at a routine examination without change in symptoms (the patient had chronic low grade rectal bleeding and had had a grade 1 mucosal appearance at entry to the trial). The remainder of relapses were diagnosed on the basis of worsening symptoms or increasing corticosteroid requirements.

The only side effect observed during the trial was transient bone marrow suppression in two patients taking azathioprine. In one of these patients a low white cell count ($2{\cdot}7\times10^9/l$) at four months responded to dose reduction from 100 to 50 mg, and the patient was subsequently stabilised at 75 mg. The other patient had a low platelet count ($73\times10^9/l$), which responded to temporary stopping of treatment (150 mg) with later stabilisation at 50 mg daily.

Discussion

Our study has shown that maintenance treatment with azathioprine is beneficial as withdrawal resulted in a doubling of the relapse rate in patients who had achieved complete remission. These patients represent a selected but substantial group who had poorly controlled colitis as well as a good response to (and tolerance of) azathioprine. The likely size of this group is not clear; in Nottingham at least 35 patients are currently taking azathioprine for ulcerative colitis. Our results also raise the possibility that a wider group of patients with ulcerative colitis might benefit from initial treatment with azathioprine.

Our study shows that patients in prolonged remission of six months or more still benefit from continuing maintenance treatment. The total duration of benefit is unclear. The duration of remission before entry to the trial was a median of 12 months, so maintenance treatment seems to be beneficial for a minimum of two years. Most patients in this study were taking sulphasalazine or mesalazine, and these drugs were continued during the trial. The benefit from azathioprine maintenance treatment in preventing relapse is thus additive to the effects of these drugs.

The group of patients who had not achieved complete remission and stopped taking corticosteroids after six months' treatment with azathioprine was small. Our trial was therefore unable to reliably determine whether azathioprine should be continued in these patients. Although there seemed to be no benefit from continuing azathioprine, the concept of remission in these patients is somewhat artificial, and an end point of relapse can be difficult to decide, often being based on a patient's perception of worsening symptoms. These patients may have been non-compliant with treatment but there was no evidence for this on the basis of diary record of tablet consumption or changes in lymphocyte counts. For whatever reason not all patients will respond to azathioprine, and if patients are not in remission within six months after starting taking the drug our data suggest there is little value in continuing it.

Azathioprine has not been widely used in ulcerative colitis because of the lack of clear evidence of its value and concern about its toxicity. Two controlled trials have shown a corticosteroid sparing effect in chronic active disease,[2,3] but no significant benefit was seen over one month in patients with acute relapse.[4] This was, perhaps, predictable in view of the slow onset of action of azathioprine,[7] and the high response rate to the concomitant corticosteroids. Although the continuation of this trial into a maintenance phase failed to detect an overall significant benefit, there was a strong trend in favour of azathioprine in a subgroup of patients admitted with a relapse of established disease, suggesting likely therapeutic benefit.[4] The use of azathioprine and its metabolite 6-mercaptopurine is better established in Crohn's disease, with evidence of benefit in chronic active disease,[8-10] and in the prevention of relapse. This was seen both in patients who had just achieved remission on the drug,[11] and in patients in established remission in whom azathioprine was withdrawn according to a protocol similar to that used in our study.[12] Azathioprine can cause serious adverse drug reactions[5] such as nausea, bone marrow depression, or diarrhoea.[13] However, these are either idiosyncratic and evident early in treatment or, in the case of bone marrow depression, can be avoided by regular monitoring of the blood count.

We conclude that patients with ulcerative colitis who have achieved remission with azathioprine benefit from continuing azathioprine in addition to aminosalicylic acid preparations for a minimum of two years. Although azathioprine is not widely used in ulcerative colitis, there is a growing awareness of its value in inflammatory bowel disease, as evidenced by an increasing number of recent reports of experience with the drug.[14-17] Our results give these observations a sound basis and suggest that azathioprine should be used more widely in patients with poorly controlled ulcerative colitis.

1 Bean RHD. The treatment of chronic ulcerative colitis with 6-mercaptopurine. *Med J Aust* 1962;2:592-3.
2 Kirk AP, Lennard-Jones JE. Controlled trial of azathioprine in chronic ulcerative colitis. *BMJ* 1982;**284**:1291-2.
3 Rosenberg JL, Wall AJ, Levin B, Binder HJ, Kirsner JB. A controlled trial of azathioprine in the management of chronic ulcerative colitis. *Gastroenterology* 1975;**69**:96-9.
4 Jewell DP, Truelove SC. Azathioprine in ulcerative colitis: final report on controlled therapeutic trial. *BMJ* 1974;iv:627-30.
5 Hawthorne AB, Logan RFA, Hawkey CJ. Azathioprine in resistant ulcerative colitis. *Gastroenterology* 1989;**96**:A201.
6 Baron JH, Connell AM, Lennard-Jones JE. Variation between observers in describing mucosal appearances in proctocolitis. *BMJ* 1964;i:89-92.
7 Hawthorne AB, Hawkey CJ. Immunosuppressive drugs in inflammatory bowel disease: a review of their mechanisms of efficacy and place in therapy. *Drugs* 1989;**38**:267-88.
8 Present DH, Korelitz BI, Wisch JL, Glass JL, Sachar DB, Pasternack BS. Treatment of Crohn's disease with 6-mercaptopurine. *N Engl J Med* 1980;**302**:981-7.
9 Rosenberg JL, Levin B, Wall AJ, Kirsner JB. A controlled trial of azathioprine in Crohn's disease. *American Journal of Digestive Diseases* 1975;**20**:721-6.
10 Willoughby JMT, Thomas JM, Sudweeks DM. Azathioprine and levamisole in Crohn's disease: a double blind controlled trial of one year's treatment with long follow up. *Gut* 1990;**31**:A1193.
11 Willoughby JMT, Beckett J, Kumar P, Dawson AM. Controlled trial of azathioprine in Crohn's disease. *Lancet* 1971;ii:944-6.
12 O'Donoghue DP, Dawson AM, Powell-Tuck J, Bown RL, Lennard-Jones JL. Double-blind withdrawal trial of azathioprine as maintenance treatment for Crohn's disease. *Lancet* 1978;ii:955-7.
13 Cox JA, Daneshmend TK, Hawkey CJ, Logan RFA, Walt RP. Devastating diarrhoea due to azathioprine—management difficulty in inflammatory bowel disease. *Gut* 1989;**29**:686-8.
14 O'Brien JJ, Bayless JA. Use of azathioprine or 6-mercaptopurine in the treatment of Crohn's disease. *Gastroenterology* 1991;**101**:39-47.
15 Lobo AJ, Foster PN, Burke DA, Johnston D, Axon ATR. The role of azathioprine in the management of ulcerative colitis. *Dis Colon Rectum* 1990;**33**:182-5.
16 Verhave M, Winter HS, Grand RJ. Azathioprine in the treatment of children with inflammatory bowel disease. *Pediatrics* 1990;**117**:809-14.
17 Adler DJ, Korelitz BI. The therapeutic efficacy of 6-mercaptopurine in refractory ulcerative colitis. *Am J Gastroenterol* 1990;**85**:717-22.

(Accepted 29 April 1992)

© *Gut* 1993; 34: 503–508

Inter-relationships between inflammatory mediators released from colonic mucosa in ulcerative colitis and their effects on colonic secretion

T D Wardle, L Hall, L A Turnberg

Abstract

Metabolites of arachidonic acid have been implicated in the pathophysiology of ulcerative colitis – they can stimulate intestinal secretion, increase mucosal blood flow, and influence smooth muscle activity. The influence on the mucosal transport function of culture medium in which colonic mucosal biopsy specimens had been incubated was investigated using rat stripped distal colonic mucosa in vitro as the assay system. Colonic tissue from patients with colitis and from control subjects was cultured. Medium from inflamed tissue contained more prostaglandin E_2 (PGE_2) and leukotriene D_4 (LTD_4) and evoked a greater electrical (secretory) response in rat colonic mucosa than control tissue medium. In inflamed tissue, cyclo-oxygenase inhibition (indomethacin) attenuated PGE_2 but increased LTD_4 production; conversely lipoxygenase inhibition (ICI 207968) inhibited LTD_4 production but enhanced PGE_2 output. Each inhibitor alone enhanced the electrical response in the rat colon. Inhibition of both enzymes (indomethacin plus ICI 207968) caused a fall in both PGE_2 (82%) and LTD_4 (89%) production and in the electrical response (57%). Inflamed tissue treated with a phospholipase A_2 inhibitor (mepacrine) produced less PGE_2, LTD_4, and electrical responses when compared with inflamed tissue, either untreated (91%, 92%, and 79% respectively) or treated with cyclo-oxygenase and lipoxygenase inhibition. Incubation with bradykinin stimulated eicosanoid release and electrical response, while a bradykinin antagonist caused a modest inhibition. Analysis of these observations suggests that a combination of arachidonic acid derivatives accounts for about half the secretory response. Other products of phospholipase A_2 activity are probably responsible for much of the remainder, leaving up to 20% the result of types of mediator not determined in this study.

(*Gut* 1993; **34:** 503–508)

Department of Medicine and the Epithelial Membrane Research Centre, University of Manchester, Hope Hospital, Salford, Manchester
T D Wardle
L Hall
L A Turnberg

Correspondence to:
T D Wardle, Department of Medicine, Clinical Sciences Building, Hope Hospital, Eccles Old Road, Salford M6 8HD.

Accepted for publication
31 August 1992

High concentrations of prostaglandins and leukotrienes have been found in stool water and colonic mucosal biopsy specimens from patients with ulcerative colitis[1-7] and these have been implicated in the pathophysiology of inflammatory bowel disease. They may not only be involved in the mediation and amplification of the immune response but several have also been shown to stimulate mucosal secretion, increase mucosal blood flow, and influence smooth muscle activity, each of which may be relevant to the diarrhoea that these patients suffer.[8-10]

Because such a wide variety of inflammatory mediators is liberated in colitis it is difficult to ascertain which, either alone or in combination, might be responsible for the associated changes in intestinal function.

We describe studies of the influence on intestinal secretion of inflammatory mediators released into the medium in which biopsy specimens of inflamed colonic mucosa were cultured. We used rat colonic mucosa in vitro as our 'assay' system for determining secretory responses. Studies of the effect of a variety of inhibitors on these responses, and on the release of a number of mediators, have allowed us to show that a combination of prostaglandins and leukotrienes are probably responsible for over half of the secretory response, and that other products of phospholipase A_2 activity are probably responsible for much of the remainder.

Methods

PATIENT DETAILS

Thirty patients underwent colonoscopy after bowel preparation. Preparation consisted of a three day low residue diet, and one day before the examination a combination of X prep (purified senna extract; 1 ml/kg body weight) and 10% mannitol (500 ml) modified according to the patient's symptoms.

Ten of the patients (four men and six women, median age 36 years) had a clinical diagnosis of irritable bowel syndrome. They all had endoscopically and histologically normal mucosa.

Twenty patients (13 men and seven women median age 39·4 years) with active distal proctosigmoiditis had biopsy specimens taken from inflamed mucosa. Six patients were taking mesalazine (400 mg three times daily), four prednisolone (5 to 15 mg once daily), and seven topical steroids at the time of colonoscopy. All biopsy specimens were taken with non-spiked forceps to minimise tissue trauma.

Ethical approval for these studies was given by the Salford Health Authority Ethics Committee.

EXPLANT CULTURE

A series of cultures was performed for each patient. Mucosal biopsy specimens were immediately placed in transport medium (L15, with added penicillin G and streptomycin sulphate), transferred to the laboratory, washed gently three times in the L15 medium, carefully blotted, weighed (range 3–8 mg), and placed in a 5 cm culture dish containing 1 ml of culture medium (CMRL) 1066, plus glucose 5 μg/ml, methionine 1 μM/ml, Tris buffer 20 mM, glutamine 3 μM/ml, β-retinyl acetate 1 μg/ml, penicillin G 100 units/ml, streptomycin sulphate 100 μg/ml, gentamicin 50 μg/ml, and amphoteracin β 0·25 μg/ml). Individual mucosal biopsy specimens were cultured with either no additives or in the presence of one of the following: indomethacin (cyclo-oxygenase inhibitor); ICI 207968 (lipoxygenase inhibitor); a combination of indomethacin and ICI 207968; mepacrine (phospholipase A_2 inhibitor) (all at 10^{-5}M); and bradykinin, or des arg leu bradykinin (bradykinin antagonist) (both at 10^{-8}M). The culture dishes were placed in a humidified chamber maintained at 37°C, supplied with a mixture of 95% oxygen/5% carbon dioxide, and rotated at 10 cycles/minute. After 4 hours of culture the medium was removed and divided into three aliquots for measurement of PGE_2, LTD_4, and electrical responses in rat colonic mucosa.

EICOSANOID MEASUREMENTS

PGE_2 and LTD_4 were measured using commercially available radioimmunoassay kits (PGE_2, du Pont UK, Stevenage, Herts, UK[11]; LTD_4, Amersham, Aylesbury, Bucks, UK[12]). Eicosanoids were extracted from the culture medium using solid phase sorbant extraction (mini columns, Amersham). The resultant sample competes with a fixed amount of radioactively labelled eicosanoid analogue (iodinated PGE_2 or tritiated LTD_4) for a limited number of binding sites. The sample PGE_2 antibody complex is separated from the free antigen by polyethylene glycol precipitation and centrifugation, and then counted in a gamma counter. Separation of the leukotriene bound antibody complex was facilitated using dextran coated charcoal. After centrifugation the quantity of antibody bound radioactive ligand was measured on a beta counter.

Assay performance characteristics

Assay performance characteristics were as follows. PGE_2 intra and interassay variation values were 11 pg/ml and 60 pg/ml respectively; recovery was 96% and sensitivity 0·8 pg/ml. Cross reactivity (non-E prostaglandins) was <0·4%.[11] LTD_4 intra and interassay variation values were 14 pg/ml and 39 pg /ml respectively; recovery was 91% and sensitivity 5 pg/ml. Cross reactivity (non-sulphidopeptide leukotrienes) was <0·001%.[12]

Eicosanoid concentrations were calculated by interpolation from a standard curve. All results were expressed in pmol/mg wet tissue/hour.

RAT DISTAL COLON PREPARATION

An in vitro technique modified from that of Ussing and Zerahn was used.[13] Unfasted male Sprague-Dawley rats were killed and the distal colon was removed immediately and bathed in oxygenated buffer. Muscle layers were stripped and the two most distal pieces of mucosa were mounted as sheets, between Perspex flux chambers, with a surface area of 0·64 cm^2 (VT Plastics Ltd, Warrington, UK).

The spontaneous, basal transmucosal potential difference (PD) was measured, on a high impedance digital volmeter via fine tipped electrode bridges (3M KCl in 3% agar) connected to matched calomel half cells. The short circuit current (Isc) was delivered by silver/silver chloride electrodes via 1M NaCl in 1% agar bridges. The electrodes were connected to a voltage clamp for automatic short circuiting. The clamp was corrected for fluid resistance between the PD sensing bridges. Tissue conductance and resistance were calculated from the PD and Isc according to Ohm's law.

Each mucosal sheet was bathed on both sides with 5 ml of isotonic buffer containing: Na 146 mM; K 4·2 mM; Cl 125·8 mM; HCO_3 26·6 mM; H_2PO_4 0·2 mM; HPO_4 1·2 mM; Ca 1·2 mM; Mg 1·2 mM; and glucose 10 mM, at pH 7·4. The bathing media were stirred and oxygenated via a bubble lift system using 95% O_2/5% CO_2 and were maintained at a constant temperature of 37°C.

Culture medium (100 μl) was added to the bathing fluid on the serosal aspect of rat colonic mucosa after electrical stability had been reached, usually after 30 minutes.

SECRETORY AGONISTS

Eicosanoids

PGE_2 or LTD_4, in final concentrations ranging from 10^{-10} to 10^{-4}M, were added to the serosal aspect of stripped rat distal colon. Changes in PD, Isc, and resistance were recorded.

Culture medium

Culture medium (100 μl) was added to the serosal aspect of stripped rat colon and electrical measurements, as described above, were recorded. The process was repeated using either medium incubated with the inhibitors to act as controls or medium from biopsy specimens cultured with the inhibitors as detailed above. The resultant rise in Isc was compared with the PGE_2 and LTD_4 dose response curves.

CHEMICALS

The 5 lipoxygenase inhibitor, ICI 207968, was kindly supplied by Dr R Dowell, Imperial Chemical Company, Alderley Edge, UK. Prostaglandin E_2, bradykinin, des arg leu bradykinin, mepacrine, and indomethacin were obtained from Sigma Chemical Co, Poole, Dorset, UK. LT D_4 was purchased from Cascade Biochem Ltd, University of Reading, Berks, UK.

CALCULATIONS

All values are expressed as the mean (SEM). Statistical comparisons were performed using paired and unpaired *t* tests.[14]

© Gut 1993; 34: 503–508

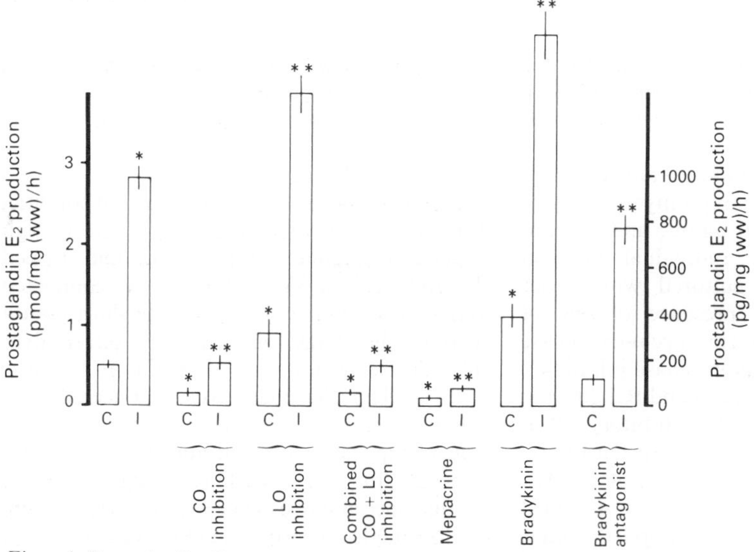

Figure 1: Prostaglandins E_2 production by cultured colonic mucosa (pmol and pg/mg wet tissue/hour mean (SEM)). n=10 cultures/column. C=control mucosa; I=inflamed mucosa; CO=cyclo-oxygenase inhibition (indomethacin); LO=lipoxygenase inhibition (ICI 207968). *Significantly different from untreated control tissue, $p<0·01$; **significantly different from untreated inflamed tissue, $p<0·01$.

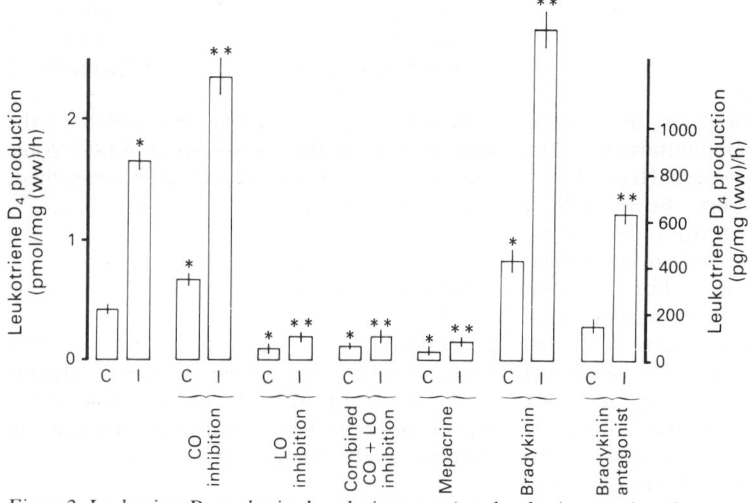

Figure 2: Leukotriene D_4 production by colonic mucosa (pmol and pg/mg wet tissue/hour mean (SEM)) n=10 cultures/column. C=control mucosa; I=inflamed mucosa; CO=cyclo-oxygenase inhibition (indomethacin), LO=lipoxygenase inhibition (ICI 207968). *Significantly different from untreated control tissue, $p<0·01$; **significantly different from untreated inflamed tissue, $p<0·01$.

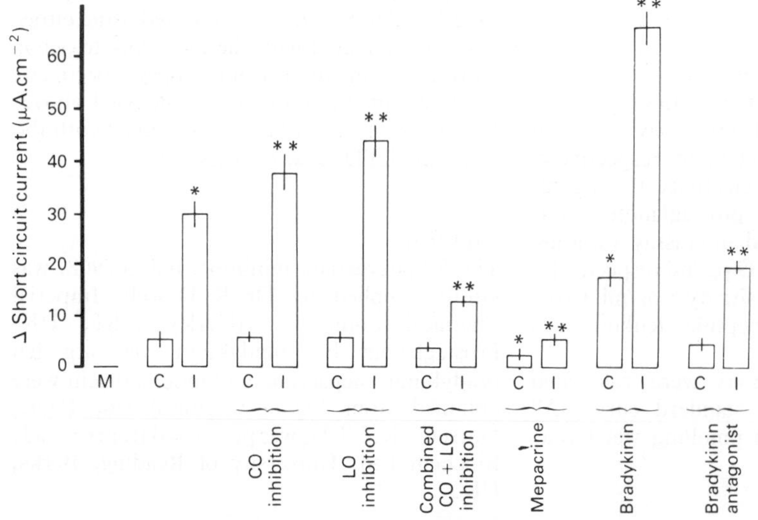

Figure 3: The effect of inflammatory mediators liberated from cultured colonic tissue on the secretory response of rat colonic mucosa; the effect of agonists and antagonists. Isc=short circuit current ($\mu A.cm^{-2}$, mean (SEM)). n=4 pieces of stripped rat distal colonic mucosa/column. M=medium alone, C=control mucosa; I=inflamed mucosa; CO=cyclo-oxygenase inhibition (indomethacin); LO=lipoxygenase inhibition (ICI 207968). *Significantly different from untreated control tissue, $p<0·01$; **significantly different from untreated inflamed tissue, $p<0·01$.

Results

EICOSANOID MEASUREMENTS

Inflamed tissue produced significantly more PGE_2 and LTD_4 than control tissue (2·79 (0·11) *v* 0·54 (0·04); :1·73 (0·11) *v* 0·44 (0·04) respectively, $p<0·01$) (all values are given in pmol/mg wet tissue weight/hour). The production rate of eicosanoids is also expressed graphically in both pmol and pg/mg wet tissue weight/hour; for example in inflamed tissue PGE_2 production is 2·79 pmol or 1012 pg/mg wet weight/hour and LTD_4 is 1·73 pmol or 837 pg/mg wet weight/hour. (Figs 1 and 2). Cyclo-oxygenase inhibition (indomethacin, 10^{-5}M) significantly reduced PGE_2 production when values were compared with those in the untreated groups (inflamed 0·511 (0·06) *v* 2·79 (0·11); control 0·17 (0·02) *v* 0·54 (0·04); $p<0·01$), whereas the yield of LTD_4 was increased (inflamed 2·4 (0·17) *v* 1·73 (0·11): control 0·74 (0·07) *v* 0·44 (0·04), $p<0·01$).

A significant increase in PGE_2 production, by all groups, followed lipoxygenase inhibition (ICI 207968, 10^{-5}M) (inflamed 3·9 (0·22) *v* 2·79 (0·11); control 0·91 (0·13) *v* 0·54 (0·04), $p<0·01$), while LTD_4 generation was reduced (inflamed 0·16 (0·07) *v* 1·73 (0·11); control 0·1 (0·01) *v* 0·44 (0·04), $p<0·01$).

Combined inhibition of cyclo-oxygenase and lipoxygenase produced almost identical PGE_2 results to those found after indomethacin alone (Fig 1), and LTD_4 results to those found after ICI 207968 alone (Fig 2).

In inflamed tissue, phospholipase A_2 inhibition (mepacrine) appreciably reduced the production of both PGE_2 and LTD_4 when compared with values in untreated mucosa (PGE_2 0·21 (0·03) *v* 2·79 (0·11); LTD_4 0·14 (0·04) *v* 1·73 (0·11) respectively; $p<0·001$). The reduction after mepacrine was also greater than that after combined cyclo-oxygenase and lipoxygenase inhibition (PGE_2 0·21 (0·03) *v* 0·5 (0·05); LTD_4 0·14 (0·04) *v* 0·19 (0·03) respectively, $p<0·04$). Mepacrine also significantly attenuated eicosanoid output by control tissue (PGE_2 0·11 (0·014) *v* 0·54 (0·04); LTD_4 0·1 (0·08) *v* 0·44 (0·04); $p<0·01$).

In comparison with the untreated group, bradykinin stimulated a significant increase in both PGE_2 production (control 1·1 (0·18) *v* 0·54 (0·04); inflamed 4·1 (0·24) *v* 2·79 (0·11); $p<0·001$) and LTD_4 production (control 1·1 (0·12) *v* 0·44 (0·4); inflamed 4·1 (0·17) *v* 1·7 (0·11); $p<0·001$).

Inhibition of bradykinin resulted in a fall in PGE_2 and LTD_4 generation by all groups but only the reduction found in the inflamed group reached statistical significance (inflamed PGE_2 2·3 (0·14) *v* 2·79 (0·11); LTD_4 1·1 (0·1) *v* 1·73 (0·11) respectively; $p<0·01$, control PGE_2 0·34 (0·05) *v* 0·54 (0·04); LTD_4 0·29 (0·05) *v* 0·44 (0·04); NS).

EFFECT OF CULTURE MEDIUM ON STRIPPED RAT DISTAL COLON

Fresh culture medium applied to the serosal half chamber did not produce any change in baseline electrical activity (Fig 3). Culture medium incubated with the inhibitors did not influence the basal Isc. Culture fluid from inflamed tissue evoked a significantly larger Isc increase than fluid from control mucosa (31 (2·6) *v* 6·3 (1·3) $\mu A.cm^{-2}$; $p<0·001$).

Cyclo-oxygenase inhibition
Medium from control biopsy specimens cultured with or without indomethacin produced similar rises in electrical measurements. However, a significantly greater increase in Isc occurred with fluid derived from inflamed mucosal biopsy specimens treated with indomethacin, compared with the untreated group (40 (2·5) *v* 31 (2·6) $\mu A.cm^{-2}$; $p<0·01$).

Lipoxygenase inhibition
Lipoxygenase inhibition with ICI 207968 did not influence the modest rise in electrical activity seen with the control biopsy medium. However, after lipoxygenase inhibition medium from inflamed tissue produced a significantly greater Isc response than that from untreated control tissues (43·5 (5) *v* 31 (2·6) $\mu A.cm^{-2}$; $p<0·01$).

Combined lipoxygenase and cyclo-oxygenase inhibition
There was no significant difference between the short circuit response evoked by culture medium from untreated control tissue and control biopsy specimens exposed to combined cyclo-oxygenase and lipoxygenase inhibition. Culture medium from inflamed tissue treated in the same way, however, produced a significantly lower Isc response than medium from untreated tissues (13·4 (2·1) *v* 31 (2·6) $\mu A.cm^{-2}$; $p<0·005$).

Phospholipase A_2 inhibition
Control biopsy specimens incubated with mepacrine produced media which provoked a significantly smaller Isc response than untreated mucosal media (2·5 (1) *v* 6·3 (1·3) $\mu A.cm^{-2}$; $p<0·01$). Medium from inflamed tissue exposed to mepacrine evoked an Isc response that was significantly lower than that from either medium from untreated tissue or from tissues exposed to the combined effects of cyclo-oxygenase and lipoxygenase inhibition. (6·4 (1·1) *v* 31 (2·6) and 13·4 (2·1) $\mu A.cm^{-2}$; respectively, $p<0·005$).

Bradykinin agonist
The addition of bradykinin to the culture medium bathing both types of tissue produced a highly significant increase in Isc compared with values in the untreated groups (control 17·5 (2·8) *v* 6·3 (1·3): inflamed 66·1 (4·9) *v* 31 (2·6) $\mu A.cm^{-2}$; $p<0·001$).

Bradykinin antagonism
Bradykinin receptor blockade produced a fall in the Isc for both tissue types, but only in the inflamed group did the change reach statistical significance (31 (2·6) *v* 19·3 (3·1) $\mu A.cm^{-2}$; $p<0·01$).

DOSE RESPONSE CURVES

PGE_2
PGE_2 added to the serosal, but not the mucosal, side of stripped rat distal colon caused a rapid increase in Isc, which peaked after 2½ to 3 minutes. The dose response curve for PGE_2 gave an EC_{50} of $5\times10^{-7}M$ (Fig 4). PGE_2 generated a parallel but smaller increase in PD and a modest rise in tissue conductance.

LTD_4
LTD_4 added to the serosal aspect of stripped rat distal colon, evoked a rapid rise in Isc, which peaked after 2½ minutes (Fig 5). The EC_{50} for this response was $8\times10^{-7}M$. The transmucosal PD also increased while conductance rose to a modest extent.

Combined PGE_2 and LTD_4
At the peak Isc response to PGE_2 at $10^{-5}M$ and $10^{-8}M$, LTD_4 $10^{-5}M$ and $10^{-8}M$ respectively were added to the serosal chamber. The combined Isc for $10^{-5}M$ was 43.4 $\mu A.cm^2$ and for $10^{-8}M$ it was 20·8 $\mu A.cm^2$. These values were not significantly different from those expected from the dose response curves (41·5 $\mu A.cm^2$:

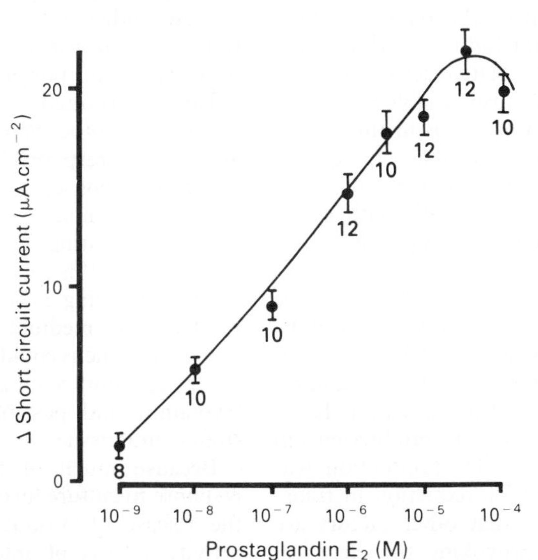

Figure 4: Prostaglandin E_2 dose response curve in stripped rat distal colon. Values are mean (SEM). Number of rat mucosal preparations under each point.

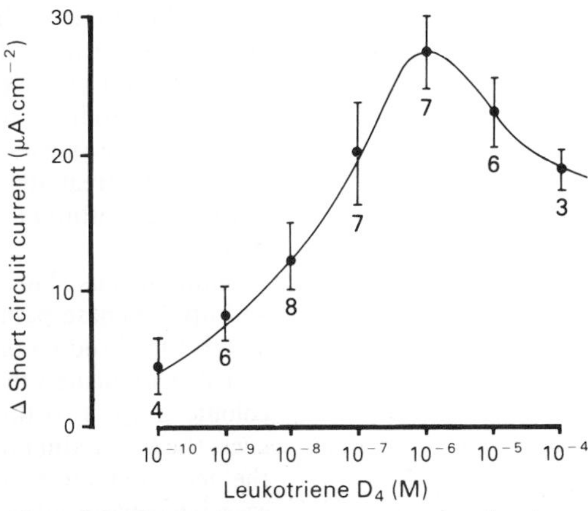

Figure 5: Leukotriene D_4 dose response curve in stripped rat distal colon. Values mean (SEM). Number of rat mucosal preparations under each point.

© Gut 1993; 34: 503–508

18·5 μA.cm^2 respectively – that is, there was no evidence of potentiation at either maximal or half maximal concentration.

Discussion

In these studies we have shown that inflamed tissue releases more eicosanoids into the culture medium than control mucosa, and that medium from any of the tissues will evoke an electrical response in stripped rat distal colon. A rise in electrical potential difference and Isc in this mucosal preparation is associated with secretion of chloride ions and we have used a rise in electrical measurements as a proxy for anion secretion.

Inflamed tissue produced significantly more PGE_2 and LTD_4 than control mucosa, but the difference was not as great as that shown by rectal dialysis.[15,16] Although the degree of indomethacin induced cyclo-oxygenase inhibition is variable,[17] all groups showed significant attenuation of PGE_2 production and a reciprocal, significant increase in LTD_4 generation. Conversely, inhibition of lipoxygenase activity resulted in a suppression of LTD_4 generation and stimulation of PGE_2 synthesis. Presumably, the increased availability of arachidonate for one enzyme system when the alternative route was blocked is responsible for these reciprocal effects on PGE_2 and LTD_4 production.

Because PGE_2 and LTD_4 have each been shown to stimulate intestinal secretion[18–21] it is not surprising to find that inhibiting the production of one of these did not reduce the secretory (electrical) response to medium, in which a reciprocal rise in the other had occurred. More difficult to explain is the *greater* Isc response to medium in which one stimulant was appreciably depressed while the other was only moderately increased. It is possible that the inhibition of the lipoxygenase or cyclo-oxygenase pathways caused the synthesis of more potent secretagogues than simply the two measured in this study. Other potential contenders for this role include prostacyclin, a more potent secretagogue than PGE_2[22] in the case of lipoxygenase inhibition, and other leukotrienes (B_4, C_4) in the case of cyclo-oxygenase inhibition.[21]

This type of analysis leads to the conclusion that there is a finely balanced production of the major metabolites of arachidonic acid and that subtle alterations in the relative activities of the enzymes concerned will cause variable responses. Blockade of a major pathway, as in this study, can thus produce unpredictable changes in functional responses. The failure of early attempts to treat ulcerative colitis with cyclo-oxygenase inhibitors may be explicable on this basis.[23–27]

Simultaneous blockade of cyclo-oxygenase and lipoxygenase pathways reduced both PGE_2 and LTD_4 production, as might be expected, and also attenuated the electrical response of rat colonic mucosa to this culture medium. However, the 82% reduction in PGE_2 production and the 89% reduction in LTD_4 production was associated with only a 57% reduction in transmucosal Isc suggesting that other factors are probably involved in provoking the electrical response. One possibility is that potentiation between the effects of low concentrations of these metabolites might occur. Such a potentiation would have to be greater at low than at high concentrations to account for this observation and we did not find evidence of potentiation between PGE_2 and LTD_4 in our study. Thus, this seems a less likely explanation than the simultaneous generation of other types of secretory agonists. In favour of this are the results of phospholipase A_2 inhibition with mepacrine. Here blockade of the enzyme responsible for arachidonic acid liberation caused a much greater fall in the electrical response of rat colonic mucosa (from 57% after combined lipoxygenase and cyclo-oxygenase inhibition to 79% after phospholipase A_2 inhibition). PGE_2 and LTD_4 production were also further reduced (82% to 92% and 89% to 91% respectively), but these falls were much less impressive than the fall in Isc.

It is interesting to compare the electrical responses to culture media (with their measured eicosanoid concentrations) with the dose response curves for PGE_2 and LTD_4. It is clear that the concentrations of both eicosanoids measured in the culture media are much lower than those that might be expected to provoke the electrical responses which were observed if their effects were simply additive. The mean eicosanoid concentrations derived from culture medium from inflamed tissue were in the order of $4{\cdot}45\times10^{-11}$M for PGE_2, and $2{\cdot}77\times10^{-11}$M for LTD_4. As indicated by the dose response curves, no change in Isc would be expected with these amounts, even if these concentrations were summated. The mean rise in Isc evoked by medium from inflamed cultures was 30 μA.cm^{-2} which would be expected at concentrations of some 10^{-5}M PGE_2, or 10^{-6}M LTD_4, if these were the only mediators present. Clearly other mediators must also be involved in the electrical response, but the degree of inhibition by mepacrine (79%) suggests that most are likely to be products of phospholipase A_2 activation.

It may be concluded from these observations that cyclo-oxygenase and lipoxygenase products account for most (57%) of the electrical response induced by medium from cultured colonic mucosa. Only PGE_2 and LTD_4 were measured in these studies and since they could only be held responsible for part of the response, other cyclo-oxygenase and lipoxygenase products are likely to have contributed.

Moreover, other phospholipase A_2 metabolites are probably responsible for a further 22% of the electrical response. It seems most likely that this is due to a non-arachidonic acid derivative, platelet activating factor being a reasonable contender for this role.

The remaining 21% of the electrical response produced by medium from cultured inflamed biopsy specimens could be caused by a variety of other mediators such as histamine, 5-hydroxytryptamine and, possibly, transmitters liberated from neural tissues.

Because much of the electrical, secretory response to culture medium could be ascribed to the release of products of phospholipase A_2 activity it was of interest to investigate the influence of one potentially important stimulus to phospholipase A_2 activity. Inflammatory cells, in particular macrophages have receptors for bradykinin, a potent secretagogue acting almost entirely by stimulating arachidonic acid release via phospholipase A_2 activation. Its effect on intestinal mucosa, at least in the rat ileum, is indirect, its site of action being on subepithelial cells.[28 29] In our study bradykinin caused a noticeable rise in eicosanoid release from control and inflamed biopsy specimens and culture medium from these caused a greater rise in Isc in the rat colonic mucosa model. Bradykinin receptor blockade with des arg leu bradykinin caused a fall in eicosanoid output and the associated Isc response, suggesting that bradykinin may be a stimulus to endogenous phospholipase A_2 activity in biopsy specimens of normal and inflamed colonic mucosa. The fall in PGE_2 and LTD_4 production after bradykinin receptor blockade was, however, less than that found after direct phospholipase A_2 inhibition with mepacrine or after combined lipoxygenase and cyclo-oxygenase inhibition. Reasons for this smaller effect include the possibility that receptor blockade with des arg leu bradykin was incomplete in these specimens. It is also likely that the other stimuli to phospholipase A_2 activity such as interleukin 1,[30] interleukin 8, and other monocyte derived growth factors,[31] are liberated in these tissues.

Although we have focussed on the secretory effects of these inflammatory mediators, it is clear that they are likely to have a number of other effects that will contribute to the pathophysiology of the disease. The effects, on secretion, described here, however, provide one indicator of the tissue response in inflammatory disease.

In conclusion, we have provided evidence in favour of the view that eicosanoids are the major inflammatory mediators causing secretory responses in colonic mucosa and that their production can be significantly reduced by combined cyclo-oxygenase and lipoxygenase inhibition or by mepacrine or by a bradykinin antagonist. The maximal reduction in eicosanoid release and secretory response was achieved with mepacrine and this may warrant further clinical evaluation of its therapeutic role in inflammatory bowel disease. Care should be taken in the assessment of drugs which influence inflammatory mediator metabolic pathways since disturbance of these complex interactions and balances may produce unpredictable results.

We are grateful to Dr R Dowell of the Imperial Chemical Industries for donating the 5-lipoxygenase inhibitor. We are indebted to the Ileostomy Association for their financial support and interest in our work. We would also like to thank Carol McDonna for typing the manuscript.

1 Gould SR. Prostaglandins, Ulcerative colitis and sulphasalazine. *Lancet* 1975; ii: 988.
2 Sharon P, Ligumsky M, Rachmilewitz D, Zor U. Role of prostaglandins in ulcerative colitis. Enhanced production during active disease and inhibition by sulphasalazine. *Gastroenterology* 1978; **75:** 638–40.
3 Sharon P, Stenson WF. Enhanced synthesis of leukotriene B_4 by colonic mucosa in inflammatory bowel disease. *Gastroenterology* 1984; **86:** 435–60.
4 Ligumsky M, Karmeli F, Sharon P, Zor U, Cohen F, Rachmilewitz D. Enhanced thromboxane A_2 and prostacyclin production by cultured rectal mucosa in ulcerative colitis and its inhibition by steroids and sulfasalazine. *Gastroenterology* 1981; **81:** 444–9.
5 Boughton-Smith NK, Hawkey CJ, Whittle BJR. Biosynthesis of lipoxygenase and cyclo-oxygenase products from ^{14}C arachidonic acid by human colonic mucosa. *Gut* 1983; **24:** 1176–86.
6 Peskar BM, Dreyling KW, Peskar BA, May B, Goebell H. Enhanced formation of sulfidopeptide leukotrienes in ulcerative colitis and Crohn's disease: inhibition by sulfasalazine and 5-aminosalicyclic acid. *Agents Action* 1986; **18:** 381–3.
7 Wardle TD, Turnberg LA. Co-culture of colonic mucosa – a novel technique for investigating the role of soluble mediators in inflammatory bowel disease. *Gastroenterology* 1990; **98:** A499.
8 Hawkey CJ, Rampton DS. Prostaglandins and the gastrointestinal mucosa, are they important in its function, disease or treatment? *Gastroenterology* 1985; **89:** 1162–88.
9 Rask-Madsen J. Eicosanoids and their role in the pathogenesis of diarrhoeal diseases. *Clin Gastro* 1986; **15:** 545–66.
10 Bennett A, Eleg KG, Scholes GB. Effects of prostaglandin E_1 and E_2 on human, guinea pig and rat isolated small intestine. *Br J Pharm* 1968; **34:** 630–8.
11 NEN Research. *Instruction manual for measurement of prostaglandin E_2 in plasma and tissue samples.* 1988.
12 *Leukotriene $C_4/D_4/E_4$ assay system.* Hertford: Du Pont, Amersham: Amersham International, 1988.
13 Ussing HH, Zerahn K. Active transport of sodium as a source of the electric current in short circuited isolated frog skin. *Acta Physiol Scan* 1951; **23:** 110–27.
14 Snedecor GW, Cochran WG. *Statistical methods,* 7th Edition. Ames, Iowa; Iowa State University, 1980.
15 Lauritsen K, Laursen LS, Bukhave K, Rask-Madsen J. Intra luminal colonic levels of arachidonic acid metabolites in ulcerative colitis. *Advances in Prostaglandin Thromboxane Leukotriene Research* 1987; **17:** 347–52.
16 Lauritsen K, Laursen LS, Bukhave K, Rask-Madsen J. In vivo profiles of eicosanoids in ulcerative colitis, Crohn's colitis and clostridium difficle colitis. *Gastroenterology* 1988; **95:** 11–7.
17 Moore PK. Effect of drugs on arachidonic acid metabolism. In eds: *Prostanoids: pharmacological, physiological and clinical relevance.* Cambridge, Cambridge University Press, 1988, 41–68.
18 Smith PL, Montzka DP, McCafferty GP, Wasserman MA, Fondacaro JD. Effect of sulphidopeptide leukotrienes D_4 and E_4 on ileal ion transport in vitro in the rat and rabbit. *Am J Physiol* 1988; **255:** G175–83.
19 Kimberg DV, Field M, Johnson J, Henderson A, Gershon E. Stimulation of intestinal mucosa adenylate cyclase by cholera enterotoxin and prostaglandin. *J Clin Invest* 1971; **50:** 1218–30.
20 Field M, Musch MW, Steff JS. Role of prostaglandins in the regulation of intestinal electrolyte transport. *Prostaglandins* 1987; **21:** 73–9.
21 Musch MW, Miller RJ, Field M, Siegel MI. Stimulation of colonic secretion by lipoxygenase metabolites of arachidonic acid. *Science* 1982; **217:** 1255–6.
22 Moriarty K, Wardle T, Higgs NB, Tonge A, Warhurst G. Prostacyclin regulates secretion in mammalian colon via dual calcium and cyclic AMP dependent mechanisms – comparison with PGE_2. *Gastroenterology* 1990; **98:** A549.
23 Gould SR, Brash AR, Conolly ME, Lennard-Jones JE. Studies of prostaglandins and sulfalazine in ulcerative colitis. *Prostaglandins Med* 1981; **6:** 165–82.
24 Gilat T, Ratan J, Rosen P, Peled Y. Prostaglandins and ulcerative colitis. *Gastroenterology* 1978; **76:** 1083.
25 Campieri M, Lanfranchi GA, Bazzochi G. Prostaglandins, indomethacin and ulcerative colitis. *Gastroenterology* 1980; **78:** 193.
26 Rampton DS, Sladen GE. Prostaglandin synthesis inhibitors in ulcerative colitis: flurbiprofen compared with conventional treatment. *Prostaglandins* 1987; **21:** 417–25.
27 Rampton DS, Sladen GE. Relapse of ulcerative proctitis during treatment with non-steroidal anti-inflammatory drugs. *Postgrad Med J* 1981; **57:** 297–9.
28 Warhurst G, Higgs NB, Lees M, Tonge A, Turnberg LA. Site and mechanisms of action of kinins in rat ileal mucosa. *Am J Physiol* 1987; **252:** G293–300.
29 Lawson LD, Powell DW. Bradykinin stimulated eicosanoid synthesis and secretion by rabbit ileal components. *Am J Physiol* 1987; **252:** G783–90.
30 Cominelli F, Nast CC, Dinarello CA, Gentilini P, Sipser RD. Regulation of eicosanoid production in rabbit colon by interleukin 1. *Gastroenterology* 1989; **97:** 1400–5.
31 Cominelli F, Dinarello CA. Interleukin 1 in the pathogenesis of and protection from inflammatory bowel disease. *Biotherapy* 1989; **1;** 369–75.

Multiple G-Protein–dependent Pathways Mediate the Antisecretory Effects of Somatostatin and Clonidine in the HT29-19A Colonic Cell Line

G. Warhurst, L. A. Turnberg, N. B. Higgs, A. Tonge, J. Grundy, and K. E. Fogg
The Epithelial Membrane Research Centre and Department of Medicine, University of Manchester, Hope Hospital, Salford M6 8HD, United Kingdom

Abstract

Using the functionally differentiated colonic cell line, HT29-19A, we have examined sites at which inhibitory G-proteins mediate the antisecretory actions of somatostatin (SST) and the α_2-adrenergic agonist, clonidine (CLON) at the epithelial level. Both agents caused a dose-dependent inhibition (EC_{50}: SST 35 nM; CLON 225 nM) of Cl^- secretion (assessed by changes in short circuit current) activated by cAMP-mediated agonists, PGE_2 and cholera toxin. Inhibition was accompanied by a reduction in intracellular cAMP accumulation and could be blocked by pretreatment with pertussis toxin at a concentration (200 ng/ml) which activated ADP-ribosylation of a 41-kD inhibitory G protein in HT29-19A membranes. Secretion stimulated by the permeant cAMP analogue, dibutyryl cAMP, was also inhibited by SST and CLON (30–50%; $P < 0.005$), indicating additional inhibitory sites located distal to cAMP production. Both agents were effective inhibitors of secretion mediated through the Ca^{2+} signaling pathway. SST (1 μM) and CLON (10 μM) reduced the Isc response to the muscarinic agonist, carbachol, by 60–70%; inhibition was reversed in pertussis toxin–treated cells. These effects did not, however, involve inhibition of the carbachol-induced increase in cellular inositol 1,4,5-trisphosphate levels or the rise in cytosolic calcium, $[Ca]_i$. Inhibition by SST of secretion induced by phorbol 12,13 dibutyrate but not by the calcium agonist, thapsigargin, suggests that SST may act at a distal inhibitory site in the Ca^{2+}-dependent secretory process activated by protein kinase C. We conclude that SST and α_2-adrenergic agonists can act directly on intestinal epithelial cells to exert a comprehensive inhibition of Cl^- secretion mediated through both cAMP and Ca^{2+}/protein kinase C signaling pathways. Inhibition is mediated via pertussis toxin–sensitive G-proteins at sites located both proximal and distal to the production of second messengers. (*J. Clin. Invest.* 1993. 92:603–611.) Key words: α_2-adrenergic • cyclic adenosine monophosphate • inhibitory G-protein • intestinal epithelial cell • ion secretion • somatostatin

J. Clin. Invest.

0021-9738/93/08/0603/09 $2.00
Volume 92, August 1993, 603–611

© *Lancet* 1993; 342: 575–577

Regression of primary low-grade B-cell gastric lymphoma of mucosa-associated lymphoid tissue type after eradication of *Helicobacter pylori*

Andrew C Wotherspoon, Claudio Doglioni, Timothy C Diss, Langxing Pan, Alvise Moschini, Michele de Boni, Peter G Isaacson

Summary

Certain features of primary low-grade B-cell gastric lymphoma of mucosa-associated lymphoid tissue (MALT) suggest the tumour is antigen-responsive. Given the close association between gastric MALT lymphoma and *Helicobacter pylori*, these organisms might be evoking the immunological response, and eradication of *H pylori* might inhibit the tumour. 6 patients in whom biopsies showed histological and molecular-genetic evidence of low-grade gastric B-cell MALT lymphoma with *H pylori* infection were treated with antibiotics. In all cases *H pylori* was eradicated and in 5, repeated biopsies showed no evidence of lymphoma. These results suggest that eradication of *H pylori* causes regression of low-grade B-cell gastric MALT lymphoma, and that anti-*H-pylori* treatment should be given for this lymphoma.

Lancet 1993; **342:** 575–77

Introduction

Primary low-grade B-cell lymphomas of the stomach have features of mucosa-associated lymphoid tissue (MALT).[1] The paradox of lymphoma arising in the stomach, which normally contains no organised lymphoid tissue, has been explained by observations that MALT appears in the stomach in response to infection by *Helicobacter pylori*[2,3] and that the organism is also present in over 90% of gastric MALT lymphomas.[4] In low-grade gastric MALT lymphoma, blast transformation,[1] subepithelial plasma-cell differentiation[1], and the specific colonisation of lymphoid follicle centres by neoplastic cells[5] suggest that the tumour is immunologically responsive. Given its close association with gastric MALT lymphoma, *H pylori* might evoke immune responses and, in so doing, stimulate tumour growth. If this were the case, eradication of *H pylori* should inhibit the growth of low-grade gastric lymphoma.

Patients and methods

Patients

6 patients (3 male, age 37–76) with primary gastric low-grade B-cell MALT lymphoma and *H pylori* infection on endoscopic biopsy were selected. 4 had been followed up for up to 38 months before the study for dyspepsia, and gastric biopsies had shown lymphoid infiltrates thought to be lymphoma. After a diagnostic biopsy, each patient was started on ampicillin with either metronidazole and tripotassium dicitrobismuthate (cases 1–4 and 6) or omeprazole (case 5). Patients underwent endoscopy 1–2 months, and 4–10 months later, and an average of 10 paired biopsies (range 3–15) for molecular genetic studies and routine histology were taken from the same area (antrum, 5; fundus, 1) on each occasion.

Histopathology

Haematoxylin and eosin sections from formalin-fixed wax-embedded biopsies were examined for features characteristic of MALT lymphoma, including centrocyte-like cells within the lamina propria infiltrating the glandular epithelium to form lymphoepithelial lesions. The sections were reviewed by 3 histopathologists (ACW, CD, and PGI). As a measure of change on repeated biopsy, the confidence of a diagnosis of lymphoma was expressed on a scale 0–5 (table 1). Lymphoepithelial lesions, essential to the diagnosis of gastric MALT lymphoma, were defined as unequivocal partial destruction of gastric glands or crypts by groups of centrocyte-like cells. The presence of *H pylori* was initially assessed on haematoxylin and eosin sections; negative findings were confirmed by a modified Giemsa stain.

Molecular biology

High-molecular-weight DNA was extracted from fresh tissue, when available, by a modification of standard procedures.[6] The restriction enzymes *Eco*R1, *Hind*III, and either *Bam*H1 or *Pst*-1 were used in separate digestion reactions and the resulting digests size-fractionated on 0·8% agarose gels and transferred to Hybond N-plus membranes by Southern blotting. The membranes were hybridised with a probe to the joining region of the immunoglobulin heavy-chain gene which had been labelled with ^{32}P-dCTP. Following hybridisation the membranes were washed and exposed to pre-fogged X-ray film at −70°C.

Amplification of DNA from both fresh and wax-embedded tissue was done with semi-nested PCR[7,8] in which primers were directed to the joining region and to either the framework 2 or 3 part of the variable region of the immunoglobulin heavy-chain gene. Test samples were run in parallel with positive and negative controls and products analysed on 10% polyacrylamide gels, stained with ethidium bromide, and viewed under UV light.

Results

Endoscopic appearances, histological evidence of lymphoma, presence of *H pylori*, and molecular results are

Grade	Description	Histological features
0	Normal	Scattered plasma cells in lamina propria. No lymphoid follicles
1	Chronic active gastritis	Small clusters of lymphocytes in lamina propria. No lymphoid follicles. No LELs
2	Chronic active gastritis with florid lymphoid follicle formation	Prominent lymphoid follicles with surrounding mantle zone and plasma cells. No LELs
3	Suspicious lymphoid infiltrate in lamina propria, probably reactive	Lymphoid follicles surrounded by small lymphocytes that infiltrate diffusely in lamina propria and occasionally into epithelium
4	Suspicious lymphoid infiltrate in lamina propria, probably lymphoma	Lymphoid follicles surrounded by CCL cells that infiltrate diffusely in lamina propria and into epithelium in small groups
5	Low-grade B-cell lymphoma of MALT	Presence of dense diffuse infiltrate of CCL cells in lamina propria with prominent LELs

CCL = centrocyte-like, LEL = lymphoepithelial lesion.

Table 1: **Histological scoring for diagnosis of MALT lymphoma**

Department of Histopathology, UCL Medical School, University Street, London WC1E 6JJ, UK (A C Wotherspoon MB, T C Diss MSc, L Pan PhD, P G Isaacson FRCPath); **and Ospedale Civile, Feltre, Italy** (C Doglioni MD, A Moschini MD, M de Boni MD)

Correspondence to: Prof P G Isaacson

© Lancet 1993; 342: 575–577

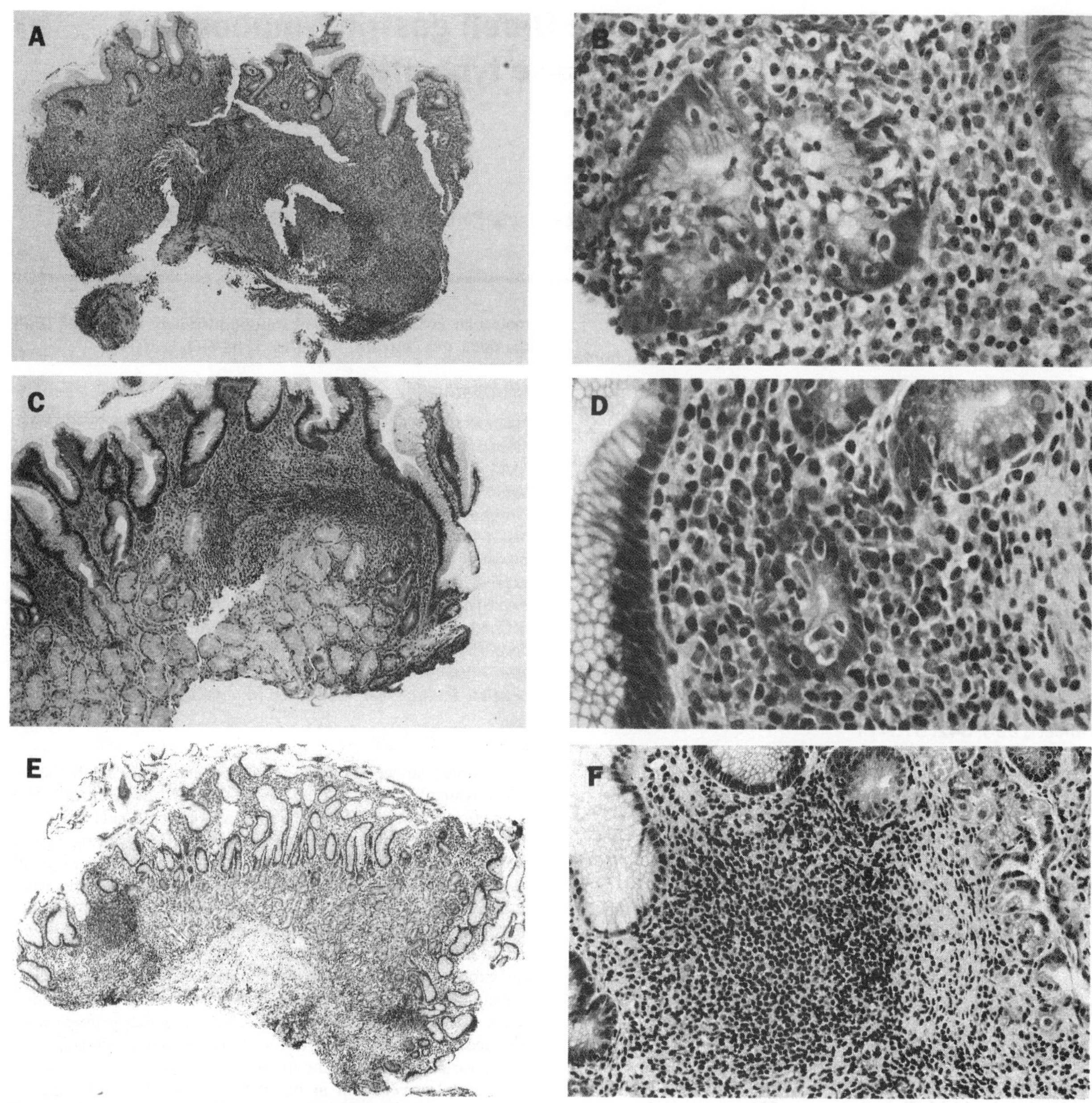

Figure 1: **Case 1—sequential gastric biopsy specimens**

A = heavy lymphoid infiltrate. B = higher magnification of A; mucosal infiltration by plasma and centrocyte-like cells that form prominent lymphoepithelial lesions (score 5). C = 1 mo after antibiotics; only focal lymphoid infiltration. D = higher magnification of C; plasma cells in lamina propria with single gland containing intra-epithelial B-cells (score 3). E = 7 mo after start of therapy; small lymphoid aggregates. F = higher magnification of E; single lymphoid aggregate (score 2).

shown in table 2. In each case a diagnosis of low-grade B-cell MALT lymphoma was made before anti-*H-pylori* treatment (figure 1). In 5 of 6 patients, lymphoma was confirmed by demonstrating immunoglobulin gene rearrangement by Southern blot or PCR (figure 2). The 6th failed to amplify by PCR (a feature reported in up to 20% of B-cell lymphomas[9,10]). Colonisation of the gastric mucosa by *H pylori* was seen in each case.

Follow-up biopsies showed eradication of *H pylori* in all patients. In 5, biopsies showed no morphological or molecular evidence of lymphoma (figures 1 and 2); in the 6th, biopsy showed a residual infiltrate within the lamina propria which was suspicious for lymphoma, and PCR showed persistence of a weak clonal band in the same position as before but with decreased intensity.

Discussion

Although the diagnosis of low-grade B-cell MALT lymphoma in gastric biopsies is usually straightforward, early or borderline cases can be confused with follicular gastritis seen with *H pylori*. We therefore devised a scoring system to provide a measure of diagnostic confidence. In doubtful cases, lymphoma can be confirmed by demonstrating B-cell monoclonality by either immunocytochemical or molecular methods. We have found PCR can detect a monoclonal B-cell population to a level as low as 1% of total cell numbers.[9]

Stolte[11] suggested that eradication of *H pylori* in borderline cases results in loss of lymphoid tissue in reactive conditions but accentuation of the features of lymphoma. By contrast, Genta et al[12] have shown acquired MALT in all cases of *H-pylori*-associated gastritis and persistence of

Case	Age	Sex	Biopsy	Start of Rx (mo)	Symptoms	Endoscopic appearances	Hist L	Hist HP	PCR P	PCR F	SB F
1	37	M	A	0	Dyspepsia	Abnormal "granular" antral mucosa	5	+	B	ND	ND
			B	1	Asymptomatic	Normal	3	–	S	ND	ND
			C	4	Asymptomatic	Normal	1	–	S	ND	ND
			D	7	Asymptomatic	Normal	2	–	S	ND	ND
2[a]	76	M	A	0	Dyspepsia	AG, healed antral ulcer	5	+	S	S	R
			B	2	Dyspepsia	AG	4	–	ND	B	R
			C	9	Asymptomatic	Small antral erosions	1	–	ND	S	G
3	42	M	A	0	Epigastric pain	AG, small antral erosions	5	+	B	ND	ND
			B	2	Dyspepsia	AG	3	+	B	ND	ND
			C	6	Dyspepsia	Small antral erosions	2	–	S	S	G
4[b]	75	F	A	0	Dyspepsia	Fundic gastritis	5	+	B	B	ND
			B	2	Dyspepsia	Fundic gastritis	3	–	B	B	ND
			C	9	Dyspepsia	Fundic gastritis	4	–	B	B	ND
5[c]	60	F	A	0	Epigastric pain	Pyloric ulcer	5	+	B	ND	ND
			B	3	Asymptomatic	Healed ulcer	3	–	B	ND	ND
			C	8	Asymptomatic	Healed ulcer	2	–	ND	S	G
6[d]	57	F	A	0	Epigastric pain	Healed DU, AG	4	+	S	ND	ND
			B	2	Asymptomatic	Normal	4	–	ND	ND	ND
			C	9	Asymptomatic	Normal	2	–	ND	ND	ND
			D	15	Asymptomatic	Normal	2	–	ND	S	G

Rx = treatment, Hist = histological appearances, L = lymphoma, HP = *H pylori*, PCR = polymerase chain reaction, SB = Southern blot, P = paraffin, F = frozen, AG = antral gastritis, DU = duodenal ulcer, ND = not done, B = monoclonal band, S = polyclonal smear pattern, R = rearranged band, and G = germline configuration.
Previous biopsies, mo before, score: a = 3, 38, 3–5; b = 2, 18, 5; c = 3, 34–38, 3; and d = 3, 11, 3–5; *H pylori* always present.

Table 2: **Clinical, endoscopic, histological, and molecular-genetic features of sequential gastric biopsies after antibiotics**

lymphoid follicles up to a year after eradication of the organism. In 5 of our 6 cases, antibiotic treatment eradicated *H pylori* and caused regression of the lymphoma. The possibility that the anitbiotics alone, directly or via some other mechanism, were responsible for the regression is unlikely given our in-vitro studies showing a specific effect of *H pylori* on tumour-associated T cells.[13]

There are parallels between the effects of antibiotics on gastric MALT lymphomas and their use to induce remissions in early stages of immunoproliferative small intestinal disease,[14] a subtype of MALT lymphoma which shares many of the histological features of low-grade B-cell gastric lymphoma.[1] Low-grade B-cell lymphoma of lymph nodes, including follicular, lymphocytic, and lymphoplasmacytic lymphoma, may also be antigen-responsive. All show some immunological organisation and contain a variety of non-neoplastic cells, including accessory cells, compatible with an immune response. This group of lymphomas is largely incurable and a search for relevant antigens might be more rewarding than chemotherapy.

Long-term follow-up of our low-grade gastric lymphoma patients is clearly indicated. Nevertheless, these results are encouraging. Even with conventional treatments (partial gastrectomy or chemotherapy), which are known to lead to long disease-free survival, long-term follow-up is indicated since gastric MALT lymphoma is an unusually indolent neoplasm, as shown by the 4 cases in this study retrospectively diagnosed as MALT lymphoma and followed up for 11–38 months without progression. Compared with surgery or chemotherapy, antibiotic treatment for *H pylori* is harmless and inexpensive. There is no urgency for radical treatment, and anti-*H-pylori* treatment should, therefore, be the first line of treatment.

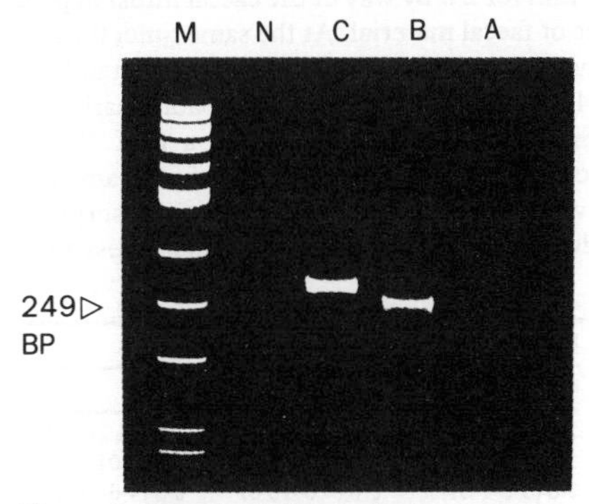

Figure 2: **Case 1—PCR products**

M = molecular weight markers, N = negative control (no DNA template), C = monoclonal control (Raiji B-cell line), B = gastric biopsy before treatment and A = after eradication of *H pylori*.

We thank Dr M S Al-Jafari and Dr B D Linaker for allowing us access to material from case 1. This work was supported by the Cancer Research Campaign and the Leukaemia Research Fund.

References

1 Isaacson PG, Spencer J. Malignant lymphoma of mucosa-associated lymphoid tissue. *Histopathology* 1987; **11:** 445–62.

2 Wyatt JI, Rathbone BJ. Immune response of the gastric mucosa to *Campylobacter pylori. Scand J Gastroenterol* 1988; **23:** 44–49.

3 Stolte M, Eidt S. Lymphoid follicles in the antral mucosa: immune response to *Campylobacter pylori. J Clin Pathol* 1989; **42:** 1269–71.

4 Wotherspoon AC, Ortiz-Hidalgo C, Falzon MF, Isaacson PG. *Helicobacter pylori*-associated gastritis and primary B-cell gastric lymphoma. *Lancet* 1991; **338:** 1175–76.

5 Isaacson PG, Wotherspoon AC, Diss T, Pan L. Follicular colonization in B-cell lymphoma of mucosa-associated lymphoid tissue. *Am J Surg Pathol* 1991; **15:** 819–28.

6 Maniatis T, Fritsch EF, Sambrook J. Molecular cloning: a laboratory manual. New York: Cold Spring Harbour, 1982.

7 Ramasamy I, Brisco M, Morley A. Improved PCR method for detecting monoclonal immunoglobulin heavy chain rearrangement in B cell neoplasms. *J Clin Pathol* 1992; **45:** 770–75.

8 Wan JH, Trainor KJ, Brisco MJ, Morley AA. Monoclonality in B-cell lymphoma detected in paraffin wax embedded sections using the polymerase chain reaction. *J Clin Pathol* 1990; **43:** 888–90.

9 Trainor KJ, Brisco MJ, Story CJ, Morley AA. Monoclonality in B-lymphoproliferative disorders detected at the DNA level. *Blood* 1990; **75:** 2220-22.

10 Diss TC, Peng H, Wotherspoon AC, Isaacson PG, Pan L. Detection of monoclonality in low-grade B-cell lymphomas using the polymerase chain reaction is dependent on primer selection and lymphoma type. *J Pathol* 1993; **169:** 291–95.

11 Stolte M. *Helicobacter pylori* and gastric MALT lymphoma. *Lancet* 1992; **339:** 745–46.

12 Genta RM, Hamner HW, Graham DY. Gastric lymphoid follicles in *Helicobacter pylori* infection: frequency, distribution and response to triple therapy. *Human Pathol* 1993; **24:** 577–83.

13 Hussell T, Isaacson PG, Crabtree JE, Spencer J. The response of cells from low-grade B-cell gastric lymphoma of mucosa-associated lymphoid tissue to *Helicobacter pylor*. *Lancet* 1993; **342:** 571–74.

14 Ben-Ayed F, Halphen M, Najjar T, et al. Treatment of α-chain disease: results of a prospective study in 21 Tunisian patients by the Tunisian-French intestinal lymphoma study group. *Cancer* 1989; **63:** 1251–56.

Reversal by short-chain fatty acids of colonic fluid secretion induced by enteral feeding

Timothy E Bowling, Ana H Raimundo, George K Grimble, David B A Silk

Summary

Diarrhoea complicates enteral feeding in up to 25% of patients. In-vivo perfusion studies in healthy subjects have shown secretion of salt and water in the ascending colon in response to enteral feeding. This study investigated the effect of short-chain fatty acids (SCFA) on this secretory response.

Six healthy volunteers underwent segmental in-vivo colonic perfusion. First, baseline fasting colonic water and electrolyte movement was established, then a standard polymeric enteral diet was infused into the stomach while the colon was perfused with either a control electrolyte solution or a test solution containing SCFA. The electrolyte concentrations and osmolality of the two perfusates were identical. In the fasting state water was absorbed throughout the colon. During the control infusion there was significant ($p<0·05$) secretion of water in the ascending colon (median rate 1·0 mL per min [95% CI 2·8 mL per min secretion to 0·8 mL per min absorption]). During the SCFA infusion the secretion was significantly reversed ($p<0·05$) and there was net absorption (1·6 [0·8–3·7] mL per min). In the distal colon water absorption was significantly greater during the control infusion than during fasting (3·7 [2·5–4·6] vs 1·3 [0·3–2·2] mL per min); during the test infusion this absorption persisted (2·8 [1·3–3·6] mL per min). Movement of sodium, chloride, and potassium ions was similar to that of water in all stages of the study. Bicarbonate movement did not significantly change at any stage.

Infusion of SCFA directly into the caecum reverses the fluid secretion seen in the ascending colon during enteral feeding. This finding could have implications for the management of diarrhoea related to enteral feeding.

Lancet 1993; **342:** 1266–68

Introduction

Diarrhoea is the commonest complication of enteral feeding, occurring in up to 25% of patients.[1] This problem not only limits the efficacy of enteral feeding, but also makes other complications more likely, distresses patients and staff, and increases costs.[2] Several factors have been implicated in the pathogenesis of this diarrhoea, including infusion of contaminated diet, lactose intolerance,[3] concomitant antibiotic therapy,[4,5] and co-existing hypoalbuminaemia.[6,7] Attention to these factors has reduced the incidence of diarrhoea, but it still occurs, in our experience, in at least 15% of patients.

In studies of the function of the small intestine during enteral feeding, diarrhoea invariably occurred during intragastric feeding, even though the volume of fluid entering the colon (colonic in-flow) was the same as that during fasting.[8] During intraduodenal infusion of the same diet, despite an increase in colonic in-flow volume, the subjects did not develop diarrhoea.[9] These findings implied that an abnormality of colonic function may be involved in the pathogenesis of diarrhoea related to enteral feeding.

We therefore carried out in-vivo segmental colonic perfusion in healthy volunteers, and measured water and electrolyte movement simultaneously in the ascending and distal colon in response to the intragastric and intraduodenal infusion of enteral diets of differing strengths.[10,11] There was excessive secretion of water, sodium, and chloride in the ascending colon during the intragastric infusion of low-load or high-load diet, and during the intraduodenal infusion of high-load diet.[10,11]

Short-chain fatty acids (SCFA) are by-products of carbohydrate fermentation in the colon[12,13] and have an important role in salt and water absorption.[14,15] We have investigated the effects of a caecal infusion of SCFA on the secretory response to intragastric enteral feeding.

Patients and methods

The method of in-vivo steady-state colonic perfusion used is a modification of the four-lumen technique of Devroede and Phillips.[16] The tube comprises seven lengths of polyvinyl tubing cemented together along their length with tetrahydrofluoran, with internal diameters ranging from 0·6 to 1·5 mm. Colonic in-flow volumes were calculated from the dilution of a non-absorbable marker infused under steady-state conditions through a 20 cm segment of the terminal ileum just proximal to the ileocaecal valve. We assessed colonic segmental water and electrolyte movement by infusing a second non-absorbable marker into the caecum and sampling at the hepatic flexure and rectum. Full details of the perfusion tube and experimental methods have been reported elsewhere.[17]

Six studies were carried out in healthy volunteers with no history of gastrointestinal disease or metabolic disorders. Approval was granted by the Parkside Health Authority Ethics Committee.

After fasting overnight, the subjects were intubated with the seven-lumen tube, which was allowed to pass caudally so that the distal end was just proximal to the hepatic flexure of the colon. The final position was verified by fluoroscopy. In addition to this orocolonic tube, a nasogastric feeding tube (6 FG, 93 cm; Corpak, Illinois, USA) was inserted. 0·9% normal saline at 37°C was infused at 16 mL per min for 2 h by way of the caecal infusion port to flush the colon free of faecal material. At the same time, the test solution for the terminal ileal segment (18·5 kBq/L tritiated [^{3}H] polyethylene glycol 4000 [PEG] as the non-absorbable marker in 150 mmol/L sodium chloride) was infused into a port 30 cm proximal to the ileocaecal valve at 1 mL per min by means of a peristaltic pump. 2 h was allowed so that a steady state of absorption could be achieved, defined as variation in ^{3}H counts of less than

	Median (95% CI) value		
	Fasting	Control	SCFA
Water (mL per min)	1·75 (1·10–2·10)	1·65 (1·10–2·00)	1·65 (1·20–2·00)
Sodium (mmol/L)	142 (137–147)	144 (128–147)	137 (101–142)
Potasssium (mmol/L)	5·8 (3·9–7·5)	6·0 (4·6–10·8)	6·3 (4·6–10·2)
Chloride (mmol/L)	124 (86–147)	122 (104–137)	114 (82–123)
Bicarbonate (mmol/L)	15 (11–22)	19 (14–24)	19 (8–37)

Table 1: **Colonic in-flow**

Department of Gastroenterology and Nutrition, Central Middlesex Hospital Trust, London NW10 7NS, UK (T E Bowling MRCP, A H Raimundo MD, G K Grimble PhD, D B A Silk FRCP)

Correspondence to: Dr David B A Silk

© *Lancet* 1993; 342: 1266–1268

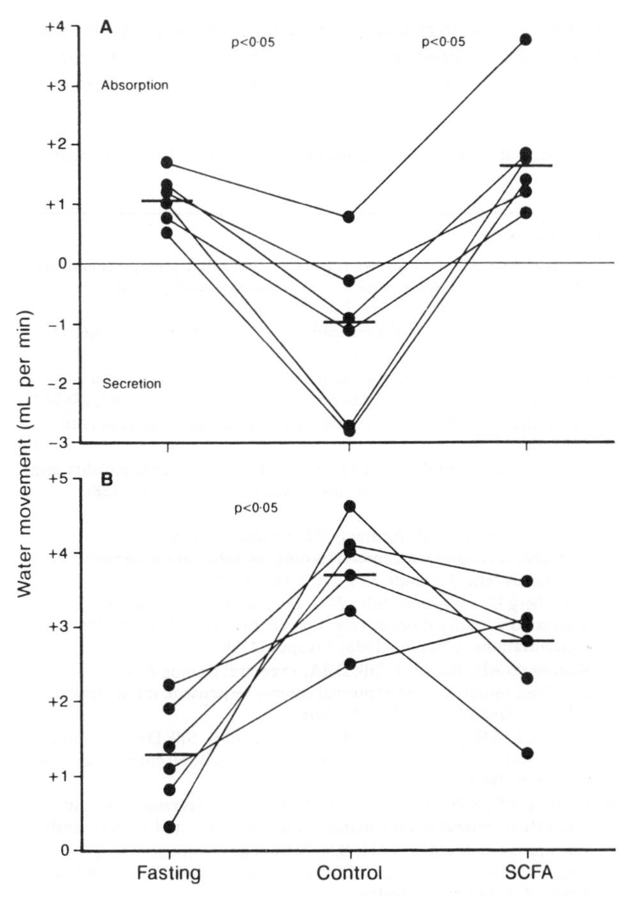

Figure: **Water movement in the ascending colon (A) and distal colon (B)**

5%.[14,16] Thereafter, aspirates were collected every 20 min from the distal end of the 20 cm ileal test segment for the duration of the study. The first 1 mL of each sample was discarded, since this was the calculated dead space within the tube; the subsequent 1 mL was kept for analysis.

Once the colon had been flushed of faecal material, a soft 24 FG tube was placed in the rectum. The control solution for the colon, containing 18·5 kBq/L carbon-14-labelled PEG 4000 in an iso-osmotic electrolyte solution at pH 7 (sodium 120 mmol/L, potassium 30 mmol/L, chloride 40 mmol/L, bicarbonate 20 mmol/L, sulphate 45 mmol/L, mannitol 45 mmol/L) was infused into the caecum at 10 mL per min by means of a peristaltic pump. Again, 2 h of colonic infusion was allowed for a steady state of absorption to be reached; then three collections separated by 10 min intervals were taken from a port at the hepatic flexure and from the rectal fluid. The first 5 mL of each hepatic flexure sample (calculated dead space) was discarded and the subsequent 2 mL kept for analysis. The rectal effluent, however, was allowed to drain freely, and 5 mL was collected every 10 min.

After these fasting collections had been made, the intragastric infusion of enteral diet was started at 1·39 mL per min (1·39 kcal or 5·8 MJ per min, 8·75 mg nitrogen per min). 2 h of feeding was allowed for the new steady state to be reached. Samples from the hepatic flexure port and from the rectal effluent were then taken every 20 min for 3 h. At this stage, SCFA were substituted for the control solution being infused into the caecum. This solution was also iso-osmotic with a pH of 7, and contained the same concentrations of electrolytes as the control solution, but SCFA in physiological concentrations (acetate 50 mmol/L, propionate 20 mmol/L, butyrate 20 mmol/L) replaced the sulphate and mannitol. After another 2 h, samples from the same ports were taken every 20 min for 3 h. The study was terminated and the positions of the orocolonic and nasoenteral tubes were checked by fluoroscopy.

^{3}H and ^{14}C PEG concentrations were measured by double-channel liquid scintillation counting (Beckman LS 7500, High Wycombe, UK) with the H-number method of determination of quenching. Electrolyte contents of perfusion solutions and intestinal aspirates were measured by standard automated clinical methods. The methods used to calculate colonic in-flow volumes and electrolyte concentrations and ascending and distal colonic water and electrolyte flows have been described elsewhere,[17] and are similar to those used in the original perfusion studies.[18-20].

The statistical analysis was planned to be a comparison of colonic in-flow volumes and regional colonic water and electrolyte flows during fasting and during caecal infusion of control and test (SCFA) solutions. The Wilcoxon matched-pairs signed-ranks test was used.

Results

Six successful studies were done (five men, one woman, of mean age 25 years). The median total colonic in-flow during fasting was 1·75 (95% CI 1·10–2·10) mL per min (table 1). There was no significant change during either control or SCFA infusion. Similarly, there were no significant changes in electrolyte concentrations during the study.

In the ascending colon during the fasting state there was water absorption at a median rate of 1·1 (0·5–1·7) mL per min (figure, A).

During the control infusion there was a significant change ($p<0·05$) to a median net secretion of −1·0 (−2·8 to +0·8) mL per min, but during SCFA infusion the secretion was reversed ($p<0·05$) and there was net absorption of median rate 1·6 (0·8–3·7) mL per min. Sodium, chloride, and potassium movement was similar to water movement in the ascending colon throughout the study, with net secretion of all three during the control infusion and net absorption during SCFA infusion (table 2). There was no significant change in bicarbonate secretion during the study.

In the distal colon there was net absorption of water throughout the study, at significantly greater rates during the control infusion than in the fasting state (figure, B).

	Median (95% CI) value mmol per min		
	Fasting	Control	SCFA
Ascending colon			
Sodium	+0·15 (+0·1 to +0·2)	−0·20 (−0·8 to +0·1)*	+0·30 (+0·1 to +0·5)†
Potassium	+0·08 (0 to +0·14)	−0·01 (−0·06 to +0·03)	+0·10 (+0·02 to +0·2)†
Chloride	+0·20 (+0·02 to +0·2)	−0·10 (−0·3 to +0·2)*	+0·07 (−0·2 to +0·2)
Bicarbonate	−0·01 (−0·15 to +0·1)	−0·07 (−0·3 to −0·01)	−0·13 (−0·4 to −0·04)
Distal colon			
Sodium	+0·30 (+0·1 to +0·45)	+0·40 (+0·1 to +0·7)	+0·12 (+0·02 to +0·5)
Potassium	+0·04 (−0·07 to +0·08)	+0·10 (−0·04 to +0·26)	+0·06 (0 to +0·17)
Chloride	+0·05 (−0·1 to +0·13)	+0·45 (+0·2 to +0·6)*	+0·24 (+0·1 to +0·4)†
Bicarbonate	−0·03 (−0·08 to +0·08)	+0·06 (−0·17 to +0·28)	+0·05 (−0·04 to +0·14)

Positive values indicate net absorption, negative values net secretion.
Significance of differences: *$p<0·05$ for control vs fasting; †$p<0·05$ for SCFA vs control.

Table 2: **Electrolyte movement in the colon**

Chloride absorption increased significantly (table 2, $p<0.05$) during the control infusion, and then fell during SCFA infusion ($p<0.05$). The absorption of sodium and potassium also increased during the control infusion, but not significantly. Bicarbonate absorption did not change.

Discussion

We have shown that the fluid secretion that occurs in the ascending colon during intragastric feeding can be reversed by a caecal infusion of SCFA. Endogenous bacteria in the large bowel produce SCFA by anaerobic fermentation of carbohydrates.[21] SCFA are predominantly found in the caecum at concentrations of about 120 mmol/L under physiological conditions.[13] The principal components are acetate, propionate, and butyrate, which are produced in a nearly constant molar ratio of 60/20/20.[13,15]

SCFA have several biological functions. They are important in maintaining the integrity of the colonic epithelium[22] and in stimulating mucosal proliferation.[23] They are avidly absorbed in the colon,[13] and their absorption enhances water and electrolyte absorption.[14,22,24] Their importance in the pathogenesis of diarrhoea probably derives from this feature, although the mechanisms by which they affect water and electrolyte absorption are still unclear. SCFA are absorbed by both ionic and non-ionic diffusion. SCFA ions are probably exchanged for bicarbonate,[14] and non-ionic diffusion takes place after protonation of SCFA by Na^+, K^+, or H^+ provided by the Na^+/H^+ exchange mechanism on the apical membrane.[23]

Ruppin and colleagues[14] examined water and electrolyte movement in response to SCFA. They perfused the whole colon with isotonic solutions directly into the caecum; the solutions contained only one SCFA at 0, 30, 60, or 90 mmol/L. All three SCFA enhanced water, sodium, and potassium absorption and bicarbonate secretion, mainly in a dose-dependent way. Our study followed on from Ruppin's work, since we perfused the colon segmentally, which allowed us to examine ascending colonic function separately, and used all three SCFA in physiological concentrations and ratios.

Our experimental design does not allow us to speculate in detail on mechanisms of electrolyte movement. We did, however, show that sodium, chloride, and potassium absorption was significantly enhanced and bicarbonate secretion increased, although not significantly, in the ascending colon during SCFA infusion. These findings would be consistent with an SCFA/bicarbonate exchange mechanism for non-ionic diffusion and also with recycling of ionised SCFA across the apical membrane in exchange for sodium and chloride.[24]

Many clinicians prescribe fibre-containing diets to patients with diarrhoea related to enteral feeding, because of the theoretical benefit of SCFA on colonic water and electrolyte absorption (unpublished). There are anecdotal reports that such diets can improve the diarrhoea, but no controlled clinical trials have confirmed this belief. We believe that colonic secretion has a fundamental role in the pathogenesis of diarrhoea related to enteral feeding. This is the first study to show that SCFA infused directly into the caecum can reverse this secretion. It is possible that fibre-supplemented enteral diets, which increase the caecal concentration of SCFA, may lower the frequency of diarrhoea.

This study was supported by a grant from the Sir Jules Thorn Charitable Trust.

References

1 Jones BJM, Lees R, Andrews J, Frost P, Silk DBA. Comparison of an elemental and polymeric enteral diet in patients with normal gastrointestinal function. *Gut* 1983; **24:** 78–84.
2 Dobb GJ. Diarrhoea in the critically ill. *Intensive Care Med* 1986; **12:** 113–15.
3 O'Keefe SJD, Adam JK, Cakata E, et al. Nutritional support of malnourished lactose intolerance in African patients. *Gut* 1984; **25:** 942.
4 Silk DBA. Towards the optimization of enteral nutrition. *Clin Nutr* 1987; **6:** 61–74.
5 Keohane PP, Attrill H, Love M, et al. Relation between osmolality and gastrointestinal side effects in enteral nutrition. *BMJ* 1984; **288:** 678–81.
6 Ford EG, Jennings M, Andrassy RJ. Serum albumin (oncotic pressure) correlates with enteral feeding tolerance in the pediatric surgical patient. *J Pediatr Surg* 1987; **22:** 597–99.
7 Waitzberg D, Teixera de Silva ML, Borges VC, et al. Factors associated with diarrhoea in tube fed patients. Role of serum albumin concentrations. *Clin Nutr* 1988; 7 (suppl 1): 58.
8 Raimundo AH, Rogers J, Silk DBA. Is enteral feeding related diarrhoea initiated by an abnormal colonic response to intragastric diet infusion? *Gut* 1990; **31:** A1195 (abstr).
9 Raimundo AH, Rogers J, Grimble GK, Cahill E, Silk DBA. Colonic inflow and small bowel motility during intraduodenal enteral nutrition. *Gut* 1988; **29:** A1469 (abstr).
10 Bowling TE, Raimundo AH, Silk DBA. Colonic secretory effect in response to enteral feeding in man. *Gut* 1993; **34** (suppl 1): A54 (abstr).
11 Bowling TE,, Raimundo AH, Silk DBA. The colonic secretory response to enteral feeding: influence of high strength diet. *Clin Nutr* 1993; **12** (suppl 2): 23 (abstr).
12 Cummings JH. Colonic absorption; the importance of short chain fatty acids in man. *Scand J Gastroenterol* 1984; **19** (suppl 93): 89–99.
13 Cummings JH, Pomare EW, Branch WJ, Naylor CPE, MacFarlane GT. Short chain fatty acids in human large intestine, portal, hepatic and venous blood. *Gut* 1987; **28:** 1221–27.
14 Ruppin H, Bar-Meir S, Soergel KH, Wood CM, Schmitt MG. Absorption of short chain fatty acids by the colon. *Gastroenterology* 1980; **78:** 1500–07.
15 MacFarlane GT, Gibson GR, Cummings JH. Comparisons of fermentation reactions in different regions of the human colon. *J Appl Bacteriol* 1992; **72:** 57–64.
16 Devroede GJ, Phillips SF. Studies of the perfusion technique for colonic absorption. *Gastroenterology* 1969; **56:** 92–100.
17 Bowling TE, Raimundo AH, Silk DBA. In vivo segmental colonic perfusion in man: a new technique. *Eur J Gastroenterol Hepatol* 1993; **5:** 809–15.
18 Levitan R, Fordtran JS, Burrows BA, Ingelfinger FJ. Water and salt absorption in the human colon. *J Clin Invest* 1962; **41:** 1754–59.
19 Whalen GE, Harris JA, Geenen JE, Soergel KH. Sodium and water absorption from the human small intestine. *Gastroenterology* 1966; **51:** 975–84.
20 Phillips SF, Giller J. The contribution of the colon to electrolyte and water conservation in man. *J Lab Clin Med* 1973; **81:** 733–46.
21 Cummings JH, Branch WJ. Fermentation and production of short chain fatty acids in the human large intestine. In: Vahouny GB, Kritchevsky D, eds. Dietary fibre: basic and clinical aspects. New York: Plenum Press, 1986: 131–52.
22 Roediger WEW. Role of anaerobic bacteria in the metabolic welfare of the colonic mucosa in man. *Gut* 1980; **21:** 793–98.
23 Jacobs LR. Effects of dietary fiber on mucosal growth and cell proliferation in the small intestine of the rat: a comparison of oat bran, pectin and guar with total fiber deprivation. *Am J Clin Nutr* 1983; **37:** 954–60.
24 Binder HJ, Mehta P. Short chain fatty acids stimulate active sodium and chloride absorption in vitro in the rat distal colon. *Gastroenterology* 1989; **96:** 989–96.

© *Lancet* 1993; 341: 843–848

Effect of luminal growth factor preservation on intestinal growth

R. J. Playford A. C. Woodman P. Clark P. Watanapa
D. Vesey P. H. Deprez R. C. N. Williamson J. Calam

Intestinal atrophy contributes to the clinical difficulties of patients who cannot eat normally. Atrophy is prevented by luminal food proteins but not by the equivalent aminoacids. This observation is not explained by current theories of intestinal physiology. Epidermal growth factor (EGF) and transforming growth factor α (TGFα) are secreted into the gut lumen. We speculated that these are digested by pancreatic enzymes in fasting juice, but preserved when food proteins block the active sites of these enzymes.

Studies based on molecular size and bioactivity confirmed that fasting human jejunal juice destroys EGF and TGFα. EGF, but not TGFα, was preserved when the milk protein casein or an enzyme inhibitor were present; elemental diets were ineffective. Diversion of pancreatic juice to the mid point of the small intestine in rats significantly increased luminal EGF-like bioactivity and all variables of growth in the proximal enzyme-free segment.

Our findings support a novel mechanism of control of intestinal growth, which has important clinical implications. The addition of enzyme-inhibiting proteins such as casein to elemental diets may preserve intestinal integrity and function.

Lancet 1993; **341**: 843–48.

Introduction

Patients who cannot eat normally may be fed intravenously, although enteral feeds are preferred. One reason is that intravenous feeding causes intestinal atrophy that delays weaning onto normal foods and permits systemic entry of bacteria and toxins.[1] Design of enteral feeds is hindered by ignorance of the mechanism of atrophy. Popular theories are based on nutrition of enterocytes and release of hormones but these do not explain why atrophy is prevented by feeding whole proteins rather than the aminoacids that they contain.[2]

We examined a new idea: that proteins can act as enzyme inhibitors by occupying active sites of pancreatic proteases. In this way they preserve growth factors such as epidermal growth factor (EGF) and transforming growth factor α (TGFα), which are secreted into the lumen but otherwise are digested by luminal proteases. To test this hypothesis we examined the fate of EGF and TGFα added to human jejunal juice with and without food proteins. We then studied the effect of diverting pancreatic enzymes distally on luminal EGF concentrations and intestinal growth in rats.

Materials and methods

Growth factors in human jejunal juice

EGF (human purified, Amersham International, Amersham, UK) and TGFα (recombinant, kindly donated by W. Gulick, RPMS, UK) were labelled with ^{125}I and incubated for 1 h at 37°C in "tris" buffer pH 7·6 either alone or with small intestinal juice from 6 fasting volunteers. Intestinal juice had a trypsin content of 195 μg/mL and a chymotrypsin content of 120 μg/mL. To mimic postprandial conditions the proteins casein (1–20 mg/mL), soya bean trypsin inhibitor (0·1–2 mg/mL), and lactalbumin (1–20 mg/mL, Sigma, UK), together with two elemental diets Elemental 028 (5–400 mg/mL, Scientific Hospital Supplies, Liverpool, UK) and Flexical (5–550 mg/mL, Mead Johnson Nutritionals, Slough, UK) were added separately to the juice before incubation. Samples

ADDRESSES: **Departments of Medicine** (R. J. Playford, MRCP, A. C. Woodman, PhD, D. Vesey, PhD, P. H. Deprez, MD, J. Calam, FRCP), **Surgery** (P. Watanapa, FRCS, Prof R. C. N. Williamson, FRCS), **and Physics** (P. Clark, PhD), **Royal Postgraduate Medical School, London, UK.** Correspondence to Dr R. J. Playford, Gastroenterology Unit, Royal Postgraduate Medical School, Du Cane Road, London W12 0NN, UK.

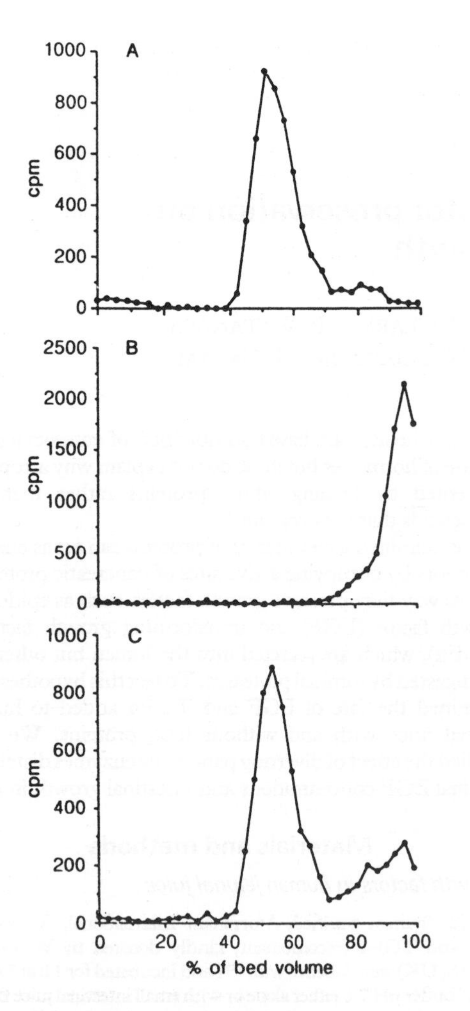

Fig 1—Stability of [^{125}I]EGF in jejunal juice.

Column chromatography separates molecules according to size, the largest eluting first. Typical elution profiles under the various conditions are shown. Cpm, counts per minute.

A: Intact [^{125}I]EGF elutes on a Sephadex G75 column as a single peak at 54 (2)% (n=12) of bed volume.

B: Incubation of the [^{125}I]EGF with fasting jejunal juice results in displacement of the ^{125}I to 96 (2)% (n=6), suggesting destruction of the [^{125}I]EGF.

C: Addition of soya bean trypsin inhibitor (1 or 2 mg/mL) or casein (10 or 20 mg/mL) to the jejunal juice before addition of the [^{125}I]EGF results in the ^{125}I eluting at 54 (2)% (n=8), the position of intact [^{125}I]EGF, suggesting preservation of EGF by food proteins.

were then run on a Sephadex G75 size-exclusion column. The pattern of elution of ^{125}I was noted. To determine which of the proteases present in intestinal juice were responsible for the destruction of EGF and TGFα, the purified enzymes trypsin, chymotrypsin, carboxypeptidase A, carboxypeptidase B, enterokinase, and elastase (at a final concentration of 1 mg/mL), were each incubated with EGF and TGFα under identical conditions. All column runs were done in duplicate unless otherwise stated. In addition, [^{125}I]EGF and [^{125}I]TGFα were regularly run on the column to ensure that their elution position did not change with time.

Preservation of bioactivity in intestinal juice was studied by incubating 50 µg of EGF or TGFα in buffer alone or with fasting jejunal juice with or without the various proteins and elemental diets as for the column chromatography studies. All samples were then diluted 1 in 4 in growth medium and remaining bioactivity was then estimated by a EGF/TGFα bioassay that was based on uptake of [^{3}H]thymidine into rat hepatocytes.[3] To ensure that food proteins were not stimulating thymidine uptake, hepatocytes were

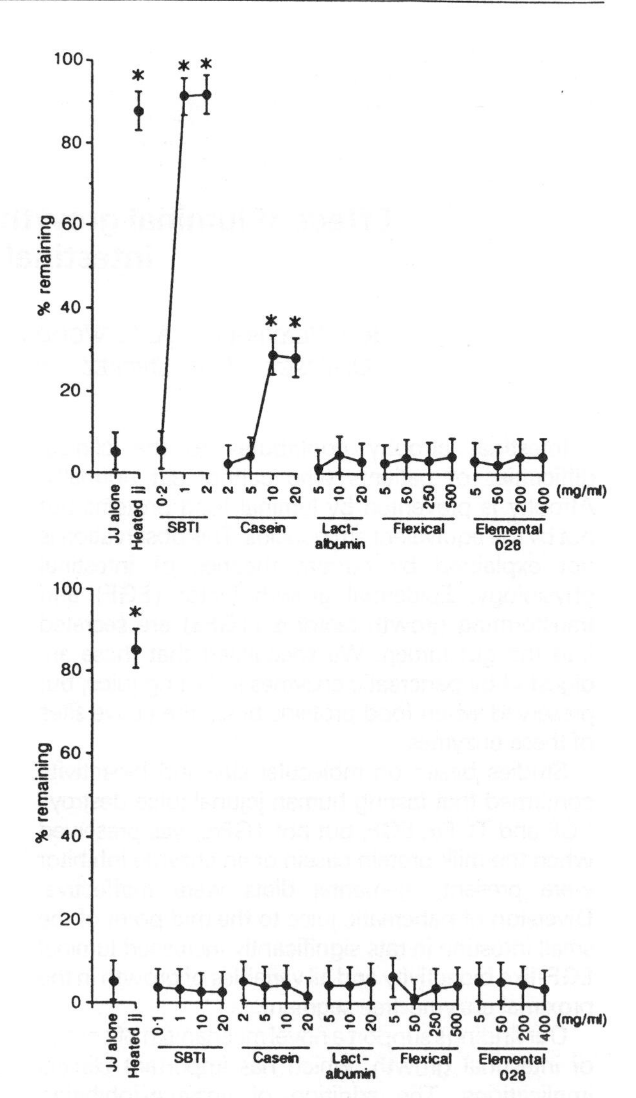

Fig 2—Stability of bioactivity of EGF and TGFα in jejunal juice in vitro

50 µg EGF (upper) or TGFα (lower) were incubated in jejunal juice (jj) with and without various food products at varying concentrations. The food products were three proteins (soya bean trypsin inhibitor, casein, and lactalbumin) and two elemental diets (Flexical and Elemental 028). Incubation of EGF or TGFα in jejunal juice alone destroyed about 95% of biological activity. Heat-inactivated juice only destroyed about 10% of activity. Over 90% of biological activity of EGF was preserved by soya bean trypsin inhibitor at concentrations ≥1 mg/mL and about 30% was preserved by casein at concentrations ≥10 mg/mL. By contrast, lactalbumin, Flexical, and Elemental 028 did not preserve EGF biological activity. No preservation of TGFα by any of the diets was seen. Results are expressed as means and 95% CI for those means.

*$p<0.001$ *vs* incubation in jejunal juice alone.

Detailed statistical comparisons are given in tables I and II.

incubated with various food compounds in jejunal juice under identical conditions but without added EGF or TGFα. For studies of the stability of EGF/TGFα in vitro, thymidine uptake under each condition was measured five times. Measurements of EGF-like bioactivity in rat intestinal juice were done in quadruplicate. The presence of jejunal juice did not affect cell viability as assessed by exclusion of trypan blue from cells, incorporation of [^{3}H] aminoacids into protein, and baseline thymidine incorporation.

Pancreatic juice diversion

If our theory is correct, diversion of pancreatic enzymes from the bowel would increase luminal growth factor activity and intestinal

© Lancet 1993; 341: 843–848

TABLE I—STABILITY OF THE BIOLOGICAL ACTIVITY OF EGF IN JEJUNAL JUICE

Group	Incubation conditions	% EGF survived (mean)	Additional % survival with heat or diet compared with group 1 (mean, 95% CI)	p
1	EGF in jejunal juice	5	..	
2	EGF in heat-treated jejunal juice	88	83 (76, 89)	<0·001
3	EGF in jejunal juice + SBTI			
	(0·2 mg/mL)	6	1 (−6, 7)	0·90
	(1 mg/mL)	91	86 (80, 93)	<0·001
	(2 mg/mL)	92	87 (80, 93)	<0·001
4	EGF in jejunal juice + casein			
	(2 mg/mL)	2	−3 (−9, 4)	0·40
	(5 mg/mL)	4	−1 (−7, 6)	0·81
	(10 mg/mL)	29	24 (17, 30)	<0·001
	(20 mg/mL)	28	23 (17, 30)	<0·001
5	EGF in jejunal juice + lactalbumin			
	(5 mg/mL)	1	−4 (−10, 3)	0·25
	(10 mg/mL)	5	0 (−7, 6)	0·90
	(20 mg/mL)	3	−2 (−9, 4)	0·50
6	EGF in jejunal juice + Flexical			
	(5 mg/mL)	3	−2 (−9, 4)	0·47
	(50 mg/mL)	4	−1 (−7, 5)	0·72
	(250 mg/mL)	3	−2 (−8, 5)	0·58
	(500 mg/mL)	4	−1 (−7, 6)	0·81
7	EGF in jejunal juice + Elemental 028			
	(5 mg/mL)	3	−2 (−9, 5)	0·54
	(50 mg/mL)	2	−3 (−9, 4)	0·40
	(200 mg/mL)	4	−1 (−8, 6)	0·76
	(400 mg/mL)	4	−1 (−8, 6)	0·76

SBTI, soya bean trypsin inhibitor.

TABLE II—STABILITY OF THE BIOLOGICAL ACTIVITY OF TGFα IN JEJUNAL JUICE

Group	Incubation conditions	% TGFα survived (mean)	Additional % survival with heat or diet compared with group 1 (mean, 95% CI)	p
1	TGFα in jejunal juice	5	..	
2	TGFα in heat-treated jejunal juice	85	80 (73, 87)	<0·001
3	TGFα in jejunal juice + SBTI			
	(0·1 mg/mL)	3	−2 (−9, 5)	0·61
	(1 mg/mL)	3	−2 (−9, 5)	0·57
	(10 mg/mL)	2	−3 (−10, 4)	0·42
	(20 mg/mL)	2	−3 (−10, 4)	0·46
4	TGFα in jejunal juice + casein			
	(2 mg/mL)	5	0 (−7, 7)	1·00
	(5 mg/mL)	4	−1 (−8, 6)	0·69
	(10 mg/mL)	4	−1 (−8, 6)	0·77
	(20 mg/mL)	1	−4 (−11, 3)	0·28
5	TGFα in jejunal juice + lactalbumin			
	(5 mg/mL)	4	−1 (−8, 6)	0·77
	(10 mg/mL)	4	−1 (−8, 6)	0·73
	(20 mg/mL)	5	0 (−7, 7)	0·95
6	TGFα in jejunal juice + Flexical			
	(5 mg/mL)	6	1 (−6, 8)	0·73
	(50 mg/mL)	1	−4 (−11, 3)	0·23
	(250 mg/mL)	4	−1 (−9, 5)	0·65
	(500 mg/mL)	4	−2 (−8, 6)	0·73
7	TGFα in jejunal juice + Elemental 028			
	(5 mg/mL)	5	0 (−7, 7)	1·00
	(50 mg/mL)	5	0 (−7, 7)	1·00
	(200 mg/mL)	5	−1 (−8, 6)	0·82
	(400 mg/mL)	3	−2 (−9, 5)	0·61

SBTI, soya bean trypsin inhibitor.

growth. We tested this in three groups of rats (six per group). Two groups had operations that caused pancreatic juice and bile to enter the small bowel about half way down its length; in one group, the ampullary opening with a small cuff of intestine was transplanted. The second group had a roux-en-y procedure in which a 10 cm segment of bowel containing the ampulla was connected to the midpoint of the bowel by an end-to-side anastomosis.[4] The third group had sham operation with the upper intestine and the midpoint of the bowel divided and re-anastomosed. Two weeks later, juice was collected by lavage from 8 cm segments above and below the midpoint of the small intestine for measurement of EGF/TGFα-like bioactivity. The contribution of EGF was examined by adding an EGF-specific blocking antibody.[5] Intestinal growth was assessed at the same sites by estimation of the weight and content of protein, RNA, and DNA per cm by standard methods.[6]

Statistics

For in-vitro studies, thymidine uptake into hepatocytes incubated with the various samples of jejunal juice was compared with an EGF or TGFα standard curve. This approach allowed the determination of the percentage survival of the added growth factors under each condition. These data were then analysed by a one-way ANOVA of the percentage survival. Means, 95% confidence intervals for means, and 95% CI for differences from control (EGF or TGFα in jejunal juice) were based on mean square error and degrees of freedom derived from the ANOVA. The significance of differences from control was assessed by *t* tests with the mean square error and degrees of freedom from the ANOVA. Figure 2 shows the means and 95% CI for the survival of EGF and TGFα. Tables I and II show the differences from control (EGF/TGFα in jejunal juice) and 95% CI for those differences.

The thymidine uptake of hepatocytes incubated with samples from the intestinal washings were compared with an EGF standard curve. Results from washings were therefore expressed in terms of total EGF-like bioactivity per cm of intestinal length. These data were analysed as a split plot design using the GLIM statistical package (Generalised Linear Interactive Modelling, Numerical Algorithms Group, Oxford, UK). Rats were taken as the plots, the operation groups (control, ampullary diversion, and roux en Y) as a between-plot factor, and the position (above and below) as a within-plot factor. Residuals from the ANOVA were checked for normal distribution with the Shapiro Francia W test and for equal variance with the Schweder test.[8,9] To achieve a satisfactory distribution, log (EGF + 1) and log DNA transformations were

TABLE III—EFFECT OF PANCREATICO-BILIARY DIVERSION ON GROWTH VARIABLES AND LUMINAL EGF CONCENTRATIONS IN THE PROXIMAL SEGMENT (NOT PERFUSED WITH PANCREATIC JUICE)

Growth variable	Operation	n	Mean	Difference from control (95% CI)	p
Intestinal weight (mg/cm)	Control	5	55·1		
	Ampulla	6	118·5	63·3 (46·5, 80·2)	<0·0001
	R-en-Y	6	95·9	40·8 (23·9, 57·7)	<0·0001
DNA (μg/cm)	Control	5	513·6		
	Ampulla	6	1225·4	712 (383, 1161)	<0·0001
	R-en-Y	6	1040·1	527 (246·1, 910·3)	0·0001
RNA (μg/cm)	Control	5	339·4		
	Ampulla	6	637·0	298 (132, 463)	0·001
	R-en-Y	6	516·0	177 (11, 342)	0·037
Protein (mg/cm)	Control	5	6·64		
	Ampulla	6	13·68	7·04 (5·12, 8·97)	<0·0001
	R-en-Y	6	10·98	4·34 (2·42, 6·27)	0·0001
Luminal EGF (ng/cm)	Control	6	0·49		
	Ampulla	6	2·48	2·00 (0·36, 5·09)	0·0010
	R-en-Y	6	3·80	3·31 (1·05, 7·58)	0·0007

TABLE IV—EFFECT OF PANCREATICO-BILIARY DIVERSION ON GROWTH VARIABLES AND LUMINAL EGF CONCENTRATION IN THE DISTAL SEGMENT (STILL PERFUSED WITH PANCREATIC JUICE)

Growth variable	Operation	n	Mean	Difference from control (95% CI)	p
Intestinal weight (mg/cm)	Control	5	54·0		
	Ampulla	6	66·1	12·2 (−4·8, 29·0)	0·15
	R-en-Y	6	67·8	13·9 (−3·0, 30·7)	0·10
DNA (μg/cm)	Control	5	501		
	Ampulla	6	539	38 (−107, 236)	0·64
	R-en-Y	6	780	279 (70, 566)	0·007
RNA (μg/cm)	Control	5	305		
	Ampulla	6	342	37 (−129, 203)	0·65
	R-en-Y	6	536	231 (65, 396)	0·008
Protein (mg/cm)	Control	5	6·18		
	Ampulla	6	7·78	1·60 (−0·32, 3·53)	0·10
	R-en-Y	6	7·77	1·59 (−0·34, 3·52)	0·10
Luminal EGF (ng/cm)	Control	6	0·23		
	Ampulla	6	0·25	0·02 (−0·57, 1·14)	0·96
	R-en-Y	6	0·91	0·67 (−0·23, 2·37)	0·17

used in the ANOVA; other comparisons (weight, protein, and RNA) were analysed without transformation. Comparisons of the variables for growth and luminal EGF concentrations in the above and below segments were then compared with the relevant control (sham operation) values by *t* testing with a weighted average of the between-group and within-group variations to calculate both the standard errors used in these tests and confidence intervals. For EGF and DNA, results were transformed back from the log scale to their observed scales for presentation in tables and figures. Results displayed in tables III and IV are expressed as means, differences between means, and 95% CI for those differences. Results in figure 3 are expressed as means and 95% CI for those means.

Results

Growth factors in human jejunal juice

[^{125}I]EGF eluted as a single peak at a mean (SD) 54 (2)% (n = 12) of bed volume (fig 1A). [^{125}I]TGFα eluted as a single peak at 70 (2)% (n = 15). Incubation of [^{125}I]EGF or [^{125}I]TGFα with jejunal juice resulted in displacement of the ^{125}I to 90–100% bed volume suggesting hydrolysis of EGF and TGFα (fig 1B). Pre-heating the jejunal juice to 85°C for 6 min prevented the displacement of ^{125}I. Incubation of [^{125}I]EGF or [^{125}I]TGFα with the pure proteases chymotrypsin and elastase led to elution of ^{125}I at 90–100%, suggesting that these enzymes may have contributed to the destruction of [^{125}I]EGF and [^{125}I]TGFα in jejunal juice. Incubation with trypsin, carboxypeptidase A, carboxypeptidase B, or enterokinase did not alter the elution position of either [^{125}I]EGF or [^{125}I]TGFα. Co-incubation of [^{125}I]EGF with jejunal juice and soya bean trypsin inhibitor (1 mg/mL and 2 mg/mL) or casein (10 mg/mL and 20 mg/mL) resulted in elution of tracer at 54%,

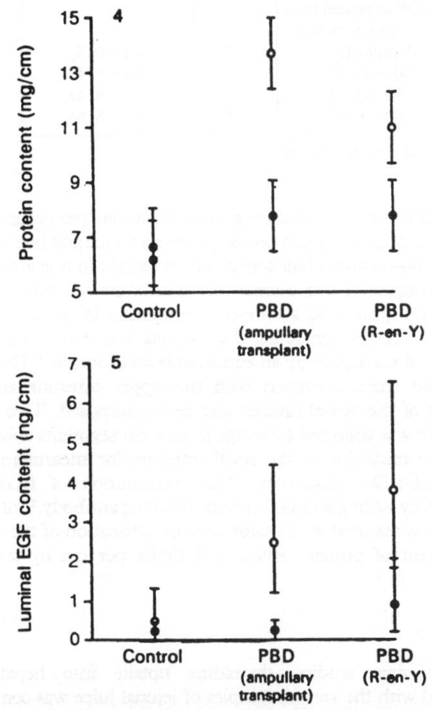

Fig 3—Effects of pancreatico-biliary diversion on intestinal growth.

Three groups of laboratory animals underwent operation: control (sham) and two groups with pancreatico-biliary diversions (PBD) by ampullary transplantation or roux en y. Results from the segment of bowel above the entry of pancreatic juice in PBD-treated animals and the equivalent segment of control animals are shown as open circles (○). Results from segments of bowel below the entry of pancreatic juice are shown as closed circles (●). Results are expressed as mean and 95% CI for the means.

Both methods of diversion caused increased intestinal growth in the segment above entry of pancreatic juice compared with control animals, (all p < 0·01 *vs* control group) but this procedure only had a minor effect on the segment below. PBD also caused a five-fold (ampullary transplanted) and eight-fold (R en Y) increase in luminal EGF bioactivity in the segment above the entry of pancreatic juice (p < 0·01 *vs* control) but not in the segment below. Statistical comparisons are given in tables III and IV.

suggesting protection of EGF (fig 1C). Lower concentrations of soya bean trypsin inhibitor (0·1 mg/mL) and casein (1 mg/mL), as well as all concentrations of lactalbumin (1, 10, and 20 mg/mL), Elemental 028 (5–400 mg/mL), and Flexical (5–550 mg/mL), did not protect [^{125}I]EGF from destruction, with ^{125}I eluting at 90–100%. However, [^{125}I]TGFα behaved differently to [^{125}I]EGF in jejunal juice. Co-incubation of TGFα with jejunal juice and SBTI at 1 mg/mL or 10 mg/mL, casein at 1, 10, and 20 mg/mL, lactalbumin at 1, 10, or 20 mg/mL, Elemental 028 at 5–400 mg/mL, or Flexical at 5–550 mg/mL resulted in the ^{125}I eluting at 90–100%, suggesting destruction of TGFα.

Over 95% of the bioactivities of EGF and TGFα were destroyed by fasting jejunal juice (group 1) (tables I and II, fig 2). By contrast, only about 10% of the bioactivity of EGF and TGFα was destroyed by heat-inactivated intestinal juice (group 2). SBTI in concentrations ≥ 1 mg/mL preserved about 90% of EGF biological activity and casein at concentrations ≥ 10 mg/mL preserved about 30% of biological activity. No protection of TGFα by SBTI or casein was seen. The presence of lactalbumin or elmental diets did not preserve EGF or TGFα. Incubation of hepatocytes with food compounds without added EGF or TGFα did not stimulate thymidine uptake above baseline (data not shown). All of these results are consistent with those obtained using column chromatography.

Pancreatic juice diversion

As can be seen from tables III and IV and figure 3, the main effect of pancreaticobiliary diversion was to increase all measured variables of growth in the segment above the entry of pancreatic juice compared with controls. By contrast, the segments below the entry of pancreatic juice showed only a small, usually non-significant, change in growth compared with controls.

The segments of bowel that were not perfused with pancreatic juice also had about five-fold (ampullary transplantation) and eight-fold (roux en Y) higher intraluminal EGF content than controls. By contrast, segments below the entry of pancreatic juice showed a much smaller, non-significant, increase in intraluminal EGF content than controls. In all samples, >90% of bioactivity was removed by adding the specific EGF-neutralising antiserum.

Discussion

Our results show that human EGF and TGFα are destroyed by fasting human intestinal juice, but EGF is preserved in the presence of casein or SBTI. Elemental diets did not have this effect. Diversion of pancreatic juice distally increased luminal EGF bioactivity and all variables of intestinal growth in the segment above the entry of pancreatic juice, but not in the segment below.

Intestinal atrophy is clinically important but why it occurs is not completely understood. Current theories are largely based on the notion that luminal nutrients provide epithelial nutrition and stimulate hormone release. These ideas might explain why atrophy develops in the absence of luminal nutrients, but do not explain the region-specific changes that we found. In addition, they do not explain why atrophy is prevented by intact proteins but not by the equivalent aminoacids present in elemental diets. Our results support our hypothesis that food proteins prevent the digestion of luminal growth factors, thus allowing them to stimulate intestinal growth. This effect of food protein is expected to depend on kinetic factors including concentration and affinity. Thus, growth factors might not be digested if food proteins were sufficiently concentrated to saturate the enzymes present.

Furthermore, a food protein may or may not have greater affinity for the enzyme than other substrates, including growth factors. Our results agree with those which showed that casein acts as an enzyme inhibitor whereas lactalbumin does not.[10] Our theory also explains a discrepancy in published findings on effects of exogenous EGF on epithelial growth. EGF stimulates growth of human intestinal tissue in vitro.[11] However, administration of EGF into the gut lumen stimulated growth in rats fed normally but not in rats fed intravenously.[12,13] Food proteins may have prevented digestion of EGF in the former but not the latter experiments.

Modern nutritional strategies aim to avoid intestinal atrophy for two main reasons. First, atrophy causes malabsorption that necessitates gradual reintroduction of normal foods over several days.[14,15] Second, by increasing intestinal permeability, atrophy can cause translocation of luminal substances such as endotoxin and even enteric microorganisms into the circulation.[1] Understanding of the molecular mechanisms that prevent atrophy should allow a rational approach to therapy. Our results suggest that the addition of specific proteins such as casein to diets might be of benefit.

Recombinant EGF will soon be available for clinical trials and may prove valuable in the treatment of inflammatory and ulcerative disorders of the intestine, especially since such conditions increase binding of EGF to the mucosa.[16] Oral administration of EGF to rats has been shown to promote healing of chronic duodenal ulcers.[17] Based on our results, the addition of proteins or protease inhibitors or the development of protease-resistant recombinant EGF may improve clinical efficacy.

We thank the Medical Research Council for funding R. J. P. and A. C. W.

REFERENCES

1. Alverdy JC, Aoys E, Moss GS. Total parenteral nutrition promotes bacterial translocation from the gut. *Surgery* 1988; **104:** 185–90.
2. Morin CL, Ling V, Bourassa D. Small intestinal and colonic changes induced by a chemically defined diet. *Dig Dis Sci* 1980; **25:** 123–28.
3. Selden AC, Hodgson HJF. Further characterisation of hepatotropin, a high molecular weight hepatotrophic factor in rat serum. *J Hepatol* 1989; **9:** 167–76.
4. Newman BM, Brooks S, Tajiri H, Cooney DR, Lebenthal E, Lee PC. Long term pancreaticobiliary diversion in the rat: persistent loss of enterokinase with reintroduction by delayed oral pancreatic biliary supplementation. *Digestion* 1988; **41:** 172–79.
5. Vesey DA, Selden AC, Woodman AC, Hodgson HJF. Effect of in vivo administration of an antibody to epidermal growth factor on the rapid increase in DNA-synthesis induced by partial hepatectomy in the rat. *Gut* 1992; **33:** 831–35.
6. Terpstra OT, Dahl EP, Williamson RCN, Ross JS, Malt RA. Colostomy closure promotes cell proliferation and dimethyl hydrazine-induced carcinogenesis in rat distal colon. *Gastroenterology* 1981; **81:** 475–80.
7. Winer BJ. In: Statistical principles in experimental design, 2nd edition. New York: McGraw-Hill. 1971: 201.
8. Royston JP. A simple method for evaluating the Shapiro Francia W test of non normality. *Statistician* 1983; **32:** 297–300.
9. Schweder T. A simple test for a set of sums of squares. *Appl Stat* 1981; **30:** 16–21.
10. Liddle RA, Green GM, Conrad CK. Proteins but not amino acids, carbohydrates or fats stimulate cholecystokinin secretion in the rat. *Am J Physiol* 1986; **251:** G243–48.
11. Challacombe DN, Wheeler EE. Trophic effect of epidermal growth factor on human duodenal mucosa cultured in vitro. *Gut* 1991; **32:** 991–93.

12. Goodlad RA, Wilson TJG, Lenton W, Gregory H, Mccullagh KG, Wright NA. Intravenous but not intragastric urogastrone (EGF) is trophic to the intestine of parenterally fed rats. *Gut* 1987; 28: 573–82.
13. Ulshen MH, Lyn-Cook LE, Raasch RH. Effects of intraluminal epidermal growth factor on mucosal proliferation in the small intestine of adult rats. *Gastroenterology* 1986; 91: 1134–40.
14. Bragg LE, Thompson JS, Rikkers LF. Influence of nutrient delivery on gut structure and function. *Nutrition* 1991; 7: 237–43.
15. Miura S, Tanaka S, Yoshioka M, et al. Changes in intestinal absorption of nutrients and brush border glycoproteins after total parenteral nutrition in rats. *Gut* 1992; 33: 484–89.
16. Poulsen SS. On the role of epidermal growth factor in the defence of gastroduodenal mucosa. *Scand J Gastroenterol* 1987; 22 (suppl 128): 20–21.
17. Skov-Olsen P, Poulsen SS, Therkelsen K, Nexo E. Oral administration of synthetic human urogastrone promotes healing of chronic duodenal ulcers in rats. *Gastroenterology* 1986; 90: 911–17.

© *Gut* 1993; 34: 1060–1065

Eradicating *Helicobacter pylori* infection lowers gastrin mediated acid secretion by two thirds in patients with duodenal ulcer

E El-Omar, I Penman, C A Dorrian, J E S Ardill, K E L McColl

Abstract

***Helicobacter pylori* (*H pylori*) raises serum gastrin but it is unclear whether this stimulates increased acid secretion. Gastrin mediated acid secretion and plasma gastrin after the intravenous infusion of gastrin releasing peptide was studied in nine *H pylori* negative and nine *H pylori* positive healthy volunteers, and in 11 duodenal ulcer patients. Nine of the last group were re-examined one month after eradication of *H pylori*. The median acid output (mmol/h) to gastrin releasing peptide (40 pmol/kg/h) in the *H pylori* positive healthy volunteers was 15·1 (range 3·3–38·3), which was three times that of the *H pylori* negative healthy volunteers (median=5·5, range 1·0–9·0) ($p<0·02$). The median acid output in the duodenal ulcer patients with *H pylori* was 37 (range 8·5–57), which was >six times that of the *H pylori* negative healthy volunteers. Eradication of *H pylori* in the duodenal ulcer patients lowered their acid secretion by a median of 66% (range 30%–80%) ($p<0·01$) and to values equivalent to the *H pylori* positive healthy volunteers. The pepsin output in response to gastrin releasing peptide followed the same pattern as the acid output. The median plasma gastrin concentrations during gastrin releasing peptide were similar in the *H pylori* positive duodenal ulcer patients (150 ng/l, range 95–400) and *H pylori* positive healthy volunteers (129 ng/l, range 23–420) and both were appreciably higher than *H pylori* negative healthy volunteers (60 ng/l, range 28–135) ($p<0·005$ for each). Eradication of *H pylori* lowered the plasma gastrin in the duodenal ulcer patients to values equivalent to the *H pylori* negative healthy volunteers. These findings show a threefold increase in acid secretion in *H pylori* positive healthy volunteers that is explained by *H pylori* induced hypergastrinaemia and a sixfold increase in acid secretion in the duodenal ulcer patients that is explained by the combination of *H pylori* induced hypergastrinaemia and an exaggerated acid response to stimulation by gastrin. Eradicating *H pylori* lowers gastrin mediated acid secretion by 66% in duodenal ulcer patients as a result of the resolution of the hypergastrinaemia. Increased gastrin mediated acid secretion seems to be the key factor in the pathophysiology of duodenal ulceration and explains the role of *H pylori* infection in the disorder.**

(*Gut* 1993; **34:** 1060–1065)

University Department of Medicine and Therapeutics,
E El-Omar
I Penman
K E L McColl

and Pathological Biochemistry, Western Infirmary, Glasgow
C A Dorrian

Queen's University, Belfast
J E S Ardill

Correspondence to:
Dr E L McColl, University Department of Medicine and Therapeutics, Western Infirmary, Glasgow G11 6NT.

Helicobacter pylori (*H pylori*) infection is now recognised to be the main acquired factor in the pathogenesis of duodenal ulcer disease. It is present in >95% of duodenal ulcer patients and numerous studies have shown that eradicating the infection dramatically lowers the ulcer relapse rate.[1–4] The mechanism by which this infection, which predominantly affects the antral mucosa, predisposes to ulceration of the duodenum is unknown. Also, the reason why only a small proportion of subjects with this common infection develop duodenal ulceration is unclear.

We and others have shown that both duodenal ulcer patients and healthy volunteers with *H pylori* have increased basal and meal stimulated gastrin concentrations that fall after eradication of the infection.[5–9] Though gastrin is recognised to be the main mediator of meal stimulated acid secretion,[10] the effect of *H pylori* on acid secretion remains unclear. A major reason for this is the technical difficulty of reliably determining acid output in response to a meal. To overcome this problem we have measured gastrin mediated acid secretion after the intravenous infusion of gastrin releasing peptide. This stimulates the release of endogenous gastrin, which in turn stimulates acid secretion, and thus makes it possible to measure accurately the combined functional response of the antrum and body of the stomach. Gastrin releasing peptide like peptides also stimulate the release of cholecystokinin[11] and somatostatin[12] as well as other gastric inhibitory hormones[11] and in this way simulate the response to eating.

To elucidate the effect of *H pylori* on gastric function, we have examined basal and gastrin mediated acid secretion in healthy volunteers with and without *H pylori* and also in duodenal ulcer patients before and after eradicating the infection.

Patients and methods

Eleven *H pylori* positive patients (eight men) with chronic duodenal ulcer disease proved by endoscopy, nine *H pylori* positive healthy volunteers (seven men), and nine *H pylori* negative healthy volunteers (six men) were studied. The three groups were matched for age and body weight. There were eight smokers in the duodenal ulcer group and three in each of the other two groups. Duodenal ulcer patients were asked to stop any antisecretory treatment two weeks before the secretory studies. None of the healthy volunteers were taking any drug and none reported major gastrointestinal symptoms. *H pylori* infection was confirmed in the duodenal ulcer patients by microscopic examination of antral biopsy rapid urease test (CLO test) on antral biopsy, and by ^{14}C urea breath test. In

© Gut 1993; 34: 1060–1065

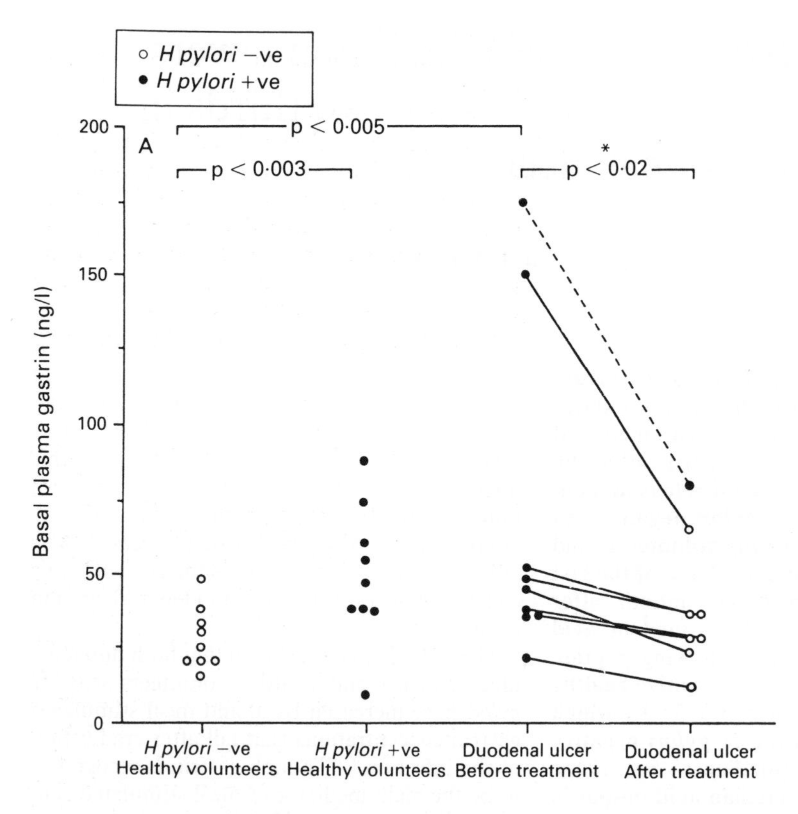

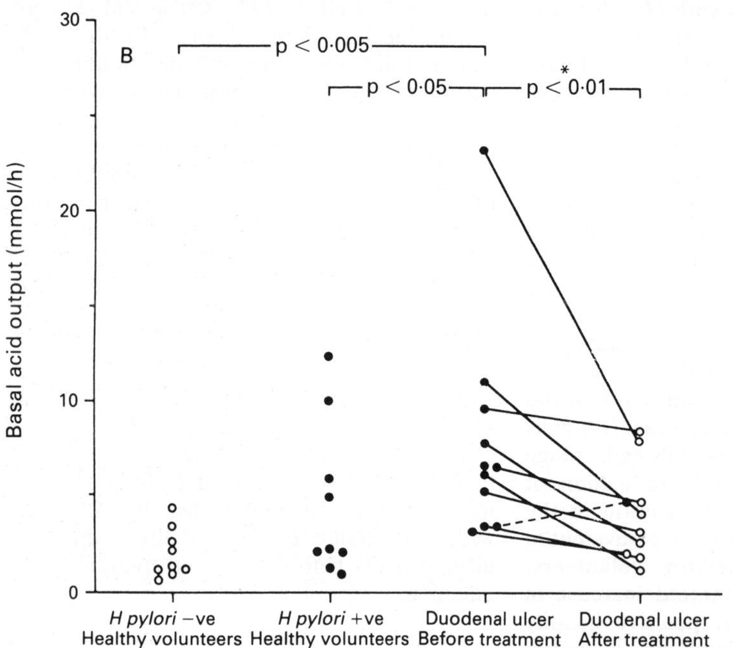

Figure 1: Basal plasma gastrin concentrations (A) and basal acid output (B) in healthy volunteers with and without H pylori, *and in duodenal ulcer patients before and after* H pylori *eradication treatment. The before and after treatment values in the patient in whom the infection was not eradicated are joined by broken line. *Statistics applies only to the patients in whom the infection was eradicated.*

healthy volunteers, *H pylori* state was determined by the ^{14}C urea breath test.

SECRETORY STUDIES

All subjects reported at 0900 after a 12 hour fast. An orogastric tube (Anderson Inc, New York) was swallowed and its position in the dependent part of the stomach checked by the water recovery test. After emptying the stomach, intermittent suction was applied using an intermittent suction unit (Ohmeda, Columbia, USA) that applies suction for 20 seconds in each 32 second cycle. Three 15 minute collections were obtained basally and at each of the following rates of intravenous infusion of gastrin releasing peptide: 10, 40, 100, and 200 pmol/kg/hr. Blood samples were collected every 15 minutes for gastrin determination and the plasma stored at −20°C. The secretory studies were all performed with the investigator blind to the subjects' *H pylori* state.

Gastrin releasing peptide was purchased from Cambridge Research Biochemicals (Cheshire, England) in 0·5 mg aliquots. Each aliquot was made up into a stock solution by dissolving in sterile water. 0·1 ml of 50% acetic acid solution was added to stablilise the solution. Aliquots were stored at −80°C. For each study the aliquot was further diluted in 0·9% NaCl solution.

The volume and pH of each gastric juice collection was recorded and its hydrogen ion concentration measured by titration with 0·1 N NaOH to pH 7 using an autotritrator (Radiometer ETS 822). Gastric juice aliquots for pepsin measurement were centrifuged at 4°C. One ml of each aliquot was added to 0·3 ml of a Glycerol/HCl (10 mmol) solution 50/50 vol/vol). Samples were stored at −80°C before determination of pepsin activity by the method of Gray and Billings.[13]

Basal acid output was calculated by taking the mean of all three 15 minute samples before gastrin releasing peptide infusion. Acid and pepsin outputs for each gastrin releasing peptide infusion rate were calculated by taking the mean of the second and third 15 minute collections. Pepsin measurements were not performed in two of 10 duodenal ulcer patients after treatment.

Gastrin was measured by radioimmunoassay with antiserum R98[14] that has a sensitivity of 5 ng/l. The basal gastrin value for each subject was measured by taking the mean of the three samples obtained before the start of gastrin releasing peptide infusion. The gastrin value at each infusion rate of gastrin releasing peptide was measured by taking the mean of the two values at 30 and 45 minutes of each infusion. To ensure accuracy, gastrin measurements were performed in the same assay batch. For this reason, gastrin results are not available in two of 11 duodenal ulcer patients before treatment and two of 10 duodenal ulcer patients after treatment who entered the study later.

ERADICATION OF H PYLORI

After the above secretory studies, 10 duodenal ulcer patients were treated with tripotassium dicitratobismuthate 120 mg three times daily, metronidazole 400 mg three times daily, and amoxycillin 500 mg three times daily for three weeks. One month after completion of this treatment their ^{14}C-urea breath test was repeated to assess the *H pylori* state. Their secretory studies were also repeated at this point.

STATISTICS

Statistical analysis of unpaired data was performed using the Mann-Whitney U test and of paired data using the Wilcoxin test. A p value of

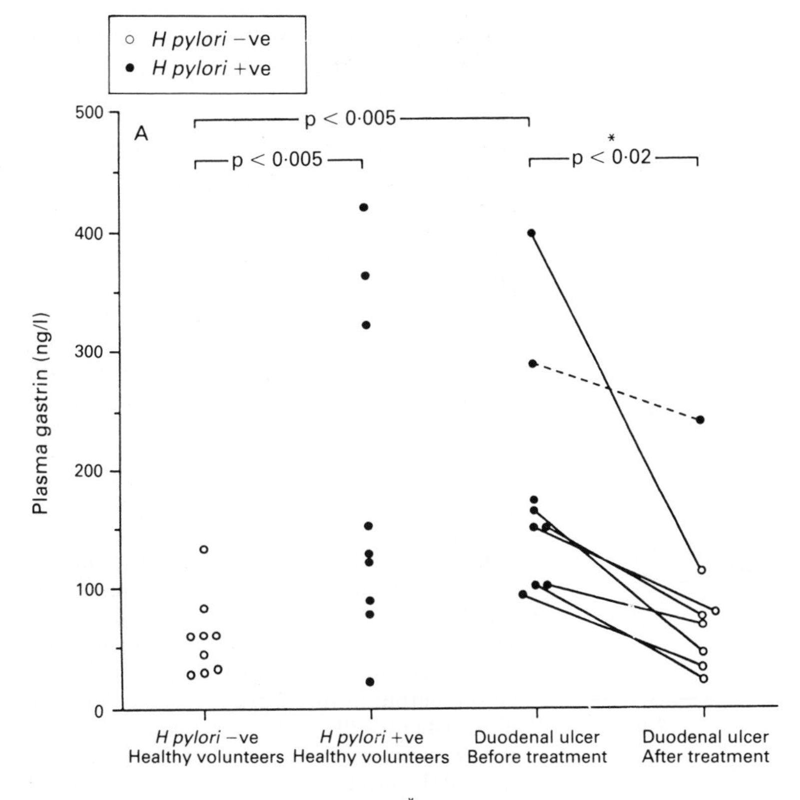

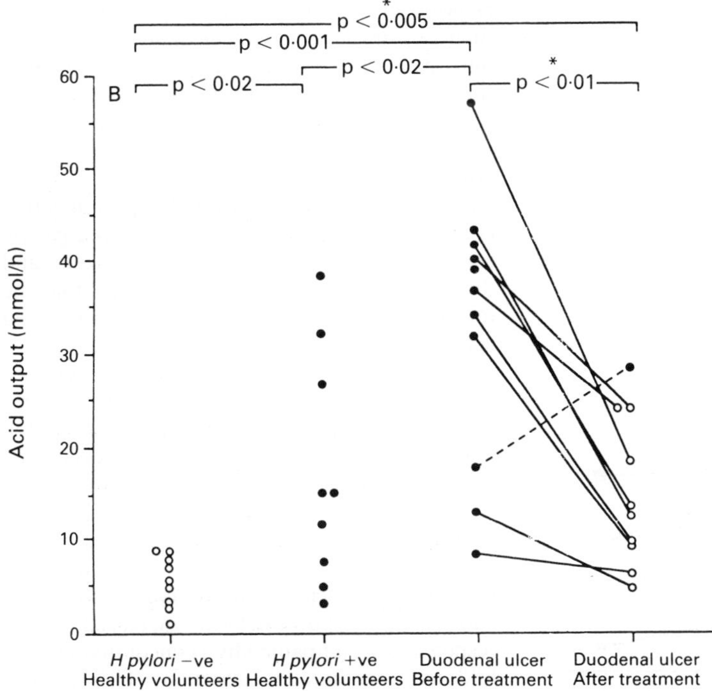

*Figure 2: Plasma gastrin concentrations (A) and acid output (B) during intravenous infusion of gastrin releasing peptide (40 pmol/kg/h). The before and after treatment values in the patient in whom the infection was not eradicated are joined by broken line. *Statistics applies only to the patients eradicated of* H pylori.

<0·05 was taken as significant. The study was approved by the Western Infirmary Ethical Committee.

Results

The repeat ^{14}C-urea breath test at one month after completion of the triple anti-*H pylori* treatment showed that the infection had been eradicated in nine of 10 duodenal ulcer patients.

BASAL GASTRIN

The medium basal gastrin (ng/l) was increased by a similar extent in the *H pylori* positive healthy volunteers (45, range 10–88) and *H pylori* positive duodenal ulcer patients (47, range 22–175) compared with the *H pylori* negative healthy controls (25, range 15–48) (p<0·005 for both) (Fig 1A). After eradication of *H pylori* the median serum gastrin in the duodenal ulcer patients fell to 28 (range 12–65) (p<0·02 *v* before eradication), which was similar to the value in the *H pylori* negative healthy volunteers.

BASAL ACID SECRETION

The median basal acid output (mmol/h) was similar in the *H pylori* negative (1·3, range 0·7–4·6) and positive (2·2, range 1·0–13·3) healthy volunteers (Fig 1B). It was increased in the *H pylori* positive duodenal ulcer patients (6·6, range 3·1–23·2), however, compared with both the *H pylori* negative healthy volunteers (p< 0·005) and *H pylori* positive healthy volunteers (p<0·05). Eradication of *H pylori* lowered the median basal acid output in the nine duodenal ulcer patients to 3·6 (range 1·2–8·4) (p<0·01 *v* before eradication), representing a median reduction of 50% (20%–80%). The basal acid output in the one duodenal ulcer subject in whom *H pylori* infection was not eradicated was similar before (3·7) and after (4·8) the triple treatment.

GASTRIN RESPONSE TO GASTRIN RELEASING PEPTIDE

At the gastrin releasing peptide infusion rate of 40 pmol/kg/h the median plasma gastrin concentration (ng/l) was increased to a similar value in the *H pylori* positive healthy volunteers (129, range 23–420) and *H pylori* positive duodenal ulcer patients (150, range 94–400) and each was higher than that of the *H pylori* negative healthy volunteers (60, range 28–135) (p<0·005 for each) (Fig 2A). After eradication of *H pylori* the median gastrin concentration in response to gastrin releasing peptide 40 pmol/kg/h in the nine duodenal ulcer patients fell to 68 (range 23–115) (p<0·02 *v* before eradication), which was similar to the value in the *H pylori* negative healthy volunteers.

Though the gastrin concentration increased with increasing gastrin releasing peptide infusion rates, the four groups of subjects showed the same pattern of response at each infusion rate (Fig 3A). The statistical differences between the groups were the same at each infusion rate as that seen at 40 pmol/kg/h. We chose to present the results of the individual data points for the 40 pmol/kg/h gastrin releasing peptide rate as the gastrin concentrations stimulated by this are closest to those seen after a meal.

ACID RESPONSE TO GASTRIN RELEASING PEPTIDE

At gastrin releasing peptide 40 pmol/kg/h the median acid output (mmol/h) in the *H pylori* positive healthy volunteers (15·1, range 3·3–38·3) was about three times that of the *H pylori* negative healthy volunteers (5·5, range

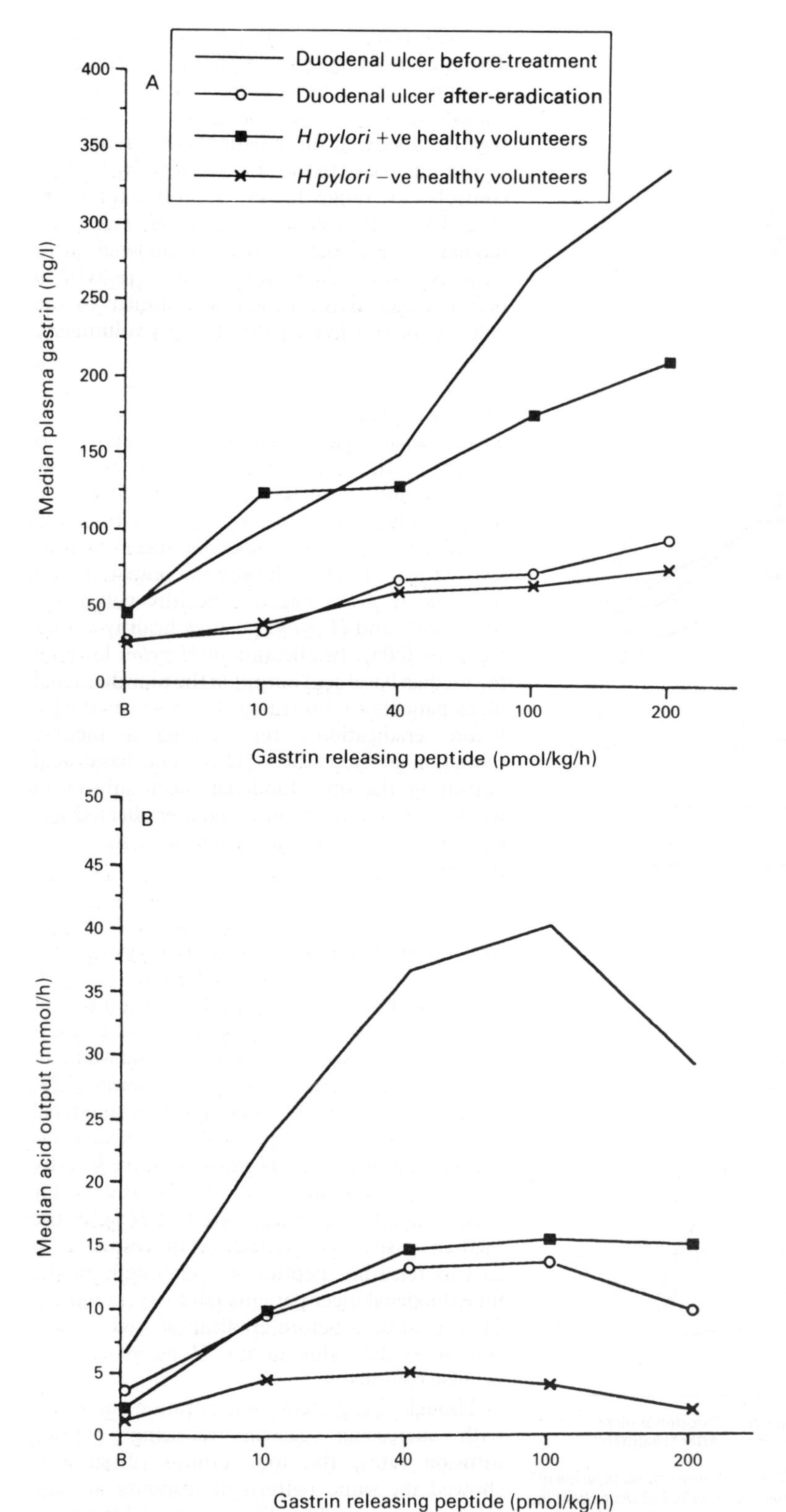

Figure 3: Median plasma gastrin concentration (A) and median acid output (B) in response to increasing infusion rates of gastrin releasing peptide in the different groups examined.

1·0–9·0) (p<0·02) (Fig 2B). At this infusion rate the median acid output in the *H pylori* positive duodenal ulcer patients was 37 (range 8·5–57), which was about twice that of the *H pylori* positive healthy volunteers (p<0·02) and six times that of the *H pylori* negative healthy volunteers (p<0·001). After eradication of *H pylori* the acid output in the nine duodenal ulcer patients fell by a median of 66% (range 30%–80%) to a median value of 13·7 mmol/h (range 6·2–24) (p<0·01) and thus became similar to that of the *H pylori* positive healthy volunteers but remained higher than the *H pylori* negative healthy volunteers (p<0·005). Gastrin mediated acid secretion did not fall in the one patient whose infection was not eradicated (Fig 2B).

The acid response to gastrin releasing peptide was again consistent in the four groups at each of the infusion rates of gastrin releasing peptide studied (Fig 3B).

PEPSIN RESPONSE TO GASTRIN RELEASING PEPTIDE

The pepsin response to gastrin releasing peptide showed the same pattern as the acid response at each infusion rate of gastrin releasing peptide. The differences between the groups, however, were most evident at the gastrin releasing peptide infusion rate of 100 pmol/kg/h (Fig 4).

In response to gastrin releasing peptide 100 pmol/kg/h the median pepsin output (units/h) in the *H pylori* positive healthy volunteers (18, 15–43) was higher than the *H pylori* negative volunteers (12, 6–25) (p<0·02). The median pepsin output in the *H pylori* positive duodenal ulcer patients (29, 19–60) was higher than both the *H pylori* positive (p<0·005) and negative (p<0·001) healthy volunteers. Eradication of *H pylori* in the duodenal ulcer patients lowered their pepsin output by a median of 55% to 17 units/h (11–55) (p<0·03) making them similar to the *H pylori* positive healthy volunteers.

Discussion

This study shows that chronic *H pylori* infection is accompanied by appreciably increased gastric acid output in both healthy volunteers and duodenal ulcer patients. It also shows that the infection increases both basal and stimulated acid secretion.

In the healthy volunteers with *H pylori* both their basal gastrin and gastrin response to gastrin releasing peptide were increased compared with the *H pylori* negative healthy volunteers. The two–threefold increase in gastrin response to gastrin releasing peptide in the *H pylori* positive healthy volunteers is consistent with their previously reported two–threefold increased gastrin response to a meal.[6 9] The design of this study allowed us to show that this increased gastrin response is accompanied by a concomitant threefold increase in acid secretion. This is consistent with the recent studies showing that the increased gastrin concentration in *H pylori* infection is due to a rise in the biologically active G17 form of the hormone.[15 16]

The duodenal ulcer patients with *H pylori* infection resembled the *H pylori* positive healthy volunteers with respect to their serum gastrin concentrations both basally and at each infusion rate of gastrin releasing peptide. This is consistent with our previous finding that the gastrin response to a meal is exaggerated by a similar extent in *H pylori* positive duodenal ulcer patients and *H pylori* positive healthy volunteers.[6] The *H pylori* positive duodenal ulcer patients and *H pylori* positive healthy volunteers differed, however, with respect to gastrin mediated acid secretion, which was increased sixfold

© Gut 1993; 34: 1060–1065

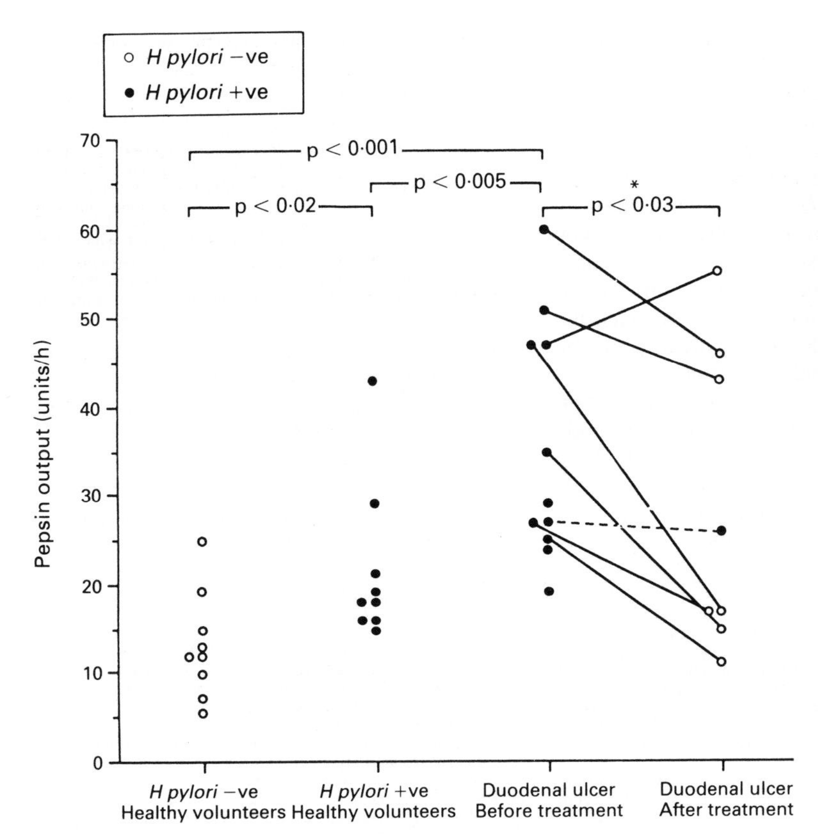

Figure 4: Pepsin output during intravenous infusion of gastrin releasing peptide (100 pmol/kg/h) in healthy volunteers with and without H pylori *and in duodenal ulcer patients before and after* H pylori *eradication treatment. The before and after treatment values in the patient in whom the infection was not eradicated are joined by broken line. *Statistics applies only to the patients in whom the infection was eradicated.*

in the first but only threefold in the second when compared with *H pylori* negative healthy volunteers. The fact that the duodenal ulcer patients secreted more than twice as much acid as the *H pylori* positive healthy volunteers despite having equivalent gastrin concentrations shows that the duodenal ulcer patients have an exaggerated acid response to stimulation by gastrin. This finding is consistent with the previous studies showing that duodenal ulcer patients have an increased sensitivity to pentagastrin[17–19] as well as to endogenous gastrin released in response to a peptone meal.[20]

Our data, therefore, show that subjects with *H pylori* infection who develop duodenal ulceration have two disturbances of gastric function: (1) increased release of gastrin by the antral mucosa and (2) an exaggerated acid response to stimulation by gastrin. It is this dual defect that causes their considerable sixfold increase in gastrin mediated acid secretion. The increased antral gastrin release is explained by the *H pylori* infection though the mechanism by which the infection stimulates gastrin release is unknown. It may be secondary to the recent findings of reduced somatostatin concentrations in the presence of *H pylori* infection.[21 22] The exaggerated acid response to gastrin can be explained by the increased parietal cell mass present in duodenal ulcer patients.[23] The increased parietal cell mass may be due to the longterm trophic effects of *H pylori* induced hypergastrinaemia on the oxyntic mucosa,[24 25] due to smoking,[26] represent the genetic factor in duodenal ulcer, or be due to any combination of these.

After eradication of *H pylori* infection in the duodenal ulcer patients their gastrin fell to the same value as the *H pylori* negative healthy volunteers and this was accompanied by a 66% fall in their gastrin mediated acid secretion after gastrin releasing peptide. This brought acid secretion in the duodenal ulcer patients into the range of the *H pylori* positive healthy volunteers but it did not fall to the values of *H pylori* negative healthy volunteers. This is explained by the fact that eradicating *H pylori* resolved the increased acid secretion caused by the increased antral gastrin release but did not resolve that caused by their exaggerated acid response to gastrin. The second finding is consistent with our previous study showing that the response to pentagastrin stimulation in duodenal ulcer patients is not changed after eradication of *H pylori*.[27] The fact that the exaggerated acid response to gastrin did not resolve after eradication of *H pylori* does not exclude it being due to trophic effects of *H pylori* induced hypergastrinaemia on the oxyntic mucosa. The half life of the parietal cell is 23 days in rats[28] and presumably much longer in man and therefore it could take many months for resolution of an increased parietal cell mass.

Increased basal and nocturnal acid output are also important features of duodenal ulcer disease[29 30] and in this study the median basal acid output of the *H pylori* positive duodenal ulcer patients was five times that of the *H pylori* negative healthy volunteers. After eradication of *H pylori* in the duodenal ulcer patients both their basal acid output and basal gastrin fell by 50%. Though gastrin is considered to be the main mediator of food stimulated acid secretion,[10] its role in the regulation of basal acid output is unclear. The fact that the fall in basal gastrin with eradication of *H pylori* in the duodenal ulcer patients was accompanied by a fall in basal acid secretion suggests that the increased basal gastrin was stimulating gastric secretion in the absence of food. Further evidence of this is the fact that the value of gastrin that increased acid secretion after gastrin releasing peptide in the *H pylori* negative healthy volunteers was equivalent to the basal gastrin value in the *H pylori* positive duodenal ulcer patients. Though basal gastrin was increased to a similar extent in *H pylori* positive healthy volunteers and *H pylori* positive duodenal ulcer patients the first did not have a significantly increased basal acid output. This may be explained by the fact that the increased basal acid output in duodenal ulcer patients was due to their combination of increased basal gastrin and exaggerated acid response to gastrin. It is probable that the increased basal gastrin is also stimulating increased basal acid secretion in the *H pylori* positive healthy volunteers, which will become discernible after lowering of the gastrin by eradicating the infection.

In addition to increased acid secretion, duodenal ulcer patients are known to have increased pepsin secretion[31] and it is the increased exposure to this combination of acid and pepsin that is likely to be injurious to the duodenal mucosa. In our studies pepsin output correlated closely with acid output. The beneficial effect of eradicating *H pylori* in duodenal ulcer patients is therefore explained by the consequent lowering of gastric acid and pepsin secretion to the values present in non-ulcer (*H pylori* positive) subjects.

The finding in this study that gastrin mediated acid secretion is so appreciably increased (six-fold) in duodenal ulcer patients compared with true normal subjects (*H pylori* negative healthy volunteers) implies that it is likely to be the key factor in the pathophysiology of duodenal ulcer disease. The effect of *H pylori* on gastrin mediated acid secretion provides a scientific explanation for the role of the infection in the pathogenesis of duodenal ulceration.

Because of the fact that permanent reduction of acid secretion can be achieved by a single course of *H pylori* eradication treatment, there seems little justification to continue to treat duodenal ulcer patients with repeated courses of expensive acid suppressive agents.

This work was supported by grants from the Biomedical Research Committee of the Scottish Home and Health Department and the Research Support Group of the Greater Glasgow Health Board. The authors gratefully acknowledge the assistance of the staff of the Department of Nuclear Medicine, Western Infirmary; the statistical advice of Miss Catherine Howie; the technical assistance of Mrs Devina Fillmore, Sister Liz Spence, and Mrs Jennifer Harwood and the invaluable secretarial assistance of Mrs Dorothy Ronney.

This work was presented at the 1992 Autumn Meeting of the British Society of Gastroenterology and appeared as an abstract in *Gut*.

1 Marshall BJ, Goodwin CS, Warren JR, Murray R, Blincow ED, Blackburn SJ, *et al.* Prospective double-blind trial of duodenal ulcer relapse after eradication of Campylobacter pylori. *Lancet* 1988; ii: 1437–41.
2 Coghlan JG, Gilligan D, Humphries H, McKenna D, Dooley C, Sweeney E, *et al.* Campylobacter pylori and recurrence of duodenal ulcers – a 12 month follow-up study. *Lancet* 1987; ii: 1109–11.
3 Rauws EAJ, Tytgat GNJ. Cure of duodenal ulcer associated with eradication of Helicobacter pylori. *Lancet* 1990; **335:** 1233–5.
4 Fiocca R, Solcia E, Santoro B. Duodenal ulcer relapse after eradication of *Helicobacter pylori*. *Lancet* 1991; i: **337**, 1614.
5 McColl KEL, Fullarton GM, Chittajallu R, El Nujumi AM, Macdonald AMI, Dahill SW, *et al.* Plasma gastrin, daytime intragastric pH, and nocturnal acid output before and at 1 and 7 months after eradication of *Helicobacter pylori* in duodenal ulcer subjects. *Scand J Gastroenterol* 1991; **26: 3:** 339–46.
6 Chittajallu RS, Ardill JES, McColl KEL. The degree of hypergastrinaemia induced by *Helicobacter pylori* is the same in duodenal ulcer patients and asymptomatic volunteers. *Eur J Gastroenterol Hepatol* 1992; **4:** 49–53.
7 Levi S, Bearsdshall K, Swift I, Foulkes W, Playford R, Ghosh P, *et al.* Antral Helicobacter pylori, hypergastrinaemia and duodenal ulcer: effect of eradicating the organism. *BMJ* 1989; **299:** 1504–5.
8 Graham DY, Opekum A, Lew GM, Evans DJ, Klein PD, Evans DG. Ablation of exaggerated meal-stimulated gastrin release in duodenal ulcer patients after clearance of Helicobacter (Campylobacter) pylori infection. *Am J Gastroenterol* 1990; **85 4:** 394–8.
9 Prewett EJ, Smith JTL, Nwokolo CU, Hudson M, Sawyerr AM, Pounder RE. Eradication of *Helicobacter pylori* abolishes 24-hour hypergastrinaemia: a prospective study in healthy subjects. *Aliment Pharmacol Therap* 1991; **5:** 283–90.
10 Kovacs TOG, Walsh JH, Maxwell V, Wong HC, Azuma T, Katt E. Gastrin is a major mediator of the gastric phase of acid secretion in dogs: proof by monoclonal antibody neutralization. *Gastroenterology* 1989; **97:** 1406–13.
11 Ghatei MA, Jung RT, Stevenson JC, Hillyard CJ, Adrian TE, Lee YC, *et al.* Bombesin: action on gut hormones and calcium in man. *J Clin Endocrinol Metab* 1982; **54:** 980–5.
12 Guo Y-S, Thompson JC, Singh P. Role of gastrin in bombesin-stimulated somatostatin release. *Gastroenterology* 1990; **99:** 1297–302.
13 Gray SP, Billings JA. Kinetic assay of human pepsin with albumin-bromophenol blue as substrate. *Clin Chem* 1983; **29:** 447–51.
14 Ardill JES. Radioimmunoassay of GI hormones. *Clin Endocrinol Metab* 1979; **8:** 265–80.
15 Beardshall K, Moss S, Gill J, Levi S, Ghosh P, Playford RJ, *et al.* Suppression of *Helicobacter pylori* reduces gastrin releasing peptide stimulated gastrin release in duodenal ulcer patients. *Gut* 1992; **33:** 601–3.
16 Mulholland G, Ardill JES, Fillmore D, Chittajallu RS, Fullarton GM, McColl KEL. *Helicobacter pylori* related hypergastrinaemia is the result of a selective increase in gastrin 17. *Gut* 1993; **34:** 757–61.
17 Johnson D, Jepson K. Use of pentagastrin in a test of gastric acid secretion. *Lancet* 1967; ii: 585.
18 Petersen H, Myren J. Pentagastrin-dose response in peptic ulcer disease. *Scand J Gastroentrol* 1975; **10:** 705–14.
19 Isenberg JI, Grossman MI, Maxwell V, Walsh JH. Increased sensitivity to stimulation of acid secretion by pentagastrin in duodenal ulcer. *J Clin Invest* 1975; **55:** 330–7.
20 Lam SK, Isenberg JI, Grossman MI, Lane WH, Walsh JH. Gastric acid secretion is abnormally sensitive to endogenous gastrin released after peptone test meals in duodenal ulcer patients. *J Clin Invest* 1980; **65:** 555–62.
21 Kaneko H, Nakada K, Mitsuma T, Uchida K, Furusawa A, Maeda Y, *et al.* Helicobacter pylori infection induces a decrease in immunoreactive-somatostatin concentrations of human stomach. *Dig Dis Sci* 1992; **37:** 409–16.
22 Moss SF, Legon S, Bishop HE, Polak JM, Calam J. Effect of Helicobacter pylori on gastric somatostatin in duodenal ulcer disease. *Lancet* 1992; **340:** 930–3.
23 Cox AJ. Stomach size and its relation to chronic peptic ulcer. *Arch Pathol* 1952; **54:** 407.
24 Willems G, Lehy T. Radioautographic and quantitative studies on parietal and peptic cell kinetics in the mouse. A selective effect of gastrin on parietal cell proliferation. *Gastroenterology* 1975; **69:** 416–26.
25 Crean GP, Marshall MW, Ramsey RDE. Parietal cell hyperplasia induced by the administration of pentagastrin (ICI 50, 123) to rats. *Gastroenterology* 1969; **57:** 147–55.
26 Lanas A, Hirschowitz BI. Influence of smoking on basal and on vagally and maximally stimulated gastric acid secretion and pepsin secretion. *Scand J Gastroenterol* 1992; **27:** 208–13.
27 Chittajallu RS, Howie CA, McColl KEL. Effect of Helicobacter pylori on parietal cell sensitivity to pentagastrin in duodenal ulcer subjects. *Scand J Gastroenterol* 1992; **27:** 857–62.
28 Ragins H, Wincze F, Liu SM, Dittbrenner M. The origin and survival of gastric parietal cells in the mouse. *Anat Rec* 1968; **162:** 99–110.
29 Dragstedt LR. Gastric secretion tests. *Gastroenterology* 1967; **52:** 587.
30 Feldman M, Richardson CT. Total 24-hour gastric acid secretion in patients with duodenal ulcer. *Gastroenterology* 1986; **90:** 540.
31 Walker V, Taylor WH. Pepsin I secretion in chronic peptic ulceration. *Gut* 1980; **21:** 766–71.

© *Lancet* 1993; 342: 1131–1134

Treatment of active Crohn's disease by exclusion diet: East Anglian Multicentre Controlled Trial

A M Riordan, J O Hunter, R E Cowan, J R Crampton, A R Davidson, R J Dickinson, M W Dronfield, I W Fellows, S Hishon, G N W Kerrigan, H J Kennedy, R C M McGouran, G Neale, J H B Saunders

Summary

Elemental diet is as effective in producing remission of Crohn's disease (CD) as is corticosteroid treatment, but most patients relapse soon after resumption of a normal diet. We have investigated the efficacies of dietary modification and oral corticosteroids in maintaining remission achieved with elemental diet.

In a multicentre trial, 136 patients with active CD were started on elemental diet and other treatment was withdrawn. 43 (31%) declined to continue elemental diet for 14 days, but 78 (84%) of the remaining 93 achieved remission and were randomly assigned corticosteroids (38) or diet (40). Corticosteroid treatment started at 40 mg prednisolone daily, which was tapered and stopped after 12 weeks; that group received dietary advice on healthy eating. The diet group received "tapered" placebo and were instructed to introduce one new food daily, excluding any that precipitated symptoms. Assessment of progress for up to 2 years was made by physicians unaware of group assignment.

Intention-to-treat analysis showed median lengths of remission of 3·8 (interquartile range 5·0) months in the corticosteroid group and 7·5 (15·3) months on diet, and relapse rates at 2 years, adjusted for withdrawals, of 79% and 62%, respectively ($p=0{\cdot}048$). Clinical improvement in the diet group was associated with significant changes in plasma albumin and α_1-antichymotrypsin concentrations and erythrocyte sedimentation rate. Food intolerances discovered were predominantly to cereals, dairy products, and yeast. Diet provides a further therapeutic strategy in active Crohn's disease.

Lancet 1993; **342:** 1131–34

Department of Gastroenterology, Addenbrooke's Hospital, Cambridge (A M Riordan SRD, J O Hunter FRCP, J R Crampton MRCP, G Neale FRCP); **Colchester General Hospital** (R E Cowan FRCP); **Kettering and District General Hospital** (A R Davidson FRCP); **Hinchingbrooke Hospital, Huntingdon** (R J Dickinson FRCP); **Peterborough District Hospital** (M W Dronfield FRCP); **Norfolk and Norwich Hospital** (I W Fellows MRCP, H J Kennedy MRCP); **James Paget Hospital, Gorleston** (S Hishon FRCP); **West Suffolk Hospital, Bury St Edmunds** (G N W Kerrigan FRCP); **Queen Elizabeth Hospital, Kings Lynn** (R C M McGouran FRCP); **and Bedford Hospital, UK** (J H B Saunders FRCP)

Correspondence to: Dr J O Hunter, Gastroenterology Research Unit, Addenbrooke's Hospital, Cambridge CB2 2QQ, UK

Introduction

The treatment of Crohn's disease (CD) remains unsatisfactory. Many drugs in routine use, such as corticosteroids, azathioprine, and sulphasalazine, have dangerous side-effects and are not always effective. So surgery is necessary in many cases. Elemental diet is as reliable as corticosteroids in producing remission in acute CD, with success rates as high as 90%.[1-6] However, most patients relapse shortly after resumption of a normal diet. Although the mechanism of action of elemental diet is poorly understood, it has been claimed that remissions so induced can be prolonged by dietary modification.[7,8] However, this suggestion has yet to be proven in a large trial of unselected patients. We have investigated the value of elemental diet in active CD and the efficacies of dietary modification and oral corticosteroids.

Patients and methods

All patients with active CD seen in the participating hospitals were considered for inclusion provided that they were permanent residents of the health districts where the hospitals were situated. The diagnosis of CD was confirmed by standard radiological and histological tests within 2 months of entry. Disease activity was confirmed by a Harvey and Bradshaw index (HBI)[9] of greater than 6, and the only indications for exclusion were pregnancy, lactation, surgical complications (such as intestinal obstruction, abscesses, and symptomatic fistulae), and severe complications necessitating corticosteroids, such as uveitis. Patients with CD of the rectum only were excluded, as were those with perianal disease more severe than simple fissures or skin tags. Patients unwilling to take part in the study were noted.

Patients were treated with elemental diet (E028, Scientific Hospital Supplies, Liverpool, UK) as inpatients or outpatients, according to the physician's choice. All other CD treatment was withdrawn. Remission was defined as a fall in the HBI to less than 3. Patients who achieved remission were randomly allocated to treatment with corticosteroids or with diet. Those who did not achieve remission took no further part in the study. Randomisation codes were separate for each participating centre and were stratified for the extent of the disease (small-bowel disease only, colonic disease only, or both small-bowel and large-bowel involvement).

Patients in the corticosteroid group were prescribed prednisolone (Prednesol, Glaxo) 40 mg daily. They received general dietary advice from a dietitian. If they remained in remission, the prednisolone dose was reduced to 30 mg after 1 week, to 20 mg after 1 month, and to 10 mg after 2 months; prednisolone was withdrawn after 3 months.

Patients in the diet group were instructed to reintroduce a single food each day and to exclude any food that provoked symptoms such as diarrhoea and pain.[7] In an attempt to make the trial double-blind they were given placebo tablets identical to the prednisolone and instructed to reduce the dose in the same way. Both groups saw the dietitians at every clinic visit and were free to telephone for advice if necessary. Patients in both groups were told

© *Lancet* 1993; 342: 1131–1134

	Mean (SE) value	
	Diet	Corticosteroids
HBI		
Before ED	8·25 (0·30)	8·95 (0·42)
After ED	1·70 (0·18)	1·92 (0·19)
Haemoglobin (g/dL)		
Before ED	11·8 (0·3)	11·8 (0·3)
After ED	12·0 (0·3)	11·9 (0·2)
Albumin (g/L)		
Before ED	36·1 (1·1)	34·6 (1·0)
After ED	36·6 (1·2)	36·9 (0·9)
ESR (mm/h)		
Before ED	33·2 (4·2)	43·2 (4·8)
After ED	29·6 (4·1)	33·9 (4·4)
CRP (mg/L)		
Before ED	51·0 (10·7)	62·3 (9·5)
After ED	27·1 (10·4)	24·2 (4·7)
α_1-antichymotripsin (g/L)		
Before ED	1·12 (0·07)	1·14 (0·09)
After ED	1·70 (0·84)	0·95 (0·05)

ESR = erythrocyte sedimentation rate, CRP = C-reactive protein.

Table 1: **HBI and blood variables before and after elemental diet (ED) in patients randomised to diet or corticosteroids**

that they had entered a trial of diet in CD and that the tablets might be corticosteroids or a harmless placebo.

The group assignment was known to the dietitians who advised the patients but not to the physicians who assessed their progress. Clinic visits were made monthly until 6 months, every 2 months to 1 year, then every 4 months to 2 years, or at any time if severe symptoms developed. Only assessing physicians were allowed to withdraw patients from the trial. An HBI of greater than 6 was taken as a relapse. Other criteria for treatment failure included: unwillingness by the patient to continue; a diet found on computer analysis to be deficient in energy, protein, or any other nutrient that could not be replaced by simple supplements; surgery for CD; serious medical complications; and steroid side-effects severe enough to warrant withdrawal of therapy. Withdrawn patients were subsequently treated at their physicians' discretion. Blood samples were taken for measurement of erythrocyte sedimentation rate and concentrations of haemoglobin, serum C-reactive protein, α_1-antichymotrypsin, and albumin at entry to the trial and at each visit. Laboratory tests were done at the local hospitals, except for C-reactive protein and α_1-antichymotrypsin which were measured at the Department of Biochemistry, Addenbrooke's Hospital.

Data were analysed by the SPSS statistical package (version 5.0.1). Means were compared by *t* tests for paired or independent samples, as appropriate. Where necessary, non-parametric tests were used. Life-tables were calculated and used to assess the progress of the two groups. We took $p<0·05$ to indicate statistical significance.

Results

224 eligible patients were seen in the participating hospitals during the trial. 88 were not enrolled (35 were unwilling to undergo randomisation or follow the trial protocol, 8 had started on other treatment from their general practitioners, 4 declined for social reasons, 13 were unwilling to try the elemental diet, 11 asked for steroids and 7 for diet, 6 had contraindications to steroid use, 3 required total parenteral nutrition, and 1 was mentally subnormal).

136 patients started on the elemental diet but 43 (31%) refused to continue for longer than 7 days. After 14 days on the elemental diet 78 (84%) of the remaining 93 patients had achieved remission. There were significant improvements in the group as a whole in erythrocyte sedimentation rate and serum albumin and C-reactive protein concentrations ($p<0·01$, Wilcoxon signed-rank test) but not in haemoglobin or α_1-antichymotrypsin (table 1).

	Demography	
	Corticosteroid group (n=38)	Diet group (n=40)
M/F	11/27	15/25
Mean (SD) age in yr	36·4 (12·9)	31·1 (11·1)
Smoking status		
Current smoker	17	10
Ex-smoker	16	23
Never smoked	5	7
Mean (SD) time since diagnosis (mo)	40·0 (87·8)	26·1 (43·2)
Site of disease		
Small bowel	14	17
Large bowel	10	11
Small and large bowel	14	12
Previous treatment		
Surgery	7	4
Azathioprine	4	1
Mean (SD) time to remission on ED	12·5 (4·0)	10·8 (3·6)

ED = elemental diet.

Table 2: **Demographic and clinical details of corticosteroid and diet groups**

There was no significant difference between the patients who responded to the elemental diet and those who did not in severity of disease, age, sex, site or duration of disease, smoking habits, or previous drug treatment or surgery. Similarly, there were no differences in these variables between the 38 patients assigned corticosteroid treatment and the 40 patients assigned diet treatment (table 2).

On reintroduction of normal foods the patients discovered many intolerances (corn [7 patients]; wheat, milk, yeast [6 each]; egg, potato, rye, tea, coffee [4 each]; apples, mushrooms, oats, chocolate [3 each]). 26 patients were intolerant of more than 3 foods.

25 patients (66%) were withdrawn from the corticosteroid group because of clinical relapse compared with 12 (30%) in the diet group. In addition, 7 patients from the diet group were withdrawn for non-compliance. They were all counted as failures, even if they were in full remission at the time of withdrawal. 2 patients were withdrawn from the diet group because of intercurrent illness. Withdrawals from the steroid group included 1 patient with intercurrent illness, 2 with steroid side-effects (diabetes mellitus and severe furunculosis), and 2 who became pregnant. All withdrawals (except the pregnant women) were counted as treatment failures in an intention-to-treat analysis.

There was no significant change in weight during the study in either the diet group (57·6 [SE 8·8] kg on entry and

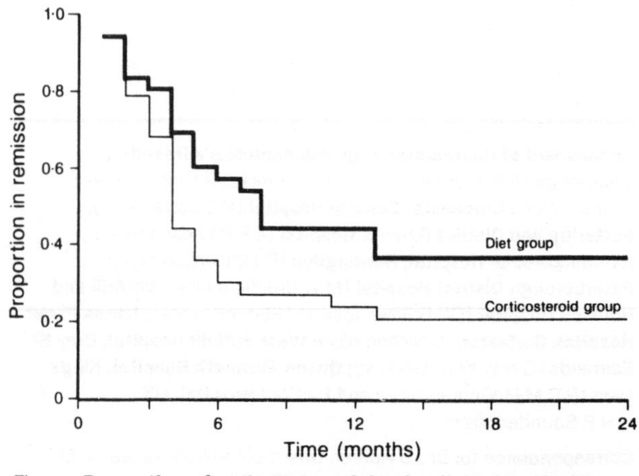

Figure: **Proportion of patients remaining in clinical remission**

	Corticosteroid group						Diet group					
	On recruitment		Last visit before relapse		Withdrawal		On recruitment		Last visit before relapse		Withdrawal	
	Mean (SE)	n	Mean (SE)	n	Mean (SE)	n	Mean (SE)	n	Mean (SE)	n	Mean (SE)	n
Relapse												
HBI	9·1 (0·5)	30	2·4 (0·4)	16	8·7 (0·5)	29	8·8 (0·4)	21	2·4 (0·5)	14	8·5 (0·8)	21
Haemoglobin (g/dL)	11·6 (0·3)	30	12·0 (0·4)	13	12·2 (0·3)	27	11·5 (0·3)	20	11·6 (0·3)	3	11·3 (0·3)	19
Albumin (g/L)	33·8 (1·1)	29	37·4 (1·3)	14	36·9 (1·1)	25	35·8 (1·2)	20	36·2 (1·4)	14	36·3 (1·5)	18
ESR (mm/h)	43·5 (5·1)	28	32·4 (4·7)	13	32·5 (3·8)	24	29·0 (5·3)	20	30·1 (3·3)	12	30·1 (4·6)	18
CRP (mg/L)	56·5 (9·1)	25	24·8 (5·9)	14	42·5 (8·6)	26	39·6 (9·0)	15	22·1 (3·7)	13	54·2 (13·8)	17
α_1-antichymotrypsin (g/L)	1·13 (0·10)	25	1·62 (0·65)	14	1·07 (0·07)	25	1·07 (0·08)	14	0·87 (0·03)	13	1·24 (0·1)	14
No relapse												
HBI	8·4 (0·9)	8	1·4 (0·6)	8	..		7·7 (0·4)	19	0·9 (0·4)	15	..	
Haemoglobin (g/dL)	12·7 (0·6)	8	12·9 (0·7)	8	..		12·2 (0·4)	18	13·1 (0·5)	15	..	
Albumin (g/L)	37·9 (1·6)	7	40·1 (1·9)	8	..		36·5 (2·0)	18	40·5 (3·4)	13	..	
ESR (mm/h)	42·1 (12·5)	8	28·0 (17·1)	7	..		37·9 (6·6)	18	19·7 (4·7)	15	..	
CRP (mg/L)	80·6 (27·4)	8	16·0 (11·0)	6	..		61·8 (19·0)	16	19·7 (6·4)	15	..	
α1-antichymotrypsin (g/L)	1·17 (0·22)	6	0·72 (0·15)	5	..		1·16 (0·12)	14	0·74 (0·07)	13	..	

Table 3: **Changes in HBI and blood variables during trial**

60·3 [7·4] kg at 3 months) or the corticosteroid group (59·3 [11·4] kg and 63·8 ([12·2] kg, respectively). The median remission times were 7·5 (interquartile range 15·3) months in the diet group and 3·8 (5·0) months in the steroid group, and the respective relapse rates at 2 years were 62% and 79% (Wilcoxon [Gehan] statistic 3·920, df 1, $p=0·048$, figure).

Changes in the clinical state of the patients and in their various blood tests are summarised in table 3. Patients in the diet group who remained well until the end of the trial showed significant improvements in albumin, erythrocyte sedimentation rate, and α_1-antichymotrypsin concentration in comparison with values on entry to the trial. Haemoglobin and C-reactive protein concentrations tended to improve, but the changes did not reach statistical significance.

Discussion

This trial confirms the value of elemental diet in acute CD; 84% of patients willing to limit their food intake to elemental diet were symptom-free after 2 weeks. However, the overall success rate was only 57%, since 43 (31%) patients were unwilling to continue elemental diet for more than a week. It seems that the different success rates in previous trials[1-6] relate to patients' selection, with higher rates reported by groups who are known to believe that elemental diet is valuable in CD and whose patients are referred to them specifically for this treatment. Such patients are more likely to persevere with elemental diet than are unselected patients, such as those in our trial.

Despite its proven efficacy, elemental diet is still not used widely, partly because it is not pleasant to ingest. Palatability has improved lately. Earlier forms had to be given by nasogastric tube but most of the patients in our study were able to drink E028 from a cup. Peptide-based and polymeric diets may prove more palatable but seem to be less effective.[10-12]

The second difficulty is that many doctors are uncertain how best to manage patients after they have reached remission on elemental diet. The administration of potentially toxic drugs, such as corticosteroids and antimetabolites, seems unwarranted in patients who have become symptom-free and yet most patients relapse rapidly on resumption of normal eating.[8,13]

Our study shows that in CD patients who have achieved remission on elemental diet, the process of food testing[7,8] provides an effective strategy for long-term management. Food testing and reintroduction is not easy, but even if we take patients who were unwilling to comply as failures, the group treated by diet had a significant advantage over those who received steroids in terms of time of relapse.

It is not possible to design a trial of diet that is perfectly double-blind unless artificial foods are used. We have attempted to overcome this difficulty in patients eating every-day foods by ensuring that all were given dietary advice and visited the dietitian with equal frequency. Furthermore, all received indistinguishable medication, with the dose tapered in the same way in both groups. The assessment of a patient's progress was made, not by the dietitians who were unavoidably aware of his or her treatment, but by the physician, who was not.

Although the assessment of the patients made by their physicians at each visit was based on the HBI, which is derived entirely from clincial variables, the changes in the various blood tests provided objective confirmation that the patients were in remission, and that the improvement was not merely symptomatic.

Many CD patients report that the course of their illness is affected by what they eat, but this study is the first to demonstrate this association in a large-scale controlled trial of unselected patients. There are many reasons for the difficulty of proving such a simple relation. Many and varied foods were implicated and the resulting diets differed substantially. When a food is eaten daily, it can be difficult to realise that it is provoking symptoms. The process of food testing was slow and difficult and required much skilled dietetic support. Some patients did not have enough determination to continue.

Although there was a significant benefit in the group treated with diet, the percentage still in remission at 2 years was nonetheless disappointing. Alun Jones et al[8] reported that as many as two-thirds of patients were well at 2 years. The difference in result is probably related to the type of patients studied; self-selected patients inevitably prove more compliant of dietary regimens than an unselected group.

Diet provides a further method of treatment for CD that may enable well-motivated and determined patients to avoid unnecessary surgery and the complications of drug therapy. Clearly, however, it does not provide the final answer to the treatment of CD. It is difficult for the patients and requires skilled dietetic support. Also, since staple foods must be avoided by many patients, the diet may be costly and socially inconvenient. Nevertheless, it may well point the way to further research. Discovery of the mechanisms underlying food intolerance may lead to more successful treatment of CD in the future.

This study was supported by the East Anglian Regional Health Authority. Prednisolone and matching placebo tablets were provided by Glaxo Ltd. We thank the dietitians, pharmacists, and clinical biochemists of the hospitals involved in the study for their help and support, Dr R Hanka (Medical Informatics Department, University of Cambridge) for statistical advice, and Miss A J Lee for preparation of the paper.

References

1 O'Morain C, Segal AW, Levi AJ. Elemental diet as primary treatment of acute Crohn's disease: a controlled trial. *BMJ* 1984; **288:** 1859–62.
2 Saverymuttu S, Hodgson HJF, Chadwick VS. Controlled trial comparing prednisolone with an elemental diet plus non-absorbable antibiotics with active Crohn's disease. *Gut* 1985; **26:** 994–98.
3 Kelly SM, Thuluvath, P Fotherby K, Crampton J, Hunter JO. Elemental diet is an effective treatment of acute Crohn's disease. *Scand J Gastroenterol* 1989; **24** (suppl 158): 149.
4 Sanderson IR, Boulton P, Menzie I, Walker-Smith JA. Improvement of abnormal lactulose/rhamnose permeability in active Crohn's disease of the small bowel by an elemental diet. *Gut* 1987; **28:** 1073–76.
5 Malchow H, Steinhardt HJ, Lorenz-Meyer H, et al. Feasibility and effectiveness of a defined formula diet regimen in treating active Crohn's disease: European Cooperative Crohn's disease study III. *Scand J Gastroenterol* 1990; **25:** 235–44.
6 Lochs H, Steinhardt HJ, Klaus-Wentz B, et al. Comparison of enteral nutrition and drug treatment in active Crohn's disease: results of the European Cooperative Crohn's disease study IV. *Gastroenterology* 1991; **101:** 881–88.
7 Workman EM, Alun Jones V, Wilson AJ, Hunter JO. Diet in the management of Crohn's disease. *Hum Nutr Appl Nutr* 1984; **38A:** 469–73.
8 Alun Jones V, Workman E, Dickinson RJ, Wilson AJ, Freeman AH, Hunter JO. Crohn's disease: maintenance of remission by diet. *Lancet* 1985; ii: 177–80.
9 Harvey RF, Bradshaw JM. A simple index of Crohn's disease activity. *Lancet* 1980; i: 514.
10 Giaffer MH, North G, Holdsworth CD. Controlled trial of polymeric diet in the treatment of active Crohn's disease. *Lancet* 1990; **335:** 816–19.
11 Rigaud D, Cosnes J, Le Quintrec Y, Rene E, Gendre JP, Mignon M. Controlled trial comparing two types of enteral nutrition in treatment of active Crohn's disease: elemental vs polymeric diet. *Gut* 1991; **32:** 1492–97.
12 Middleton SJ, Riordan AM, Hunter JO. Peptide based diet: an alternative to elemental diet in the treatment of acute Crohn's disease. *Gut* 1991; **32:** A578.
13 Teahon K, Bjarnason L, Pearson M, Levi AJ. Ten years experience with an elemental diet in the management of Crohn's disease,. *Gut* 1990; **31:** 1133–37.

Printed in Great Britain by Robquest Ashford Kent

© Gut 1993; 34: 537–543

Cephalic phase of colonic pressure response to food

J Rogers, A H Raimundo, J J Misiewicz

Department of Gastroenterology and Nutrition, Central Middlesex Hospital, London
J Rogers
A H Raimundo
J J Misiewicz

Correspondence to:
Mr J Rogers, Academic Surgical Unit, The Royal London Hospital, Whitechapel, London E1 1BB.

Accepted for publication 7 September 1992

Abstract

A cephalic phase of colonic pressure response to food was sought in five normal subjects (mean age (22·6) years, 22–24), studied on six separate occasions by recording intraluminal pressures in the unprepared sigmoid colon. Gastric acid secretion was measured simultaneously by continuous aspiration through a nasogastric tube. After a 60 minute basal period, one of five 30 minute food related cephalic stimuli, or a control stimulus was given in random order; records were continued for a further 120 minutes. The cephalic stimuli were: food discussion, sight and smell of food without taste, smell of food without sight or taste, sight of food without smell or taste, and modified sham feeding; the control stimulus was a discussion of neutral topics. Colonic pressures were expressed as study segment activity index (area under curve, mm Hg.min) derived by fully automated computer analysis. Gastric acid output was expressed as mmol/30 min. Food discussion significantly ($p<0·02$, Wilcoxon's rank sum test) increased colonic pressure activity compared with control or basal activity. Smell of food without sight or taste also significantly ($p<0·03$) increased the colonic pressure activity compared with control and basal periods. Sham feeding and sight and smell of food without taste significantly ($p<0·02$ and $p<0·03$) increased colonic pressures compared with control but not basal activity. The increase in colonic activity after sight of food without smell or taste was not significantly different from control or basal activity ($p=0·44$ and $p=0·34$). Food discussion was the strongest colonic stimulus tested. Food discussion and sham feeding significantly ($p<0·02$) stimulated gastric acid output above control and basal values. Sight and smell of food without taste significantly ($p<0·02$) increased acid output above basal. Smell of food without sight or taste and sight of food without smell or taste did not significantly ($p=0·06$, $p=0·34$) increase acid output. In contrast with the effect on colonic pressures, sham feeding was the best stimulus of acid output. Increased colonic pressure activity after food discussion correlated significantly ($r=0·45$, $p<0·02$) with gastric acid output. There was no correlation ($r=-0·1$, $p>0·5$) between colonic pressure activity and gastric acid output in the control study. These data show that there is a cephalic phase of the colonic response to food.

(*Gut* 1993; **34:** 537–543)

Characterisation of neuronal, endocrine, and paracrine pathways that affect intracolonic pressures is important because abnormal colonic motility plays a part in irritable bowel syndrome, colonic diverticular disease, ulcerative colitis, and similar diseases. Colonic pressure responses may be mediated by a variety of pathways: neural, hormonal, and local reflexes may be involved. The main physiological stimulus for colonic segmenting pressures is the ingestion of food, but they are also affected by acute experimental stress and by drugs. It is generally thought that the colonic pressure response to eating is initiated by the local effect of nutrients or products of digestion on receptors in the mucosa of the upper digestive tract. Some of the possible mechanisms of the response, in particular the effect of calorie load and the constituents of meals,[1-3] have been investigated by experimental studies in man.

The presence of a cephalic phase of colonic pressure response to food has never been formally investigated: on the contrary, its existence has been doubted.[4] By contrast, the cephalic phase of gastric acid secretion is fully accepted and documented.[5-7] Teleologically, the cephalic phase could be important in preparing the alimentary tract for receiving food when it is eventually swallowed. By analogy with the physiological mechanisms known to operate in the cephalic phase of gastric acid secretion, the hypothesis that a cephalic phase of the colonic pressure response to food exists was postulated, and tested experimentally in this study. Thought, sight, smell, sight and smell, and also sight and smell and taste of food were used separately as candidate cephalic stimuli of the colonic pressure response to food.

The cephalic stimuli used in this study were derived from those developed by Feldman and Richardson[8] for their studies of the cephalic phase of gastric acid secretion. They systematically studied the relative importance of five food related cephalic stimuli: thought of food without sight or taste (food discussion), sight of food without smell or taste, smell of food without sight or taste, sight and smell of food without taste, and thought, sight, smell, and taste (sham feeding). A neutral cephalic stimulus, discussion about topics unrelated to food was used as a control. All food related cephalic stimuli significantly increased gastric acid output and serum gastrin concentrations. Modified sham feeding was the most potent agonist, followed by food discussion, sight and smell, sight alone, and smell alone. The neutral discussion did not change acid output or serum gastrin concentrations. These well researched cephalic stimuli of gastric acid secretion were tested with respect to their effect on colonic pressure activity.

Subjects

Five normal male volunteers (mean age (22·6) years, 22–24) were studied on six separate occasions. They had no history of gastro-

© Gut 1993; 34: 537–543

intestinal, anorectal, or metabolic disorder and all had a regular bowel habit. One subject was a regular smoker and all drank moderate amounts of alcohol. Informed consent was obtained from all subjects and the study was approved by the Brent Health Authority Ethical Committee.

Methods

QUESTIONNAIRE

All subjects completed a general questionnaire four weeks before the study which collected details of the subject's day to day activities, dietary preferences, and bowel habit. Details of the subject's favourite meal, hobbies, and general interests were also recorded. The questionnaire was very general so as not to disclose the aim of the study and to ensure that the subject's attention was not focused on food. It provided the information necessary for the neutral, or control, discussion.

MEALS

Each subject's favourite meal, derived from the questionnaire to ensure maximal cephalic effect, was prepared in advance in identical batches of five by high class professional caterers. The five meals for each subject were mass cooked and then divided into five servings, thus ensuring uniformity. The meals were prepared to a high standard, so that they could be presented in an attractive and appetising manner. The meals were deep frozen until needed for use. All the meals in a batch were and looked exactly the same. As none of the meals were eaten during the experiments, standardisation of the calorie, carbohydrate, protein, and fat content of the food between the five subjects was unnecessary.

INVESTIGATORS

The experimental protocol was too complex to be managed by one person. To ensure uniformity throughout the experiments each investigator had the same responsibilities in each study. One investigator (JR) performed all intubations, supervised the motility recording, and aspirated the gastric juice and was present in the laboratory at all times. Conversation with the subject was kept to a minimum and popular music was played to prevent boredom. The other investigator (AHR) was responsible for the control and food discussions and for all the other cephalic stimuli and was present in the laboratory only during the stimulus periods.

STIMULI

Subjects were instructed to keep to their normal dietary routine during the study. They were not encouraged to attempt defecation before fibreoptic flexible sigmoidoscopy. Each subject was studied the same time of day in the morning after fasting from midnight and five to seven days apart. Each cephalic stimulus was given on a separate day, in random order, after basal colonic pressure activity had been recorded for 60 minutes.

The stimuli were as follows:

Control discussion: thought of subject unrelated to food

The investigator conducting the interview entered the room and discussed a variety of neutral topics unrelated to food with the subject. Emotionally loaded subjects were not discussed.

Food discussion: thought of food without sight, smell or taste

The investigator discussed the subject's favourite foods as detailed in the questionnaire. The subject was encouraged to talk about the food he liked, how he liked it prepared, and which restaurants served this food. He was asked to describe the smell, appearance, and the taste when eating his favourite meal. Care was taken to ensure that the subject did not see, smell, or taste food during the study, nor were food related topics mentioned during other periods of the study. The interviewer had no difficulty in maintaining the food discussion for the whole of the 30 minute period.

Sight only: sight of food without smell or taste

The subject's favourite meal was reheated in a microwave oven in a kitchen remote from the laboratory, so that he could not hear, see, or smell the meal being cooked. It was presented at a normal distance from the subject in an attractive fashion with table cloth, cutlery, wine glass, and bottle of white wine on a decorated plate sealed with transparent film, so that no food odours could escape. The subject was asked to look and think about the food without discussion for 30 minutes, after which the meal was removed. Subjects were told at the time of presentation of the meal that they would be allowed to eat the meal at the end of the study.

Smell only: smell of food without sight or taste

The subject's favourite meal was partly cooked by microwave oven in the kitchen remote from the laboratory and then brought into the laboratory concealed behind a screen, so the subject could hear and smell, but not see, the meal while it was fully reheated on a conventional hot plate. The meal was kept simmering for the 30 minute period of stimulation. The subject was asked to think about the smell of the food for this 30 minute period. After 30 minutes the meal and cooker were removed. The windows were opened and the room sprayed with a commercial air freshener to remove the conscious olfactory stimuli. Subjects were told that they would be allowed to eat the meal at the end of the study.

Sight and smell: sight and smell of food without taste

The subject's favourite meal was partly reheated in the kitchen by microwave oven remote from the laboratory and then brought into the laboratory on the hot plate cooker so that the subject could see and smell the meal being cooked. The meal was simmered for 30 minutes and

© Gut 1993; 34: 537–543

the subject was encouraged to take part in the cooking by moving the food around on the hot plate of the cooker. The subject was asked to think about the food during this 30 minute period. After the stimulus period the meal and cooker were removed, the windows opened, and the room sprayed with air freshener. Subjects were told that they could eat the meal at the end of the study.

Sham feeding: 'chew and spit' modified sham feeding

A 'chew and spit' modified sham feeding technique was used over the whole 30 minute period, using the subject's favourite meal. The subjects were encouraged to chew the food slowly and enjoy the taste of the meal, but not to swallow the food. Boluses of food were spat out into a container and covered by a layer of thick tissue so that the previously chewed bolus could not be seen by the subject. At the end of the 30 minute period the subject rinsed his mouth with cold water, which he then spat out. The windows of the room were then opened and the room sprayed with air freshener.

COLONIC PRESSURE ACTIVITY

The colon was intubated without bowel preparation with laxatives or enemas. The standard intubation technique using a flexible sigmoidoscope as described previously[9] was used to place four manometric tubes into the descending, proximal sigmoid, distal sigmoid, and rectum 50, 40, 30, and 15 cm from the anus, respectively. Each tube was connected to a pressure transducer (Type P23ID, Statham, Hato Rey, PR, USA) and was perfused with distilled water at a constant rate of 0·25 ml/min^{-1} using a pneumohydraulic pump (Mui Scientific, Mississauga, Ontario, Canada). Pressures were recorded on a polygraph (Grass 7PD) calibrated at ambient temperature and pressure to 100 mm Hg.cm^{-1} by mercury manometer. The electrical signal driving each pen galvanometer was also passed to a custom built analogue to digital converter (PC-Polygraf, Synectics Medical, Sweden) and the digitised data stored on an IBM PC computer for automated analysis. A 30 minute rest period followed intubation before recordings were made. After a 60 minute basal period one of the cephalic stimuli was given to the subject for 30 minutes and pressure recordings were continued for a further 90 minutes.

ANALYSIS OF PRESSURE RECORDS

Pressure records were analysed by custom written fully automated computer analysis software (PC-Polygram, Gastrosoft, Sweden) in 10 minute periods. The main variable derived for analysis was the study segment activity index (mm Hg.min), as previously described in this laboratory.[9] Synchronous hard copy records were also made on the polygraph. The details of pressure trace analysis and the design and validation of the computer system used have been fully described previously.[10] Hard copy records were also visually analysed for segmental and propagative contractions.

GASTRIC ACID OUTPUT

Before the sigmoidoscopy, all the subjects were intubated transnasally with a 12 FG nasogastric tube and positioned in the gastric antrum under fluoroscopic control: the resting gastric contents were aspirated and discarded. Throughout the study gastric juice was continuously aspirated by manual syringe suction and collected in 15 minute aliquots. Subjects were encouraged to spit saliva onto tissue paper to prevent contaminating gastric juice.

The hydrogen ion concentration in the gastric aspirates was determined by titration against 0·1 M NaOH to pH 7·00 using an Autoburette system (Radiometer, Copenhagen, PHM62 – pH meter, TTT80 – Titrator, ABU80 – Autoburette, and TTA60 – Titration assembly). The Autoburette system was calibrated using reference pH buffers at pH 4·02 and 7·00 (Radiometer, Copenhagen). Gastric acid output was expressed in mmol H^+/30 min.

Statistical analysis

The data pertaining to the colonic study segment activity index and to gastric acid output were analysed by comparisons with the control studies (control discussion) and also with the basal values of each study, using Wilcoxon's signed rank test.

Results

Tables I and II show medians and ranges of colonic study segment activity index and gastric acid output, respectively.

TABLE I *Colonic study segment activity index*

Colonic activity index (mm Hg.min)	*Median (range)*					
	Basal		*Stimulus*		*After stimulus*	
30 minute periods	1	2	3	4	5	6
Control	903 (353–3519)	955 (553–1711)	634 (286–2683)	805 (539–2041)	669 (256–1758)	716 (533–2004)
Food discussion	1074 (783–1828)	2037 (355–2705)	*†2845 (1103–5222)	*2130 (671–4213)	*1921 (575–5067)	1216 (352–4818)
Sham feeding	1208 (532–258)	1379 (957–2194)	*1483 (1006–5516)	1773 (138–3450)	1845 (12–5712)	*1720 (112–4074)
Sight only	1121 (838–1618)	1427 (375–2400)	1472 (450–3334)	1764 (707–2216)	1175 (464–2775)	949 (177–2734)
Smell only	668 (164–1761)	1729 (303–2700)	†2035 (798–2497)	*†2406 (1171–3402)	*1724 (805–5737)	1539 (275–4528)
Sight and smell	1831 (857–2950)	1478 (1384–2362)	*1903 (1238–4565)	1788 (680–3970)	1107 (673–1924)	1066 (646–2743)

* p<0·03 compared with control; † p<0·03 compared with basal.

TABLE II *Gastric acid output*

Acid output (mmol H^+/30 min)	*Median (range)*					
	Basal		*Stimulus*		*After stimulus*	
30 minute periods	1	2	3	4	5	6
Control	1·53 (0·18–4·20)	0·82 (0·08–5·30)	2·03 (0·14–3·98)	2·69 (0·26–3·11)	0·64 (0·17–3·95)	0·86 (0·41–6·30)
Food discussion	0·49 (0·11–3·46)	1·08 (0·17–8·58)	*†6·59 (1·51–13·36)	2·53 (1·09–4·47)	1·44 (0·60–3·98)	1·37 (0·24–8·35)
Sham feeding	1·43 (1·01–5·52)	0·97 (0·94–2·79)	*†9·03 (4·10–15·64)	*†9·92 (4·49–14·36)	*†6·45 (4·96–7·57)	*†3·10 (2·83–5·47)
Sight only	1·67 (0·13–3·30)	1·02 (0·50–4·01)	2·80 (0·96–4·32)	1·86 (0·61–2·52)	1·63 (0·59–5·06)	0·55 (0·34–1·61)
Smell only	0·79 (0·29–3·41)	1·75 (0·43–6·85)	2·10 (0·39–9·68)	1·10 (0·29–4·25)	1·76 (0·33–5·00)	1·04 (0·45–5·54)
Sight and smell	0·91 (0·32–5·49)	1·36 (0·67–2·40)	†3·30 (0·85–8·23)	0·73 (0·25–5·05)	*1·26 (0·35–4·16)	0·82 (0·48–4·32)

* p<0·03 compared with control; † p<0·03 compared with basal.

© Gut 1993; 34: 537–543

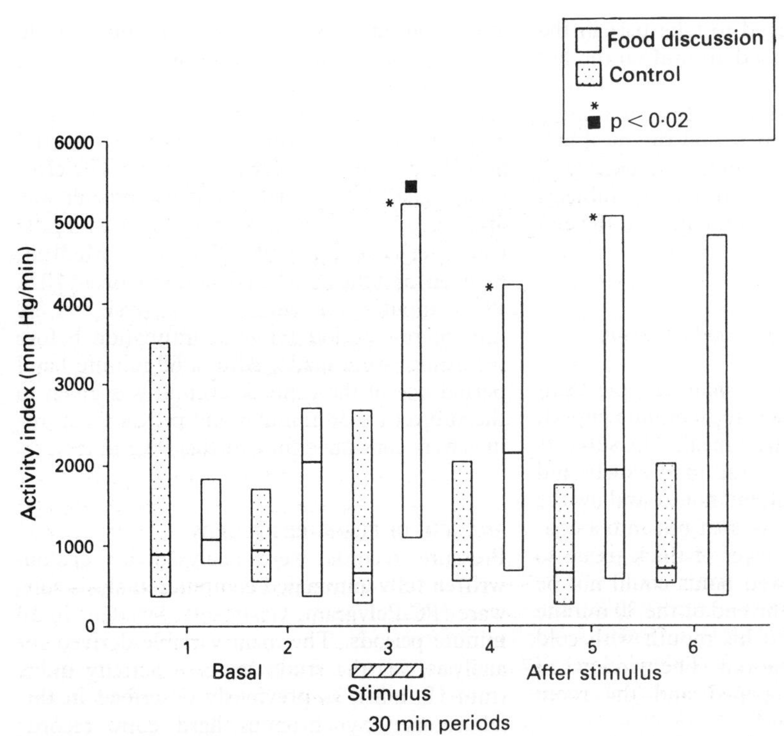

Figure 1: The effect of control and food discussions on study segment colonic pressure activity. The median (bar), and range (box) of activity index is plotted on the Y axis for each 30 minute period plotted on the X axis. Period of stimulation(▨).

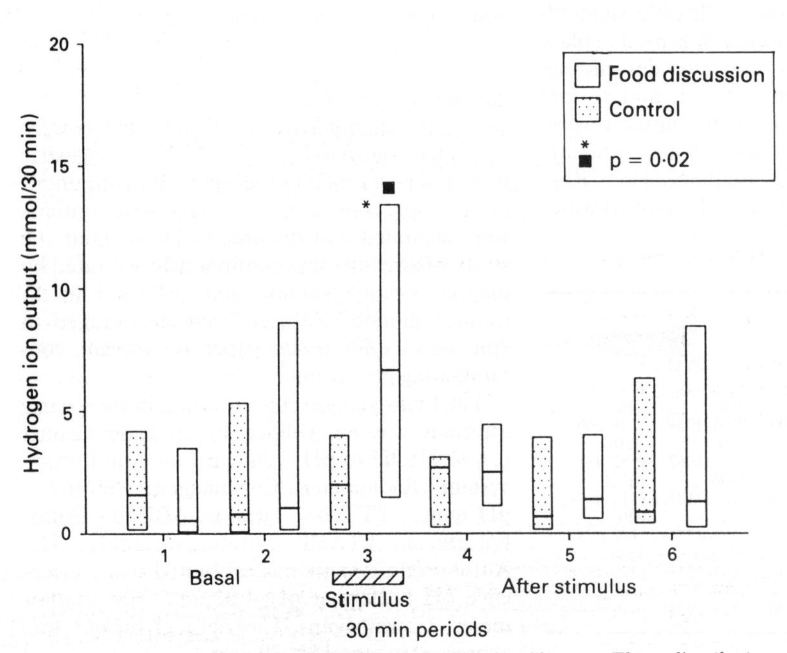

Figure 2: The effect of control and food discussions on gastric acid output. The median (bar), and range (box) of acid output is plotted on the Y axis for each 30 minute period plotted on the X axis. Period of stimulation (▨)

TABLE III *Quantitative pressure data from pressure trace (Fig 6). Basal and food discussion 30 minute periods*

	Channel 1 50 cm		*Channel 2 40 cm*		*Channel 3 30 cm*		*Channel 4 15 cm*	
	Basal	*Food discussion*	*Basal*	*Food discussion*	*Basal*	*Food discussion*	*Basal*	*Food discussion*
Maximum pressure (mm Hg)	111·1	255·8	150·8	115·4	207·9	278·6	31·4	253·7
Mean pressure (mm Hg)	7·4	54·8	27·7	36·8	31·8	43·2	1·1	22·9
Activity index (mm Hg min)	222	1656	831	1111	954	1306	47·6	694

CONTROL DISCUSSION

There was no significant change in colonic study segment activity index or in gastric acid output during, or after the control discussion (Figs 1 and 2), suggesting that the control discussion was a neutral cephalic stimulus to colonic pressure activity and gastric acid output.

FOOD DISCUSSION

Basal colonic pressure activity in the study segment during food discussion studies was not significantly (p=0·34) different from control. Food discussion produced an immediate and significant (p<0·02) increase in colonic study segment activity index above basal and control values which was maintained for the remainder of the study (Fig 1). Basal gastric acid output during food discussion studies was not significantly (p=0·22) different from control but increased significantly (p<0·02) during food discussion above basal and control values, returning to basal levels at the end of the stimulus period (Fig 2). Increased colonic pressure activity correlated significantly (r=0·45, p<0·02) with gastric acid output during food discussion (Fig 3) but not in the control study (r=−0·1, p>0·5).

MODIFIED SHAM FEEDING

Basal colonic pressure activity during sham feeding was not different from control (p=0·34). Modified sham feeding significantly (p<0·02) increased colonic study segment activity index during the stimulus and the after stimulus periods compared with control, but not with basal periods (p=0·25; Fig 4). Basal gastric acid output during sham feeding studies was not different (=0·34) from control. Modified sham feeding significantly (p<0·02) increased acid secretion above control and basal outputs, and this was sustained for 90 minutes after the sham feeding stimulus (Fig 5).

SIGHT ONLY

Basal pressure data during sight only studies were not different from control (p=0·34). The sight only stimulus did not increase colonic study segment activity index in comparison with control (p=0·44) or basal (p=0·34) periods. Basal gastric acid output during sight only studies was not (p=0·89) different from control, and this stimulus did not increase gastric acid output in comparison with either control (p=0·25) or basal (p=0·06) periods.

SMELL ONLY

Basal colonic pressure activity during smell only studies was not different from control (p=0·17). The smell only stimulus significantly increased colonic study segment activity index compared with control (p<0·02) and basal (p<0·03) data. Basal gastric acid output during smell only studies was not different from control (p=0·22). In contrast with the results of colonic activity, the increase in acid output which occurred during the smell only stimulus was not signific-

© Gut 1993; 34: 537–543

antly different from control ($p=0\cdot44$), or basal ($p=0\cdot06$) data.

SIGHT AND SMELL

Basal colonic pressure activity during sight and smell studies was not different from control ($p=0\cdot25$). Colonic study segment activity index increased significantly ($p=0\cdot03$) above control data during the 30 minute period following the stimulus. There was no increase ($p=0\cdot11$), however, in colonic activity index above basal during the stimulus or, after stimulus periods. During the basal periods gastric acid output was not significantly ($p=0\cdot89$) different from control.

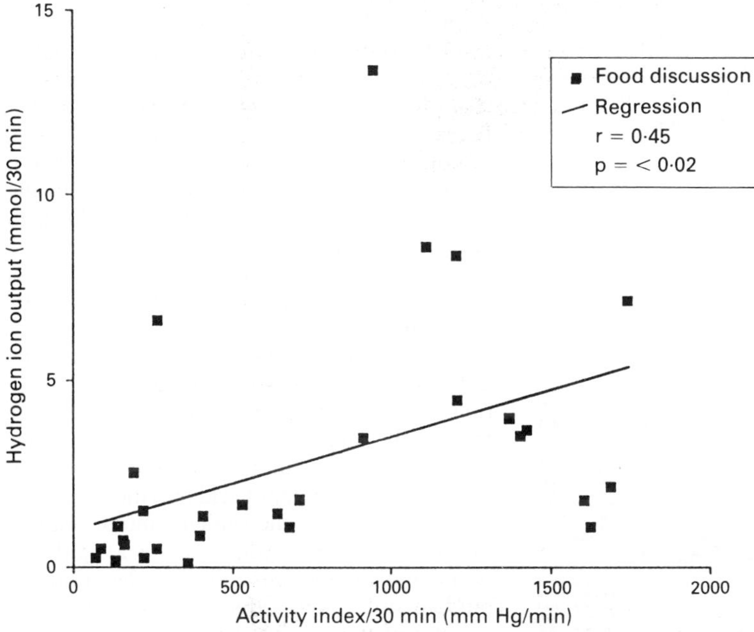

Figure 3: The relation between colonic activity index and gastric acid output during the food discussion studies.

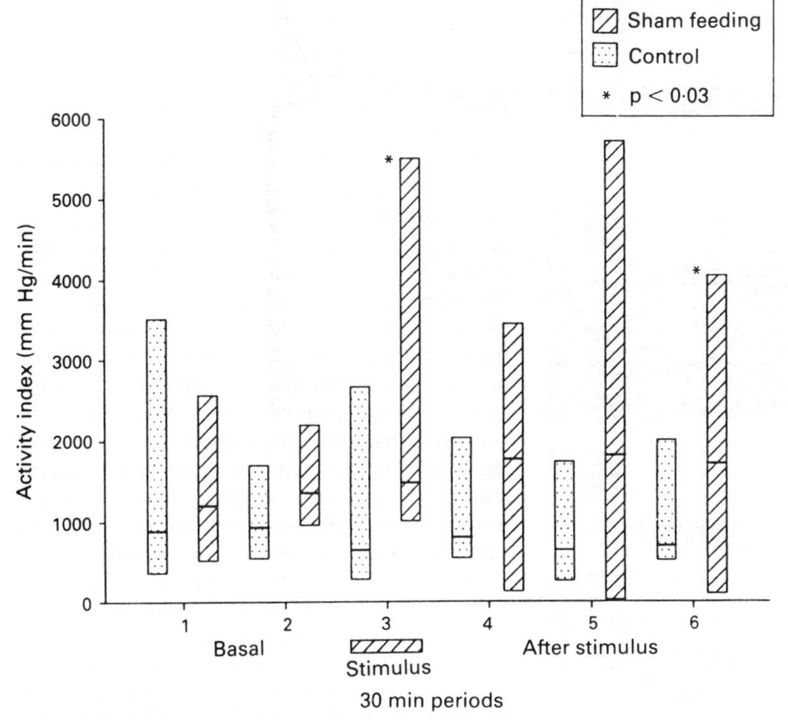

Figure 4: The effect of control discussion and sham feeding on study segment colonic pressure activity. The median (bar), and range (box) of activity index is plotted on the Y axis for each 30 minute period plotted on the X axis. Period of stimulation (▨)

The sight and smell stimulus significantly increased gastric acid output above basal ($p<0\cdot02$), but not control ($p=0\cdot06$) levels.

QUALITATIVE ANALYSIS OF COLONIC PRESSURE RECORDS

The increased colonic activity index during the food discussion stimulus was associated with a number of qualitative changes in colonic pressure activity as illustrated in Figure 6, which shows the 4 channel pressure trace for the 30 minute periods before (top) and during food discussion (bottom). There was a predominance of segmental contractions throughout the study in both the basal and food discussion periods. No propagating contractions or rectal motor complexes were seen. During food discussion there was a qualitative increase in segmental activity in all channels associated with quantitative increases in maximum amplitude, mean amplitude, and activity index (Table III). There was no change in the baseline pressure to account for the quantitative increases in pressure activity seen during food discussion.

Discussion

The existence of a cephalic phase of the colonic response to food was sought for and found in this study, which further investigated the relative potency of thought, sight, smell, and taste of food as agonists in this reflex. The hypothesis that a cephalic phase of colonic response to food may exist was suggested by previous observations in this laboratory, which indicated that the colonic response was synchronous with the start of the meal, that significantly increased colonic pressures occurred during sham feeding, and that the colonic response was affected by the route of administration of the meal.[11]

Procedures in this study followed the model developed by Feldman and Richardson[8] for the investigation of the cephalic phase of gastric acid secretion. The present experiments conducted under similar conditions showed that discussion of food, a pure cephalic stimulus, significantly increased colonic pressure activity and stimulated gastric acid secretion, confirming the previous studies. The increased colonic pressure activity was the result of stimulation of segmenting contractions, without any evidence of propulsive wave forms. Control discussion which was not food related and devoid of emotional content, did not alter colonic pressure activity or gastric acid secretion.

Food discussion was the most potent stimulus of colonic pressure activity. The other pure cephalic stimuli – sight, smell, and sight and smell – were less potent as stimulants of colonic pressure activity. Their effectiveness, expressed as a percentage of the response to food discussion, was 51% for sight, 71% for smell, and 66% for sight and smell. The reasons for these variations must remain conjectural at present. It may be noteworthy, however, that food discussion required the subject's complete concentration and participation during the 30 minute stimulus period. In the case of the sight, smell, and sight and smell stimuli the concen-

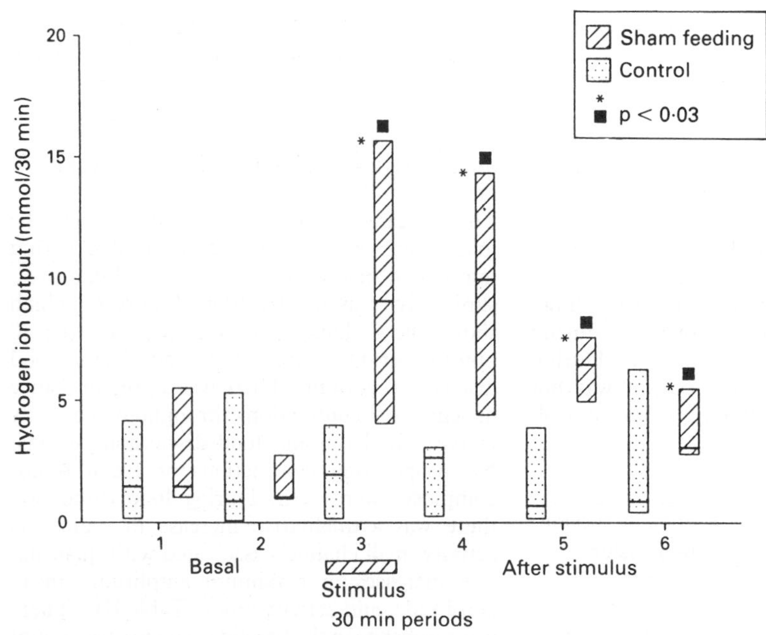

Figure 5: The effect of control discussion and sham feeding on gastric acid output. The median (bar), and range (box) of acid output is plotted on the Y axis for each 30 minute period plotted on the X axis. Period of stimulation (▨)

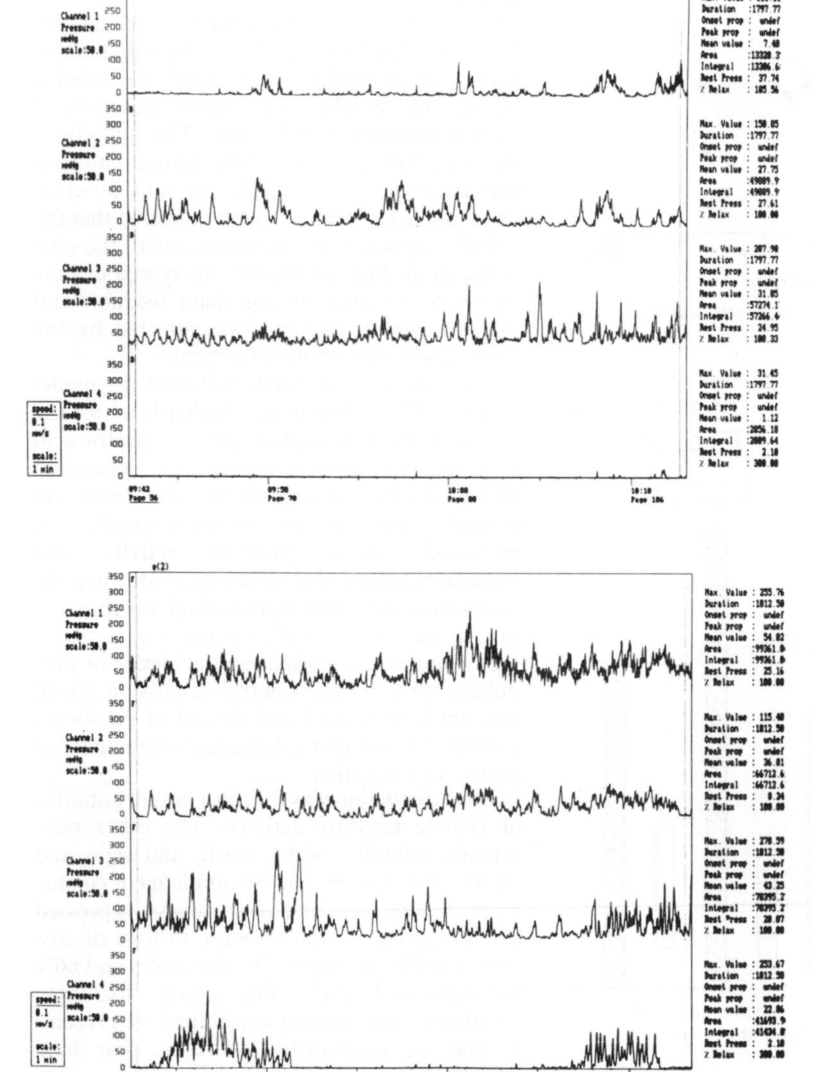

Figure 6: Shows the 4 channel pressure trace for the 30 minute period before (top) and 30 minute period during food discussion (bottom). There was an increase in segmental pressure activity during the food discussion period.

tration of the subjects during the stimulus period was more difficult to monitor, as they were asked to think about the food without discussion with the investigators.

Sham feeding increased colonic pressures and produced the greatest increase in gastric acid output, which persisted into the after stimulus observation period. This was probably because particles of food, which were seen in gastric aspirates, were inadvertently swallowed by the subjects despite all reasonable precautions. In our hands therefore, this stimulus can not be considered purely cephalic in nature. The colonic response to sham feeding, which was only 52% of that to food discussion, may have been modulated by the presence of food in the stomach. The relative potencies of the other cephalic stimuli in terms of gastric acid output expressed as a percentage of the response to sham feeding were remarkably similar to those reported by Feldman and Richardson.[8] Mean responses in this study (their results in parenthesis) were: 66% (66%) for food discussion, 39% (33%) for sight and smell, 29% (28%) for sight only, and 32% (23%) with smell only.

Acid was continuously aspirated in our experiments, and although it is unlikely that the aspiration was entirely complete, transpyloric losses were probably very small. Thus, the influence of cephalically stimulated acid secretion on more distal gut motor function, including that of the large intestine, needs to be determined. Further studies in our laboratory indicate that the entry of acid into the duodenum does not influence the cephalic motor stimulation of the colon.[12] Adherence to a rigid time frame and the administration of the stimuli in random order were adopted to minimise bias because of the possible habituation of the subjects to the conditions of the study or to circadian variations in gut function.[13–16]

Studies of the relation between the central nervous system and the colon have mainly been concerned with the effects of acute experimental stress[17–19] or of sleep.[13 16] The present data show another aspect of the way in which the central nervous system can modulate the function of the distal large intestine. The pathways through which this effect is mediated is unclear. The vagus mediates the gastric cephalic response[6] but there is no direct evidence that the vagus mediates the cephalic colonic response. Although anatomical dissection limits the distribution of this nerve to the proximal two thirds of the colon,[20] there is physiological evidence that a neural mechanism plays a part in the distal colonic motor responses to food,[21] which is present in patients with complete transection of the spinal cord.[22] On the other hand, recent studies in primates suggests that the vagus innervates the whole colon.[23] Interestingly, the small intestine seems to be unaffected by cephalic influences[24] despite the well documented differences in small intestinal motility between the fed and fasted states.

Results of this study show the existence of a cephalic phase of the colonic pressure response to food in healthy subjects. The pathways involved in the mediation of the response remain to be determined.

Some of the data were presented to the British Society of Gastroenterology, Sheffield, September 1988.

Our thanks are due to Ms Annie O'Dell of 'Hotstuff' for her expert cookery. This work was funded by a project grant from the Medical Research Council.

1 Wright SH, Snape WJ Jr, Battle WM, Cohen S, London RL. Effect of dietary components on gastrocolonic response. *Am J Physiol* 1980; **238:** G228–32.
2 Battle WM, Cohen S, Snape WJ Jr. Inhibition of postprandial colonic motility after ingestion of amino acid mixture. *Dig Dis Sci* 1980; **25:** 647–52.
3 Levinson S, Bhasker M, Gibson TR, Morin R, Snape WJ Jr. Comparison of intraluminal and intravenous mediators of colonic response to eating. *Dig Dis Sci* 1985; **30:** 33–9.
4 Sun EA, Snape WJ Jr, Cohen S, Renny A. The role of opiate receptors and cholinergic neurons in the gastrocolonic response. *Gastroenterology* 1982; **82:** 689–93.
5 Pavlov IP. The centrifugal (efferent) nerves to gastric glands and the pancreas. In: Thompson WH, transl. *The work of the digestive glands.* WH Philadelphia: Charles Griffin, 1910: 48–59.
6 Farrell JI. Contributions to the physiology of gastric secretion. The vagi as the sole efferent pathway for the cephalic phase of gastric secretion. *Am J Physiol* 1928; **85:** 685–7.
7 Grossman MI. Neural and hormonal stimulation of gastric secretion of acid. In: Code CF, ed. *Handbook of physiology.* Vol II. pp 835–63. Washington DC: American Physiology Society, 1967.
8 Feldman M, Richardson CT. Role of thought, sight, smell, and taste of food in the cephalic phase of gastric acid secretion in humans. *Gastroenterology* 1986; **90:** 428–33.
9 Rogers J, Henry MM, Misiewicz JJ. Increased segmental activity and intraluminal pressures in the sigmoid colon of patients with the irritable bowel syndrome. *Gut* 1989; **30:** 634–41.
10 Rogers J, Misiewicz JJ. Fully automated computer analysis of intracolonic pressures. *Gut* 1989; **30:** 642–9.
11 Rogers J, Raimundo AH, Misiewicz JJ. Cephalic and gastric phases of the colonic pressure response to food. *Gastroenterology* 1991; **100:** A487.
12 Rogers J, Raimundo Ana H, Misiewicz JJ. Cephalic phase of the colonic response to food is not secondary to increased gastric acid output, *Gut* 1989; **30:** A735.
13 Narducci F, Bassotti G, Gaburri M, Morrelli A. Twenty four hour manometric recording of colonic motor activity in healthy man. *Gut* 1987; **28:** 17–25.
14 Kellow JE, Borody TJ, Phillips SF, Tucker RL, Haddad AC. Human interdigestive motility: variations in patterns from the oesophagus to colon. *Gastroenterology* 1986; **91:** 386–95.
15 Bassotti G, Gaburri M, Imbimbo BP, Rossi L, Farroni F, Pelli MA, *et al.* Colonic mass movements in idiopathic chronic constipation. *Gut* 1988; **29:** 1173–9.
16 Frexinos J, Bueno L, Fioramonti J. Diurnal changes in myoelectrical spiking activity of the human colon. *Gastroenterology* 1985; **88:** 1104–10.
17 Almy TP, Kern F Jr, Tulin M. Alterations in colonic function in man under stress. II. Experimental production of sigmoid spasm in healthy persons. *Gastroenterology* 1949; **12:** 425–36.
18 Misiewicz JJ, Waller SL, Fox RH, Goldsmith R, Hunt TJ. The effect of elevated body temperature and of stress on the motility of stomach and colon in man. *Clin Sci* 1968; **34:** 149–59.
19 Narducci F, Snape WJ Jr, Battle WM, London RL, Cohen S. Increased colonic motility during exposure to a stressful situation. *Dig Dis Sci* 1985; **30:** 40–4.
20 Last RJ. Anatomy, regional and applied. 6th ed. Edinburgh: Churchill Livingstone, 1978.
21 Snape WJ Jr, Wright SH, Battle WM, Cohen S. The gastrocolonic response: evidence for a neural mechanism. *Gastroenterology* 1979; **77:** 1235–40.
22 Connell AM, Frankel H, Guttmann L. The motility of the pelvic colon following complete lesions of the spinal cord. *Paraplegia* 1963; **1:** 98–115.
23 Dapoigny M, Zhu YR, Cowles VE, Condon RE. Vagal cryo-interruption and efferent stimulation effects on colonic motor activity in monkeys. *Gastroenterology* 1990; **98:** A343.
24 Raimundo AH, Rogers J, Misiewicz JJ, Silk DBA. Effect of cephalic stimulation on human small bowel motility and intestinal flows. *Gut* 1991; **32:** A590–1.

© *Lancet* 1993; 341: 1359–1362

An international association between *Helicobacter pylori* infection and gastric cancer

THE EUROGAST STUDY GROUP

Gastric infection with *Helicobacter pylori* seems to be a risk factor for gastric cancer. We have conducted a multicentre epidemiological study to investigate this relation further.

Our study was designed to look at the relation between the prevalence of *H pylori* infection and gastric cancer rates in 17 populations from 13 countries, chosen to reflect the global range of gastric cancer incidence. In each centre, about 50 males and 50 females in each of the two age groups 25–34 years and 55–64 years were selected at random from the local population and provided blood samples. Serum samples were assayed for the presence of IgG antibodies to *H pylori* in a single laboratory. Prevalence rates of *H pylori* seropositivity were related to local gastric cancer incidence and mortality rates using linear regression. There was a statistically significant relation between the prevalence of seropositivity and cumulative rates (0—74 years) for both gastric cancer incidence and mortality with regression coefficients of 2·68 (p=0·001) and 1·79 (p=0·002), respectively.

Our findings are consistent with an approximately six-fold increased risk of gastric cancer in populations with 100% *H pylori* infection compared with populations that have no infection.

Lancet 1993; **341**: 1359–62.

Introduction

There is increasing evidence to suggest that gastric infection with the bacterium *Helicobacter pylori* is a risk factor for gastric cancer. Prospective epidemiological studies have shown seropositivity to *H pylori* associated with a three-to-six-fold increased risk of gastric cancer,[1-3] findings that are compatible with pathological links between *H pylori*-associated gastritis, precancerous lesions, and subsequent cancer of the stomach. Because the prevalence of seropositivity to *H pylori* in adult populations is normally high (47–76%),[1-3] even modestly raised relative risks imply that around 40–60% of gastric cancers could be attributed to infection with this organism.[4]

If the *H pylori*-gastric cancer hypothesis was true, the geographic pattern of cancer incidence would be expected, at least in part, to be correlated with the geographic pattern of *H pylori* infection. Although there have been many studies of the prevalence of *H pylori* infection among patient populations in different countries, together with a few studies of general populations,[5] there has been no systematic attempt to relate the prevalence of *H pylori* infection to international gastric cancer rates.

The EUROGAST study was designed to investigate the relation between gastric cancer and prevalence of *H pylori* infection, as assessed by the detection of *H pylori* IgG antibodies in randomly selected samples of different international populations.

Subjects and methods

The methodology for the EUROGAST study will be described in detail elsewhere. Briefly, 14 populations were initially chosen to be representative of the range of gastric cancer incidence in Europe. Populations from the US and Japan were added later to extend this range. About 200 individuals were selected at random from population-based registers, from general practitioners' lists (UK), drivers' licence rosters (USA), or health-screening programmes (Greece) and were invited by letter and/or telephone to take part. We aimed to recruit 50 males and 50 females in each of the two age-groups 25–34 years and 55–64 years. Non-respondents were followed up with further letters, telephone calls, and home visits. Individuals who could not be contacted or who refused to participate were, in general, replaced by additional subjects in the same age and sex group. All subjects provided a blood sample and answered a short questionnaire by personal interview about sociodemographic details. Serum was collected, stored, and transported according to an identical protocol in each centre. Analysis for *H pylori* IgG antibodies was done in a single laboratory using an ELISA assay,[6] as slightly modified,[7] with duplicate measurements. A threshold of 10 μg/mL was chosen to discriminate *H pylori*-positive from *H pylori*-negative subjects. The sensitivity and specificity of this test was 96% and 93%, respectively, as determined in a trial using sera from the USA.[7]

Cumulative sex-specific gastric cancer incidence and mortality rates[8] for the age range 0–74 years (and, for some analyses, 0–54

ADDRESSES: **Contributors to the EUROGAST study are listed in the appendix at the end of the article.** Correspondence to Dr D. Forman, PhD, Imperial Cancer Research Fund, Cancer Epidemiology Unit, Gibson Building, Radcliffe Infirmary, Oxford OX2 6HE, UK.

© *Lancet* 1993; 341: 1359–1362

CUMULATIVE (0–74 YEARS) GASTRIC CANCER MORTALITY AND INCIDENCE RATES AND PREVALENCE OF *H PYLORI* SEROPOSITIVITY

Country	Centre	Mortality rate %		Incidence rate %		*H pylori* seropositivity prevalence (%)				Total sample size
						25–34 years		55–64 years		
		Male	Female	Male	Female	Male	Female	Male	Female	
Algeria	Algiers	NA	NA	1·6	0·7	42	44	49	69	200
Belgium	Ghent	1·1	0·7	1·2	0·6	20	17	60	47	208
Denmark	Copenhagen	1·3	0·6	1·4	0·9	23	5	34	27	157
Germany	Augsburg	2·2	1·1	NA	NA	14	22	57	65	187
	Deggendorf	2·6	1·3	NA	NA	40	40	74	76	198
	Mosbach	2·3	0·8	NA	NA	24	33	65	75	158
Greece	Crete	0·6	0·4	NA	NA	53	54	80	70	229
Iceland	S Region*	2·5	0·7	3·2	1·2	31	40	56	62	206
Italy	Florence	3·0	1·2	3·8	1·9	17	14	38	57	205
Japan	Miyagi	4·2	2·1	9·9	4·0	55	64	88	87	186
	Yokote	5·7	2·0	NA	NA	70	54	90	80	200
Poland	Adamowka	3·6	1·3	NA	NA	69	70	79	93	171
Portugal	Gaia	3·9	1·8	5·3	2·6	57	57	73	65	132
Slovenia	Ljubljana	2·3	0·8	2·9	1·1	51	27	71	70	201
UK	Oxford	1·4	0·4	2·6	0·9	8	8	49	42	158
	Stoke	3·4	1·3	3·4	1·3	27	10	49	41	200
US	Minneapolis-St Paul	0·6	0·2	0·9	0·3	13	16	36	32	198

*National figures used for cancer mortality and incidence rates. NA = Not available.

years and 55–74 years) were calculated for each study area for a period during the early-mid 1980s. For the Algerian centre, mortality data were not available, while for six centres (three in Germany and one each in Japan, Poland, and Greece) incidence data were not available. The dependency of the cumulative gastric cancer rates on *H pylori* seroprevalence was evaluated by linear regression completed separately for each sex and in a combined model, in which seroprevalence and sex (male = 1, female = 0) were fitted together. Regression coefficients were calculated to represent the slope of the line which best fitted the data under the given model. Cancer rates were log-transformed and the seroprevalence for each centre was calculated as the average of the two age-groups, 25–34 years and 55–64 years.

Results

The table shows the sex-specific, cumulative 0–74 years incidence and mortality rates for gastric cancer, together with the percentage of *H pylori*-positive subjects in the two age groups, for each of the 17 populations. Gastric cancer incidence and mortality rates were lowest in the population from Minneapolis-St Paul (USA) and highest in the two Japanese populations. For males there was an eleven-fold range in gastric cancer incidence and a ten-fold range in mortality, while for females there was a thirteen-fold range in incidence and an eleven-fold range in mortality.

Overall, 1563 of 3194 subjects tested (49%) were *H pylori* seropositive; 543 of 1558 (35%) at 25–34 years and 1020 of 1636 (62%) at 55–64 years. At 25–34 years the prevalence (both sexes combined) of *H pylori* seropositivity varied from 8% in Oxford (UK) to 70% in Adamowka (Poland), while at 55–64 years the prevalence varied from 31% in Copenhagen (Denmark) to 87% in both Adamowka and Miyagi (Japan). There was, therefore, a nine-fold range in prevalence in the younger age group and a three-fold range in the older group. Within each of the individual populations the prevalence was higher in the older age group than in the younger one, but there was a strong correlation between the prevalence at 25–34 years and that at 55–64 years ($r = 0{\cdot}88$, both sexes combined). There was no appreciable difference between the prevalence in males and females (36% and 34%, respectively, at 25–34 years; 62% and 63%, respectively, at 55–64 years; $r = 0{\cdot}88$, both age-groups combined).

For both sexes, there was a statistically significant relation between seroprevalence of *H pylori* and log-transformed cumulative (0–74 years) gastric cancer mortality and incidence rates (figure). In the combined model, the coefficients for *H pylori* seroprevalence were 1·79 ($p = 0{\cdot}002$) for mortality and 2·68 ($p = 0{\cdot}001$) for incidence—ie, a 10% increase in infection prevalence was associated with approximately an 18% increase in log cancer mortality and a 27% increase in log cancer incidence. When the analyses were sub-divided into two age groups, the coefficient estimates and their significance level for combined models were higher for the effect of *H pylori* seroprevalence at 25–34 years on gastric cancer rates from 0–54 years (2·30 [$p = 0{\cdot}001$] for mortality; 3·60 [$p = 0{\cdot}0001$] for incidence) than for the effect of *H pylori* seroprevalence at 55–64 years on gastric cancer rates from 55–74 years (1·73 [$p = 0{\cdot}003$] for mortality; 2·53 [$p = 0{\cdot}003$] for incidence).

For Algiers (Algeria), cancer incidence data were substituted because of the unavailability of mortality data and thus regressions on cancer mortality were based on 34 data points (17 populations, both sexes). Exclusion of the Algiers data had virtually no effect on the estimates of the coefficients or their significance. The regression on cancer incidence was based on 22 data points (11 populations).

Although the regression on cancer incidence rates showed higher coefficients for *H pylori* antibody prevalence than those for cancer mortality, these differences resulted from enforced selection of those 11 centres for which incidence data were available and not from a stronger relation in itself. Analyses of the mortality data restricted to the same 11 centres resulted in very similar coefficients as for the analysis of incidence.

The distribution of data points around the regression line can be seen in the figure, which shows that although there was a clear association between *H pylori* seropositivity and gastric cancer incidence and mortality, there was also considerable scatter. In particular, the populations from Minneapolis-St Paul (USA) and Crete (Greece) had substantially lower cancer rates than would be predicted from the regression model, while the populations from Florence (Italy), Stoke (UK), and Miyagi (Japan) had cancer rates that were higher than predicted. The statistical significance of the regression analyses was not affected by the removal of any single centre. After accounting for sex, the proportion of the variance in the log-transformed cancer

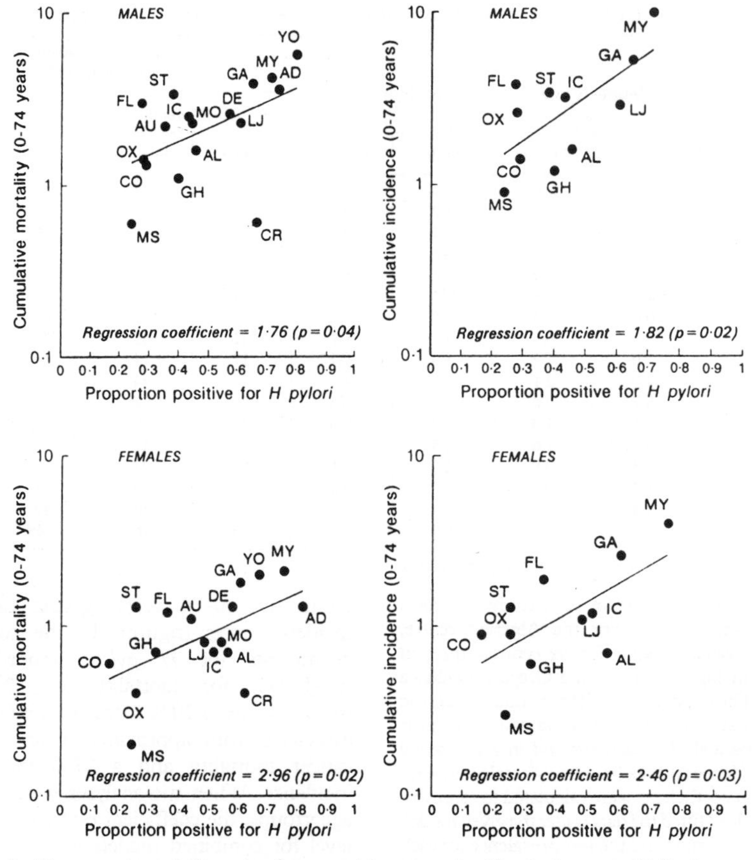

Incidence and mortality rates from gastric cancer by *H pylori* seropositivity (mean of 25–34 years and 55–64 years).

In models in which males and females were combined, regression coefficients were 1·79 (p=0·002) for mortality and 2·68 (p=0·001) for incidence.

Centre codes: AL,, Algiers; GH, Ghent; CO, Copenhagen; AU, Augsburg; DE, Deggendorf; MO, Mosbach; CR, Crete; IC, Iceland; FL, Florence; MY, Miyagi; YO, Yokote; AD, Adamowka; GA, Gaia; LJ, Ljubljana; OX, Oxford; ST, Stoke; MS, Minneapolis-St Paul.

rates explained by *H pylori* seropositivity was 18·3% for mortality and 31·4% for incidence.

Discussion

Our study has shown a statistically significant association between the gastric cancer incidence and mortality rates and the prevalence of *H pylori* seropositivity in 17 populations. These data suggest that the ten-fold range in gastric cancer rates in these populations is due, at least in part, to the prevalence of *H pylori* infection. Geographical correlation studies such as ours do not provide firm evidence of cause and effect, since the variation in both gastric cancer rates and *H pylori* seroprevalence could be influenced by confounding factors. Socio-economic status was a potential confounder in our study because it is strongly related to the risk of both gastric cancer[9] and *H pylori* infection.[5] After adjustment for average level of education (as a surrogate measure of socio-economic status) the regression coefficients changed from 1·79 to 1·53 (p=0·009) for mortality and from 2·68 to 2·60 (p=0·003) for incidence. Although average level of education will only partly reflect socio-economic status, the lack of any appreciable effect of the adjustment on the regression coefficients or their statistical significance weighs against a major confounding influence. Apart from socio-economic status we do not know of any potential confounding factors that correlate as strongly with both gastric cancer risk and *H pylori* infection. Nevertheless, the possibility of confounding by an unknown factor cannot be dismissed.

Our results are consistent with a study that reported a significant correlation between gastric cancer mortality rates and the prevalence of *H pylori* seropositivity in 46 counties in rural China[10] and with a study in Colombia[11] which found a significantly higher infection rate among the adult population of one city than another, gastric cancer rates also being higher in the former. By contrast, a study in Italy[12] found no difference in *H pylori* seropositivity between regions at high and low risk for gastric cancer.

There are certain to be other risk factors involved in the aetiology of gastric cancer apart from *H pylori* infection. Dietary factors are especially important[9] and consideration of these might help explain the scatter of individual populations around the regression line. That certain populations can have a high prevalence of *H pylori* infection yet relatively low rates of gastric cancer has been reported previously,[10] especially in Africa.[13]

A weakness of our study is the implicit assumption that, within a population, the prevalence of *H pylori* seropositivity in the age groups 25–34 and 55–64 years will reflect levels of seropositivity in older generations who contribute most to current gastric cancer rates. Although this assumption may be valid for some populations in the study, it is unlikely to be uniformly true for them all. The transmission of *H pylori* is known to be heavily dependent on socio-economic conditions[5] and the different rates of change of such conditions among the study populations may have resulted in differential rates of change in *H pylori* infection prevalence over time. This might explain why, for example, the population in Florence had a higher gastric cancer rate in the 1980s than would be predicted from the regression on current *H pylori* prevalence—ie, if improvements in social conditions in recent decades had resulted in lower *H pylori* infection rates than was the case elsewhere.

A closer temporal concordance between cancer rates and *H pylori* seroprevalence rates, with less possibility of differential change in social conditions, is obtained by using cumulative cancer rates for the age range 0–54 years rather than for 0–74 years and relating these to seroprevalence in the 25–34 year age group. The coefficient estimates and their significance are increased in this regression model. However, the strong age-dependency of gastric cancer means that cumulative rates for 0–54 years were based on substantially fewer events than the rates for 0–74 years. The number of cancer registrations and deaths on which the 0–74 years' incidence and mortality rates are based ranged from 73 and 61, respectively, in Copenhagen to 1296 and 565, respectively, in Miyagi.

We believe that the most reliable analysis is for cumulative cancer mortality from 0–74 years (a coefficient of 1·79 [p = 0·002]). Although there are theoretical reasons to favour analyses based on registration data or on cancer rates accumulated to 54 years, we prefer to emphasise the estimate based on the maximum data available using all the study populations to minimise random errors introduced by small numbers. Based on this estimate, one could predict that mortality from gastric cancer in a population with 100% prevalence of *H pylori* infection would be about six times higher than in a population with no infection. This value is consistent with the relative risks in the range 3–6 obtained in prospective studies comparing the gastric cancer risk in seropositive and seronegative individuals.[1-3]

Our study has several strengths derived from the use of a common protocol to collect blood from several populations for analysis in a single laboratory. However, there were limitations in the study design, most of which were unavoidable in this type of collaborative exercise. Thus, the cancer mortality and incidence data, although broadly comparable, varied in detail (period covered, age groupings) and probably also in quality. Also, the participation rate varied from 39% in Gaia (Portugal) to 93% in Algiers (overall average 64%) and it was impossible to estimate directly the effect of different rates of participation.

Our results show a statistically significant relation between *H pylori* infection, as determined by serum antibody positivity, and gastric cancer mortality and incidence. This finding adds further weight to the hypothesis that *H pylori* infection is a risk factor for gastric cancer.

This study was financially partly supported as a Concerted Action by contract no: MR4-086-UK from the Directorate Biology, Directorate-General for Science, Research and Development Joint Research Centre, Commission of the European Communities.

THE EUROGAST STUDY GROUP

Project leader

D. Forman (Cancer Epidemiology Unit, Imperial Cancer Research Fund, Oxford, UK).

Project management group

M. Coleman (Unit of Descriptive Epidemiology, International Agency for Research on Cancer, Lyon, France); G. De Backer (Department of Hygiene and Social Medicine, Univesity Hospital, Ghent, Belgium); J. Elder (Department of Surgery, University of Keele, Stoke on Trent, UK); H. Møller (Danish Cancer Registry, Institute of Cancer Epidemiology, Danish Cancer Society, Copenhagen, Denmark).

EEC COMAC-EPIDEMIOLOGY liaison officer

L. Cayolla da Motta (National School of Public Health, Lisbon, Portugal).

Study co-ordinators

IARC: P. Roy (Unit of Descriptive Epidemiology, International Agency for Research on Cancer, Lyon, France); Algeria: L. Abid (Registry of Digestive Tract Cancers, Bologhine Hospital, Algiers); Belgium: G. de Backer (Department of Hygiene and Social Medicine, University Hospital, Ghent); Denmark: A. Tjönneland (Danish Cancer Registry, Institute of Cancer Epidemiology, Danish Cancer Society, Copenhagen); Germany: H. Boeing, T. Haubrich, J. Wahrendorf (Institute of Epidemiology and Biometry, German Cancer Research Centre, Heidelberg); Greece: O. Manousos (Department of Gastroenterology, University General Hospital, Heraklion, Crete); Iceland: H. Tulinius, H. Ogmundsdottir (Icelandic Cancer Society, Reykjavik); Italy: D. Palli, F. Cipriani (Epidemiology Unit, Centre for the Study and Prevention of Cancer, Florence); Japan: A. Fukao (Department of Public Health, Tohoku University, Sendai), S. Tsugane (Environmental Epidemiology Section, National Cancer Centre Research Institute, Tokyo), Y. Miyajima (Yokote Health Centre, Akita); Poland: W. Zatonski, J. Tyczynski (Department of Cancer Control and Epidemiology, Institute of Oncology, Warsaw); Portugal: J. Calheiros (Epidemiology Unit, Institute of Biomedical Sciences Abel Salazar, University of Oporto, Oporto); Slovenia: M. Primic Zakelj (Epidemiology Unit, Institute of Oncology, Ljubljana), M. Potocnik (Blood Transfusion Centre of Slovenia, Ljubljana); UK: P. Webb (ICRF Cancer Epidemiology Unit, Oxford), T. Knight, A. Wilson (Department of Surgery, University of Keele, Stoke on Trent); USA: S. Kaye, J. Potter (Division of Epidemiology, University of Minnesota, Minneapolis).

Assay laboratory

D. G. Newell (Department of Pathology, PHLS Centre for Applied Microbiology and Research, Porton Down, UK).

Writing group

D. Forman, P. Webb, D. Newell, M. Coleman, D. Palli, H. Møller, K. Hengels, J. Elder, G. De Backer.

REFERENCES

1. Forman D, Newell DG, Fullerton F, et al. Association between infection with *Helicobacter pylori* and risk of gastric cancer: evidence from a prospective investigation. *BMJ* 1991; **302:** 1302–05.
2. Nomura A, Stemmermann GN, Chyou P-H, Kato I, Perez-Perez GI, Blaser MJ. *Helicobacter pylori* infection and gastric carcinoma among Japanese Americans in Hawaii. *N Engl J Med* 1991; **325:** 1132–36.
3. Parsonnet J, Friedman GD, Vandersteen DP, et al. *Helicobacter pylori* infection and the risk of gastric carcinoma. *N Engl J Med* 1991; **325:** 1127–31.
4. Forman D. *Helicobacter pylori* infection: a novel risk factor in the aetiology of gastric cancer. *J Natl Cancer Inst* 1991; **83:** 1702—03.
5. Taylor DN, Blaser MJ. The epidemiology of *Helicobacter pylori* infection. *Epidemiol Rev* 1991; **13:** 42–59.
6. Steer HW, Hawtin PR, Newell DG. An ELISA technique for the serodiagnosis of *Campylobacter pyloridis* infection in patients with gastritis and benign duodenal ulceration. *Serodiagnosis Immunol* 1987; **1:** 253–59.
7. Talley NJ, Newell DG, Ormand JE, et al. Serodiagnosis of *Helicobacter pylori*: comparison of enzyme linked immunosorbent assays. *J Clin Microbiol* 1991; **29:** 1635–39.
8. Muir C, Waterhouse J, Mack T, Powell J, Whelan S. Cancer incidence in five continents (volume 5). Lyon: International Agency for Research on Cancer, 1987.
9. Howson CP, Hiyama T, Wynder EL. The decline in gastric cancer: epidemiology of an unplanned triumph. *Epidemiol Rev* 1986; **8:** 1–27.
10. Forman D, Sitas F, Newell DG, et al. Geographic association of *Helicobacter pylori* antibody prevalence and gastric cancer mortality in rural China. *Int J Cancer* 1990; **46:** 608–11.
11. Correa P, Fox J, Fontham E, et al. *Helicobacter pylori* and gastric carcinoma: serum antibody prevalence in populations with contrasting cancer risks. *Cancer* 1990; **66:** 2569–74.
12. Palli D, Decarli A, Cipriani F, et al. *Helicobacter pylori* antibodies in areas of Italy at varying gastric cancer risk. *Cancer Epid Biomarkers Prev* 1993; **2:** 37–40.
13. Holcombe C. *Helicobacter pylori:* the African enigma. *Gut* 1992; **33:** 429–31.

© Gut 1993; 34: 1075–1080

Failure of colonoscopic surveillance in ulcerative colitis

D A F Lynch, A J Lobo, G M Sobala, M F Dixon, A T R Axon

Abstract

A prospective surveillance programme for patients with longstanding (>=8 years), extensive (>=splenic flexure) ulcerative colitis was undertaken between 1978 and 1990. It comprised annual colonoscopy with pancolonic biopsy. One hundred and sixty patients were entered into the programme and had 739 colonoscopies (4·6 colonoscopies per patient; 709 patient years follow up). Eighty eight per cent of examinations reached the right colon. There was no procedure related death. One Dukes's A cancer was detected. Forty one patients (25%) defaulted. Of these 25 remain well; 13 are unaccounted for, and one died from colonic cancer. One patient had colectomy for medical reasons, and another died of carcinoma of the pancreas. Retrospectively an additional 16 eligible patients were identified who had not been recruited. Of these, 14 remain well, two are unaccounted for. None developed colonic cancer. Four patients refused colonoscopy. All remain well. Over the same period seven other cases of colonic cancer were found in association with ulcerative colitis, two in patients who had erroneously been diagnosed as having only proctitis and were therefore not entered into the programme, but were found at operation to have total colitis, one in a patient with colitis of seven years duration, and four patients who had previously attended the clinic but had been lost to follow up before 1978 and then had represented with new symptoms during the surveillance period. Thus, of the nine colitis related cancers diagnosed in this centre during the study period only one was detected by the surveillance programme. The results of this large study, and a review of published works, cast doubts on the effectiveness of colonoscopic surveillance programmes in detecting colorectal cancer in patients with ulcerative colitis.

(*Gut* 1993; **34:** 1075–1080)

Colorectal carcinoma was recognised as a complication of ulcerative colitis over 65 years ago.[1] The risk of developing cancer is increased in those individuals who have had extensive colitis for more than 10 years after the first attack, the cumulative cancer rate being 7% at 20 years and 17% at 30 years disease duration.[2] Such was the perceived risk of a patient developing cancer that prophylactic colectomy has been recommended.[3-6]

The strong association between colorectal dysplasia and cancer in ulcerative colitis was described in 1967.[7] The development of flexible endoscopy, which allows pancolonic biopsy, has supported this finding[8-15] and has led to a change in practice such that in many centres at risk patients are examined at intervals, with colonoscopy and biopsy, to detect premalignant dysplasia or early cancer.

These cancer surveillance programmes are now widely implemented despite not having been subjected to clinical trial. A number of reports[8-17] have supported the use of colonoscopic surveillance in ulcerative colitis, but doubts have also been expressed about its efficacy.[18,19]

Surveillance programmes are expensive, time consuming, and unpleasant for patients and should be shown to be effective before implementation. Colonoscopic surveillance in colitis should reduce cancer related death compared with routine clinical care, by detecting early curable cancer. It might be deemed unethical, however, to perform a controlled trial. Gastroenterologists, therefore, have a responsibility to review their results to show whether or not this form of surveillance is effective.

In 1978 a prospective surveillance programme was started[9,14] whereby all patients with longstanding extensive ulcerative colitis were invited to have annual colonoscopy with biopsy. In this paper the results of this large programme and other reported series are reviewed to discover if colonoscopic surveillance works.

Methods

SURVEILLANCE PROGRAMME

From 1978 to December 31 1990 all patients with longstanding (>=8 years) and extensive (disease extending to or beyond the splenic flexure) ulcerative colitis were advised to have annual colonoscopy with pancolonic biopsy.

Patients were seen at routine clinic follow up and the reasons for surveillance explained. If the patient failed to attend for their clinic/colonoscopy then a repeat appointment was made. If a second reminder was unsuccessful no further action was taken. If patients were known to be moving away a letter detailing their surveillance history was sent to their doctor or next supervising consultant.

The duration of disease was taken from the date of diagnosis except where obvious symptoms of colitis came before the diagnosis by a matter of years. Disease extent was verified by barium enema or colonoscopy, or both. Patients older than 75 years were not entered and those reaching 75 during surveillance were withdrawn.

Colonoscopy was carried out under light sedation after standard laxative and bowel enema preparation. Biopsy specimens were taken with forceps from flat mucosa at about 10 cm intervals

Centre for Digestive Diseases, The General Infirmary, Leeds
D A F Lynch
A J Lobo
G M Sobala
M F Dixon
A T R Axon

Correspondence to:
Dr D A F Lynch,
Gastroenterology Unit,
The General Infirmary, Leeds
LS1 3EX.

Accepted for publication
26 November 1992

© Gut 1993; 34: 1075–1080

along the colorectum and from any identifiable 'mass lesions'. These correspond to the following descriptive sites: caecum; proximal ascending colon; distal ascending colon; proximal transverse colon; distal transverse colon; proximal descending colon; distal descending colon; sigmoid colon; rectum. Biopsy specimens were mounted on filter paper or placed in cassettes before fixation in formalin and after routine processing were sectioned at three levels and stained with haematoxylin and eosin.

If dysplasia was present it was classified as low grade, high grade, or carcinoma. If high grade dysplasia was found, repeat biopsies were performed within six months. Surgery was performed in cases of persistent high grade dysplasia, or carcinoma.

DETERMINING OUTCOME OF SURVEILLANCE PROGRAMME

Our review of the surveillance programme had three distinct goals: (a) to obtain full follow up of all patients who had participated at any time in the surveillance programme; (b) to identify any other patients who attended the department over this time and who should have been recruited into the surveillance programme; and (c) to identify all cases of colonic carcinoma occurring in association with ulcerative colitis presenting to the department over this period.

These goals were achieved as follows: (a) the outcome of patients entered into the surveillance programme was obtained from departmental records, patient case notes, histopathology reports, doctor, supervising consultant or patient by clinic, letter or telephone; (b) eligible patients with ulcerative colitis were identified from index cards used to document all colitis clinic patients, and review of notes of all patients attending the clinic for a 12 month period. Using this information notes were obtained from the records departments. Information extracted included date of birth, relevant medical and surgical history, date of onset of symptoms, date of diagnosis (histological/radiological), disease extent (barium enema/colonoscopy), surveillance colonoscopy date and findings, biopsy site and histological findings, and present status if known; (c) cases of cancer in association with colitis were identified from histopathology department records that document all colitis patients who developed dysplasia, cancer, or had colonic surgery since 1978.

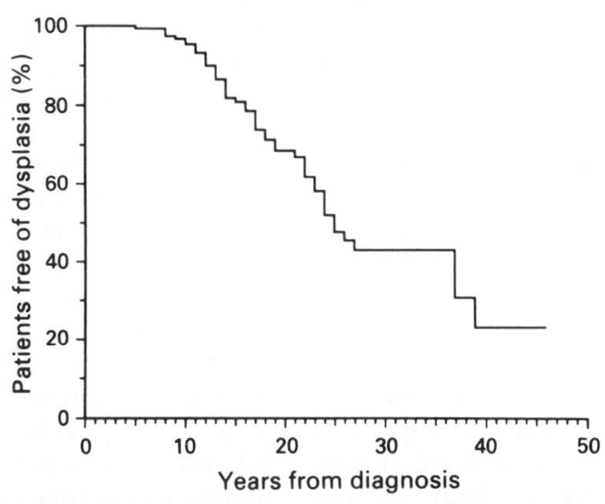

A low grade dysplasia free survival curve shows that 25% of patients with ulcerative colitis had exhibited low grade dysplasia at least once by 17 years after diagnosis of ulcerative colitis, 50% at 25 years, and 75% by 38 years.

Results

One hundred and eighty patients fulfilled the criteria for entry into the surveillance programme.

RECRUITMENT FAILURES

Sixteen patients were erroneously not entered into the programme by the supervising physician because they were unaware that the patient was eligible for surveillance. Fourteen of these patients are well, a mean of 9·4 years (range 3–12) after what should have been their programme entry date. Two are unaccounted for after a mean of three years.

SURVEILLANCE REFUSALS

Four patients refused colonoscopic surveillance, but continue with regular clinical supervision. All are well, a mean of 9·75 years (range 6–12) after programme entry date.

PATIENTS STARTING SURVEILLANCE

One hundred and sixty patients entered the surveillance programme and had 739 colonoscopies (4·6 colonoscopy/patient; 709 years follow up). The mean length of duration of colitis was 14·1 years (range 8–46). Eighty eight per cent of examinations reached the right colon. There was no procedure related death. Biopsy specimens (5695) were taken giving a mean of 7·8 per colonoscopy (range 1–9).

SURVEILLANCE DEFAULTERS

Forty one patients who started surveillance defaulted. Twenty five remain well, a mean of 2·5 years (range 2–10) after default. Thirteen patients are unaccounted for, mean 6·5 years (range 2–12) later. One patient died of disseminated colonic cancer after three years (see Table I, patient E), the three previous complete annual colonoscopies had been negative for dysplasia. One patient had colectomy for medical reasons six years later. No cancer was found. One patient died of pancreatic cancer seven years later.

LOW GRADE DYSPLASIA

Forty patients were found to have low grade dysplasia in at least one biopsy. The mean age at first diagnosis of low grade dysplasia was 45·2 years (SD 13·64) and mean duration of colitis to diagnosis of low grade dysplasia 17·7 years (SD 7·33).

These 40 patients had a further 201 colonoscopies (223 patient years follow up). Twenty (50%) had no further dysplasia (mean 4·0 colonoscopies per patient over 4·7 years). Nineteen continued to exhibit low grade dysplasia in at least one subsequent biopsy (mean 6·3 follow up colonoscopies per patient over 6·9 years). One of

© Gut 1993; 34: 1075–1080

TABLE I *Colorectal cancer in ulcerative colitis 1978–1990*

Year of cancer diagnosis	*Age*	*Sex*	*Duration of ulcerative colitis (years)*	*Extent of colitis/ method of determination*	*Presentation*	*Dukes's stage*	*Patient group*
Patient A							
1979	60	M	7	Total/ colonoscopy	Previous history of colonic polyps. Colonoscopy performed at 7 years duration to determine extent plus polypectomy (Barium enema showed recurrence of polyps)	A	Did not fulfil eligibility criteria
Patient B							
1983	49	F	20	Rectum/ sigmoidoscopy	Patient believed to have proctitis. Diagnosed 1963. Lost to follow up. Presented with symptoms 1983. Found to have rectal carcinoma	B	Did not fulfil eligibility criteria
Patient C							
1984	45	M	21	Total/ colonoscopy	Patient entered surveillance 1979 at 17 years duration. High grade dysplasia at fifth colonoscopy. Colectomy performed	A	Surveillance
Patient D							
1984	33	M	12	Total/barium	Lost to follow up 1972. Re-presented 1984 with colitic symptoms. Barium enema showed sigmoid polyp. Colonoscopy showed high grade dysplasia. Colectomy performed	A	Lost to follow up before programme
Patient E							
1985	36	M	18	Total/barium enema	Normal surveillance 1980–82. Moved away 1982/83. Died with a disseminated colon carcinoma 1985	>=C	Defaulter
Patient F							
1987	42	F	19	Total/ colonoscopy	Diagnosed 1968. Lost to follow up. Presented with rectal bleeding 1987. Sigmoidoscopy showed polypoid, rectal carcinoma. Anterior resection performed. Patient entered into surveillance	C	Lost to follow up before programme
Patient G							
1988	47	M	20	Unknown	Lost to follow up in 1970. Re-presented in 1987 with rectal bleeding. Colonoscopy showed carcinoma in situ at 80 cm	C	Lost to follow up before programme
Patient H							
1990	62	M	21	Unknown	Believed to have proctitis. Diagnosed 1969. Lost to follow up 1972. Presented with changed bowel habit 1990. Ascending colon and sigmoid cancer on barium enema	C	Did not fulfil eligibility criteria
Patient I							
1990	44	M	26	Unknown	Diagnosed colitis 1964. Lost to follow up in 1976. Presented with dysphagia and anaemia in 1990, Colonoscopy at that time showed sigmoid polyp (cancer)	C	Lost to follow up before programme

This table shows the year of diagnosis, age at diagnosis, sex, duration of disease, disease extent (method used), presentation, Dukes's staging, and patient group for each of the nine cancers found in association with ulcerative colitis between 1978 and 1990.

these developed an adenoma six years later, which was removed at colonoscopy and has remained free of dysplasia since (6 years). One patient (patient C) who had low grade dysplasia in the distal descending and sigmoid colon was found to have high grade dysplasia in the sigmoid colon at the next colonoscopy 14 months later. At colectomy two Dukes's A cancers were found; one in the sigmoid and one in the transverse colon. This patient was the only case of cancer detected by the surveillance programme.

Thus, follow up of patients with low grade dysplasia found one cancer in 223 patient years. The Figure shows that 25% of patients with ulcerative colitis exhibited low grade dysplasia on at least one occasion by 17 years after diagnosis of ulcerative colitis, 50% by 25 years, and 75% by 38 years.

NON-CANCER SURGERY

Fifteen patients had colectomy for failed medical treatment after a mean of 15·6 years (range 9–32) disease duration. Nine had subtotal colectomy, six had panproctocolectomy. Four of the patients who had low grade dysplasia previously were negative for dysplasia at colectomy. Two patients who had been negative for dysplasia were found to have low grade dysplasia in their colectomy specimens.

CANCER COMPLICATING ULCERATIVE COLITIS OUTSIDE THE SURVEILLANCE PROGRAMME

During the 12 year period there have been seven other cases of colonic cancer in association with ulcerative colitis at this centre. Two patients (patient B and patient H) were believed to have had proctitis but were subsequently found to have total colitis at colonoscopy with biopsy or histological examination of the colectomy specimen (one Dukes's B, one Dukes's C) (Table I). One patient (patient A) had several colonic polyps removed endoscopically two years earlier. A barium enema performed at seven years disease duration showed recurrent polyps. Colonoscopy was performed to remove the colonic polyps and determine disease extent. Total colectomy was performed because of incomplete removal of a large tubular adenoma with intra-epithelial malignant change. At colectomy a Dukes's A cancer was found on a background of total colitis. There were no other areas of dysplasia (Table I). Four patients (D, F, G, and I) had been seen in the Leeds colitis clinic before the policy of surveillance had been started

© Gut 1993; 34: 1075–1080

TABLE II *Breakdown of 12 (11 published) studies on cancer surveillance in ulcerative colitis*

Year	Author	No of patients	Colonoscopies per patient	Dukes's >=C*	Dukes's A/B exclude†	Dukes's A/B success‡
1980	Fuson[10]	75	1·1	4	7	0
1981	Blackstone[22]	112	1·5	2	4	0
1985	Rosenstock[12]	248	1·5	3	4	0
1988	Jones[20]	313	?	5	2	2
1988	Rutegard[15]	93	3·6	0	1	0
1989	Lashner[21]	99	4·2	5	0	3
1990	Lennard-Jones[22]	344	2·4	8	13	1
1990	Lofberg[24]	72	4·0	0	1	1
1991	Nugent[8]	213	?	6	3	1
1991	Leidenius[16]	66	2·8	0	0	0
1992	Woolrich[17]	121	3·7	2	3	2
Sub total		1756		35	38	10
1993	Lynch	160	4·3	5	3	1
Total		1916		40	41	11

*Patients found to have cancer, but stage Dukes's C or worse. †Patients found to have Dukes's A/B cancer, but not as part of the colonoscopic surveillance policy detailed in the discussion. ‡Patients found to have cancer as part of surveillance programme.

and were lost to follow up. They re-presented during the surveillance period with new symptoms.

CANCER SURGERY

Thus, altogether, there were nine cases of colonic cancer in association with ulcerative colitis at this centre over this time period (Table I); mean age 46·4 years (range 33–62), mean disease duration 18·2 years (range 7–26), six men. Six patients developed cancer under the age of fifty. Seven patients had total colectomy (three Dukes's A, one Dukes's B, three Dukes's C). One patient (patient F) who had been lost to follow up, had an anterior resection for a rectal carcinoma (one Dukes's C). Because of the high risk of developing a further cancer the patient was entered into the surveillance programme. Three subsequent colonoscopies have been negative for dysplasia.

Therefore, of 180 patients eligible for colonic cancer surveillance in ulcerative colitis 160 were entered into the programme. During the 12 year period 1978–1990 nine colonic cancers were found in association with ulcerative colitis, but only one was detected by the surveillance programme.

Discussion

Many gastroenterologists consider that patients with ulcerative colitis with longstanding, extensive disease should have annual colonoscopy and biopsy to detect dysplasia or early cancer. If high grade dysplasia or carcinoma is detected the patient can be treated at an early stage.

It is important to define what is 'success' and what is 'failure' in a surveillance programme to allow critical analysis of the outcome. An early cancer – that is, Dukes's A or B found as a result of the programme represents a success. A Dukes's C cancer or worse should be regarded a failure of surveillance because of the uncertain outlook.

It is also important to consider the method of cancer detection when reviewing the results of a surveillance policy. The generally accepted surveillance policy in most centres today is regular colonoscopy for patients with longstanding extensive colitis. If this definition is applied when reviewing surveillance studies the result is that cancers found earlier than eight years from onset or found in left sided colitis or a cancer found at colonoscopy performed for any reason other than surveillance (such as rectal bleeding), cannot be regarded as a success. Colorectal cancer presenting as an abdominal mass or perforation,[20 21] cancers found on sigmoidoscopy and barium enema,[20 22] or colonoscopy performed because of an abnormal barium enema[10 12 22 23] are outside protocols that use regular colonoscopic examination as the surveillance technique.

Similarly, if a cancer is found at a screening colonoscopy in a patient presenting to a unit years after the programme entry date for example, colitis of 17 years duration or when referred from another centre[8 10 22 24] it cannot be counted a success becaue these cancers represent a selected group detected outside the regular surveillance protocol. Cancers found at surgery performed for reasons other than high grade dysplasia or early carcinoma, such as debility or failed medical treatment,[12 22] or low grade dysplasia,[8 12 23] (not a generally recognised indication for surgery) cannot be counted as successes of the surveillance policy either.

Applying these criteria to our results, one of nine colonic cancers that arose in association with ulcerative colitis during the surveillance period was detected by the surveillance programme. Analysis of 12 published studies of colonoscopic surveillance programmes (Tables II and III) shows that 93 cases of colonic cancer were found. Twelve (13%) of these represent successes for the colonoscopic surveillance programmes – that is, Dukes's A/B cancers detected by regular colonoscopic surveillance.

It could be argued that these criteria are too rigid. Some surveillance programmes entail routine clinical follow up, regular sigmoidoscopy, and barium enema examination as well as regular colonoscopy and biopsy.[22] These methods of cancer detection are equally valid if they are laid down as part of a surveillance protocol. Also, cancers found at the screening (first) colonoscopy may be regarded as a success

TABLE III *Ulcerative colitis surveillance papers (amalgamated results of 1916 patients). Method of cancer diagnosis*

Dukes's stage	Mass/ perforation. Other signs/ symptoms	Barium enema/ sigmoidoscopy	Barium enema leading to colonoscopy	Operation or necropsy	Operation for low grade dysplasia	Colonoscopy without entry criteria fulfilled	Screen colonoscopy	Surveillance colonoscopy
>=C	13	10	5	1	1		2	8
B		6	5	5	2		1	5
A		4	2	6		3	7	6

Of the 1916 patients from the 12 studies, 92 cancers were found.
This table indicates the Dukes's staging and the method of diagnosis of the colonic cancers.

© Gut 1993; 34: 1075–1080

when the examination is performed according to the protocol. Adopting this approach the number of successes in the 12 published studies is 24 (26%).

A workable surveillance programme requires defined entry criteria and a cheap simple test, which is acceptable to the patient and which has a sound discriminatory basis.[25] Current surveillance colonoscopy programmes in ulcerative colitis fall short in a number of ways.

There are no universally accepted entry criteria for cancer surveillance.[26–28] There is a general feeling in published studies that colitis extending beyond the splenic flexure can be regarded as extensive in terms of cancer risk.[2] Assessment of extent, however, may be by barium enema, colonoscopy or both. Barium studies seem to be insensitive to microscopic involvement[29] and may detect only more severe cases. In our study two patients were originally diagnosed as having proctitis. If colonoscopy had been done the extensive nature of the disease might have been recognised and the patient would have entered the programme. Colitis for at least eight years is considered to be longstanding. In this series, however, one patient developed cancer after seven years disease duration so perhaps the criteria for entry should be widened.

Colonscopic surveillance programmes cause a heavy clinical workload as well as a substantial capital outlay[19 20] – that is, the test is not simple or cheap.

Patient recruitment is a recognised problem; 12% were not recruited into our programme. Some were lost to follow up from clinic before fulfilling the entry criteria for longstanding disease; others despite being eligible, were not entered. Once recruited, patients had a regular, uncomfortable examination that requires a day off work. In our study four patients refused colonoscopy, and 41 (27%) patients defaulted from the programme – strong evidence that annual colonoscopy is unacceptable to many.

There are problems with the discriminatory power of colonoscopy and biopsy. Colonic epithelial dysplasia is patchy.[30 31] Multiple biopsies sample much less than 1% of the surface area of the colon. The evidence for the association of dysplasia and cancer is conflicting. Twenty to fifty per cent of cancers are thought to arise de novo.[32 30] Fozard *et al* found a weak association between colon cancer and distant dysplasia.[33] By contrast two other studies conclude that the association is invariable.[12 34] The histological interpretation of biopsy specimens and diagnosis of dysplasia is fraught with the problems of inter and intraobserver variation[35 36] – that is, the diagnostic test does not have a sound discriminatory basis. The histological recognition of dysplasia is the very cornerstone of surveillance yet it would seem that the process of tissue collection to final diagnosis is susceptible to a number of pitfalls.

It can be argued that the finding of high grade dysplasia without cancer should be considered to be a success of surveillance. This argument is not straightforward. The diagnosis of dysplasia is beset with problems, as discussed above, furthermore the significance and outcome of high grade dysplasia is unpredictable. Colon cancer was found in 25% of patients with high grade dysplasia but another 25% had a negative colectomy specimen or colonoscopy on follow up.[22] In another study while 33% of patients with high grade dysplasia developed cancer within six years 33% were not operated on and were alive and well five years later so not all authors have advised operation even when high grade dysplasia has been diagnosed.[10 12 15] Low grade dysplasia was a common finding in ulcerative colitis surveillance in our study and in others[21] and has little prognostic significance.

All but one of the colorectal cancers in this series occurred in patients outside the surveillance programme. This experience is not unique.[20 22] This cannot be construed as a criticism of the surveillance protocol itself. Only one of these patients had been recruited and had then defaulted. We are not aware of any extensive cancer arising in patients who had regular surveillance colonoscopy. It is apparent, however, that a number of patients who needed surveillance did not receive it. It is probable that these individuals were well and asymptomatic or had minimal symptoms. This might explain why they did not attend for clinical review. A review of the notes of our cancer patients suggests that virtually none of them were taking disease suppressant drugs, such as salazopyrin, regularly or at all. It may be that unsuppressed inflammation, while causing few or no symptoms, places these patients at increased risk of developing colonic cancer.

The main criticism that can be levelled at our study (and those in published works) is that the finding of one patient with high grade dysplasia (and carcinoma) does not justify the great expense and the effort for staff and patients involved in 739 colonscopies and 709 years of follow up. In 10 of 12 surveillance studies it is possible to calculate the number of colonoscopies performed and the number of early cancers detected by them. Including this study eight early cancers were found by colonoscopic surveillance and 3807 colonoscopies were performed: one cancer per 476 examinations.

There are 38 deaths per 100 000[37] from colorectal cancer annually in the United Kingdom. As nearly all of these occur in the 40–80 age group (and not everyone with colorectal cancer dies of it) the annual incidence in this group is greater than 38 per 50 000.[37] If, therefore, the normal population in this age group was screened at five year intervals, and assuming that the polyp/carcinoma sequence takes longer than five years, 190 cases of cancer or premalignant polyp would be found per 50 000 examinations – that is, 1 in 263: a higher detection rate in the normal population than that achieved by annual colonoscopic surveillance of extensive longstanding ulcerative colitis. In a recent study colonoscopy was performed on 210 asymptomatic subjects aged 50–75 years with negative faecal occult bloods. Two Dukes's A cancers were detected giving a yield of one cancer per 105 colonoscopies.[38]

We conclude that in our experience annual colonoscopic surveillance for cancer has been unsuccessful; eight of nine colonic cancers occurred in ulcerative colitis patients not having surveillance. Our results and a review of published works cast doubts on the value of annual colonoscopic surveillance in this condition when considering its cost effectiveness and the definition of a workable programme.[24]

Lashner *et al*[39] monitored two groups of 90 patients with longstanding, extensive ulcerative colitis, one with regular colonoscopy, the other with regular clinical follow up. There was no difference in the cancer detection rate. Though the numbers affected are small colonoscopic biopsy and histological examination for dysplasia seems to hold no advantage over routine clinical management.

How then should we manage these patients who are known to be at an increased risk of developing cancer?

The published data show that most cancers are detected as a result of clinical follow up, where new symptoms are investigated at an early stage. Many cancers were found in patients who had defaulted the clinic before they were eligible for surveillance returning with new symptoms years later. 'Screening' colonoscopy (as opposed to 'surveillance' colonoscopy) detected a number of cancers.

All patients with ulcerative colitis should be screened at eight years. This will allow them to be assessed microscopically as 'total', 'extensive', or 'left sided' providing important information about their cancer risk. All patients with colitis should be followed up indefinitely. It is difficult to justify regular colonoscopy thereafter.

Clinicians faced with a patient with longstanding colitis, at increased risk of developing colonic cancer, feel compelled to do, or be seen to do, something. There is also an obligation, however, to use effective methods. The argument for colonoscopic surveillance is not convincing. While it has been deemed unethical to perform a controlled clinical trial, it could be argued that the use of limited resources on surveillance programmes of unproved value is also unethical. The funds released by ending surveillance are considerable. They could be channelled into a more cost effective cancer prevention scheme. It is time to review cancer surveillance in ulcerative colitis.

We would like to thank Mrs Olive Bell, Miss Julie Mackintosh and Mrs Andrea Scales for their help in the preparation and typing of this paper.

These data were published in abstract form in *Gut* 1991; **32:** A556 and A561.

1 Crohn BB, Rosenberg H. The sigmoidoscopy picture of chronic ulcerative colitis (non-specific). *Am J Med Sci* 1925; **170:** 220–8.
2 Gyde SN, Prior P, Allan RN, Stevens A, Jewell DP, Truelove SC, *et al.* Colorectal cancer in ulcerative colitis: a cohort study of primary referrals from three centres. *Gut* 1988; **29:** 206–17.
3 de Dombal FT, Watts JMcK, Watkinson G, Goligher JC. Local complications of ulcerative colitis: stricture, pseudopolyposis, and carcinoma of the colon and rectum. *BMJ* 1966; **1:** 1442–7.
4 Devroede GJ, Taylor WF, Sauer WG, Jackman RJ, Stickler GB. Cancer risk and life expectancy of children with ulcerative colitis. *N Engl J Med* 1971; **285:** 17–21.
5 Kewenter J, Ahlman H, Hulten L. Cancer risk in extensive colitis. *Ann Surg* 1987; **188:** 824–7.
6 MacDougal IPM. The cancer risk in ulcerative colitis. *Lancet* 1964; ii: 655–8.
7 Morson BC, Pang LSC. Rectal biopsy as an aid to cancer control in ulcerative colitis. *Gut* 1967; **8:** 423–34.
8 Nugent FW, Haggit RC, Gilpin PA. Cancer surveillance in ulcerative colitis. *Gastroenterology* 1991; **100:** 1241–8.
9 Dickinson RJ, Dixon MF, Axon ATR. Colonoscopy and the detection of dysplasia in patients with longstanding ulcerative colitis. *Lancet* 1980; ii: 620–2.
10 Fuson JA, Farmer RG, Hawk WA, Sullivan BH. Endoscopic surveillance for cancer in chronic ulcerative colitis. *Am J Gastroenterol* 1980; **73:** 120–6.
11 Lennard Jones JE, Morson BC, Ritchie JK, Williams C. Cancer surveillance in ulcerative colitis: experience over 15 years. *Lancet* 1983; ii: 149–52.
12 Rosenstock E, Farmer RG, Petras R, Sivak MV, Rankin GB, Sullivan BH. Surveillance for colonic carcinoma in ulcerative colitis. *Gastroenterology* 1985; **89:** 1342–6.
13 Brostrom O, Lofberg R, Ost A, Reichard H. Cancer surveillance of patients with longstanding ulcerative colitis: a clinical, endoscopical, and histological study. *Gut* 1986; **27:** 1408–13.
14 Manning AP, Bulgim OR, Dixon MF, Axon ATR. Screening by colonoscopy for colonic epthelial dysplasia in inflammatory bowel disease. *Gut* 1987; **28:** 1489–94.
15 Rutegard J, Ahsgren L, Stenling R, Janunger KG. Ulcerative colitis. Cancer surveillance in an unselected population. *Scand J Gastroenterol* 1988; **23:** 139–45.
16 Leidenius M, Killokumpu I, Husa A, Riitula M, Sipponen P, Dysplasia and carcinoma in longstanding ulcerative colitis: an endoscopic and histological surveillance programme. *Gut* 1991; **32:** 1521–5.
17 Woolrich AJ, DaSilva MD, Korelitz BI. Surveillance in the routine management of ulcerative colitis: the predictive value of low-grade dysplasia. *Gastroenterlogy* 1992; **103:** 431–8.
18 Gyde S. Screening for colorectal cancer in ulcerative colitis: dubious benefits and high costs. *Gut* 1990; **31:** 1089–97.
19 Collins RH, Feldman M, Fordtran JS. Colon cancer, dysplasia, and surveillance in patients with ulcerative colitis. A critical review. *N Engl J Med* 1987; **316:** 1654–8.
20 Jones HW, Grogono J, Hoare AM. Surveillance in ulcerative colitis: burdens and benefit. *Gut* 1988; **29:** 325–31.
21 Lashner BA, Silverstein MD, Hanaver SB. Hazard rates for dysplasia and cancer in ulcerative colitis. *Dig Dis Sci* 1989; **34:** 1536–41.
22 Lennard-Jones JE, Melville DM, Morson BC, Ritchie JK, Williams CB. Precancer and cancer in extensive ulcerative colitis: findings among 401 patients over 22 years. *Gut* 1990; **31:** 800–6.
23 Blackstone MO, Riddell RH, Rogers BHG, Levin B. Dysplasia-associated lesion or mass (DALM) detected by colonoscopy in longstanding ulcerative colitis: an indication for colectomy. *Gastroenterology* 1981; **80:** 366–74.
24 Lofberg R, Brostrom O, Karlen P, Tribukait B, Ost A. Colonoscopic surveillance in longstanding total ulcerative colitis – a 15 year follow-up study. *Gastroenterology* 1990; **99:** 1021–31.
25 Weil J, Langman MJS. Screening for gastrointestinal cancer: an epidemiological review. *Gut* 1991; **32:** 220–4.
26 Lennard Jones JE, Morson BC, Ritchie JK, Shove DC, Williams CB. Cancer in colitis: assessment of the individual risk by clinical and histological criteria. *Gastroenterology* 1977; **73:** 1280–9.
27 Anonymous. Colorectal carcinoma in ulcerative colitis [Editorial]. *Lancet* 1986; ii: 197–8.
28 Morson BC. Precancer and cancer in inflammatory bowel disease. *Pathology* 1985; **17:** 173–80.
29 Lennard-Jones JE. Compliance, cost, and common sense limit cancer control in colitis. *Gut* 1986; **27:** 1403–7.
30 Ransohoff DF, Riddell RH, Levin B. Ulcerative colitis and colonic cancer: problems in assessing the diagnostic usefulness of mucosal dysplasia. *Dis Colon Rectum* 1985; **26:** 382–8.
31 Cook MG, Goligher JC. Carcinoma and epithelial dysplasia complicating ulcerative colitis. *Gastroenterology* 1975; **68:** 1127–36.
32 Riddell RH. The precarcinomatous phase of ulcerative colitis. *Curr Top Pathol* 1976; **63:** 179–219.
33 Fozzard JBJ, Griffiths SB, Dixon MF, Axon ATR, Giles GR. Lectin and mucin histochemistry as an aid to cancer surveillance in ulcerative colitis. *Histopathology* 1987; **11:** 385–94.
34 Cuvelier CA, Morson BC, Roels HJ. The DNA content in cancer and dysplasia in chronic ulcerative colitis. *Histopathology* 1987; **11:** 927–39.
35 Dixon MF, Brown CTR, Gilmore HM, *et al.* Observer variation in the assessment of dysplasia in ulcerative colitis. *Histopathology* 1988; **13:** 385–97.
36 Melville DM, Jass JR, Shepherd NA, Northover JMA, Capellano D, Richman PI, *et al.* Dysplasia and deoxyribonucleic acid aneuploidy in the assessment of precancerous changes in chronic ulcerative colitis. Observer variation and correlations. *Gastroenterology* 1988; **95:** 668–75.
37 Fielding LP, Blesovsky L. Clinical features of colorectal cancer. In: Misiewicz JJ, Pounder RE, Venables CW, eds. *Diseases of the gut and pancreas.* Oxford: Blackwell Scientific Publications, 1987.
38 Rex DK, Lehman GH, Hawes RH, Ulbright TM, Smith JJ. Screen colonoscopy in asymptomatic average – risk persons with negative occult blood tests. *Gastroenterology* 1991; **100:** 64–7.
39 Lashner BA, Kane SV, Hanauer SB. Colon cancer surveillance in chronic ulcerative colitis: historical cohort study. *Am J Gastroenterol* 1990; **85:** 1083–7.

© N Engl J Med 1993; 329: 1905–1911

ANAL-SPHINCTER DISRUPTION DURING VAGINAL DELIVERY

ABDUL H. SULTAN, M.B., CH.B., MICHAEL A. KAMM, M.D., CHRISTOPHER N. HUDSON, M.CHIR., JANICE M. THOMAS, M.SC., AND CLIVE I. BARTRAM, F.R.C.P.

Abstract *Background.* Lacerations of the anal sphincter or injury to sphincter innervation during childbirth are major causes of fecal incontinence, but the incidence and importance of occult sphincter damage during routine vaginal delivery are unknown. We sought to determine the incidence of damage to the anal sphincter and the relation of injury to symptoms, anorectal physiologic function, and the mode of delivery.

Methods. We studied 202 consecutive women six weeks before delivery, 150 of them six weeks after delivery, and 32 with abnormal findings six months after delivery. Symptoms of anal incontinence and fecal urgency were assessed, and anal endosonography, manometry, perineometry, and measurement of the terminal motor latency of the pudendal nerves were performed.

Results. Ten of the 79 primiparous women (13 percent) and 11 of the 48 multiparous women (23 percent) who delivered vaginally had anal incontinence or fecal urgency when studied six weeks after delivery. Twenty-eight of the 79 primiparous women (35 percent) had a sphincter defect on endosonography at six weeks; the defect persisted in all 22 women studied at six months. Of the 48 multiparous women, 19 (40 percent) had a sphincter defect before delivery and 21 (44 percent) afterward. None of the 23 women who underwent cesarean section had a new sphincter defect after delivery. Eight of the 10 women who underwent forceps delivery had sphincter defects, but none of the 5 women who underwent vacuum extractions had such defects. Internal-sphincter defects were associated with a significantly lower mean (±SD) resting anal pressure (61±11 vs. 48±10 mm Hg, $P<0.001$) six weeks post partum, and external-sphincter defects were associated with a significantly lower squeeze pressure (increase above resting pressure, 70±38 vs. 44±13 mm Hg; $P<0.001$). There was a strong association ($P<0.001$) between sphincter defects and the development of bowel symptoms.

Conclusions. Occult sphincter defects are common after vaginal delivery, especially forceps delivery, and are often associated with disturbance of bowel function. (N Engl J Med 1993;329:1905-11.)

CHILDBIRTH may be accompanied by mechanical or neurologic injury to the anal sphincter. Overt sphincter damage due to a third-degree or fourth-degree tear[1] occurs in approximately 0.7 percent of women undergoing vaginal delivery in centers where posterolateral episiotomy is practiced.[2,3] Inadequate primary repair of these sphincter injuries can lead to early fecal incontinence.[3,4] Pudendal-nerve conduction can also become impaired after vaginal delivery,[5] and the later development of fecal incontinence has been attributed to progressive denervation of the anal-sphincter muscles.[6-8] Some women sustain both mechanical and neurologic trauma during vaginal delivery.[9]

Until recently, defects of the external anal sphincter were detected by electromyography,[10] and defects of the internal sphincter were inferred from measurement of a low resting anal pressure.[11] Anal endosonography, however, has allowed accurate imaging of both sphincter muscles,[12,13] leading to the recognition of unsuspected defects of the external sphincter in women thought to have purely neurogenic fecal incontinence[14] and the detection of internal-sphincter damage when only an external-sphincter defect was suspected.[15] In a study of 62 women with fecal incontinence related to obstetrical procedures, anal endosonography revealed an external-sphincter defect in 90 percent and an internal-sphincter defect in 65 percent.[15]

Because most previous studies of anal-sphincter function were either retrospective[14,15] or attributed the development of fecal incontinence directly to pudendal-nerve damage,[5,6,16] we undertook a prospective study of women before and after delivery, using anal endosonography and anorectal neurophysiologic tests to establish the incidence of mechanical and neurologic trauma during childbirth.

From St. Mark's Hospital (A.H.S., M.A.K., C.I.B.) and St. Bartholomew's (Homerton) Hospital (A.H.S., C.N.H., J.M.T., C.I.B.), both in London. Address reprint requests to Dr. Bartram at St. Mark's Hospital, City Rd., London EC1V 2PS, United Kingdom.

Supported by the Joint Research Board of St. Bartholomew's Hospital, a travel grant from the Wellcome Trust (Dr. Sultan), and St. Mark's Research Foundation (Dr. Kamm).

Presented at the annual meeting of the American Gastroenterological Association, San Francisco, May 10–13, 1992, and published in abstract form (Gastroenterology 1992;102(4):A522).

METHODS

Subjects

We studied 202 unselected, consecutive women (median age, 28 years; range, 18 to 43) who had been pregnant for more than 34 weeks. Of the 202 women, 135 had never had a vaginal delivery (including 2 who had had a cesarean section) and 67 had had one or more vaginal deliveries.

This study was approved by the Research Ethics Committee of the City and Hackney District Health Authority, and all the women gave informed consent.

Delivery and Evaluation

All women were examined during the last six weeks of pregnancy and were asked to return for reevaluation six to eight weeks after delivery. At each assessment an interviewer completed a detailed questionnaire that reported any symptoms of fecal urgency (the inability to defer defecation for more than five minutes) and anal incontinence. Anal endosonography, manometry, studies of pudendal-nerve terminal motor latency, and perineometry were then performed. Information on labor and delivery was obtained from hospital records.

Delivery was managed as deemed appropriate by the attending physician. All episiotomies were posterolateral. Uncomplicated episiotomies were repaired by senior house officers and qualified midwives, whereas complicated episiotomies were repaired by more senior physicians. Tears related to delivery were classified as follows: first-degree tears involved only vaginal epithelium (women with such tears were included among those with no laceration); second-degree tears involved the perineal body but not the external sphincter; third-degree tears involved the external sphincter; and fourth-degree tears involved both the external sphincter and the anal epithelium.

Women with defects on ultrasonography or prolonged terminal motor latency of the pudendal nerves six weeks after delivery were asked to return for reevaluation six months post partum.

Anal Endosonography

Endosonography was performed with an ultrasound scanner with a rotating rectal probe, a 7-MHz transducer (focal range, 2 to 4.5 cm), and a hard sonolucent plastic cone (Bruel and Kjaer, Naerum, Denmark),[12] while the woman lay on her left side. Serial images of the upper, middle, and lower anal canal were recorded (Umatic video recorder, Sony, Tokyo, Japan). The endosonographic interpretation of the appearance of muscle layers has been previously validated[13]: an external-sphincter defect appears as a break in the normal texture of this muscle ring[17,18] (Fig. 1), and an internal-sphincter defect as a gap in the hypoechoic ring[18,19] (Fig. 2). All investigations were performed and the results interpreted by one operator; the results were reviewed independently by a second observer unaware of the first interpretation.

Anal Manometry

Anal manometry was performed with an intracompartmental-pressure monitor (Stryker, Kalamazoo, Mich.) attached to an air-filled microballoon.[20] The maximal resting pressure and the maximal squeeze pressure (i.e., the maximal increase above the resting pressure) were measured according to a stationary pull-through technique.[21]

Measurement of Terminal Motor Latency of the Pudendal Nerves

The terminal motor latency of each pudendal nerve was measured after an electronic stimulus (Medelec stimulator, Old Woking, United Kingdom) from an electrode (Dantec, Skovlunde, Denmark) mounted on a gloved index finger.[22,23] Latency is the time between stimulation of the pudendal nerve at the level of the ischial spine and contraction of the anal sphincter. Prolongation of latency is indicative of damage to the fastest conducting nerve fibers.[24]

Perineometry

The perineal plane (the level of the perineal soft tissues at the point of the anal verge, relative to the bony ischial tuberosities) was measured with a perineometer at rest and during maximal straining effort in the left lateral position.[25] The difference between the two measurements indicates the degree of perineal descent. Descent of the perineum below the level of the ischial tuberosities at rest or on straining was considered abnormal.[25]

Statistical Analysis

Antepartum measurements were compared with postpartum measurements by paired t-tests. Associations between categorical variables were assessed with the chi-square test or Fisher's exact test. Continuous variables in independent groups were compared by two-tailed t-tests. A P value of less than 0.05 was considered to indicate statistical significance. All results are reported as means ±SD.

All variables shown to be significantly associated with sphincter defects on univariate analysis were then entered in a multiple logistic-regression analysis in a stepwise fashion to determine the combination of variables that best predicted sphincter damage. An odds ratio was also calculated.

The statistical analyses were performed with software from Minitab Data Analysis (Minitab, State College, Pa.) and SAS (SAS Institute, Cary, N.C.).

Results

One hundred fifty women (of whom 100 were primiparous and 50 multiparous) returned for postpartum examination a median of 49 days (range, 35 to 105) after delivery. Twenty-three women (21 primiparous and 2 multiparous) had delivered by cesarean section, and 127 vaginally (73 women were white, 71 black, and 6 of other races).

Vaginal Delivery

Of the 127 women who had a vaginal delivery, 79 were considered primiparous (including 2 women who had had previous children, but by cesarean section) and 48 multiparous, of whom 38 (79 percent) had only one previous vaginal delivery. Two primiparous women (3 percent) and 10 multiparous women (21 percent) had symptomatic urinary stress incontinence on examination at six weeks.

Bowel Symptoms

None of the 79 primiparous women had diabetes mellitus or neurologic or anorectal disease. Post partum, 10 women (13 percent) reported having one or more new bowel symptoms; 8 (10 percent) had fecal urgency, and 4 (5 percent) had anal incontinence (3 had flatus, and 1 had flatus and liquid stool). Two women had temporary incontinence of flatus for less than three weeks post partum. Among the 48 multiparous women, 9 (19 percent) had one or more bowel symptoms before delivery. These symptoms began after a previous vaginal delivery (seven women had fecal urgency, three were incontinent of flatus, and five were incontinent of liquid stool). After delivery, three women (6 percent) had new symptoms (two had urgency and incontinence of flatus, and one had urgency alone). One woman with incontinence of liquid stool before delivery had no symptoms afterward. Therefore, after delivery, 11 (23 percent) of the multiparous women had bowel symptoms.

Altogether, of the 127 women who delivered vagi-

© *N Engl J Med* 1993; 329: 1905–1911

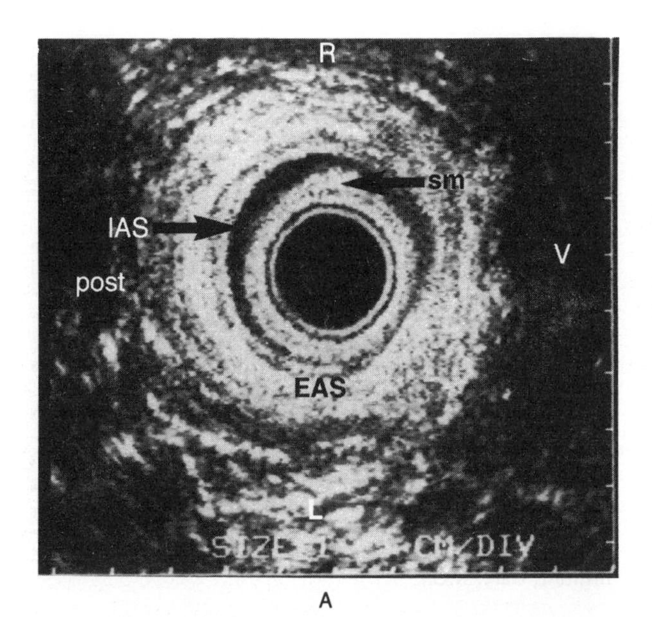

A

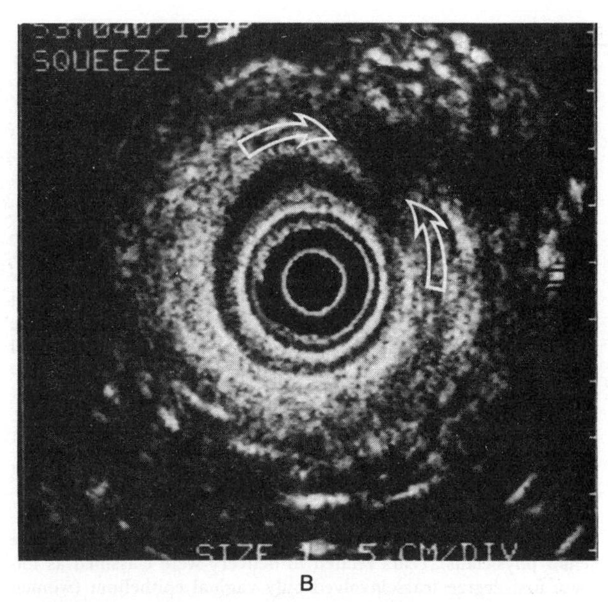

B

Figure 1. Results of Anal Endosonography before and after Delivery in a Primiparous Woman with a Postpartum Defect of the External Anal Sphincter.

Panel A shows a normal image of the middle portion of the anal canal at 34 weeks of pregnancy. R denotes right, L left, IAS internal anal sphincter (hypoechoic), EAS external anal sphincter (hyperechoic), post posterior, sm submucosa (hyperechoic), and V vagina. The probe lies medial to the submucosa. Panel B shows the canal six weeks after delivery. The woman had incontinence of flatus after a forceps delivery with an episiotomy. A hypoechoic defect of the external anal sphincter is present between the open arrows. The damage to the anal sphincter was not recognized during repair of the episiotomy.

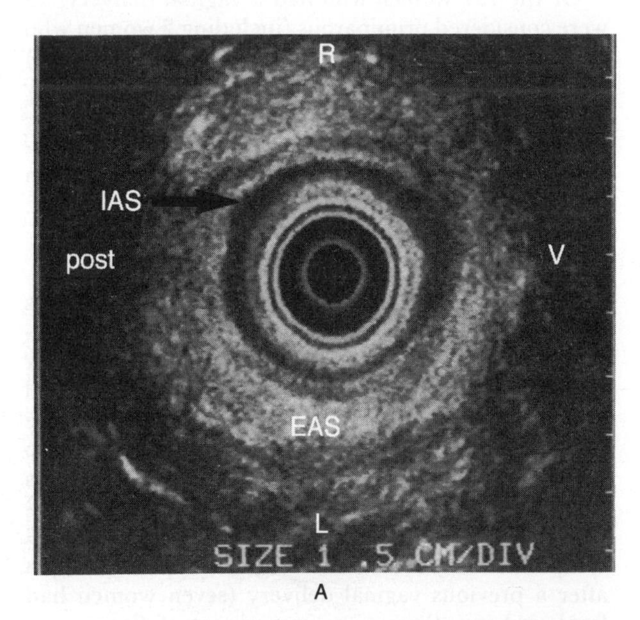

A

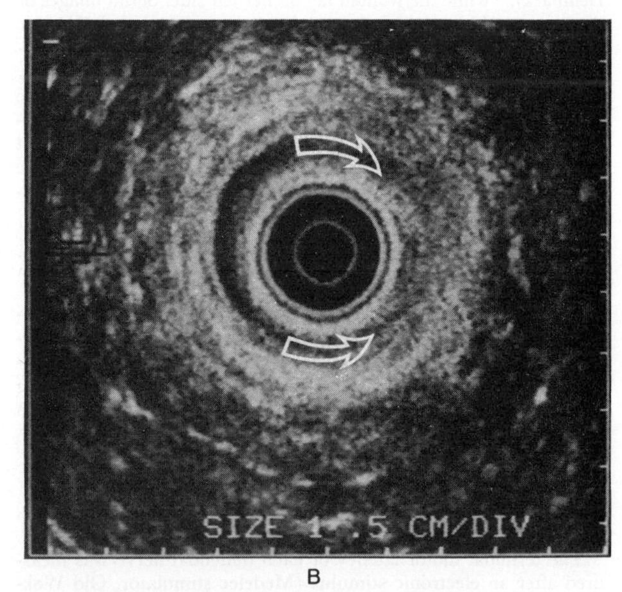

B

Figure 2. Results of Anal Endosonography before and after Delivery in a Primiparous Woman with a Postpartum Defect of the Internal Anal Sphincter.

Panel A shows the middle portion of the anal canal at 34 weeks of pregnancy. R denotes right, L left, IAS internal anal sphincter, EAS external anal sphincter, post posterior, and V vagina. Panel B shows the canal six weeks after delivery. The woman had no symptoms after a spontaneous vaginal delivery but had a second-degree tear (not involving the anal sphincter). The hyperechoic defect in the internal anal sphincter is present between the open arrows.

© N Engl J Med 1993; 329: 1905–1911

nally, 13 (10 percent) had one or both bowel symptoms (urgency and incontinence) after delivery.

Anal Endosonography

No sphincter defect was detected before delivery in any primiparous woman. Six weeks after delivery, 28 women (35 percent) had defects of either the internal sphincter (Fig. 2B), the external sphincter (Fig. 1B), or both (Table 1). Twenty-three women (29 percent) had a defect of the internal sphincter; the defect involved the entire length of the internal sphincter in 14 women and the distal portion in 9. Among the 15 women (19 percent) with a defect of the external sphincter, the defect involved the full length of the sphincter in 11 women, the proximal portion in 2, and the distal portion in 2. Nine women had only partial thickness defects, and six had complete defects. Ten of the 15 women with an external-sphincter defect also had an internal-sphincter defect.

Nineteen (40 percent) multiparous women had a sphincter defect before delivery, and 21 (44 percent) after delivery (Table 1). Two women had a new defect, and two with an internal-sphincter defect before delivery had a new, external-sphincter defect after delivery. All three multiparous women who reported new bowel symptoms after delivery had combined sphincter defects, which were new in two of the women. All these defects occurred in the anterior portion of the sphincter.

Manometry

The maximal resting anal pressure fell significantly after delivery in both the primiparous and the multiparous women (Table 2). It was also significantly lower in women with an internal-sphincter defect than in those without such a defect (Table 3). The decrement in resting pressure (the difference between the value after delivery and the value before delivery) was significantly greater in women with an internal-sphincter defect than in those without (Table 3). The relation between resting pressure and external-sphincter defects was not significant (Table 3).

The squeeze pressure fell significantly after delivery in both the primiparous and the multiparous women (Table 2). It was also lower in women with an external-sphincter defect than in those without such a defect (Table 3). The decrement in squeeze pressure after delivery was greater in the women with an external-sphincter defect than in those without (Table 3). There was no relation between the squeeze pressure and internal-sphincter defects (Table 3).

The 23 women in whom an internal-sphincter defect developed had a significantly shorter anal canal before delivery than the 56 women in whom such a defect did not develop (36±5 vs. 39±5 mm, P = 0.01). No such relation was found among the women with external-sphincter defects.

Pudendal-Nerve Terminal Motor Latency

The terminal motor latency of each pudendal nerve was measured in 63 primiparous and 33 multiparous women. Latency was significantly increased in both nerves in women from both groups who underwent vaginal delivery (Table 2). The values were higher

Table 1. Incidence of Anal-Sphincter Defects in Women Evaluated by Anal Endosonography after Vaginal Delivery, According to Parity.

Parity Group	Anal-Sphincter Defects			
	Internal Sphincter	External Sphincter	Internal and External	Total
	no. with defect (%)			
Primiparous women (n = 79)				
Before delivery	0	0	0	0
After delivery	13 (16)	5 (6)	10 (13)	28 (35)
Multiparous women (n = 48)				
Before delivery	8 (17)	2 (4)	9 (19)	19 (40)
After delivery	7 (15)	2 (4)	12 (25)	21 (44)

Table 2. Anal Pressure, Perineal Descent, and Pudendal-Nerve Terminal Motor Latency before and Six Weeks after Childbirth, According to Type of Delivery.*

Type of Delivery†	Antepartum Value	Postpartum Value	P Value
Vaginal delivery			
Primiparous women (n = 79)			
Anal pressure (mm Hg)			
Resting	61±10	57±12	<0.001
Squeeze	88±41	64±36	<0.001
Perineal descent (mm)	11±6	14±7	<0.001
Pudendal-nerve latency (msec)			
Right nerve (n = 63)	1.9±0.2	2.0±0.2	<0.001
Left nerve (n = 64)	2.0±0.2	2.1±0.2	<0.001
Multiparous women (n = 48)			
Anal pressure (mm Hg)			
Resting	57±12	53±14	0.004
Squeeze	60±31	52±22	0.006
Perineal descent (mm)	14±6	17±7	<0.001
Pudendal-nerve latency (msec)			
Right nerve (n = 33)	1.9±0.2	2.0±0.2	0.002
Left nerve (n = 33)	2.0±0.2	2.1±0.2	0.009
Cesarean section (n = 23)			
All women			
Anal pressure (mm Hg)			
Resting	62±12	61±13	0.29
Squeeze	72±32	71±32	0.69
Women with elective procedure (n = 7)			
Perineal descent (mm)	9±2	10±2	0.19
Pudendal-nerve latency (msec)			
Right nerve	2.0±0.2	2.0±0.2	1.00
Left nerve	1.9±0.2	2.0±0.2	0.08
Women with indicated procedure (n = 9)‡			
Perineal descent (mm)	11±6	12±5	0.39
Pudendal-nerve latency (msec)			
Right nerve	1.9±0.1	2.0±0.2	0.12
Left nerve	1.9±0.1	2.1±0.3	0.01

*Plus–minus values are means ±SD.

†Resting denotes maximal resting anal pressure; squeeze, maximal increase above resting pressure; and perineal descent, the difference between the plane of the perineum at rest and its plane during a straining effort.

‡An indicated procedure was performed after the onset of labor.

© N Engl J Med 1993; 329: 1905–1911

Table 3. Anal Pressure in Relation to the Presence or Absence of Sphincter Defects in 79 Women Six Weeks after Vaginal Delivery.*

Type of Pressure†	Defect	No Defect	P Value
	anal pressure (mm Hg)		
Internal sphincter	(n = 23)	(n = 56)	
Resting (post partum)	48±10	61±11	<0.001
Change	−9±9	−2±11	0.01
Squeeze (post partum)	61±32	66±37	0.49
Change	−29±36	−22±25	0.37
External sphincter	(n = 15)	(n = 64)	
Resting (post partum)	52±13	59±12	0.07
Change	−8±8	−3±11	0.15
Squeeze (post partum)	44±13	70±38	<0.001
Change	−47±27	−18±26	<0.001

*Plus–minus values are means ±SD.

†Resting denotes maximal resting pressure; squeeze, maximal squeeze pressure; and change, the difference between postpartum and antepartum values.

than the upper limit of the antepartum normal range in 10 primiparous women (16 percent) and 5 multiparous women (15 percent) six weeks post partum; only 1 multiparous woman (3 percent) had abnormal values before delivery.

There was no relation between the change in the pudendal-nerve terminal motor latency and the development of symptoms or the results of anal manometry. However, there was a significant association (P = 0.02) between abnormal latency and the development of a sphincter defect in primiparous women.

Perineometry

Perineal descent increased significantly after vaginal delivery in both primiparous and multiparous women (Table 2). The 36 women with abnormal perineal descent on straining after delivery had a significantly longer mean pudendal-nerve motor latency post partum than the 35 with normal descent (2.1±0.2 vs. 2.0±0.2 msec, P = 0.01).

The duration of active pushing during the second stage of labor correlated significantly with the plane of the perineum at rest (P = 0.04, r = 0.23) and during straining (P = 0.008, r = 0.30): the women with a longer active second stage of labor had a greater descent.

Sphincter Defects in Relation to Obstetric Variables

A defect involving at least one of the sphincter muscles occurred in 8 of the 10 women (80 percent) who had forceps deliveries (9 with outlet [low] deliveries and 1 with a rotational delivery), but in none of the 5 who had vacuum-extractor deliveries (Table 4). All instrumental deliveries were carried out when the infant presented below the ischial spines.

The deliveries of two women were complicated by shoulder dystocia; one of these women had a forceps delivery and was later found to have an external-sphincter defect. In addition, one woman underwent a twin delivery (no defects), another a breech delivery (internal-sphincter and external-sphincter defects), and a third an occipitoposterior delivery (external-sphincter defect).

Internal-sphincter defects developed in three women although their perineum was intact after delivery. External-sphincter defects were detected only in women who underwent episiotomy or sustained a spontaneous perineal tear.

Univariate analysis showed that internal-sphincter defects were significantly associated with forceps delivery (P = 0.004), epidural analgesia (P = 0.005), and the presence of an episiotomy (P = 0.04). Stepwise logistic-regression analysis revealed that forceps delivery was associated with a significant risk of an internal-sphincter defect (odds ratio, 7.0). When this factor was controlled for, epidural analgesia was not found to contribute to the development of an internal-sphincter defect.

External-sphincter defects were associated with augmentation of labor (P = 0.03), epidural analgesia (P = 0.03), posterolateral episiotomy (P = 0.02), and forceps delivery (P = 0.001) on univariate analysis. On stepwise logistic-regression analysis, the single independent factor associated with the development of an external-sphincter defect was forceps delivery (odds ratio, 11.1).

The infant's weight, the infant's head circumference, induction of labor, the length of each stage of labor, spontaneous perineal tears, the mother's age, and race were not significantly related to the development of sphincter defects.

Sphincter Defects in Relation to Bowel Symptoms

All women except one (a primiparous woman) who had either fecal urgency or anal incontinence after delivery had sphincter defects. There was a strong

Table 4. Obstetrical Variables in Relation to the Development of Anal-Sphincter Defects in 79 Women with Vaginal Deliveries.

Variable — No. of Women (%)*	No. of Women with Sphincter Defects			
	Internal Sphincter	External Sphincter	Internal and External	Total
Noninstrumental delivery — 64				
Induction — 6 (9)	2	0	0	2
Augmentation — 20 (31)	4	2	2	8
Epidural analgesia — 16 (25)	5	1	2	8
Episiotomy — 22 (34)†	4	2	3	9
Second-degree tears — 24 (38)	4	2	0	6
Third-degree tears — 2 (3)	0	0	2	2
No laceration — 17 (27)	3	0	0	3
Instrumental delivery — 15				
Forceps — 10 (67)	2	1	5	8
Vacuum extractor — 5 (33)	0	0	0	0
Induction — 8 (53)	0	1	4	5
Augmentation — 8 (53)	1	1	4	6
Epidural analgesia — 10 (67)	1	1	5	7
Episiotomy — 14 (93)†	2	1	5	8

*Some women in each group (noninstrumental delivery and instrumental delivery) underwent more than one procedure.

†All episiotomies were posterolateral.

© N Engl J Med 1993; 329: 1905–1911

association (P<0.001) between the development of either symptom and sphincter defects (Table 5).

Cesarean Section

No woman who underwent cesarean section had any bowel symptom after delivery or any significant change in anal pressure (Table 2). Pudendal-nerve terminal motor latency was measured in 16 of these women. None of the seven in whom this procedure was elective had a significant change in latency; however, the nine women in whom the procedure was indicated after labor had begun had a significant increase in the latency of the left pudendal nerve (Table 2).

There was no significant change in perineal descent in 16 of these women (Table 2). However, the perineal plane on straining was significantly lower after delivery in the nine women who underwent a cesarean section after the onset of labor (P = 0.05).

Follow-up Evaluation at Six Months

Thirty-two women returned a mean of six months after delivery for a third evaluation. This group included 10 women with fecal urgency and 7 with anal incontinence six weeks post partum. Fecal urgency was no longer a problem in 4 of the 10 women with this symptom, but it developed in 2 others. Two of the seven women with anal incontinence had improvement, and another woman (with no sphincter defect) had had no further episodes of incontinence.

Repeat anal endosonography performed at six months in women with sphincter defects six weeks after delivery showed no change in the defects. Anal manometry did not reveal any significant change from the values recorded six weeks post partum. Measurement of pudendal-nerve terminal motor latency was repeated in 22 women and showed a significant decrease in latency in both the right (P = 0.002) and left (P = 0.04) pudendal nerves. Latency had returned to normal in 8 of the 12 women who had abnormal values six weeks after delivery.

Discussion

We found that vaginal delivery is frequently associated with mechanical disruption of the anal sphincters. Three percent of the primiparous women studied, but none of the multiparous women, sustained an injury to the anal sphincters during delivery that was apparent on clinical examination — i.e., a third-degree or fourth-degree tear. Endosonography, however, revealed sphincter damage in 35 percent and 44 percent, respectively. The incidence of sphincter defects among the primiparous women six weeks after delivery was comparable to that among the multiparous women before delivery, most of whom had had only one previous vaginal delivery. There was only a slight increase in the incidence among the multiparous group post partum (4 percent), suggesting that the risk of sphincter damage is greatest during the first vaginal delivery.

Table 5. Symptoms of Fecal Urgency or Anal Incontinence in Relation to the Presence of Any Anal-Sphincter Defect after Vaginal Delivery in 127 Women.

Symptom	Defect (N = 49)	No Defect (N = 78)	P Value*
	no. of women		
Fecal urgency			
Yes (n = 18)	18	0	<0.001
No (n = 109)	31	78	
Anal incontinence			
Yes (n = 11)	10	1	<0.001
No (n = 116)	39	77	

*By Fisher's exact test. Both symptoms were strongly associated with the presence of a defect.

External-sphincter damage occurred only in the presence of a tear or episiotomy, suggesting that it occurs as part of a direct continuation of perineal disruption. As others have reported,[1] a posterolateral episiotomy did not appear to protect the patient against the development of sphincter defects (Table 4). Midline episiotomies are associated with a higher incidence of third-degree or fourth-degree tears than posterolateral episiotomies.[1,26] There is therefore no reason to suspect that our findings would have been any different in women who underwent a midline episiotomy.

The internal sphincter was injured more frequently than the external sphincter and was sometimes damaged when the perineum remained intact. Shearing forces produced by the descent of the infant's head may cause isolated damage to the internal sphincter, a mechanism different from that causing injury to the external sphincter. Women with a shorter anal canal may be more prone to this form of trauma, since internal-sphincter disruption was positively associated with a shorter canal before delivery.

Endosonographic examination suggested that the structural damage to the sphincters was permanent, since the defects were present at six months, and the incidence of defects among the primiparous women after delivery was similar to that among the multiparous women before delivery.

There was a definite relation between the presence of sphincter defects, anal pressure (Table 3), and bowel symptoms (Table 5). These ultrasonographically identified sphincter defects therefore appear to have physiologic and clinical importance. The single best predictive test of clinical dysfunction was anal endosonography. Although anal pressures were reduced in women with sphincter defects, there was considerable overlap of values between the women with symptoms and those without them.

Only about one third of the women with sphincter defects had bowel symptoms. Women with defects who do not have symptoms may have sufficient residual sphincter function to maintain continence. Long-term follow-up of such women will be necessary to determine whether they are at greater risk for incontinence later in life. Since the peak incidence of fecal incontinence among women occurs in the fifth and sixth decades,[27] the cumulative effect of subsequent deliveries, the effects of aging,[27,28] the menopause,[27,28] and the progression of a neuropathy[6] may all contribute to sphincter weakness in the long term. Women with an occult sphincter defect may be at greater risk.

None of the women with disturbances of bowel function had spontaneously reported their symptoms or sought medical attention. Underreporting of such symptoms is well known[29] and may explain why these problems are not widely recognized in obstetrical practice.

Sphincter defects developed in 8 of the 10 primiparous women who had a forceps delivery but in none of the 5 who had a vacuum-extractor delivery. These findings are consistent with those of other reports indicating that vacuum extraction is associated with less trauma to the perineum than forceps delivery.[30,31]

In two previous studies,[5,16] pudendal-nerve terminal motor latency in women who delivered vaginally was not increased two months post partum, as compared with latency in a control group of women[5]; latency had not been measured before delivery. When we compared postpartum values directly with antepartum values, we found that vaginal delivery, particularly a first vaginal delivery, resulted in a significant increase in pudendal-nerve terminal motor latency and in perineal descent six weeks after delivery. There was no association between bowel symptoms and prolonged pudendal-nerve terminal motor latency or abnormal perineal descent, which is not the case with idiopathic fecal incontinence[32] that develops in middle age and is believed to be related to neuropathy.[8] The association of a prolonged pudendal-nerve terminal motor latency with a sphincter defect probably reflects a traumatic cause common to these two factors, rather than a causal relation between them.

In conclusion, vaginal delivery causes bowel symptoms, mechanical trauma to the anal sphincter, and injury to the pudendal nerve in many women. The use of the obstetrical forceps is particularly associated with a higher risk of sphincter damage.

We are indebted to Professor Tim Chard (Department of Reproductive Physiology, St. Bartholomew's Hospital) for his helpful advice, to the obstetrical consultants who allowed us to study their patients, and to the women who participated in this study.

References

1. Thacker SB, Banta HD. Benefits and risks of episiotomy: an interpretative review of the English language literature, 1860–1980. Obstet Gynecol Surv 1983;38:322-38.
2. Haadem K, Ohrlander S, Lingman G. Long-term ailments due to anal sphincter rupture caused by delivery — a hidden problem. Eur J Obstet Gynecol Reprod Biol 1988;27:27-32.
3. Sultan AH, Kamm MA, Bartram CI, Hudson CN. Third degree tears: incidence, risk factors and poor clinical outcome after primary sphincter repair. Gut 1992;33:Suppl 2:S29. abstract.
4. Nielsen MB, Hauge C, Rasmussen OO, Pedersen JF, Christiansen J. Anal endosonographic findings in the follow-up of primarily sutured sphincteric ruptures. Br J Surg 1992;79:104-6.
5. Snooks SJ, Setchell M, Swash M, Henry MM. Injury to innervation of pelvic floor sphincter musculature in childbirth. Lancet 1984;2:546-50.
6. Snooks SJ, Swash M, Mathers SE, Henry MM. Effect of vaginal delivery on the pelvic floor: a 5-year follow-up. Br J Surg 1990;77:1358-60.
7. Neill ME, Swash M. Increased motor unit fibre density in the external anal sphincter muscle in ano-rectal incontinence: a single fibre EMG study. J Neurol Neurosurg Psychiatry 1980;43:343-7.
8. Beersiek F, Parks AG, Swash M. Pathogenesis of ano-rectal incontinence: histometric study of the anal sphincter musculature. J Neurol Sci 1979;42:111-27.
9. Snooks SJ, Henry MM, Swash M. Faecal incontinence due to external sphincter division in childbirth is associated with damage to the innervation of the pelvic floor musculature: a double pathology. Br J Obstet Gynaecol 1985;92:824-8.
10. Swash M. Electromyography in pelvic floor disorders. In: Henry MM, Swash M, eds. Coloproctology and the pelvic floor. 2nd ed. Oxford, England: Butterworth–Heinemann, 1992:184-95.
11. Sun WM, Read NW, Donnelly TC. Impaired internal anal sphincter in a subgroup of patients with idiopathic faecal incontinence. Gastroenterology 1989;97:130-5.
12. Law PJ, Bartram CI. Anal endosonography: technique and normal anatomy. Gastrointest Radiol 1989;14:349-53.
13. Sultan AH, Nicholls RJ, Kamm MA, Hudson CN, Beynon J, Bartram CI. Anal endosonography and correlation with in vitro and in vivo anatomy. Br J Surg 1993;80:508-11.
14. Law PJ, Kamm MA, Bartram CI. Anal endosonography in the investigation of faecal incontinence. Br J Surg 1991;78:312-4.
15. Burnett SJD, Spence-Jones C, Speakman CTM, Kamm MA, Hudson CN, Bartram CIB. Unsuspected sphincter damage following childbirth revealed by anal endosonography. Br J Radiol 1991;64:225-7.
16. Allen RE, Hosker GL, Smith ARB, Warrell DW. Pelvic floor damage and childbirth: a neurophysiological study. Br J Obstet Gynaecol 1990;97:770-9.
17. Sultan AH, Kamm MA, Talbot IC, Nicholls RJ, Bartram CI. Anal endosonography: precision of identifying external sphincter defects confirmed histologically. Br J Surg (in press).
18. Sultan AH, Kamm MA. Ultrasound of the anal sphincter. In: Schuster MM, ed. Atlas of gastrointestinal motility. Baltimore: Williams & Wilkins, 1993:115-21.
19. Sultan AH, Kamm MA, Nicholls RJ, Bartram CI. Prospective study of the extent of internal sphincter division during lateral sphincterotomy. Dis Colon Rectum (in press).
20. Orrom WJ, Williams JG, Rothenberger DA, Wong WD. Portable anorectal manometry. Br J Surg 1990;77:876-7.
21. Cherry DA, Rothenberger DA. Pelvic floor physiology. Surg Clin North Am 1988;68:1217-30.
22. Rogers J, Henry MM, Misiewicz JJ. Disposable pudendal nerve stimulator: evaluation of the standard instrument and new device. Gut 1988;29:1131-3.
23. Swash M, Snooks SJ. Motor nerve conduction studies of the pelvic floor innervation. In: Henry MM, Swash M, eds. Coloproctology and the pelvic floor. 2nd ed. Oxford, England: Butterworth–Heinemann, 1992:196-206.
24. Jones PN, Lubowski DZ, Swash M, Henry MM. Relation between perineal descent and pudendal nerve damage in idiopathic faecal incontinence. Int J Colorectal Dis 1987;2:93-5.
25. Henry MM, Parks AG, Swash M. The pelvic floor musculature in the descending perineum syndrome. Br J Surg 1982;69:470-2.
26. Coats PM, Chan KK, Wilkins M, Beard RJ. A comparison between midline and mediolateral episiotomies. Br J Obstet Gynaecol 1980;87:408-12.
27. Laurberg S, Swash M. Effects of aging on the anorectal sphincters and their innervation. Dis Colon Rectum 1989;32:737-42.
28. Haadem K, Dahlstrom JA, Ling L. Anal sphincter competence in healthy women: clinical implications of age and other factors. Obstet Gynecol 1991;78:823-7.
29. Browning GGP, Motson RW. Results of Parks operation for faecal incontinence after anal sphincter injury. BMJ 1983;286:1873-5.
30. Vacca A, Keirse MJNC. Instrumental vaginal delivery. In: Chalmers I, Enkin M, Keirse MJNC, eds. Effective care in pregnancy and childbirth. Vol. 2. Childbirth. Oxford, England: Oxford University Press, 1989:1216-33.
31. Johanson RB, Rice C, Doyle M, et al. A randomised prospective study comparing the new vacuum extractor policy with forceps delivery. Br J Obstet Gynaecol 1993;100:524-30.
32. Caputo RM, Benson JT. Idiopathic fecal incontinence. Curr Opin Obstet Gynecol 1992;4:565-70.

© *Lancet* 1994; 344: 707–711

Role of circumferential margin involvement in the local recurrence of rectal cancer

I J Adam, M O Mohamdee, I G Martin, N Scott, P J Finan, D Johnston, M F Dixon, P Quirke

Summary

Local recurrence after resection for rectal cancer remains common despite growing acceptance that inadequate local excision may be implicated. In a prospective study of 190 patients with rectal cancer, we examined the circumferential margin of excision of resected specimens for tumour presence, to examine its frequency and its relation to subsequent local recurrence.

Tumour involvement of the circumferential margin was seen in 25% (35/141) of specimens for which the surgeon thought the resection was potentially curative, and in 36% (69/190) of all cases. After a median 5 years' follow-up (range 3·0–7·7 years), the frequency of local recurrence after potentially curative resection was 25% (95% CI 18–33%). The frequency of local recurrence was significantly higher for patients who had had tumour involvement of the circumferential margin than for those without such involvement (78 [95% CI 62–94] vs 10 [4–16]%). By Cox's regression analysis tumour involvement of the circumferential margin independently influenced both local recurrence (hazard ratio = 12·2 [4·4–34·6]) and survival (3·2 [1·6–6·53]).

These results show the importance of wide local excision during resection for rectal cancer, and the need for routine assessment of the circumferential margin to assess prognosis.

Lancet 1994; **344:** 707–11

Academic Units of Surgery (I J Adam FRCS, I G Martin FRCS, P J Finan MD, Prof D Johnston MD) **and Pathological Sciences** (M O Mohamdee MRCPath, N Scott MRCPath, M F Dixon MD, P Quirke PhD), **Centre for Digestive Diseases, The General Infirmary at Leeds, Leeds LS1 3EX, UK**

Correspondence to: Dr P Quirke

Introduction

Local recurrence of rectal cancer after surgery is common and probably influences survival. The frequency of local recurrence varies according to the treating surgeon.[1,2]

Several mechanisms have been postulated as the cause of local recurrence, including the implantation of exfoliated tumour cells at the anastomosis during resection[3] and the promotional effects of the anastomosis on tumour growth.[4] However, these factors do not explain that in many cases tumour recurrence is not mucosal but intramural or extramural,[5] the difference in frequency of local recurrence in rectal and colonic cancer, or the variation of frequency between surgeons.

In a series of 52 patients we found that tumour involvement of the circumferential resection margin was a powerful predictor of subsequent local recurrence.[6] We concluded that most local recurrences occurred as a direct result of inadequate tumour resection and that this factor may explain variation in local recurrence rates between surgeons.[1,2]

Since that study[6] support for wide local surgical clearance of rectal cancer has grown. However, two other studies have yielded conflicting results: one study[7] did not confirm the association with local recurrence, although it found a significant influence on survival, whereas the other confirmed the results in 80 patients by meticulous whole-mount sections, but could only present data based on 2 years' follow-up. In our study, 190 patients were followed up for a median of 5 years with the aim of clarifying the importance of complete local excision at the circumferential margin.

Patients and methods

Between October, 1985, and June, 1990, specimens from all rectal cancer patients who had had resection at the Leeds General Infirmary were examined by pathologists who routinely recorded the Dukes'[9] and Jass[10] stages and various pathological variables.

Examination for tumour at the circumferential resection margin has been reported in detail.[11] It involved slicing the resected specimen transversely to provide multiple coronal sections through the tumour and the associated mesorectum. The mesorectum above the tumour was also coronally sliced from the posterior aspect and examined for deposits of tumour at the circumferential margin. 3 or 4 tissue blocks were taken where tumour approached

© Lancet 1994; 344: 707–711

Operation	Number (%) (n = 190)
Anterior resection	82 (43)
Abdominoperineal excision of rectum	95 (50)
Hartmann's procedure	9 (5)
Local resection (transanal)	4 (2)

Table 1: **Operative details**

closest to the margin. We measured the closest point of the tumour to the circumferential margin microscopically, and any specimen that had tumour 1 mm or less from the circumferential margin of excision was recorded as having tumour involvement.

In July, 1993, one researcher (IJA) independently reviewed the patients' clinical details and subsequent outcome. Any patient who had had preoperative radiotherapy was excluded from the trial because of reports that it may downstage the tumour.[11] Information about patient survival, cause of death, and local recurrence was retrieved from patients' notes and general practitioner records. All patients were followed up in general surgical clinics. Only one consultant specifically and routinely looked for local recurrence in the absence of symptoms. All other consultants investigated only patients with symptoms. The surgeon who routinely looked for local recurrence found a lower frequency of local recurrence than that seen overall in the study. The presence or absence of information about circumferential resection margin status did not affect management. All information was cross-checked against the death certificate and files of the Yorkshire Regional Cancer Organisation. Local recurrence was defined as any recurrence within the pelvis and was recorded only when confirmed by positive histology or by radiographic imaging. Cancer-specific survival was determined in all cases. Information was collected from the hospital notes and the individual notes of the surgeon to identify whether the original resection was palliative or potentially curative. A potentially curative resection was defined as one in which all macroscopic tumour tissue had been excised and there was no evidence of distal margin involvement.

Statistical analysis

Data on the pathological variables plus survival and local recurrence were entered into the computer programme Database III (Ashton-Tate). For the purpose of the analysis, the following pathological variables were used: tumour penetration through the muscularis propria, penetration of the serosa, presence of involved lymph nodes, presence of distant metastases, involvement of the apical lymph node, histological grade, presence of a lymphocytic infiltrate, appearance of the tumour border, presence of extramural venous invasion, involvement of the distal margin of excision by tumour, involvement of the circumferential margin of excision by tumour (involved ≤1 mm, or clear >1 mm).

The initial analysis examined the influence of circumferential margin involvement by tumour on local recurrence in all patients in the study, irrespective of whether they had had a palliative or potentially curative resection. This analysis was repeated for both groups separately.

In a subsequent analysis of survival, patients who died from non-cancer-related illness were censored from further analysis from the time of death. All results are expressed in terms of

	Number (%)	Local recurrence (%)
All patients	190	55 (29)
CRM involved	69 (36)	44 (64)
CRM not involved	121 (64)	11 (9)
Potentially curative resection	141	32 (23)
CRM involved	35 (25)	23 (66)
CRM not involved	106 (75)	9 (8)
Palliative resection	49	23 (47)
CRM involved	34 (69)	21 (62)
CRM not involved	15 (31)	2 (13)

CRM = circumferential resection margin

Table 2: **Local recurrence: influence of circumferential resection margin (CRM) involvement by tumour**

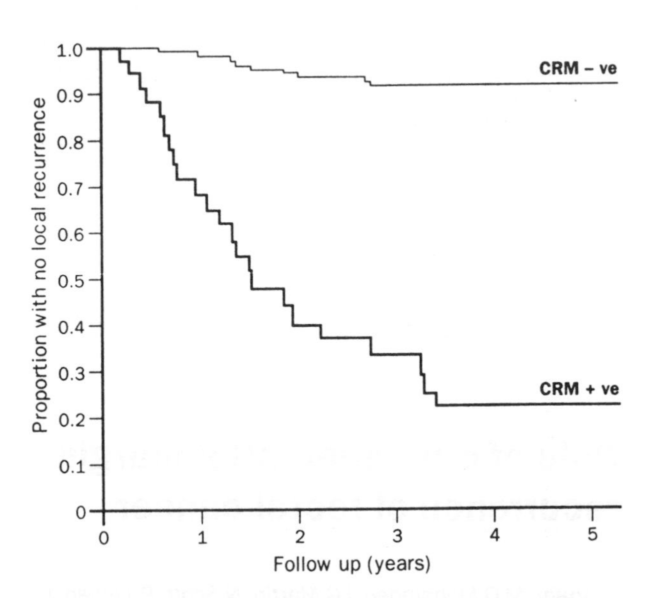

Figure 1: **Cumulative frequency of local recurrence comparing presence or absence of tumour at circumferential resection margin (CRM) in patients who had potentially curative resection**

cancer-specific survival. Data for the influence of tumour involvement of the circumferential resection margin on overall survival on all patients, and its effects on survival and the cumulative risk of local recurrence was tested with the log-rank method.[13] We then analysed the data to find out how each pathological variable influenced either the cumulative risk of local recurrence or survival by log-rank method. Variables that had a significant effect were compared with Cox's regression analysis[14] to determine which had an independent effect on prognosis.

Results

190 patients (104 male, 86 female) with a median age of 69 years (range 32–88) were enrolled in our prospective study between October, 1985, and June, 1990. 6 patients were excluded from analysis—3 received preoperative radiotherapy and 3 were lost to follow-up. The median follow-up was 5·3 years (3·0–7·7 years). The patients were operated on by 23 different surgeons, and the operative procedures used are shown in table 1. In 141 patients (74%) the operation was potentially curative. Residual tumour remained of the pelvis at time of operation in 23 patients (12%). Operative mortality (30 day) was 6% (11 patients) and was greater in patients who had a palliative procedure. 11 patients received postoperative radiotherapy (6%).

Tumour involvement of circumferential resection margin

Involvement of the circumferential resection margin was found in 69 specimens (36%). 35 (25%) of the 141 patients who were considered to have had potentially curative resections had involvement of the circumferential margin.

Local recurrence

Local recurrence was diagnosed in 55 patients (29%). Of the 69 patients who had tumour involvement of the circumferential margin, 44 had subsequent local recurrence, whereas recurrence developed in only 11 patients without such involvement. Local recurrence developed in 32 of 141 patients who had a potentially curative resection (23%) and in 23 of 49 who had a palliative procedure (47%). For patients with a clear circumferential margin who had potentially curative resection, the percentage without local recurrence at 5 years was 90%

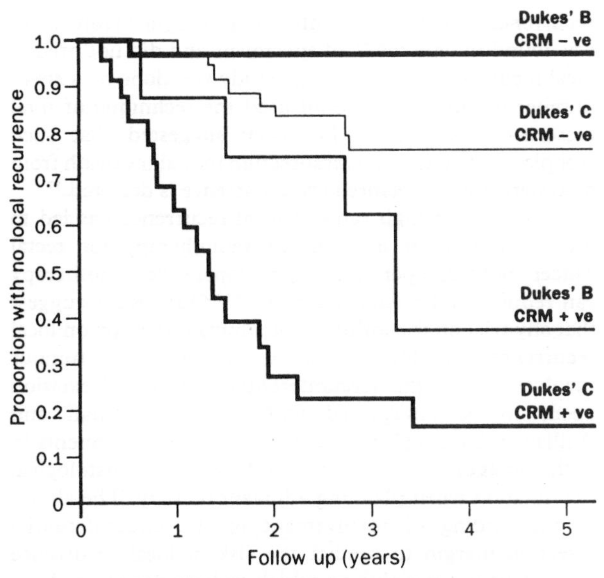

Figure 2: **Cumulative frequency of proportion of patients with no local recurrence comparing presence or absence of tumour at circumferential resection margin (CRM) in patients who underwent potentially curative resection for Dukes' B or C tumours**

(95% CI 84–96); patients with tumour at the circumferential margin did significantly worse, with a cumulative percentage without recurrence at 5 years of only 22% (6–38, log rank p<0·001, figure 1).

Figure 2 shows the life tables for cumulative percentage without local recurrence for patients who had a potentially curative resection for Dukes' B or Dukes' C tumour. Of the 55 patients who had local recurrence, 7 had a second operative procedure (13%).

Survival

The cancer-specific overall 5-year survival was 48% (40–56). Figure 3 shows the life table for survival by Dukes' stage (5-year survival Dukes' A 86%, B 64%, C 40%, C1 44%, C2, 23%). The 5-year survival percentage in the 69 patients with tumour involvement at the circumferential margin was 15% (6–25), compared with 66% (57–75) in those without such involvement (log rank p<0·001). For

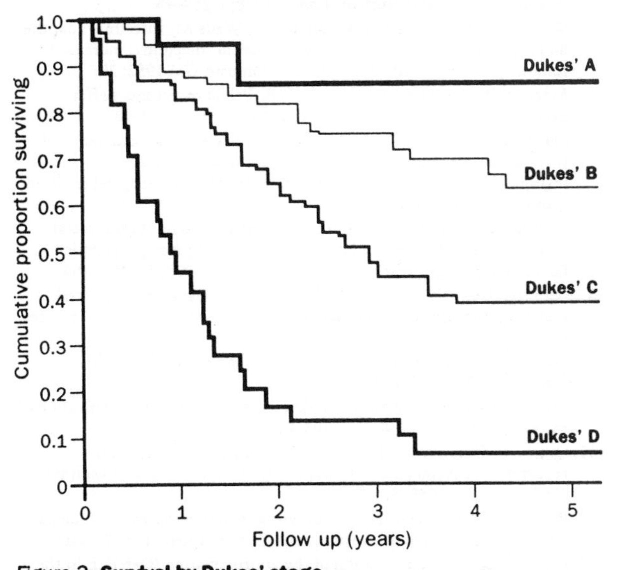

Figure 3: **Survival by Dukes' stage**
Proportion of cases: 13% A, 31% B, 39% C, 17% D.

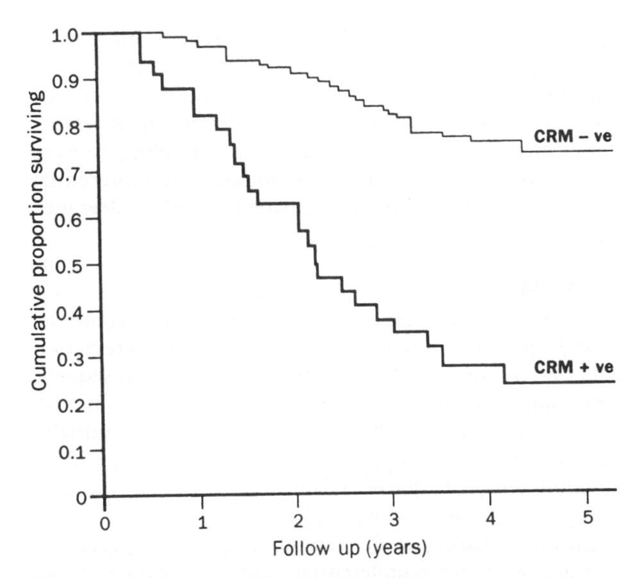

Figure 4: **Survival comparing presence or absence of tumour at the circumferential resection margin (CRM) in patients who underwent potentially curative resection**

the 141 patients who had a potentially curative resection, overall 5-year survival was 62% (53–70). Again, patients who had tumour involvement of the circumferential margin of excision (n=35) had significantly poorer 5-year survival than those without such involvement (24 [8–39] *vs* 74 [65–83]%, log rank p<0·001). The life tables for these two groups are shown in figure 4.

Multivariate analysis

To assess the effects of circumferential margin involvement in patients with no residual disease, the effect on outcome of each pathological variable was assessed for patients who had a potentially curative resection (table 3). Variables that had a significant result in this univariate analysis were then used in a multivariate analysis to see if they had an independent effect.

We found that the same three variables were of independent significance to determine poor survival and a higher cumulative percentage of local recurrence: the

Pathological variable	p for survival	p for local recurrence
Lymph-node involvement	<0·001	<0·001
Involvement of C2 node	>0·2	>0·06
Penetration of muscularis propria	<0·01	>0·4
Infiltrating tumour margin	<0·001	<0·005
Conspicuous lymphocytic response	<0·02	>0·4
Poor histological grade	<0·03	<0·01
Extramural venous invasion	<0·001	<0·001
Serosal penetration	>0·4	>0·4
Distal margin involvement	>0·4	>0·4
CRM involvement	<0·001	<0·001

Studies done on potentially curative resections only.

Table 3: **Univariate analysis: influence of pathological variables on prognosis**

	Estimate	SE	Hazard ratio (95% CI)
Overall survival			
Lymph-node involvement	0·827	0·319	2·28 (1·20–4·77)
Infiltrating tumour margin	0·864	0·319	2·37 (1·14–4·95)
CRM involvement	1·173	0·305	3·23 (1·60–6·53)
Cumulative local recurrence			
Lymph-node involvement	1·198	0·459	3·31 (1·15–9·55)
Infiltrating tumour margin	1·016	0·417	2·76 (1·06–7·22)
CRM involvement	2·504	0·451	12·23 (4·32–34·6)

Table 4: Multivariate analysis: pathological variables independently influencing prognosis

presence of tumour at the circumferential margin of excision; lymph node involvement by tumour; and an infiltrating appearance of the tumour border (table 4). Patients with circumferential margin involvement were 3 times more likely to die and 12 times more likely to have local recurrence than patients without circumferential margin involvement, despite apparent complete clearance of tumour at operation.

Discussion

The results of our prospective study support the hypothesis that the presence of tumour at the circumferential resection margin is important in determining the subsequent development of local recurrence in many patients. The risk of a local recurrence after a resection that was initially regarded as potentially curative was 12 times greater if the circumferential margin of excision was involved by tumour. Furthermore, along with lymph-node involvement and an infiltrating margin at the tumour edge, the presence of tumour at the circumferential resection margin is an important independent determinant of overall survival. The multivariate analysis suggests that for potentially curative resections, the critical factor is the involvement of the circumferential margin rather than penetration of the muscularis propria by tumour. The message for the surgeon is clear—wide local excision of a rectal cancer is important in determining a good prognosis for the patient.

Although circumferential margin involvement was a powerful predictor of local recurrence, our study also shows that local recurrence develops in a few patients without circumferential resection margin involvement. Previous studies have looked at other mechanisms for the development of local recurrence in rectal cancer, such as free exfoliated tumour cells[3] and the promotional effects of the anastomosis.[4] These mechanisms may have brought about local recurrence in the patients without circumferential margin involvement. A further possibility is the presence of discontinuous local spread of tumour into an area of the mesorectum not removed by the surgeon.[15] In our study some patients had circumferential resection margin involvement, but did not develop local recurrence. In most of these patients, widespread tumour dissemination was diagnosed during follow-up, but intensive investigation specifically to identify local recurrence was not indicated. Other possible reasons for the apparent non-progression to local recurrence are inadequate follow-up or the effects of postoperative adjuvant radiotherapy. A further possibility is the creation of an artifactual circumferential margin during removal or subsequent handling of the tumour.

Our finding that the circumferential margin was involved by tumour in 25% of resections at which the surgeon had considered the margins of excision to be clear is important. The reported frequency of local recurrence varies widely from 6% in specialist units to more than 50%. Recurrence rates between 15 and 35% are not unusual in routine surgical practice, which has led to calls for rectal cancer to be treated by specialist surgeons only.[16] We suggest that the variation of local recurrence may be due to the frequency of unsuspected involvement of the circumferential resection margin. In this study, 23 different surgeons were involved, no doubt with consequent variations in surgical technique, and there was a high frequency of local recurrence (23%) among patients who had potentially curative resection. Our results confirm those of Ng et al[8] but not those of Cawthorn and colleagues.[7] In that study,[7] the frequency of local recurrence was 8%: circumferential margin involvement was found in only 6·6% of specimens and did not predict local recurrence. However, the study was done by a small number of surgeons who all used the technique of total mesorectal excision; it has been suggested that such complete excision of the mesorectum may allow death from metastatic disease before local recurrence is detected.[17]

Concern over high rates of local recurrence has led to increasing interest in adjuvant radiotherapy for rectal cancer. Both preoperative and postoperative radiotherapy can reduce local recurrence rates.[18,19] Our results suggest that any trial on the influence of adjuvant therapy on local recurrence that does not allow for unexpected tumour involvement of the circumferential margin of excision needs to be interpreted with caution. Abulafi and Williams[20] have highlighted the need for improvements in both imaging techniques and routine histological examination when planning adjuvant therapy. The ability of the finding of involvement of the circumferential resection margin to predict the risk of local recurrence suggests it is a variable on which to base decisions about postoperative adjuvant radiotherapy. Indeed, we would question the need for any adjuvant therapy in the apparently excised Dukes' B tumour when the circumferential margin is clear. Good surgical technique can result in cure in most of these patients.[15,22] Improvements in surgical technique that lead to a reduction in local recurrence may benefit the patient more than adjuvant therapy alone.[1]

The pathological method itself is designed to be simple and rapid. It adds no more than 10 min to the assessment of a rectal cancer, it is easy to teach, and is very cost-effective, adding no more than four blocks to a case.

This work was supported by the Yorkshire Cancer Research Campaign and the Special Trustees of Leeds General Infirmary. Secretarial assistance was provided by Mrs J Fearnly.

References

1 McArdle CS, Hole D. Impact of variability amongst surgeons in post-operative morbidity and mortality and ultimate survival. *BMJ* 1991; **302:** 1501–05.

2 Phillips RKS, Hittinger R, Blesovsky L, Fry JS, Fielding LP. Local recurrence following "curative" surgery for large bowel cancer: I, the overall picture. *Br J Surg* 1984; **71:** 12–16.

3 Gordon-Watson C. Origin and spread of cancer of the rectum in relation to surgical treatment. *Lancet* 1938; i: 239–45.

4 Williamson RCN, Davis PW, Bristol JB, Wells M. Intestinal adaption and experimental carcinogenesis after partial colectomy: increased tumour yields are confined to the anastomosis. *Gut* 1982; **23:** 316–25.

5 Morson BC, Vaughn EG, Bussey HJR. Pelvic recurrences after excision of the rectum for carcinoma. *BMJ* 1963; **2:** 13–18.

6 Quirke P, Durdey P, Dixon MF, Williams NS. Local recurrence of rectal adenocarcinoma due to inadequate surgical resection: histopathological study of lateral tumour spread and surgical excision. *Lancet* 1986; ii: 996–99.

7 Cawthorn SJ, Parums DV, Gibbs NM, et al. Extent of mesorectal spread and involvement of lateral resection margin as prognostic factors after surgery for rectal cancer. *Lancet* 1990; **335:** 1055–59.

8 Ng IOL, Luk ISC, Yuen ST, et al. Surgical clearance in resected rectal carcinomas; a multivariate analysis of clinicopathologic features. *Cancer* 1993; **71:** 1972–76.

9 Dukes CE. Classification of carcinoma of the rectum. *J Pathol Bacteriol* 1932; **35:** 330–32.

10 Jass LR, Love SB, Northover JMA. A new prognostic classification of rectal cancer. *Lancet* 1987; i: 1303–06.

11 Quirke P, Dixon MF. How do I do it: the prediction of local recurrence in rectal adenocarcinoma by histopathological examination. *Int J Colon Dis* 1988; **3:** 127–31.

12 Powers WE, Tolmach LJ. Preoperative radiation therapy: biological basis and experimental investigations. *Nature* 1964; **201:** 172–204.

13 Peto R, Pike M. Conservation of the approximation (O-E)2/E in the log rank test for survival data or tumour recurrence data. *Biometrics* 1973; **29:** 579–84.

© *Lancet* 1994; 344: 707–711

14 Cox DR. Regression models and life tables. *J Roy Stat Soc* 1972; **34:** 187–219.

15 Heald RJ, Ryall RD. Recurrence and survival after total mesorectal excision for rectal cancer. *Lancet* 1986; i: 1479–82.

16 Fielding LP, Stewart-Brown S, Dudley HAF. Surgeon-related variables and the clinical trial. *Lancet* 1978; ii: 778–79.

17 Editorial. Breaching the mesorectum. *Lancet* 1990; **335:** 1067–68.

18 Stockholm Rectal Cancer Study Group. Short-term preoperative radiotherapy for adenocarcinoma of the rectum. *Am J Clin Oncol* 1987; **10:** 369–75.

19 Fisher B, Wolmark N, Rockette H, et al. Post-operative adjuvant chemotherapy or radiation therapy for rectal cancer: results from NSABP Protocol R-01. *J Natl Cancer Inst* 1988; **80:** 21–29.

20 Abulafi AM, Williams NS. Local recurrence of colorectal cancer: the problem, mechanisms, management and adjuvant therapy. *Br J Surg* 1994; **81:** 7–19.

21 Chan KW, Boey J, Wong SKC. A method of reporting radial invasion and surgical clearance of rectal carcinoma. *Histopathology* 1985; **9:** 1319–27.

22 MacFarlane JK, Ryall RDH, Heald RJ. Mesorectal excision for rectal cancer. *Lancet* 1993; **341:** 457–60.

Randomised trial of single-dose ciprofloxacin for travellers' diarrhoea

Imroz Salam, Peter Katelaris, Simon Leigh-Smith, Michael J G Farthing

Summary

Diarrhoea is the most common illness affecting travellers to developing countries. Our study was designed to compare the efficacy of a single 500 mg dose of ciprofloxacin with placebo for treatment of acute diarrhoea in travellers. British troops who were within their first 8 weeks of deployment in Belize and who presented within 24 h of the onset of diarrhoea, were randomised to receive either ciprofloxacin 500 mg or placebo. Every subject recorded the number and consistency of stools and presence of any other associated symptoms for 72 h or until recovery.

Of 88 subjects enrolled, 83 were evaluable, of whom 45 received ciprofloxacin and 38 placebo. Groups did not differ with regard to duration or severity of diarrhoea at randomisation. Mean (SE) duration of diarrhoea, as assessed by time to the last liquid and last unformed stool, was reduced from 50·4 (4·5) h and 53·5 (4·4) h, respectively, in the placebo group to 20·9 (3·4) h and 24·8 (3·8) h in those receiving ciprofloxacin ($p<0·0001$). Mean number of liquid stools was reduced from 11·4 (1·2) in the placebo group to 5·0 (0·7) in the ciprofloxacin-treated group ($p<0·0001$). The cumulative percentages of subjects with no unformed stool after 24 h, 48 h, and 72 h were, respectively, 64%, 82%, and 93% in the ciprofloxacin group and 11%, 42%, and 79% in the placebo group ($p<0·0001$, $p<0·001$, and not significant, respectively).

A single 500 mg dose of ciprofloxacin was an effective empirical treatment for reducing the duration and severity of diarrhoea in travellers. The regimen should maximise compliance and reduce the cost and duration of therapy.

Lancet 1994; **344:** 1537–39

See Commentary page 1520

Department of Medicine and Gastroenterology, Queen Elizabeth Military Hospital, Woolwich, London (I Salam MRCPI); **Department of Gastroenterology, St Bartholomew's Hospital, London EC1 7BF, UK** (P Katelaris FRACP, Prof M J G Farthing FRCP); **and 45 Commando Royal Marines, Arbroath** (S Leigh-Smith MB)

Correspondence to: Prof Michael J G Farthing

Introduction

Acute diarrhoea is the most common illness of travellers from industrialised to developing countries,[1] with an attack rate between 30 and 50%.[2] Although it is rarely a serious illness, more than a third of travellers with diarrhoea will be confined to bed and another 40% will have to modify their travel plans.[3] Travellers' diarrhoea is usually self-limiting even without specific therapy, although a 3–5-day course of a broad-spectrum antibiotic is effective in reducing the duration and severity of illness.[4–10] Treatment is recommended if three or more unformed stools are passed within 24 h.[11] However, early empirical treatment at the onset of symptoms with a single dose of antibiotic would, if effective, be more desirable, because such an approach would reduce duration of illness, minimise adverse effects, reduce the duration and cost of treatment, and optimise the chances of full compliance. The 4-fluoroquinolone antibiotic ciprofloxacin is effective against all bacterial enteropathogens known to cause travellers' diarrhoea and 3–5-day courses have successfully been used in the treatment of this condition.[6–7]

We have therefore studied the efficacy of early empirical therapy with a single 500 mg dose of ciprofloxacin in a prospective, placebo-controlled, double-blind trial in British troops deployed on military exercise in Belize.

Patients and methods

Between May and November, 1993, British marines who developed diarrhoea within the first 8 weeks of arrival in Belize were eligible to be included in the trial. The trial was conducted in five different parts of Belize. Ethical approval for the study was obtained from the Army Medical Research Executive Committee and informed consent was obtained from all participants before enrolment. Diarrhoea was defined as passage of one or more unformed stools. We did not wait for 24 h or three loose stools before inclusion in the study because such criteria would imply that travellers should endure three episodes or 24 h of diarrhoea before resorting to therapy.

Subjects with blood in their stools, high fever (>38·5°C), or severe dehydration requiring intravenous fluid therapy were excluded. All subjects were taking weekly chloroquine and daily proguanil for malaria prophylaxis. Subjects were assigned in a double-blind, random fashion to receive either a single 500 mg dose of ciprofloxacin or an identical placebo. For the 72 h after starting therapy or until complete recovery, subjects recorded in a diary the number of watery, loose, soft, or normal stools, the presence of cramps, abdominal pain, vomiting, nausea, or anorexia, and any other symptoms. Subjects were followed-up for 3 days or until recovery. Those who did not fully recover or whose symptoms worsened after 3 days received additional treatment if clinically indicated.

Duration of illness was measured to the nearest hour within two end points: last liquid stool, and last unformed stool (semi-solid or soft). Severity of illness was assessed by the cumulative

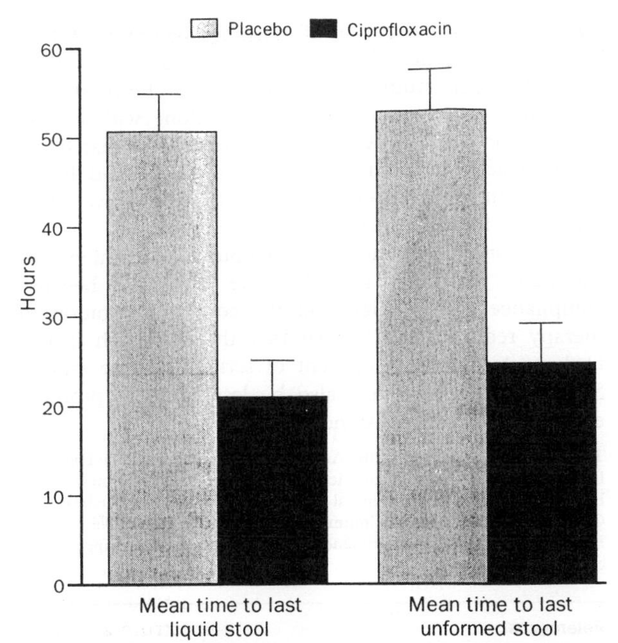

Figure 1: **Duration of diarrhoea (time from onset of symptoms to last liquid or unformed stool) in subjects who had received a single 500 mg dose of ciprofloxacin or placebo**
Data shown as mean (SE).

numbers of liquid and unformed stools at 24 h, 48 h, and 72 h after enrolment. Numbers of stools passed and duration of diarrhoea (hours) were expressed as mean (SE). Comparison of these variables between the two groups was with the two-tailed Student's *t* test. The cumulative proportions of subjects recovering at 24 h, 48 h, and 72 h in each group were compared by χ^2 or Fisher's exact tests, with Bonferroni adjustment applied for multiple comparison.

Results

During their first 8 weeks in Belize, 180 of 500 marines developed diarrhoea, giving an acute diarrhoea attack rate of 36%. Of the 180 subjects, 88 (49%) were seen on the day of first loose stool and were thus eligible for enrolment in the study. Reduced accessibility to a medical centre while on exercise in the jungle, indifference to a single episode of diarrhoea, and self-treatment with an antidiarrhoeal agent prevented inclusion in the study of all the subjects who developed diarrhoea. Of the 88 subjects enrolled, 5 had record sheets that provided insufficient data (4 placebo, 1 ciprofloxacin) and thus they were excluded from the final analysis. Of the remaining 83 subjects, 45 received ciprofloxacin and 38 placebo. The groups did not differ with respect to age or duration or frequency of diarrhoea before treatment. Duration of diarrhoea before randomisation was 8·9 (0·9) h in the ciprofloxacin group and 8·9 (0·8) h in the placebo group. Mean numbers of stool on presentation were 3·0 (0·3) in the ciprofloxacin group and 3·1 (0·2) in the placebo group.

	Ciprofloxacin (n=45)	Placebo (n=38)	p (*t* test)
Number of liquid stools			
Total	5·0 (0·7)	11·4 (1·2)	<0·0001
Number of unformed stools			
Total	5·3	11·7 (1·2)	<0·0001
0–24 h	3·8 (0·5)	5·8 (0·6)	<0·0166
24–48 h	1·1 (0·3)	3·2 (0·4)	<0·0001
48–72 h	0·5 (0·2)	2·0 (0·4)	<0·0003

Data presented as mean (SE).

Table 1: **Severity of diarrhoea in subjects who received ciprofloxacin or placebo during first 72 h**

	Ciprofloxacin (n=45)	Placebo (n=38)	p (χ^2)
No liquid stool after:			
24 h	31 (68·9)	6 (15·8)	<0·0001
48 h	39 (86·7)	19 (50·0)	<0·0001
72 h	44 (97·8)	32 (81·5)	0·01
No unformed stool after:			
24 h	29 (64·4)	4 (10·5)	<0·0001
48 h	37 (82·2)	16 (42·1)	<0·0001
72 h	42 (93·3)	30 (78·9)	0·1

Data presented as number (%) of subjects.

Table 2: **Recovery from diarrhoea in subjects who received ciprofloxacin or placebo**

Duration of illness was significantly (p<0·001) reduced from over 2 days in the placebo group (mean [SE] time to last liquid stool 50·4 [4·5] h, mean time to last unformed stool 53·5 [4·4] h) to less than 1 day in the group who received ciprofloxacin (20·9 [3·4] h and 24·8 [3·8] h, respectively) (figure 1). Severity of illness (as measured by the cumulative numbers of unformed and liquid stools) was reduced by half in the ciprofloxacin group. Mean number of unformed stools in the first, second, and third 24 h of illness were reduced to nearly half, a third, and a quarter, respectively, in the ciprofloxacin group compared with placebo (table 1). No liquid stools were reported after 24 h, 48 h, and 72 h in 69%, 87%, and 98% of subjects, respectively, who were treated with ciprofloxacin compared with 16%, 50%, and 81% of subjects who received placebo. After 24 h, 48 h, and 72 h of therapy, no unformed stools were reported in 29, 37, and 42 subjects, respectively, in the ciprofloxacin group compared with 4, 16, and 30 subjects in the placebo group (table 2). Duration and severity of diarrhoea are clearly not independent of one another; thus the results presented in tables 1 and 2 are related. 8 subjects in the ciprofloxacin group had no further diarrhoea after intervention, whereas all receiving placebo continued to have diarrhoea after intervention. No adverse effects were reported after treatment with ciprofloxacin or placebo. All subjects who received placebo recovered within 5 days, confirming that their illness was self-limiting and almost certainly travellers' diarrhoea (figure 2). There were no differences in the reported associated symptoms in the two treatment groups: abdominal cramps and pain were reported by 49% of subjects in the ciprofloxacin group

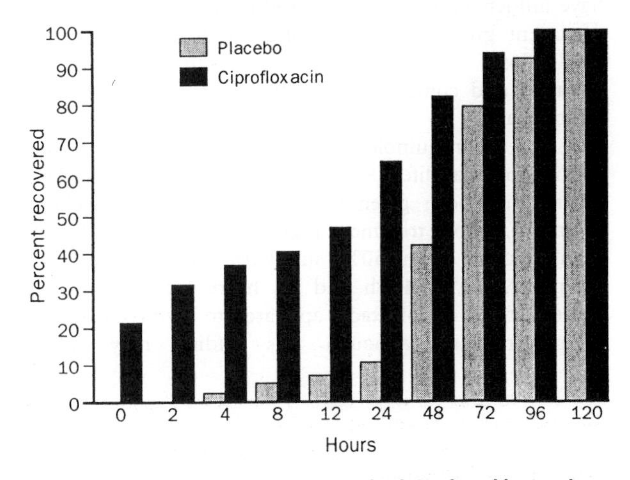

Figure 2: **Cumulative recovery from diarrhoea in subjects who had received a single 500 mg dose of ciprofloxacin or placebo**

and 45% in the placebo group, nausea was present in 28% and 24%, and vomiting was experienced by 16% and 17%, respectively. However, associated symptoms in all subjects in the ciprofloxacin group had resolved before the passage of the last unformed stool.

Discussion

Although acute diarrhoea in travellers is usually a self-limiting illness, it can cause considerable disruption of professional and business activities and great inconvenience to holidaymakers.[4,11] For voluntary aid workers and military personnel on exercise, relief operation, or United Nations missions, a high attack rate could mean failure to carry out such duties owing to temporary incapacitation.[12] Thus the reason for using a specific therapy such as an antibiotic is to reduce the severity and duration of diarrhoea and minimise the hours lost due to illness.

Our study demonstrates that when acute travellers' diarrhoea is empirically treated at the onset of symptoms with a single 500 mg dose of ciprofloxacin, the duration and severity of diarrhoea are significantly reduced. The natural history of diarrhoea in this setting can be ascertained from the placebo group who had on average more than eleven stools in the course of their illness and a mean duration of the illness exceeding 50 h. Because we wanted to minimise the period of illness and temporary incapacitation, we did not wait for three loose stools or for 24 h before starting treatment—a standard definition of travellers' diarrhoea[2,11,13]—and therefore maximised the chances of observing the efficacy of early intervention with a single-dose regimen.

We did not attempt to establish a microbiological diagnosis in this study, treatment being given empirically as would usually happen in the self-therapy of travellers' diarrhoea. However, we know from previous studies of travellers' diarrhoea in Central America that enterotoxigenic, enteroadherent, and enteroinvasive *Escherichia coli, Shigella* sp, *Salmonella* sp, and *Campylobacter jejuni* are the main bacterial enteropathogens in this region.[14-16] Ciprofloxacin has proven activity against all of these organisms.[17,18]

A study of US military personnel in central Thailand showed that the duration of acute diarrhoea was similar whether ciprofloxacin was given as a single dose of 750 mg or as 500 mg twice daily for 3 days.[6] However, use of doxycycline for malarial prophylaxis in this study may have influenced the results by reducing diarrhoea in both treatment groups and obscuring the true efficacy of a single dose. Our study was free of other confounding variables and confirmed the efficacy of a single dose of ciprofloxacin.

A new fluoroquinolone, fleroxacin, which has a long elimination half-life (8–12 h) designed for once-daily dosing, has been given for 1 or 2 days in travellers' diarrhoea.[19] Both treatment regimens were more effective than placebo, with 50% and 80% of patients being symptom free at 48 h and 72 h, respectively. In the present study, ciprofloxacin appeared to be more effective than fleroxacin, although this finding may reflect differences in the duration of diarrhoea before entry into the study, being up to 24 h in our study but up to 6 days in the fleroxacin study. Our study indicates, however, that it is unnecessary to use a fluoroquinolone with a long half-life for single-dose therapy of travellers' diarrhoea. Ciprofloxacin, which is universally available and has a short elimination half-life (3·5–4·5 h), is effective when given early in the course of disease.

Our simple regimen for empirical treatment of travellers' diarrhoea should prove attractive because compliance will be high and the cost and duration of therapy reduced. We believe that this approach is less likely to lead to development of serious adverse effects. Short-term therapy may also be less likely to promote emergence of drug resistance.

This study was supported by the Army Medical Services and the Digestive Disease Research Centre at the Medical College of St Bartholomew's Hospital. We thank Major General G O Cowan, Royal Army Medical College, Millbank, Surgeon Commander A R O Miller, Royal Naval Hospital, Hasler, and 45 Commando Royal Marines for their support in conducting this study.

References

1 Steffen R, Boppart I. Travellers' diarrhoea. *Bailliere's Clin Gastroenterol* 1987; **1:** 361–76.
2 Arduino RC, DuPont HL. Travellers' diarrhoea. *Bailliere's Clin Gastroenterol* 1993; **7:** 365–85.
3 Gorbach SL. Travelers' diarrhea. *N Engl J Med* 1982; **307:** 881–83.
4 Farthing MJ. Travellers' diarrhoea. *Br J Hosp Med* 1992; **48:** 82–92.
5 Ericsson CD, DuPont HL, Mathewson JJ, et al. Treatment of travellers' diarrhea with sulphamethoxazole and trimethoprim and loperamide. *JAMA* 1990; **263:** 257–61.
6 Petruccelli BP, Murphy GS, Sanchez JL, et al. Treatment of travelers' diarrhea with ciprofloxacin and loperamide. *J Infect Dis* 1992; **165:** 557–60.
7 Taylor DN, Sanchez JL, Chandler W, et al. Treatment of travelers' diarrhea: ciprofloxacin plus loperamide compared with ciprofloxacin alone. *Ann Intern Med* 1991; **114:** 731–34.
8 Pichler HE, Diridl G, Stickler K, et al. Clinical efficacy of ciprofloxacin compared with placebo in bacterial diarrhea. *Am J Med* 1987; **82** (suppl 4A): 329–32.
9 Ericsson CD, Johnson PC, DuPont HL, et al. Ciprofloxacin or trimethoprim-sulfamethoxazole as initial therapy for travelers' diarrhea: a placebo controlled randomised trial. *Ann Intern Med* 1987; **106:** 216–20.
10 Goodman LJ, Trenholme GM, Kaplan RL, et al. Empirical antimicrobial therapy of domestically acquired acute diarrhea in urban adults. *Arch Intern Med* 1990; **150:** 541–46.
11 DuPont HL, Ericsson CD. Prevention and treatment of travelers' diarrhea. *N Engl J Med* 1993; **328:** 1821–27.
12 Hyams KC, Bourgeois AL, Merrel BR, et al. Diarrheal disease during Operation Desert Shield. *N Engl J Med* 1991; **325:** 1423–28.
13 Farthing MJG. Travellers' diarrhoea. *Gut* 1994; **35:** 1–4.
14 Black RE. Pathogens that cause travelers' diarrhea in Latin America and Africa. *Rev Infect Dis* 1986; **8:** 131–35.
15 Steffen R, Mathewson JJ, Ericsson CD, et al. Travelers' diarrhea in West Africa and Mexico: faecal transport systems and liquid bismuth subsalicylate for self therapy. *J Infect Dis* 1988; **157:** 1008–13.
16 Black RE. Epidemiology of travelers' diarrhea and relative importance of various pathogens. *Rev Infect Dis* 1990; **12:** 573–79.
17 Wolfson JS, Hooper DC. The fluoroqinolones: structures, mechanisms of action and resistance and spectra of activity in vitro. *Antimicrob Agents Chemother* 1985; **28:** 581–86.
18 Goodman LJ, Fliegelman RM, Trenholme GM, et al. Comparative *in vitro* activity of ciprofloxacin against campylobacter sp and other bacterial enteric pathogens. *Antimicrob Agents Chemother* 1984; **25:** 504–06.
19 Steffen R, Jori J, DuPont HL, Mathewson JJ, Sturchler D. Treatment of travellers' diarrhoea with fleroxacin: a case study. *J Antimicrob Chemother* 1993; **31:** 767–76.

© N Engl J Med 1994; 330: 811–815

TRANSDERMAL NICOTINE FOR ACTIVE ULCERATIVE COLITIS

Rupert D. Pullan, B.M., B.Ch., John Rhodes, M.D., Subramanian Ganesh, M.B., B.S., Venk Mani, M.B., B.S., John S. Morris, M.D., Geraint T. Williams, M.D., Robert G. Newcombe, Ph.D., Michael A.H. Russell, B.M., B.Ch., Colin Feyerabend, Ph.D., Gareth A.O. Thomas, M.B., B.S., and Urbain Säwe, M.D., Ph.D.

Abstract *Background.* Ulcerative colitis is largely a disease of nonsmokers. Because anecdotal reports suggest that smoking and nicotine may improve the symptoms of the disease, we examined the effect of nicotine as a supplemental treatment for ulcerative colitis.

Methods. We treated 72 patients with active ulcerative colitis with either transdermal nicotine patches or placebo patches for six weeks in a randomized, double-blind study. Incremental doses of nicotine were given; most patients tolerated doses of 15 to 25 mg per 24 hours. All the patients had been taking mesalamine, and 12 were receiving low doses of glucocorticoids; these medications were continued without change during the study. Clinical, sigmoidoscopic, and histologic assessments were made at base line and at the end of the study; symptoms were recorded daily on a diary card, and the clinician made a global assessment. Side effects and plasma nicotine and cotinine concentrations were monitored throughout the study.

Results. Seventeen of the 35 patients in the nicotine group had complete remissions, as compared with 9 of the 37 patients in the placebo group ($P = 0.03$). The patients in the nicotine group had greater improvement in the global clinical grade of colitis ($P<0.001$) and the histologic grade ($P = 0.03$), lower stool frequency (a difference of 1.6 stools daily; $P = 0.008$), less abdominal pain ($P = 0.05$), and less fecal urgency ($P = 0.009$). More patients in the nicotine group had side effects (23, vs. 11 in the placebo group; $P = 0.002$), the most common of which were nausea, lightheadedness, headache, and sleep disturbance. Withdrawals due to ineffective therapy were more common in the placebo group (3 vs. 8, $P = 0.12$).

Conclusions. The addition of transdermal nicotine to conventional maintenance therapy improves symptoms in patients with ulcerative colitis. (N Engl J Med 1994; 330:811-5.)

Most patients with ulcerative colitis are nonsmokers, and patients with a history of smoking usually acquire their disease within a few years after they have stopped smoking.[1-4] Among patients who continue to smoke, symptoms may improve, suggesting that smoking may have a beneficial effect.[5,6] Given the possibility that nicotine is the ingredient of tobacco smoke responsible for improvement, we treated 16 patients with active ulcerative colitis in an uncontrolled fashion with transdermal nicotine patches, and symptoms improved in 12.[7] We report here the results of a randomized, double-blind, controlled trial of transdermal nicotine in patients with active ulcerative colitis.

Methods

Patients

Seventy-seven patients with known left-sided ulcerative colitis who had relapsed, as confirmed by rigid sigmoidoscopic examination, were invited to participate in the study of treatment with transdermal nicotine or placebo for six weeks. Patients were not enrolled if they had enteric infection or other medical problems (particularly of the cardiovascular system), were pregnant or lactating, had changed their maintenance anticolitis therapy during the previous four weeks, or currently smoked. Both former smokers and lifelong nonsmokers were enrolled; the two groups were not stratified separately in the randomization.

From the Department of Gastroenterology, University Hospital of Wales, Cardiff, United Kingdom (R.D.P., J.R., G.A.O.T.); Leigh Infirmary, Leigh, Greater Manchester, United Kingdom (S.G., V.M.); Princess of Wales Hospital, Bridgend, Mid Glamorgan, United Kingdom (J.S.M.); the Departments of Pathology (G.T.W.) and Medical Computing and Statistics (R.G.N.), University of Wales College of Medicine, Cardiff, United Kingdom; the Health Behaviour Unit, Institute of Psychiatry and Maudsley Hospital, London (M.A.H.R.); the Nicotine Laboratory, Poisons Unit, New Cross Hospital, London (C.F.); and Kabi Pharmacia Therapeutics, Helsingborg, Sweden (U.S.). Address reprint requests to Dr. Rhodes at the Dept. of Gastroenterology, Ward A7, University Hospital of Wales, Heath Park, Cardiff, United Kingdom.

Supported in part by Kabi Pharmacia, which provided the transdermal nicotine patches.

The study was approved by the appropriate review committees at each of the three study hospitals, and all the patients gave informed written consent.

Nicotine Patches

We used two sizes of transdermal nicotine patch that released 5 or 15 mg of nicotine over a period of 16 hours (the average smoker absorbs about 1 mg of nicotine per cigarette smoked).[8,9] The patients applied the patches before going to bed to limit side effects and wore them for 24 hours.

Since the therapeutic trial involved the administration of nicotine to patients who had never smoked, we studied the tolerance and pharmacokinetics of transdermal nicotine in 12 normal subjects (7 men and 5 women) who were lifelong nonsmokers. The nicotine doses were increased in a stepwise manner over a period of five days to minimize side effects. On days 1 and 2 single 5-mg patches were worn, on days 3 and 4 two 5-mg patches, and on days 5 and 6 single 15-mg patches. Three of these subjects were intolerant of nicotine, but in the remaining nine the mean (±SD) plasma nicotine concentrations eight hours after the application of the patches on days 2, 4, and 6 were 3.4±1.0, 7.3±2.1, and 13.3±5.6 ng per milliliter, respectively.

Nicotine Dose in the Therapeutic Trial

The incremental dose regimen used in the preliminary studies was repeated in the patients with ulcerative colitis, most of whom tolerated a dose of 15 mg. If no clinical benefit was evident after two weeks the dose was increased to 25 mg daily. The patients who were unable to tolerate 15-mg patches were given a lower-dose patch. The mean (±SD) dose in the nicotine group was 17±6 mg. The placebo patches were identical to the nicotine patches in appearance and were increased in size in a similar manner. The mean patch "dose" for patients in the placebo group was 19±5 mg. Changes in treatment were monitored by one physician at each hospital; none of the three physicians were aware of the patients' treatment assignments.

Study Design

All the patients had relapsed despite treatment with their usual medication. During the trial the patients continued to take the same doses of anticolitis drugs (oral formulations of mesalamine and glucocorticoids) that they had taken during the previous four weeks. Those who were taking glucocorticoids were randomized separately. The effect of transdermal nicotine on the course of the patients' disease was evaluated by analyzing changes in clinical, sigmoidoscopic, and histologic indexes during the six-week study period.

Evaluation Procedures

The severity of disease was assessed clinically at the start of the trial and after two, four, and six weeks; at each center one physician saw every patient and made a global clinical assessment using the grading system described by Truelove and Witts (Table 1).[10] The patients were asked to complete a daily diary recording stool frequency and consistency, the presence of blood or mucus, and episodes of abdominal pain. Pain, fecal urgency, and the degree of general well-being were also noted. Fecal urgency was scored daily by the patient on a scale from 1 (no urgency) to 10 (incontinent of stool), and general well-being on a scale from 1 (poor) to 10 (very well). Each day the patients also recorded the occurrence of nine common side effects and any others.

At the beginning of the study all the patients underwent sigmoidoscopy and rectal biopsy. When the proximal extent of disease could not be seen, colonoscopy or barium enema was performed. Sigmoidoscopy and biopsy were repeated by the same physician at the end of the study or at the time of a premature withdrawal. The extent of inflammation of the rectal mucosa was graded visually,[11] and biopsy specimens stained with hematoxylin and eosin were graded histologically according to a system described by Truelove and Richards (Table 1).[12] Biopsies were performed at the start and end of the trial in all but one patient, and the specimens were examined without knowledge of treatment assignment.

Plasma nicotine and cotinine concentrations were measured at base line and after two, four, and six weeks. Most of the blood samples were obtained 12 hours after the nicotine patch had been applied, and they were stored at −20°C until analysis.[13] Nicotine and cotinine concentrations are maximal about eight hours after application of the patch. To determine whether any patient had resumed smoking, breath carbon monoxide was measured with a Bedfont MicroSmokerlyzer at each clinic visit.

Table 1. Grading Systems for the Assessment of Patients with Ulcerative Colitis.

System and Grade	Criteria
Global clinical grade*	
0	1–3 bowel motions per day; formed, without blood or mucus; no constitutional symptoms
1	1 or 2 more bowel motions per day than usual, change in consistency, or both; no constitutional symptoms
2	6 bowel motions daily; blood or mucus more than 3 times per week; no constitutional symptoms
3	More than 6 bowel motions daily; gross blood or mucus; constitutional symptoms
Sigmoidoscopy†	
0	Normal, smooth, glistening mucosa with visible vascular pattern; not friable
1	Granular mucosa; vascular pattern not visible; not friable; hyperemia
2	As grade 1, with friable mucosa but no spontaneous bleeding
3	As grade 2, but mucosa bleeding spontaneously
4	As grade 3, but clear ulceration and denuded mucosa
Histology (acute inflammatory activity)‡	
0	No polymorphs
1	Small number of polymorphs in the lamina propria with minimal infiltration of crypts
2	Prominent polymorphs in the lamina propria with infiltration of >50% of crypts
3	Florid polymorph infiltrate with crypt abscesses
4	Florid acute inflammation with ulceration

*The system is described by Truelove and Witts.[10]

†The system is described by Baron et al.[11]

‡The system is described by Truelove and Richards.[12]

Side Effects and Mood

The side effects of treatment were recorded at each visit and graded as absent, mild, moderate, severe, or severe enough to cause withdrawal from the study; they were scored from 0 (none) to 4 (severe) for analysis. Mood was assessed by questionnaire before, during, and at the end of the trial and 6 to 12 weeks later to identify any change after nicotine withdrawal.

Statistical Analysis

The base-line characteristics of the patients in the two study groups were compared by the chi-square test, Mann–Whitney test, Fisher's test, or unpaired t-test as appropriate. All P values are two-tailed. The changes in clinical, sigmoidoscopic, and histologic scores in the two groups were compared by analysis of covariance of the results for all patients who remained in the study for more than three days; the corresponding base-line value was the covariate. The effect of active treatment was assessed by the corresponding adjusted mean difference. Changes in the proportion of patients reporting mucus were compared by the Mantel–Haenszel method.[14]

Results

Base-Line Data

Seventy-seven patients entered the trial, but five in the nicotine group withdrew within three days and are not included in the analysis. One of the five had colitis of the entire colon, another did not use any patches, and three had severe side effects. Of the remaining 72 patients, 15 (5 in the nicotine group and 10 in the placebo group) withdrew before the end of the trial. The reasons for the premature withdrawals were side effects (two patients in the nicotine group and one in the placebo group), a change of mind (none and one, respectively), worsening symptoms (two and three), and ineffective treatment (one and five); all these patients had end-of-treatment assessment measures. Analyses of the 72 patients were based on the principle of intention to treat. Of the 72, 35 received nicotine and 37 placebo. The base-line characteristics of the two groups were similar (Table 2), as were their symptomatic and sigmoidoscopic findings (Table 3). The initial general well-being and histologic scores were both significantly higher in the nicotine group than in the placebo group (Table 3).

Outcome

The global clinical score, other clinical scores, and sigmoidoscopic and histologic scores improved in both groups, but the improvements were greater and more consistent in the nicotine group (Table 3). Comparisons of the improvement in the two groups by analysis of covariance, taking into account differences in disease activity at base line, revealed greater improvement in the nicotine group in global clinical grade, stool frequency, abdominal pain, fecal urgency, and histologic score (Table 3).

Seventeen of the 35 patients in the nicotine group had complete symptomatic relief and a global clinical grade of 0, as compared with 9 of the 37 patients in the placebo group (P = 0.03). The proportion of patients reporting no stool mucus at the end of the trial was 57

© N Engl J Med 1994; 330: 811–815

Table 2. Clinical Characteristics of 72 Patients with Ulcerative Colitis.*

Characteristic	Nicotine (N = 35)	Placebo (N = 37)
Sex (M/F)	20/15	21/16
Age (yr)	43±14	45±14
Weight (kg)	73±14	68.5±14
Duration of disease (mo)	77±67	76±57
Duration of flare-up (wk)	17±25	9±9
No. taking oral mesalamine	28	31
No. taking oral glucocorticoids†	7	6
No. withdrawn from study	5	10
No. completing study	30	27
Smoking history (no.)		
Lifelong nonsmoker	11	18
Former smoker	24	19
Smoking and onset of colitis (no.)		
Stopped smoking before onset	16	14
Stopped smoking after onset	4	3
Timing unknown	4	2

*Plus–minus values are means ±SD.

†The daily dose of glucocorticoids was 10 mg or less in all but one patient, who took 20 mg per day throughout the study period.

percent (20 patients) in the nicotine group and 22 percent (8 patients) in the placebo group (P = 0.002). The mean changes in each treatment group and the differences between groups are shown in Table 3.

Influence of Smoking History, Age, and Sex

The smoking history of the patients in the two groups was similar (Table 2). There was no difference in the severity of ulcerative colitis at base line between the former smokers and the lifelong nonsmokers. There was also no significant relation between age, sex, or smoking history and the response to nicotine, although the small numbers of patients in the subgroups limited the power of these analyses.

Nicotine Dose and Side Effects

Twenty-three patients in the nicotine group and 11 patients in the placebo group had side effects during the study (P = 0.002). Three patients, two in the nicotine group and one in the placebo group, withdrew because of side effects. Six patients in the nicotine group, five of whom were lifelong nonsmokers, had side effects within the first few days that improved when the dose was reduced to 5 or 10 mg daily. Most of the other patients in the nicotine group had some side effects in the first few days, which subsequently subsided. During the first four weeks of the study 20, 15, 12, and 6 patients, respectively, in the nicotine group had side effects, as compared with 10, 7, 6, and 4 patients in the placebo group. The side effects in the nicotine group were more severe; of the 20 patients with side effects in the first week, 12 had moderate or severe effects and 8 mild effects. The side effects in the placebo group included headache, nausea, and dizziness and were mild, with one exception that led to premature withdrawal. The most common side effects in the nicotine group, in order of frequency, were nausea, lightheadedness, headache, sleep disturbance or vivid dreams, dizziness, skin irritation, sweating, vomiting, and tremor. The occurrence of side effects in the nicotine group was related to the patients' smoking history; they occurred in 10 of the 11 lifelong nonsmokers as compared with 13 of the 24 former smokers (P = 0.04). There were no significant correlations between side effects in the first two weeks and plasma nicotine or cotinine concentrations.

Plasma Nicotine and Cotinine Concentrations

Plasma nicotine and cotinine concentrations reflect the dose of nicotine given. By the fourth week, when the doses of nicotine had become acceptable, 2 patients were using 5 mg per 24 hours, 1 was using 7.5 mg, 3 were using 10 mg, 19 were using 15 mg, and 10 were using 25 mg; the respective mean plasma nicotine concentrations in these five groups were 1.2, 1.0, 8.7, 8.3, and 12.1 ng per milliliter. The mean value in the patients using 15-mg patches (8.3 ng per milliliter) was lower than the mean value of 13.3 ng per milliliter in the pilot study, which was similar to the values reported by others.[15] Altogether, the patients using 15 or 25 mg of nicotine daily had plasma nicotine and cotinine concentrations that were approximately 35 percent of the average for smokers.[16]

The plasma nicotine and cotinine concentrations before the trial and after two, four, and six weeks of treatment reflected the patients' treatment assignments (Table 4). There was considerable variation between patients in the nicotine group, but the concentrations in individual patients were more consistent. Four patients in the nicotine group had low plasma nicotine concentrations at the end of the trial, suggesting poor compliance; subsequent inquiry revealed that they had not worn patches in the last few

Table 3. Results of Clinical, Sigmoidoscopic, and Histologic Assessments at Base Line and at the End of the Trial.*

Grade	Nicotine (N = 35)		Placebo (N = 37)		Difference†	P Value
	base line	end	base line	end		
Global clinical grade (0–3)	1.5±0.7	0.6±0.8‡	1.4±0.6	1.2±0.8§	−0.7	<0.001
Daily stool frequency	5.8±3.6	3.7±3.4‡	5.5±2.5	5.1±3.6	−1.6	0.008
Blood in stool (0–2)	1.3±0.8	0.5±0.8‡	1.3±0.7	0.8±0.8¶	−0.3	0.09
Stool consistency (0–2)	1.4±0.7	0.7±0.8‡	1.4±0.7	0.9±0.8‡	−0.2	0.20
Abdominal pain (0–2)	0.8±0.6	0.3±0.5‡	0.9±0.6	0.6±0.6§	−0.3	0.05
Fecal urgency (1–10)	5.5±2.6	3.3±2.7‡	6.3±2.3	5.3±2.7§	−1.7	0.009
Well-being (1–10)	6.7±1.4	7.2±1.8	5.8±1.8	6.1±2.3	+0.8	0.13
Sigmoidoscopy (0–4)	1.9±0.6	1.1±0.9‡	1.9±0.6	1.3±1.0‡	−0.3	0.19
Histology (0–4)	2.6±1.1	1.7±1.2‡	2.0±1.1	2.0±1.2	−0.6	0.03

*Plus–minus values are means ±SD. Changes were analyzed by analysis of covariance.

†Differences are grades in the nicotine group minus grades in the placebo group. A negative difference indicates a greater benefit from nicotine than from placebo for all measures except well-being.

‡P<0.001 for the comparison with base line.

§P<0.05 for the comparison with base line.

¶P<0.01 for the comparison with base line.

Table 4. Plasma Nicotine and Cotinine Concentrations in Patients with Ulcerative Colitis Given Transdermal Nicotine or Placebo for Six Weeks.*

Variable	Base Line	2 Weeks	4 Weeks	6 Weeks
Plasma nicotine (ng/ml)				
Nicotine group				
No. of patients	35	35	35	30
Mean (±SD) concentration	0.5±1.1	7.2±5.9	9.6±8.8	8.2±7.1
Range	<0.1–5.6	<0.1–18.4	0.4–36.8	<0.1–21.8
Placebo group				
No. of patients	37	35	33	27
Mean (±SD) concentration	0.4±0.8	0.3±0.5	0.3±0.2	0.8±2.5
Range	<0.1–4.7	<0.1–2.7	<0.1–1.0	<0.1–12.6
Plasma cotinine (ng/ml)				
Nicotine group				
No. of patients	35	35	35	30
Mean (±SD) concentration	2.5±6.6	102.1±52.3	149.3±86.0	120.4±97.6
Range	0.1–13.7	1.3–222.0	3.1–355.2	2.3–459.6
Placebo group				
No. of patients	37	35	33	27
Mean (±SD) concentration	1.6±3.7	5.0±14.9	2.9±8.8	3.3±9.9
Range	0.1–17.5	0.1–76.6	0.1–40.6	0.1–48.0

*Most samples were drawn about 12 hours after the application of the patch.

days of the trial. The plasma nicotine and cotinine concentrations in the placebo group were uniformly low in all but two patients, who had plasma cotinine concentrations of 48 and 76 ng per milliliter throughout the trial, including the base-line measurements. The cutoff point for distinguishing smokers from nonsmokers is 14 ng per milliliter.[17] On average, in steady state, each increase of 11 ng per milliliter in the plasma cotinine concentration reflects a nicotine intake of 1 mg (about one cigarette) in 24 hours.[18]

Mood Changes

During the trial most former smokers in the nicotine group felt well, but the lifelong nonsmokers tolerated treatment with more difficulty. After the trial none reported a craving for smoking, and none reported any smoking during the subsequent 12 weeks.

Discussion

We found that the condition of patients with active ulcerative colitis improved when they were treated for six weeks with transdermal nicotine. This positive outcome may be a step toward clarifying the relation between smoking status and colitis.

Although the patients in both the nicotine group and the placebo group improved, the improvement in clinical and histologic grades was greater in the nicotine group. These results are based on the study of a substantial number of patients. Most were able to tolerate nicotine given in stepwise increments, although many had side effects; three patients withdrew within three days of beginning treatment because of intolerable side effects, two withdrew later, and the dose was reduced in another six. The greater frequency of side effects in the nicotine group may have suggested that they were receiving nicotine and may have influenced the subjective assessments of colitis. However, many patients had no side effects, and the physicians responsible for the clinical assessments remained unaware of the group assignments.

Our results suggest that nicotine may be a suitable treatment in patients able to tolerate the drug, and they provide information on the proportion of patients who are able to tolerate transdermal nicotine. There may be a subgroup of patients with colitis who are more likely to respond to nicotine therapy, but our data do not provide a definitive answer because of the small size of the subgroups classified according to age, sex, smoking history, and duration of relapse. In some epidemiologic studies the relation between smoking and colitis has been stronger in men than in women.[4,19-21]

Our results are consistent with epidemiologic findings that ulcerative colitis is a disease of nonsmokers and those who have recently stopped smoking.[3,4] In previous uncontrolled studies, nicotine patches,[7] nicotine chewing gum, and smoking appeared to improve symptoms,[5,22,23] and a survey of 30 intermittent smokers with colitis revealed that half of them thought their colitis improved when they smoked.[24] Nicotine is probably the active agent and may act through an effect on inflammatory mediators[25] or by changing adherent surface mucus in the colon.[26-31] Whether nicotine will become an established treatment for patients with ulcerative colitis awaits further investigation. We have shown that it is tolerated by most patients and has a beneficial clinical effect. Better understanding of its mode of action could open the way to the development of alternative therapeutic approaches more acceptable than nicotine itself. Although addiction is a major problem associated with smoking, our patients did not have recognizable withdrawal symptoms after six weeks of treatment with nicotine, although many had absorbed doses equivalent to 35 percent of those absorbed by smokers. Addiction may depend on the sharp increases in plasma nicotine concentrations that follow smoking, which are unlike the steady release from transdermal patches.[32-34]

Currently available treatment for ulcerative colitis is far from satisfactory; there are only two major drugs, glucocorticoids and mesalamine, either of which may be poorly tolerated or ineffective in regular use. Alternative safe and effective treatments would be useful. Nicotine or agents that have similar effects on colonic mucosa may emerge as useful therapeutic agents for colitis.

We are indebted to Miss Bel Adamson, pharmacist, University Hospital of Wales, for trial randomization and prescriptions.

References

1. Harries AD, Baird A, Rhodes J. Non-smoking: a feature of ulcerative colitis. BMJ 1982;284:706.
2. Logan RFA, Edmond M, Somerville KW, Langman MJ. Smoking and ulcerative colitis. BMJ 1984;288:751-3.
3. Motley RJ, Rhodes J, Ford GA, et al. Time relationships between cessation of smoking and onset of ulcerative colitis. Digestion 1987;37:125-7.
4. Motley RJ, Rhodes J, Kay S, Morris TJ. Late presentation of ulcerative colitis in ex-smokers. Int J Colorectal Dis 1988;3:171-5.

5. Roberts CJ, Diggle R. Non-smoking: a feature of ulcerative colitis. BMJ 1982;285:440.
6. de Castella H. Non-smoking: a feature of ulcerative colitis. BMJ 1982;284: 1706.
7. Srivastava ED, Russell MAH, Feyerabend C, Williams GT, Masterson JG, Rhodes J. Transdermal nicotine in active ulcerative colitis. Eur J Gastroenterol 1991;3:815-8.
8. Benowitz NL, Jacob P III. Daily intake of nicotine during cigarette smoking. Clin Pharmacol Ther 1984;35:499-504.
9. Feyerabend C, Ings RMJ, Russell MAH. Nicotine pharmacokinetics and its application to intake from smoking. Br J Clin Pharmacol 1985;19:239-47.
10. Truelove SC, Witts LJ. Cortisone in ulcerative colitis: final report on a therapeutic trial. BMJ 1955;2:1041-8.
11. Baron JH, Connell AM, Lennard-Jones JE. Variation between observers in describing mucosal appearances in proctocolitis. BMJ 1964;1:89-92.
12. Truelove SC, Richards WCD. Biopsy studies in ulcerative colitis. BMJ 1956;1:1315-21.
13. Feyerabend C, Russell MAH. A rapid gas-liquid chromatographic method for the determination of cotinine and nicotine in biological fluids. J Pharm Pharmacol 1990;42:450-2.
14. Fleiss JL. Statistical methods for rates and proportions. 2nd ed. New York: John Wiley, 1981.
15. Tønnesen P, Nørregaard J, Simonsen K, Säwe U. A double-blind trial of a 16-hour transdermal nicotine patch in smoking cessation. N Engl J Med 1991;325:311-5.
16. Russell MAH, Jarvis MJ, Feyerabend C, Saloojee Y. Reduction of tar, nicotine and carbon monoxide intake in low tar smokers. J Epidemiol Community Health 1986;40:80-5.
17. Jarvis MJ, Tunstall-Pedoe H, Feyerabend C, Vesey C, Saloojee Y. Comparison of tests used to distinguish smokers from nonsmokers. Am J Public Health 1987;77:1435-8.
18. Galeazzi RL, Daenens P, Gugger M. Steady-state concentration of cotinine as a measure of nicotine-intake by smokers. Eur J Clin Pharmacol 1985;28:301-4.
19. Benoni C, Nilsson A. Smoking habits in patients with inflammatory bowel disease. Scand J Gasteroenterol 1984;19:824-30.
20. *Idem.* Smoking habits in patients with inflammatory bowel disease: a case-control study. Scand J Gastroenterol 1987;22:1130-6.
21. Srivastava ED, Newcombe RG, Rhodes J, Avramidis P, Mayberry JF. Smoking and ulcerative colitis: a community study. Int J Colorectal Dis 1993;8:71-4.
22. Hickey RJ. Nicotine and ulcerative colitis. Gut 1989;30:416-8.
23. Lashner BA, Hanauer SB, Silverstein MD. Testing nicotine gum for ulcerative colitis patients: experience with single-patient trials. Dig Dis Sci 1990;35:827-32.
24. Rudra T, Motley R, Rhodes J. Does smoking improve colitis? Scand J Gastroenterol Suppl 1989;170:61-3.
25. Motley RJ, Rhodes J, Williams G, Tavares IA, Bennett A. Smoking, eicosanoids and ulcerative colitis. J Pharm Pharmacol 1990;42:288-9.
26. Allen A, Bell A, McQueen S. Mucus and mucosal protection. In: Allen A, Flemström G, Garner A, Silen W, Turnberg LA, eds. Mechanisms of mucosal protection in the upper gastrointestinal tract. New York: Raven Press, 1984:195-201.
27. Allen A, Hutton DA, Pearson JP, Sellers LA. The colonic mucus gel barrier: structure, gel formation and degradation. In: Peters TJ, ed. The cell biology of inflammation in the gastrointestinal tract. Hull, England: Corners Publications, 1990:113-25.
28. Cope GF, Heatley RV, Kelleher J. Does cigarette smoking protect against ulcerative colitis by affecting colonic mucus production? Gut 1986;27: A618-A619. abstract.
29. Cope GF, Heatley RV, Kelleher J, Axon ATR. In vitro mucus glycoprotein production by colonic tissue from patients with ulcerative colitis. Gut 1988;29:229-34.
30. Pullan RD, Thomas GAO, Rhodes M, et al. Human colonic mucus: measurement of adherent layer in 'normals' and in inflammatory bowel disease. Gut (in press).
31. Zijlstra FJ, Srivastava ED, Rhodes M, et al. Effect of nicotine on rectal mucus and mucosal eicosanoids. Gut 1994;35:247-51.
32. Russell MAH, Feyerabend C. Cigarette smoking: a dependence on high-nicotine boli. Drug Metab Rev 1978;8:29-57.
33. Dubois JP, Sioufi A, Muller P, Mauli D, Imhof PR. Pharmacokinetics and bioavailability of nicotine in healthy volunteers following single and repeated administration of different doses of transdermal nicotine systems. Methods Find Exp Clin Pharmacol 1989;11:187-95.
34. Russell MAH. Nicotine intake and its control over smoking. In: Wonnacott S, Russell MAH, Stolerman IP, eds. Nicotine psychopharmacology: molecular, cellular, and behavioural aspects. Oxford, England: Oxford University Press, 1990:374-418.

Peanut Lectin Stimulates Proliferation in Colonic Explants From Patients With Inflammatory Bowel Disease and Colon Polyps

STEPHEN D. RYDER,* NEIL PARKER,* DAVID ECCLESTONE,† MUSTAFA T. HAQQANI,† and JONATHAN M. RHODES*

*Department of Medicine, University of Liverpool, and †Department of Histopathology, Walton Hospital, Liverpool, England

<u>*Background/Aims:*</u> The TF antigen (galactose-β 1,3-*N*-acetylgalactosamine α) is overexpressed in malignant and premalignant colonic epithelium. Previous studies have shown that peanut lectin (PNA), which binds TF, is mitogenic for normal human colonic epithelium. This study aimed to determine its effect on abnormal colonic epithelium. <u>*Methods:*</u> Crypt cell proliferation rate (CCPR) was measured using vincristine arrest and mucus synthesis by incorporation of radiolabeled *N*-acetyl glucosamine in colonoscopic biopsy specimens cultured with and without PNA. <u>*Results:*</u> Unstimulated CCPR was greater in patients with ulcerative colitis than in patients with histologically normal colon. PNA (25 μg/mL) produced a 25% average increase in CCPR in tissues from patients with ulcerative colitis, Crohn's disease, and colonic polyps. In ulcerative colitic biopsy specimens incubated with PNA, CCPR increased to more than double that of unstimulated normal colonic epithelium. In controls, the response to PNA was greater when adjacent specimens were positive for PNA (avidin-biotin) histochemistry than when they were negative. Mucus synthesis was increased by an average 75% over 24 hours by PNA. <u>*Conclusions:*</u> Increased TF expression by premalignant epithelia may allow stimulation of proliferation by dietary galactose *N*-acetylgalactosamine–binding lectins. If the hyperplasia-dysplasia cancer hypothesis is correct, this could explain the increased colon cancer risk in ulcerative colitis.

0016-5085/94/$3.00

© Lancet 1994; 343: 1075–1078

Clinical practice

Risks of bleeding peptic ulcer associated with individual non-steroidal anti-inflammatory drugs

M J S Langman, J Weil, P Wainwright, D H Lawson, M D Rawlins, R F A Logan, M Murphy, M P Vessey, D G Colin-Jones

Summary

Treatment with non-steroidal anti-inflammatory drugs (NSAIDs) is associated with an increased risk of peptic ulcer complications, but it is not clear whether some drugs are more likely than others to cause such complications.

We compared previous use of NSAIDs in 1144 patients aged 60 and older admitted to hospitals in five large cities with peptic ulcer bleeding and in 1126 hospital controls and 989 community controls matched for age and sex. Peptic ulcer bleeding was strongly associated with use of non-aspirin NSAIDs of any type during the 3 months before admission (411 cases, 351 controls; odds ratio 4·5 [95% CI 3·6 to 5·6]). The odds ratios for peptic ulcer bleeding were lowest for ibuprofen (2·0 [1·4–2·8]) and diclofenac (4·2 [2·6–6·8]), and intermediate for indomethacin, naproxen, and piroxicam (11·3 [6·3–20·3], 9·1 [5·5–15·1], and 13·7 [7·1–26·3]). Azapropazone and ketoprofen carried the highest risks (31·5 [10·3–96·9] and 23·7 [7·6–74·2]). Risks also increased with drug dose (low dose 2·5 [1·7–3·8], intermediate 4·5 [3·3–6·0], and high 8·6 [5·8–12·6]) for all drugs combined.

Appropriate clinical strategies could prevent many episodes of peptic ulcer bleeding: NSAIDs should be used only in patients who do not respond to other analgesics; the lowest possible doses should be used; and the least toxic NSAIDs should be selected.

Lancet 1994; **343:** 1075–78

See Commentary page 1051

University of Birmingham (Prof M J S Langman FRCP, J Weil MRCP, P Wainwright BSc), **Glasgow Royal Infirmary** (D H Lawson FRCPE); **University of Newcastle upon Tyne** (M D Rawlins FRCP); **University of Nottingham** (R F A Logan FRCP); **University of Oxford** (M Murphy MFPHM, M P Vessey FRS); **and Queen Alexandra Hospital, Portsmouth, UK** (D G Colin-Jones FRCP)

Correspondence to: Prof M J S Langman, Department of Medicine, Queen Elizabeth Hospital, Birmingham B15 2TH, UK

Introduction

Treatment with non-steroidal anti-inflammatory drugs (NSAIDs) is associated with liability to peptic ulcer complications.[1-4] Individual risks are low, of the order of 1 episode for every 10 000 NSAID prescriptions issued to people of 60 and older in the UK. However, because many such prescriptions are issued, there are many episodes: about two-thirds of the estimated 3500–4000 treatment-associated episodes can be attributed to treatment. These findings are consonant with the number of serious adverse reaction (yellow card) reports, to the UK Committee on Safety of Medicines.[5]

The reasons for individual reactions are unclear. Some clinical data and reports of suspected adverse reactions suggest that there may be large differences in individual NSAID toxicity,[2,4,5] whereas others indicate that there may be no substantial differences.[3,6]

Interpretation of findings is difficult. Spontaneous reports cannot be assumed to reflect accurately the frequency of adverse reactions in the community, and data collected in computerised prescription data-bases will not contain information about concurrent non-prescribed NSAID use or about potential confounding factors. Experimental clinical data, predominantly on endoscopic abnormalities in younger individuals, may have little relevance to serious disease in older people. We have carried out a large case-control study in which we compared previous anti-inflammatory drug use and various putative risk factors in older people admitted to hospital with peptic ulcer bleeding and in matched hospital and community controls.

Patients and methods

Patients aged 60 and older with confirmed diagnoses by endoscopy or at operation of acute upper gastrointestinal bleeding due to gastric or duodenal ulceration admitted to hospitals in Glasgow (200 patients), Newcastle (124), Nottingham (506), Oxford (143), and Portsmouth (170) between 1987 and 1991 were questioned by trained research associates. Standard questionnaires were used to seek details of all previous drug intake, whether prescribed or self-administered, and various other features including smoking habits, alcohol consumption, and history of gastrointestinal disease. Drug histories volunteered were compared with those recorded in hospital notes and by general practitioners where obtainable.

Each patient was matched wherever possible with 2 controls of the same sex and age (within 5 years) who were asked the same questions by the same research associate in relation to the period before the interview. 1 control was a hospital control, chosen from among acute medical inpatients (excluding those with acute myocardial infarction, acute rheumatic diseases, and active non-bleeding ulcers). The second control for each case was a community control, selected from the register of the same general practitioner as the case—the next person of the same sex and age (within 5 years) on the alphabetically ordered register. An

© *Lancet* 1994; 343: 1075–1078

	% of group		
	Cases (n=1144)	Hospital controls (n=1126)	Community controls (n=989)
Male	55·4	55·3	56·5
Aged (yr)			
60–69 yr	34·4	34·2	33·6
70–79 yr	39·2	40·6	40·7
≥80 yr	26·1	25·0	25·6
Social class			
I-II	22·1	18·7	22·9
III	51·3	52·7	58·6
IV-V	20·1	23·2	17·1
Home circumstances			
At home alone	30·5	33·0	29·2
At home with spouse	41·7	41·4	50·4
Sheltered accommodation	7·8	10·3	6·1
With home help	17·8	24·3	10·6
Risk factors			
Current smoker*	28·3	21·7	22·3
Current drinker†	16·1	10·7	12·9
Osteoarthritis	30·7	25·6	28·9
Rheumatoid arthritis	5·7	2·6	2·2

*Smoking at least one cigarette daily. †Drinking at least 7 units of alcohol per week.

Table 1: **Demographic characteristics of cases and controls**

interview with the community control was requested by letter, and, if necessary, by a second letter. Approval was given by local ethics committees.

To adjust for confounding factors, unconditional logistic regression was carried out with SAS software. Results for each non-aspirin NSAID were individually adjusted for: previous history of proven peptic ulcer disease, history of dyspepsia, smoking, and alcohol intake. Age and sex were not found to be confounders. Statistical significance tests for comparison of logistic regression models were based on the difference between −2 log likelihood scores. The reference category for all odds ratios was cases and controls not exposed to non-aspirin NSAIDs or aspirin.

For analyses of risk according to drug dose, categories were defined on the basis of recommendations in the *British National Formulary* (cut-off points for low, medium, and high dose categories for azapropazone <600, 600–899, ≥900 mg/day; diclofenac and indomethacin <75, 75–149, ≥150 mg/day; ibuprofen <1200, 1200–1799, ≥1800 mg/day; ketoprofen <100, 100–199, ≥200 mg/day; naproxen <500, 500–999, ≥1000 mg/day; piroxicam <10, 20, ≥30 mg/day).

Initial calculations suggested that if, as seemed likely, the bulk of prescribing was limited to four or five individual NSAIDs, a study of 1200 patients and their controls had a power of 80% to detect risks differing by three-fold between the drugs.

Results

We questioned 1144 patients, 1126 hospital controls, and 989 community controls. Cases and controls were generally well matched for social class and circumstances (table 1). Cases were slightly more likely than controls to be current smokers or drinkers and to have rheumatoid arthritis self-classified as active; there was no difference for osteoarthritis.

	Cases	Hospital controls	Community controls	Odds ratio (95% CI)*
Azapropazone	22	2	2	31·5 (10·3–96·9)
Diclofenac	71	30	31	4·2 (2·6–6·8)
Ibuprofen	88	61	75	2·0 (1·4–2·8)
Indomethacin	57	16	14	11·3 (6·3–20·3)
Ketoprofen	31	2	4	23·7 (7·6–74·2)
Naproxen	90	23	21	9·1 (5·5–15·1)
Piroxicam	57	13	11	13·7 (7·1–26·3)
Any non-aspirin NSAID	411	169	182	4·5 (3·6–5·6)
Not on NSAID or aspirin†	457	807	657	1·0

*All odds ratios from unconditional logistic regression model with terms for aspirin use, smoking, alcohol, previous peptic ulcer, and history of dyspepsia. For azaproprazone, to obtain convergence, aspirin use was not included. †Reference category.

Table 3: **Risks of ulcer complications associated with individual non-aspirin NSAID use during previous 3 months**

The diagnosed site of the bleeding ulcer was gastric in 506 patients and duodenal in 547. 52 had combined gastric and duodenal ulcers, 5 had combined bleeding and perforated ulcers, and 11 had perforated but non-bleeding ulcers (4 gastric, 7 duodenal). The remaining 23 had no evidence of peptic ulceration and were excluded from further analyses.

Non-aspirin NSAIDs were taken at some time in the 3 months before admission by 411 (36·7%) of the cases, and in the 3 months before interview by 169 (15·0%) of hospital controls and 182 (18·4%) of community controls.

Data were primarily assessed on whether subjects themselves said they had been taking the drug in question, but when possible this information was checked against hospital and general practice records. The information came from the patient and at least one other source in 338 (82%), from the patient only in 27 (7%), and from general practice or hospital records only in 46 (11%). The corresponding figures for hospital controls taking NSAIDs were 138 (82%), 19 (11%), and 12 (7%). For the community controls no hospital records were used and the information came from the patient and general practitioner notes in 124 (69%) and from the patient alone in 58 (31%).

Matched analyses were possible in only 836 of the 989 complete triplets because the codes detailing matching were stolen from a researcher's car. Matched analyses examining the association between the intake of any non-aspirin NSAID and ulcer complications gave an odds ratio of 3·5 (95% CI 2·4–5·3) with 1:2 matching for dichotomous exposures, whereas an unmatched analysis gave an odds ratio of 3·8 (3·1–4·5) compared with hospital and community controls combined (table 2). There was also a significant association of ulcer complications with aspirin, but not with paracetamol use. Odds ratios for matched and unmatched analyses agreed closely, but confidence intervals were wider for matched analyses because of the smaller numbers. All subsequent analyses were done with the combined control groups unmatched.

Six NSAIDs (aspirin, diclofenac, ibuprofen, indomethacin, naproxen, and piroxicam) were each taken during the 3 months before admission by at least 50 cases

Drug use in previous 3 mo	Cases (n=1121)	Hospital controls (n=1126)	Community controls (n=989)	Odds ratio (95% CI)‡	
				Matched	Unmatched
Any non-aspirin NSAID*	411	169	182	3·5 (2·4–5·3)	3·8 (3·1–4·5)
Aspirin†	324	175	179	3·1 (2·0–4·8)	2·9 (2·4–3·5)
Paracetamol (no NSAID)	140	229	199	1·1 (0·7–1·7)	1·1 (0·8–1·3)
No NSAID or aspirin§	457	807	657	1·0	1·0

*Irrespective of concurrent aspirin use.
†Irrespective of concurrent non-aspirin NSAID use.
‡For cases vs combined controls; unmatched analysis by crossed odds ratios.
§Reference category.

Table 2: **Risks of ulcer complications associated with drug use during previous 3 mo**

	Odds ratio (95% CI)			
	A	B	C	D
Diclofenac	4·4 (2·7–7·3)	3·6 (1·8–7·2)	3·7 (2·2–6·3)	35·6 (7·5–169·8)*
Ibuprofen	1·8 (1·2–2·7)	1·1 (0·6–1·9)	1·5 (1·0–2·3)	4·3 (1·6–11·8)*
Indomethacin	12·2 (6·6–22·4)	12·8 (5·4–30·5)	10·8 (5·5–21·2)	12·2 (2·8–52·7)*
Naproxen	9·8 (5·8–16·5)	5·8 (3·0–11·4)	10·0 (5·6–17·7)	14·8 (3·6–60·2)
Piroxicam	13·1 (6·8–25·5)	18·0 (7·2–45·0)	13·6 (6·9–27·0)	21·6 (2·2–213·5)*
Any non-aspirin NSAID	4·8 (3·8–6·0)	3·8 (2·9–5·1)	4·4 (3·4–5·5)	9·6 (5·5–16·8)

Unconditional logistic regression model with terms for aspirin use, smoking, alcohol, previous peptic ulcer, and dyspepsia. *Aspirin omitted from covariates convergence.
A = taken in previous month, irrespective of whether taken previously or with other non-aspirin NSAIDs.
B = taken in previous month, duration of use at least 3 months.
C = taken in previous month, irrespective of whether taken previously, excluding those taking a second non-aspirin NSAID.
D = started in previous month.

Table 4: **Risks of ulcer complications associated with use of selected non-aspirin NSAIDs in previous month according to duration of use and other concurrent NSAID use**

and two (azapropazone and ketoprofen) were taken by more than 20 cases each. No other NSAID was taken by more than 10 cases. The odds ratios for ulcer complications associated with the seven most commonly taken non-aspirin NSAIDs varied more than ten-fold from the highest (azapropazone and ketoprofen) to the lowest (ibuprofen; table 3). All risks were significantly greater than 1. Substitution of NSAID use in the previous month (irrespective of duration) did not substantially alter the risks (table 4, column A). Nor did odds ratios differ much among long-term users (column B) or when we excluded individuals who had taken both the relevant NSAID and another non-aspirin NSAID (column C).

Risks were generally greater among subjects who had started taking a NSAID during the previous month (table 4, column D). For the drugs combined, risks were significantly greater among those who had started a non-aspirin NSAID in the previous month than in those who had taken one both in the previous month and in the past year.

Among subjects who took a non-aspirin NSAID during the previous month risk increased with dose (table 5).

There were no consistent differences in risks associated with bleeding from gastric (odds ratio 4·0 [3·1–5·3]) or duodenal (4·7 [3·5–6·1]) ulceration for overall non-aspirin NSAID use or the five most frequently used NSAIDs. The same was true for aspirin (gastric ulcer 3·3 [2·5–4·4]; duodenal ulcer 3·1 [2·3–4·2]). Paracetamol use was not associated with either gastric or duodenal ulcer bleeding.

Dose*	Cases	Controls	Odds ratio (95% CI)†
Low	63	88	2·5 (1·7–3·8)
Medium	194	165	4·5 (3·3–6·0)
High	147	63	8·6 (5·8–12·6)
Not on NSAID or aspirin‡	457	1464	1·0

*For definitions of dose categories, see methods section.
†Odds ratios by unconditional logistic regression controlling for aspirin use, alcohol, smoking, previous peptic ulcer disease, and dyspepsia.
‡Reference category.

Table 5: **Risks of ulcer complications associated with use of non-aspirin NSAIDs within previous month according to dose**

Odds ratios for ulcer complications associated with NSAIDs did not differ substantially between age groups in the study (4·2 [2·7–6·4] for age 60–69; 4·4 [3·1–6·2] for age 70–79; and 4·8 [3·2–7·3] for age 80 or older).

Discussion

We have shown that in patients with bleeding ulcers there are clinically important differences in exposure rates to various NSAIDs. None of the NSAIDs for which we have sufficient data was free of risk. The risks could be calculated in two ways. First, results for each drug could be compared with the full set of other data, whether or not other NSAIDs or aspirin were taken concurrently. Second, the comparison could be restricted by contrasting findings for each individual drug with those for non-takers of other NSAIDs or aspirin.

The first method would be appropriate if only one agent were associated with risk but is inappropriate when several agents act as risk factors. The second method allows the selection of one particular drug so that takers of this drug can be contrasted with an appropriate base of non-takers of other non-aspirin NSAIDs. Its use gives higher (but appropriate) odds ratios, because takers of other NSAIDs have been removed from the "non-exposed" comparison group.

This study is one of the largest so far and therefore confidence intervals around estimates of risk are small. The data give consistent conclusions with similar rank orders for risk whether drug exposure was of short or long duration.

	Adjusted for non-prescribed drug use and social habits						No data on non-prescribed drugs, social habits, or both			
	International[11]	New Zealand[12]	Spain[4]	UK*	Italy[14]	Australia[15]	Canada[13]	UK[1]	UK[16]	USA[2]
Drug										
Azapropazone	..	..	..	31·5	..	..	..	..	23·4	..
Diclofenac	0·9/2·4†	3·3	7·9	4·2	4·4	1·7	4·0	..	3·9	..
Diflunisal	..	..	..	..	..	1·0	..	..	..	..
Fenoprofen	..	..	..	..	..	..	..	..	2·9	4·3
Ibuprofen	1·0	1·9	..	2·0	..	0·7	..	1·0	6·3	2·3
Indomethacin	..	13·9	4·9	11·3	9·2	2·5	5·1	4·1	5·4	3·8
Ketoprofen	..	..	2·6	23·7	..	3·6	..	..	3·1	..
Meclofenamate	..	..	..	..	..	..	..	..	18·0	8·7
Naproxen	4·0/12·0†	5·1	6·5	9·1	..	2·8	3·8	2·7	..	4·3
Piroxicam	..	6·6	19·1	13·7	7·7	4·8	4·2	6·5	..	6·4
Sulindac	..	3·6	..	..	..	2·1	3·1	..	..	4·2
Tolmetin	..	..	..	..	..	..	..	..	..	8·5
Total non-aspirin NSAID	74/50†	205	125	411	97	252	685	80	247	465
Controls										
Hospital	Yes‡	Yes	Yes	Yes	Yes	Yes	No	Yes	No	No
Population	Yes‡	No	No	Yes	No	Yes	Yes	Yes	Yes	Yes

*This study. †Gastric/duodenal ulcers. ‡One or the other according to study site.

Table 6: **Risks of ulcer complications or gastrointestinal hospital admission associated with non-aspirin NSAIDs in case-control studies**

Similar patterns were seen for gastric and for duodenal ulcer and for various age groups. The results cannot be explained by the operation of confounding influences; allowance for concurrent aspirin or other NSAID intake, smoking habits, alcohol consumption, or previous peptic ulcer disease did not substantially change the findings. We have previously failed to find evidence that smoking, alcohol consumption, poor social circumstances, or a history of ulcer affect the risk of NSAID-associated ulcer bleeding.[7] Recall or interviewer bias seem unlikely because there was good concordance between question outcome and hospital or practitioner records of drug prescribing. We are led to believe that non-steroidal anti-inflammatory activity is important by the observed dose-response effect and by evidence that paracetamol analgesic intake was not associated with risk.

Risk for most of the drugs, and overall, tended to be greater in those who had lately started treatment. New users may be more likely to take full recommended doses than those who have been taking drugs long term. Other explanations of this pattern include adaptive protective responses to injury during continued treatment, or withdrawal of a population susceptible to damage, for instance with dyspepsia, with time.

The high risks associated with azapropazone and ketoprofen exposure were unexpected. We checked for lost cases of exposure to these drugs in the control groups but found none. The risk for azapropazone was especially associated with treatment of gout, but no such differential risk was detected for ketoprofen or indomethacin nor NSAIDs in general. Numbers of control users of azapropazone and ketoprofen were small, however, so confidence intervals round these estimates of risk are large.

Fifteen studies have compared rates of non-aspirin NSAID exposure in patients who had peptic ulcer complications or required admission to hospital for upper gastrointestinal disease. Two[5,6] considered spontaneous reports of adverse reactions in the UK and the USA, and risks associated with individual drugs cannot be calculated. Another[8] used ibuprofen takers as the reference group, so overall rate ratios are unclear, and two[9,10] included very small numbers.

Table 6 summarises findings in the remaining ten studies.[1,2,4,11-16] Six took account of non-prescribed drug use and of potential for confounding due to individual social habits: ours is the largest of these. The other four did not take account of non-prescribed drug use, social habits, or both. The seven sets of data for ibuprofen show low rate ratios compared with those for indomethacin, naproxen, and piroxicam (nine data sets each). Results for sulindac and diclofenac are intermediate.

Rate ratios above 20 were found in the only two studies of azapropazone and in one of three of ketoprofen, and ratios approaching 20 were found in two of nine of piroxicam. Much lower risks were detected in the other two studies of ketoprofen, but all except two of the nine studies of piroxicam gave ratios higher than 5. Formal meta-analysis is inappropriate because comparable data sets cannot be extracted from all studies. Concurrent users of other NSAIDs are not generally separated, and use of over-the-counter aspirin or other drugs is not always known.

Among the 10 million people aged 60 and older in England and Wales, the overall risk of ulcer bleeding (10 000 episodes per year) is 1 in 1000. From our data, about 35% will be associated with non-aspirin NSAID use and another 28% with aspirin use. Expected population use rates for our data would be 15% for each. We can then (assuming no overlapping use) calculate that 3500 episodes occur in 1·5 million non-aspirin NSAID recipients, 2800 in 1·5 million aspirin recipients, and 3700 in 7 million receiving neither drug. If the use of aspirin and non-aspirin NSAIDs were abandoned, about 4000 episodes might be prevented. A more realistic strategy would be to use the NSAIDs with the lowest risk. This approach could halve the number of drug-associated events, with a persisting excess of 2000 episodes. The number of episodes could be cut further if all NSAIDs were used in low doses (table 5).

Few of our patients had rheumatoid disease. Others have found that many patients are unclear about why they are taking NSAIDs. We conclude that substantial risks of ulcer complications are associated with NSAID use and that appropriate clinical strategies could prevent many episodes. These strategies include administration of NSAIDs only to patients who do not respond adequately to non-NSAID analgesics, selection of the least toxic NSAIDs when such treatment is needed, and starting treatment with low doses.

We thank the Medical Research Council for support, our professional colleagues for their ready cooperation, and our monitors Ms Clare Clifford, Ms Gail Faulkner, Ms Gillian Paice, Ms Ellen Thompson, Ms Shirley Wood, and Ms Shirley Powell, without whom the study would not have been possible.

References

1 Somerville K, Faulkner G, Langman MJS. Non-steroidal anti-inflammatory drugs and bleeding peptic ulcer. *Lancet* 1986; i: 452–54.
2 Griffin MR, Piper JM, Daugherty JR, Snowden M, Ray WA. Non-steroidal anti-inflammatory drug use and increased risk for peptic ulcer disease in elderly persons. *Ann Intern Med* 1991; **114:** 257–63.
3 Carson JL, Strom BL, Soper KA, West SL, Morse ML. The association of non-steroidal anti-inflammatory drugs with upper gastrointestinal tract bleeding. *Arch Intern Med* 1987; **146:** 85–88.
4 Laporte JR, Carne X, Vidal X, Morena M, Juan J. Upper gastrointestinal bleeding in relation to previous use of analgesics and non-steroidal anti-inflammatory drugs. *Lancet* 1991; **337:** 85–89.
5 CSM Update 1. Non-steroidal anti-inflammatory drugs and serious gastrointestinal adverse reactions. *BMJ* 1985; **292:** 614.
6 Rossi SC, Hsu JP, Faich CA. Ulcerogenicity of piroxicam: an analysis of spontaneously reported data. *BMJ* 1987; 294: 147–50.
7 Somerville K, Faulkner G, Langman MJS. Risk factors for non-steroidal anti-inflammatory drug-associated upper gastrointestinal bleeding. *Eur J Gastroenterol Hepatol* 1992; **4:** 645–49.
8 Carson JL, Strom BL, Morse ML, et al. The relative gastrointestinal toxicity of the non-steroidal anti-inflammatory drugs. *Arch Intern Med* 1987; **147:** 1054–59.
9 Beard K, Walker AM, Perera DR, Jick H. Non-steroidal anti-inflammatory drugs and hospitalization for gastrointestinal bleeding in the elderly. *Arch Intern Med* 1987; **147:** 1621–23.
10 Holvoet J, Terriere L, Van Hee W, Verbist L, Fierens E, Hautekeete ML. Relation of upper gastrointestinal bleeding to non steroidal anti-inflammatory drugs and aspirin: a case-control study. *Gut* 1991; **32:** 730–34.
11 Kaufman DW, Kelly JP, Sheehan JE, et al. Non-steroidal anti-inflammatory drug use in relation to major upper gastrointestinal bleeding. *Clin Pharmacol Ther* 1993; **53:** 485–94.
12 Savage RL, Moller PW, Ballantyne CL, Wells JE. Variation in the risk of peptic ulcer complications with non steroidal anti-inflammatory drug therapy. *Arthritis Rheum* 1993; **36:** 84–90.
13 Garcia Rodriguez LA, Walker AM, Perez Gutthann S. Non-steroidal anti-inflammatory drugs and gastrointestinal hospitalizations in Saskatchewan: a cohort study. *Epidemiology* 1992; **3:** 337–42.
14 Nobili A, Mosconi P, Franzosi MG, Tognoni G. Non-steroidal anti-inflammatory drugs and upper gastrointestinal bleeding, a postmarketing surveillance case-control study. *Pharmacoepidemiol Drug Safety* 1992; **1:** 65–72.
15 Henry D, Dobson A, Turner C. Variability in the risk of major gastroinestinal complications from non aspirin non steroidal anti-inflammatory drugs. *Gastroenterology* 1993; **105:** 1978–88.
16 Garcia Rodriguez LA, Jick K. Risk of upper gastrointestinal bleeding and perforation associated with individual non-steroidal anti-inflammatory drugs. *Lancet* 1994; **343:** 769–72.

© Gastroenterology 1994; 107: 934–944

Factors Affecting the Outcome of Endoscopic Surveillance for Cancer in Ulcerative Colitis

WILLIAM R. CONNELL,* JOHN E. LENNARD-JONES,* CHRISTOPHER B. WILLIAMS,*
IAN C. TALBOT,† ASHLEY B. PRICE,§ and KAY H. WILKINSON*
*St. Mark's Hospital; †Colorectal Cancer Unit, Imperial Cancer Research Fund; and §Department of Pathology, Northwick Park Hospital, London, England

See editorial on page 1196.

Background/Aims: Cancer surveillance in patients with ulcerative colitis is of unproven benefit. This study assesses the efficacy and analyzes factors limiting the success of a surveillance program during a 21-year period in 332 patients with ulcerative colitis to the hepatic flexure and disease duration exceeding 10 years. _Methods:_ Clinical assessment and sigmoidoscopy with biopsy was undertaken yearly. Colonoscopy and biopsy every 10 cm throughout the colon was performed every 2 years or more often if dysplasia was found. Only biopsy specimens reported as showing dysplasia were reviewed. _Results:_ Surveillance contributed to detection of 11 symptomless carcinomas (8 Dukes A, 1 Dukes B, and 2 Dukes C), but 6 symptomatic tumors (4 Dukes C and 2 disseminated) presented 10–43 months after a negative colonoscopy. Dysplasia without carcinoma was confirmed in 12 symptomless patients who underwent colectomy. The 5-year predictive value of low-grade dysplasia for either cancer or high-grade dysplasia was 54% using current criteria. _Conclusions:_ Surveillance identified some patients at a curable stage of cancer or with dysplasia. Limiting factors were failure to include patients with presumed distal colitis, biennial colonoscopy, the number of biopsy specimens at each colonoscopy, and variation in histological identification and grading of dysplasia.

How best to manage cancer risk in patients with ulcerative colitis is controversial. Proctocolectomy during the first 10 years of disease eliminates the possibility of carcinoma. However, many patients are unwilling to undergo major surgery if their current quality of life is satisfactory. If an operation is later undertaken for symptomatic colorectal cancer, the 5-year survival rate is reportedly 31%–42%.[1–4] With the aim of reducing this mortality, the patient may be offered regular endoscopic surveillance for malignancy, the purpose of which is to detect patients at an especially high risk of cancer or to diagnose cancer at a symptomless, curable stage. No controlled study has compared the outcome of such regular investigation with a policy of investigation only when indicated by symptoms.

The results of seven prospective surveillance programs have been reported.[5–12] Advanced malignancy has occurred despite surveillance in some programs,[5,8,9] whereas the incidence of cancer in others has been so small that the cost-effectiveness of surveillance has been questioned.[11]

Previous reports from this hospital included patients undergoing only sigmoidoscopic surveillance before colonoscopy became available.[12–15] This report assesses the results of a surveillance program in which every patient was investigated by colonoscopy. In addition, the clinical significance of dysplasia as originally reported was compared with that diagnosed using current criteria.[16]

Materials and Methods

Patient Selection and Enrollment

Patients with disease duration from onset of symptoms exceeding 10 years who had evidence of macroscopic inflammation to the hepatic flexure at colonoscopy or previous double-contrast barium enema were enrolled in the program from 1971. The entrance date of this study is that of the initial colonoscopy undertaken after at least 10 years of ulcerative colitis.

Colonoscopic examinations and biopsies were performed every 2 years or more frequently if dysplasia was found. Patients also underwent clinical assessment during the intervening year, at which time rigid sigmoidoscopy and mucosal biopsy was performed. Reminder letters were sent to those patients who failed to attend the clinic or colonoscopy. Colonoscopy was undertaken after full bowel preparation and single biopsy specimens obtained at 10-cm intervals corresponding approxi-

Abbreviations used in this paper: **HGD, high-grade dysplasia; ID, indefinite dysplasia; LGD, low-grade dysplasia; ND, negative for dysplasia.**

0016-5085/94/$3.00

Long-term neoplasia risk after azathioprine treatment in inflammatory bowel disease

William R Connell, Michael A Kamm, Mark Dickson, Angela M Balkwill, Jean K Ritchie, John E Lennard-Jones

Summary

The incidence of various cancers, especially non-Hodgkin lymphoma (NHL), is higher among patients who receive azathioprine for immunosuppression after organ transplants than in the general population. We have studied the risk of neoplasia after azathioprine in 755 patients treated for inflammatory bowel disease.

The patients received 2 mg/kg daily for a median of 12·5 months (range 2 days to 15 years) between 1962 and 1991; median follow-up was 9 years (range 2 weeks to 29 years). Overall there was no significant excess of cancer: 31 azathioprine-treated patients developed cancer before age 85 compared with 24·3 expected from rates in the general population (observed/expected ratio 1·27, p=0·186). There was a difference in the frequency of colorectal (13) and anal (2) carcinomas (expected 2·27; ratio 6·7, p=0·00001); these tumours are recognised complications of chronic inflammatory bowel disease. There were 2 cases of invasive cervical cancer (expected 0·5), but no case of NHL. Among patients with extensive chronic ulcerative colitis there was no difference in cancer frequency between 86 who had received azathioprine and 180 matched patients who had never received it.

Thus, azathioprine treatment does not substantially increase the risk of cancer in inflammatory bowel disease.

Lancet 1994; **343:** 1249–52

St Mark's Hospital, City Road, London EC1V 2PS (W R Connell FRACP, M A Kamm FRACP, J K Ritchie MRCP, Prof J E Lennard-Jones FRCP); **and Cancer Research Campaign Epidemiology Group, Department of Public Health, University of Oxford, Radcliffe Infirmary, Oxford, UK** (M Dickson BSc, A M Balkwill MSc)

Correspondence to: Dr Michael A Kamm

Introduction

It is well established that the risk of various malignant disorders is higher in transplant recipients than in the general population. Two prospective studies of transplant recipients on immunosuppressive therapy (mainly azathioprine) reported significant excesses of non-Hodgkin lymphoma (NHL), squamous-cell skin cancer, and primary liver cancer.[1,2] Non-transplant patients who receive immunosuppressive drugs (mainly azathioprine) also show increased frequencies of these malignant disorders.[3] Even though the frequency of NHL is higher in rheumatoid arthritis than in the general population, the rate associated with immunosuppressive treatment is significantly greater.[4]

The risk of neoplasia in patients treated with azathioprine for inflammatory bowel disease has not been studied specifically. The increasing use of azathioprine (or its metabolite 6-mercaptopurine) in this setting makes such a study important. We have investigated the frequency of malignant disorders in a large population of patients with

Patient	Sex	Age (yr)	Diagnosis	Extent	Disease duration (yr)	Azathioprine duration (mo)	Follow-up (yr)	Carcinoma
1	M	79	CD	A, R	10	86	8	SCC anal canal
2	F	40	CD	A, R	22	99	16	SCC anal canal
3	F	67	CD	A, R	22	26	9	Adenocarcinoma R*
4	M	47	UC	Extensive	22	2	11	Adenocarcinoma R*
5	M	63	CD	C, A, R	28	31	11	Adenocarcinoma R*
6	M	52	CD	C, A, R	23	64	17	Adenocarcinoma R
7	F	44	CD	C, A, R	16	6	1	Adenocarcinoma R
8	M	62	UC	Extensive	14	84	12	Adenocarcinoma R
9	M	36	UC	Extensive	23	16	8	Adenocarcinoma R
10	M	26	UC	Extensive	13	39	9	Adenocarcinoma C*
11	F	63	UC	Distal	24	6	5	Adenocarcinoma C*
12	M	37	UC	Extensive	17	<1	10	Adenocarcinoma C*
13	M	72	UC	Extensive	52	14	42	Adenocarcinoma C
14	M	63	UC	Extensive	31	12	2	Adenocarcinoma C
15	M	63	UC	Extensive	16	79	8	Adenocarcinoma C
16	F	60	UC	Extensive	26	24	19	Stomach*
17	M	84	UC	Distal	11	5	4	Stomach
18	M	77	CD	Colitis	27	183	16	Carcinomatosis*
19	F	58	CD	Extensive	24	27	14	Bronchus*
20	F	74	CD	C, A	2	1	1	Bronchus*
21	M	60	CD	A, R	23	125	10	Bronchus*
22	F	46	CD	Colitis	19	4	10	Breast*
23	F	48	CD	I, C	21	12	14	Breast
24	F	49	CD	I, C	4	2	1	Cervix*
25	F	35	CD	TI	18	138	12	Cervix
26	F	32	UC	Extensive	13	4	3	AML
27	M	74	UC	Distal	6	5	6	BCC
28	F	39	CD	Colitis	1	<1	17	Dysgerminoma
29	F	60	UC	Extensive	5	10	3	PRV
30	M	54	CD	Colitis	32	20	2	SCC skin
31	M	68	UC	Distal	13	108	10	Secondary adenocarcinoma

CD = Crohn's disease; UC = ulcerative colitis; A = anal; R = rectal; C = colonic; I = ileal; TI = terminal ileum; SCC = squamous-cell carcinoma; AML = acute myeloid leukaemia; BCC = basal-cell carcinoma; PRV = polycythaemia rubra vera.
*Died from cancer before age 85.

Table 1: **Clinical details of 31 azathioprine-treated patients who developed malignant disorders**

inflammatory bowel disease who received a standard dose of azathioprine at one hospital and were followed up for a median of 9 years (range 2 weeks to 29 years).

Patients and methods

Since the introduction of azathioprine for treatment of inflammatory bowel disease at St Mark's Hospital, London, in 1962, a prospective register has been maintained of all patients who receive the drug and any complications are noted. We abstracted from case records details of the primary disease, including extent and duration of azathioprine treatment. A standard dose of 2 mg/kg daily was used. Details of any malignant disorder and deaths were noted. We sought information about patients who no longer attended the hospital from the referring general practitioner or current consultant physician. If cancer was present, relevant pathology reports were sought. If the required details could not be obtained in this way, the patient's current general practitioner was traced through the local Family Health Service Authority. When we could not find out whether a patient was still alive, he or she was identified in the National Health Service Central Register, which records death and cancer registration. Details of all causes of deaths were sought.

Observed numbers of deaths from all causes and from all neoplastic disorders before the age of 85 and before Dec 31, 1991, were compared with the numbers expected, calculated by applying national mortality rates specific for age, sex, and calendar period to the corresponding person-years at risk up to age 85. Numbers of cancer cases before age 85 were compared with those expected, calculated in the same way as for deaths but with rates recorded by the South Thames Cancer Registry as reference rates. Events after age 84 were excluded from the analysis, as is customary, because of the unreliability of applying reference rates to this open-ended age group.

We also compared rates of colorectal cancer in the subgroup of patients with chronic extensive ulcerative colitis (disease duration longer than 10 years and inflammation extending proximal to the hepatic flexure); 86 azathioprine-treated patients were compared with a similar group who had not received the drug (180). This group was identified from a separate register maintained prospectively at St Mark's Hospital since 1971 of patients with chronic extensive ulcerative colitis undergoing both clinical and endoscopic surveillance. Details of colorectal cancer are routinely recorded in this register. In this analysis of person-years at risk, the date of colectomy formed an additional endpoint. No such prospective register has been maintained for patients with Crohn's disease.

Observed and expected numbers were compared and tested for significance by two-sided *t* tests, assuming a Poisson distribution; 95% CI were calculated.

Results

Between 1962 and 1991, 755 patients with inflammatory bowel disease received azathioprine; 15 patients received lower doses than the standard 2 mg/kg daily because of myelosuppression. There were 366 female and 389 male patients; 450 had Crohn's disease, 282 ulcerative colitis, and 23 indeterminate colitis. The median duration of therapy was 12·5 months (range 2 days to 15 years). The median duration of follow-up from starting azathioprine was 9·0 years (2 weeks to 29 years), which gave 6975 patient-years of follow-up. 189 patients received azathioprine for less than 3 months because of short-term side-effects, poor response to treatment, or a decision to carry out colectomy.

At the end of the study (Dec 31, 1991) 671 patients were known to be alive in the UK, 11 had emigrated, and 6 were lost to follow-up. The remaining 67 had died before age 85, compared with 58·3 expected; this difference is not significant (observed/expected ratio 1·15 [95% CI 0·89–1·46, p = 0·264). There were 13 deaths from cancer (3 rectum, 3 colon, 1 carcinomatosis, 1 stomach, 1 breast, 3 lung, 1 cervix) compared with 16·4 expected (ratio 0·79, p = 0·459).

Cancer was recorded in 31 azathioprine-treated patients (table 1). This excess over the 24·3 expected was not

Site	Observed number	Expected number	O/E ratio	p†
Colon	6	1·40	4·29	0·0032
Rectum	7	0·84	8·33	0·0001
Anal canal	2	0·03	66·7	0·0004
Stomach	2	0·98	2·04	0·257
Lung	3	4·01	0·75	0·648
Breast	2	2·92	0·68	0·776
Cervix	2	0·50	4·00	0·090
NHL	0	0·52	..	0·691
Other neoplasms*	7	13·12	0·53	0·097
All neoplasms	31	24·3	1·27	0·186

*1 case each of: dysgerminoma ovary, basal-cell carcinoma, squamous-cell cancer of skin, carcinomatosis (primary tumour unknown), secondary adenocarcinoma of lymph node (primary tumour unknown), acute myeloid leukaemia, polycythaemia rubra vera.
†Two-sided p value.

Table 2: **Cases of carcinoma in azathioprine-treated patients compared with numbers expected from general population rates**

significant (table 2). There was, however, a significant excess of colorectal tumours (13 *vs* 2·24, p=0·00001). 8 of the colorectal tumours were associated with extensive ulcerative colitis, 1 with distal colitis, and 4 with long-standing complicated anorectal Crohn's disease. 2 patients with chronic complicated Crohn's disease developed squamous-cell cancer of the anal canal (expected 0·03, p<0·001). There were 2 cases of invasive cervical cancer (expected 0·5) and 2 skin cancers. The only case of NHL was in a man aged 89 (outside the age range of the study) who had chronic distal ulcerative colitis and had completed a 24-month course of azathioprine 3 years earlier.

There was a deficit of cancers other than those of the cervix, rectum, and anus (16 *vs* 22·05 expected) but the difference did not achieve significance.

Table 3 shows the observed and expected numbers of all neoplasms and of colorectal cancers according to the underlying disease and duration of treatment with azathioprine. The excess of malignant disorders is due to an increase in colorectal cancers, irrespective of the duration of azathioprine treatment.

We then compared the frequencies of colorectal cancer among patients who had had extensive ulcerative colitis for longer than 10 years and had or had not received azathioprine. 86 patients who had received azathioprine were matched with 180 patients who had not received the drug by sex, age (within 10 years), and duration of disease (within 1 year). Among azathioprine-treated patients there were 8 cases of colorectal carcinoma (expected 0·26), whereas among 180 non-treated patients there were 15 cases (expected 0·63); this difference is not significant (observed 8, expected from non-azathioprine rates 6·19, p=0·54).

Treatment period (yr)	Observed/expected cases (O/E ratio)		
	Crohn's disease	Ulcerative colitis	All patients
All neoplasms			
<1	6/6·71 (0·89)	8/6·59 (1·21)	14/13·30 (1·05)
1–2	4/3·24 (1·23)	3/1·51 (1·99)	7/4·75 (1·47)
2–5	0/1·91	1/0·99 (1·01)	1/2·90 (0·34)
>5	6/2·74 (2·19)*	3/0·63 (4·76)†	9/3·37 (2·67)‡
Total	16/14·6 (1·10)	15/9·72 (1·54)	31/24·32 (1·27)
Colorectal cancers			
<1	1/0·64 (1·56)	4/0·66 (6·06)	5/1·30 (3·85)
1–2	2/0·29 (6·90)	2/0·13 (15·4)	4/0·42 (9·52)
2–5	0/0·18	1/0·08 (12·5)	1/0·26 (3·85)
>5	3/0·25 (12·0)	2/0·04 (50·0)	5/0·29 (17·2)
Total	6/1·36 (4·41)	9/0·91 (9·89)	15/2·27 (6·61)

*p=0·06; †p=0·026; ‡p=0·008.

Table 3: **Cases of all types of cancer and colorectal cancer by underlying disease and duration of treatment**

Discussion

An excess of colorectal carcinoma is recognised in long-standing inflammatory bowel disease,[5-10] though not in transplant and non-transplant patients treated with azathioprine. Moreover, we found no significant difference in the frequency of colorectal cancer among patients with extensive ulcerative colitis between those who had and had not received azathioprine. Squamous-cell carcinoma of the anus has been reported previously in patients with chronic complicated anorectal Crohn's disease.[11-13]

Few studies have examined the frequency of malignant disorders in non-transplant patients treated with immunosuppressive drugs. One study of more than 1600 patients[3] found 6 cases of NHL compared with 0·55 expected, and another, of 396 patients treated with mercaptopurine and followed up for a mean of 5·4 years, found 12 cases of cancer, 1 of which was NHL of the brain.[14] The rarity of NHL in the brain in the general population and the very high frequency of the disorder among transplant recipients point to this case's being treatment-related. We know of only two other case-reports of NHL in inflammatory bowel disease treated with immunosuppressive drugs;[15,16] neither was of cerebral lymphoma.

We found no excess of NHL, though our study's power to detect an increased risk of this disorder is small (expected 0·5). It may also be relevant that among transplant recipients, who show the most striking excesses, the need for immunosuppressive therapy for graft survival means that the follow-up period usually approximates to the treatment period. If the increased risk of NHL were mainly related to current treatment (a possibility consistent with the unusually short latent interval), the power of our study to detect an increase would be even smaller, the corresponding expected value being only 0·1.

The slight excess of invasive cervical cancer is interesting since a significant increase in frequency has been reported in transplant recipients.[17,18] Both patients in our study developed the cervical cancer while receiving azathioprine. The overall deficiency of malignant disorders outside the large bowel is not statistically significant and may reflect underascertainment, chance, or both.

The potential risk of malignant disorders from azathioprine should be weighed against its proven efficacy and the effectiveness and side-effects of other medical therapy for inflammatory bowel disease. In ulcerative colitis, when other treatment has failed, azathioprine may defer or avoid the need for surgery. Colectomy, of course, is curative and eliminates the risk of carcinoma in patients with extensive disease. For patients with Crohn's disease who do not need or will not accept surgical treatment, other options are long-term corticosteroid therapy, which is associated with significant long-term morbidity, or other drugs that may be less effective, such as mesalazine or metronidazole.

WRC is supported by grants from the Wellcome Foundation and the British Council.

References

1 Hoover R, Fraumeni JF. Risk of cancer in renal-transplant recipients. *Lancet* 1973; ii: 55–57.

2 Kinlen LJ, Sheil AGR, Peto J, Doll R. Collaborative United Kingdom-Australasian study of cancer in patients treated with immunosuppressive drugs. *BMJ* 1979; ii: 1461–66.

3 Kinlen LJ. Incidence of cancer in rheumatoid arthritis and other

disorders after immunosuppressive treatment. *Am J Med* 1985; **78:** 44–49.
4 Kinlen LJ. Malignancy in autoimmune diseases. *Autoimmunity* 1992; **5:** 363–71.
5 Gyde SN, Prior P, Allan RN, et al. Colorectal cancer in ulcerative colitis: a cohort study of primary referrals from three centres. *Gut* 1988; **29:** 206–17.
6 Ekbom A, Helmick C, Zack M, Adami HO. Increased risk of large bowel cancer in Crohn's disease with colonic involvement. *Lancet* 1990; **336:** 357–59.
7 Greenstein AJ, Sachar DB, Smith H, Janowitz HD, Aufses AH. A comparison of cancer risk in Crohn's disease and ulcerative colitis. *Cancer* 1981; **48:** 2742–45.
8 Weedon DD, Shorter RG, Ilstrup DM, Huizenga KA, Taylor WF. Crohn's disease and cancer. *N Engl J Med* 1973; **289:** 1099–103.
9 Korelitz BI. Carcinoma of the intestinal tract in Crohn's disease: results of a survey conducted by the National Foundation for Ileitis and Colitis. *Am J Gastroenterol* 1993; **78:** 44–46.
10 Gyde SN, Prior P, Macartney JC, Thompson H, Waterhouse JAH, Allan RN. Malignancy in Crohn's disease. *Gut* 1980; **21:** 1024–29.
11 Somerville KW, Langman MJS, Da Cruz DJ, Balfour TW, Sully L. Malignant transformation of anal skin tags in Crohn's disease. *Gut* 1984; **25:** 1124–25.
12 Slater G, Greenstein A, Aufses AH. Carcinoma in patients with Crohn's disease. *Ann Surg* 1984; **199:** 348–50.
13 Church JM, Weakley FL, Fazio VW, Sebek BA, Achkar E, Carwell M. The relationship between fistulas in Crohn's disease and associated carcinoma. *Dis Colon Rectum* 1985; **26:** 361–66.
14 Present DH, Meltzer SJ, Krumholz MP, Wolke A, Korelitz BI. 6-mercaptopurine in the management of inflammatory bowel disease: short- and long-term toxicity. *Ann Intern Med* 1989; **111:** 641–49.
15 Gelb A, Zalusky R. Lymphoma in Crohn's disease occurring in a patient on 6-MP. *Am J Gastroenterol* 1983; **78:** 316.
16 Glick SN, Teplick SK, Goodman LR, Clearfield HR, Shanser JD. Development of lymphoma in patients with Crohn disease. *Radiology* 1984; **153:** 337–39.
17 Halpert R, Fruchter RG, Sedlis A, Butt K, Boyce JG, Sillman FH. Human papillomavirus and lower genital neoplasia in renal transplant patients. *Obstet Gynaecol* 1986; **68:** 251–58.
18 Alloub MI, Barr BB, McLaren KM, Smith IW, Bunney MH, Smart GE. Human papillomavirus infection and cervical intraepithelial neoplasia in women with renal allografts. *BMJ* 1989; **298:** 153–56.

Hepatitis C Virus Genotypes: An Investigation of Type-specific Differences in Geographic Origin and Disease

GEOFFREY DUSHEIKO,[1] HEMDA SCHMILOVITZ-WEISS,[1] DAVID BROWN,[1] FIONA MCOMISH,[2] PONG-LEE YAP,[2] SHEILA SHERLOCK,[1] NEIL MCINTYRE[1] AND PETER SIMMONDS[3]

[1]Department of Medicine, Royal Free Hospital and School of Medicine, London NW3 2QG, [2]Edinburgh and Southeast Scotland Blood Transfusion Service, Royal Infirmary of Edinburgh, and [3]Department of Medical Microbiology, Medical School, University of Edinburgh, Edinburgh EH8 9AG, United Kingdom

Because of the nucleotide sequence diversity of different isolates of hepatitis C virus, it has become important to clarify whether distinct genotypes of hepatitis C virus vary with respect to pathogenicity, infectivity, response to antiviral therapy and geographic clustering. We assessed nucleotide sequence variability in the 5′ noncoding region of hepatitis C virus, using restriction enzymes to analyze the distribution of hepatitis C virus genotypes, in 80 patients with chronic hepatitis C virus infection. Genotypes were correlated with demographic, clinical and histological features. Thirty-seven patients were infected with type 1, 10 had type 2 and 8 had type 3, and another 23 were infected with a new distinct hepatitis C virus type now classified as type 4. Two were infected with variants whose classification are uncertain. Types 1, 2 and 3 were found in patients from the United Kingdom, southern Europe, Asia, Africa and South America. Nineteen of 23 type 4 genotype isolates were from Middle Eastern patients, compared with 0 of 37 type 1 isolates ($p < 0.001$). Of 21 Middle Eastern patients, 19 (90.4%) had type 4 hepatitis C virus ($p = 0.001$, odds ratio = 9). We found no significant difference between the mean ages or mean serum aminotransferase concentrations between the various types. Types 1, 2, 3 and 4 were found in patients with mild-to-moderate disease or severe disease. However, 21 of 29 (72.4%) patients with type 1 who underwent liver biopsy had severe chronic hepatitis, cirrhosis or hepatocellular carcinoma histologically; 8 had mild or moderate chronic hepatitis without cirrhosis ($p = 0.03$, odds ratio = 2.6). Poor response to interferon-α was noted in patients with type 1 disease. Our data suggest significant geographic clustering of type 4 disease in the Middle East area. Although different hepatitis C virus genotypes can be encountered in both mild and severe disease, type 1 hepatitis C virus may have important clinical implications. The prognostic importance of these genotypes will require prolonged follow-up studies. (HEPATOLOGY 1994;19:13-18.)

Hepatitis C virus (HCV) can cause chronic liver disease: Chronic hepatitis, cirrhosis or HCC may ensue (1). Several isolates of HCV have been sequenced, and distinct genotypes have been proposed on the basis of sequence difference in both the coding and noncoding regions of the virus (2-8). A spectrum of disease ranging from mild and indolent disease to rapidly progressive cirrhosis has been observed in chronic HCV infection. It is therefore important to clarify whether particular genotypes of HCV correlate with pathogenicity, infectivity, response to antiviral therapy and geographic prevalence.

In this study, we used restriction fragment length polymorphism analysis of amplified viral sequences in the 5′ noncoding region (5′NCR) to study HCV genotypes in 80 viremic patients with chronic HCV infection (9). The observed genotypes correlated with demographic, clinical and histological features in patients from different regions and with differing grades of disease.

Our data suggest that the several HCV genotypes may be associated with benign or severe disease when patients are studied at one point in time. However, patients with type 1 HCV tend to have severe disease and to respond poorly to interferon (IFN). There is marked geographic clustering of distinct viral genotypes in these patients.

PATIENTS AND METHODS

One hundred one serum or plasma samples were collected from 95 patients with chronic HCV infection. The patients studied were consecutively referred for the investigation, diagnosis and possible treatment of chronic hepatitis. We found all patients to have chronic liver disease on the basis of their histories, physical examinations, past serum aminotransferase levels and histological status. The ethnic composition of this cohort reflects the cross-section of patients with chronic hepatitis referred to the Royal Free Hospital. As part of the investigation, we tested them for HCV antibody (anti-HCV). We selected patients for genotyping from serum samples stored in the previous 12 mo. Eighty patients were HCV RNA

Received March 1, 1993; accepted August 10, 1993.

Address reprint requests to: Dr. G.M. Dusheiko, Department of Medicine, Royal Free Hospital and School of Medicine, Pond Street, Hampstead, London NW3 2QG, UK.

0270-9139/94 $1.00 + .10 **31/1/51173**

positive and could be genotyped. Second serum samples from four HCV RNA–positive patients were included under code so that we might assess reproducibility of typing. Demographic and clinical details, including age, birthdate, ethnic origin, suspected mode of acquisition, associated diseases, serum ALT, AST, bilirubin, albumin, prothrombin time, treatment and response to treatment were obtained for these patients. The group comprised 55 men and 25 women (mean ages = 47.5 and 47.3 yr, respectively). These patients originated from the United Kingdom (n = 20), Italy (n = 20), Greece (n = 6), Egypt (n = 16) and other Middle Eastern countries (one each from Bahrain, Saudi Arabia, Iraq, Lebanon, Yemen), other European countries (n = 8) (Spain, Portugal, Cyprus, France, Turkey), Asia (n = 1) (Pakistan), Africa (n = 1) (Ghana) and South America (n = 1) (Brazil). Samples were coded, and the investigators undertaking the genotyping had no knowledge of the clinical status or the ethnic origin of the patients. Most of the patients who were not from the United Kingdom lived in their countries of origin and had been referred to the Royal Free Hospital for investigation or treatment. Four patients (ethnic Middle Eastern, Italian and Greek) resided in the United Kingdom but had emigrated as adults to the United Kingdom from their countries of birth. These patients were classified according to country of origin. The noteworthy difference in the epidemiological pattern was the fact that a relatively high proportion of United Kingdom patients (47.3%) had used intravenous drugs reflecting the main pathogenesis of disease in the United Kingdom. Seven of this cohort of patients had received blood transfusions that could be linked to the acquisition of hepatitis C. Four patients had received blood products. In the absence of definite exposure in the remainder, the exact onset and hence the duration of chronic hepatitis were difficult to ascertain in patients who were born in countries where the disease is more prevalent and who may have acquired their disease through community transmission.

Liver biopsies were performed in 68 patients for diagnostic reasons. Twelve patients did not undergo biopsies; four had hemophilia, and three had only minimally increased serum aminotransferase levels. Biopsy specimens were coded for the purposes of this analysis into five categories according to previously recognized morphological features of chronic hepatitis C (10): (a) histological mild chronic hepatitis, (b) moderate or severe chronic hepatitis, (c) CAH and cirrhosis, (d) inactive cirrhosis and (c) HCC. Four patients had clinical stigmata of cirrhosis and portal hypertension (f). One patient had hepatic lymphoma. To correlate genotypes with histological and clinical severity of disease, we graded patients in categories 1 and 2 as having mild-to-moderate disease and patients in categories 3, 4, 5 or 6 as having severe disease. Most biopsies were performed around the time of serum sampling. Plasma samples were collected in EDTA, and all serum samples were stored at −20° C until they could be studied under code. Anti-HCV was measured by means of second-generation immunoassay (Ortho Diagnostic Systems, Raritan, NJ).

One-way ANOVA and Fisher's exact test were used to determine the statistical significance of differences between groups.

Extraction of RNA. RNA was extracted from 100-μl aliquots of plasma by means of addition of 1 ml RNAzol solution (2 mol/L guanidinium thiocyanate, 12.5M sodium citrate [pH 7.0], 0.25% [wt/vol] N-lauroylsarcosine, 0.05 mol/L 2-mercaptoethanol, 100 mmol/L sodium acetate [pH 4.0] and 50% [wt/vol] water-saturated phenol) as previously described and mixed until the precipitate dissolved (11). After addition of 100 μl chloroform, each sample was spun for 5 min at 14,000 *g*; the aqueous phase was reextracted with 0.5 ml chloroform. RNA was precipitated by means of addition of an equal volume of isopropanolol and incubated at −20° C for at least 1 hr. An RNA pellet was produced on centrifugation at 14,000 *g* for 15 min at 4° C; it was washed in 1 ml 70% cold ethanol solution, dried and resuspended in 20 μl diethylpyrocarbonate-treated distilled water. Two-milliliter volumes of HCV RNA–negative samples were subjected to ultracentrifugation at 200,000 *g* for 2 hr; and the pellet was reextracted as described above. Extraction from the larger volume of plasma yielded another three positive samples.

PCR and Typing. RNA was reverse-transcribed with primer 940, and cDNA was amplified in a two-stage nested PCR reaction with primers 940/939, followed by primers 209/211, as described previously (12). The PCR product was radiolabeled with [^{35}S]dATP and analyzed by means of restriction endonuclease cleavage as previously described (9). We ensured the completeness of restriction endonuclease digestion by adding an excess of enzyme to a small amount of radiolabeled DNA. Samples were cleaved with *Scr*FI and a combination of *Hae*III/*Rsa*I in two separate reactions so that we might identify HCV types 1/4, 2 and 3. Sequence analysis in the 5′NCR of HCV from some patients revealed a relatively homogenous group of novel sequence variants in both the 5′NCR and the core region distinct from HCV types 1, 2 and 3; this group has been provisionally designated HCV type 4 (13). Type 4 variants show the same cleavage patterns with *Hae*III/*Rsa*I and *Scr*FI as type 1 but can be further differentiated by a further cleavage reaction with *Hinf*I. All type 1 sequences are uncleaved by *Hinf*I (pattern a), whereas all type 4 sequences contained one or two potential cleavage sites with this enzyme (pattern b: fragments 107 and 142 bp [in order, 5′ to 3′]; pattern c: fragments of 56, 51 and 142 bp) (13).

All but two samples from the patients with chronic hepatitis C in this study could be designated as type 1, 2, 3 or 4 with the method described above. However, the remaining two samples showed unusual cleavage patterns for *Hae*III/*Rsa*I. One produced bands of 44 bp, 172 bp, 9 bp and 26 bp (pattern h), and one produced bands of 216 bp, 9 bp and 26 bps (pattern i). The samples were sequenced and found to be similar to each other. They were unlike any of the known HCV types (data not shown) and also distinct from EG-28, the other sequence showing pattern i with *Hae*III/*Rsa*I (14). Because they cannot be classified, they will subsequently be referred to as *type U.*

RESULTS

Typing of Study Subjects. RNA was extracted from 101 samples from patients with chronic hepatitis C and amplified with primers in the 5′NCR. Of these, 84 samples from 80 patients were PCR positive, enabling us to perform HCV typing with restriction fragment length polymorphism analysis. This was initially carried out with *Hae*III/*Rsa*I and *Scr*FI, permitting identification of 10 type 2 and 8 type 3 variants. Samples showing electrophoretic patterns aA/B or bA/B (type 1 or type 4) were further analyzed by means of cleavage with *Hinf*I. Using the criteria described in Materials and Methods, we found that 37 patients had type 1, 10 had type 2 and 8 had type 3. A further 23 were infected with the distinct HCV type provisionally termed type 4; two patients were infected with a yet-uncharacterized type with new restriction patterns with *Hae*III/*Rsa*I (U). Samples from the four patients tested twice under code yielded the same patterns in both tests.

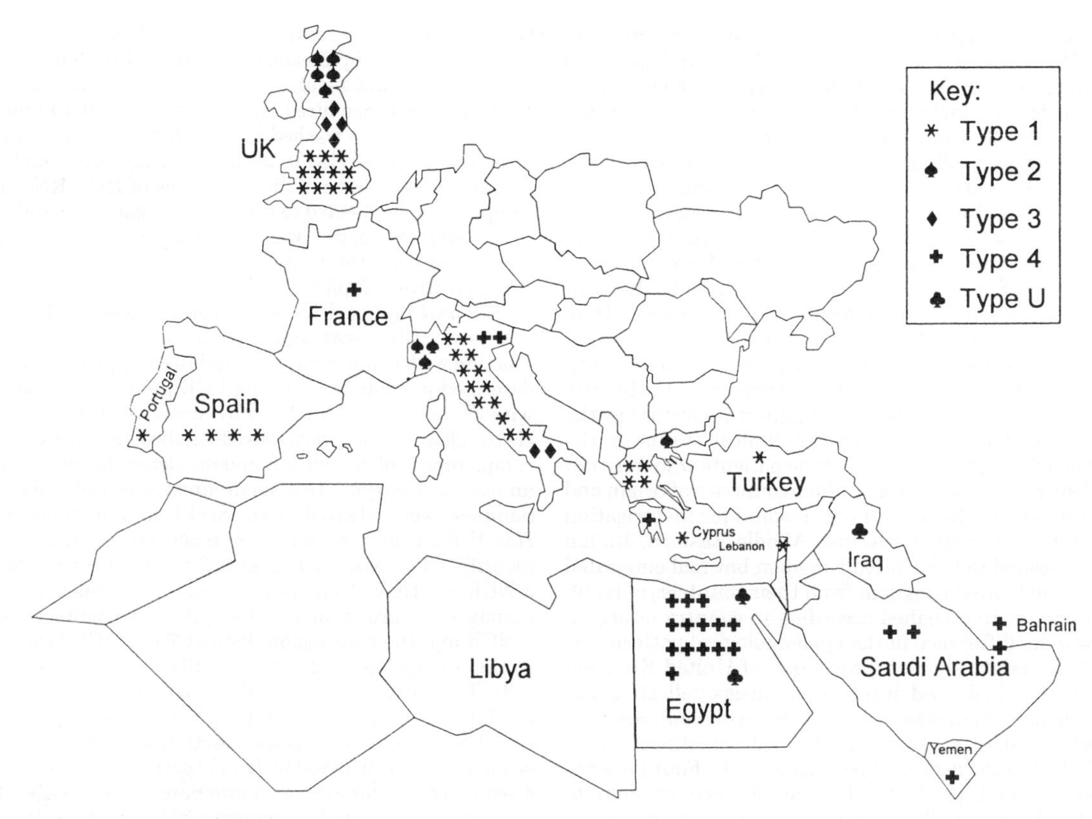

FIG. 1. Geographic distribution of viral genotypes in European and Middle Eastern patients. Three patients—one each from Ghana (type 1), Brazil and Pakistan (type 3)—are not included in the map.

We noted a significant association between geographic origin and genotype (Fig. 1). Types 1, 2 and 3 were found in patients from the United Kingdom, southern Europe, Asia, Africa and South America but were rare in Middle Eastern patients. However, we found a significant association between type 4 and Middle Eastern patients: 19 of 23 type 4 isolates were from Middle Eastern patients, compared with 0 of 37 with type 1 ($p < 0.001$). The Middle Eastern patients originated from Bahrain, Egypt, Saudi Arabia, Yemen, Lebanon and Iraq. The remaining four with type 4 were of Greek, Italian ($n = 2$) and Indo-French origin. Interestingly, one of the Italian patients had lived in Egypt for 20 yr. Conversely, 19 of 21 (90.4%) Middle Eastern patients were infected with type 4. Two were infected with type U ($p < 0.005$, odds ratio = 9).

Other Parameters. The mean ages of patients with genotypes 1, 2, 3, 4 and U were 48.1, 52.6, 42.0, 47.2 and 34.8 yr, respectively. We found no significant difference between these means (ANOVA). The mean serum ALT concentrations (128.7, 160.6, 105.2, 140.6 and 127 IU/L) did not differ significantly between different genotypes; nor were there significant differences between the serum albumin values.

Histology. Types 1, 2, 3, 4 and U were found in patients with mild-to-moderate severe disease (Table 1). However, 21 of 29 patients (72.4%) with type 1 who had undergone liver biopsy (or in whom the stage of disease could be assessed clinically) had severe disease (i.e., severe CAH, cirrhosis or HCC); the other 8 patients had mild or moderate chronic hepatitis histologically ($p < 0.03$, odds ratio = 2.6). No such difference within each type was seen in patients with type 2, 3 or 4. However, the number of patients with type 2 or 3 was small. We found no statistically significant difference in disease severity in patients with type 1 compared with those with type 4: 21 of 29 vs. 11 of 19 had severe chronic hepatitis (one-tailed p value = 0.4, Fisher's exact test).

Treatment Responses. Treatment responses, defined as normal or more than 50% reduction of serum ALT during treatment, are detailed in Table 2. Forty patients had been treated with IFN-α or ribavirin. Twenty-two (55%) responded with decreased or normal serum transaminases. One of eight type 1 patients responded to interferon, compared with three of seven patients with type 4 ($p = 0.33$, Fisher's exact test). Two of five patients with type 1 responded to ribavirin, compared with nine of nine with type 4 ($p = 0.30$). Seven of the ribavirin-treated patients with type 4 had cirrhosis. Three of 13 with type 1 responded to treatment with ribavirin or IFN-α, vs. 12 of 16 with type 4 ($p = 0.09$) and 19 of 30 with types 2, 3 and 4 combined ($p = 0.12$, odds ratio = 0.364).

TABLE 1. HCV genotypes and grade of liver disease

Genotype	Mild-to-moderate chronic hepatitis (%)	Severe chronic hepatitis (%)	p Value[a]
1	8 (27.5)	21 (72.4)	0.03
2	4 (44.4)	5 (55.5)	NS
3	5 (62.5)	3 (37.5)	NS
4	8 (42.1)	11 (57.8)	0.39
U	1 (50)	1 (50)	NS
TOTAL	26 (38%)	41 (61.1)	

Twelve patients did not undergo biopsies. One patient had hepatic lymphoma and is not included.
[a]Fisher's exact test for 2 × 2 tables (one-tailed p value).

TABLE 2. HCV genotype and response to antiviral therapy

Genotype	IFN-treated	IFN response	Ribavirin-treated	Ribavirin response	TOTAL treated	TOTAL response
1	8	1	5	2	13	3
2	3	3	1	1	4	4
3	3	2	2	1	5	3
4	7	3	9	9	16	12
U	2	0	0	0	2	0
TOTAL	23	9	17	13	40	22

Response to treatment was evaluated for patients with types 1 and 4. IFN: type 1 vs. type 4, $p = 0.33$; ribavirin: type 1 vs. type 4, $p = 0.30$; IFN or ribavirin: type 1 vs. type 4, $p = 0.09$.

DISCUSSION

HCV is typical of RNA viruses in having a quasispecies nature due to relatively high mutation rates, particularly in the envelope regions of the genome (15, 16). Indeed, its genetic heterogeneity may be involved in persistence of infection (17-19). Comparison of the sequences of the American prototype and Japanese isolates indicated that these viruses are genetically distinguishable (8, 20, 21). Subsequent cloning and sequencing of European and Asian isolates suggested further heterogeneity in isolates of HCV worldwide (22-26). Several genotypes have been proposed on the basis of nucleotide sequence variation or typing by means of specific primer amplification (4, 27). Direct sequence analysis of PCR products after reverse transcription has indicated that several of the observed genotypes coexist in several geographic regions (5, 7, 12).

We previously reported a phylogenetic analysis of sequence in the 5′NCR, core and nonstructural 3′ and 5′ regions, the results of which suggested an alternate classification of HCV into types 1, 2, 3 and 4 (12, 13). In this study we analyzed HCV variants in 80 patients with chronic hepatitis C from different geographic regions by means of restriction enzyme cleavage. We found type 4 to be significantly more prevalent in Middle Eastern patients. A high prevalence of hepatitis C has previously been reported in Middle Eastern countries, including Egypt, Saudi Arabia and Yemen (28, 29). Most of the patients we studied were likely infected in their countries of origin. It was of interest that one Italian patient with type 4 HCV had lived in Egypt for 20 yr. Our study does not rule out the possibility that type 4 HCV may be encountered in regions other than the Middle East, and further point-prevalence studies will be required. The French patient we studied was infected with type 4. However, as in other parts of Europe, type 1 is actually predominant in France (30).

HCV genotypes may correlate with severity of liver disease, cirrhosis in particular. Our analysis suggests that different HCV genotypes can be found in patients with mild or severe disease. We noted, however, a trend toward more advanced hepatic lesions in patients infected with type 1. Higher serum ALT concentrations have previously been reported in asymptomatic Scottish blood donors with type 3 HCV compared with donors with type 1 (9). However, this finding was not confirmed in this study of patients who were referred for disease, and it may reflect the fact that serum aminotransferase levels at one point in time are a poor indicator of the long-term natural history of HCV infection. In a disease with a long natural history, we believe it important to consider histological liver disease as a marker of cumulative damage to the liver and disease severity rather than serum aminotransaminase levels.

The issue of genotype pathogenicity in a disease such as chronic HCV infection is complex. Other host and viral factors will also influence the outcome. In some patients, disease severity may be related to the duration of disease, but this is frequently difficult to establish in patients who may have acquired the disease by inapparent transmission in childhood. Other factors, including viral load, mode of acquisition, reinfections, host immunity, genetic factors, age, coexistent viral and parasitic infection and alcohol may conceivably determine the outcome of infection (31-34). Our study did not address these factors but points to a possible relationship between geographic origin and the histological range of the disease for a given genotype. Future studies of the significance of HCV genotypes will need to take other variables into account. The significance of genotypes determining the clinical features of acute hepatitis C might also be of interest, but it was not addressed in this study of chronic disease.

We also examined the correlation of HCV genotypes and response to IFN or ribavirin. These two agents have different antiviral actions against HCV; we have examined their efficacy separately and together. It is possible that viral load is one determinant of response to therapy with either of these agents. Our data support the possibility that patients with type 1, who tended to have more advanced disease, respond poorly to IFN-α. Japanese patients infected with HCV type 1b (Okamoto II) have lower response rates to IFN-α than do patients with HCV type 2a (Okamoto III) (27, 35, 36). However, logarithmic concentrations of HCV RNA were higher in the latter group, and the patients were older. These variables, rather than genotype, may be independent predictors of response. It has also been suggested that infection by multiple species, rather than by a specific genotype, determines outcome of treatment (37). Response in our patients was measured according to decreases in serum aminotransferase levels, but this should be qualified as not necessarily indicative of a virological response because it does not preclude later relapse. Although a high proportion of type 4 patients had improved serum ALT levels with ribavirin treatment, the antiviral effect of this drug is uncertain (38). Understanding the restricted responsiveness of patients may be of critical importance in the selection of patients for IFN therapy; however, many patients will need to be carefully studied with appropriate definitions of virological response and prolonged follow-up (27).

The recognition of specific genotypes will become important in designing primers for optimal diagnostic testing of HCV RNA; the latter test is increasingly used as a measure of infectivity, disease, viremia and response to therapy (39, 40). Moreover, the recognition of specific genotypes will be useful in studying the epidemiology, transmission, clinical manifestations and pathogenesis of the disease. However, clinical evaluation of the virulence of genotypes is complex. These studies will require standardized nomenclature and typing for evaluation and prolonged follow-up studies, including histological assessment, in view of the relatively long natural history of the disease. Indeed sequential studies of the emergence of mutant types during the course of the disease may be necessary to understand the role of genotypes in disease (16, 41).

REFERENCES

1. Dusheiko GM. Hepatitis C virus. In: Pounder RE, ed. Recent advances in gastroenterology. 9th ed. Edinburgh: Churchill Livingstone, 1992:195-216.
2. Chen P-J, Lin M-H, Tu S-J, Chen D-S. Isolation of a complementary DNA fragment of hepatitis C virus in Taiwan revealed significant sequence variations compared with other isolates. HEPATOLOGY 1991;14:73-78.
3. Choo QL, Richman KH, Han JH, Berger K, Lee C, Dong C, Gallegos C, et al. Genetic organization and diversity of the hepatitis C virus. Proc Natl Acad Sci USA 1991;88:2451-2455.
4. Okamoto H, Kurai K, Okada S-I, Yamamoto K, Lizuka H, Tanaka T, Fukuda S, et al. Full-length sequence of a hepatitis C virus genome having poor homology to reported isolates: comparative study of four distinct genotypes. Virology 1992;188:331-341.
5. Bukh J, Purcell RH, Miller RH. Sequence analysis of the 5′ noncoding region of hepatitis C virus. Proc Natl Acad Sci USA 1992;89:4942-4946.
6. Cuypers HTM, Winkel IN, Van der Poel CL, Reesink HW, Lelie PN, Houghton M, Weiner A. Analysis of genomic variability of hepatitis C virus. J Hepatol 1991;13:(suppl 4):S15-S19.
7. Cha T-A, Beall E, Irvine B, Kolberg J, Chien D, Kuo G, Urdea MS. At least five related, but distinct, hepatitis C viral genotypes exist. Proc Natl Acad Sci USA 1992;89:7144-7148.
8. Enomoto N, Takada A, Nakao T, Date T. There are two major types of hepatitis C virus in Japan. Biochem Biophys Res Commun 1990;170:1021-1025.
9. McOmish F, Chan S-W, Dow BC, Gillon J, Frame WD, Crawford RJ, Yap P-L, et al. Detection of three types of hepatitis C virus in blood donors: investigation of type-specific differences in serologic reactivity and rate of alanine aminotransferase abnormalities. Transfusion 1993;33:7-13.
10. Scheuer PJ, Ashrafzadeh P, Sherlock S, Brown D, Dusheiko GM. The pathology of hepatitis C. HEPATOLOGY 1992;15:567-571.
11. Chomczynski P, Sacchi N. Single-step method of RNA isolation by acid guanidinium thiocyanate-phenol-chloroform extraction. Anal Biochem 1987;162:156-159.
12. Chan S-W, McOmish F, Holmes EC, Dow B, Peutherer JF, Follett E, Yap PL, et al. Analysis of a new hepatitis C virus type and its phylogenetic relationship to existing variants. J Gen Virol 1992; 73:1131-1141.
13. Simmonds P, McOmish F, Yap PL, Chan S-W, Lin CK, Dusheiko G, Saeed AA, et al. Sequence variability in the 5′ non-coding region of hepatitis C virus: Identification of a new virus type and restrictions on sequence diversity. J Gen Virol 1993;74:661-668.
14. Williams BRG, Kerr IM. Inhibition of protein synthesis by 2′-5′ linked adenine oligonucleotides in intact cells. Nature 1978;276: 88-89.
15. Murakawa K, Esumi M, Kato T, Kambara H, Shikata T. Heterogeneity within the nonstructural protein 5-encoding region of hepatitis C viruses from a single patient. Gene 1992;117: 229-232.
16. Martell M, Esteban JI, Quer J, Genescà J, Weiner A, Esteban R, Guardia J, et al. Hepatitis C virus (HCV) circulates as a population of different but closely related genomes: quasispecies nature of HCV genome distribution. J Virol 1992;66:3225-3229.
17. Kato N, Ootsuyama Y, Tanaka T, Nakagawa M, Nakazawa T, Muraiso K, Ohkoshi S, et al. Marked sequence diversity in the putative envelope proteins of hepatitis C viruses. Virus Res 1992;22:107-123.
18. Abe K, Inchauspe G, Fujisawa K. Genomic characterization and mutation rate of hepatitis C virus isolated from a patient who contracted hepatitis during an epidemic of non-A, non-B hepatitis in Japan. J Gen Virol 1992;73:2725-2729.
19. Weiner AJ, Geysen HM, Christopherson C, Hall JE, Mason TJ, Saracco G, Bonino F, et al. Evidence for immune selection of hepatitis C virus (HCV) putative envelope glycoprotein variants: potential role in chronic HCV infections. Proc Natl Acad Sci USA 1992;89:3468-3472.
20. Kubo Y, Takeuchi K, Boonmar S, Katayama T, Choo QL, Kuo G, Weiner AJ, et al. A cDNA fragment of hepatitis C virus isolated from an implicated donor of post-transfusion non-A, non-B hepatitis in Japan. Nucleic Acids Res 1989;17:10367-10372.
21. Tanaka T, Kato N, Nakagawa M, Ootsuyama Y, Cho M-J, Nakazawa T, Hijikata M, et al. Molecular cloning of hepatitis C virus genome from a single Japanese carrier: sequence variation within the same individual and among infected individuals. Virus Res 1992;23:39-53.
22. Delisse AM, Descurieux M, Rutgers T, D'Hondt E, De Wilde M, Arima T, Barrera-Sala JM, et al. Sequence analysis of the putative

structural genes of hepatitis C virus from Japanese and European origin. J Hepatol 1991;13(suppl 4):S20-S23.

23. Inchauspe G, Zebedee S, Lee D-H, Sugitani M, Nasoff M, Prince AM. Genomic structure of the human prototype strain H of hepatitis C virus: Comparison with American and Japanese isolates. Proc Natl Acad Sci USA 1991;88:10292-10296.
24. Chen P-J, Lin M-H, Tai K-F, Liu P-C, Lin C-J, Chen D-S. The Taiwanese hepatitis C virus genome: sequence determination and mapping the 5′ termini of viral genomic and antigenomic RNA. Virology 1992;188:102-113.
25. Fuchs K, Motz M, Schreier E, Zachoval R, Deinhardt F, Roggendorf M. Characterization of nucleotide sequences from European hepatitis C virus isolates. Gene 1991;103:163-169.
26. Kremsdorf D, Porchon C, Kim JP, Reyes GR, Bréchot C. Partial nucleotide sequence analysis of a French hepatitis C virus: implications for HCV genetic variability in the E2/NS1 protein. J Gen Virol 1991;72:2557-2561.
27. Takada N, Takase S, Enomoto N, Takada A, Date T. Clinical backgrounds of the patients having different types of hepatitis C virus genomes. J Hepatol 1992;14:35-40.
28. Scott DA, Constantine NT, Callahan J, Burans JP, Olson JG, Al-Fadeel M, Al-Ozieb H, et al. The epidemiology of hepatitis C virus antibody in Yemen. Am J Trop Med Hyg 1992;46:63-68.
29. Ayoola EA, Huraib S, Arif M, Al-Faleh FZ, Al-Rashed R, Ramia S, Al-Mofleh IA, et al. Prevalence and significance of antibodies to hepatitis C virus among Saudi haemodialysis patients. J Med Virol 1991;35:155-159.
30. Li J, Tong S, Vitvitski L, Lepot D, Trépo C. Two French genotypes of hepatitis C virus: Homology of the predominant genotype with the prototype American strain. Gene 1991;105:167-172.
31. Farinati F, Fagiuoli S, De Maria N, Chiaramonte M, Aneloni V, Ongaro S, Salvagnini M, et al. Anti-HCV positive hepatocellular carcinoma in cirrhosis: prevalence, risk factors and clinical features. J Hepatol 1992;14:183-187.
32. Garson JA, Wicki AN, Ring CJA, Joller H, Zala G, Schmid M, Buehler H. Detection of hepatitis C viraemia in Caucasian patients with hepatocellular carcinoma. J Med Virol 1992;38:152-156.
33. Fattovich G, Tagger A, Brollo L, Giustina G, Pontisso P, Realdi G, Alberti A, et al. Hepatitis C virus infection in chronic hepatitis B virus carriers. J Infect Dis 1991;163:400-402.
34. Sheen I-S, Liaw Y-F, Chu C-M, Pao C-C. Role of hepatitis C virus infection in spontaneous hepatitis B surface antigen clearance during chronic hepatitis B virus infection. J Infect Dis 1992;165: 831-834.
35. Kanai K, Kako M, Okamoto H. HCV genotypes in chronic hepatitis C and response to interferon. Lancet 1992;339:1543.
36. Yoshioka K, Kakumu S, Wakita T, Ishikawa T, Itoh Y, Takayanagi M, Higashi Y, et al. Detection of hepatitis C virus by polymerase chain reaction and response to interferon-α therapy: relationship to genotypes of hepatitis C virus. HEPATOLOGY 1992;16:293-299.
37. Okada S, Akahane Y, Suzuki H, Okamoto H, Mishiro S. The degree of variability in the amino terminal region of the E2/NS1 protein of hepatitis C virus correlates with responsiveness to interferon therapy in viremic patients. HEPATOLOGY 1992;16:619-624.
38. Reichard O, Andersson J, Schvarcz R, Weiland O. Ribavirin treatment for chronic hepatitis C. Lancet 1991;337:1058-1061.
39. Bukh J, Purcell RH, Miller RH. Importance of primer selection for the detection of hepatitis C virus RNA with the polymerase chain reaction assay. Proc Natl Acad Sci USA 1992;89:187-191.
40. Alberti A, Morsica G, Chemello L, Cavalletto D, Noventa F, Pontisso P, Ruol A. Hepatitis C viraemia and liver disease in symptom-free individuals with anti-HCV. Lancet 1992;340: 697-698.
41. Okamoto H, Kojima M, Okada S-I, Yoshizawa H, Iizuka H, Tanaka T, Muchmore EE, et al. Genetic drift of hepatitis C virus during an 8.2-year infection in a chimpanzee: variability and stability. Virology 1992;190:894-899.

© Gut 1994; 35: 1590–1592

Ulcerative colitis and Crohn's disease: a comparison of the colorectal cancer risk in extensive colitis

C D Gillen, R S Walmsley, P Prior, H A Andrews, R N Allan

Abstract

The risk of developing colorectal cancer has been compared in two identically selected cohorts of patients with extensive Crohn's colitis (n=125) and extensive ulcerative colitis (n=486). In both groups the effects of selection bias have been reduced wherever possible. There was an 18-fold increase in the risk of developing colorectal cancer in extensive Crohn's colitis and a 19-fold increase in risk in extensive ulcerative colitis when compared with the general population, matched for age, sex, and years at risk. The absolute cumulative frequency of risk for developing colorectal cancer in extensive colitis was 8% at 22 years from onset of symptoms in the Crohn's disease group and 7% at 20 years from onset in the ulcerative colitis group. The relative risk of colorectal cancer was increased in both ulcerative colitis and Crohn's disease among those patients whose colitis started before the age of 25 years. Whether the absolute risk is greater in the younger age group or merely reflects that the expected number of carcinomas increases with age is uncertain. While there is an increased risk of developing colorectal cancer in extensive colitis the number of patients with Crohn's disease who actually develop colorectal cancer is small because many patients with extensive Crohn's colitis undergo colectomy early in the course of their disease to relieve persistent symptoms unresponsive to medical treatment.

(*Gut* 1994; 35: 1590–1592)

Queen Elizabeth Hospital, Birmingham
C D Gillen
R S Walmsley
H A Andrews
R N Allan

Cancer Epidemiology Research Unit, University of Birmingham, Birmingham
P Prior

Correspondence to: Dr R N Allan, Queen Elizabeth Hospital, Edgbaston, Birmingham B15 2TH.

Accepted for publication 4 February 1994.

Patients with ulcerative colitis have an increased risk of developing colorectal cancer when compared with the general population[1] and the excess risk is almost entirely confined to patients with longstanding extensive colitis.[2 3] Although population based studies are the preferred epidemiological method for determining the colorectal cancer incidence in ulcerative colitis we have shown that the incidence of colorectal cancer in ulcerative colitis can be estimated by studying a cohort of hospital patients, after reducing the effects of bias whenever possible inherent in any hospital based study.[4] The cancer risk in Crohn's disease is less well defined. Several statistical studies have shown an increased risk of colorectal cancer in Crohn's disease.[5-8] Three have found no such association,[9-11] but this lack of association might be explained by short follow up,[9] a large proportion of patients undergoing panproctocolectomy for symptomatic colitis,[10] or small numbers of patients with short follow up.[11] In this study of patients with extensive colitis we have, for the first time, compared the colorectal cancer risk in Crohn's disease with the risk in an identically selected series of patients with ulcerative colitis.[4]

Methods

CROHN'S DISEASE COHORT

A total of 281 patients were selected for this study from among those first seen at the General and Queen Elizabeth Hospitals, Birmingham between 1945–1975. The patients were selected if they were resident in the West Midlands region, were 15 or more years of age, and within five years of onset of symptoms when first seen at the index centre. A total of 5213 patient years at risk (PYR) was observed for all patients (mean 20·2 years from onset). When this cohort was divided by extent of colitis there were 125 patients (44·5%) with extensive Crohn's colitis. These data formed the basis of our study of the colorectal cancer risk in Crohn's disease.[12] Extensive colitis was defined as disease involving the whole colon as far proximally as the hepatic flexure and total colitis as colitis involving all the large intestine including the ascending colon.

ULCERATIVE COLITIS COHORT

A total of 823 patients were initially included in this study from among those first seen at one of three centres (Birmingham, Oxford, Stockholm county).[4] All patients were resident in a strictly defined geographical area, and when first seen at the index centre were 15 or more years of age and were within five years of symptomatic onset of ulcerative colitis. A total of 16 928 PYR was observed for all patients (mean 20·5 years from onset). Among these patients 486 (59%) had extensive colitis.

COMPUTATION

The number of cancers expected to occur was computed using the person years programme (PYRS).[13] The procedure applied age, sex, and site specific cancer incidence rates, derived from data from the Regional Cancer Registry, applicable to each subgroup, to age and sex

© Gut 1994; 35: 1590–1592

TABLE I *Extensive colitis: colorectal cancer morbidity 5+ years from onset (corrected for operation)*

	Site	*O*	*E*	*Relative risk*	*95% Confidence intervals*
Ulcerative colitis (n=486)	Colon	22	0·90	24·4***	15·3 to 37·0
	Rectum	7	0·61	11·5***	4·6 to 23·6
	Total	29	1·51	19·2***	12·9 to 27·5
Crohn's disease (n=125)	Colon	6	0·16	37·5***	13·7 to 81·6
	Rectum	2	0·28	7·1*	0·8 to 25·8
	Total	8	0·44	18·2***	7·8 to 35·8

O=observed cancers, E=expected cancers. *$p<0·05$, ***$p<0·001$.

specific years at risk (PYR). For sites of cancer other than large bowel, PYR were accumulated to date of death or to the end of the study periods for survivors. PYR were truncated at the date when total colectomy or proctectomy, or both, had been completed to compute expected numbers for colon and rectum respectively. The results for 'all sites of cancer' were then modified to allow for the effect of this truncation on the estimates of expected cancers.

STATISTICAL TESTING

The relative risk of cancer (RR) is defined as the observed/expected number, the risk being relative to that of the general population. The significance of the difference between the RR and 1·0 was assessed by assuming that the observed number followed a Poisson distribution, with a mean equal to the expected number. Exact Poisson probabilities were computed for a one tailed significance test. The method of Rothman and Boice[14] was used to obtain 95% confidence intervals (95% CI) for the RRs. Estimates of cumulative risk of colorectal cancer were computed by the product limit method (Kaplan and Meier).[15]

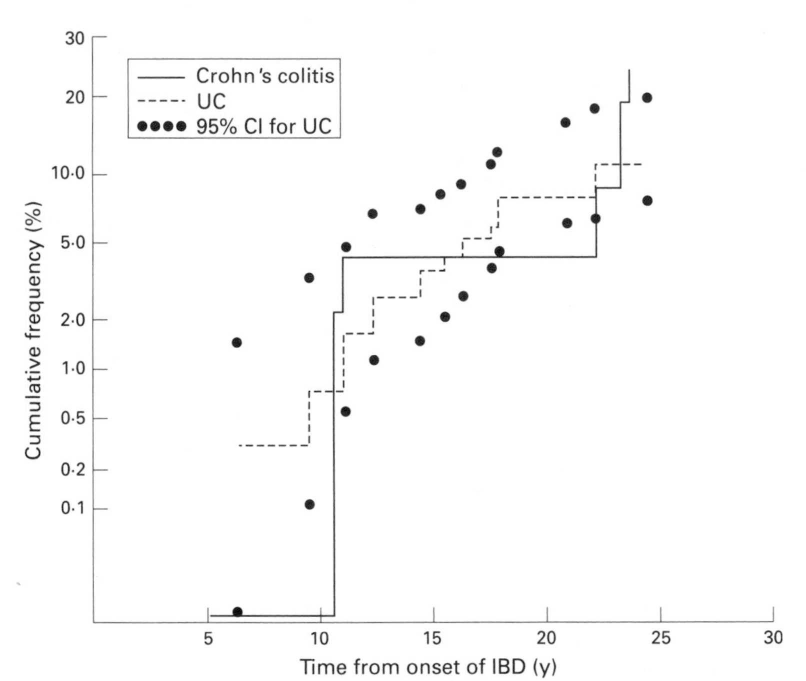

The cumulative frequency of colorectal cancer in patients with extensive ulcerative colitis (UC) and extensive Crohn's colitis.

Results

EXTENSIVE COLITIS: COLORECTAL CANCER MORBIDITY, ALL PATIENTS, 5+ YEARS FROM ONSET (CORRECTED FOR OPERATION)

Extensive ulcerative colitis – the 29 colorectal cancers (22 colonic, 7 rectal) represent a highly significant 19-fold excess when assessed against the expectation for the whole series. Rectal carcinoma was only seen in those patients with extensive ulcerative colitis (0=29, E=1·51, RR=19·2, $p<0·001$).

Extensive Crohn's colitis – colorectal cancers were only found in patients with extensive colitis. The eight colorectal cancers (6 colonic, 2 rectal) represent a highly significant 18-fold excess which is similar to the risk in patients with extensive ulcerative colitis (0=8, E=0·44, RR=18·2, $p<0·001$). Inevitably, given the small numbers of patients studied the 95% CI are wide (Table I).

CUMULATIVE FREQUENCY OF COLORECTAL CANCERS

The absolute cumulative frequency of colorectal cancer in patients with extensive colitis was 8% at 22 years from onset in the patients with Crohn's disease and 7% at 20 years from onset in the patients with ulcerative colitis (Figure).

RELATIVE RISK AND AGE AT ONSET

The relative risk of colorectal cancer was considerably increased in both ulcerative colitis and Crohn's disease among those patients whose colitis started before the age of 25 years (Table II).

Discussion

Effective comparison of the cancer risk in Crohn's disease and ulcerative colitis is difficult because the extent of macroscopic disease in the two disorders is often so different. As the excess colorectal cancer risk in ulcerative colitis is, however, largely confined to patients with extensive or total colitis and the observed pattern is similar in Crohn's disease (apart from a small excess in the small intestine) it seemed appropriate to compare the colorectal cancer risk in these two groups. While a population based group of patients provides the ideal basis for such a study, in practice such series are rarely available and their value limited by short follow up.

We have already shown that once the known biases in a hospital series have been reduced wherever possible, the colorectal cancer risk in a hospital based series is similar to that in a population based group of patients with ulcerative colitis.[4] In this study we therefore compared the colorectal cancer risk in extensive or total ulcerative colitis, using the data from three centres (Birmingham, Oxford, and Stockholm) with the risk of extensive or total Crohn's colitis from the Birmingham series.[12] Ideally we would have liked to increase the size of the cohort of patients

TABLE II *Extensive colitis: cancer of the large bowel by age at onset of ulcerative colitis and Crohn's disease, 5+ years after onset (corrected for operation)*

	Age group	*O*	*E*	*Relative risk*	*95% Confidence intervals*
Ulcerative colitis	<25	12	0·11	109·1***	56·3 to 190·6
	25–39	14	0·50	28·0***	15·3 to 47·0
	40+	3	0·90	3·33	0·7 to 9·7
Total		29	1·51	19·2***	12·9 to 27·6
Crohn's disease	<25	4	0·07	57·1***	15·4 to 146·3
	25–39	2	0·22	9·1**	1·0 to 32·8
	40+	2	0·15	13·3	1·5 to 48·1
Total		8	0·44	18·2***	7·8 to 35·8

**p<0·01, ***p<0·001. Abbreviations as in Table I.

with extensive Crohn's colitis, but it proved difficult to obtain complete data from the other two centres.

The same criteria were used to define the patient cohorts to ensure a valid comparison; that is patients over 15 years of age at onset of symptoms drawn from a defined geographical area and seen within five years of onset of symptoms. The completeness of follow up was 97% in the patients with ulcerative colitis and 100% in the patients with Crohn's disease. The relative risk of developing colorectal cancer is remarkably similar in the two groups when compared with the general population, corrected for age, sex, and years of follow up. The cumulative risk over time in patients with extensive ulcerative colitis and Crohn's disease is also similar. The relative rectal sparing, seen in Crohn's disease, has not reduced the risk of developing colorectal cancer in Crohn's disease. Inevitably, given the relatively small numbers the confidence intervals in the Crohn's disease study are relatively wide. An even larger study would be required to reduce the confidence intervals in the group of patients with Crohn's disease.

While a statistically significant trend over age could not be shown either for ulcerative colitis or Crohn's disease when age band was used as a stratifying variable in the product limit analysis or in a Cox regression analysis, the absolute risk is broadly the same. Age at onset of the underlying colitis as an independent risk factor for the development of colorectal cancer, however, has also been suggested by earlier studies in both Crohn's disease[5 8] and ulcerative colitis.[16] Whether the absolute risk is greater in the younger age group or merely reflects that the expected number of carcinomas increases with age is uncertain. If the relative risk is a measure of association between Crohn's disease and cancer, then the high relative risk in young people could be interpreted to mean that most cancers at this age are associated with Crohn's disease, whereas in older age groups a smaller proportion of incident cancers can be attributed to the association.

Stahl *et al* have suggested that younger patients with Crohn's disease should be considered for colonic surveillance to permit earlier diagnosis and treatment of colorectal cancer.[17] The number of patients with Crohn's disease developing colorectal cancer is small, however, as many patients with extensive Crohn's colitis required colectomy to relieve persistent symptomatic disease early in the course of their illness, thus eliminating the colorectal cancer risk. It would be difficult to justify a surveillance policy for all patients with extensive or total Crohn's colitis, particularly as the value of surveillance for colorectal cancer in ulcerative colitis has been questioned recently.[18 19] The data presented here suggest that it might be sensible to consider a surveillance programme for those few patients with extensive colitis of long standing with an intact colon whose Crohn's disease started at a young age.

The authors are grateful for the generous financial support from the Cancer Research Campaign and the National Association for Colitis and Crohn's Disease.

1 Butt JH, Lennard-Jones JE, Ritchie JK. A practical approach to the risk of cancer in inflammatory bowel disease. *Med Clin North Am* 1980; **64:** 1203–20.
2 Kewenter J, Ahlman H, Hulten L. Cancer risk in extensive colitis. *Ann Surg* 1978; **188:** 824–7.
3 Hendriksen C, Kreiner S, Binder V. Long term prognosis in ulcerative colitis – based on results from a regional patient group from the county of Copenhagen. *Gut* 1985; **26:** 158–63.
4 Gyde SN, Prior P, Allan RN, *et al.* Colorectal cancer in ulcerative colitis: a cohort study of primary referrals from three centres. *Gut* 1988; **29:** 206–17.
5 Weedon DD, Shorter RG, Ilstrup DM, *et al.* Crohn's disease and cancer. *N Engl J Med* 1973; **289:** 1099–103.
6 Greenstein AJ, Sachar DB. Cancer in Crohn's disease. In: Allan RN, Keighley MRB, Alexander-Williams J, Hawkins CF, eds. *Inflammatory bowel diseases.* Edinburgh: Churchill Livingstone, 1983: 332–7.
7 Greenstein AJ, Sachar DB, Smith H, *et al.* A comparison of cancer risk in Crohn's disease and ulcerative colitis. *Cancer* 1981; **48:** 2742–5.
8 Ekbom A, Helmick C, Zack M, Hans-Olov A. Increased risk of large bowel cancer in Crohn's disease with colonic involvement. *Lancet* 1990; **336:** 357–9.
9 Binder V, Hendriksen C, Kreiner S. Prognosis in Crohn's disease – based on results from a regional patient group from the county of Copenhagen. *Gut* 1985; **26:** 146–50.
10 Kvist N, Jacobsen O, Norgaard P, *et al.* Malignancy in Crohn's disease. *Scand J Gastroenterol* 1986; **21:** 82–6.
11 Gollop JH, Phillips SF, Melton LJ III, Zinsmeister AR. Epidemiologic aspects of Crohn's disease. *Gut* 1988; **29:** 49–56.
12 Gillen CD, Andrews HA, Prior P, Allan RN. Crohn's disease and colorectal cancer. *Gut* 1994; **35:** 651–6.
13 Coleman M, Douglas A, Hermon C, Peto J. Cohort study analysis with a FORTRAN computer program. *Int J Epidemiol* 1986; **15:** 134–7.
14 Rothman KT, Boice JD Jr. *Epidemiologic analysis with a programmable calculator.* NIH Publication No 79-1649. Washington DC: US Government Printing Office, 1979.
15 Kaplan EL, Meier P. Non-parametric estimates from incomplete observations. *Am Stat Assoc J* 1958; **10:** 457–81.
16 Ekbom A, Helmick C, Zack M, Adami HO. Ulcerative colitis and colorectal cancer. A population based study. *N Engl J Med* 1990; **323:** 1228–33.
17 Stahl TJ, Schoetz DJ Jr, Roberts PL, *et al.* Crohn's disease and carcinoma: increasing justification for surveillance? *Dis Colon Rectum* 1992; **35:** 850–6.
18 Collins RH, Feldman M, Fordran JS. Colon cancer, dysplasia and surveillance in patients with ulcerative colitis: a critical review. *N Engl J Med* 1987; **316:** 1654–8.
19 Gyde SN. Screening for colorectal cancer in ulcerative colitis: dubious benefits and high costs. *Gut* 1990; **31:** 1089–92.

© Lancet 1994; 343: 758–761

Wheat peptide challenge in coeliac disease

Richard Sturgess, Paul Day, H Julia Ellis, Knut E A Lundin, Henrik A Gjertsen, Maria Kontakou, Paul J Ciclitira

Summary

The exact nature of the cereal moiety that exacerbates coeliac disease is unknown. In-vitro studies have implicated both the N-terminal and far C-terminal domains of one of the wheat prolamins, A-gliadin. Peptides within these regions may act as epitopes that trigger immune events leading to enteropathy.

We synthesised three peptides corresponding to aminoacids 3-21, 31-49, and 202-220 of A-gliadin. Four patients with coeliac disease were challenged by intraduodenal infusion of 1 g of gliadin or 200 mg of the synthetic peptides. Jejunal biopsies were taken before and at hourly intervals for 6 h after the infusion. Morphometric variables were measured and intraepithelial lymphocytes counted. Significant histological changes occurred in the small intestinal mucosa after challenge with a synthetic peptide corresponding to amino acids 31-49 of A-gliadin. The N-terminal peptide, residues 3-21 of A-gliadin, did not cause histological changes in any of the patients. In one of the four patients, minor histological changes following challenge with the peptide corresponding to residues 202-220 of A-gliadin were seen.

Our results suggest that the oligopeptide corresponding to aminoacids 31-49 of A-gliadin is toxic in vivo, but there is no evidence of toxicity of the far N-terminal peptide, residues 3-21. The C-terminal peptide 202-220 may contain an epitope to which patients with coeliac disease display variable sensitivity. Since the oligopeptide corresponding to amino-acids 31-49 of A-gliadin is recognised by HLA DQ2-restricted T cells, the observed effects may be due to immune activation within the intestinal mucosa.

Lancet 1994; **343:** 758–61

Rayne Institute Division of Pharmacology, St Thomas' Hospital, London SE1 7EH, UK (R Sturgess MRCP, P Day MRCP, H J Ellis PhD, M Kontakou PhD, Prof P J Ciclitira FRCP); **and Institute of Transplantation Immunology, The National Hospital, Oslo, Norway** (K E A Lundin MD, H A Gjertsen MD)

Correspondence to: Prof Paul J Ciclitira

Introduction

Coeliac disease occurs as a result of an autodestructive response to certain dietary cereals and is probably mediated by T lymphocyte-driven immunological activation within the gastrointestinal mucosa.[1,2] The causative agent in wheat is in the ethanol-soluble prolamin fraction, the gliadins,[3] whose toxicity remains after peptic-tryptic digestion.[4]

Coeliac disease is closely associated with the HLA class II α/β heterodimer, HLA-DQ(α1*0501, β1*0201)(DQ2).[5] It has been shown that gliadin-specific CD4 T cells in the small intestinal mucosa of patients with coeliac disease are predominantly restricted by this DQ heterodimer.[6] It is possible that presentation of gliadin-derived peptides to T cells in the small intestinal mucosa is important for the pathogenesis of the disease. The epitopes for T cell clones from the intestinal mucosa have not been identified. However, with CD4 T cells from the blood of a patient with coeliac disease, a peptide epitope corresponding to residues 31-49 of A-gliadin, one of the α-gliadins, was shown to be recognised when presented by the coeliac-disease-associated DQ heterodimer.[7]

One of the difficulties in testing toxicity of prolamin fractions has been the lack of a suitable test system. The only true test of toxicity is in-vivo challenge. The invasive nature of challenge studies, however, and the difficulties in obtaining sufficiently large quantities of pure protein fractions has led to the use of in-vitro systems in the assessment of cereal fractions.[8] Most studies have focused on the N-terminal region of A-gliadin[9,10] but the C-terminal region has also been studied.[9,11,12]

We synthesised three 19-aminoacid oligopeptides from the A-gliadin sequence.[13] The length of peptides selected was such that they would be ideally suited for HLA class II restricted T-cell recognition.[14] We used these synthetic peptides for in-vivo challenge studies.

Patients and methods

Oligopeptides (table 1) were synthesised with a solid-phase peptide synthesiser (Model 431A, Applied Biosystems Inc, CA, USA). The peptides were analysed by high performance liquid chromatography (HPLC) and plasma desorption mass spectrometry (BioIon Spectrometer, Applied Biosystems Inc), sequenced by automated phenyl-thiohydantoin gas phase sequencing (ABI 475, Applied Biosystems Inc), and purified on a gel exclusion column (Sephadex G15, Pharmacia LKB, Uppsala, Sweden). The fractions were collected with a UV-1 single path monitor (Pharmacia LKB) and FRAC-100 fraction collector (Pharmacia LKB). Peptide solutions were frozen in liquid nitrogen and double lyophilised. Undigested gliadin was prepared from Kolibri wheat flour by standard methods.[15] The flour was defatted with butanol, extracted with ethanol, dialysed against acetic acid, and lyophilised.

We studied four unrelated white patients with coeliac disease, diagnosed according to European Society of Paediatric Gastroenterology and Nutrition (ESPGAN) criteria[16] (table 2). Patients gave written informed consent to the study, which was approved by the hospital ethics committee. Patients had four challenges—gliadin first, followed by the peptides in random

Peptide	Sequence*	A-gliadin homology†
A	LGQQQPFPPQQPYPQPQPF	31–49
B	QQYPLGQGSFRPSQQNPQA	202–220
C	VPVPQLQPQNPSQQQPQEQ	3–21

*Single letter code.
†Numbers represent residues within the 266 aminoacid, A-gliadin protein.

Table 1: **Aminoacid sequence of challenge peptides**

Patient	Age (yr)	Sex	Time on gluten-free diet (yr)
I	63	M	24
II	76	F	23
III	30	F	2
IV	29	F	4

Table 2: **Patient characteristics**

order, with at least one week between to allow for recovery of the jejunal mucosa.

A cannula was taped to a Quinton hydraulic biopsy tube with the tip lying 10 cm proximal to the suction port of the capsule. Following midazolam sedation, the biopsy tube was positioned in the proximal jejunum under fluoroscopic control. For the challenge, the peptides were dissolved in 50 mL of 0·5% bovine serum albumin in distilled water. Gliadin, 1000 mg, was dissolved in 250 mL of 0·5% bovine serum albumin. The solutions were infused into the distal duodenum over 2 h by syringe-driver pump. Biopsies were taken before and at hourly intervals for 6 h after starting the infusion.

Upon recovery from the Quinton tube, the biopsies were orientated epithelial surface upwards on filter paper and fixed in formol saline. Biopsies taken before and at 4 h after starting the infusion were snap frozen for analysis of CD3 intraepithelial lymphocytes (IEL). A streptavidin-biotin immunoperoxidase method was used. Anti-CD3 (Dako, High Wycombe, UK) was the primary monoclonal antibody and the second layer was biotinylated rabbit anti-mouse immunogobulin (Dako). The density of cells expressing CD3 in the epithelium was determined by counting the number of stained cells as a percentage of all epithelial cells, both IEL and enterocytes, since in frozen sections it is not always possible to determine whether a negative cell is epithelial or lymphoid. Over 1000 cells were counted.

Morphometric measurements were done on 5 μm wax-mounted sections. Measurements were made of the height of five separate villi and of the depth of the adjoining crypt, and the villus-height/crypt-depth ratio (VH/CD) calculated. Under 400× magnification, the heights of five separate enterocytes (EH) in the middle third of the villus were measured.

Changes in VH/CD and EH were analysed by repeated measures analysis of variance. Bonferroni post hoc analysis was used to examine time points of significant change. Individuals' CD3 IEL counts before and 4 h after the start of the challenge were compared by the Mann-Whitney *U* test. Results are expressed as means (SE). Significance was $p<0·05$.

Results

Before each challenge, all subjects had normal villae. In response to gliadin, three developed significant changes in VH/CD and all had significant changes in EH and CD3 IEL counts (figure). Challenge with peptide A produced significant changes in VH/CD, EH, and CD3 IEL counts in all patients (figure). Combined data from all patients showed significant change for the group in VH/CD, EH, and CD3 IEL counts for both gliadin and peptide A (table 3).

Patient III had a reduction in VH/CD ratio and EH when challenged with peptide B, but no increase in CD3 IEL counts. Analysis of grouped data showed no significant change in any of the histological variables following challenge with peptide B. None of the subjects showed any mucosal response to peptide C.

Time (h)	Gliadin	Peptide A	Peptide B	Peptide C
VH/CD ratio				
0	3·1 (0·2)	3·3 (0·2)	3·3 (0·1)	3·2 (0·1)
1	2·9 (0·2)	2·9 (0·2)	3·0 (0·1)	3·2 (0·1)
2	2·5 (0·2)	2·7 (0·3)	3·1 (0·1)	3·0 (0·1)
3	2·4 (0·2)	2·3 (0·2)	3·0 (0·1)	3·2 (0·1)
4	2·3 (0·3)*	2·2 (0·2)*	3·0 (0·2)	3·0 (0·1)
5	2·3 (0·3)*	2·7 (0·2)	3·0 (0·1)	3·1 (0·1)
6	2·9 (0·3)	2·9 (0·1)	3·1 (0·1)	3·0 (0·1)
EH (μm)				
0	38 (1)	37 (1)	36 (1)	36 (1)
1	35 (1)	33 (1)*	36 (1)	35 (1)
2	32 (1)	33 (1)*	35 (1)	34 (1)
3	31 (2)*	33 (2)*	35 (1)	34 (1)
4	28 (2)*	32 (1)*	34 (2)	35 (1)
5	30 (3)*	34 (1)	35 (1)	36 (1)
6	37 (1)	36 (1)	36 (1)	35 (1)
CD3 IEL counts				
0	25 (2)	23 (3)	23 (1)	23 (1)
4	36 (3)*	33 (4)*	24 (2)	23 (1)

Mean (SE). *$p<0·05$ compared with time 0.

Table 3: **Mean values of enteropathic variables for oligopeptides**

Discussion

We confirmed our previous finding of a significant reduction in VH/CD ratio and EH together with an increase in IEL count within 4 h of infusion of 1 g of unfractionated gliadin into the duodenum of patients with coeliac disease in remission.[17] It is accepted that there is considerable variation in the response of patients with coeliac disease to gluten and its components. Challenge with unfractionated gliadin acted as a positive control in our subjects for subsequent challenge with the synthetic oligopeptides. All had been on a gluten-free diet for at least two years and thus gliadin challenge may have reprimed the intestinal mucosal immune system to subsequent challenge. The identities of our peptides were confirmed by mass spectrometry, HPLC, and sequencing. They were purifed by gel exclusion chromatography to remove reagents remaining after synthesis, so observed responses were unlikely to be due to chemical toxicity.

All three peptides tested contain the putatively active tetrapeptide motifs QQQP and/or PSQQ, and all contain potentially antigenic β-reverse turns, both of which have been proposed as models for peptide toxicity in coeliac disease.[9,18] Recent evidence suggests, however, that HLA class II molecules bind peptides in an extended conformation and thus secondary peptide structure may be of lesser importance.[19] This evidence is consistent with our study which suggests that such structures do not themselvees confer toxicity to gliadin peptides, since they are almost certainly present in peptides B and C.[18]

Peptide A was designed to resemble peptides that have shown in-vitro toxicity (table 4).[9,10,20] However, the PSQQ

Peptide	Sequence*	A-gliadin homology†
A	LGQQQPFPPQQPYPQPQPF	31–49
Gjertsen et al	LGQQQPFPPQQPYPQPQPF	31–49
Wieser et al	VQQQQFPGQQQPFPPQQPYPQPQPFPSQQPY	25–55
De Ritis et al	LGQQQPFPPQQPYPQPQPFPSQQPY	31–55
Auricchio et al	LGQQQPFPPQQPY	31–43
C	VPVPQLQPQNPSQQQPQEQ	3–21
Wieser et al	VPVPQLQPQNPSQQQPQEQVPL	3–24
De Ritis et al	VRVPVPQLQPQNPSQQQPQEQVPLVQQQQF	1–30
Devery et al	CPQLQPQNPSQQQPQEQG	5–22

*Single letter amino acid code.
†Numbers represent residues within A-gliadin.

Table 4: **Aminoacid sequence of gliadin peptides**

© *Lancet* 1994; 343: 758–761

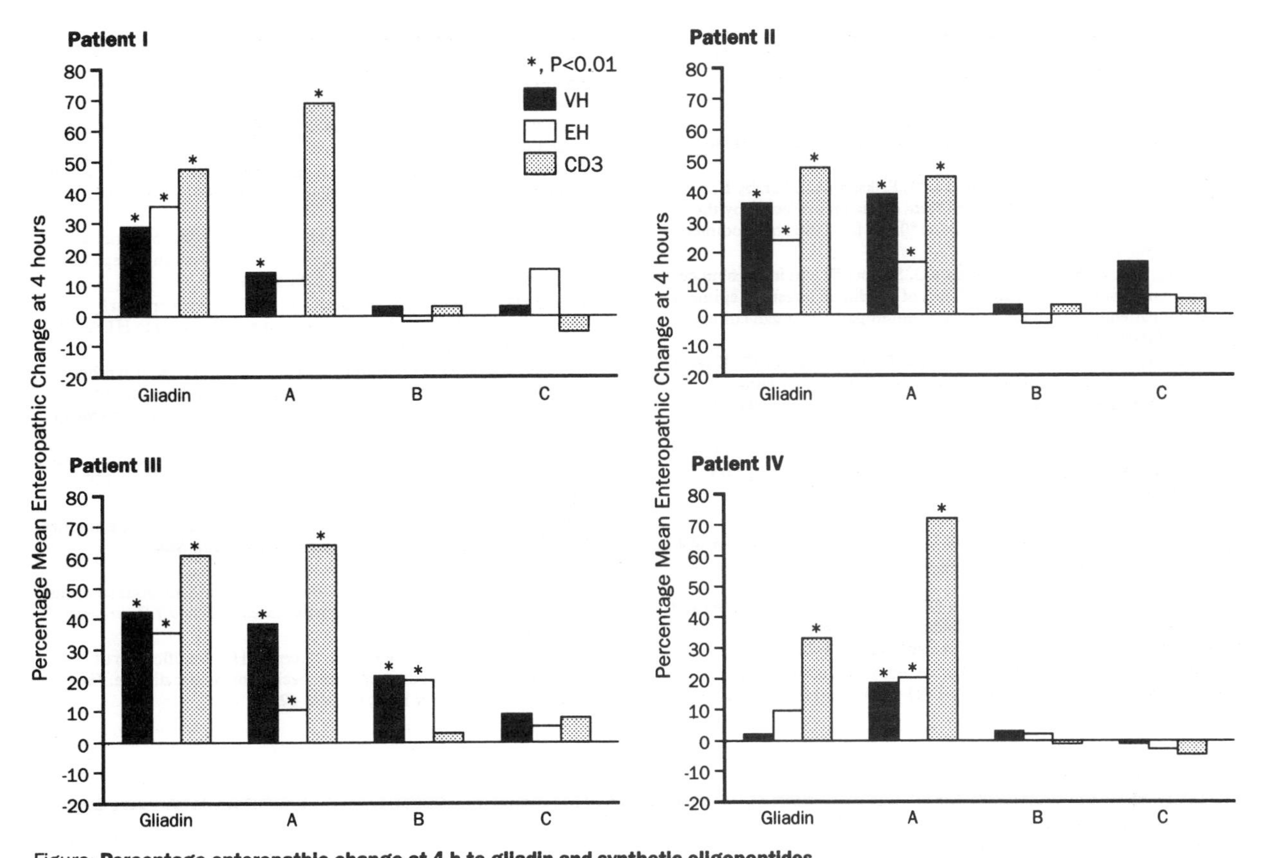

Figure: **Percentage enteropathic change at 4 h to gliadin and synthetic oligopeptides**

Percentage change in morphometric variables and CD3 IEL counts at 4 h compared with 0 h. VH = villous-height to crypt-depth ratio; EH = enterocyte height; CD3 = CD3 IEL count per 100 epithelial cells; A = peptide A; B = peptide B; C = peptide C. Variables are plotted as enteropathic change—ie, decrease in VH and EH are positive enteropathic change.

motif found in the active peptides described by Wieser et al[10] and de Ritis et al[9] has been omitted from our peptide A. Thus, this study does not support toxicity of the PSQQ motif. We have recently shown that a monoclonal antibody against an active peptide, residues 3-56 of α-gliadin,[21] cross-reacts with only those cereal prolamins thought to exacerbate coeliac disease and appears to be restricted by the proline residue at position 36, which is incorporated by peptide A.[22] Peptide A also corresponds to a peptide that we have shown to be recognised by an HLA-DQ2-restricted T-cell clone isolated from the blood of a patient with coeliac disease.[7]

Peptide B was selected because of its homology with the E1b protein of adenovirus 12,[11] the presence of PSQQ motif, and a probable β-reverse turn centred on the proline residue 213. The lack of histological change caused by this peptide in three of the four patients studied argues against a role for adenovirus 12 in the aetiology of coeliac disease. Patient III developed significant morphometric changes in response to peptide B but CD3 IEL count—regarded as a sensitive indicator of gluten enterotoxicity—did not increase. A previous study, which did not include gliadin control infusions, showed minor histological abnormalities in the jejunal mucosae of two patients with coeliac disease after infusion with 100 mg of peptide corresponding to aminoacid residues 206-217 of A-gliadin.[23] This raises the possibility that there may be a toxic epitope within this peptide to which the sensitivity of patients with coeliac disease varies.

Peptide C was selected on the basis of the motifs PSQQ and QQQP,[9] the presence of β-reverse turns,[18] and partial identity with peptides displaying in-vitro toxicity.[9,10,24] No significant changes were seen in any of the four patients following infusion with peptide C. The C-terminal motif VPL represents the only difference between the in-vitro active peptide of Wieser et al[10] and peptide C (table 4). It is possible that the omission of this motif has diminished the toxicity of petide C. However, there was in-vitro evidence of cellular immunity in blood to a peptide corresponding to aminoacids 5-22 of A-gliadin, which also lacks the motif VPL (table 4).[24]

It is possible that other regions of A-gliadin, and probable that regions of the other gliadins and prolamins, may be shown to exacerbate coeliac disease. This study has, however, shown for the first time in-vivo toxicity of a synthetic oligopeptide corresponding to residues 31-49 of A-gliadin in patients with treated coeliac disease.

We thank Dr Gerard Evan and Miss Nicola O'Reilly, the Imperial Cancer Research Fund, London, for use of their facility and assistance in peptide synthesis, and Mr J M Nelufer for technical assistance with histological work. Grant support was provided by St Thomas' Hospital Research (endowments) Committee, Nutricia Research Foundation, AB Semper, the Jean Shanks Research Foundation, Pronova, the Research Council of Norway, and the Association des Amidonneries de Cereale de la CE.

References

1 Trier JS. Celiac sprue. *N Engl J Med* 1991; **325:** 1709–19.
2 Marsh MN. Gluten, major histocompatibility complex, and the small intestine. *Gastroenterology* 1992; **102:** 330–54.
3 Van de Kamer JH, Weijers HA, Dicke WK. Coeliac disease IV. An investigation into the injurious constituents of wheat in connection with their action on patients with coeliac disease. *Acta Paediatr* 1953; **42:** 223–31.
4 Frazer AC, Fletcher RF, Ross CAC, Shaw B, Sammons HG, Schneider R. Gluten-induced enteropathy. The effect of partially digested gluten. *Lancet* 1959; ii: 252–55.

5 Sollid LM, Markussen G, Ek G, Gjerde H, Vartbal F, Thorsby E. Evidence for a primary association of celiac disease to a particular HLA-DQ α/β heterodimer. *J Exp Med* 1989; **169:** 345–50.

6 Lundin KEA, Scott H, Hansen T, et al. Gliadin-specific, HLA-DQ(α1*0501,β1*0201) restricted T cells isolated from the small intestinal mucosa of celiac disease patients. *J Exp Med* 1993; **178:** 187–96.

7 Gjertsen HA, Lundin KEA, Sollid LM, Eriksen JA, Thorsby E. T cells recognize a peptide derived from α-gliadin presented by the celiac disease associated HLA-DQ (α1*0501, β1* 0201) heterodimer. *Hum Immunol* (in press).

8 Falchuk ZM, Gebhard RL, Sessoms C, Strober W. An in vitro model of gluten sensitive enteropathy. Effect of gliadin on intestinal epithelial cells of patients with gluten sensitivity enteropathy in organ culture. *J Clin Invest* 1974; **53:** 487–500.

9 de Ritis G, Auricchio S, Jones HW, Lew EJ-L, Bernardin JE, Kasarda DD. In vitro (organ culture) studies of the toxicity of specific A-gliadin peptides in celiac disease. *Gastroenterology* 1988; **94:** 41–49.

10 Wieser H, Belitz HD, Idar D, Ashkenzai A. Coeliac activity of gliadin peptides CT-1 and CT-2. *Z Lebensm Unters Forsch* 1986; **182:** 115–17.

11 Kagnoff MR, Raleigh KA, Hubert JJ, Bernadin JF, Kasarda DD. Possible role of a human adenovirus in the pathogenesis of coeliac disease. *J Exp Med* 1984; **160:** 1544–47.

12 Karagiannis JA, Priddle JD, Jewell DP. Cell-mediated immunity to a synthetic gliadin peptide resembling a sequence from adenovirus 12. *Lancet* 1987; i: 884–86.

13 Kasarda DD, Okita TW, Bernadin JE, et al. Nucleic acid (cDNA) and amino acid sequences of α-type gliadins from wheat (*Triticum aestivum*). *Proc Natl Acad Sci USA* 1984; **81:** 4712–16.

14 Chicz RM, Urban RG, Lane WS, et al. Predominant naturally processed peptides bound to HLA-DR1 are derived from MHC-related molecules and are heterogenous in size. *Nature* 1992; **358:** 764–68.

15 Patey AL, Evans DJ. Large scale preparation of gliadin proteins. *J Sci Food Agric* 1973; **24:** 1229–93.

16 Meeuwisse G. Diagnostic criteria in coeliac disease. *Acta Paediatr Scand* 1970; **59:** 461–63.

17 Ciclitira PJ, Evans DJ, Fagg NLK, Lennox ES, Dowling RH. Clinical testing of gliadin fractions in coeliac patients. *Clin Sci* 1984; **66:** 357–64.

18 Tatham AS, Marsh MN, Wieser H, Shewry PR. Conformational studies of peptides corresponding to the coeliac-activating regions of wheat α-gliadin. *Biochem J* 1990; **270:** 313–18.

19 Brown JH, Jardetsky TS, Gorga JC, et al. Three-dimensional structure of the human class II histocompatibility antigen HLA-DR1. *Nature* 1993; **364:** 33–39.

20 Auricchio S, de Ritis G, Maiuri L, et al. A-gliadin related synthetic peptides: damaging effects on in vitro cultured atrophic coeliac intestinal mucosa and developing fetal rat intestine. *Gastroenterology* 1991; **100:** A194.

21 Wieser H, Blitz H-D, Ashkenazi A. Amino-acid sequence of the coeliac active gliadin peptice B3142. *Z Lebensm Unters Forsch* 1984; **179:** 371–76.

22 Ellis HJ, Doyle AP, Wieser H, Sturgess RP, Ciclitira PJ. Specificities of monoclonal antibodies to domain 1 of α-gliadin. *Scand J Gastroenterol* 1993; **28:** 212–16.

23 Mantzaris G, Jewell DP. In vivo toxicity of a synthetic dodecapeptide from A-gliadin in patients with coeliac disease. *Scand J Gastroenterol* 1991; **26:** 392–98.

24 Devery JM, Bender V, Penttila I, Skerritt JH. Identification of reactive synthetic gliadin peptides specific for coeliac disease. *Int Arch Allergy Appl Immunol* 1991; **95:** 356–62.

© Gastroenterology 1994; 107: 1503–1513

The Role of Bile Composition and Physical Chemistry in the Pathogenesis of Octreotide-Associated Gallbladder Stones

S. HYDER HUSSAINI,* GERARD M. MURPHY,* COLETTE KENNEDY,† G. MICHAEL BESSER,§ JOHN A. H. WASS,§ and R. HERMON DOWLING*

*Gastroenterology Unit, Division of Medicine, and †Department of Diagnostic Radiology, Guy's Hospital and Campus, United Medical and Dental Schools of Guy's and St. Thomas' Hospitals, London; and §Department of Endocrinology, Medical College of St. Bartholomew's Hospital, London, England

Background/Aims: Treatment of acromegaly with octreotide inhibits cholecystokinin release and gallbladder contraction and induces gallbladder stones. However, little is known about the effects of octreotide on bile composition. **_Methods:_** Fresh gallbladder bile was obtained from three groups: (1) 11 nonacromegalic patients with cholesterol gallstones, (2) 6 acromegalic patients with octreotide-associated stones (treatment, 300–600 μg/day for 3–66 months), and (3) 8 acromomegalic patients with no stones before octreotide treatment, 5 of whom were reexamined after 3–24 months of therapy. **_Results:_** Compared with stone-free acromegalic patients untreated with octreotide, bile from patients with cholesterol stones and from acromegalic patients with octreotide-associated stones had greater saturation indices (mean ± SEM) (1.52 ± 0.17 and 1.32 ± 0.14 vs. 0.90 ± 0.05, respectively; $P < 0.01$); more cholesterol in vesicles (61.2% ± 4.5% and 67.7% ± 7.2% vs. 37.7% ± 3.5%; $P < 0.009$); more unstable vesicles (cholesterol/phospholipid ratios, 0.97 ± 0.12 and 0.81 ± 0.16 vs. 0.52 ± 0.05; $P < 0.02$); more rapid nucleation (<5 and <5 days vs. >18 days; $P < 0.003$); and more deoxycholic acid (22.8% ± 2.4% and 23.6% ± 4.8% vs. 13.9% ± 1.4%; $P < 0.05$). In the paired studies, the saturation indices increased from 0.89 ± 0.07 before octreotide treatment to 1.12 ± 0.03 during octreotide treatment ($P < 0.02$), as did the percentage of deoxycholic acid from 13.3% ± 2.1% to 24.9% ± 2.7% ($P < 0.03$). **_Conclusions:_** Acromegalic patients with octreotide-associated gallstones and stone-free acromegalic patients treated with octreotide have similar changes in bile composition to those in patients with "conventional" cholesterol gallstone disease.

0016-5085/94/$3.00

Selective Stimulation of Bifidobacteria in the Human Colon by Oligofructose and Inulin

GLENN R. GIBSON, EMILY R. BEATTY, XIN WANG, and JOHN H. CUMMINGS
Medical Research Council, Dunn Clinical Nutrition Centre, Cambridge, England

Background/Aims: Oligofructose and inulin are naturally occurring indigestible carbohydrates. In vitro they selectively stimulate the growth of species of *Bifidobacterium,* a genus of bacteria considered beneficial to health. This study was designed to determine their effects on the large bowel microflora and colonic function in vivo. *Methods:* Eight subjects participated in a 45-day study during which they ate controlled diets. For the middle 15 days, 15 $g \cdot day^{-1}$ oligofructose was substituted for 15 $g \cdot day^{-1}$ sucrose. Four of these subjects went on to a further period with 15 $g \cdot day^{-1}$ inulin. Bowel habit, transit time, stool composition, breath H_2 and CH_4, and the predominant genera of colonic bacteria were measured. *Results:* Both oligofructose and inulin significantly increased bifidobacteria from 8.8 to 9.5 $\log_{10}$ g $stool^{-1}$ and 9.2 to 10.1 $\log_{10}$ g $stool^{-1}$, respectively, whereas bacteroides, clostridia, and fusobacteria decreased when subjects were fed oligofructose, and gram-positive cocci decreased when subjects were fed inulin. Total bacterial counts were unchanged. Fecal wet and dry matter, nitrogen, and energy excretion increased with both substrates, as did breath H_2. Little change in fecal short-chain fatty acids and breath CH_4 was observed. *Conclusions:* A 15-$g \cdot day^{-1}$ dietary addition of oligofructose or inulin led to *Bifidobacterium* becoming the numerically predominant genus in feces. Thus, small changes in diet can alter the balance of colonic bacteria towards a potentially healthier microflora.

0016-5085/95/$3.00

Grading of Cellular Rejection After Orthotopic Liver Transplantation

SIDDHARTHA DATTA GUPTA,[1,6] MARK HUDSON,[2] ANDREW K. BURROUGHS,[3] RICHARD MORRIS,[4] KEITH ROLLES,[3] PETER AMLOT,[5] PETER J. SCHEUER,[1] AND AMAR P. DHILLON[1]

All 684 post-orthotopic liver transplantation (OLT) liver biopsies performed at the Royal Free Hospital (RFH) between 1988 and 1993, from 120 patients, were reviewed in order to try to define the relative importance of the histological features of immunosuppression-responsive cellular rejection. Twenty histological features considered to be possible contributors to the diagnosis of cellular rejection were documented in a binary (present/absent) fashion. These features in 106 biopsy specimens obtained 1 to 8 days after OLT were analyzed using stepwise logistic discriminant analysis. All clinical and treatment records were reviewed, and each biopsy specimen was assigned to a diagnostic category depending on these records and follow-up information. Important determinants of the histological diagnosis of cellular rejection (which occurred in 84 of the 106 cases) were moderate/severe mixed portal inflammation, eosinophils, endotheliitis, and bile duct damage. When these all occurred together, the odds of rejection increased 3.6-fold. The original histological diagnosis was recorded, and each biopsy specimen showing cellular rejection was regraded according to the specific criteria of Snover et al., Demetris et al., and a novel RFH scoring system. The latter consists of evaluating portal inflammation, endotheliitis, eosinophils, and bile duct damage, each on a 0 to 3 scale (none, mild, moderate, or severe, respectively) and summation. The resulting cellular rejection score thus can range from 0 to 12. The agreement between the different scoring systems was analyzed using K statistics, and there was good concordance (K, 0.64 to 0.78), despite different histological criteria being used to derive each score. Each system showed a similar degree of sensitivity (87% to 96%). The specificity ranged from 59% to 77%. We conclude that the histological diagnosis of cellular rejection relies mainly on the previously described features of mixed portal inflammation, endotheliitis, eosinophils, and duct damage. There is scope for unification and simplification of the existing grading systems, which depend on differing criteria, and we suggest one such scheme. (HEPATOLOGY 1995;21:46-57.)

Abbreviations: OLT, orthotopic liver transplantation; RFH, Royal Free Hospital; PAS, periodic acid-Schiff; CMV, cytomegalovirus; HBs, hepatitis B surface antigen; HBc, hepatitis B core antigen; HDV, hepatitis delta virus; HCV, hepatitis C virus; PCR, polymerase chain reaction; ALG/ATG, antilymphocyte globulin/antithymocyte globulin; TP, true-positives; TN, true-negatives; FP, false-positives; FN, false-negatives; MHC, major histocompatibility complex.

From the University Departments of [1]Hisopathology, [2]Medicine, [3]Hepatobiliary and Liver Transplantation Unit (University Departments of Medicine & Surgery), [4]Public Health & Primary Care, and [5]Immunology, Royal Free Hospital School of Medicine, Hampstead, London, United Kingdom; and [6]Department of Pathology, All India Institute of Medical Sciences, Ansari Nagar, New Delhi, India.

Received October 26, 1993; accepted June 29, 1994.

A.P.D. is partly supported by the Frances and Augustus Newman Foundation (London, England).

Address reprint requests to: Amar P. Dhillon, MA, MD, MRCP, MRCPath, University Department of Histopathology, Royal Free Hospital, School of Medicine, Rouland Hill St, Hampstead, London NW3 2PF, United Kingdom.

0270-9139/95/2101-0009$3.00/0

Changes in the intragastric distribution of *Helicobacter pylori* during treatment with omeprazole

R P H Logan, M M Walker, J J Misiewicz, P A Gummett, Q N Karim, J H Baron

Abstract

Omeprazole is a powerful inhibitor of gastric acid and may suppress *Helicobacter pylori* by effecting the pKa of *H pylori* urease, by altering the pattern of infection, or by promoting overgrowth of other bacteria. At routine endoscopy *H pylori* was detected by histology and culture before and after four weeks' treatment with omeprazole, 40 mg each morning. A ^{13}C-urea breath test was also done at t=0, 2, 4, and 6 weeks. Thirty nine patients with duodenal ulcer (n=25) or reflux oesophagitis (n=14) were studied, of whom 29 of 39 had *H pylori* infection. During omeprazole treatment, ^{13}C-urea breath test values fell significantly – mean (SEM) values before treatment and at four weeks were 23·0 (2·1) and 15·5 (2·7) per mil respectively, $p<0·001$. Before treatment *H pylori* was seen in 28 of 29 antral, 29 of 29 corpus, and 28 of 29 fundic biopsy specimens. After four weeks of omeprazole treatment, the histological density of *H pylori* in the antrum and corpus was reduced ($p<0·001$), while that in the fundus was increased. The migration of *H pylori* from the antrum to the fundus was associated with a corresponding decrease in the activity of antral gastritis. *H pylori* was not seen in antral biopsy specimens from 12 of 29 patients whose median excess δ $^{13}CO_2$ excretion fell from 23·0 to 9·9 per mil. In the body mucosa, 26 of 29 specimens were still positive for *H pylori* and there was no significant change in the gastritis type. Two weeks after finishing treatment, the mean (SEM) excess δ $^{13}CO_2$ excretion returned to levels before treatment. Omeprazole decreases antral *H pylori* colonisation but increases that in the fundus. The changes in the intragastric distribution of the organism are associated with concomitant changes in the activity of gastritis and are matched by a progressive fall in the excretion of δ $^{13}CO_2$.

(*Gut* 1995; **36:** 12–16)

Keywords: *Helicobacter pylori,* intragastric distribution, omeprazole, ^{13}C-urea breath test.

Parkside Helicobacter Study Group, Central Middlesex and St Mary's Hospitals, London
R P H Logan
M M Walker
J J Misiewicz
P A Gummett
Q N Karim
J H Baron

Correspondence to:
Dr R P H Logan, Division of Gastroenterology, Department of Therapeutics, University Hospital, Nottingham NG7 2UH.

Accepted for publication 29 April 1994

Helicobacter pylori causes non-autoimmune gastritis[1] and is an important factor in the aetiology of recurrent duodenal ulcer disease.[2 3] *H pylori* colonises only gastric type epithelium. Its powerful urease activity is probably essential for colonisation and the base produced by urease may protect the organism from gastric acid.[4 5] Omeprazole inhibits H+/K+ ATPase, and 40 mg can suppress over 80% of gastric acid secretion.[6] Initial reports of the effect of omeprazole on *H pylori* were inconclusive.[7 8] Although eradication has been claimed in some reports,[8–10] *H pylori* status was assessed prematurely and on antral biopsy specimens alone. More recent reports using either the ^{13}C or ^{14}C-urea breath test suggest that omeprazole partly suppresses, but does not eradicate *H pylori*.[11 12] This prospective study examines the effect of omeprazole on the distribution and persistence of *H pylori* within the stomach using the ^{13}C-urea breath test and antral, corpus, and fundic histology.

Methods

Patients attending for routine diagnostic gastroscopy and likely to need omeprazole were invited to take part in, and give written consent to this study, which was approved by the Parkside Ethical Committee. Patients with previous gastric surgery, known bleeding diathesis, taking oral anticoagulants, or who had been treated with bismuth compounds, omeprazole, or antibiotics known to be active against *H pylori* within the previous two months, were excluded. To determine *H pylori* status biopsy specimens were taken from the antrum (within 2 cm of the pylorus, two for histology and two for microbiology), corpus (half way along greater curvature, two for histology), and fundus (two for histology).

After each examination the endoscopes were disinfected by an automatic washing machine (Olympus EW20)[13] and the biopsy forceps were sterilised by autoclaving.

A ^{13}C-urea breath test[14] was performed within 24 hours of the initial endoscopy before starting treatment with omeprazole 40 mg each morning for four weeks in all patients in whom it was clinically indicated.

Grade of acute gastritis and grade of Helicobacter pylori *colonisation in patients before and after treatment with omeprazole 40 mg in the morning*

	Antrum				*Body*				*Fundus*			
	0	*1*	*2*	*3*	*0*	*1*	*2*	*3*	*0*	*1*	*2*	*3*
Grade of acute gastritis												
Before treatment (no)	6	4	14	4	11	2	14	1	11	8	2	1
After treatment (no)	14	3	10	1	7	3	18	0	7	6	9	3
(p)		<0·05								<0·05		
Grade of H pylori *colonisation*												
Before treatment (no)	1	6	11	11	0	12	11	5	1	19	1	0
After treatment (no)	12	9	5	1	5	11	8	4	3	15	4	5
(p)		<0·001										

FOLLOW UP

The ^{13}C-urea breath test was repeated in the *H pylori* positive patients after two weeks' treatment with omeprazole. A second endoscopy and a third breath test were completed after a further two weeks' therapy, and a fourth breath test was done two weeks after finishing omeprazole. If this breath test was negative, it was repeated two weeks later to document possible eradication at one month after finishing the drug.

Patients without *H pylori* were also studied to examine the possibility that overgrowth of other urease producing bacteria might yield a false positive breath test and to act as negative controls.

DETERMINATION OF *H PYLORI* STATUS

The presence of *H pylori* was determined by ^{13}C-urea breath test, culture of two antral biopsy specimens on selective and unselective media in microaerobic conditions for up to 10 days, and by histological examination of two specimens from the gastric antrum, corpus, and fundus. Patients were classified as *H pylori* positive by a positive breath test (excess δ $^{13}CO_2$ >5 per mil) together with either positive antral culture of positive histology from any site.

Clearance of *H pylori* was defined as a negative breath test (excess δ $^{13}CO_2$ <5 per mil) at the end of treatment, and eradication as a negative breath test one month after the end of treatment.[14]

^{13}C-UREA BREATH TEST

Semiquantitative assessments of the severity of *H pylori* infection were made with the ^{13}C-urea breath test (European standard protocol).[14] Briefly, a baseline sample of expired breath was obtained before drinking a fatty liquid test meal designed to delay gastric emptying. After 10 minutes, ^{13}C-urea (100 mg (99% pure, Cambridge Isotopes, Boston, USA) in 50 ml of tap water) was swallowed and distributed within the stomach by turning the patient to the left and right decubitus position. Two litre serial breath samples were collected every five minutes into a large reservoir collecting bag, from which a single 20 ml sample (pooled sample) was taken at the end of the test and analysed by mass spectrometry (BSIA, Brentford, London). The results were expressed as excess δ $^{13}CO_2$ excretion per mil by subtracting the baseline from the pooled sample.

HISTOLOGY

Biopsy specimens were processed routinely, embedded in paraffin wax, and stained (haematoxylin and eosin, and Gimenez method) for *H pylori*. In each patient the histologist examined two biopsy specimens at three levels (six sections) from the gastric antrum, body, and fundus and assessed the overall grade (0–3) according to the Sydney system of the activity (numbers of neutrophils) and chronicity (number of lymphocytes) of the gastritis.[15] For illustrative purposes the means of the overall grades for the three sites of all patients were then calculated. All histological assessments were made by the same experienced histopathologist (MMW), who was unaware of the other results, or of the patient's treatment. Ten biopsy specimens were selected at random for replicate histological examination, in order to assess observer variation.

STATISTICAL ANALYSIS

The Wilcoxon rank sum test and Spearman's rank correlation coefficient were used for statistical analysis of the histological data; the paired Student's t test was used for ^{13}C-urea breath test results.

Results

Thirty nine patients (24 men, median age 48 years, range 16–72 years) with moderate to severe reflux oesophagitis (n=14) or duodenal ulcer unhealed by H_2 antagonists (n=25) entered the study. In 29 of 39 patients *H pylori* was detected by a positive ^{13}C-urea breath test (mean excess δ $^{13}CO_2$ excretion=23·0 per mil), which was confirmed by either positive antral culture (n=26), or positive antral biopsy, or both (n=28). In all patients *H pylori* was also present in the corpus biopsy specimens and in 28 of 29 it was present in fundic specimens.

In 10 patients with reflux oesophagitis there was no evidence of *H pylori* infection on ^{13}C-urea breath test (mean (SEM) excess δ $^{13}CO_2$ excretion=1·9 (0·24) per mil), antral culture, or on antral, corpus, and fundic histology.

H PYLORI POSITIVE PATIENTS

Histology

Before starting omeprazole *H pylori* was found in all the biopsy specimens, except those from two patients. One patient had no antral *H pylori* (but mild chronic antral gastritis and *H pylori* in the corpus and fundus). Another patient had no fundic *H pylori* (but mild chronic fundal gastritis and *H pylori* in the corpus and antrum). The mean density scores for *H pylori* in the antrum, body, and fundus were 2·1, 1·75, and 1·04 respectively. The presence of *H pylori* was often associated with active (presence of neutrophils) antral (26 of 29) or corpus gastritis (18 of 28). There were features of chronic inflammation in all the

© Gut 1995; 36: 12–16

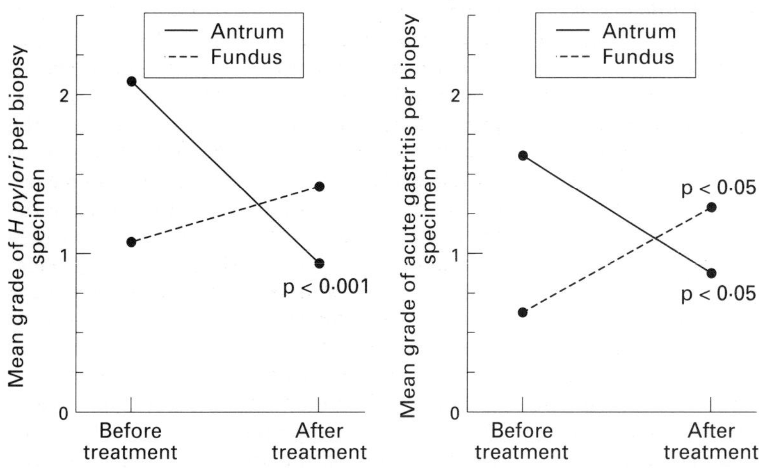

Figure 1: Changes in antral and fundal Helicobacter pylori *colonisation and severity of acute antral and fundal gastritis before and after omeprazole, 40 mg mane for four weeks.*

remaining, *H pylori* positive antral, corpus, and fundal specimens.

After four weeks' treatment with omeprazole, *H pylori* could no longer be detected in the antral specimen of 12 patients. Moreover, in three of these, *H pylori* could no longer be detected in the corpus specimens, but all three still had organisms in the fundus. In the patients who were *H pylori* positive before starting treatment, the mean density score of antral *H pylori* was significantly lower after four weeks' omeprazole (0·90 *v* 2·1 before treatment, $p<0·001$, Fig 1) with a similar, but not significant, trend in the corpus (1·75 *v* 1·3, $p>0·05$). In contrast, there was a small increase in the density of fundal *H pylori* (from 1·0 to 1·4, $p>0·05$). These changes in the distribution of *H pylori* were associated with a decreased mean grade of active antral gastritis (from 1·6 to 0·9, $p<0·05$) and an increased mean grade of active fundal gastritis (from 0·6 to 1·3, $p<0·05$, Fig 1). The decreased density of antral and corpus *H pylori* in biopsy specimens correlated with a decreased excess $\delta\ ^{13}CO_2$ excretion measured by the urea breath test (rank Spearman correlation, $r=0·45$, $p<0·05$). There was no change in the grade of chronic gastritis in the antrum, corpus, or fundus after omeprazole treatment. In one patient, unusual morphological forms of bacteria, not typical of *H pylori*, were detected after four weeks' omeprazole treatment.

Replicate histological examination assessments of gastritis and *H pylori* were the same (n=5), or varied by no more than one grade (n=5).

^{13}C-urea breath test

The excess $\delta\ ^{13}CO_2$ excretion fell progressively in *H pylori* positive patients (n=29) after treatment with omeprazole 40 mg daily. The mean (SEM) excess $\delta\ ^{13}CO_2$ excretion fell from 23·0 (2·1) per mil before starting omeprazole to 17·2 (2·1) after two weeks' treatment ($p<0·05$, compared with before treatment), and to 15·5 (2·7) per mil after four weeks ($p<0·25$, compared with two weeks) (Fig 2).The fall in $\delta\ ^{13}CO_2$ at four weeks was closely correlated with the decrease in the semiquantitative histological assessments of *H pylori* ($r=0·6$, $p<0·001$). In four patients the excess $\delta\ ^{13}CO_2$ excretion fell to <5 per mil after four weeks, but in all four the breath test was positive two weeks after finishing omeprazole. In the 12 patients with an antrum histologically cleared of *H pylori*, the fall in excess $\delta\ ^{13}CO_2$ excretion was more pronounced than in the remainder: the (mean (SEM) excess $\delta\ ^{13}CO_2$ excretion fell from 23·0 (2·1) to 9·9 (4·2) per mil, $p<0·001$ from mean value before treatment), compared with 18·3 (3·3) per mil in those without antral clearance of *H pylori*.

Two weeks after finishing treatment the excess $\delta\ ^{13}CO_2$ excretion returned to values before treatment (mean excess $\delta\ ^{13}CO_2$ excretion=23·0 (3·8) per mil, $p>0·5$ *v* value before treatment, Fig 2).

H PYLORI NEGATIVE PATIENTS

In the *H pylori* negative patients there was no significant change in the excess $\delta\ ^{13}CO_2$ excretion after two weeks' treatment with omeprazole (mean excess $\delta\ ^{13}CO_2=2·4$ (0·37) per mil *v* 1·9 (0·24) per mil before treatment, $p>0·25$).

Discussion

Omeprazole, given in a dose of 40 mg daily for four weeks, significantly decreased histological evidence of *H pylori* in the antral mucosa and the corpus, and significantly reduced the activity of antral gastritis. In the fundic mucosa, however, *H pylori* increased as did the activity of fundic gastritis; but overall the ^{13}C-urea breath test results decreased progressively with treatment. The breath test became transiently negative in only four of 29 patients but *H pylori* was not eradicated by omeprazole in any patient.

These results confirm previous reports

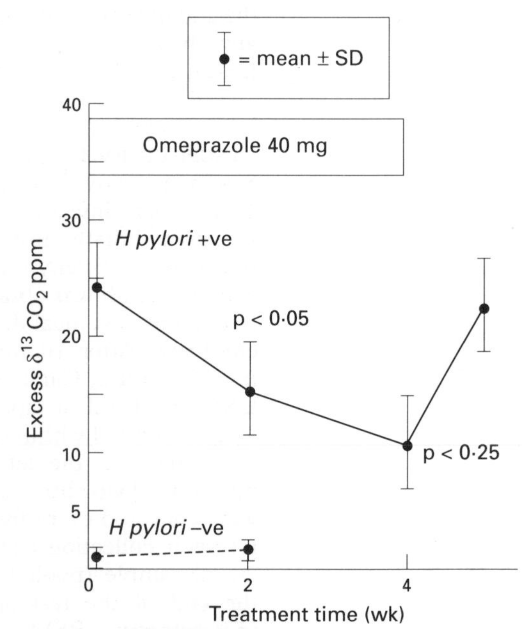

Figure 2: ^{13}C-urea breath test results (mean (SD)) in patients who were positive and negative for Helicobacter pylori *before, during, and after two and four weeks' omeprazole 40 mg daily.*

© Gut 1995; 36: 12–16

that omeprazole suppresses *H pylori* infection.[11 12 17–19] In a small study using the ^{14}C-urea breath test, Bell *et al*[12] cleared the organism in half the patients given omeprazole 40 mg for four weeks, while a dose of 20 mg cleared *H pylori* in only one quarter. No biopsy assessments of *H pylori* infection were made in this study. After four weeks' treatment with omeprazole 20 mg, Daw *et al*[16] reported 50% clearance from the antrum using culture as the criterion (the associated gastritis improved in 54% of patients), but over half the patients who had been negative on culture at the end of treatment had *H pylori* in the gastric pits visible on transmission electron microscopy. Similarly, 40% clearance of antral *H pylori* was reported after only two weeks of omeprazole 20 mg, but histology was used to assess the *H pylori* status.[18] Similar results were also reported in a large study dealing with duodenal ulcer patients after four weeks of either ranitidine 150 mg bd or omeprazole 10 or 20 mg daily: in patients receiving omeprazole 20 mg daily, antral *H pylori* was cleared in 68% of cases, with a concurrent improvement in the activity of the gastritis.[19] These changes were not dose related.

The highest (72%) clearance of antral *H pylori* was reported by Vigneri *et al* after four weeks' omeprazole 40 mg per day.[20] Thus, clearance of antral *H pylori* based on biopsy findings occurs in 40% to 80% of patients after either two or four weeks' treatment. This effect does not seem to be dose-related, although two retrospective studies have suggested that prolonged treatment might produce higher clearance rates.[17] Only our study and that of Vigneri *et al* have documented the increase and shift of *H pylori* to the fundic mucosa with increased colonisation of this area.

The pathogenic effects of *H pylori* may depend on the pattern of colonisation, but factors that determine the distribution of the organism within the stomach are unknown. *H pylori* is most often isolated from the gastric antrum, but loss of normal gastric type epithelium (for example, with gastric antral atrophy or intestinal metaplasia) or the loss of the adherent layer of mucus because of bile reflux is associated with lower levels of antral colonisation. Data from this study suggest that the distribution of *H pylori* can be changed by omeprazole, so far the only agent shown to influence the distribution of *H pylori* within the stomach.

One possible explanation for the suppression of *H pylori* by omeprazole is bacterial overgrowth. In this study neither mucosal biopsy specimens nor gastric juice were assessed microbiologically for bacterial overgrowth because of the inherent problems of accurately reproducing the in vivo microenvironment in vitro. Preliminary data suggest, however, that bacterial overgrowth does not correlate with the suppression of *H pylori*.[21] A possible explanation for this observation is that *H pylori* and other bacteria do not share the same habitat: *H pylori* is generally found beneath the mucus layer or in the gastric pits, while other bacteria colonise the gastric lumen and surface mucus. In addition, loss of antral *H pylori* in patients with atrophic antral gastritis (but in whom *H pylori* persists in the corpus) is seldom associated with bacterial overgrowth (J Wyatt, personal communication).

Omeprazole and lansoprazole are potent inhibitors of *H pylori* in vitro, with minimum inhibitory concentrations that compare favourably with bismuth salts.[22–24] After the preliminary results of our study had been reported, Bugnoli *et al* discovered that omeprazole was a powerful inhibitor of *H pylori* urease. Although these data may seem to explain our findings, mutant urease negative *H pylori* and *H mustelae* were also inhibited by omeprazole. In addition inhibition of urease is an ineffective treatment for *H mustelae*,[25] which suggests that omeprazole's urease inhibition alone does not account for our findings.

Although omeprazole heals duodenal ulcers more rapidly than H_2 antagonists do,[19] the incidence of recurrence in the absence of maintenance treatment is similar.[26] Duodenal ulcer healing rates are related to the extent of acid suppression.[27] It has also been shown that duodenal ulcer healing rates may increase when H_2 antagonists are combined with anti-*H pylori* treatment.[28] It is possible, therefore, that more rapid duodenal ulcer healing with omeprazole may depend on suppression of *H pylori* as well as greater inhibition of gastric acid. Because omeprazole does not eradicate *H pylori*, the incidence of duodenal ulcer recurrence after initial healing with omeprazole is similar to those recorded with other antisecretory agents.[26]

We have shown that during treatment with omeprazole, *H pylori* may be suppressed sometimes simulating clearance of the antrum and corpus, or both, but with relapse of *H pylori* after the end of treatment. This effect of omeprazole considerably impairs the sensitivity of antral biopsy tissue for detecting *H pylori* in patients who are taking this drug. The practical consequences of this observation are that if breath tests are not available biopsies should also be taken from the corpus and fundus in order to determine if *H pylori* is still present in the stomach. In addition for patients unable to temporarily stop treatment with omeprazole, a negative breath test result should be interpreted with caution.

How omeprazole suppresses *H pylori* is not clear. We hypothesise that our findings may be due to *H pylori*'s chemotaxis for H+, however, further studies of the relationship between H+, *H pylori*, and the role of urease are needed.

The authors thank the endoscopy staff at the Central Middlesex and St Mary's Hospitals for help with this study. Dr R Logan was supported by a grant from Glaxo Group Research.
An abstract of this study was presented at the European Digestive Diseases Week in Amsterdam in September 1991.

1 Rauws EA, Langenberg W, Houthoff HJ, Zanen HC, Tytgat GNJ. Campylobacter pyloridis-associated chronic active antral gastritis. A prospective study of its prevalence and the effects of antibacterial and antiulcer treatment. *Gastroenterology* 1988; **94:** 33–40.
2 Rauws EAJ, Tytgat GNJ. Cure of duodenal ulcer with eradication of Helicobacter pylori. *Lancet* 1990; **335:** 1233–5.
3 Axon AR. Duodenal ulcer: the villain unmasked? *BMJ* 1991; **302:** 919–21.

4 Eaton KA, Brooks CL, Morgan DR, Krakowka S. Essential role of urease in pathogenesis of gastritis induced by Helicobacter pylori in gnobiotic piglets. *Infect Immun* 1991; **59:** 2470–5.
5 Mobley HLT, Hausinger RP. Microbial ureases: significance, regulation and molecular characterisation. *Microbiol Rev* 1989; **53:** 85–108.
6 Maton PN. Omeprazole. *N Engl J Med* 1991; **324:** 965–75.
7 Mainguet P, Delmee M, Debongnie J-C. Omeprazole, Campylobacter pylori and duodenal ulcer. *Lancet* 1989; ii: 389–90.
8 Ghelani AM, Hale S, Coleman H, Radziwonik H, Robertson C, Atkinson M. Lack of in vitro activity of omeprazole against Campylobacter pylori. *J Clin Pathol* 1990; **43:** 171–2.
9 Biasco G, Miglioli M, Barbara L, Corinaldesi R, Di Febo G. Omeprazole, Helicobacter pylori, gastritis and duodenal ulcer. *Lancet* 1989; ii: 1403.
10 Tessaro P, Di Mario M, Rugge M, Baffa R, Pasqualetti P, Vio A, *et al.* Efficacy of omeprazole in eradicating Helicobacter pylori from the gastric mucosa. *Eur J Gastroenterol Hepatol* 1990; **2** (1): S117–8.
11 Sharp J, Logan RPH, Walker MM, Gummett PA, Misiewicz JJ, Baron JH. Effect of omeprazole on Helicobacter pylori. *Gut* 1991; **32:** A565.
12 Weil J, Bell DG, Powell K, Morden A, Harrison G, Gants PW, *et al.* Omeprazole and Helicobacter pylori: temporary suppression rather than true eradication. *Alimentary Pharmacology and Therap* 1991; **5:** 309–13.
13 Weller IVD, Williams CB, Jeffries DJ, Leicester RJ, Gazzard BG, Axon ATR, *et al.* Cleaning and disinfection of equipment for gastrointestinal flexible endoscopy: interim recommendations of a Working Party of the British Society of Gastroenterology. *Gut* 1988; **29:** 1134–51.
14 Logan RPH, Dill S, Bauer FE, Walker MM, Hirschl AM, Gummett PA, *et al.* The European ^{13}C-urea breath test for the detection of Helicobacter pylori. *European Journal of Gastroenterology and Hepatology* 1991; **3:** 915–21.
15 Misiewicz JJ. The Sydney system: a new classification of gastritis. *J Gastroenteral Hepatol* 1991; **6:** 207–52.
16 Daw MA, Deegan P, O'Morain C. The effect of omeprazole on Helicobacter pylori and associated gastritis. *Alimentary Pharmacology and Therapy* 1991; **5:** 435–39.
17 Stolte M, Bethke B. Elimination of Helicobacter pylori under treatment with omeprazole. *Z Gastroenterol (Verh)* 1990; **28:** 271–4.
18 Arachimandritis C, Tjivras M, Davaris P, Fertakis A. Effect of omeprazole of H pylori after 2 weeks of treatment. *Italian Journal of Gastroenterology* 1991; **23:** 357–8.
19 Hui WM, Lam SK, Ho J, Lai CL, Lok ASF, Ng MMT, *et al.* Effect of omeprazole on duodenal ulcer-associated antral gastritis and Helicobacter pylori. *Dig Dis Sci* 1991; **36:** 577–82.
20 Vigneri S, Termini R, Scialabba A, Pisciotta G, Di Mario F. Omeprazole therapy modifies the gastric localisation of Helicobacter pylori. *Am J Gastroenterol* 1991; **86:** 1276.
21 Fraser R, Thorens J, Froelich F, Gonvers JJ, Bille J, Blum A, *et al.* Relationship between Helicobacter pylori infection and gastric and duodenal bacterial overgrowth. *Gastroenterology* 1993; **104:** A81.
22 Iwahi T, Satoh H, Nakao M, Iwasaki T, Yamazaki T, Kubo K, *et al.* Lansoprazole, a novel benzimidazole proton pump inhibitor, and its related compounds have selective activity against Helicobacter pylori. *Antimicrobial Agents and Chemotherapy* 1991; **35:** 490–6.
23 Bugnoli M, Bayeli PF, Rappuoli R, Pennatini C, Figura N, Crabtree JE. Inhibition of Helicobacter pylori urease by omeprazole. *European Journal of Gastroenterology Hepatology* 1993; **5:** 683–5.
24 Nagata K, Satoh H, Iwahi T, Shimoyama T, Tamura T. Potent inhibitory action of the gastric proton pump inhibitor lansoprazole against urease activity of Helicobacter pylori: unique action selective for H pylori cells. *Antimicrobial Agents and Chemotherapy* 1993; **37:** 769–74.
25 McColm AA, Bagshaw JA, O'Malley CFO. Development of a ^{14}C-urea breath test in ferrets colonised with Helicobacter mustelae: effects of treatment with bismuth, antibiotics and urease inhibitors. *Gut* 1993; **34:** 181–6.
26 Schiller KFR, Axon ATR, Carr-Locke DL, Cockel R, Donovan IA, Edmonstone WM, *et al.* Duodenal ulcer recurrence after healing with omeprazole or cimetidine treatment: a multicentre study in the UK. *Gut* 1989; **30:** A1490.
27 Hunt RH, Howden CW, Jones DB, Burget DW, Kerr GD. The correlation between acid suppression and peptic ulcer healing. *Scan J Gastroenterol* 1986; **21** (suppl 125): 22–9.
28 Graham DY, Ginger M, Lew PA-C, Evans DG, Evans DJ, Klein PD, *et al.* Effect of triple therapy (antibiotics plus bismuth) on duodenal ulcer healing. *Ann Intern Med* 1991; **115:** 266–9.

© *Lancet* 1996; 347: 995–999

Postoperative morbidity and mortality after D_1 and D_2 resections for gastric cancer: preliminary results of the MRC randomised controlled surgical trial

*A Cuschieri, P Fayers, J Fielding, J Craven, J Bancewicz, V Joypaul, P Cook, for the Surgical Cooperative Group**

Summary

Background In Japan the surgical approach to treatment of potentially curable gastric cancer, including extended lymphadenectomy, seems in retrospective surveys to give better results than the less radical procedures favoured in Western countries. There has, however, been no evidence from randomised trials that extended lymphadenectomy (D_2 gastric resection) confers a survival advantage. This question was addressed in a trial involving thirty-two surgeons in Europe.

Methods In a prospective randomised controlled trial, D_1 resection (level 1 lymphadenectomy) was compared with D_2 resection (levels 1 and 2 lymphadenectomy). Central randomisation (200 patients in each arm) followed a staging laparotomy.

Findings The D_2 group had greater postoperative hospital mortality (13% *vs* 6·5%; p=0·04 [95% CI 9–18% for D_2, 4–11% for D_1] and higher overall postoperative morbidity (46% *vs* 28%; p<0·001); their postoperative stay was also longer. The excess postoperative morbidity and mortality in the D_2 group was accounted for by distal pancreatico-splenectomy and splenectomy. In the whole group (400 patients), survival beyond three years was 30% in patients whose gastrectomy included en-bloc pancreatico-splenic resection versus 50% in the remainder.

Interpretation D_2 gastric resections are followed by higher morbidity and mortality than D_1 resections. These disadvantages are consequent upon additional pancreatectomies and distal splenectomies, and in long-term follow-up the higher mortality when the pancreas and spleen are resected may prove to nullify any survival benefit from D_2 procedures.

Lancet 1996; **347:** 995–99

*Members of group listed at end of article

Department of Surgery, Ninewells Hospital & Medical School, Dundee DD1 9SY, UK (Prof A Cuschieri MD, V Joypaul FRCS); **MRC Cancer Trials Office, Cambridge, UK** (P Fayers BSc, P Cook BA); **Queen Elizabeth Hospital, Birmingham, UK** (J Fielding FRCS); **Kingstown General Hospital, St Vincents, Jamaica** (J Craven FRCS); **Hope Hospital, Salford, UK** (J Bancewicz FRCS)

Correspondence to: Prof A Cuschieri, Chairman, MRC Gastric Cancer Working Party, Department of Surgery, Ninewells Hospital & Medical School, University of Dundee, Dundee DD1 9SY, UK

Introduction

Despite the steady decline in its incidence, carcinoma of the stomach remains one of the common lethal malignancies in the West. In the United Kingdom, the disease affects 12 000 people a year, causing 11 000 deaths.[1] Surgical resection is the only effective therapy but the locoregional recurrence and five-year survival rates after resection for gastric cancer in the West remain poor[2] and distinctly inferior to the reported experience from Japan.[3-5] Although Japanese patients with advanced gastric cancer (infiltrating the muscularis propria) differ from Western patients in being younger and having less cardiorespiratory disease,[6] the crucial factors in their better outcome may be the higher resectability rate and the performance in Japan of extended lymphadenectomy. These radical (D_2) resections, based on knowledge of lymph flow from the stomach, entail removal of the level 2 nodes (N_2) in addition to the perigastric nodes within 3 cm of the tumour (N_1).[7] Several centres in the West have practised and reported favourably on the Japanese surgical approach,[8-11] but there is no evidence from randomised studies that D_2 gives better long-term survival than D_1. The reluctance of surgeons in Western countries to adopt the more extensive operations, which often involve distal pancreatectomy and splenectomy and require major dissections of the vascular pedicles down to the aortic level, has stemmed from the fear of increasing the early morbidity and mortality. Other considerations that may have influenced the decision to continue with the D_1 approach include the longer operating time and the costs of intensive care in these patients. It is against this background that the Medical Research Council (MRC) Gastric Cancer Surgical Trial (ST01) was set up.

Patients and methods

Registration

Patients enrolled in MRC ST01 were to have histologically proven and potentially curable gastric adenocarcinoma. The

Panel: **Assessment of resections**

Absolute curative resection
No residual intraperitoneal disease
Histological tumour-free resection margins
Level of dissection (D) greater than the level of lymph node involvement (N)

Relative curative resection
No residual intraperitoneal disease
Histologically tumour free resection margins
Level of dissection (D) equals the level of lymph node involvement (N)

Relative non-curative
Obvious residual peritoneal disease
or
Involved resection margin(s) on histology

	D_1 resection	D_2 resection
Sex		
Male	132 (66%)	138 (69%)
Female	68 (34%)	62 (31%)
Age, yr		
Median	67	67
Range	38–86	26–83
Tumour location		
C, CM	61 (31%)	56 (28%)
M, MA, MC	31 (16%)	42 (21%)
A, AM	88 (44%)	94 (47%)
CMA	20 (10%)	8 (4%)
Gastric resection*		
Distal	88 (44%)	91 (46%)
Total	110 (56%)	108 (54%)
Disease stage†		
pT_1 (lamina propria/submucosa)	32 (20·3%)	32 (18·6%)
pT_2 (muscularis propria)	58 (36·7%)	20 (37·2%)
pT_3 (serosa/localised infiltration)	68 (43%)	76 (44%)

C=cardia; M=middle third; A=antrum. *No resection was performed on 2 patients in the D_1 group and 1 patient in the D_2 group.
†Based on 330 out of 400 where the tumour histopathology was reviewed and staged by an independent Pathology Review Panel.

Table 1: **Comparison of the two randomised groups**

study was directed from a central office, which was also responsible for randomisation. Potentially eligible patients were registered with the office provided they did not require emergency surgery, had not undergone previous gastric surgery, and did not harbour a coexisting cancer. Also excluded were young patients (<20 yr) and those with serious co-morbid cardiorespiratory disease which precluded safe D_2 resections.

Staging laparotomy and randomisation

Following the preoperative work-up, all registered patients underwent staging laparotomy to define potentially curative disease. This staging included exposure of the infracolic aorta, with biopsy and frozen section if enlarged lymph nodes were detected in the region of the left renal vein. Eligible cases were those that fell within the Japanese clinical staging S_{0-2}, P_0, H_0 N_{0-2}[7]—ie, stage I–III gastric cancer except those with positive infracolic aortic nodes. Patients fulfilling these criteria were randomised centrally (over the phone) to either D_1 or D_2 gastrectomy at the same operating session.

Treatment arms

The operative details of the two procedures were defined in terms of the extent of gastric resection, the macroscopic tumour-free resection margins, and the level of lymphadenectomy (N_1 or N_2). In essence, D_1 resections entailed removal of the lymph nodes within 3 cm of the tumour en bloc with the greater omentum and the stomach. D_2 resections necessitated the additional extirpation of the omental bursa and the lymph nodes along the coeliac axis down to the aorta, the hepatoduodenal and retroduodenal nodes, and the splenic and retropancreatic nodes, depending on the exact location of the tumour. In both arms, a distal gastrectomy up to and including the duodenal bulb with a minimum of 2·5 cm proximal tumour margin was performed for antral neoplasms, whereas a total gastrectomy was undertaken for middle and proximal tumours. The surgeon was asked to categorise the operation performed (in both treatment arms) into absolute curative, relative curative, and relative non-curative (panel). A total of 400 patients were randomised subsequent to the staging laparotomy.

Quality control

To ensure standardisation of the two procedures, an operative booklet and videotapes of the procedures were produced and agreed upon by the participating surgeons. In addition the "operative form" was designed to enable the data managers and the trials coordinator (AC) to establish the extent of the procedure performed relative to the randomised option for each patient. Where discrepancies were found between the randomised option and the operative report, the case details were

Gastrectomy	D_1	D_2	p
No resection	1/2 (50%)	0/1 (0%)	
Distal	2/88 (2%)	9/91 (10%)	
Total	10/110 (9%)	17/108 (16%)	
Overall	13/200 (6·5%)	26/200 (13%)	0·04

Table 2: **Hospital mortality**

checked with the respective surgeon. A trial monitoring committee supervised the progress of the study throughout the entire period of recruitment.

Statistical aspects

Eligible patients were randomised centrally by use of random permuted blocks and with stratification for centre, nodal status, and tumour location (antral, middle, proximal, total, mixed). Sample size calculations were based upon a pre-study survey of 26 gastric surgeons, which indicated that the baseline five-year survival rate for D_1 surgery was expected to be 20%, and improvement in survival to 34% (14% change) with D_2 resection would be a realistic expectation and one that would justify the anticipated increase in surgical morbidity and mortality. Thus 400 patients were randomised (200 in each arm), providing 90% power to detect such a difference with $p<0·05$.

The data were analysed according to the intention-to-treat principle. Significance tests were performed by Fisher's exact test for 2×2 tables. Survival curves were analysed by use of the log-rank test. Confidence intervals for percentages are 95% intervals based on exact binomial probabilities.

Results

In total, 737 patients with histologically proven adenocarcinoma were registered from thirty-two surgeons over seven years. Of these, 337 (46%) patients were found to be ineligible at staging laparotomy, which indicated that their disease was more advanced than that specified in the protocol; treatment of these patients was left to the individual surgeon. Table 1 shows demographic, surgical, and histopathological data on the patients who were randomised. The two groups were similar with respect to age, sex ratio, tumour location, extent of surgical resection, and stage of disease. There were three protocol violations: one patient proved to have a gastric lymphoma (D_1) and in two (one each in D_1 and D_2) the staging laparotomy was incorrect (posterior aortic invasion, positive pre-aortic nodes) and the neoplasm was not resected but intubated.

Early mortality

Early death included deaths within 30 days of surgery and also deaths in patients who died after 30 days but never left hospital (hospital mortality). The usual definition of postoperative mortality includes only patients who die within 30 days of surgery; however, in view of the ability of modern intensive care to delay death, this will underestimate the true mortality consequent upon radical surgery. Hospital mortality as defined above was adopted by the Surgical Cooperative Group in 1990 as being the only acceptable definition of postoperative mortality.

Treatment allocated	Post-op course/complications				Total morbidity
	None	Minor*	Serious	Fatal	
D_1	145 (72·5%)	30 (15%)	12 (6%)	13 (6·5%)	55 (28%)
D_2	108 (54%)	45 (22·5%)	21 (10·5%)	26 (13%)	92 (46%)

*Minor complications included wound infections without wound dehiscence, minor chest infections/pulmonary collapse, deep vein thrombosis without pulmonary embolism or leg oedema.

Table 3: **Categorisation of postoperative morbidity in first 371 randomised patients**

Complication	D_1	D_2	p
Haemorrhage	6	4	
Anastomotic leakage	11	26*	0·015
Cardiac	2	8	
Respiratory	5	8	
Pulmonary embolism	1	1	

*Includes 2 patients where the dehiscence was associated with severe pancreatitis and pancreatic fistula and 1 patient with necrosis of gastric remant.

Table 4: **Serious/fatal morbidity**

Table 2 gives the data on hospital mortality. The overall hospital mortality was 39/400 (9·8%). This was significantly higher after D_2 (13%, CI 9%–18%) than after D_1 resections (6·5%, CI 4%–11%) (p=0·04). Both to allow comparison with other studies and to eliminate any possibility of bias from D_2 patients being at greater risk of cancer-related (non-operative) mortality during their longer hospital stay, additional analyses were done on postoperative mortality by the conventional 30-day definition. There were 21 D_2 deaths (10·5%) and 9 D_1 deaths (4·5%), p<0·04. Hence our results cannot be ascribed to bias.

In the two groups, there were more deaths after total gastrectomy than after distal resections, but this difference was not statistically significant. Nor did the age of the patients (above or below 70 years) or the curative intent of the procedure influence mortality.

Postoperative hospital morbidity

All the postoperative complications were assessed independently by three surgeons (AC, JF, and JC) as serious and potentially fatal (eg, severe pancreatitis, necrosis of gastric remnant, haemorrhage, anastomotic leakage, major cardiorespiratory incidents requiring intensive care) or minor (wound infection, urinary tract infection, minor patchy pulmonary collapse, prolonged ileus, uncomplicated calf vein thrombosis); the results are shown in table 3. The overall morbidity was significantly higher (p<0·001) in the D_2 group (46%, CI 39%–53%) than in the D_1 group (28%, CI 21%–34%). Table 4 summarises the serious and fatal complications. The outstanding difference was the much higher incidence of anastomotic dehiscence in the D_2 group. In addition, major cardiorespiratory complications requiring intensive care support were more often encountered in the D_2 arm although the difference here was not significant.

The wound infection rate was low in both arms (D_1 4%, D_2 5%) and there were only two instances of deep vein thrombosis (uncomplicated).

Effect of distal pancreatico-splenectomy

Distal pancreatico-splenectomy had a significant adverse effect on both morbidity and mortality (table 5). Logistic regression analysis showed that the difference in mortality and morbidity between D_1 and D_2 became non-significant after allowance for pancreatico-splenectomy. In the D_2 group both morbidity and mortality rates were 100% higher when distal pancreatectomy and splenectomy formed part of the resection. Severe (necrotic) pancreatitis and necrosis of the gastric remnant was encountered in 2 and 1 patients, respectively, within the fatal subgroup (all of whom had anastomotic dehiscence). Splenectomy without pancreatic resection was likewise associated with morbidity and mortality (table 6). Again the difference between D_1 and D_2 became non-significant after allowance for removal of the spleen. The increased morbidity after splenectomy was not due to a higher incidence of serious infections.

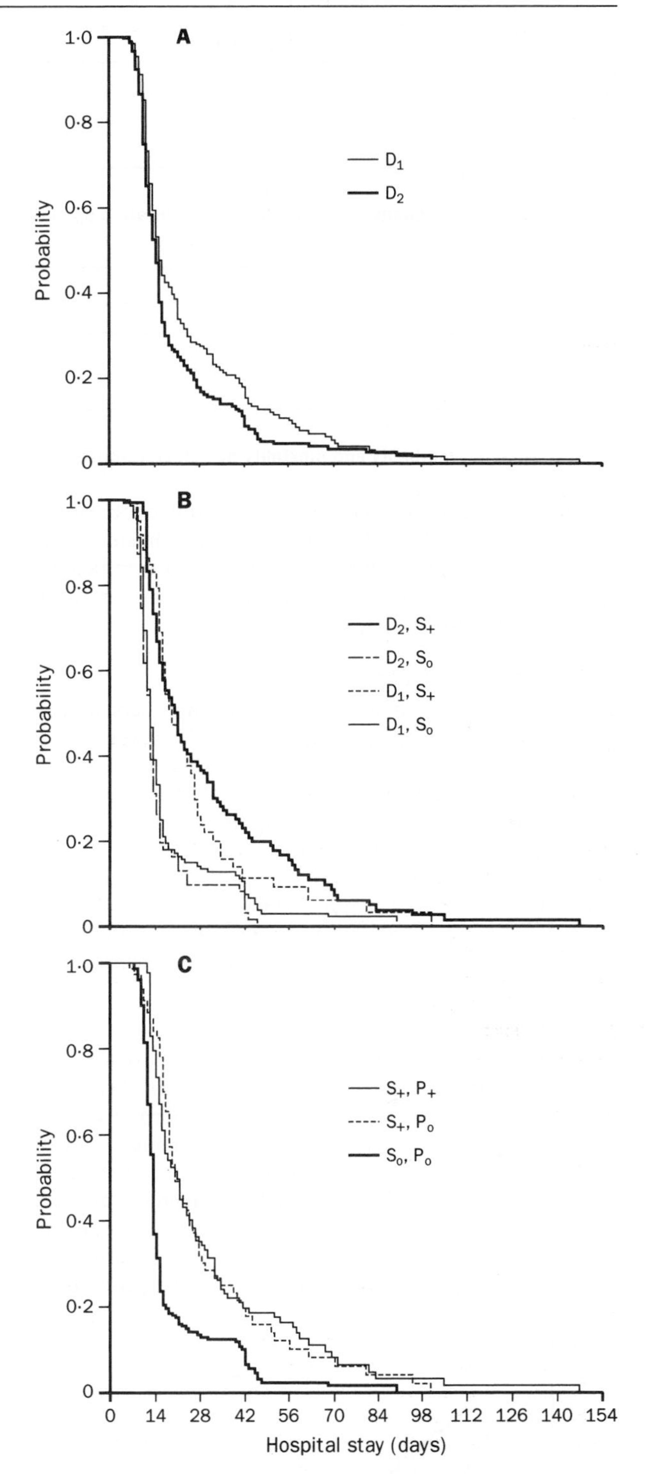

Figure 1: **Lengths of hospital stay (a) by treatment D_1 *vs* D_2, (b) by treatment and spleen group, (c) by spleen and pancreas group**

S_+=spleen removed, S_0=spleen not removed, P_+=pancreas removed, P_0=pancreas not removed.

Postoperative hospital stay

The data on hospital stay exclude all early deaths and are therefore based on 355 patients. For D_1 surgery, the median time spent in hospital after operation was 14 days (mean 18, range 6–101). For the D_2 group, the median postoperative stay was 14 days (mean 23, range 10–147 days). A better appreciation of the difference in postoperative hospital stay between the two arms is obtained when the probability data are displayed

© *Lancet* 1996; 347: 995–999

	No pancreas or spleen removal			Pancreas and spleen removal			p
	D_1	D_2	D_1+D_2	D_1	D_2	D_1+D_2	
Morbidity	53 (28%)	26 (30%)	79 (28%)	2 (–)	66 (58%)	68 (56%)	<0·001
Mortality	12 (6%)	8 (9%)	20 (7%)	1 (–)	18 (16%)	19 (16%)	0·01
Total patients	192	87	279	8	113	121	

p values relate to D_1+D_2.

Table 5: **Hospital morbidity and mortality by pancreatico-splenectomy**

	No spleen removal			Spleen removal			p
	D_1	D_2	D_1+D_2	D_1	D_2	D_1+D_2	
Morbidity	28 (20%)	15 (22%)	43 (28%)	27 (44%)	77 (59%)	104 (54%)	<0·001
Mortality	5 4%)	4 (6%)	9 (4%)	8 (13%)	22 (17%)	30 (16%)	<0·001
Total patients	138	69	207	62	131	193	

p values relate to D_1+D_2.

Table 6: **Hospital morbidity and mortality by spleen removal**

graphically (figure 1). The effect of distal pancreatico-splenectomy or splenectomy on duration of hospital stay is clear. The length of hospital stay differed significantly ($p=0·01$) for D_1 versus D_2 and for splenectomy versus no splenectomy ($p<0·001$).

Collective survival rate

The follow-up period to date with the numbers at risk precludes any valid inter-group analysis. However, figure 2 shows the collective survival of the total randomised cohort up to March, 1995. The survival in patients who had pancreatico-splenectomy has been consistently lower than that of the remaining patients beyond three years (30% *vs* 50%). The survival curves show a significant effect (Cox model) for removal of pancreas ($p=0·05$), but after allowance for removal of pancreas the overall curves do not differ significantly with respect to the spleen.

Discussion

The surgical management of resectable potentially curative gastric cancer is a balance between maximum locoregional control and acceptable morbidity and mortality. Cure by surgical treatment alone is then dependent on the absence of occult systemic disease. A radical procedure with extended lymphadenectomy will confer little material benefit if its potential for reducing locoregional recurrence in the gastric bed is offset by higher mortality. Over the years, Japanese surgeons have performed extensive D_2 and D_3 resections for gastric cancer with impressive survival figures and mortality rates lower than 3%.[3-5] Operative experience is clearly important; and in Japan, with its high incidence of gastric cancer, management is centralised so that designated surgeons deal with it. In Europe, where regional specialisation is uncommon, such experience and technical skill can seldom be matched. Second, Japanese patients presenting with gastric cancer are younger by an average of 6 years than their Western counterparts and have a lower prevalence of vascular and cardiorespiratory disease.[6] The third factor concerns the large number of centres and surgeons involved in the present MRC trial. Although surgical skills and quality of postoperative care cannot be ignored, subset analysis of the mortality per centre did not show any specific trend. Indeed we could argue that this trial was pragmatic and therefore likely to reflect real life.

Our finding that D_2 resections carry a higher mortality and morbidity than D_1 resections is in total agreement with the outcome of the equivalent Dutch trial.[12] The two studies were run in parallel and the data monitoring teams cooperated freely. The results of these two randomised prospective trials are at variance with other recent reports.[8-11] The German study demonstrated a much lower mortality for D_2 resections (5%) than that in the Dutch and MRC trials. However, the German study was a prospective audit and not a randomised trial. The lowest combined morbidity and mortality rates after D_2 resections in the West have been reported from the Sloan Kettering Institute (US)[9] and Leeds (UK),[11] but both are retrospective single-centre series.

Subset analysis of the MRC and Dutch trials indicates that the higher morbidity in the D_2 arm is due not to the extended lymphadenectomy but largely to pancreatic resection and splenectomy. In this context, the Japanese have lately stressed that extended lymphadenectomy should whenever possible be undertaken without distal pancreatectomy.[13] The adverse consequences of distal pancreatico-splenectomy resection may be related to subclinical leakage of pancreatic juice, which would accumulate in close proximity to the proximal reconstructive anastomosis. In the MRC study, instances of severe pancreatitis and overt pancreatic fistulae were encountered in the subgroup of patients who developed anastomotic dehiscence. Another possible factor is vascular compromise of the stomach remnant following proximal ligature of the arterial pedicles and the extensive clearance of tissue and lymph nodes in the gastric bed.

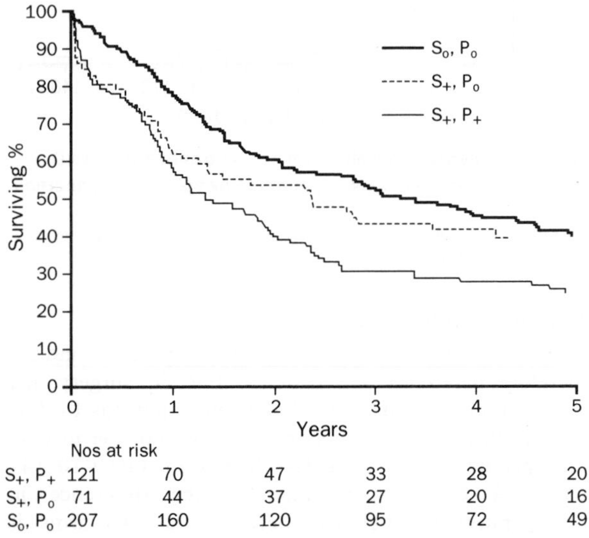

Figure 2: **Collective survival (both arms) up to March, 1995**

One instance of total necrosis of the gastric stump was also recorded in the present study. The adverse effect of splenectomy on morbidity and mortality after gastric resection for cancer observed in this trial is not explained by a higher incidence of serious infection. However, these subset analyses were not based upon a randomised comparison and, pending a randomised controlled study, they should be interpreted with some caution.

We must stress that the reported data on postoperative outcome from the Dutch and the MRC trials cannot be taken as proof that D_2 resections give lower survival; in the MRC study the 5-year follow-up period has not been reached. However, the collective long-term survival rate reported in here renders it unlikely that any survival advantage for D_2 resection will be detected in the future.

The question raised by this analysis is whether D_2 resection with regional lymphadenectomy (N_2) but without splenectomy or pancreatic resection might be the best management for potentially curable advanced gastric cancer. This hypothesis needs to be addressed by a separate trial. Meanwhile, gastrectomy with N_2 lymphadenectomy but without splenectomy or pancreatectomy seems to be the safest option. The lesser magnitude of the procedure will permit trials of neoadjuvant perioperative chemotherapy.[14]

Members of the Surgical Cooperative Group are: D Alderson (UK), W Allum (UK), J Bancewicz (UK), H D Becker (Germany), A Broughton (UK), F C Campbell (UK), J Clark (UK), J Craven (UK), A Cuschieri (UK), A Cook (UK), I Donovan (UK), N Dorricot (UK), D Ellis (UK), J Fielding (UK), P Finan (UK), D Fossard (UK), A Hall (UK), M Hallisey (UK), T Hennessey (Ireland), D Kumar (UK), J Magnusson (Iceland), M Mughal (UK), G Sagor (UK), O Soreide (Norway), R Stedeford (UK), S Stipa (Italy), C Stoddard (UK), T Taylor (UK), W Thomas (UK), D Tweedle (UK), A Viste (Norway), D Webster (UK), R A B Wood (UK).

References

1 Cancer Statistics: registrations. England and Wales. London: MH Stationery Office, 1989.

2 Allum WH, Powell DJ, McConkey CC, Fielding JWL. Gastric cancer. A 25 year review. *Br J Surg* 1989; **76:** 535–40.

3 Miwa K. Cancer of the stomach in Japan. *Gann Monogr Cancer Res* 1979; **22:** 61–75.

4 Maruyama K, Okabayashi K, Kinoshita T. Progress in gastric cancer surgery and its limits of radicality. *World J Surg* 1987; **11:** 418–26.

5 Nakajima T, Nishi M. Surgery and adjuvant chemotherapy for gastric cancer. *Hepatogastroenterology* 1989; **36:** 79–85.

6 Bonenkamp JJ, Van de Velde CJH, Kampschoer GHM, et al. A comparison of factors influencing the prognosis of Japanese and Western gastric cancer patients. *World J Surg* 1993; **17:** 410–15.

7 Kajitani T. Japanese Research Society for the Study of Gastric Cancer. The general rules for gastric cancer study in surgery and pathology. *Jap J Surg* 1981; **11:** 127–45.

8 Diggory MT, Cuschieri A. R2/3 gastrectomy for gastric carcinoma: an audited experience of a consecutive series. *Br J Surg* 1985; **72:** 146–48.

9 Smith JW, Shiu MH, Kelsey L, Brennan MF. Morbidity of radical lymphadenectomy in the curative resection of gastric carcinoma. *Arch Surg* 1991; **126:** 1469–73.

10 Roder JD, Böttcher K, Siewert JR, et al. Prognostic factors in gastric carcinoma: results of the German Gastric Carcinoma Study 1992. *Cancer* 1993; **72:** 2089–97.

11 Sue-Ling HM, Johnston D, Martin IG, Dixon MF, et al. Gastric cancer: a curable disease in Britain. *BMJ* 1993; **307:** 591–96.

12 Bonenkamp JJ, Songun J, Hermans J, et al. Randomised comparison of morbidity after D1 and D2 dissection for gastric cancer in 996 Dutch patients. *Lancet* 1995; **345:** 745–48.

13 Yoshino K, Ogawa S, Tanaka T, et al. Controversy regarding extended lymphadenectomy for gastric cancer. In: Nishi M, Sugano H, Takahasi T, eds. International Gastric Cancer Congress Bologna: 1995: vol I, 91–95.

14 Findlay M, Cunningham D, Norman A, et al. A phase II study in advanced gastro-oesophageal cancer using epirubicin and cisplatin in combination with continuous infusion 5-fluorouracil (ECF). *Ann Oncol* 1994; **5:** 609–16.

A randomised prospective comparison of percutaneous endoscopic gastrostomy and nasogastric tube feeding after acute dysphagic stroke

B Norton, M Homer-Ward, M T Donnelly, R G Long, G K T Holmes

Abstract

***Objective*—To compare percutaneous endoscopic gastrostomy and nasogastric tube feeding after acute dysphagic stroke.**

***Design*—Randomised prospective study of in-patients with acute stroke requiring enteral nutrition.**

***Setting*—One university hospital (Nottingham) and one district general hospital (Derby).**

***Subjects*—30 patients with persisting dysphagia at 14 days after acute stroke: 16 patients were randomised to gastrostomy tube feeding and 14 to nasogastric tube feeding.**

***Main outcome measures*—Six week mortality; amount of feed administered; change in nutritional state; treatment failure; and length of hospital stay.**

***Results*—Mortality at 6 weeks was significantly lower in the gastrostomy group with two deaths (12%) compared with eight deaths (57%) in the nasogastric group (P<0·05). All gastrostomy fed patients (16) received the total prescribed feed whereas 10/14 (71%) of nasogastric patients lost at least one day's feed. Nasogastric patients received a significantly (P<0·001) smaller proportion of their prescribed feed (78%; 95% confidence interval 63% to 94%) compared with the gastrostomy group (100%). Patients fed via a gastrostomy tube showed greater improvement in nutritional state, according to several different criteria at six weeks compared with the nasogastric group. In the gastrostomy group the mean albumin concentration increased from 27·1 g/l (24·5 g/l to 29·7 g/l) to 30·1 g/l (28·3 g/l to 31·9 g/l). In contrast, among the nasogastric group there was a reduction from 31·4 g/l (28·6 g/l to 34·2 g/l) to 22·3 g/l (20·7 g/l to 23·9 g/l) (P<0·003). In addition, there were fewer treatment failures in the gastrostomy group (0/16 versus 3/14). Six patients from the gastrostomy group were discharged from hospital within six weeks of the procedure compared with none from the nasogastric group (P<0·05).**

***Conclusion*—This study indicates that early gastrostomy tube feeding is greatly superior to nasogastric tube feeding and should be the nutritional treatment of choice for patients with acute dysphagic stroke.**

Derbyshire Royal Infirmary, Derby DE1 2QY
B Norton, *senior registrar in gastroenterology*
M Homer-Ward, *senior house officer in general medicine and gastroenterology*
G K T Holmes, *consultant physician and gastroenterologist*

Nottingham City Hospital, Nottingham NG5 1PB
M T Donnelly, *registrar in gastroenterology*
R G Long, *consultant physician and gastroenterologist*

Correspondence to: Dr Holmes.

BMJ 1996;312:13-6

Introduction

It has been suggested that up to 45% of all cerebrovascular accidents (strokes) are complicated by dysphagia.[1,2] Gordon has demonstrated that dysphagia complicates 35% of first episode monohemispheric strokes and has an associated mortality at six weeks of around 50%.[2] The natural history of dysphagia after an acute cerebrovascular accident, however, is poorly understood, and the time at which a swallowing deficit becomes irreversible is not clearly defined.[3,4] Consequently, it is common practice to delay enteral feeding in such patients for several weeks. In the United Kingdom most patients admitted after a cerebrovascular accident are eventually fed, at least in the initial stage, through a nasogastric tube. There are well recognised problems associated with nasogastric tube feeding,[5-7] notably the inadvertent removal of the tube with an inherent risk of pulmonary aspiration.[7,8] In addition, frequent unintentional removal of the nasogastric tube leads to a discontinuation of nutritional intake, and the amount of feed lost to the patient is often underestimated.[9] Percutaneous endoscopic gastrostomy is a relatively new method of enteral feeding[10,11] and is associated with low morbidity and mortality.[12] It can be safely performed in patients after a recent stroke[13,14] who would otherwise represent a considerable anaesthetic risk.

We performed a prospective randomised comparison of endoscopic gastrostomy versus nasogastric tube feeding after acute dysphagic stroke.

Patients and methods

Patients were recruited after an acute cerebrovascular accident with persisting dysphagia for eight or more days. Patients were recruited for a one year period commencing February 1994. At the start of the study period we circulated a request to consultant colleagues from both general medical and geriatric departments for referral of potential patients as above. Each patient was then assessed by one of the authors. We recruited the first 30 patients who fulfilled the criteria admitted to either the Nottingham City hospital (eight) or the Derbyshire Royal Infirmary (22) during this period. Twenty five out of 30 patients had computed axial tomography of the brain to confirm the diagnosis of stroke, but in all cases a firm diagnosis could be made on clinical grounds. All patients had clinical evidence of a severe stroke, primarily dense hemiplegia, and were unconscious at the time of admission. At the time of recruitment patients were assessed by using the Barthel activities of daily living index (range 0-20), which is an assessment of disability after a stroke and a guide to how much care a patient is likely to require.[15] Dysphagia was demonstrated by the absence of a normal gag reflex or the inability to swallow 50 ml of sterile water easily without choking, or both. Each patient by this stage was in a stable condition and enteral feeding considered appropriate by the referring clinician. Those patients with a previous history of gastrointestinal disease which would preclude siting a gastrostomy tube or who were unfit for upper gastrointestinal endoscopy and intravenous sedation were excluded. If patients fulfilled the above criteria informed consent was obtained from the next of kin after a full explanation. Patients were randomly allocated by closed envelopes at 14 (plus or minus 3) days to receive enteral nutritional support via either a fine bore nasogastric tube (Flocare 500) or a gastrostomy tube (12 French gauge Fresenius or 24 French gauge Wilson Cook). Nasogastric tubes were passed by experienced senior nursing staff from the ward on which the patient was being cared for. Gastrostomy tubes were inserted by using a percutaneous approach and pull through technique.[10] Sedation was induced by using 5-10 mg of diazepam, and a prophylactic antibiotic (cefuroxime 750 mg intravenously) was administered at the same time. Patients in both groups were assessed by a dietitian and received a standard enteral feed (Nutrison). The feeds were administered by using a Flocare 500 system, and the rate of delivery of the feed was 50 ml per hour for the first 24 hours gradually increasing to an average of 100 ml per hour for both groups of patients. Patients were fed in a semirecumbent position.

Treatment efficacy was assessed by several methods. The principal outcome measures were mortality at six weeks after initiation of feed and changes in nutritional state during this period. Nutritional state was assessed by recording anthropometric data including weight, upper arm skin fold thickness, mid-arm circumference, and concentrations of haemoglobin, serum total protein, and serum albumin at the start of the trial and weekly during the trial. Nursing staff on the ward where the patients were being cared for were asked to keep a record of any tube resitings, the number of days on which feed was administered or omitted with reasons, and the development of any complications. Treatment failure was defined as failure to site the feeding tube or recurrent displacement of the feeding tube in those patients in whom it was thought inappropriate to persevere with treatment. The length of hospital stay was monitored in the two groups. Results were expressed as means, and differences between the two groups were compared by using the χ^2 test with Yates's correction for continuity. Changes in nutritional state were assessed by using the Mann-Whitney U test. P values less than 0·05 were regarded as significant.

Table 1—*Mortality at six weeks in patients with acute dysphagic stroke randomised to receive gastrostomy (n=16) or nasogastric (n=14) tube feeding**

Group	Sex	Age (years)	Cause of death	Time of death (days after procedure)
Gastrostomy:				
1	M	76	Initial cerebrovascular accident	27
2	M	85	Bronchopneumonia	23
Nasogastric:				
1	F	80 years†	Initial cerebrovascular accident	13 (2-25)†
2	F		Initial cerebrovascular accident	
3	M		Initial cerebrovascular accident	
4	M		Initial cerebrovascular accident	
5	F	79 years†	Bronchopneumonia	24 (13-37)†
6	F		Bronchopneumonia	
7	F		Bronchopneumonia	
8	M		Bronchopneumonia	

*χ^2 for numbers alive/dead according to group, P<0·05.
†Mean or mean (range).

Results

Thirty patients (11 men, 19 women; mean age 77 years) were recruited to the study. Sixteen patients (seven men, nine women; mean age 76 years) received gastrostomy feeding and 14 patients (four men, 10 women; mean age 79 years) received nasogastric feeding. Assessment with the Barthel activities of daily living index did not show a significant difference in residual disability. The two groups scored a mean value of less than 3 at the time of recruitment. Table 1 illustrates the six week mortality for each group together with the causes of death and the length of survival after the procedure for those patients who died within six weeks. There were two deaths (12·5%) in the gastrostomy group compared with eight (57%) in the nasogastric group. The χ^2 analysis demonstrated a significant difference in mortality at six weeks between the two groups (P<0·05).

Each patient in the gastrostomy group required only one tube insertion compared with a mean of six (range 1 to 10) in the nasogastric fed group. There were no instances of omitted feed among the gastrostomy patients whereas 10 (71%) of the nasogastric fed group lost at least one day's feed due to delay in resiting of the tube (range 1 to 10 days with a mean of 5 days; P<0.001). This represented a mean loss of 22% (95% confidence interval 6% to 37%) of the total prescribed feed for this group of nasogastrically fed patients. Table 2 shows the mean changes in nutritional state for each category. Follow up laboratory data were not available for one patient from the gastrostomy group and four patients from the nasogastric fed group because of either early abandonment of the study or death. It was not possible for medical reasons to obtain weights in three patients from each group. Table 2 demonstrates the mean values for various nutritional parameters for each group at recruitment and after a period of follow up of at least one week.

The mean initial weight at randomisation was 58·8 kg (51·0 kg to 66·7 kg) for the gastrostomy fed patients and 60·4 kg (54·2 kg to 66·6 kg) for those fed by nasogastric tube (a non-significant difference). At follow up 10/13 (77%) of the patients fed by gastrostomy had gained weight, with a mean increase of 2·2 kg (−0·6 kg to 5·2 kg). Only one of the eight (12%) nasogastric fed patients showed any weight gain with a mean at follow up of 57·8 kg (49·4 kg to 66·2 kg), which represents an average deficit of 2·6 kg (−5·1 kg to 0·38 kg) per patient. This difference in weight gain was significant (P<0·03). In the gastrostomy group there was an overall modest reduction in haemoglobin concentration, and a similar pattern was observed in

Table 2—*Measurement of nutritional state at week 0 and at follow up of at least one week for patients with acute dysphagic stroke randomised to receive gastrostomy or nasogastric tube feeding*

Group	Weight (kg)				Haemoglobin (g/l)*				Albumin (g/l)†				Mid-arm circumference (cm)			
	No of patients	Mean (SD) weight	95% Confidence interval	No (%) of patients improved	No of patients	Mean (SD) value	95% Confidence interval	No (%) of patients improved	No of patients	Mean (SD) value	95% Confidence interval	No (%) of patients improved	No of patients	Mean (SD) value	95% Confidence interval	No (%) of patients improved
Gastrostomy:																
Week 0	13	58·8 (13·0)	51·0 to 66·7		16	127 (12)	121 to 133		16	27·1 (4·9)	24·5 to 29·7		16	25·3 (4·0)	23·2 to 27·4	
Follow up	13	61·0 (11·0)	54·4 to 67·6	10/13 (77%)‡	15	123 (12)	116 to 130	4/15 (27%)	15	30·1 (3·6)	28·3 to 31·9	9/15 (60%)§	13	26·3 (5·3)	23·1 to 29·5	6/13 (46%)‖
Nasogastric:																
Week 0	11	60·4 (9·2)	54·2 to 66·6		14	130 (26)	115 to 145		14	31·4 (4·9)	28·6 to 34·2		14	26·8 (2·7)	25·2 to 28·4	
Follow up	8	57·8 (10·0)	49·4 to 66·2	1/8 (12%)	10	119 (20)	105 to 133	2/10 (20%)	10	22·3 (2·2)	20·7 to 23·9	1/10 (10%)	8	23·8 (1·8)	22·3 to 25·3	0/8 (0%)

*Normal range 135-180 g/l for men; 115-165 g/l for women.
†Normal range 30-45 g/l.
‡P<0·03 compared with nasogastric group.
§P<0·003 compared with nasogastric group.
‖P<0·03 compared with nasogastric group.

the nasogastric group with no significant difference observed between the two. Six out of 13 patients in the gastrostomy group showed a mean improvement in anthropometric measurements at follow up. In contrast, almost all the patients (7/8) in the nasogastric fed group showed a fall in anthropometric measurements ($P<0\cdot03$). There was a clear difference in mean serum albumin concentration at follow up between the two groups. The gastrostomy fed group (n=15) achieved an increase of 2·7 g/l (−0·1 g/l to 5·6 g/l) whereas those fed nasogastrically (n=10) showed a mean reduction of 9·5 g/l (−13·6 g/l to −5·4 g/l) ($P<0\cdot003$). One patient in the gastrostomy (24 French gauge Wilson Cook) fed group developed a peristomal infection that resolved with antibiotics and continuation of feeding. All other gastrostomy placements were without complications. There were no treatment failures in the gastrostomy fed group but three in the nasogastric fed group (inability to resite the nasogastric tube in one patient and recurrent removal of the tube in two patients). This difference was not significant.

There was a significant difference in discharge rates at six weeks. Six patients fed by gastrostomy were discharged within six weeks (all to nursing homes) compared with none from the nasogastric fed group ($P<0\cdot05$). A further six patients from the gastrostomy fed group were discharged within a three month period compared with none from the nasogastric fed group. Two additional patients from each group have now died (all secondary to bronchopneumonia as the terminal event) within six months of the initial procedure. Three patients from the gastrostomy fed group can now swallow normally and have had their tubes removed. No patients from the nasogastric fed group have regained normal swallowing.

Discussion

We believe this study to be the first to compare prospectively the efficacy of gastrostomy tube feeding with nasogastric tube feeding at such an early stage after acute dysphagic stroke. The two study groups were well matched in terms of age, sex, and residual disability. The most striking difference was in mortality, and we have shown that early gastrostomy feeding produced a significant reduction in mortality at six weeks. There was one early death (at two days) in the nasogastric fed group, and it could be reasonably assumed that this patient would have been unlikely to survive regardless of which feeding method was used. Even if we exclude this patient, however, the difference in mortality between the two groups remains significant. The difference in mortality is probably a reflection of the superiority of gastrostomy feeding over nasogastric feeding after acute dysphagic stroke. Several factors might account for this. It is well recognised that a major cause of death after a dysphagic stroke is bronchopneumonia.[7] Several studies have shown that enteral tube feeding is associated with an increased risk of pulmonary aspiration and pneumonia, which under these conditions has a mortality of over 50%.[7 12 13 16 17] Patients fed by a nasogastric tube are at greater risk of pulmonary aspiration, which is inherent on recurrent removal and resiting of the nasogastric tube and which will clearly increase proportionately with the number of times this occurs. We have demonstrated that even over a short time period patients in the nasogastric group frequently removed their feeding tubes. In contrast there were no instances of inadvertent removal of a gastrostomy tube. The final recorded terminal event for most of the patients in the nasogastric fed group was bronchopneumonia.

At the time of randomisation patients from both groups had evidence of poor nutritional state, reflected in below average body weight and low mean albumin concentration. This is in keeping with other studies that have indicated that undernutrition in hospital inpatients is common and has an associated increase in mortality.[18] This study has shown that gastrostomy feeding has the advantage of more certain provision of adequate continuous nutritional support. Those in the gastrostomy fed group enjoyed the benefit of uninterrupted feeding whereas 71% of the nasogastric fed group missed at least one day's feed with a mean loss of 22% of their total prescribed feed. Patients fed through a gastrostomy showed a greater overall improvement in nutritional state compared with the nasogastric group (table 2). This difference was most clear in the measurement of serum albumin at follow up. Those patients in the gastrostomy group showed a mean increase of 3 g/l compared with the nasogastric group who had a mean reduction of almost 10 g/l. Although some phenomena such as the distinct reduction in serum albumin concentration may represent a separate effect—that is, a fall secondary to pneumonia or other acute illness—the changes in the various parameters suggest a global impairment of nutritional state in the nasogastric group compared with the gastrostomy group.

There were no treatment failures in the gastrostomy group. Other benefits of gastrostomy feeding were reflected in discharge rates, with six patients discharged within six weeks compared with none from the nasogastric fed group. Furthermore, in our areas, nursing homes will more readily accept patients who are fed via a gastrostomy rather than a nasogastric tube. This is because gastrostomy tubes tend to be much easier to manage in the community. The improved prospects of earlier discharge for gastrostomy fed patients has obvious financial benefits for the NHS as a whole.

Malnutrition among hospital inpatients is a common problem which contributes to mortality and morbidity.[18] It must be recognised that the provision of adequate nutrition is an integral part of management at least as important as giving specific treatment. This is not widely appreciated. A recent article giving a 15 point guide to ideal stroke management failed to mention nutritional support at all.[19] It is incumbent on all health workers to change attitudes toward nutrition and to recognise it as an essential and basic part of patient care. Patients who are already severely ill who are then deprived of adequate nutrition are much more likely than well nourished patients to develop complications and have a reduced survival rate.

In conclusion, this study has demonstrated that early gastrostomy feeding after acute dysphagic stroke is associated with a significant reduction in mortality at six weeks. The use of a gastrostomy results in improved nutritional state compared with nasogastric

Key messages

- Gastrostomy tube feeding is associated with a reduction in six week mortality compared with nasogastric feeding
- Patients fed through a gastrostomy are more likely to receive more of their prescribed feed and show a greater improvement in nutritional state
- Gastrostomy tube feeding is associated with fewer treatment failures
- Patients fed through a gastrostomy are more likely to be discharged earlier from hospital
- Gastrostomy feeding is superior to nasogastric tube feeding after acute dysphagic stroke

feeding and will improve the prospects of early hospital discharge. We are carrying out further work to determine the effects on long term quality of life in such patients, and our preliminary results have so far been encouraging. In addition, further work is required to determine the ideal timing at which to institute gastrostomy feeding after an acute dysphagic stroke.

Funding: None.
Conflict of interest: None.

1 Walton JN. *Brain's diseases of the nervous system.* 10th ed. Oxford: Oxford University Press, 1993.
2 Gordon C, Langton Hewer R, Wade DT. Dysphagia in acute stroke. *BMJ* 1987;**295**:411-4.
3 Barer DH. Lower cranial nerve motor function in unilateral vascular lesions of the cerebral hemisphere. *BMJ* 1984;**289**:1622.
4 Veis SL, Logemann JA. Swallowing disorders in persons with cerebrovascular accident. *Arch Phys Med Rehabil* 1985;**66**:372-5.
5 Wolfsen H, Kozarek R. Percutaneous endoscopic gastrostomy. Ethical considerations. *Gastroenterol Clin North Am* 1993;2:259-71.
6 Ciocon JO, Silverstone FA, Graver M, Foley CJ. Tube feeding in elderly patients. *Arch Intern Med* 1988;**148**:429-33.
7 Wicks C, Gimson A, Vlavianos P, Lombard M, Panos M, Macmathuna P, *et al.* Assessment of the percutaneous endoscopic gastrostomy feeding tube as part of an integrated approach to enteral feeding. *Gut* 1992;33:613-6.
8 Rees RGP, Payne-James JJ, King C, Silk DBA. Spontaneous transpyloric passage and performance of fine bore polyurethane feeding tubes: a controlled clinical trial. *Journal of Parenteral and Enteral Nutrition* 1988;**12**: 469-72.
9 Abernathy G, Heizer W, Holcombe B, Raasch R, Schlegel K, Hak L, *et al.* Efficacy of tube feeding in supplying energy requirements of hospitalised patients. *Journal of Parenteral and Enteral Nutrition* 1989;**13**:387-91.
10 Ponsky JL, Gauderer MWL. Percutaneous endoscopic gastrostomy: a non-operative technique for feeding gastrostomy. *Gastrointest Endosc* 1981;**27**: 9-11.
11 Jones M, Santanello SA, Falcone RE. Percutaneous endoscopic versus surgical gastrostomy. *Journal of Parenteral and Enteral Nutrition* 1990;**14**:533-4.
12 Peters RA, Westaby D. Percutaneous endoscopic gastrostomy. Indications, timing and complications of the technique. *Br J Int Care* 1994;4:88-95.
13 Larson DE, Burton DD, Schroeder KW, DiMagno EP. Percutaneous endoscopic gastrostomy. Indications, success, complications, and mortality in 314 consecutive patients. *Gastroenterology* 1987;**93**:48-52.
14 Raha SK, Woodhouse K. The use of percutaneous endoscopic gastrostomy (PEG) in 161 consecutive elderly patients. *Age Ageing* 1994;**23**:162-3.
15 Mahoney FI, Barthel DW. Functional evaluation: the Barthel index. *Md Med J* 1965;**14**:61-5.
16 Grant J. Comparison of percutaneous endoscopic gastrostomy with Stamm gastrostomy. *Ann Surg* 1988;**207**:598-603.
17 Park RHR, Allison MC, Lang J, Spence E, Morris A J, Danesh BJZ, *et al.* Randomised comparison of percutaneous endoscopic gastrostomy and nasogastric tube feeding in patients with persisting neurological dysphagia. *BMJ* 1992;**304**:1406-9.
18 *A positive approach to nutrition as treatment. Kings Fund report on the role of enteral and parenteral feeding in hospital and at home.* London: King's Fund Centre, 1992.
19 Stone SP, Whincup P. Standards for the hospital management of stroke patients. *J R Coll Physicians Lond* 1994;**28**:52-8.

(Accepted 24 October 1995)

© Lancet 1996; 347: 1212–1217

Contribution of genes of the major histocompatibility complex to susceptibility and disease phenotype in inflammatory bowel disease

Jack Satsangi, Ken I Welsh, Mike Bunce, Cecile Julier, J Mark Farrant, John I Bell, Derek P Jewell

Summary

Background Despite strong evidence implicating immune dysfunction and genetic predisposition in the pathogenesis of the chronic inflammatory bowel diseases Crohn's disease and ulcerative colitis, the importance of the genes of the major histocompatibility complex remains uncertain. We have investigated the contribution of HLA DRB1 and DQB genes by the strategies of non-parametric linkage analysis (affected sibling pair method) as well as association study. The relation between genotype and phenotype was examined in detail.

Methods For linkage analysis 74 families in whom two or more siblings had inflammatory bowel disease were studied. A total of 83 affected sibling pairs were involved: in 42 pairs both siblings had Crohn's disease; in 29 both had ulcerative colitis; in 12 one sibling had Crohn's disease, the other ulcerative colitis. For the association study there were 175 patients with ulcerative colitis, 173 with Crohn's disease, and 472 controls. Details of sex, age of onset, disease extent, and family history were analysed. 24 patients with ulcerative colitis and 92 with Crohn's disease required surgery for refractory disease. HLA DRB1 and DQB1 gene-typing was performed by polymerase chain reaction with sequence-specific primers.

Findings In ulcerative colitis, the sharing of alleles among affected sibling pairs provided evidence for linkage with DRB1 locus (p=0·017, χ^2=5·32). Of 29 affected sibling pairs studied, only one pair shared no DRB1 DQB haplotypes. 15 shared two DRB DQB haplotypes. In contrast, no linkage was noted for Crohn's disease (42 sibling pairs; p=0·30, χ^2=0·16) or for inflammatory bowel disease overall (83 sibling pairs, p=0·16, χ^2=2·28). In the association study the rare DRB1*103 (8·3% *vs* 3·2% in controls) and DRB1*12 (8·6% *vs* 2·1% in controls) alleles were associated with ulcerative colitis (p=0·0074, χ^2=7·22, odds ratio OR=2·9 [95% CI 1·3–6·4] and p=0·0056, χ^2=12·63, OR=4·33 [1·8–11·0] respectively). No association with alleles representing DR2 (p=0·55, χ^2=0·34) was noted. No overall association was seen in Crohn's disease. In ulcerative colitis, the frequency of DRB1*0301 DQB*0201 (DR3 DQ2) was reduced in females (9·8% *vs* 26·3% in controls, p=0·037, χ^2=8·39 OR=0·34 [0·15–0·71]), particularly in those with distal disease (2·3%, p=0·001 *vs* controls, χ^2=11·35, OR=0·07 [0·00–0·39]). In both males and females, the DR3 DQ2 haplotype was predictive of extensive ulcerative colitis (32·9% *vs* 10·7% in distal disease, p<0·01, χ^2=10·94, OR 4·09 [1·70–10·6]) but not of need for surgery (p=0·93, χ^2=0·01).

Interpretation These data provide strong evidence for genetic heterogeneity in inflammatory bowel disease. Genes of the major histocompatibility complex are implicated as important inherited determinants of susceptibility to ulcerative colitis and may also influence the pattern of disease. In Crohn's disease, important susceptibility genes are likely to exist outside the HLA region.

Lancet 1996; **347:** 1212–17

See Commentary page 1198

Gastroenterology Unit (J Satsangi MRCP, J M Farrant MRCP, D P Jewell FRCP), **Nuffield Departments of Medicine** (J I Bell FRCP) **and Surgery** (K I Welsh PhD, M Bunce), **Oxford Radcliffe Hospitals, Oxford; and Wellcome Trust Centre for Human Genetics** (C Julier PhD), **Oxford, UK**

Correspondence to: Dr Jack Satsangi and Dr Derek P Jewell, Gastroenterology Unit, Radcliffe Infirmary, Woodstock Road, Oxford OX2 6HE, UK

Introduction

The aetiology of Crohn's disease and ulcerative colitis remains unknown, but strong evidence has accumulated from studies of different ethnic groups, families of patients, and twin pairs to implicate genetic susceptibility in pathogenesis.[1,2] For Crohn's disease in particular, the coefficient of heritability calculated from concordance rates in twin pairs is greater than for insulin-dependent diabetes, asthma, or schizophrenia.[3]

The mode of inheritance is unknown, but there is very limited support for a simple mendelian inheritance pattern in either disease. Complex segregation analysis suggests that simple models of inheritance are, at best, pertinent to only a small fraction of patients.[4,5] It is more likely that inflammatory bowel disease is multifactorial in aetiology, and, in view of the variability of clinical phenotypes, the term inflammatory bowel disease may represent several related polygenic conditions. Susceptibility genes, or environmental stimuli, may be shared between subtypes, accounting for the concurrence of different phenotypes within one family. However, at present, the extent of heterogeneity and the relation between genotype and phenotype is uncertain.

Previous attempts to identify susceptibility genes in inflammatory bowel disease by means of linkage analysis or population-based studies have generally been inconclusive. Few linkage studies involving multiply affected families have been reported and all have serious methodological defects—small numbers of families investigated, reliance on parametric linkage analysis, or assumptions regarding disease homogeneity.[1,4–6] The complexity of inflammatory bowel disease demands large studies involving robust non-parametric methods of analysis such as the affected sibling pair method.[7,8]

Several investigators have conducted association studies, usually focused on genes involved in the regulation of the immune response, in particular the

© Lancet 1996; 347: 1212–1217

major histocompatibility complex (in man, the HLA human leucocyte antigen region).[9,10] With the exception of the small subgroups of patients with primary sclerosing cholangitis[9] or ankylosing spondylitis,[9] results of previous HLA association studies have been confusing and inconsistent. Even molecular genotyping has produced conflicting results. Particular controversies concern putative class II gene associations in ulcerative colitis with the alleles representing the serological DR2 antigens[9,10] and in Crohn's disease with the DR1 DQ5 haplotype.[10,11]

A repository of clinical material (DNA, plasma, and frozen lymphocytes) from more than 400 European patients with non-familial inflammatory bowel disease and from members of 250 multiply affected families has been established in Oxford. Details of clinical history have also been obtained and are stored on a computer database. This resource, the Crohn's and Colitis Gene Bank, will allow investigation of the importance of genetic factors in disease susceptibility. We report here a detailed study of the contribution of HLA DRB1 and DQB genes to the pathogenesis of inflammatory bowel disease.

Methods

This investigation was approved by the Central Oxford Research Ethics Committee and all participants gave informed consent. Clinical data were obtained by questionnaire, by personal interview, and from case records.

Linkage analysis: affected sibling pair method

74 families, all European caucasoid and resident in the UK, in which two or more siblings had inflammatory bowel disease, were identified with the help of the National Association for Crohn's and Colitis (NACC) and cooperating physicians. Advertisements were placed in the NACC newsletter asking suitable families to contact the investigators. Interviews (either in person or by telephone) and collection of blood from affected siblings and all willing healthy first-degree relatives (parents, offspring, siblings) were arranged. Clinical details were obtained from hospital physicians or family doctors.

Crohn's disease families—In 30 families, two siblings had Crohn's disease; in a further four families, three siblings were affected (12 sibling pairs). Hence, a total of 42 affected sibling pairs with Crohn's disease, together with their healthy first-degree relatives, were studied. In 18 pairs both affected siblings were female, in five both were male, and in 19 pairs one sibling with Crohn's disease was male, the other female. Clinical details of disease extent were available for 41 pairs. In 27 both siblings had ileo-colonic disease; in 2 pairs both siblings had exclusively colonic disease; and in one pair both siblings had jejunal disease only. In the other 11 pairs for whom clinical data were available, one sibling had colonic and one ileo-colonic Crohn's disease.

Ulcerative colitis—In 27 families, two siblings had ulcerative colitis; and in one family two pairs of siblings in different generations were affected. 29 pairs of affected siblings together with their healthy relatives were therefore studied. In 11 pairs both affected siblings were female, and in 12 pairs both were male.

"Mixed disease" pairs—In twelve sibling pairs one sibling had Crohn's disease, the other ulcerative colitis. In two pairs both were male; in three pairs both were female. Of note, seven of the siblings with Crohn's disease had exclusively colonic disease, with no small-bowel involvement. Fuller clinical details and pedigrees are available from the authors.

Association study

An allelic association study was performed, involving 348 unrelated patients (175 ulcerative colitis, 173 Crohn's disease). For this purpose, patients with no family history of inflammatory bowel disease were selected at random from adult outpatients attending the gastroenterology clinics at the John Radcliffe Hospital, Oxford, between January and November, 1994. Patients having affected first-degree relatives were selected from the Crohn's and Colitis Gene bank database in Oxford, which now contains details of 250 multiply affected families throughout the UK. No two members from one family were included in the association study. In any family the affected individual chosen was the first in the family to develop disease. For both Crohn's disease and ulcerative colitis, disease phenotype was defined by sex, age at onset of symptoms, familial disease, disease extent, and need for surgery (see below). Ethnic biases have been minimised by exclusion of all Asian and South European patients. The proportion of Jewish persons among the patient groups and controls is about 5%.

Ulcerative colitis—175 patients with definitive ulcerative colitis were studied (92 male), chosen as described above. 52 had one or more affected first-degree relative; 123 patients had no family history. Disease extent was defined by the most proximal extent of disease at the most recent investigation performed (barium enema or colonoscopy). If macroscopic extent differed from the microscopic assessment, the microscopic extent was recorded. Thus, disease was classified as extensive (inflammation proximal to the splenic flexure) in 85 patients (37 female, 48 male; 65 non-familial, 20 familial) and as distal in 84 patients (40 male, 44 female; 56 sporadic, 28 familial). In six patients, the disease extent was uncertain. 24 patients (ten female; six familial) had required colectomy for severe disease refractory to medical therapy. Five patients (three extensive, two distal) had primary sclerosing cholangitis; one had primary biliary cirrhosis; all others had normal liver biochemistry. One patient had vitiligo and one had multiple sclerosis.

The median age of onset in ulcerative colitis was 35·0 years (interquartile range [IQR] 25·0–48·0 years). Median age of onset was lower in familial disease (28·5 years [IQR 23·0–42·0] *vs* 37·5 years [26·0–38·0] in patients with non-familial disease, $p<0·02$, Kruskal-Wallis analysis) and in patients with extensive disease (31·5 years [IQR 22·0–48·0] *vs* 36 years [28·0–47·0] in patients with distal disease, not significant).

Crohn's disease—The association study included 173 unrelated patients with definite Crohn's disease. 68 were male. 67 patients had a positive family history of inflammatory bowel disease; 106 had no affected relatives. Disease extent was defined from clinical, radiological, endoscopic, and histological data. 107 patients (40 male) had both small-bowel and large-bowel involvement, predominantly ileo-caecal disease. Patients with limited terminal ileal disease were included in this group.[12] 42 patients (18 male) had exclusively colonic disease (including perianal disease alone). 18 patients (ten male) had exclusively jejunal or proximal ileal disease. In six patients (all female) disease extent was uncertain. 13 patients had predominantly fistulising disease, 31 had stricturing disease, and the remainder were judged to have predominantly inflammatory disease. 92 patients had required surgery for refractory disease (excluding perianal sepsis alone). In 13 of these laparotomy had revealed perforating disease. Two patients had developed carcinomas (one adenocarcinoma of the small bowel, one adenocarcinoma of the rectum). One patient with extensive Crohn's colitis had primary sclerosing cholangitis. The median age of onset of Crohn's disease was 24·2 years (IQR 20·0–33·0 years; $p<0·00001$ *vs* ulcerative colitis patients). Patients with colonic disease had a higher median age of onset (32·0 years [IQR 24·5–47·5] *vs* 22·0 years [19·0–30·0] in ileo-colonic disease, $p<0·001$, Kruskal-Wallis analysis).

Controls—During 1992–94, 472 unrelated European caucasoid individuals were HLA genotyped by molecular methods. These controls were recruited from hospital workers and prospective blood and organ donors. No one in the control group had a disease with known genetic predisposition. All were Oxfordshire residents.

© Lancet 1996; 347: 1212–1217

	Pairs identical for 0, 1, or 2 haplotypes		
	0	1	2
All sibling pairs			
Ulcerative colitis (29)	1	13	15
Crohn's disease (42)	8	22	12
Mixed diseases (12)	2	7	3
Sibling pairs informative for all parenteral haplotypes			
Ulcerative colitis (19)	1	8	10
Crohn's disease (28)	5	15	8
Mixed diseases (9)	2	5	2

Table 1: **DRB1 DQB haplotype sharing in affected sibling pairs**

Laboratory techniques

DNA was extracted from 10 mL venous blood by a modified "salting-out" technique[13] and was resuspended in sterile distilled water at a final concentration of 0·1–1·0 μg/μL before use.

HLA DRB and DQB genotyping was performed by polymerase chain reaction amplification with sequence-specific primers (PCR-SSP). Methodological details have been published previously.[14–16] Briefly, each group of alleles or individual allele making up a serological defined specificity was amplified by a primer pair specific for the template. Stringent conditions for PCR avoided non-specific amplification. Details of the amplification primers, with annealing sites and alleles detected, are available from the authors. Amplification control primers giving rise to a 796 base-pair fragment from the third intron of HLA DRB1 were included in each reaction. 13 μL amplification reaction mixtures consisted of 67 mmol/L Tris base pH 8·8, 16·6 mmol/L ammonium sulphate, 2 mmol/L magnesium chloride, 0·01% (vol/vol) Tween-20, 200 mmol/L of each dNTP, 1–3 mmol/L allele-specific primers, 0·1 mmol/L DRB1 control primers, and 0·025 units *taq* polymerase (Advanced Biotechnology, London). Amplifications were done with Gene Amp PCR system 9600 (Perkin-Elmer Corporation) or MJ Research 96 V machines. The cycling parameters for 13 μL reactions in rapid cycling PCR machines with a heated lid were: 1 min at 96°C followed by five cycles of 20 s at 96°C, 45 s at 70°C, 25 s at 72°C, followed by 20 cycles of 20 s at 96°C, 50 s at 65°C, 30 s at 72°C, followed by five cycles of 20 s at 96°C, 60 s at 55°C, 120 s at 72°C. PCR products were separated by electrophoresis in 1% agarose gels containing ethidium bromide.

	HLA antigen	Crohn's disease n=173	Ulcerative colitis n=175	Controls n=472
DRB1				
*0101/2/4	*DR1*	16·2	19·4	18·9
*0103	*DR103*	4·6	8·6 (p=0·0074)	3·2
*15	*DR2(15)*	33·5	32	29·2
*16	*DR2(16)*	0·6	1·1	0·8
*0301	*DR3(17)*	22·0	22·3	26·3
*04	*DR4*	32·4	27·4 (p=0·046)	35·8
*11	*DR5(11)*	15·6	16	13·6
*12	*DR5(12)*	2·9	8·6 (p=0·056)	2·1
*13	*DR6(13)*	17·9	16·6	18
*14	*DR6(14)*	1·7	4·6	4·4
*07	*DR7*	23·1	20	25·4
*08	*DR8*	6·4	5·7	4
*09	*DR9*	3·5	2·3	1·9
*10	*DR10*	3·5	0	1·7
DQB1				
*02	*DQ2*	38·2	37·1	41·9
*04	*DQ4*	4·6	5·7	3·6
*05	*DQ5*	28·9	34·3	28·2
*06	*DQ6*	47·4	46·9	40·7
*0301/4	*DQ7*	35·8	32·6	35
*0302	*DQ8*	12·1	10·3	18
*03031/2	*DQ9*	11·6	4	8·3

Probability values (comparison with controls) are those where p<0·05.

Table 2: **HLA-DRB1 and DQB1 allele frequency (%) in inflammatory bowel disease**

The gels were run for 18 min at 15 V per cm in 0·5×TBE buffer. About 5% of DNA samples were typed on two occasions to establish reproducibility (no discrepancies were present). All the results were checked independently by two of the investigators.

Data analysis and statistics

Linkage analysis—Linkage between susceptibility to inflammatory bowel disease and HLA class II genes was assessed by comparing the sharing of alleles among affected siblings. Complete information regarding parental haplotypes was available for 56 affected sibling pairs, allowing attribution of haplotypes and alleles identical by descent. To utilise information from all 83 affected sibling pairs, sharing of haplotypes identical by state was also assessed,[8] with corrections derived from the DRB1 and DQB allele frequency in the control population. The numbers of affected sibling pairs sharing no haplotypes and two haplotypes were compared by χ^2 testing. Probability values of p<0·05 were taken as evidence of significant linkage. In four families with Crohn's disease, three siblings all were affected. In the results presented, these siblings have been included as three independent pairs.

Association study—Interim analysis was performed in May, 1994. 74 patients with ulcerative colitis had been genotyped. On interim analysis, significant differences in the frequency of the DRB1*0301 DQB*0201 haplotype (representative of the serologically defined DR3 DQ2 haplotype) were apparent between subgroups of patients with ulcerative colitis (male *vs* female; distal *vs* extensive disease). The frequencies of the DRB1*0103 allele and the DRB1*12 allele were both increased in patients with ulcerative colitis. Hence, preliminary hypotheses were generated. All comparisons of allele frequency between groups were made by use of a 2×2 contingency table and χ^2 statistics. Corrections were made where necessary for small sample numbers (Fisher's exact test). All comparisons and derived probability values were subject to correction for multiple testing, except for the comparisons made on the basis of pre-existing hypotheses.[10] Subgroup analyses were done with the Knowledge Seeker data analysis package.

Results

Linkage results

Ulcerative colitis—Of 29 affected sibling pairs with ulcerative colitis, 15 shared two HLA DRB1 DQB haplotypes and only one pair of siblings shared zero haplotypes (table 1). Comparison of the number of sibling pairs with ulcerative colitis sharing zero and two haplotypes identical by state (29 sibling pairs) provided strong evidence of linkage in ulcerative colitis with the DRB1 DQB haplotype (χ^2=5·27, p=0·016, 1 df), and the DRB1 locus (χ^2=5·32, p=0·017, 1 df). Only one pair of siblings were discordant for both haplotypes. This method of analysis, which takes into account control frequencies of DRB1 and DQB alleles, is conservative. Of the 19 affected sibling pairs with ulcerative colitis for whom full parental information was available, ten shared two DRB1 DQB haplotypes identical by descent, and only one pair shared none. By use of these data and previously reported relative risks in siblings and twins, it is possible to estimate the contribution of the HLA class II region to overall genetic susceptibility in ulcerative colitis. By either the method of Risch[17] or that of Rotter and Landaw,[18] it appears that important genetic determinants of susceptibility to ulcerative colitis are linked to the HLA class II region. On the assumption of an empirical risk of ulcerative colitis in siblings of between 2% and 4% and a monozygotic twin concordance rate of 6·3%,[3] the derived coefficent of genetic contribution[18] for the HLA genes is between 64% and 100%. This estimated value is reliant

	n	Allele(s)		
		*0301 DR3	*0103 DR103	*04 DR4
Controls	472	26·3%	3·2%	35·8%
Ulcerative colitis	175	22·3%	8·6%	27·4% (p=0·046)
Extensive colitis	85	32·9%	11·8% (p=0·012)	22·4% (p=0·022)
Distal colitis	84	10·7% (p=0·032)	6·0%	32·1%
Distal colitis (females)	44	2·3% (p=0·001)	6·8%	30·0%
Colectomy	24	37·5%	12·5% (p=0·050)	12·5%

In the association study, DRB1*0301 was in linkage disequilibrium with DQB1*0201. Probability values shown (those with p<0·05) have been corrected for multiple analyses. The DRB1*0301 DQB1*0201 haplotype frequency was lower in females with ulcerative colitis than in controls (9·8% *vs* 26·3%, p=0·0037, χ^2=8·39, OR=0·34 [0·15–0·71]).

Table 3: **HLA DRB1 allele frequency (%) in ulcerative colitis: genotype-phenotype analysis**

on the accuracy of the twin concordance rate and on the sibling relative risk data.[18] Of the 15 pairs of affected siblings with ulcerative colitis sharing two haplotypes, 13 were of the same sex (eight both male, five both female).

Crohn's disease—In contrast with the findings in ulcerative colitis, there was no evidence for linkage with DRB1, DQB loci, or the DRB1 DQB haplotype when allele sharing among sibling pairs with Crohn's disease was compared. In total, 42 sibling pairs were available for identity by state analysis, and 28 for identity by descent analysis. Formal identity by state analysis showed no significant linkage with the HLA DRB1 DQB loci or HLA DRB1 DQB haplotype with Crohn's disease (p=0·30, χ^2=0·15, 1 df). The contribution of the HLA region to overall genetic susceptibility in Crohn's disease derived from the allele sharing in affected sibling pairs is no more than 10%.[18] Of the 12 pairs of affected siblings sharing two haplotypes, eight were of the same sex (two male; six female). Four families in which three siblings each had Crohn's disease were studied. In all four families, two affected siblings were identical for both HLA types, with the other sibling sharing only one of his siblings' haplotypes.

Association study

The association study involved 175 patients with ulcerative colitis, 173 patients with Crohn's disease, and 472 controls. Interim analysis was conducted in May, 1994, at which time 74 patients with ulcerative colitis and 75 patients with Crohn's disease had been genotyped. On the basis of this analysis, interim hypotheses were generated: these were tested at final analysis. At the final analysis in November, 1994, all comparisons and probability values were corrected for multiple testing, except for specific comparisons made on the basis of pre-existing hypotheses.

Table 2 shows the class II HLA allele frequencies in patients with Crohn's disease and ulcerative colitis. Comparisons have been made with the control population. The expected linkage disequilibrium in white people between the DRB1 and DQB loci was noted in patients and in controls.

Ulcerative colitis—In ulcerative colitis, no overall association was present with the alleles corresponding to the DR2 antigen (32·0% *vs* 29·2% in controls, p>0·5). Associations were noted, both at interim and at final analyses, with the rare DRB1*0103 allele (8·6% *vs* 3·2% in controls, p=0·0074, χ^2=7·22, OR 2·86 [95% CI 1·27–6·42]) and the DRB1*12 allele (serological equivalent DR12; 8·6% *vs* 2·1%, p=0·0056, χ^2=12·63, OR 4·33 [1·77–10·98]). The DRB1*04 alleles (serological equivalent DR4) were modestly reduced (27·4% *vs* 35·8% in controls, p=0·046, χ^2=4·01, p=0·045, OR 0·68 [0·45–1·01]) at interim and final analysis. In subgroup analysis with the Knowledge Seeker package, which incorporates a partial Bonferroni correction for multiple testing, several strong associations were observed at both interim and final analyses (table 3). Thus, the DR3-DQ2 haplotype was reduced in females with ulcerative colitis (9·8% *vs* 32·6% in males, p=0·008, χ^2 12·22, 1 df). This difference was most pronounced in females with limited distal disease (only one of 44 had this haplotype, 2·3%, p=0·001 compared with control population, χ^2=11·35, OR 0·07 [0·00–0·39]). For both males and females, the DR3 DQ2 haplotype was predictive of extensive rather than distal disease (32·9 *vs* 10·7%, p<0·01, χ^2=10·94, OR 4·1 [1·70–10·60]). Although these differences were noted both at interim and final analysis, the data have nevertheless all been corrected for multiple analysis. Knowledge Seeker incorporates a partial Bonferroni correction for the number of alleles tested: probability values derived from this package were subsequently multiplied by ten to correct for the number of subgroups. Nine of the 24 patients requiring surgery possessed the DR3 DQ2 haplotype (p=0·93, χ^2=0·01). It was noticeable that the increased frequency of the DRB1*0103 suballele and the decrease in the DR4 specificity were both most pronounced in those patients with extensive and severe disease requiring colectomy (table 3). In contrast, the increase in frequency of the DR12 specificity was most striking in distal disease. No association was seen with subgroups defined by age at onset of disease (data available, but not shown here).

Crohn's disease—In Crohn's disease, no overall association with any DRB1 or DQB allele was present. The DRB1 DQ5 haplotype was not increased (16·2% *vs* 18·9% in controls, p=0·51, χ^2=0·44, OR=0·83 [0·50–1·83]). Several differences between subgroups were statistically significant before correction for multiple testing. The frequency of the DRB1*0301 DQB*0201 haplotype (serologically DR3 DQ2) was reduced in patients with Crohn's disease in the colon (n=42 patients; 11·9% *vs* 26·3% in controls, uncorrected p=0·04, χ^2=4·23). In male patients with colonic disease, the frequency of alleles detecting the serological DR4 and DR7 specificities was lower than in controls. None of these differences retained significance after correction for the numbers of tests performed. No association was seen with subgroups, defined by age at onset, or behaviour (stricturing *vs* fistulising, perforating *vs* non-perforating).

Discussion

The results of this investigation provide strong evidence for genetic heterogeneity within inflammatory bowel disease. The comparisons of haplotype sharing in affected sibling pairs offer evidence of linkage between HLA class II genes and ulcerative colitis, but not Crohn's disease or inflammatory bowel disease overall. In view of the estimated relative risks for siblings and concordance rates in twin pairs, these data suggest that genes of the major histocompatibility complex encode important determinants of suscpeptibility in ulcerative colitis.

© Lancet 1996; 347: 1212–1217

However, no individual allele or haplotype is implicated as the primary disease susceptibility gene in ulcerative colitis. Overall associations were noted only with two uncommon alleles (DRB1*0103 and DRB1*12), accounting for 17·2% of patients with ulcerative colitis. The contrast between the very strong evidence for the presence of a susceptibility gene in the HLA region (from the affected sibling pair analysis) and the size of the associations noted is intriguing, and may signify that the primary disease susceptibility gene(s) lie not in the class II region but in linked genes in the adjacent class I or class III regions.

The association with the DRB1*0103 allele was most pronounced in male patients with extensive disease. This allele was also associated with an increased risk of colectomy for severe disease. These results are consistent with previous work in which this allele was associated not only with severe colitis necessitating colectomy but also with recurrent inflammation of the ileo-anal pouch ("pouchitis").[19]

The present study reveals no association between alleles representing DR2 and ulcerative colitis. These results are consistent with recent data from Pittsburgh,[20] but contrast sharply with findings from Japan[21] and California.[10] Ethnic differences between the populations studied probably account for these discrepancies (table 4). In Oxford and Pittsburgh, the populations were predominantly white non-Jewish, of European origin. In this ethnic group, DRB1*1501 is the only common allele of DR2,[22] and DRB1*1502 accounts for less than 5% of alleles. By contrast, DRB1*1502 is the most common allele representing DR2 in Japanese[23] and Jewish[24] populations: it is this allele (or its extended haplotype) that seems to account for the association reported between DR2 and ulcerative colitis in California, where the population was mixed Jewish/non-Jewish.

Strong associations were noted between class II genotypes and subgroups defined by phenotype. Both at interim analysis and at final analysis, the DR3 DQ2 haplotype (part of the extended HLA A1 B8 DR3 DQ2 haplotype) was implicated as an important determinant of disease behaviour. This haplotype emerges as a potential marker of extensive disease, particularly in females. Only one of 44 female patients with distal disease possessed this haplotype, compared with 26·3% of the controls overall and 32·9% of patients with extensive disease. These results are consistent with and may even explain the well-accepted association between this haplotype and primary sclerosing cholangitis, a disease most common in male patients with extensive ulcerative colitis.[25]

The region of the A1 B8 DR3 DQ2 haplotype primarily associated with disease remains unknown. In primary sclerosing cholangitis[26] and other immune-mediated diseases,[27] investigators have concentrated on the structure of the cell surface class II molecules themselves and have tried to implicate specific aminoacid residues involved in antigen presentation. Before these molecules can be implicated in the pathogenesis of ulcerative colitis, further association studies and linkage analyses are needed to assess the contribution of linked genes. Polymorphisms of genes of the class I and class III regions, including the genes encoding complement components and the tumour necrosis factor α, may be most pertinent.

	Jews[27] (Israel)	North[28] European non-Jews	Japanese[28]
DRB1*1501	27·7	96·0	39·5
DRB1*1502	55·5	1·0	57·0
DRB1*1601/2	16·8	3·0	3·5

Table 4: **Relative frequency (%) of DR2 alleles in different ethnic groups**

The results reported here are consistent with findings in systemic sclerosis[28] and rheumatoid disease[29] which have implicated class II alleles as markers of disease severity (if not overall susceptibility). In both conditions, DRB1 genotyping has already become useful in the clinical assessment of newly diagnosed patients. The striking difference in frequency of the DR3 DQ2 haplotype between male and female patients with ulcerative colitis also warrants further attention. Although the present study has not confirmed the association with the DR2 specificity reported by Toyoda and colleagues,[10] the results do confirm a reduction in the DR4 specificity in patients with ulcerative colitis. This effect is most pronounced in patients with extensive colitis and those requiring colectomy.

In contrast with the results in ulcerative colitis, the linkage analysis has provided no evidence of linkage between HLA class II genes and Crohn's disease. The sibling pair method is relatively insensitive to disease heterogeneity; and it remains possible that these genes are important in only a small subgroup of patients. Nevertheless, in view of the strong evidence from concordance rates in twin pairs that genetic factors are important in the pathogenesis of Crohn's disease, it is likely that important susceptibility genes exist outside the HLA region.

Although the association study does not confirm previously described HLA associations in Crohn's disease,[10,11] it does lend some weight to the concept of heterogeneity within Crohn's disease. The clinical as well as immunogenetic data support the idea that Crohn's disease of the colon is more closely related to ulcerative colitis than to small-bowel Crohn's disease: median age at onset of disease in patients with colonic Crohn's disease was higher than in patients with ileo-colonic or small-bowel disease. Furthermore, in patients with colonic Crohn's disease the DR3 DQ2 haplotype was implicated as a marker of disease behaviour, as in ulcerative colitis.

These results have important implications for future studies of the genetics of inflammatory bowel disease and also of other complex disorders of polygenic inheritance. Future association (or linkage) studies must be designed to permit assessment of the relation between phenotype and genotype. Subclinical as well as clinical markers should be considered. Non-HLA genes must be studied. In Crohn's disease in particular, our investigation suggests that HLA genes are only weakly involved; other susceptibility genes must be present to explain the striking concordance rate in family members and twin pairs. In ulcerative colitis, further work is needed to define more closely the genes in the HLA region that are of primary importance in determining susceptibility and disease behaviour.

We are thank all the patients and physicians who have taken part in this study, the National Association for Crohn's and Colitis, and the European Collection of Animal and Cell Cultures. Heather Holt organised the collection of blood samples and clinical data and was supported by Astro Draco. JS is a Medical Research Council training fellow. We thank G M Lathrop for his critical advice and Clare O'Neill for technical guidance.

References

1 Satsangi J, Jewell DP, Rosenberg WMC, Bell JI. Genetics of inflammatory bowel disease. *Gut* 1994; **35:** 696–700.

2 Satsangi J, Rosenberg WMC, Jewell DP. The prevalence of inflammatory bowel disease in relatives of patients with Crohn's disease. *Eur J Gastroenterol Hepatol* 1994; 6: 413–16.

3 Tysk C, Lindberg E, Järnerot G, Flodérus-Myrhed B. Ulcerative colitis and Crohn's disease in an unselected population of monozygotic and dizygotic twins. A study of heritability and the influence of smoking. *Gut* 1988; **29:** 990–96.

4 Hugot JP, Laurent-Puig P, Gower-Rousseau C, Caillat-Zucman S, Beaugerie L, Dupas J. Linkage analyses of chromosome 6 loci, including HLA, in familial aggregations of Crohn's disease. *Am J Med Genet* 1994; **52:** 207–14.

5 Naom IS, Lee JC, Ford D, et al. Genetic predisposition to ulcerative colitis: a detailed study of the HLA region by linkage analysis. *Gut* 1994; **35:** S30.

6 Lander ES, Schork NJ. Genetic dissection of complex traits. *Science* 1994; **265:** 2037–48.

7 Suarez BK, Rice J, Reich T. The generalised sib pair IBD distribution: its use in the detection of linkage. *Ann Hum Genet* 1978; **42:** 87–94.

8 Bishop DT, Williamson JA. The power of identity-by-state methods for linkage analysis. *Am J Hum Genet* 1990; **46:** 254–65.

9 McConnell RB, Vadheim CM. Inflammatory bowel disease. In: King RA, Rotter JI, Motulsky AO, eds. The genetic basis of common diseases. Oxford: Oxford University Press, 1992: 326–48.

10 Toyoda H, Wang S-J, Yang H, Redford A, Magalong D, Tyan D. Distinct association of HLA class II genes with inflammatory bowel disease. *Gastroenterology* 1993; **104:** 741–48.

11 Wassmuth R, Keller Y, Thompson G, Starck M, Lindhagen T, Holmberg E. HLA DRB1 alleles provide protection against Crohn's disease in Caucasians. *Eur J Gastroenterol Hepatol* 1994; **6:** 405–11.

12 Farmer RG, Whelan G, Fazio VW. Long-term follow-up of patients with Crohn's disease. *Gastroenterology* 1985; **88:** 1818–25.

13 Miller D, Polesky H. A salting-out procedure for extracting DNA from human nucleated cells. *Nucl Acid Res* 1988; **16:** 1215.

14 Bunce M, Taylor CJ, Welsh KI. Rapid HLA-DQB typing by eight PRC amplifications with sequence-specific primers (PCR-SSP). *Hum Immunol* 1993; **37:** 201–06.

15 Olerup O, Zetterquist H. HLA-DR typing by PCR amplifications with sequence-specific primers in 2 hours. An alternative to serological DR typing in clinical practice including donor-recipient matching in cadaveric transplantation. *Tissue Antigens* 1992; **39:** 225–35.

16 Bunce M, Fanning GC, Welsh KI. Comprehensive serologically equivalent DNA typing for HLA-B by PCR using sequence-specific primers. *Tissue Antigens* (in press).

17 Risch N. Assessing the role of HLA-linked and unlinked determinants of disease. *Am J Hum Genet* 1987; **40:** 1–14.

18 Rotter JI, Landaw EM. Measuring the genetic contribution of a single locus to a multi-locus disease. *Clin Genet* 1984; **26:** 529–42.

19 Merrett MN, Bunce M, Mortensen N, Kettlewell MGW, Jewell DP. HLA DRB1*0103 (HLA-DR-BON) may predict pouchitis in patients who have an ileal pouch-anal anastomosis (IPAA) for ulcerative colitis (UC). *Gastroenterology* 1992; **102:** A935.

20 Duerr RH, Neigut DA. Molecularly defined HLA-DR2 alleles in ulcerative colitis and an anti-neutrophil cytoplasmic antibody-positive subgroup. *Gastroenterology* 1995; **108:** 423–27.

21 Asakura H, Tsuchiya M, Aiso S, et al. Association of human leucocyte DR2 antigen with Japanese ulcerative colitis. *Gastroenterology* 1982; **82:** 413–18.

22 Reijonen H, Ilonen I, Akerblom HA, Knip M, Dosch H. Childhood diabetes in Finland study group. Multi-locus analysis of HLA class II genes in DR2-positive IDDM haplotypes in Finland. *Tissue Antigens* 1994; **43:** 1–6.

23 Hashimoto M, Kinoshita T, Yamasaki M, Tanaka H, Imanishi T, Ihara H. Gene frequencies and haplotypic associations within the HLA region in 916 unrelated Japanese individuals. *Tissue Antigens* 1994: **44:** 166–73.

24 Roitberg-Tambur A, Friedmann A, Korn S, et al. Serological and molecular analysis of the HLA system in Israeli Jewish patients with oral erosive lichen planus. *Tissue Antigens* 1994; **43:** 219–23.

25 Chapman RW. Aetiology and natural history of primary sclerosing cholangitis: a decade of progress? *Gut* 1991; **32:** 1433–35.

26 Farrant JM, Doherty DG, Donaldson PT, et al. Amino acid substitutions at position 38 of the DRB polypeptide confer susceptibility and protection from primary sclerosing cholangitis. *Hepatology* 1992; **16:** 390–95.

27 Todd JA, Bell JI, McDevitt HO. HLA-DQB gene contributes to susceptibility and resistance to insulin-dependent diabetes mellitus. *Nature* 1987; **329:** 599–604.

28 Briggs DC, Vaughan RW, Welsh KI, Myers A, Dubois RM, Black CM. Immunogenetic prediction of pulmonary fibrosis in systemic sclerosis. *Lancet* 1991; **338:** 661–62.

29 Wordsworth BP, Lanchbury JSS, Sakkas LI, Welsh KI, Panayi GI, Bell JI. HLA-DR4 subtype frequencies in rheumatoid arthritis indicate that DRB1 is the major susceptibility locus within the HLA class II region. *Proc Natl Acad Sci* 1989; **10053:** 10049–153.

© Gut 1996; 38: 316–321

Risk assessment after acute upper gastrointestinal haemorrhage

T A Rockall, R F A Logan, H B Devlin, T C Northfield, and the steering committee and members of the National Audit of Acute Upper Gastrointestinal Haemorrhage

Abstract

The aim of this study was to establish the relative importance of risk factors for mortality after acute upper gastrointestinal haemorrhage, and to formulate a simple numerical scoring system that categorises patients by risk. A prospective, unselected, multicentre, population based study was undertaken using standardised questionnaires in two phases one year apart. A total of 4185 cases of acute upper gastrointestinal haemorrhage over the age of 16 identified over a four month period in 1993 and 1625 cases identified subsequently over a three month period in 1994 were included in the study. It was found that age, shock, comorbidity, diagnosis, major stigmata of recent haemorrhage, and rebleeding are all independent predictors of mortality when assessed using multiple logistic regression. A numerical score using these parameters has been developed that closely follows the predictions generated by logistical regression equations. Haemoglobin, sex, presentation (other than shock), and drug therapy (non-steroidal anti-inflammatory drugs and anticoagulants) are not represented in the final model. When tested for general applicability in a second population, the scoring system was found to reproducibly predict mortality in each risk category. In conclusion, a simple numerical score can be used to categorise patients presenting with acute upper gastrointestinal haemorrhage by risk of death. This score can be used to determine case mix when comparing outcomes in audit and research and to calculate risk standardised mortality. In addition, this risk score can identify 15% of all cases with acute upper gastrointestinal haemorrhage at the time of presentation and 26% of cases after endoscopy who are at low risk of rebleeding and negligible risk of death and who might therefore be considered for early discharge or outpatient treatment with consequent resource savings.

(*Gut* 1996; **38:** 316–321)

Keywords: gastrointestinal haemorrhage, risk assessment.

Correspondence to:
Mr T Rockall, The Surgical Epidemiology and Audit Unit, The Royal College of Surgeons of England, 35–43 Lincoln's Inn Fields, London WC2A 3PN.

Accepted for publication
7 September 1995

Acute upper gastrointestinal haemorrhage is a common medical emergency with an incidence in England of approximately 100 per 100 000 adults per year and a mortality among unselected cases in the region of 14%.[1] The important factors influencing the outcome of acute upper gastrointestinal haemorrhage have been the focus of much research and debate since the 1940s but, although the risk factors associated with both rebleeding and death are well known, different researchers have put a different emphasis on each of these according to their experiences.[2–16] Age, comorbidity, shock, diagnosis, admission haemoglobin values, presentation, ulcer size, stigmata of recent haemorrhage, and blood transfusion requirements have all been described as significant risk factors for further haemorrhage and death. Further haemorrhage has been consistently described as the most important risk factor for mortality. It is generally accepted that the risk of rebleeding and death is related to many factors, which are not entirely independent of each other.

While previous studies have served to indicate which variables are important in determining the risk of rebleeding and death, few attempts have been made to devise a simple and therefore clinically useful risk scoring system that makes use of readily available clinical information to categorise patients by risk. We have used a large uniform database to analyse the risk factors for mortality and we have used the analysis to construct a simple numerical risk scoring system. The primary purpose of this score is to allow case mix assessment for comparative audit. An understanding of the risk associated with any particular patient is an important initial step in the management process. Most cases of acute upper gastrointestinal haemorrhage are treated by junior staff in the setting of busy casualty departments and a simple scoring system may be a useful aid to the clinical judgement of risk, especially as there is evidence of considerable disagreement as to what the important prognostic factors are, even within the British Society of Gastroenterology.[17] The development of treatment protocols and the selection of patients for clinical trials are other areas where a risk index might be of benefit.

Methods

The data presented were collected as part of a national audit of the management and outcome of acute upper gastrointestinal haemorrhage. Four health regions in England (North West Thames, South West Thames, Trent, and the West Midlands) were recruited to this prospective study, undertaken under the auspices of the British Society of Gastroenterology, the Royal College of Surgeons of England, the Royal College of Physicians of

© Gut 1996; 38: 316–321

TABLE I *Factors analysed in relation to rebleeding and mortality with odds ratios and 95% confidence intervals*

Variable	*Type of data*	*Categorisation*	*Cases*	*Rebleed No*	*Rebleed %*	*Dead No*	*Dead %*	*Odds*	*95% CI*
All cases			4185	643/4119 (66 missing)	15·6	585/4142 (43 missing)	14·1		
Age	Continuous	<60		151/1290	11·7	74/1294	5·7	Reference	
		60–79		291/1741	16·7	255/1754	14·5	2·80	2·14 to 3·67
		>=80		201/1088	18·5	256/1094	23·4	5·04	3·83 to 6·62
Sex	Categorical	Male	2376	379/2366	16·0	313/2376	13·2	Reference	
(4 missing)		Female	1762	263/1749	15·0	272/1762	15·4	1·20	1·01 to 1·43
Shock	Ordinal	No shock	2897	330	11·4	288	9·9	Reference	
(74 missing)		Tachycardia	687	164	23·9	134	19·3	2·17	1·73 to 2·71
		BP<100	347	94	27·1	95	27·1	3·37	2·58 to 4·39
		BP<70	60	30	50·0	28	45·9	7·70	4·59 to 12·9
		BP<50	34	15	44·0	27	71·1	22·3	10·9 to 45·4
Haemoglobin	Continuous	Hb>=10	2554	299	11·7	275/2554	10·8	Reference	
		Hb<10	1362	314	23·3	258/1362	18·9	1·94	1·61 to 2·33
NSAID	Categorical	No		423/2820	15·0	417/2834	14·7	Reference	
		Yes		220/1299	16·9	168/1308	12·8	0·85	0·71 to 1·04
Anticoagulants	Categorical	No	3864	595/3841	15·5	536/3864	13·9	Reference	
		Yes	278	48/278	17·3	49/278	17·6	1·33	0·96 to 1·83
SRH	Categorical	None	1976	178	9·0	103	5·2	Reference	
(all cases)	n=3047	Present	1078	298	27·8	193	17·9	3·97	3·08 to 5·10
Further haemorrhage	Categorical	No	3387	–		293	8·7	Reference	
(62 missing)		Yes	730	–		272	37·3	6·24	5·15 to 7·56
SRH	Categorical	None		66/674	9·8	25/674	3·7	Reference	
(peptic ulcer		Blood in UGIT		103/316	32·6	68/321	21·2	6·98	4·31 to 11·3
group only)		Adherent clot		79/238	33·2	39/240	16·3	5·04	2·98 to 8·53
n=1300		Visible vessel		22/97	22·7	12/97	12·3	3·66	1·78 to 7·56
		Spurting vessel		9/34	26·5	6/35	17·1	5·37	2·05 to 14·1
		Dark spot		17/115	14·8	11/117	9·4	2·69	1·29 to 5·64
Diagnosis	Categorical	None made	1014	125	12·5	200	19·7	1·75	1·45 to 2·11
		Peptic ulcer	1450	267	18·5	170	11·7	0·73	0·60 to 0·88
		Malignancy	155	47	29·7	58	37·4	3·93	2·80 to 5·50
		Varices	180	67	37·0	41	22·8	1·85	1·29 to 2·66
		Mallory-Weiss	214	8	3·7	6	2·8	0·17	0·07 to 0·38
		Erosive disease	447	36	8·1	29	6·5	0·39	0·27 to 0·58
		Oesophagitis	429	37	8·6	35	8·2	0·51	0·36 to 0·73
		Other	253	56	22·8	46	18·2	1·38	0·99 to 1·93
Comorbidity	Categorical	None	1653	184	11·2	73	4·4	Reference	
		Cardiac failure	378	84	22·6	129	34·1	7·73	5·68 to 10·5
		Ischaemic heart disease	659	107	16·5	125	19·0	4·30	3·17 to 5·81
		Asthma	136	18	13·3	19	14·0	3·16	1·85 to 5·40
		COAD	280	48	17·6	67	23·9	5·42	3·80 to 7·73
		Diabetes mellitus	277	43	15·9	62	22·4	5·07	3·53 to 7·28
		Rheumatoid arthritis	168	32	19·0	33	19·6	4·45	2·86 to 6·91
		Liver failure	178	61	35·5	68	38·2	8·65	6·01 to 12·5
		Renal failure	123	29	24·4	56	45·5	10·3	6·96 to 15·3
		Disseminated malignancy	172	53	30·0	89	51·7	11·7	8·28 to 16·6
		Other	463	83	18·0	78	16·8	3·81	2·73 to 5·33
		Pneumonia	88	12	14·1	30	34·1	7·72	4·80 to 12·4
		Dementia	176	22	12·5	28	15·9	3·60	2·27 to 5·72
		Recent major operation	120	24	20·5	27	22·5	5·09	3·16 to 8·22
		Malignancy	119	27	23·7	33	27·7	6·28	4·0 to 9·86
		CVA/TIA	253	32	13·1	54	21·3	4·83	3·30 to 7·04
		Haematological malignancy	109	28	25·7	30	27·5	6·23	3·91 to 9·94
		Hypertension	179	18	10·2	19	10·6	2·40	1·42 to 4·07
		Trauma/burns	62	4	6·9	17	27·4	6·21	3·46 to 11·2
		Other cardiac disease	141	20	14·5	20	14·2	3·21	1·9 to 5·42
		Major sepsis	42	6	14·6	13	31·0	7·01	3·61 to 13·6
		Other liver disease	69	14	23·3	5	7·2	1·64	0·64 to 4·19

SRH=stigmata of recent haemorrhage, UGIT=upper gastrointestinal tract, COAD=chronic obstructive airway disease, CVA/TIA=cerebrovascular accident/transient ischaemic attack.

London, and the Association of Surgeons of Great Britain and Ireland. Seventy four 'acute' hospitals participated in the initial audit.

A lead consultant at each site (usually a member of the British Society of Gastroenterology) represented the project locally. The identification of subjects and administration of the questionnaire was undertaken by an audit coordinator at each hospital. Patients were identified daily in the accident and emergency department, the wards, the endoscopy unit, the operating theatre, and from blood transfusion records and admission data. The questionnaire was generally completed by medical staff and the audit coordinator was then responsible for checking and returning a completed questionnaire for each patient correctly identified. The data collected incorporated patient details including known risk factors, treatment including the use of endoscopy, endoscopic findings, details of surgical involvement, diagnosis, complications, and mortality. Data were entered into a computer database using a validated optical scanning device.[18 19]

The risk scoring system was validated using data collected during the second phase of the national audit in 1994, which used an identical methodology at 45 'acute' hospitals from three health regions over a period of three months.

Statistical methods

Multiple logistic regression analysis[20] was undertaken using SPSS computer software.[21] Continuous variables were categorised to avoid multiplicative errors and variables with more than two categories were recorded using an appropriate indicator variable coding scheme. Variables were entered into the initial models if the crude odds ratios were significantly different from 1. The models were developed using a forward stepwise selection procedure. A variable was included at each step if the score statistics was less than 0·05 and was removed if

© Gut 1996; 38: 316–321

TABLE II *Significant predictor variables for mortality*

Variable	*Initial model* b	SE	Significance	Exp(B)	*Complete model* b	SE	Significance	Exp(B)
Age								
<60	Reference		<0·0001				<0·0001	
60–79	0·92	0·17	<0·0001	2·5	0·85	0·22	0·0001	2·34
80+	1·53	0·18	<0·0001	4·6	1·49	0·24	<0·0001	4·43
Shock – none	Reference		<0·0001				0·0363	
Tachycardia (p>=100)	0·76	0·13	<0·0001	2·15	0·34	0·18	0·0570	1·40
BP<100	0·89	0·16	<0·0001	2·43	0·50	0·21	0·0199	1·65
BP<70	1·75	0·30	<0·0001	5·60	0·77	0·39	0·0517	2·15
BP<50	2·75	0·43	<0·0001	15·69	0·83	0·61	0·1759	2·28
Comorbidity								
None	−1·04	0·16	<0·0001	0·35	−1·06	0·20	<0·0001	0·35
Cardiac failure	0·72	0·15	<0·0001	2·06	0·59	0·21	0·0051	1·81
Renal failure	1·55	0·21	<0·0001	4·72	1·68	0·29	<0·0001	5·40
Liver failure	1·04	0·22	<0·0001	2·84			NS	
Disseminated malignancy	1·83	0·19	<0·0001	6·22	1·43	0·28	<0·0001	4·18
Pneumonia	0·92	0·29	0·0017	2·50			NS	
Malignancy	0·59	0·28	0·0370	1·80			NS	
Haematological malignancy	0·76	0·28	0·0061	2·13	0·77	0·35	0·0292	2·15
Diagnosis								
No lesion identified, no SRH					Reference		0·0005	
No lesion identified, SRH present					−0·16	0·38	0·6710	0·85
Peptic ulcer					−0·16	0·14	0·2549	0·85
Malignancy					1·14	0·25	<0·0001	3·14
Varices					−0·40	0·28	0·1419	0·67
Mallory-Weiss					−0·33	0·47	0·4792	0·71
Erosive disease					−0·24	0·25	0·3225	0·78
Oesophagitis					0·29	0·21	0·1685	1·34
Other					−0·09	0·28	0·7589	0·91
Major SRH					1·05	0·17	<0·0001	2·87
Rebleeding					1·71	0·15	<0·0001	5·57
Constant (B_0)	−1·22	0·13	<0·0001		−2·98	0·24	<0·0001	

B represents the variable coefficient in the logistic regression equation and B_0 represents a constant. SE is the standard error of the coefficient B. Significance is the statistical significance for the hypothesis that the coefficient is different from zero. Exp(B) represents the factor change in the odds that death will occur. For the categorised variables the value should only be interpreted within each variable. The prediction of mortality is calculated using the equation $p=\frac{1}{1+e^{-(B_0+B_1X_1+B_2X_2+B_3X_3+......B_pX_p)}}$ where p is the probability of death and X represents the variable, where X=0 if absent and 1 if present. SRH=stigmata of recent haemorrhage, NS=not significant.

the log likelihood ratio test statistic was greater than 0·1. Confidence interval analysis was undertaken using CIA software.[22]

Results

Utilisation of all the principal risk factors that determine outcome necessitates the development of two related models. Important predictive variables such as diagnosis and the presence of stigmata of recent haemorrhage are usually only available once endoscopy has been performed. An initial predictive model has been developed based upon the information derived from the history, examination, and simple blood tests. A second more complete model includes, in addition, risk factors derived from endoscopic information and further haemorrhage.

Data were drawn from 4185 cases presenting with an acute upper gastrointestinal haemorrhage. Overall mortality was 14% (585 of 4142*). Further haemorrhage (continued bleeding necessitating operation or rebleeding) occurred in 18% (736) and was associated with a 37% (272 of 730*) mortality. The initial model was based upon 3981 cases for whom all investigated variables were recorded. The second complete model was based upon 2956 cases that had, in addition, undergone diagnostic endoscopy or emergency surgery.

*Mortality data were missing in a total of 43 cases and in six cases in the group sustaining further haemorrhage.

Table I lists the factors considered in this study with crude odds ratios and 95% confidence intervals. Continuous variables have been categorised.

Age, sex, comorbidity, shock, and haemoglobin had a crude odds ratio significantly different form 1 and were entered into a logistic regression analysis with death as the dependant variable. After forward stepwise analysis, 'sex' and 'haemoglobin <10 g/dl' were excluded from the model.

Diagnosis, stigmata of recent haemorrhage, and rebleeding were then entered into a second analysis together with the significant variables from the first analysis.

Table II gives the B coefficients for both models with the standard error and significance. Age, shock, comorbidity, diagnosis,

TABLE III *Numerical risk scoring system*

Variable	*Score* 0	1	2	3
Age	<60 Years	60–79 Years	>=80 Years	
Shock	'No shock', systolic BP >=100, pulse <100	'Tachycardia', systolic BP >=100, pulse >=100	'Hypotension', systolic BP <100	
Comorbidity	No major comorbidity		Cardiac failure, ischaemic heart disease, any major comorbidity	Renal failure, liver failure, disseminated malignancy
Diagnosis	Mallory-Weiss tear, no lesion identified and no SRH	All other diagnoses	Malignancy of upper GI tract	
Major SRH	None or dark spot only		Blood in upper GI tract, adherent clot, visible or spurting vessel	

Maximum additive score prior to diagnosis=7. Maximum additive score following diagnosis=11.

© Gut 1996; 38: 316–321

stigmata of recent haemorrhage, and rebleeding are all independently significant factors in the prediction of mortality in these models.

A simple risk score has been devised using only these significant variables. An integer score was attributed to each category of each variable according to its relative contribution in the logistic regression model (as determined by its regression coefficient). The score was then adapted so that the outcome in each category most closely fitted the predictions of the logistic regression model.

Age and degree of shock were categorised and each attributed a score of 0, 1, or 2. Comorbidity was categorised and attributed a score of 0, 2, or 3. This gives a maximum additive score of 7 before diagnosis.

A score of 0, 1, or 2 for diagnosis and 0 or 2 for stigmata of recent haemorrhage was then added to give a maximum score of 11. Scores of 8 or more are considered as one category as there are very few cases in these very high risk categories. Table III shows the derived scoring system.

The population experiencing further haemorrhage is considered separately from the population without further haemorrhage in the complete model.

Table IV shows the observed mortality and rebleeding rate in each category for both models. Figure 1 shows these data for the complete model. Mortality increases in a stepwise fashion as the risk score increases. The rate of rebleeding also increases as the risk score increases. There were no deaths in categories 0 and 1 of the full model and only one death (0·3%) in category 2. Twenty six per cent of the sample were in these lowest three categories. The population that rebled experienced a fivefold increase in mortality in risk group 3, which decreased to a twofold increase for risk group 8.

TABLE IV(A) *Observed mortality by initial risk score*

Score		0	1	2	3	4	5	6	7
	No	595	505	641	890	859	326	141	24
	%	14·9	12·7	16·1	22·4	21·6	8·2	3·5	0·6
Deaths	No	1	12	36	98	211	129	69	12
	%	0·2	2·4	5·6	11·0	24·6	39·6	48·9	50·0

TABLE IV(B) *Observed rebleeding and mortality by complete risk score*

Score		0	1	2	3	4	5	6	7	8+
	No	144	281	337	444	528	453	312	267	190
	%	4·9	9·5	11·4	15·0	17·9	15·3	10·6	9·0	6·4
Rebleed	No	7	9	18	50	76	83	102	113	101
	%	4·9	3·4	5·3	11·2	14·1	24·1	32·9	43·8	41·8
Deaths	No	0	0	1	8	16	30	20	23	25
(no rebleed)	%	0	0	0·3	2·0	3·5	8·1	9·5	14·9	28·1
Deaths	No	0	0	0	5	12	19	34	49	53
(rebleed)	%	0	0	0	10·0	15·8	22·9	33·3	43·4	52·5
Deaths	No	0	0	1	13	28	49	54	72	78
(total)	%	0	0	0·2	2·9	5·3	10·8	17·3	27·0	41·1

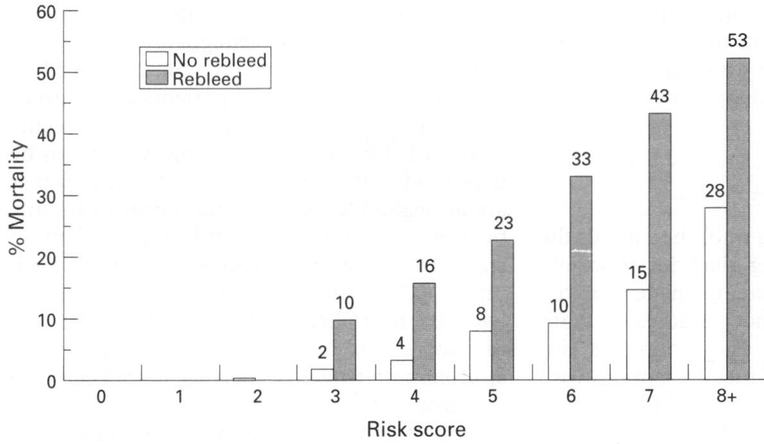

Figure 1: Mortality by risk score.

Validation

Figure 2 shows the degree of association between the predictions of the full logistical regression model and the observed mortality in each category of the risk score. The box plots represent the distribution of predicted

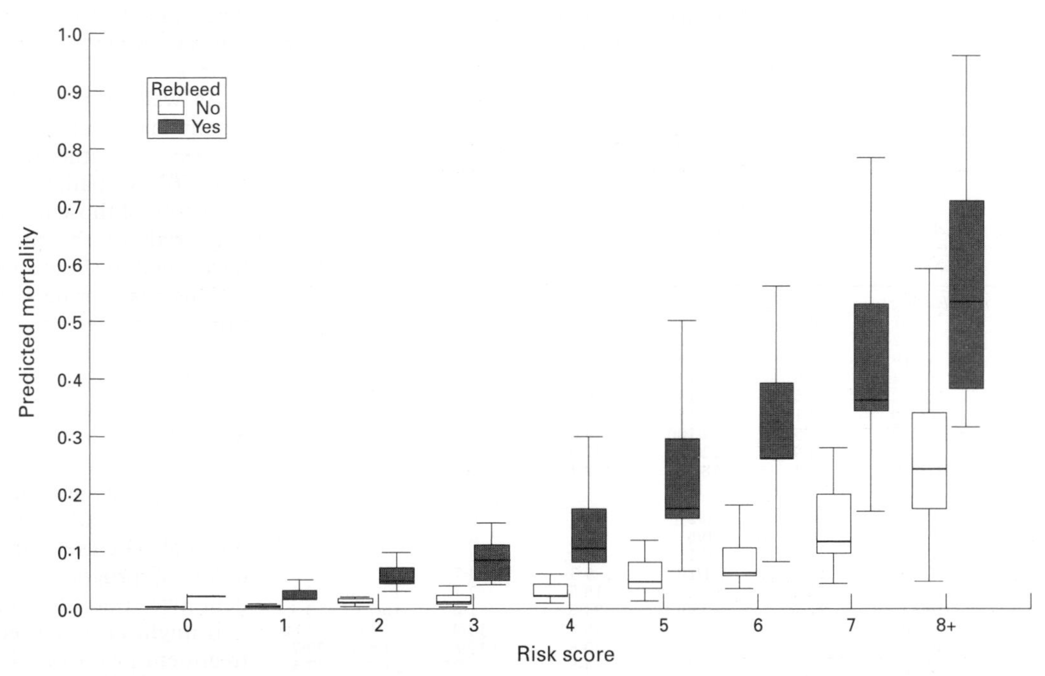

Figure 2: Boxplot of computer predicted mortality by risk score.

© Gut 1996; 38: 316–321

TABLE V(A) *Predicted and observed mortality by risk score for initial model*

Score	Mortality: Audit 1 (predicted) No	%	Audit 2 (observed) No	%	Difference with 95% CI	
0	1/595	0·2	0/246	0·0	+0·2	−0·2 to +0·5
1	12/505	2·4	6/201	3·0	−0·6	−3·3 to +2·1
2	36/641	5·6	14/249	6·1	0·0	−3·9 to +2·9
3	98/890	11·0	38/311	12·1	−1·2	−5·4 to +3·0
4	211/859	24·6	77/364	21·0	+3·4	−1·8 to +8·5
5	129/326	39·6	47/134	35·1	+4·5	−5·2 to +14·2
6	72/141	51·1	42/68	61·8	−10·7	−24·9 to +3·5
7	12/24	50·0	6/8	75·0	−25·0	−61·1 to +11·1
Total	568/3981	14·3	230/1584	14·5		

mortalities (using the logistic regression equation) for cases within each risk score category. It can be seen that there is a high degree of association between the predictions of the logistic regression model and the greatly simplified numerical score.

The risk score has been validated in a second population of 1625 cases collected using an identical methodology as part of the second phase of the National Audit. All the necessary variables were recorded in 1584 cases. In 1190 cases, variables for endoscopic diagnosis and stigmata of recent haemorrhage were also recorded. It can be seen in Table V that the predicted outcomes, based upon the observed outcome by risk category in the first audit, are not significantly different from the observed outcome in the second audit in either the initial or complete models.

Discussion

There is a great deal more published about the risk factors for rebleeding than for mortality after an acute episode of haemorrhage from the upper gastrointestinal tract. Studies of both rebleeding and mortality show that the risk factors for these two outcomes are similar, with the additional conclusion that rebleeding is itself of independent predictive value for mortality.

Univariate analyses have led us to believe that rebleeding increases mortality between five and 16-fold, and perhaps as a result it is often regarded as the harbinger of death. Indeed the thrust of modern treatment is specifically targeted at preventing rebleeding by physical means in those lesions amenable to endoscopic haemostatic therapy in the belief that a reduction in mortality should follow. Although several clinical trials have shown a significant reduction in rebleeding with these methods, however, the reduction in mortality has been much more elusive and only two trials using lasers have shown a significant reduction in mortality.[23] Meta-analysis has suggested a 30% improvement in mortality in the peptic ulcer group with visible vessels.[24] Although rebleeding is a very important sign to detect and act upon, either endoscopically or surgically, there are many other factors that determine the final outcome.

Our scoring system has been developed with a view to simplicity and ease of variable acquisition. We have shown how it can be used to broadly categorise patients by risk and there are several important conclusions for the model: firstly, that the risk of rebleeding as well as the risk of death increases as the risk score increases; secondly, that patients who rebleed have an increased mortality compared with those who do not rebleed; thirdly, that the proportional increased risk of death after a rebleed is not the same in each category.

For cases scoring 0, 1, or 2 rebleeding occurs in less than 5% of patients and mortality is virtually zero whether rebleeding occurs or not (Table IV). The scoring system can be used to identify the one quarter of patients that are at negligible risk of dying but this can only be done once a diagnosis and an assessment of stigmata of recent haemorrhage have been made. Rebleeding has its most profound influence on mortality in the middle risk groups that score 3 or 4, when it is associated with an approximately fivefold increase in mortality. In risk groups 5 to 7 rebleeding is associated with an approximately threefold increase in mortality and for risk group 8, a twofold increase. The impact of rebleeding on outcome should not be judged independently of other risk factors.

As well as the failure to investigate sufficiently large numbers of cases, the relation of rebleeding to other risk factors and the fact that only 50% of patients that die have rebled and only 40% of those that rebleed die, may explain why trials of therapy that reduce rebleeding have failed to show a reduction in mortality.

This risk scoring system has been developed primarily to determine case mix and to calculate risk standardised mortality for the hospitals taking part in the national audit of acute upper gastrointestinal haemorrhage.[25] Systems such as this are likely to become more important as the discipline of comparative audit expands and the threat of league tables looms. As an adjunct to clinical judgement, it might also be useful in the clinical setting as an index of prognosis both before and after a definitive endoscopic diagnosis.

It might also be used in the development of treatment protocols. The full array of management tools for optimal care of patients with

TABLE V(B) *Predicted and observed mortality by risk score for complete model*

Score	Mortality: Audit 1 (predicted) No	%	Audit 2 (observed) No	%	Difference with 95% CI	
Cases not rebleeding						
0	0/137	0	0/46	0	0	0
1	0/272	0	0/125	0	0	0
2	1/319	0·3	0/131	0	+0·3	−0·3 to +0·9
3	8/394	2·0	2/143	1·4	+0·6	−1·7 to +3·0
4	16/452	3·5	9/149	6·0	−2·5	−6·7 to +1·7
5	30/370	8·1	9/150	6·0	+2·1	−2·6 to +6·8
6	20/210	9·5	9/100	9·0	+0·5	−6·4 to +7·4
7	23/154	14·9	12/67	17·9	−3·0	−13·7 to +7·8
8+	25/89	28·1	18/56	32·1	−4·0	−19·4 to +11·3
Cases rebleeding						
0	0/7	0	0/2	0	0	0
1	0/9	0	0/6	0	0	0
2	0/18	0	0/11	0	0	0
3	5/50	10·0	1/19	5·3	+4·7	−8·3 to +17·8
4	12/76	15·8	5/27	18·5	−2·7	−19·5 to +14·1
5	19/83	22·9	12/49	24·5	−1·6	−16·7 to +13·5
6	34/102	33·3	7/37	18·9	+14·4	−1·17 to +30·0
7	49/113	43·4	12/39	30·8	+12·6	−4·5 to +29·7
8+	53/101	52·5	18/33	54·5	+2·07	−21·7 to +17·5

© Gut 1996; 38: 316–321

upper gastrointestinal haemorrhage is expensive. Rapid endoscopy by experienced endoscopists on call 24 hours per day, high dependency units, medicosurgical collaboration, and on call endoscopy staff all have considerable financial implications. Being able to select patients that will benefit the most from intensive treatment is one important step in the rationalisation of resources. Early discharge or even outpatient treatment of very low risk groups or the transfer to intensive care facilities of very high risk cases for whom a determined effort to save life is being made, might easily be incorporated into a treatment protocol, however, the use of such a system in selecting patients for surgery could only be promoted after evidence from clinical trials.

It is important to understand that this system, like most predictive methods cannot predict the outcome of any individual patient, except perhaps those in categories 0 and 1 in whom no deaths occurred. The risk of death is simply a measurement of the number of deaths that might be expected in a large population of cases with those risk factors. The testing of the model in a second large population has, however, allowed us to confirm the general applicability of the model based upon current standards of treatment.

This project was undertaken under the auspices of the Royal College of Physicians of London, the Royal College of Surgeons of England, the British Society of Gastroenterology, and the Association of Surgeons of Great Britain and Ireland. We gratefully acknowledge the financial support of Lederle Pharmaceuticals and the support of South West Thames, North West Thames, and Trent regional health authorities and the West Midlands Gastroenterology services committee. We also acknowledge the great deal of work performed by medical and audit staff in each of the participating units.

Members of the steering group: Professor T C Northfield (Chairman), St George's Hospital Medical School, London; Mr H B Devlin (Director), Surgical Epidemiology and Audit Unit, RCS, London; Dr R F A Logan, Queen's Medical Centre, Nottingham; Dr J Levi, Northwick Park Hospital, London; Dr K Bardhan, Rotherham District General Hospital, Rotherham; Dr A Hamlyn, Wordsley Hospital, Wordsley; Mr G Gillespie, Victoria Infirmary, Glasgow; Mr R McCloy, Manchester Royal Infirmary, Manchester; Mr D Watkin, Leicester Royal Infirmary, Leicester; Mr M Crisp, Lederle Pharmaceuticals. Also Mr R Leicester (chairman) and Mrs C Romaya (administrator) of the British Society of Gastroenterology audit committee.

1 Rockall TA, Logan RFA, Devlin HB, Northfield TC. Incidence of and mortality from acute upper gastrointestinal haemorrhage in the UK. *BMJ* 1995; **311:** 222–6.
2 Swain CP, Kirham JS, Salmon PR, Bown SG, Northfield TC. Controlled trial of Nd-YAG laser photocoagulation in bleeding peptic ulcers. *Lancet* 1986; i: 1113.
3 Storey DW, Bown SG, Swain CP, Salmon PR, Kirkham JS, Northfield TC. Endoscopic prediction of recurrent bleeding in peptic ulcers. *N Engl J Med* 1981; **305:** 915.
4 Northfield TC. Factors predisposing to recurrent haemorrhage after acute gastrointestinal bleeding. *BMJ* 1971; **1:** 26.
5 Katschinski BD, Logan RFA, Davies J, Langman MJS. Audit of mortality in upper gastrointestinal bleeding. *Postgrad Med J* 1989; **65:** 913.
6 Katschinski B, Logan R, Davies J, Faulkner G, Pearson J, Langman M. Prognostic factors in upper gastrointestinal bleeding. *Dig Dis Sci* 1994; **39:** 706.
7 Jones PF, Johnston SJ, McEwan AB, Kyle J, Needham CD. Further haemorrhage after admission to hospital for gastrointestinal haemorrhage. *BMJ* 1973; **3:** 660.
8 Hunt PS. Mortality in patients with haematemesis and melaena: a prospective study. *BMJ* 1979; **1:** 1238.
9 Griffiths WJ. The visible vessel as an indicator of uncontrolled or recurrent gastrointestinal bleeding. *N Engl J Med* 1979; **300:** 1411.
10 Kalabakas A, Xourgias B, Karamanolis D. Incidence and significance of stigmata of recent haemorrhage in ulcer patients without clinical evidence of recent bleeding. *Gut* 1990; **31:** A1206.
11 Wara P, Berg V, Amdrup E. Factors influencing mortality in patients with bleeding ulcer. A review of 7 years experience preceding therapeutic endoscopy. *Acta Chir Scand* 1983; **149:** 775.
12 Macleod IA, Mills PR. Factors identifying the probability of further haemorrhage after acute upper gastrointestinal haemorrhage. *Br J Surg* 1982; **69:** 256.
13 Bornman PC, Theodorou NA, Shuttleworth RD, Essel HP, Marks IN. Importance of hypovolaemic shock and endoscopic signs in predicting recurrent haemorrhage from peptic ulceration: a prospective evaluation. *BMJ* 1985; **291** (27 July): 245.
14 Branicki FJ, Coleman SY, Fok PJ, Pritchett CJ, Fan S, Lai ECS, *et al.* Bleeding peptic ulcer: a prospective evaluation of risk factors for rebleeding and mortality. *World J Surg* 1990; **14:** 262.
15 Clason AE, Macleod DAD, Elton RA. Clinical factors in the prediction of further haemorrhage or mortality in acute upper gastrointestinal haemorrhage. *Br J Surg* 1986; **73:** 985.
16 Morgan AG, Clamp SE. OMGE International Upper Gastrointestinal Bleeding Survey 1978–1982. *Scand J Gastroenterol Suppl* 1984; **19** (suppl 95): 41.
17 Thomas GE, Cotton PB, Clark CG, Boulos PB. Survey of management in acute upper gastrointestinal haemorrhage. *J Roy Soc Med* 1980; **73:** 90.
18 Emberton M, Meredith P. Caught in the act. *British Journal of Healthcare Computing and Information Management* 1993; **10:** 32.
19 Emberton M, Rockall TA, Meredith P. Scanning for Audit. *British Journal of Healthcare Computing and Information Management* 1994; **11:** 23.
20 Hall GH, Round AP. Logistic regression – explanation and use. *J R Coll Physicians Lond* 1994; **28** (3): 242.
21 SPSS. *Advanced statistics.* 6.0.1 ed. Chicago: SPSS Inc, 1993.
22 Gardner MJ, Altman DG. *Statistics with confidence – confidence intervals and statistical guidelines.* London: BMJ Publishing Group, 1989.
23 Steele RJC. Endoscopic haemostasis for non-variceal upper gastrointestinal haemorrhage. *Br J Surg* 1989; **76:** 219–25.
24 Sacks HS, Chalmers TC, Blum AL, Berrier J, Pagano D. Endoscopic haemostasis. An effective therapy for bleeding peptic ulcers. *JAMA* 1990; **264:** 494–9.
25 Variation in outcome after acute upper gastrointestinal haemorrhage. *Lancet* 1995; **346:** 346–50.

Genetic Mapping of the Hereditary Mixed Polyposis Syndrome to Chromosome 6q

H. J. W. Thomas,[1,2,4,*] S. C. Whitelaw,[1,2,4,*] S. E. Cottrell,[5,*] V. A. Murday,[2,5,*] I. P. M. Tomlinson,[2,5,*] D. Markie,[5] T. Jones,[6] D. T. Bishop,[7] S. V. Hodgson,[1,2] D. Sheer,[6] J. M. A. Northover,[1] I. C. Talbot,[1,3] E. Solomon,[4] and W. F. Bodmer[5]

[1]Imperial Cancer Research Fund Colorectal Unit, [2]Imperial Cancer Research Fund Family Cancer Clinic and [3]Department of Pathology, Northwick Park and St. Mark's Hospitals NHS Trust, Middlesex; [4]Somatic Cell Genetics Laboratory, [5]Cancer Genetics Laboratory, and [6]Human Cytogenetics Laboratory, Imperial Cancer Research Fund, Lincoln's Inn Fields, London; [7]Cancer Epidemiology Laboratory, Imperial Cancer Research Fund, St. James's Hospital, Leeds

Summary

Hereditary mixed polyposis syndrome (HMPS) is characterized by atypical juvenile polyps, colonic adenomas, and colorectal carcinomas. HMPS appears to be inherited in an autosomal dominant manner. Genetic linkage analysis has been performed on a large family with HMPS. Data did not support linkage to the APC locus or to any of the loci for hereditary nonpolyposis colorectal cancer. Evidence that the HMPS locus lies on chromosome 6q was, however, provided by significant two-point LOD scores for linkage between HMPS and the *D6S283* locus. Analysis of recombinants and multipoint linkage analysis suggested that the HMPS locus lies in a 4-cM interval containing the *D6S283* locus and flanked by markers *D6S468* and *D6S301*.

Introduction

Hereditary mixed polyposis syndrome (HMPS) is a rare condition in which individuals develop characteristic polyps of the large bowel. These polyps closely resemble juvenile polyps but show significant histological differences (S. C. Whitelaw, unpublished data). Affected individuals also develop colonic adenomas and colorectal carcinomas. The natural history of the disease is, however, incompletely characterized (Murday and Slack 1989): HMPS polyps may progress to adenomas and thence to carcinomas, or polyps and adenomas may arise and progress separately. HMPS patients may also have an increased propensity to develop inflammatory and metaplastic polyps.

The similarity of HMPS polyps to juvenile polyps and the possible progression of HMPS polyps to adenomas and carcinomas means that ascertainment of HMPS is unlikely to be accurate or complete. However, one large HMPS family (SM96) has been identified by St. Mark's Hospital, London (fig. 1). Accurate clinical details are available from most family members (S. C. Whitelaw, unpublished data). HMPS in this pedigree appears to be inherited as an autosomal dominant syndrome. Most older individuals presented with colorectal carcinoma; younger individuals, most of whom have undergone screening by colonoscopy, tend to present with benign colonic lesions, often the characteristic HMPS polyp (S. C. Whitelaw, unpublished data).

By analogy to familial adenomatous polyposis (FAP) (Miyaki et al. 1994), loci at which mutations predispose to rare, inherited bowel tumors may also be important to sporadic colorectal tumors (Solomon et al. 1987). We have performed genetic linkage analysis on 46 members of family SM96 (fig. 1), in order to determine the possible location of the HMPS gene. Allele loss (loss of heterozygosity [LOH]) at the putative HMPS locus has also been studied in the colorectal carcinomas of three members of family SM96 and in 100 sporadic colorectal cancers.

Methods

Collection and Preparation of Samples

Peripheral blood was collected from 43 members of the family and was Epstein-Barr virus–transformed to form permanent lymphoblastoid cell lines. DNA was extracted by use of standard techniques. Paraffin-embedded archival material was obtained from the normal tissues of two members of the family and from the colorectal carcinomas of three patients. After microdissection of the appropriate tissue and digestion in 400 μg proteinase K/ml, DNA was extracted from the par-

Received October 20, 1995; accepted for publication December 8, 1995.

Address for correspondence and reprints: Dr. I. P. M. Tomlinson, Cancer Genetics Laboratory, Imperial Cancer Research Fund, Lincoln's Inn Fields, Box 123, London WC2A 3PX, United Kingdom. E-mail: tomlinso@europa.lif.icrf.icnet.uk

*These authors contributed equally to this work.

0002-9297/96/5804-0015$02.00

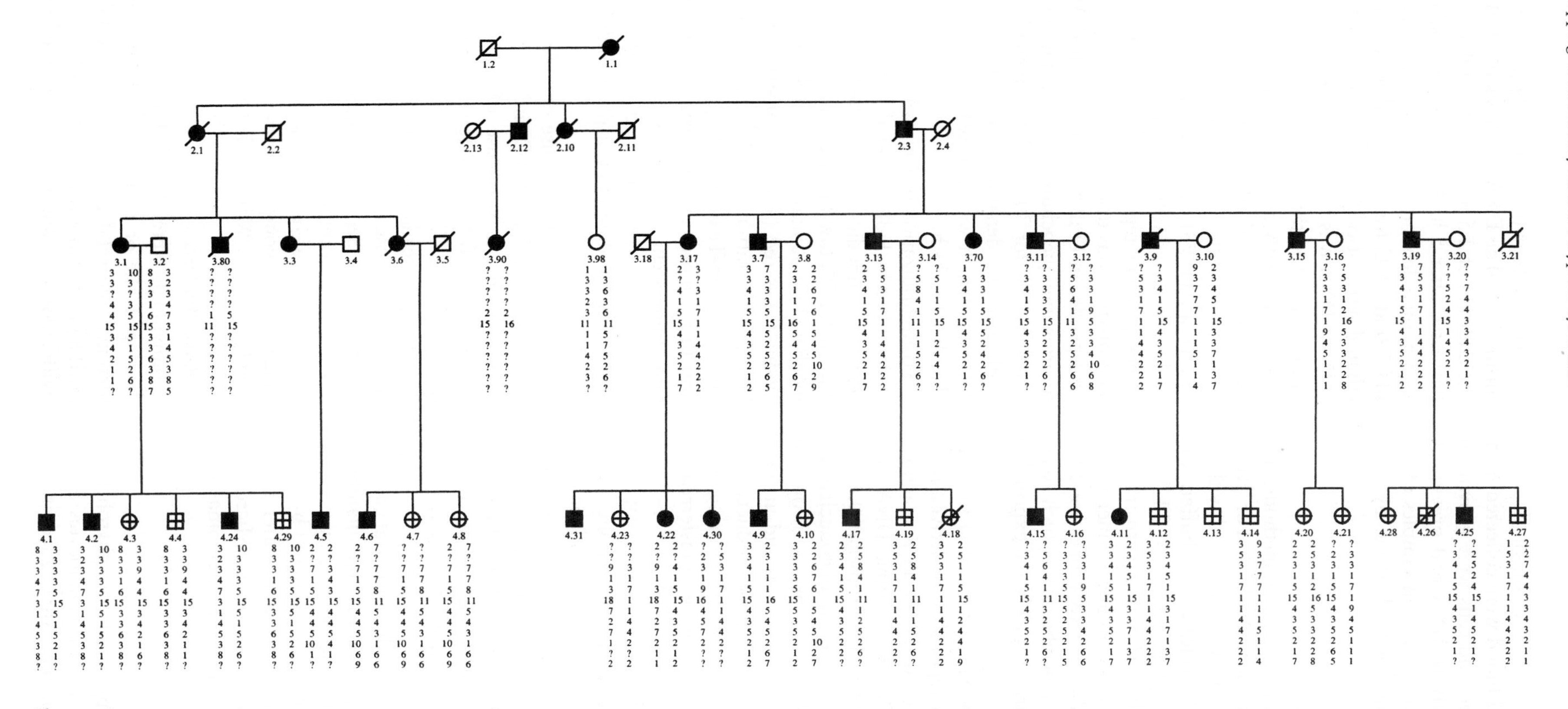

Figure 1 Pedigree of family SM96, showing haplotypes at loci near the putative HMPS locus. The full pedigree is much larger than that shown, but all genotyped individuals are illustrated. Loci are shown in the map order given in fig. 2. Affected individuals are denoted by blackened symbols, unaffected individuals are denoted by unblackened symbols, and individuals of unknown affection status are denoted by symbols that have a cross. The disease-associated haplotype 5-15-4 (or 5-15-5) at D6S283-D6S434-D6S301 can be followed throughout the family, with the exception of the postulated phenocopy 4.30. We assume that the allele "5" at D6S301 arose either by a recombination (which would place the putative HMPS locus proximal to D6S301; see multipoint LOD score analysis) or by mutation of an allele "4."

© *Am J Hum Genet* 1996; 58: 770–776

affin-embedded tissue by use of a Nucleon kit (Scotlab). Fresh samples of peripheral blood were collected from one affected family member, and cells were grown for karyotyping and FISH analysis. DNA had previously been extracted from 100 paired, frozen samples of colorectal carcinoma and blood/normal tissue, by standard methods.

Determination of Genotypes

Genotyping was performed by two methods, depending on the type of marker involved. For RFLP markers, 5–10 μg genomic DNA was digested with an appropriate restriction endonuclease and buffer. Restricted DNAs were electrophoresed for 8–24 h on 0.8%–1% agarose gels, followed by Southern transfer overnight onto Hybond N+ membranes (Amersham). α^{32}P-dATP–labeled (Amersham) DNA probes were hybridized overnight to the membranes, which were washed according to standard protocols and exposed to film (Hyperfilm) for 1–3 d.

Simple-sequence-length polymorphic (SSLP) markers (microsatellite markers, CA repeats) were derived from the Généthon set (Gyapay et al. 1994). PCR reactions were performed with 50–200 ng genomic DNA in 1 × PCR buffer (with 1.5 mM $MgCl_2$) (Promega), 0.4 mM dNTPs, and 0.4 μM of each specific oligonucleotide, according to the standard Généthon protocol: once at 94°C for 4, 35 cycles at 94°C for 1 min and at 55°C for 1 min, and once at 72°C for 5 min. Products were electrophoresed for 3–5 h on 6%–8% denaturing polyacrylamide gels. PCR products were transferred by blotting onto Hybond N+ membranes for 4–24 h. Membranes were hybridized either to a CA-repeat oligonucleotide probe or to a specific PCR-primer oligonucleotide extended with random nucleotides and labeled by use of the glutaraldehyde/horseradish peroxidase system (Amersham). Hybridization and detection of bound probes was performed by use of the enhanced chemiluminescence (ECL) method (Amersham). All autoradiographs/ECL films were scored by inspection using DNAs of known genotype as standards.

Allele loss at SSLP loci in sporadic colorectal carcinomas was scored by eye, in order only to count unambiguous cases as having lost an allele. Scoring by eye also avoided spurious cases of allele loss produced by "stutter" or conformational bands that were different, by chance, between tumor and normal DNAs. Microsatellite instability and allele loss in HMPS carcinomas were also scored by eye.

Karyotyping and FISH

Metaphase spreads were prepared from phytohemagglutinin-stimulated normal human lymphocytes by use of standard cytogenetic techniques. After 72 h of incubation, cells were exposed to 200 μg bromodeoxyuridine/ml for 17 h. The DNA synthesis block was released by the addition of 2.5 μg thymidine/ml, and the cells were harvested after 5 h. The slides were baked at 65°C for 2–3 h, then denatured in 70% formamide and 2 × SSC pH 7.0 at 75°C for 2 min and dehydrated through an ethanol series of cold 70%, 95%, and absolute ethanol.

Probe DNA was biotinylated by use of BRL's Bionick kit, then purified through a Sephadex G50 column and precipitated with 50 μg salmon sperm DNA and 50 μg *Escherichia coli* tRNA. Hybridization and detection used a modification of the technique described by Fidlerova et al. (1993). Two hundred nanograms labeled probe was mixed with 2 μg human cot-1 DNA, in order to compete out repetitive elements in the probe DNA. This mixture was dried in a vacuum centrifuge and was resuspended in 11 μl hybridization mix. After heat denaturation and quenching on ice, the mixture was preincubated at 37°C for 30 min. The preincubated probe was applied to the denatured slide under a 22 × 22-mm coverslip, which was then sealed and placed in a moist chamber for 24 h.

Posthybridization washes were performed essentially as described by Fidlerova et al. (1993). For probe detection, all antibodies were diluted in 4 × SSC, 0.05% Tween 20, 5% low-fat dried milk (Marvel), pH 7.0, and incubated for 30 min at 37°C in the following order: (1) avidin-Texas red (Vector Laboratories) (2 μg/ml), (2) biotinylated anti-avidin (Vector Laboratories) (5 μg/ml), (3) avidin-Texas red (2 μg/ml), and finally (4) with anti-BrdU-fluorescein (Boehringer) (10 μg/ml), to obtain fluorescein isothiocyanate (FITC)–stained R-bands. Slides were dehydrated and mounted in Citifluor containing 4,6-diamidino-2-phenylindole (DAPI) (0.06 μg/ml).

Slides were viewed by use of a Zeiss Axiophot fluorescence microscope. FITC and Texas red were visualized simultaneously by use of a dual pass filter set (Omega), and DAPI counterstain was visualized with filter block set 02 (Zeiss G365, FT395, and LP420). Metaphase spreads were processed by use of a Zeiss Axioscop microscope equipped with a CCD camera (Photometrics). Separate images of probe signal, banding pattern, and counterstain were captured and colored. These images were then merged by use of an Apple Macintosh IIci computer with software developed by T. Rand and D. C. Ward (Yale University, New Haven).

Linkage Analysis

Individuals were classified as "affected" if they had developed one or more of the following during their lifetime: colorectal carcinoma, colorectal adenoma, or HMPS polyp. Since the oldest affected patient presented (with colorectal cancer) at the age of 63 years, a conser-

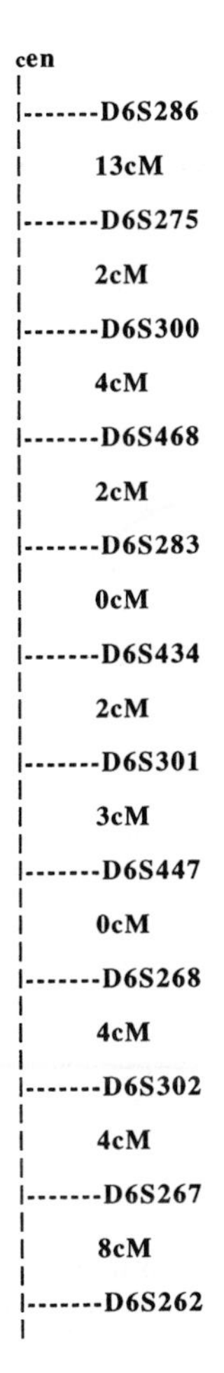

Figure 2 Genetic map of proximal part of chromosome 6q, showing markers studied.

vative approach was used to define affection status: individuals were only classified as "unaffected" if they were >65 years of age and disease free. All individuals <65 years of age were classified either as "affected" (according to the above criteria) or "unknown." Two-point LOD scores between the hypothetical disease locus and each test locus were computed by the MLINK program in the LINKAGE package, by use of published allele frequencies and standard techniques (Terwilliger and Ott 1994). Complete dominance of the disease allele (A) was assumed. LOD scores were computed at the following penetrances for each genotype at the disease locus: AA = .95; Aa = .95; and aa = .075. These values recognized the possibility of incomplete penetrance of HMPS (there being very little evidence for or against this). They also took into account the possible existence of phenocopies, at least of adenomas and carcinomas (although phenocopies of the HMPS polyp would be most unlikely). A LOD score >3.0 (corresponding to a level of significance of 5%) was considered as significant evidence of genetic linkage between disease and test loci. A LOD score <−2.0 was considered as significantly excluding linkage at that recombination fraction. Multipoint LOD scores were calculated by use of the LINKMAP program at and around loci showing significant two-point LOD scores (Terwilliger and Ott 1994).

Results

RFLP and SSLP analysis excluded close linkage of HMPS to the *APC, hMSH2, TP53,* and *DCC* loci (data not shown). No good evidence was found in favor of linkage to the *hMLH1* locus or 50 other loci associated with allele loss in sporadic colorectal carcinomas (data not shown). A genomewide search with the Généthon 1992 set of microsatellite markers (Weissenbach et al. 1992) was then performed. The only significant positive LOD score obtained was at the *D6S283* locus on the proximal part of chromosome 6q (details are given in fig. 2 and table 1). Genotyping was then performed by use of microsatellite markers closely linked to *D6S283,* in an attempt to refine the location of the putative HMPS locus. A further near-significant LOD score was found at the *D6S301* locus, 2 cM distal to *D6S283* (table 1). Analysis of haplotypes and recombinants showed the probable location of the HMPS locus as being between *D6S468* and *D6S268/D6S447* (fig. 1). Multipoint linkage analysis between and around markers *D6S468, D6S283, D6S301,* and *D6S447* gave a maximum LOD score of 3.93, between *D6S283* and *D6S301* (fig. 3), suggesting this interval as the most likely location of the putative HMPS locus. The maximum LOD score of 3.29, between *D6S468* and *D6S283* (fig. 3), also provided support for this region as a possible location for the HMPS gene.

One individual (4.30; fig. 1) was classified as "af-

Table 1

Maximum Two-Point LOD Scores at Loci on Chromosome 6q

Locus	Maximum LOD Score	Recombination Fraction
D6S468	.18	.28
D6S283	3.32	.06
D6S434	2.60	.03
D6S301	2.97	.05
D6S447	1.06	.08

NOTE.—HMPS locus penetrances are as shown in the text, and genetic distances between the marker loci are as given in fig. 2. Within realistic limits, changes in the penetrances used in the two-point LOD-score analysis (or the incorporation of age-dependence penetrances) have little effect on the values of maximum LOD score or recombination fraction obtained (details not shown).

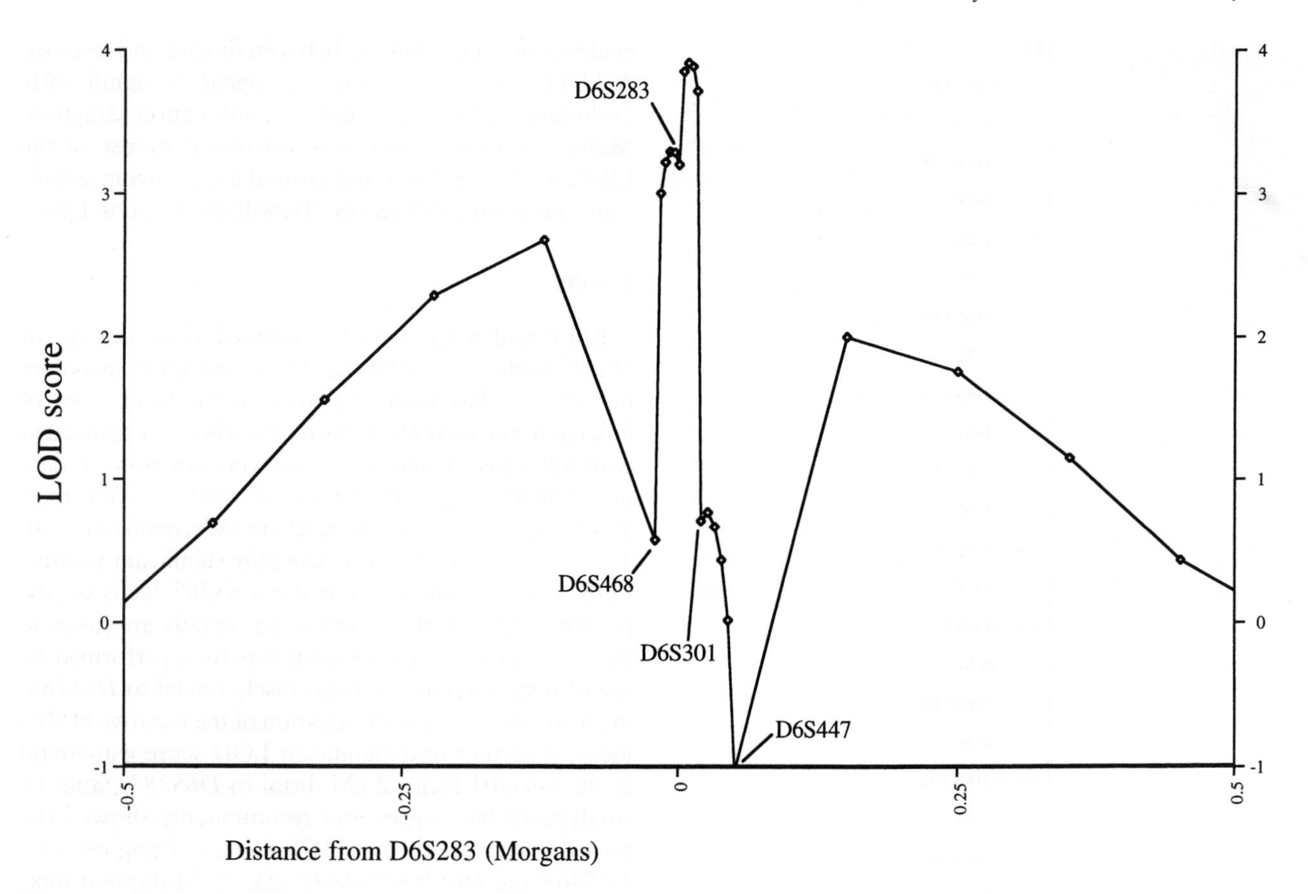

Figure 3 Multipoint linkage analysis between and outside markers D6S468 and D6S447. HMPS-locus penetrances are as shown in the text. Genetic distances between the marker loci (*x*-axis) are as given in fig. 2. LOD scores for the location of the HMPS locus are shown on the *y*-axis.

fected" for the purposes of linkage analysis but had probably inherited an "unaffected" haplotype. This individual was homozygous at the *D6S301* locus and might therefore represent a double recombination either side of *D6S301*. Given the low probability of two recombinations occurring in this interval of just 5 cM, it is possible that individual 4.30 is a phenocopy. This person was screened regularly, from age 20 years, by colonoscopy, and she developed a colonic serrated adenoma at what is probably an early age (29 years) relative to that of the general population. Most important, however, no characteristic HMPS polyp has been found in this individual, and she may therefore be a phenocopy.

By means of comparison with the *APC* locus (Solomon et al. 1987), we reasoned that significant allele loss might be expected both in HMPS tumors and in sporadic colorectal cancers near the HMPS locus. LOH was therefore searched for use of the highly polymorphic *D6S434* marker. Of three colorectal carcinomas from members of SM96, none showed LOH at *D6S434;* further analysis also showed no allele loss at *D6S301* or *D6S268* in these tumors. Of 94 sporadic carcinomas studied, 77 were informative, and only 10 (13%) had lost a *D6S434* allele. These samples had previously shown allele loss, at frequencies $\geq$40%, at other loci (I. P. M. Tomlinson, unpublished data). The three HMPS carcinomas were also analyzed for microsatellite instability, by use of the *D6S434, D6S301, D6S268, D11S29, DRD2,* and *D3S1611* loci. No allelic bands characteristic of microsatellite instability were seen.

We then investigated whether a mutation at the chromosomal level might be responsible for HMPS in family SM96. The karyotypes of two affected individuals were normal. The fact that two alleles were observed at 6q loci in all affected members of SM96 showed that a deletion of 6q (other than a very small one) was not present. FISH was then performed by use of YACs 931A10 and 961G3, which map close to the centromere on the short and long arms, respectively, of chromosome 6 (Généthon data; D. Markie, unpublished data). These YACs hybridized to their expected positions in an affected family member (3.13), thereby excluding a pericentric inversion or other gross rearrangement of chromosome 6 that was likely to involve the HMPS locus. YAC 963D6 (containing the *D6S283* locus) also

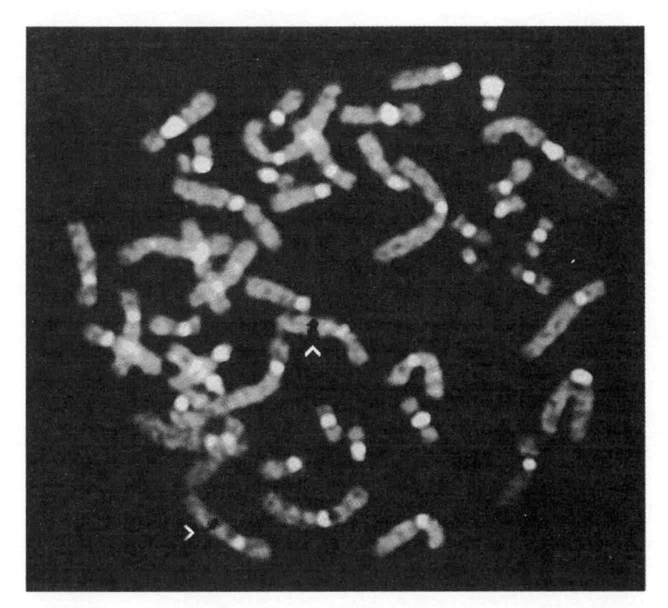

Figure 4 FISH analysis of affected member of SM96 (3.13), with use of YAC 963D6. The YAC maps to band 6q21 on both copies of this individual's chromosome 6. This position is the same as that in a normal individual (not shown).

mapped to its expected position (fig. 4) on both copies of chromosome 6 in individual 3.13.

Discussion

The results presented suggest that a gene for HMPS exists on the proximal part of the long arm of chromosome 6. Linkage analysis and study of recombinants suggest that the HMPS locus lies within a 7-cM interval flanked by the markers *D6S468* and *D6S447*, with the most probable location somewhere in the 4-cM interval between *D6S468* and *D6S301*. HMPS is not caused by mutations at either the loci responsible for FAP or the loci known to cause hereditary nonpolyposis colorectal cancer.

It is unclear whether HMPS is a variant of juvenile polyposis or a distinct disease (Murday and Slack 1989; S. C. Whitelaw, unpublished data). Certainly, it will be interesting to look for linkage between the disease and the putative HMPS locus in juvenile polyposis families. If HMPS is indeed a variant of juvenile polyposis, then the distinctive phenotype of family SM96 may result from a specific mutation in a juvenile polyposis gene, from environmental effects, or from the effects of modifier loci. Clearly, we cannot exclude the first of these possibilities. The second possibility also remains plausible. However, the family is distributed across the world and subject to many different environments, yet distant relatives have produced the characteristic HMPS polyp. The third possibility is interesting: an FAP modifier locus, *mom-1,* has been identified in the mouse (Dietrich et al. 1993; Macphee et al. 1995), showing that polyposis syndromes are affected by genetic influences additional to the locus primarily responsible. Certainly, the phenotype of juvenile polyposis is highly variable (Desai et al. 1995) and may in theory be influenced by modifying loci. Family SM96 is too small to allow us to detect the influence of modifying loci, and phenotypes are confounded by factors such as the availability of colonoscopic screening in recent years. Nevertheless, the high penetrance of HMPS in this family (in the early generations at least) and the possible phenocopy 4.30 with a colonic adenoma at a relatively early age are both factors consistent with the existence of modifying loci.

Although HMPS predisposes strongly to colorectal cancer—as do all known gastrointestinal polyposis syndromes—it does not follow that the HMPS locus is important in the development of sporadic colorectal tumors. A low proportion of sporadic colorectal carcinomas in this study showed LOH at *D6S434*. However, none of three HMPS carcinomas showed LOH at this locus. Therefore, the HMPS gene presumably acts in some way that is not analogous to that of *APC* or other colorectal tumor-suppressor genes. Its importance for colorectal tumors in general remains unknown.

Acknowledgments

Collection of data and samples from the families would have been impossible without the contribution of the late H.J. R. Bussey. We are also grateful to the members of family SM96 and to Drs. Ginsberg, Berkowitz, and Bukofzer and several other medical practitioners for collecting samples. Further technical assistance was kindly provided by Cell Production; Imperial Cancer Research Fund for transformation of lymphoblastoid cell lines; Human Genetic Resources Laboratory, Imperial Cancer Research Fund; and Mr. Hans Nicolai (Somatic Cell Genetics Laboratory, Imperial Cancer Research Fund). We gratefully acknowledge the assistance and materials provided by Généthon (Paris).

References

Desai DC, Neale KF, Talbot IC, Hodgson SV, Phillips RKS (1995) Juvenile polyposis. Br J Surg 82:14–17

Dietrich WF, Lander ES, Smith JS, Moser AR, Gould KA, Luongo C, Borenstein N, et al (1993) Genetic identification of Mom-1, a major modifier locus affecting Min-induced intestinal neoplasia in the mouse. Cell 75:631–639

Fidlerova H, Senger G, Kost M, Sanseau P, Sheer D (1994) Two simple procedures for releasing chromatin from routinely fixed cells for fluorescence *in-situ* hybridization. Cytogenet Cell Genet 65:203–205

Gyapay G, Morissette J, Vignal A, Fizames C, Millasseau P,

Marc S, Bernadi G, et al (1994) The 1993–94 Généthon human genetic-linkage map. Nat Genet 7:246–339
Macphee M, Chepenik KP, Liddell RA, Nelson KK, Siracusa LD, Buchberg AM (1995) The secretory phospholipase-a2 gene is a candidate for the mom1 locus, a major modifier of apc(min)-induced intestinal neoplasia. Cell 81: 957–966
Miyaki M, Tanaka K, Kikuchiyanoshita R, Muraoka M, Konishi M (1994) Familial polyposis—recent advances. Crit Rev Oncol Haematol 19:1–31
Murday V, Slack J (1989) Inherited disorders associated with colorectal cancer. Cancer Surv 8:139–157
Solomon E, Voss R, Hall V, Bodmer WF, Jass JR, Jeffreys AJ, Lucibello FC, et al (1987) Chromosome-5 allele loss in human colorectal carcinomas. Nature 328:616–619
Terwilliger J, Ott J (1994) Handbook of human genetic linkage. John-Hopkins University Press, Baltimore
Weissenbach J, Gyapay G, Dib C, Vignal A, Morissette J, Illasseau P, Vaysseix G, et al (1992) A 2nd-generation linkage map of the human genome. Nature 359:794–801

© Gut 1996; 38: 905–910

Predicting outcome in severe ulcerative colitis

S P L Travis, J M Farrant, C Ricketts, D J Nolan, N M Mortensen, M G W Kettlewell, D P Jewell

Abstract

***Background*—Simple criteria are needed to predict which patients with severe ulcerative colitis will respond poorly to intensive medical treatment and require colectomy.**

***Aims*—To find out if the early pattern of change in inflammatory markers or other variables could predict the need for surgery and to evaluate the outcome of medical treatment during one year follow up.**

***Patients*—51 consecutive episodes of severe colitis (Truelove and Witts criteria) affecting 49 patients admitted to John Radcliffe Hospital, Oxford.**

***Methods*—Prospective study monitoring 36 clinical, laboratory, and radiographic variables. All episodes treated with intravenous and rectal hydrocortisone and 14 of 51 with cyclosporine.**

***Results*—Complete response in 21 episodes (≤3 stools on day 7, without visible blood), incomplete response in 15 (>3 stools or visible blood on day 7, but no colectomy), and colectomy on that admission in 15. During the first five days, stool frequency and C reactive protein (CRP) distinguished between outcomes ($p<0{\cdot}00625$, corrected for multiple comparisons) irrespective of whether patients or the number of episodes were analysed. It could be predicted on day 3, that 85% of patients with more than eight stools on that day, or a stool frequency between three and eight together with a CRP >45 mg/l, would require colectomy. For patients given cyclosporine, four of 14 avoided colectomy but two continued to have symptoms. After admission, complete responders remained in remission for a median nine months and had a 5% chance of colectomy. Incomplete responders had a 60% chance of continuous symptoms and 40% chance of colectomy.**

***Conclusions*—After three days intensive treatment, patients with frequent stools (>8/day), or raised CRP (>45 mg/l) need to be identified, as most will require colectomy on that admission. The role of cyclosporine for treating severe colitis has yet to be defined. After seven days' treatment, patients with >3 stools/day or visible blood have a 60% chance of continuous symptoms and 40% chance of colectomy in the following months.**

(*Gut* 1996; **38:** 905–910)

Keywords: ulcerative colitis, cyclosporine, colectomy.

Gastroenterology Unit
S P L Travis
J M Farrant
D J Nolan
D P Jewell

and Department of Surgery
N M Mortensen
M G W Kettlewell

John Radcliffe Hospital, Oxford

School of Mathematics and Statistics, University of Plymouth
C Ricketts

Correspondence to:
Dr S P L Travis,
Gastroenterology Unit,
Derriford Hospital,
Plymouth PL6 8DH.

Accepted for publication
29 December 1995

Treatment with intravenous corticosteroids and a policy of early colectomy originally reduced the mortality in severe episodes of ulcerative colitis from 31–61% in the 1950s[1 2] to 5–9% in 1962.[2 3] Although mortality outside specialist centres in 1974 remained alarmingly high (37%, [4]), in specialist or district hospitals with an interest in colitis it is now 3% or less, including operative mortality.[5–7] These figures are pertinent because the introduction of further medical treatment such as cyclosporine[8] runs the risk of delaying colectomy inappropriately. It remains difficult, however, to predict at an early stage which patients with severe ulcerative colitis will respond poorly to intensive medical treatment and require colectomy.

There is a need for simple clinical and laboratory criteria that will predict outcome and assist the decision to operate on patients with severe ulcerative colitis. A large retrospective study in 1975 identified a persistent tachycardia, fever, hypoalbuminaemia, and radiological features (mucosal islands or dilation) after 24 hour treatment in hospital as being associated with colectomy on that admission.[9] A rising or persistently raised C reactive protein (CRP) was associated with urgent colectomy in six of eight patients,[10] but it was not clear whether more frequent measurements of CRP would be of predictive value. It has since been reported that first episodes, extensive disease,[6 11] and three or more distended loops of small bowel on the initial plain abdominal radiograph[12] are associated with a poor response to intravenous therapy.

To assess whether the early pattern of change in inflammatory markers or other variables could predict the need for surgery, 36 clinical, laboratory, and radiographic variables have been measured prospectively in patients with severe colitis. The study was performed with the option of using cyclosporine in patients not responding to intravenous corticosteroids and also examined the outcome during a one year follow up period.

Methods

PATIENTS

All patients with severe ulcerative colitis admitted to the John Radcliffe Hospital between March 1992 and September 1993 were evaluated prospectively. The diagnosis of ulcerative colitis was made on normal clinical, radiological, and pathological criteria and a severe episode defined as the passage of ≥6 bloody stools daily with one or more of the following criteria: temperature >37·8°C, pulse

© Gut 1996; 38: 905–910

>90/min, haemoglobin <10·5 g/dl, or erythrocyte sedimentation rate (ESR) >30 mm/h.[3 13]

MEASUREMENTS

In addition to the sex and date of birth of the patient, the following data were collected:

Clinical details – date of diagnosis, duration of current relapse, duration of previous remission, current maintenance therapy, number and timing of previous admissions, maximum extent of macroscopic disease, number of motions in the day prior to admission, abdominal tenderness on palpation, and rigid sigmoidoscopic appearances (loss of vascular pattern, contact bleeding, or ulceration indicated by adherent mucosal slough) on admission.

Clinical observation – daily stool frequency, consistency (unformed, semi-formed, formed), amount of blood (visible, occult blood positive, none), pulse rate, and temperature (both measured six hourly).

Laboratory investigations – blood was taken daily for five days, then as indicated for standard laboratory measurement of full blood count, ESR, CRP, potassium, creatinine, and albumin. In addition, serum was collected daily and stored at −20°C for orosomucoid analysis by nephelometry (Beckman Array, High Wycombe, Bucks). Plain abdominal radiographs were taken on admission and after two days. At the end of the study these were reported by an experienced radiologist unaware of the outcome, for the distribution of faeces (none, up to the hepatic flexure, splenic flexure, or sigmoid colon), presence of mucosal islands, colonic dilatation >5·5 cm, ⩾3 distended loops of small bowel gas,[12] or perforation.

Outcome – Complete response to intensive medical therapy was defined as a stool frequency ⩽3/day on day 7, with no visible blood in the motions. Incomplete responders were defined as those with a stool frequency >3 or visible blood on day 7 who did not require colectomy on that admission. Indications for colectomy were failure to respond or frank deterioration during the first few days of intensive medical therapy; continued diarrhoea, abdominal tenderness or a low grade fever after intensive medical therapy; and perforation, increasing colonic dilatation, or massive haemorrhage.[14]

MANAGEMENT

All patients received standard intensive medical therapy for severe colitis.[15] Fluid, electrolyte, and haemoglobin deficiencies were corrected and hydrocortisone 100 mg given intravenously six hourly, with rectal hydrocortisone 100 mg twice daily. This was continued for five to seven days with oral fluids until it was clear that the patient had responded or colectomy was needed. Parenteral nutrition was given to malnourished patients. Incomplete responders were treated with intravenous cyclosporine 4 mg/kg/day or further intravenous corticosteroids for up to six days, then converted to oral therapy (cyclosporine 5 mg/kg/day and oral corticosteroids), or referred for colectomy.

STATISTICAL ANALYSIS

Student's unpaired t test was used to compare data on admission. Both the number of episodes (51) and the number of patients (49) were analysed. All 51 episodes were analysed first, then the 49 patients excluding the initial episodes in the two patients who were entered twice and finally the 49 patients excluding the second episodes in these two patients. Repeated measures analysis of variance were used to assess differences between outcomes and to identify potential trends in data during admission in mean bowel frequency, pulse rate, haemoglobin, platelet count, ESR, CRP, orosomucoid, and albumin, using the StatGraphics statistical software package. The analyses were performed initially for five days and then for eight days after admission. As 97% of all potential data was collected, algorithms that allowed for occasional missing values were used, rather than exclude patients with missing data. Because the analysis was repeated for all eight measurements, the significance level was set at 0·00625 to correct for multiple comparisons ($p=0·05/8$, Bonferroni's correction). A classification tree[16] was then developed to try to predict patient outcome from the measures obtained on the third day of treatment.

Results

PATIENTS

Fifty one episodes were treated in 49 patients (26 male, age 21–77, median 43). Twenty one (42%) responded completely, 15 (29%) required colectomy on that admission, and 15 had an incomplete response. Analysing by patients rather than episodes changes the figures by <2%. Excluding the initial episodes, 21 patients had a complete response, 14 required colectomy, and 14 had an incomplete response. Excluding subsequent episodes, the numbers are 21, 13, and 15. Two patients had been transferred for treatment from other hospitals, neither of whom required colectomy. Two patients were subsequently found to have Crohn's disease, one at the time of surgery and another after an ileoanal pouch had been formed.

ANTECEDENT DATA

A third of episodes involved a first episode of colitis, defined as the first episode of symptoms leading to diagnosis, more commonly in complete responders (Table I). For those with a first episode (16 of 49 patients), 12 (75%) responded completely, and three (19%) required colectomy during the initial admission. For those with a previous episode of colitis, the median duration of remission tended to be shorter in those who required colectomy, as did the time since any previous admission, but the differences did not reach statistical significance. The duration of relapse

© Gut 1996; 38: 905–910

did not differ significantly. Similar proportions of patients were taking maintenance therapy in each group, but numbers are too small to identify any relation between outcome and type of salicylate therapy.

ADMISSION DATA

The number of Truelove and Witts criteria[13] on admission in addition to a bloody stool frequency ≥6/day was similar in those who responded to medical treatment or who required colectomy (Table II). One person who had a colectomy had no additional criteria on admission (and therefore technically only fulfilled the criteria for a moderate episode), but is included because she deteriorated during treatment to meet these criteria. On admission, the presence of severe rectal inflammation on sigmoidoscopy causing the appearance of ulceration was significantly more common (93%) in those who required colectomy than those who only had contact bleeding or a granular rectal mucosa (39%, p=0·002). The distribution of disease did not differ significantly between groups, although pancolitis was present in 60% who required colectomy and only in 19% of complete responders. The initial CRP was significantly higher in the colectomy group compared with those who responded completely (Table II). These data are consistent with the CRP being the most sensitive maker of colonic inflammation.

MANAGEMENT

Intravenous and rectal hydrocortisone were given for five days only in all patients who responded completely, a median of six days (range 5–8) in incomplete responders and a median of five days (range 2–8) in those who had a colectomy. In 30 of 51 episodes which did not completely respond to hydrocortisone, four had deteriorated sufficiently by five days to need urgent colectomy. Another 12 continued with hydrocortisone for up to three more days until it was clear whether improvement continued (8) or colectomy (4) was needed, and the remaining 14 received intravenous cyclosporine (4 mg/kg/day) for a median four days (range 1–6). In those who received cyclosporine, seven of 14 did not improve and proceeded to colectomy during that admission. The remaining seven of 14 were given oral cyclosporine (5 mg/kg/day) when symptoms were under sufficient control to leave hospital, but three required colectomy within three months. Of the incomplete responders, the median stool frequency on discharge was three (range 2–9), with visible blood in 60% and after a median nine days in hospital (range 7–20). Of the 15 patients who had a colectomy on the same admission, 12 had a subtotal colectomy, one a proctocolectomy, one a colectomy and mucous fistula, and the one found to have Crohn's colitis at operation had a split ileostomy.

PATTERN OF CHANGE DURING FIRST FIVE DAYS

Whether analysed by episode or by patient numbers, repeated measures analysis of variance over the first five days showed that the bowel frequency and CRP were significantly higher (p<0·00625) in patients who required colectomy than in those responding partly or completely. The bowel frequency also declined significantly more slowly in the colectomy group (Table III, Figure). At a less rigorous 5% level of significance, the mean pulse rate, haemoglobin, platelet count, serum albumin, and orosomucoids also differed between those who required colectomy and those who did not. The rate of change in pulse rate, CRP, and ESR was slower in the colectomy group when analysed by patients rather than episodes (Table III). When data were analysed over eight rather than five days, the bowel

TABLE I *Patient data prior to admission*

	Responders	*Incomplete*	*Colectomy*	*Overall*
Number of episodes	21	15	15	51
Age (SD) (y)	46·7 (19·2)	47·5 (12·3)	43·2 (15·3)	45·9 (15·3)
First episode (%)	57	7	20	31
Previous remission (range, months)	16 (5–38)	15 (5–240)	9 (3–54)	13 (3–240)
Previous admission (%)	56	43	50	49
Time since last admission (range, months)	67 (24–185)	61 (8–240)	5 (1–103)	47 (1–240)
Salicylate therapy (%)	89	93	83	89
Sulphasalazine (%)	75	23	60	48
Mesalazine (%)	25	31	10	23
Olsalazine (%)	0	46	30	29

First episode: % patients in each group presenting with a first episode of colitis; previous remission: median duration of remission in months before current relapse; previous admission: % patients previously admitted for treatment, excluding those with first episodes (n=17 of 35); time since last admission: median time in months in these patients; salicylate therapy: maintenance treatment taken by patients before admission.

TABLE II *Patient admission details*

	Responders	*Incomplete*	*Colectomy*	*Overall*
Number of episodes	21	15	15	51
Motions/day	8 (2)	8 (2)	8 (3)	8 (2)
Pulse rate	106 (15)	96 (11)	101 (14)	101 (14)
Temperature	37·7 (0·7)	37·3 (0·8)	37·6 (0·4)	37·5 (0·7)
Haemoglobin (g/dl)	12·6 (2·6)	11·3 (2·4)	11·2 (2·0)	11·8 (2·4)
ESR (mm/h)	41 (25)	48 (20)	47 (28)	45 (24)
CRP (mg/l)	43 (38)*	89 (85)	116 (102)	78 (81)
Orosomucoids (mg/dl)	117 (41)	144 (55)	158 (50)	137 (50)
Truelove and Witts criteria	2·2 (1·0)	2·1 (0·8)	2·1 (1·3)	2·2 (1·0)
Extent of disease (%)				
Distal	24	20	0	16
Left sided	19	13	20	18
Extensive	38	13	20	25
Pancolitis	19	54	60	41

Figures are mean (SD). *Significantly different from the colectomy group (p=0·005). No other differences are significant when corrected for multiple comparisons (p<0·00625). The mean number of Truelove and Witts criteria are those in addition to bloody stool frequency ≥6/day. When analysed by number of patients, the means change by <5% except for the CRP in incomplete responders, which was 100 (86) mg/l if initial episodes in two patients entered twice were excluded.

TABLE III *Analysis of serial data over five days: significance values comparing patients who required colectomy with those who did not*

	Episodes (n=51)		*Patients (n=49) Excluding first admission*		*Patients (n=49) Excluding second admission*	
	Mean	*Δ time*	*Mean*	*Δ time*	*Mean*	*Δ time*
Bowel frequency	<0·001	<0·001	<0·001	<0·001	<0·001	<0·001
Pulse rate	0·012	0·064	0·010	0·026	0·022	0·077
Haemoglobin	0·041	0·947	0·045	0·967	0·076	0·965
Platelet count	0·042	0·796	0·056	0·778	0·054	0·882
ESR	0·119	0·017	0·155	0·013	0·155	0·013
CRP	0·001	0·025	0·002	0·044	<0·001	0·018
Orosomucoids	0·011	0·904	0·013	0·902	0·011	0·761
Albumin	0·035	0·726	0·041	0·714	0·029	0·837

Significance values of the data are presented graphically (see Figure). Data have been analysed by episode and per patient, excluding either the first or second admission of two patients admitted twice. Mean: compares the means between those who required colectomy and those who did not. Δ time: compares the rate of change over time between the two groups. Over the five day period, stool frequency was significantly higher and decreased more slowly in those who required colectomy; the CRP was significantly higher in the colectomy group, but the rate of change did not differ when corrected for multiple comparisons (p<0·00625, see text).

© Gut 1996; 38: 905–910

frequency, pulse rate, and CRP were significantly higher ($p<0.00625$) in those who required surgery. Follow up analysis showed that incomplete responders were more similar to the colectomy group than the complete responders for bowel frequency, but similar to complete responders for the change in CRP.

Two days after admission, the presence of mucosal islands on the plain abdominal radiograph was significantly more common in those requiring colectomy (50%) than those who did not (10%, $p=0.013$). The extent of colitis (pancolitis, extensive, left sided, distal, proctitis) on the admission radiograph agreed within one colonic segment to that identified by barium enema, colonoscopy, or operation in 74%. The plain radiograph overestimated the extent of disease by two or more colonic

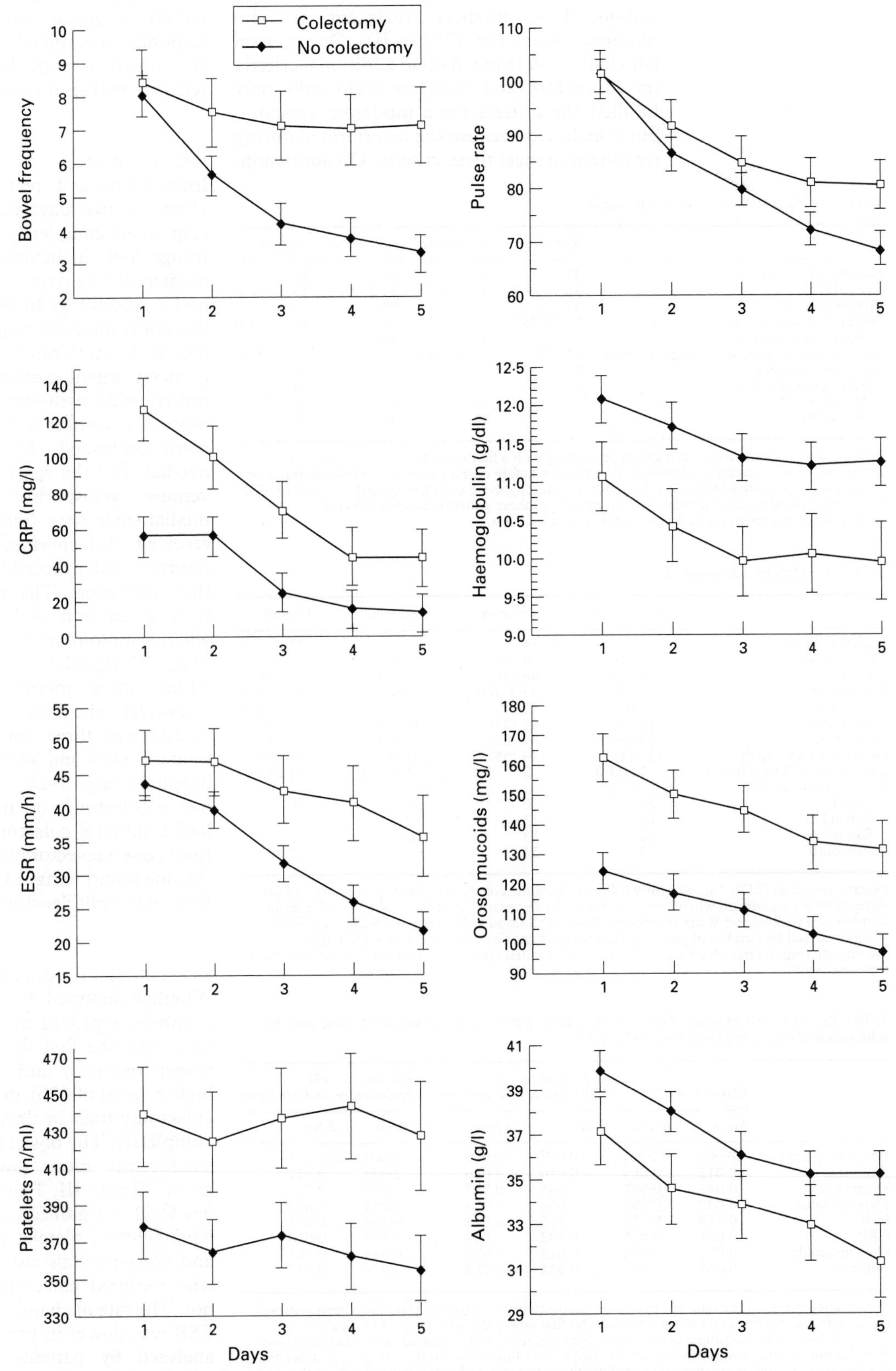

Pattern of change (mean (95% confidence limits)) for different variables in severe ulcerative colitis during the first five days of treatment (see Table III for significance values).

© Gut 1996; 38: 905–910

segments in 18% and underestimated the extent in 8%.

PREDICTING OUTCOME ON DAY 3

The simplest rule predicted with 85% success that patients with more than eight bowel actions on day 3, or with three to eight bowel actions and a CRP >45 mg/l would need colectomy on the same admission. Of those misclassified by this rule, four patients who would have been classified as surgical cases did not undergo colectomy on that admission, but required colectomy in the following months. Three patients underwent colectomy when this classification rule suggested that they should not.

FOLLOW UP DATA

Patients were followed up for a median period of 12 months (range 3·5–21). For those who had responded completely, none had continuous symptoms and the duration of remission was significantly longer than in incomplete responders (p<0·001, Table IV). Immunosuppression with prednisolone, azathioprine or cyclosporine was still necessary at the time of last follow up in 14% of complete responders, compared with 82% of incomplete responders. Among the complete responders, colectomy was subsequently needed in one patient (5%), compared with six of 15 episodes (40%) in incomplete responders. Of those who had a colectomy, 10 of 15 (67%) went on to have an ileoanal pouch (including one which later had to be excised for Crohn's disease) and three of 15 (20%) had a proctectomy after continuous symptoms from the rectal stump. One patient died from a myocardial infarction five months after colectomy.

Discussion

This study confirms that patients with severe colitis defined by the Truelove and Witts criteria[13] have a 29% chance of colectomy on the same admission.[5 14] This reflects the inadequacies of medical treatment even with cyclosporine and the prospective data show how difficult it is to predict who will require colectomy. Incomplete responders are shown to have a very high risk of continuing symptoms or colectomy in the months after a severe episode.

While the criteria for a complete response were stringent (stool frequency ≤3 without visible blood after seven days), this is a reasonable definition of remission for patients suffering the symptoms. Only 42% of episodes responded completely to intensive medical treatment. By the time that incomplete responders were discharged, 73% still had a stool frequency >3/day or visible bleeding. Of the 49 patients, 43% ultimately required colectomy. Although patients are not normally entered into a study more than once, we feel that analysis of the number of episodes rather than the number of patients is clinically most relevant. This is because a previous severe episode of colitis influences surgical decision making and the principal end point of the study was surgery on that admission. As it happens, analysis by episodes or patients (Table III) made little difference.

There is thus an urgent need for more effective medical treatment. Cyclosporine was ineffective in seven of 14 patients who had not responded to intravenous corticosteroids, and in the 50% who showed some response to cyclosporine, only four subsequently avoided colectomy and two of these continued to have symptoms. This means that only two of 14 patients (14%) can be considered to have entered remission and these two were still receiving prednisolone at the time of follow up. These figures are not encouraging and are in contrast with those described by Present.[8] It remains possible, however, that earlier use of cyclosporine might be of greater benefit. There is also a potential benefit from partial remission, in that it may allow a patient time to come to terms with the prospect of surgery, especially if the extent of disease is limited.

A severe relapse with a defined course of action (admission for intensive medical therapy) can be identified by a single Truelove and Witts' criterion[13] in addition to a bloody stool frequency ≥6/day. Table II shows that there was no difference in the number of criteria on admission between responders, incomplete responders, or those who required colectomy. Objective assessment of relapse in ulcerative colitis is essential if the severity is not to be underestimated, but there seems little need to differentiate between 'severe' and 'fulminant' colitis. Several of those who met all five criteria responded completely to medical therapy and one patient who only had a moderate episode subsequently deteriorated to need urgent colectomy. The two patients who turned out to have Crohn's colitis are included because this reflects clinical practice. Excluding these two did not change the significant variables in the repeated measures analysis of variance.

Only bowel frequency and CRP differed significantly between those responding to medical treatment and those requiring colectomy at the most rigorous level of significance (Table III). The orosomucoids tended to be higher on admission and the ESR to decline more slowly in the colectomy group, which

TABLE IV *Follow up data on patients responding completely or incompletely to medical treatment (median 12 months, range 3·5–21)*

	Responders	*Incomplete*
Number of episodes	21	15
Remission (range, months)	9 (2–21)	0 (0–12)*
Continuous symptoms (%)	0	60
Relapse (%)	43	86
Number of relapses (range)	0 (0–4)	1 (0–2)
Readmission (%)	36	50
Colectomy (%)	5	40
Immunosuppressants (n)	3/20	9/11
Prednisolone	2	8
Azathioprine	1	4
Cyclosporine	0	3

Remission: median duration of remission, *p<0·001; relapse: % relapses in those entering remission; readmission: % patients readmitted for treatment, including colectomy; immunosuppressants: patients receiving these drugs at the time of last follow up; five of nine incomplete responders were taking more than one immunosuppressant.

favours the CRP as the most useful inflammatory marker. In an attempt to find a more specific marker of colonic inflammation, the serum concentration of nitric oxide metabolites was measured in some patients. These metabolites decreased in a similar fashion to the CRP, but did not discriminate between the groups.[17] The pulse rate tended to be higher and declined more slowly in those who required colectomy, while the haemoglobin and albumin were lower. These simple measures help in the overall assessment of colitic patients. Surprisingly, the platelet count, temperature, or amount of small bowel gas did not consistently discriminate between those who required colectomy and those who did not.

It might be argued that there is circular reasoning on the premise that we have defined criteria for colectomy and then evaluated the measures that define that decision. Indeed, it has been suggested that the threshold for colectomy in severe ulcerative colitis in Oxford is lower than elsewhere. If this is the case, then published experience supports the practice.[3 5 6] By examining the change in pattern of commonly measured variables, we have tried to predict which patients make a poor response to medical treatment. In Oxford, such patients generally have a colectomy because delaying surgery increases the risk of complications, or of persistent symptoms if medical treatment is continued. No single factor (such as diarrhoea) influenced the surgical decision. All decisions considered the duration, extent and previous pattern of disease, the influence of symptoms on the patient's lifestyle, the inclination of the patient, and response to or side effects from medical treatment.

The follow up data show that there is good reason to be optimistic in those who respond completely (5% colectomy rate, 85% in remission without immunosuppressants), but every reason to be cautious in other patients. For incomplete responders, 40% required colectomy within a few months (range 3–30 weeks) and only two of 14 (14%) remained in remission without immunosuppressive therapy. These data are similar to previous reports.[3 5] Furthermore, in five patients who had an emergency sub-total colectomy and were not candidates for an ileoanal pouch, four had to have a proctectomy for continuing symptoms. Even though emergency proctocolectomy has been shown to be a safe operation in experienced hands,[5] a sub-total colectomy was initially performed in these patients because of constraints on theatre time.

What conclusions, then, can be drawn to give objective advice on the management of patients with a relapse of ulcerative colitis? Firstly, the severity of relapse should be assessed objectively. All patients with a bloody stool frequency >6/day with any additional feature (pulse >90, temperature >37·8°C, haemoglobin <10·5 g/dl, ESR >30) should be admitted for intensive treatment. Stool frequency, six hourly pulse rate, and CRP should be monitored daily as a slower rate of improvement in these variables distinguished those who required urgent colectomy from those who did not. Although one must be wary of placing values on individual variables, it is possible with reasonable confidence to predict the outcome on day 3. Patients who continue to have frequent stools (>8 on day 3), or an increased CRP on day 3 (>45 mg/l with a stool frequency of 3–8) need to be identified early, as 85% of these will require colectomy using the criteria in this study. The inadequacies of conventional treatment should be recognised, but the role of cyclosporine for treating severe ulcerative colitis has yet to be defined. After a week of treatment, those patients who have a stool frequency >3/day or visible blood in the stool have a 60% chance of continuous symptoms and 40% chance of colectomy in the months after admission.

We are particularly grateful to Sister and staff on the medical and surgical Gastroenterology wards for their care of the patients, to Dr Helen Chapel and June White, Department of Immunology, for the measurement of orosomucoids, and to Karen Hayllar, King's College Hospital, London for additional statistical evaluation.

1 Edward FC, Truelove SC. The course and prognosis of ulcerative colitis. *Gut* 1963; **4:** 299–315.
2 Gallagher ND, Goulston SSM, Wyndham N, Morrow W. The management of fulminant ulcerative colitis. *Gut* 1962; **3:** 306–11.
3 Truelove SC, Jewell DP. Intensive intravenous regimen for severe attacks of ulcerative colitis. *Lancet* 1974; i: 1067–70.
4 Ritchie JK. Results of surgery for inflammatory bowel disease: a further survey of one hospital region. *BMJ* 1974; **1:** 264–8.
5 Truelove SC, Lee EG, Willoughby CP, Kettlewell MGW. Further experience in the treatment of severe attacks of ulcerative colitis. *Lancet* 1978; ii: 1086–8.
6 Järnerot G, Rolny P, Sandberg-Gertzén H. Intensive intravenous treatment of ulcerative colitis. *Gastroenterology* 1985; **89:** 1005–13.
7 Jones HVV, Grogono J, Hoare AM. Acute colitis in a district general hospital. *BMJ* 1988; **294:** 683–4.
8 Lichtiger S, Present DH, Kornbluth A, *et al.* Cyclosporine in severe ulcerative colitis refractory to steroid therapy. *N Engl J Med* 1994; **330:** 1841–5.
9 Lennard-Jones JE, Ritchie JK, Hilder W, Spicer CC. Assessment of severity in colitis: a preliminary study. *Gut* 1975; **16:** 579–84.
10 Buckell NA, Lennard-Jones JE, Hernandez MA, Kohn J, Riches PG, Wadsworth J. Measurement of serum proteins during attacks of ultraviolet as a guide to patient management. *Gut* 1979; **20:** 22–7.
11 Meyers S, Level PK, Feuer EJ, Johnson JW, Janowitz HD. Predicting the outcome of corticoid therapy for acute ulcerative colitis. Results of a prospective randomized, double-blind trial. *J Clin Gastroenterol* 1987; **9:** 50–4.
12 Chew CN, Nolan DJ, Jewell DP. Small bowel gas in severe ulcerative colitis. *Gut* 1991; **32:** 1535–9.
13 Truelove SC, Witts LJ. Cortisone in ulcerative colitis: preliminary report on a therapeutic trial. *BMJ* 1954; **2:** 375–8.
14 Jewell DP, Caprilli R, Mortensen N, Nicholls RJ, Wright JP. Indications and timing of surgery for severe ulcerative colitis. *Gastroenterology International* 1991; **4:** 161–4.
15 Jewell DP. Medical management of severe ulcerative colitis. *Int J Colorectal Dis* 1988; **3:** 186–9.
16 Breiman L, Friedman JH, Olshen RA, Stone CJ. *Classification and regression trees.* California: Wadsworth, 1984.
17 Rees DC, Satsangi J, Cornelissen PL, Travis SPL, White J, Jewell DP. Are serum concentrations of nitric oxide metabolites useful for predicting the clinical outcome of severe ulcerative colitis. *Eur J Gastroenterol Hepatol* 1995; **7:** 227–30.

LONG-TERM OUTCOME OF HEPATITIS C INFECTION AFTER LIVER TRANSPLANTATION

EDWARD J. GANE, M.B., CH.B., BERNARD C. PORTMANN, M.D., NIKOLAI V. NAOUMOV, M.D., HEATHER M. SMITH, B.SC., JAMES A. UNDERHILL, B.SC., PETER T. DONALDSON, PH.D., GEERT MAERTENS, PH.D., AND ROGER WILLIAMS, M.D.

Abstract *Background.* End-stage cirrhosis related to hepatitis C virus (HCV) is a common reason for liver transplantation, although viremia is known to persist in most cases. We investigated the impact of persistent HCV infection after liver transplantation on patient and graft survival and the effects of the HCV genotype and the degree of HLA matching between donor and recipient on the severity of recurrent hepatitis.

Methods. A group of 149 patients with HCV infection who received liver transplants between January 1982 and April 1994 were followed for a median of 36 months; 623 patients without HCV infection who underwent liver transplantation for end-stage chronic liver disease were used as a control group. A total of 528 liver-biopsy specimens from the HCV-infected recipients were reviewed, including 82 obtained one year after transplantation as scheduled and 39 obtained at five years as scheduled. In addition, biopsy specimens were obtained from 91 of the HCV-negative patients five years after transplantation.

Results. Cumulative survival rates for the 149 patients with HCV infection were 79 percent after one year, 74 percent after three years, and 70 percent after five years, as compared with rates of 75 percent, 71 percent, and 69 percent, respectively, in the HCV-negative transplant recipients (P=0.12). Of the 130 patients with hepatitis C infection who survived more than 6 months after transplantation, 15 (12 percent) had no evidence of chronic hepatitis on their most recent liver biopsy (median follow-up, 20 months), 70 (54 percent) had mild chronic hepatitis (median, 35 months), 35 (27 percent) had moderate chronic hepatitis (median, 35 months), and 10 (8 percent) had cirrhosis (median, 51 months). Graft loss occurred after a median of 303 days in 27 of the 149 patients, including 5 with HCV-related cirrhosis and 3 with HCV-related cholestatic hepatitis. Infection with HCV genotype 1b was associated with more severe graft injury, whereas the primary immunosuppressive regimen used and the extent of HLA mismatching between donors and recipients had no significant effect on this variable.

Conclusions. After liver transplantation for HCV-related cirrhosis, persistent HCV infection can cause severe graft damage, and such damage is more frequent in patients infected with HCV genotype 1b than with other genotypes. After five years, the rates of graft and overall survival are similar between patients with and those without HCV infection. (N Engl J Med 1996;334:815-20.)

CIRRHOSIS related to infection with the hepatitis C virus (HCV) is a common reason for liver transplantation, although viremia is known to persist in over 95 percent of patients.[1] Recurrence of HCV infection in the graft can be demonstrated as early as four weeks after liver transplantation for HCV-induced cirrhosis,[2] and acute lobular hepatitis will develop in most patients during the first year.[3] Because the initial graft dysfunction usually resolves, chronic hepatitis was thought to be a rare sequela.[4,5] However, recent reports have indicated that liver-graft damage can occur at an accelerated rate, leading to recurrent cirrhosis within five years,[6-8] unlike the indolent course of HCV infection seen in patients who have not undergone transplantation.[9,10] Preliminary data suggested a detrimental effect of matching the liver donor and recipient for the HLA-DQB antigen, because of an association with a recrudescence of chronic hepatitis.[11] Certain HCV genotypes may be associated with more severe liver disease after transplantation, but reports are conflicting.[12,13]

We investigated the natural history of HCV infection in liver-transplant recipients to determine the impact of such infection on the morphologic characteristics of the graft and the long-term outcome. We also analyzed the relation of HLA mismatches between donors and recipients and viral genotypes to the severity of recurrent disease in the graft.

From the Institute of Liver Studies, King's College School of Medicine and Dentistry, London (E.J.G., B.C.P., N.V.N., H.M.S., J.A.U., P.T.D., R.W.), and Innogenetics, Ghent, Belgium (G.M.). Address reprint requests to Dr. Williams at the Institute of Liver Studies, King's College Hospital, Denmark Hill, London SE5 9RS, United Kingdom.

METHODS

Between January 1982 and April 1994, a total of 946 patients underwent orthotopic liver transplantation in the Cambridge and King's College Hospital programs. Neither pretransplantation nor post-transplantation serum samples were available for 85 patients, who were thus excluded from the study. In the remaining 861 patients, pretransplantation serum samples were tested for anti-HCV antibody. If the antibody was detected, post-transplantation serum samples were tested for HCV RNA. In addition, HCV RNA was sought in post-transplantation serum samples from all patients who were negative for anti-HCV who had histologic evidence of hepatitis in a liver-biopsy specimen obtained one year after transplantation or at the time of graft dysfunction. A total of 420 transplant recipients were tested for HCV RNA. The primary immunosuppressive regimens used in all patients consisted of a combination of either cyclosporine, azathioprine, and prednisolone or tacrolimus (FK 506) and prednisolone.

Post-transplantation HCV infection was confirmed in 149 liver-transplant recipients on the basis of persistent HCV RNA in serum (Table 1), and their long-term outcome was assessed. Twenty-five of these patients had been included in a previous prospective analysis of the factors affecting the level of viral replication after recurrent HCV infection.[14]

The patients were followed for a median of 36 months after transplantation (range, 1 to 138). Between 1 and 12 biopsy specimens of the graft (median, 4) were reviewed for each patient. Biopsies were performed at one year as part of studies of new immunosuppressive agents between 1990 and 1992 and as part of routine post-transplantation management since then, and the biopsies were performed as scheduled in 82 of the 115 patients with at least one year of follow-up. Biopsies were also performed at five years in all patients not lost to follow-up (39 of 52). A total of 528 biopsy specimens were assessed by one of us in a nonblinded fashion.

Chronic viral hepatitis was diagnosed on the basis of the presence

© N Engl J Med 1996; 334: 815–820

Table 1. Characteristics of 149 Patients with Persistent HCV Infection after Liver Transplantation.*

Characteristic	Value
Age (yr)	
Median	50
Range	22–66
Male sex — no. (%)	114 (77)
Seropositive for HBsAg — no. (%)	12 (8)
Seropositive for anti-HBs or anti-HBc — no. (%)	33 (22)
Hepatocellular carcinoma — no. (%)	44 (30)
Racial or ethnic origin — no. (%)†	
Mediterranean	63 (42)
Northern Europe	37 (25)
Arabic countries	30 (20)
Israel	10 (7)
India	4 (3)
South America	3 (2)
Asia	1 (1)
Caribbean	1 (1)

*Anti-HBs denotes antibody against hepatitis B surface antigen, and anti-HBc antibody against hepatitis B core antigen.

†Because of rounding, percentages do not total 100 percent.

of focally intense, often aggregated, lymphocytic infiltrates in portal areas with few if any eosinophils, focal infiltration of and damage to a single interlobular bile duct without duct loss, and a variable degree of piecemeal necrosis and the absence of serious portal or hepatic venular endotheliitis. The changes were subjectively graded as mild if the cellular infiltrate was mostly confined to the portal areas, or moderate to severe when extensive piecemeal necrosis was present.[15]

The diagnosis of chronic rejection was based on findings of overt ductopenia with loss of more than 50 percent of the interlobular bile ducts, perivenular cholestasis and hepatocyte loss, and inconspicuous ductular proliferation and was confirmed on biopsy of a hepatectomy specimen by a finding of associated foam-cell arteriopathy.

Patient and graft survival was analyzed for the 149 liver-transplant recipients with confirmed HCV infection after transplantation and 623 other patients who received liver transplants for chronic liver disease (primary biliary cirrhosis, primary sclerosing cholangitis, and autoimmune hepatitis) during the same period. Eighty-nine HCV-negative patients who underwent transplantation for acute liver failure were not included in the analysis. Among the 623 patients, 91 underwent a liver biopsy five years after transplantation and were found to be seronegative for HCV RNA. These 91 patients were used as a control group for the analysis of liver-biopsy specimens.

Serologic Tests

Serum samples were tested for anti-HCV antibody with a second-generation enzyme-linked immunoassay (United Biomedical, New York) and for hepatitis B surface antigen (HBsAg) and antibody against hepatitis B surface antigen and core antigen with commercial kits (Ausria II, Ausab, Corab, or IMX, Abbott, North Chicago, Ill.). Active cytomegalovirus infection was excluded on the basis of the absence of specific histopathological features (including immunostaining for immediate early antigen), negative blood cultures, and negative serologic findings. Serum levels of aspartate aminotransferase were measured.

Serum was analyzed for HCV RNA with the Amplicor assay (Roche Diagnostics, Hoffmann–LaRoche, Basel, Switzerland).[16,17] Genotyping of HCV, of which there are 6 major genotypes and 18 subtypes, was performed in serum obtained after transplantation. Briefly, a nested polymerase chain reaction (PCR) was performed with biotinylated primers from the 5′ untranslated region, and the second-round product was genotyped with a second-generation line probe assay (INNO-LiPA HCV II, Innogenetics, Ghent, Belgium).[18]

Lymphocytes were obtained from donors and recipients for HLA typing. Typing of HLA-A and B antigens was performed with a standard complement-dependent microcytotoxicity assay.[19] Typing of HLA-DR was performed with a combination of serologic techniques and either analysis involving restriction-fragment–length polymorphisms or PCR-based sequence-specific oligonucleotide typing, whereas only PCR-based oligonucleotide typing was used for the typing of HLA-DQB.[20] For HLA-A and B, only mismatches at broad specificities were considered, whereas for HLA-DR and DQ, mismatches of subspecificities (split) of DR1 through 18 and DQ1 through 9 were identified. Matches of broad antigens with mismatches of split antigens were rare.

The results of genotyping of each donor and recipient were compared to identify mismatches in the pair. For each locus, the number of mismatches was scored as 0, 1, or 2. In cases in which data on two loci were considered, the score ranged from 0 to 4, and in cases in which four loci were considered, the score ranged from 0 to 8. The mean mismatch scores were calculated for each group of patients.

Statistical Analysis

The results were compared by nonparametric tests where appropriate: the chi-square or Fisher's exact test, the Mann–Whitney test, Wilcoxon's matched-pairs test, or Kruskal–Wallis probability tests. Kaplan–Meier survival curves were calculated with the BMDP statistical package, and the groups were compared with the Mantel–Cox and Breslow log-rank methods.[21] The independent effects of host and viral factors on histologic outcome were determined with multiple logistic-regression analysis.[22]

Results

In 93 of the 149 patients with confirmed HCV infection after liver transplantation (62 percent), acute lobular hepatitis developed between 23 and 469 days after transplantation (median, 77) and subsequently resolved. Analysis of the most recent liver-graft specimen from the 130 patients who survived more than 6 months postoperatively demonstrated no evidence of chronic hepatitis in 15 patients (12 percent; median follow-up, 20 months; range, 6 to 103), mild chronic hepatitis in 70 (54 percent; median follow-up, 35 months; range, 6 to 130), moderate chronic hepatitis in 35 (27 percent; median follow-up, 35 months; range, 6 to 127), and cirrhosis in 10 (8 percent; median follow-up, 51 months; range, 24 to 138). As of the most recent follow-up, 4 of the 10 patients with recurrent HCV-induced cirrhosis remained well between 62 and 118 months after transplantation, and 1 patient had peripheral edema that was controlled with diuretics (follow-up, 138 months). Liver failure developed in the remaining five patients between 32 and 106 months after transplantation; two underwent a second, successful transplantation after 34 months in one case and 108 months in the other; one patient died of decompensated cirrhosis at 61 months and another at 84 months; and one patient was awaiting a second transplant procedure (follow-up, 39 months).

Liver-biopsy specimens were obtained as scheduled from 82 HCV-infected patients one year after transplantation and from 39 patients five years after transplantation. When the biopsy specimens obtained at one year were compared with those obtained at five years, there were no significant differences in the numbers of grafts without hepatitis (7 of 82 vs. 2 of 39), grafts with mild chronic hepatitis (51 of 82 vs. 20 of 39), and grafts with moderate chronic hepatitis (24 of 82 vs. 9 of 39). None of the patients had cirrhosis after one year, whereas eight had cirrhosis at five years ($\chi^2 = 18$, $P<0.001$). For 30 patients biopsy specimens obtained at both one and five years were available. Of the 21 patients with mild chronic hepatitis at one year, 4 had moderate chronic hepatitis at five years and 1 had cirrhosis. In compari-

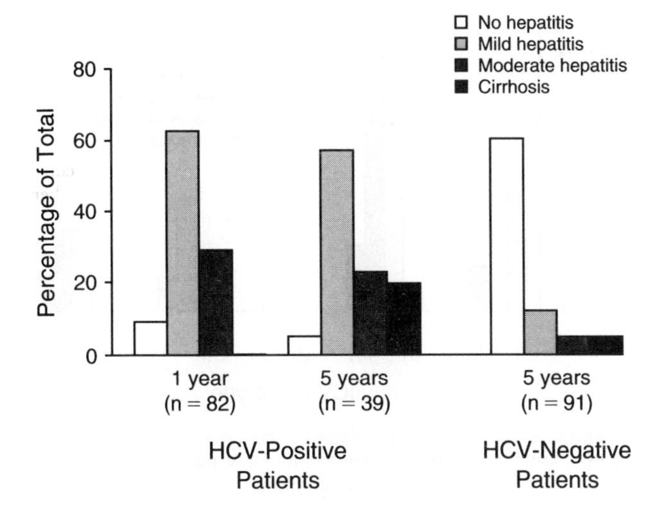

Figure 1. Biopsy Findings One and Five Years after Liver Transplantation in Recipients with HCV Infection after Transplantation and in Those without HCV Infection.

The number of patients in each group is given in parentheses. P<0.001 for the comparison of each variable between the HCV-positive and HCV-negative groups at five years.

son, six of the nine patients with moderate chronic hepatitis at one year had cirrhosis at five years (P = 0.001 by Fisher's exact test).

Of the 91 HCV-negative liver-transplant recipients who underwent liver biopsy at five years, 11 had mild chronic hepatitis, 5 had moderate chronic hepatitis, and 5 had cirrhosis. Thus, there was a significant difference at five years between the HCV-infected transplant recipients and the control group with respect to the incidence of cirrhosis and of mild and moderate chronic hepatitis (P<0.001 by the Mann–Whitney test) (Fig. 1). In 7 of the 10 HCV-negative patients with moderate chronic hepatitis or cirrhosis, the disease was caused by recurrent infection with hepatitis B virus.

Serum aspartate aminotransferase levels were a poor indicator of the severity of HCV-related graft injury. Fifty-six percent of the HCV-positive patients with mild chronic hepatitis had values in the normal range, as did 40 percent of those with moderate chronic hepatitis and 50 percent of those with cirrhosis (Fig. 2).

Of the 130 patients with hepatitis C infection who survived more than six months after transplantation, 109 received cyclosporine, azathioprine, and prednisolone as primary immunosuppressive therapy and 21 received tacrolimus and prednisolone. There was no significant difference between these two groups with respect to the distribution of histologic findings: 12 of 109 did not have hepatitis, as compared with 3 of 21; 59 of 109 had mild chronic hepatitis, as compared with 11 of 21; 30 of 109 had moderate chronic hepatitis, as compared with 5 of 21; and 8 of 109 had cirrhosis, as compared with 2 of 21 (P>0.1 for all four comparisons by the Mann–Whitney test). Similarly, there was no significant difference in the distribution of histologic findings between the 59 patients who required adjuvant high-dose corticosteroids for the treatment of acute rejection and the 71 who did not: 4 of the 59 had no evidence of hepatitis, as compared with 11 of the 71; 32 had mild chronic hepatitis, as compared with 38; 18 had moderate chronic hepatitis, as compared with 17; and 5 had cirrhosis in each group (P>0.1 for all four comparisons by the Mann–Whitney test).

Among the 149 patients with HCV infection after transplantation, chronic rejection was diagnosed in 15 (10 percent) between 28 and 1470 days after transplantation (median, 99), a value that was similar to the incidence of chronic rejection in HCV-negative patients (12 percent). Six of these 15 patients were successfully treated with tacrolimus, 6 received a second liver transplant, and 3 died of graft failure related to chronic rejection.

Graft loss occurred in 27 of the 149 patients (18 percent) between 93 and 2436 days after transplantation (median, 303) and was due to chronic rejection in 9 patients, intractable acute rejection in 1, recurrent hepatitis B virus infection in 2, recurrent hepatocellular carcinoma in 2, hepatic-artery thrombosis in 3, biliary complications in 2, HCV-related cirrhosis in 5, and HCV-related severe cholestatic hepatitis in 3. The last three patients presented with jaundice 4, 8, and 16 weeks after liver transplantation; their condition deteriorated steadily; and graft failure developed at 3, 8, and 9 months, respectively. Serial liver biopsies demonstrated a rapid progression from acute lobular hepatitis to diffuse hepatocytic ballooning, with severe intrahepatic cholestasis but only minimal inflammatory infiltrate.

The cumulative survival rates for the 149 patients with HCV infection were 79 percent after one year, 74 percent after three years, and 70 percent after five years. The corresponding rates for the 623 HCV-negative transplant recipients were 75 percent, 71 percent, and 69 percent

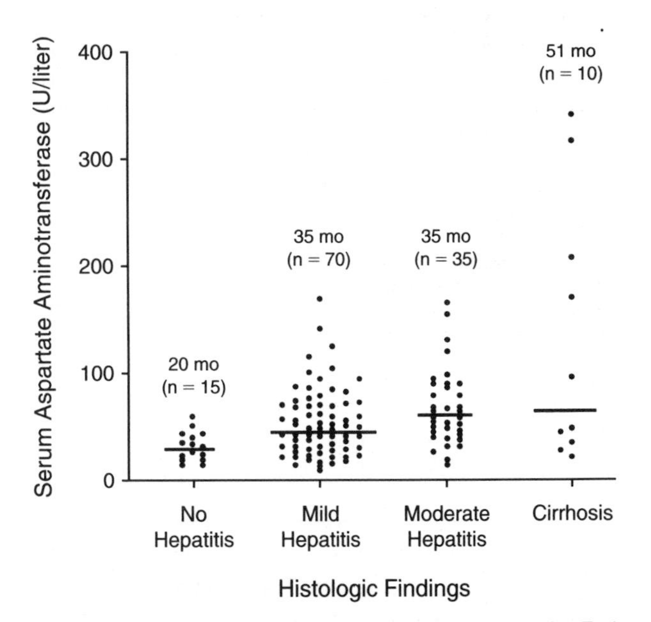

Figure 2. Serum Aspartate Aminotransferase Levels at the End of Follow-up in Relation to the Severity of Graft Injury.

The median length of follow-up and the number of patients are shown for each group. Bars indicate the median values. The normal range of values for aspartate aminotransferase is 0 to 50 U per liter.

(P=0.12 by the Mantel–Cox test and P=0.14 by Breslow's test for the difference between groups) (Fig. 3).

HLA Matching between Donors and Recipients

Lymphocytes from both members of 125 pairs of donors and recipients were available for HLA-A, B, and DR typing, including 14 cases involving a second transplantation. DNA samples from both members of 72 donor–recipient pairs were available for HLA-DR and DQ typing. No relation was found between the number of HLA-A, B, DR, or DQ mismatches and the extent of graft changes — whether absent or mild (no hepatitis or mild chronic hepatitis) or more severe (moderate chronic hepatitis or cirrhosis) at the end of follow-up. There was also no relation between the combined mismatch scores for HLA class I antigens (mean [±SD] mismatch score for HLA-A and B in the group with no hepatitis or mild chronic hepatitis, 2.88±0.90, vs. 2.94±0.86 in the group with moderate chronic hepatitis or cirrhosis) or for class II antigens (HLA-DR and DQ) (2.44±1.16 vs. 2.50±1.22) or for all four loci (5.38±1.34 vs. 5.30±1.75). There was also no association between the rate of graft loss and the extent of mismatching at individual loci or all four loci combined.

Influence of HCV Genotype

The HCV genotype was assessed in 100 patients. The most prevalent genotype was 1b, found in 43 patients. Genotype 4 was found in 14 patients, all but 2 of whom were from the Middle East. Three patients were infected with more than one subtype. The HCV genotype could not be determined in one patient. Twenty of the 43 patients who were infected with genotype 1b (46 percent) had progressive liver disease (moderate chronic hepatitis or cirrhosis) at the end of follow-up, as compared with 13 of the 53 patients (24 percent) infected with other HCV genotypes ($\chi^2=5.1$, P=0.02) (Fig. 4).

When the independent effects of the HCV genotype, the age at transplantation, sex, the type of HCV infection (recurrent or acquired), the length of time since transplantation, HBsAg status before transplantation, primary immunosuppressive regimen, use of adjuvant therapy for acute rejection, and the degree of HLA mismatching on histologic outcome were determined with multiple logistic-regression analysis, only the HCV genotype had a significant effect. Infection with HCV genotype 1b (HCV-1b) was more frequently associated with progressive graft damage than was infection with the other genotypes (P=0.01; odds ratio, 3.4; 95 percent confidence interval, 1.4 to 8.5).

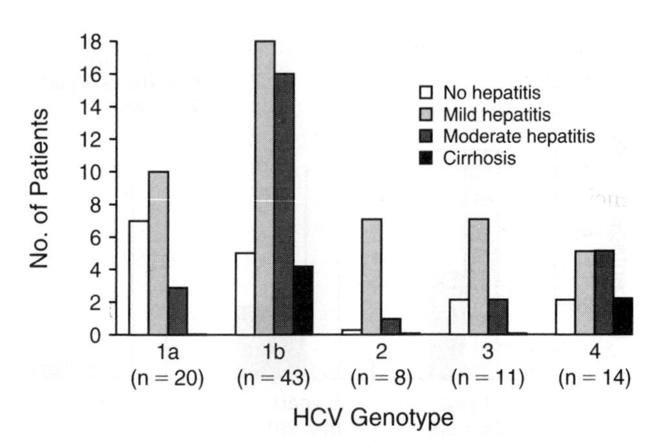

Figure 4. Effect of HCV Genotype on the Severity of Graft Injury in 96 Liver-Transplant Recipients with HCV Infection after Liver Transplantation.

The number of patients with each genotype is given in parentheses. The HCV genotype was determined in 100 patients. Three patients who were infected with two subtypes and one patient with no clear genotype pattern were excluded from the analysis.

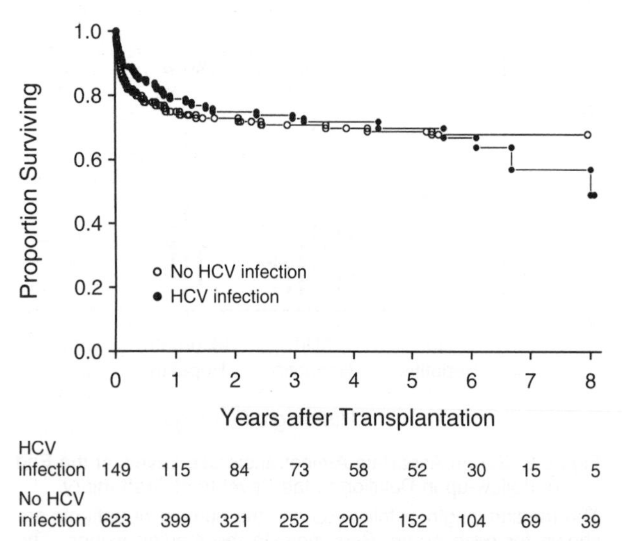

	0	1	2	3	4	5	6	7	8
HCV infection	149	115	84	73	58	52	30	15	5
No HCV infection	623	399	321	252	202	152	104	69	39

Figure 3. Kaplan–Meier Analysis of Survival According to HCV-Infection Status after Liver Transplantation.

The number of patients in each group at each point is indicated.

Discussion

Unlike previous reports suggesting that HCV infection is a relatively benign condition after liver transplantation,[1,2,4] our study found that moderate chronic hepatitis developed in 27 percent of the patients after a median of 35 months and that the disease progressed to cirrhosis in 8 percent after a median of 51 months. Although the rates of both graft survival and overall survival in patients infected with HCV were similar to those in patients without HCV infection up to five years after liver transplantation, our findings suggest that with longer follow-up the HCV-infected patients may experience more problems than the control patients.

The rapid clinical and histologic progression in the three patients in whom subacute liver failure developed within nine months after liver transplantation is similar to that described in two case reports of severe HCV infection in transplant recipients.[23,24] Although fibrosis was not a predominant feature in any of our patients, their clinical course resembled that of fibrosing cholestatic hepatitis in recurrent hepatitis B infection.[25] Serum aspartate aminotransferase levels were not correlated with the severity of chronic hepatitis in the graft, as has been observed in patients with chronic hepatitis C who have not undergone liver transplantation.[10,26]

Because cellular immune reactions restricted by both

HLA class I[27,28] and II[29,30] antigens are involved in the recognition of HCV peptides, HLA matching between donor and recipient could potentially increase damage to the graft from recurrent viral infections by facilitating host recognition of viral antigens. Recently, a beneficial effect of a complete HLA-DQ mismatch was reported in 14 patients after transplantation for hepatitis C cirrhosis.[11] We found no relation between histologic outcome and the extent of matching of either HLA-DR or DQ. This difference may be due to the higher resolution achieved through the use of PCR-based sequence-specific oligonucleotide typing, as compared with the serologic methods used in the previous study. Nonetheless, cellular immune responses restricted by HLA class II antigens may be involved in the pathogenesis of HCV-induced graft damage. The graft is repopulated by the recipient's antigen-presenting cells and effector cells (including CD4+ lymphocytes) within weeks of transplantation, allowing cellular immune responses restricted by HLA class II antigens to operate independently of the donor's HLA class II antigens.

The finding that infection with HCV-1b was associated with more severe graft injury is consistent with the more aggressive liver disease caused by this genotype in patients who have not undergone transplantation.[31-33] This finding has been attributed to an increased replicative potential of HCV-1b,[34,35] increased heterogeneity of HCV quasispecies,[12] and increased expression of viral antigen in liver tissue.[36] Alternatively, HCV-1b may be more immunogenic than other genotypes.[37] There are quantitative[17,38] and qualitative[39] differences in antibody profiles between patients infected with different HCV genotypes.

Since prednisolone enhances HCV replication in patients with chronic HCV infection who have not undergone transplantation,[40,41] our practice is to discontinue corticosteroid therapy within six months after transplantation in patients with HCV infection. High-dose therapy with intravenous methylprednisolone for acute allograft rejection is associated with a massive increase in the level of hepatitis C viremia[14] and earlier recurrence of hepatitis.[42] The need for supplemental intravenous corticosteroids and the cumulative dose of oral corticosteroids are both significantly lower in patients receiving tacrolimus-based immunosuppression than in those given cyclosporine-based therapy,[43,44] suggesting that the former regimen may have advantages in patients with HCV infection. However, we found no difference between the two regimens in either the incidence or the severity of recurrent hepatitis in the graft. The use of OKT3 in patients who underwent transplantation for HCV-induced cirrhosis was recently associated with an earlier onset of lobular hepatitis in the graft and with more severe chronic hepatitis than are seen with other immunosuppressive drugs.[45] We could not investigate this association, because none of our patients received OKT3 as induction or adjuvant immunosuppressive therapy and because tacrolimus is used in our facility as rescue therapy for episodes of rejection that do not respond to corticosteroid therapy.

In conclusion, we found that HCV infection frequently recurs after liver transplantation for HCV-induced cirrhosis and may be associated with accelerated rates of graft damage in some patients, especially those infected with HCV-1b. Liver biopsies to detect and grade the extent of HCV-related graft damage may help identify patients who would benefit from antiviral therapy.

We are indebted to N. Heaton, M. Rela, and K.C. Tan at King's College Hospital, Sir Roy Calne and his surgical team at Addenbrooke's Hospital, and other colleagues involved in the care of these patients; to E. Davis and H. Jones for valuable technical assistance; and to Karen Hayllar for assistance with the statistical analysis.

References

1. Wright TL, Donegan E, Hsu HH, et al. Recurrent and acquired hepatitis C viral infection in liver transplant recipients. Gastroenterology 1992;103:317-22.
2. Konig V, Bauditz J, Lobeck H, et al. Hepatitis C virus reinfection in allografts after orthotopic liver transplantation. Hepatology 1992;16:1137-43.
3. Ascher NL, Lake JR, Emond J, Roberts J. Liver transplantation for hepatitis C virus-related cirrhosis. Hepatology 1994;20:24S-27S.
4. Shah G, Demetris AJ, Gavaler JS, et al. Incidence, prevalence, and clinical course of hepatitis C following liver transplantation. Gastroenterology 1992;103:323-9.
5. Chazouilleres O, Kim M, Combs C, et al. Quantitation of hepatitis C virus RNA in liver transplant recipients. Gastroenterology 1994;106:994-9.
6. Weinstein JS, Poterucha JJ, Rakela J, Krom RAF, Wiesner RH. Long-term outcome of hepatitis C (HCV) infected liver transplant (OLT) recipients. Hepatology 1994;20:Suppl:133A. abstract.
7. Casavilla A, Mateo R, Rakela J, et al. Impact of hepatitis C virus (HCV) infection on survival following primary liver transplantation (OLTX) under FK506. Hepatology 1994;20:Suppl:133A. abstract.
8. Feray C, Gigou M, Samuel D, et al. The course of hepatitis C infection after liver transplantation. Hepatology 1994;20:1137-43.
9. Seeff LB, Buskell-Bales Z, Wright EC, et al. Long-term mortality after transfusion-associated non-A, non-B hepatitis. N Engl J Med 1992;327:1906-11.
10. Alter MJ, Margolis HS, Krawczynski K, et al. The natural history of community-acquired hepatitis C in the United States. N Engl J Med 1992;327:1899-905.
11. Gretch D, Wile M, Gaur L, et al. Donor-recipient match at the HLA-DQB locus is associated with recrudescence of chronic hepatitis following liver transplantation for end stage hepatitis C. Hepatology 1993;18:Suppl:108A. abstract.
12. Feray C, Gigou M, Samuel D, et al. Influence of the genotypes of hepatitis C virus on the severity of recurrent liver disease after liver transplantation. Gastroenterology 1995;108:1089-96.
13. Zhou S, Kim M, Ferrell L, Wright TL. HCV genotyping of liver transplant (OLT) recipients: relation to viremia and histology. Hepatology 1994;20: Suppl:134A. abstract.
14. Gane E, Naoumov N, Qian K, et al. A longitudinal analysis of hepatitis C virus replication following liver transplantation. Gastroenterology 1996; 110:167-77.
15. Desmet VJ, Gerber M, Hoofnagle JH, Manns M, Scheuer PJ. Classification of chronic hepatitis: diagnosis, grading and staging. Hepatology 1994;19: 1513-20.
16. Tilston P, Morris DJ, Klapper PE, Corbitt G. Commercial assay for hepatitis C virus RNA. Lancet 1994;344:201-2.
17. Izopet J, Bogard M, Costes J, et al. Multicenter evaluation of analytical performances of the Amplicor HCV RNA qualitative assay. Hepatology 1994; 20:Suppl:241A. abstract.
18. van Doorn LJ, Kleter B, Stuyver L, et al. Analysis of hepatitis C virus genotypes by a line probe assay and correlation with antibody profiles. J Hepatol 1994;21:122-9.
19. Terasaki P, McClelland JD, Park MS, McCurdy B. Microdroplet assay of human serum cytotoxins. In: Ray JG, Hare DB, Pederson PD, Kayhoe DE, eds. Manual of tissue typing techniques. Bethesda, Md.: National Institutes of Health, 1974:67-74. (DHEW publication no. (NIH) 75-548.)
20. Donaldson P, Underhill J, Doherty D, et al. Influence of human leukocyte antigen matching on liver allograft survival and rejection: "the dualistic effect." Hepatology 1993;17:1008-15.
21. Cox DR, Oakes D. Analysis of survival data. London: Chapman & Hall, 1984.
22. Armitage P, Berry G. Statistical methods in medical research. 3rd ed. Oxford, England: Blackwell Science, 1994.
23. Lim HL, Lau GK, Davis GL, Dolson DJ, Lau JY. Cholestatic hepatitis leading to hepatic failure in a patient with organ-transmitted hepatitis C virus infection. Gastroenterology 1994;106:248-51.
24. Schluger LK, Min A, Wolf DC, et al. Severe recurrent cholestatic hepatitis C following orthotopic liver transplantation. Gastroenterology 1994;106: Suppl:A978. abstract.

25. Davies SE, Portmann BC, O'Grady JG, et al. Hepatic histological findings after transplantation for chronic hepatitis B virus infection, including a unique pattern of fibrosing cholestatic hepatitis. Hepatology 1991;13:150-7.
26. DiBisceglie AM, Goodman ZD, Ishak KG, Hoofnagle JH, Melpolder JJ, Alter HJ. Long-term clinical and histopathological follow-up of chronic posttransfusion hepatitis. Hepatology 1991;14:969-74.
27. Mondelli M, Alberti A, Tremolada F, Williams R, Eddleston AL, Realdi G. In-vitro cell-mediated cytotoxicity for autologous liver cells in chronic non-A, non-B hepatitis. Clin Exp Immunol 1986;63:147-55.
28. Koziel MJ, Dudley D, Afdhal N, et al. Hepatitis C virus (HCV) specific cytotoxic T lymphocytes recognize epitopes in the core and envelope proteins of HCV. J Virol 1993;67:7522-32.
29. Botarelli P, Brunetto MR, Minutello MA, et al. T-lymphocyte response to hepatitis C virus in different clinical courses of infection. Gastroenterology 1993;104:580-7.
30. Ferrari C, Valli A, Galati L, et al. T-cell response to structural and nonstructural hepatitis C virus antigens in persistent and self-limited hepatitis C virus infections. Hepatology 1994;19:286-95.
31. Dusheiko G, Schmilovitz-Weiss H, Brown D, et al. Hepatitis C virus genotypes: an investigation of type-specific differences in geographic origin and disease. Hepatology 1994;19:13-8.
32. Qu D, Li JS, Vitvitski L, et al. Hepatitis C virus genotypes in France: comparison of clinical features of patients infected with HCV type I and type II. J Hepatol 1994;21:70-5.
33. Pozzato G, Kaneko S, Moretti M, et al. Different genotypes of hepatitis C virus are associated with different severity of chronic liver disease. J Med Virol 1994;43:291-6.
34. Yuki N, Hayashi N, Kasahara A, et al. Pretreatment viral load and response to prolonged interferon-alpha course for chronic hepatitis C. J Hepatol 1995;22:457-63.
35. Poynard T, Bedossa P, Chevallier M, et al. A comparison of three interferon alfa-2b regimens for the long-term treatment of chronic non-A, non-B hepatitis. N Engl J Med 1995;332:1457-62.
36. Ballardini G, Groff P, Pontisso P, et al. Hepatitis C virus (HCV) genotype, tissue HCV antigens, hepatocellular expression of HLA-A,B,C, and intercellular adhesion-1 molecules: clues to pathogenesis of hepatocellular damage and response to interferon treatment in patients with chronic hepatitis C. J Clin Invest 1995;95:2067-75.
37. Nagayama R, Tsuda F, Okamoto H, et al. Genotype dependence of hepatitis C virus antibodies detectable by the first-generation enzyme-linked immunosorbent assay with C100-3 protein. J Clin Invest 1993;92:1529-33.
38. Tanaka T, Tsukiyama-Kohara K, Yamaguchi K, et al. Significance of specific antibody assay for genotyping of hepatitis C virus. Hepatology 1994;19:1347-53.
39. Willems M, Sheng L, Roskams T, et al. Hepatitis C virus and its genotypes in patients suffering from chronic hepatitis C with or without a cryoglobulinemia-related syndrome. J Med Virol 1994;44:266-71.
40. Magrin S, Craxi A, Fabiano C, et al. Hepatitis C viremia in chronic liver disease: relationship to interferon-α or corticosteroid treatment. Hepatology 1994;19:273-9.
41. McHutchison JG, Wilkes LB, Pockros PJ, et al. Pulse corticosteroid therapy increases viremia (HCV RNA) in patients with chronic HCV infection. Hepatology 1993;18:Suppl:87A. abstract.
42. Sheiner PA, Schwartz ME, Mor E, et al. Severe or multiple rejection episodes are associated with early recurrence of hepatitis C after orthotopic liver transplantation. Hepatology 1995;21:30-4.
43. The U.S. Multicenter FK506 Liver Study Group. A comparison of tacrolimus (FK 506) and cyclosporine for immunosuppression in liver transplantation. N Engl J Med 1994;331:1110-5.
44. European FK506 Multicentre Liver Study Group. Randomised trial comparing tacrolimus (FK506) and cyclosporin in prevention of liver allograft rejection. Lancet 1994;344:423-8.
45. Rosen HR, Martin P, Shackleton CR, Farmer DA, Holt C, Busuttil RW. OKT3 use associated with diminished graft and patient survival in patients transplanted for chronic hepatitis C. Hepatology 1995;22:Suppl:132A. abstract.

FAMOTIDINE FOR THE PREVENTION OF GASTRIC AND DUODENAL ULCERS CAUSED BY NONSTEROIDAL ANTIINFLAMMATORY DRUGS

ALI S. TAHA, PH.D., NICHOLAS HUDSON, M.D., CHRISTOPHER J. HAWKEY, D.M., ANTHONY J. SWANNELL, M.B., PENELOPE N. TRYE, B.SC., JEREMY COTTRELL, M.SC., STEPHEN G. MANN, M.B., THOMAS J. SIMON, M.D., ROGER D. STURROCK, M.D., AND ROBIN I. RUSSELL, PH.D.

Abstract *Background.* Acid suppression with famotidine, a histamine H_2–receptor antagonist, provides protection against gastric injury in normal subjects receiving short courses of aspirin or naproxen. The efficacy of famotidine in preventing peptic ulcers in patients receiving long-term therapy with nonsteroidal antiinflammatory drugs (NSAIDs) is not known.

Methods. We studied the efficacy of two doses of famotidine (20 mg and 40 mg, each given orally twice daily), as compared with placebo, in preventing peptic ulcers in 285 patients without peptic ulcers who were receiving long-term NSAID therapy for rheumatoid arthritis (82 percent) or osteoarthritis (18 percent). The patients were evaluated clinically and by endoscopy at base line and after 4, 12, and 24 weeks of treatment. The evaluators were unaware of the treatment assignment. The primary end point was the cumulative incidence of gastric or duodenal ulceration at 24 weeks.

Results. The cumulative incidence of gastric ulcers was 20 percent in the placebo group, 13 percent in the group of patients receiving 20 mg of famotidine twice daily ($P=0.24$ for the comparison with placebo), and 8 percent in the group receiving 40 mg of famotidine twice daily ($P=0.03$ for the comparison with placebo). The proportion of patients in whom duodenal ulcers developed was significantly lower with both doses of famotidine than with placebo (13 percent in the placebo group, 4 percent in the low-dose famotidine group [$P=0.04$], and 2 percent in the high-dose famotidine group [$P=0.01$]). Both doses of famotidine were well tolerated.

Conclusions. Treatment with high-dose famotidine significantly reduces the cumulative incidence of both gastric and duodenal ulcers in patients with arthritis receiving long-term NSAID therapy. (N Engl J Med 1996; 334:1435-9.)

GASTRODUODENAL damage can be seen on endoscopy in 20 to 40 percent of people who take nonsteroidal antiinflammatory drugs (NSAIDs). In epidemiologic studies, the risks of peptic ulcer and death are three to six times higher among people who take these drugs than among those who do not.[1,2] An effective strategy to prevent these complications is needed.

Endoscopic studies have shown that misoprostol prevents NSAID-associated gastric and duodenal ulcers,[3-5] and in one study the incidence of complications from ulcers was reduced.[6] However, misoprostol may cause diarrhea and abdominal pain, it has little effect on symptoms of dyspepsia, and it is unsuitable for women of childbearing potential because of its abortifacient action.[7] Ranitidine can prevent duodenal ulceration in patients taking NSAIDs for arthritis but is relatively ineffective in preventing NSAID-associated gastric ulceration.[8,9]

Famotidine, a histamine H_2–receptor antagonist, inhibits acid secretion and provides protection against mucosal injury in normal subjects receiving short courses of aspirin or naproxen, with high doses of famotidine more effective than low doses.[10,11] The efficacy and safety of the drug have not been established in patients with arthritis receiving long-term NSAID therapy.

We compared two doses of famotidine (20 mg twice daily and 40 mg twice daily) with placebo to test the hypothesis that famotidine provides protection against NSAID-associated gastric and duodenal ulcers.

From the Departments of Gastroenterology and Rheumatology, Glasgow Royal Infirmary, Glasgow, Scotland (A.S.T., R.D.S., R.I.R.); University Hospital, Nottingham, England (N.H., C.J.H., A.J.S.); Merck Sharp & Dohme, Hoddesdon, England (P.N.T., J.C., S.G.M.); and Merck Research Laboratories, Blue Bell, Pa. (T.J.S.). Address reprint requests to Dr. Taha at the Department of Gastroenterology, Eastbourne General Hospital, King's Drive, Eastbourne, BN21 2UD, England.

Supported by a grant from Merck Research Laboratories.

METHODS

The study was a 24-week, double-blind, parallel-group, randomized comparison of placebo with low-dose famotidine (20 mg twice daily) or high-dose famotidine (40 mg twice daily) as prophylaxis against endoscopically detected gastric or duodenal ulceration. The patients were 18 years old or older and had rheumatoid arthritis or osteoarthritis. They had been receiving standard doses of an NSAID for at least one month and were likely to continue taking this medication for at least six months.

The patients were recruited from the rheumatology and orthopedic clinics at Glasgow Royal Infirmary, Glasgow, Scotland, and University Hospital, Nottingham, England. Patients were not considered eligible for the study if they had taken antiulcer drugs other than antacids within seven days before enrollment or if they were taking 7.5 mg or more of prednisolone daily (or an equivalent dose of another corticosteroid), methotrexate, or antineoplastic drugs. The other main exclusion criteria were lactation, childbearing potential in the absence of contraception, renal failure, diabetes mellitus, and clinically important abnormal values on laboratory tests.

The recruitment was conducted by two gastroenterologists, who invited all potentially eligible patients with arthritis, regardless of whether they had dyspeptic symptoms, to participate in the study. Patients who accepted the invitation underwent upper gastrointestinal endoscopy.

The study protocol was approved by the ethics committees of the two participating hospitals, and informed consent was obtained from all the patients.

Endoscopic Evaluation

Before the commencement of the study, the two endoscopists attended each other's endoscopic sessions and reviewed still and video images in order to establish standardized reporting criteria for ulcers and other lesions.

At endoscopy, ulcers, erosions, and intramucosal hemorrhages were recorded separately for the esophagus, gastric body, gastric an-

Reprinted from *The New England Journal of Medicine*
334:1435-1439 (May 30), 1996

© N Engl J Med 1996; 334: 1435–1439

trum, duodenal bulb, and second part of the duodenum. An ulcer was defined as an excavated mucosal break 3 mm or more in diameter,[3-5] as measured with biopsy forceps or a custom-made device. Erosions were defined as superficial mucosal breaks, and intramucosal hemorrhages were defined as hemorrhagic lesions without overlying mucosal breaks. The endoscopic findings were used to derive a modified Lanza score of 0 to 4 (0, no lesions, 1 nonulcerated duodenal lesion, or 1 or 2 nonulcerated gastric lesions; 1, 2 to 5 nonulcerated duodenal lesions or 3 to 5 nonulcerated gastric lesions; 2, 6 to 10 nonulcerated lesions; 3, more than 10 nonulcerated lesions; and 4, 1 or more ulcers).[9] Patients with ulcers were enrolled in a separate study of ulcer healing.

Randomization

Patients without ulcers were stratified according to the type of arthritis and, with the use of a computer-generated schedule, were randomly assigned to receive one 20-mg or 40-mg tablet of famotidine (Pepcid, Merck) twice daily or one placebo tablet twice daily. Co-magaldrox 195/220 (Maalox, Rhone–Poulenc–Rorer) tablets were provided for the relief of dyspepsia. Famotidine is not licensed anywhere for the prevention of ulcers, and the higher dose (40 mg twice daily) exceeds the dose approved for ulcer healing (40 mg once daily).

Assessments

The patients were assessed at base line and after 4, 12, and 24 weeks of treatment. In addition to the endoscopic data, we obtained information on NSAID and other drug therapy, abdominal pain, and arthritis-related physical disability as measured by the Health Assessment Questionnaire (Table 1).[12] The patients underwent a complete physical examination at base line and at the end of the study, and urinalysis and routine hematologic and biochemical tests were performed at each visit. The patients were asked to record abdominal symptoms (pain, heartburn, nausea, and vomiting) and antacid use daily on diary cards. Abdominal pain and joint pain were quantitated on a scale of 1 to 3 (1, mild; 2, moderate; and 3, severe). We assessed compliance with the study regimen by recording tablet counts. At each visit, patients were questioned about adverse events. At the time of the initial endoscopic study, the presence of *Helicobacter pylori* was determined in gastric antral biopsy specimens on the basis of both histologic examination and urease activity. Identification of the organism by either means was considered a positive result.

End Points

The primary end point was the cumulative incidence of gastric or duodenal ulceration at 24 weeks. The secondary end points were Lanza scores for lesser degrees of gastroduodenal injury, the presence or absence of abdominal pain, pain scores, and antacid consumption. The analysis of safety was based on an assessment of adverse events, the score on the Health Assessment Questionnaire, physical examinations, and laboratory tests.

Statistical Analysis

The statistical analyses were performed with the SAS statistical package (version 6.08, Cary, N.C.). The results of an intention-to-treat analysis are presented. A per-protocol analysis was also carried out on patients who could be evaluated, defined as those who took more than 80 percent of both the prescribed NSAID and the study drug, did not take additional full-dose salicylates, and underwent a final endoscopic examination no more than five days after the end of treatment with the study drug.

The primary end point (i.e., the time to the detection of a gastric or duodenal ulcer) was analyzed with the use of Kaplan–Meier curves for survival, and comparisons among the three groups were made with the log-rank test. The confidence intervals for the Kaplan–Meier curves were estimated with the binomial distribution when possible (without censoring of data) or with Greenwood's formula for the standard error, with the normal approximation.[13] Changes from base line in Lanza scores, abdominal-pain scores, and joint-pain scores were compared with the Mantel–Haenszel test (with adjustment for the study center). Changes from base line in scores on the Health Assessment Questionnaire were analyzed with the Kruskal–Wallis test.

The proportional-hazards model was used to assess the effects of potential prognostic factors on the risk of ulceration. These factors included the study center, age, sex, smoking habits, use of alcohol, type of NSAID, duration of prior NSAID therapy, rheumatologic diagnosis, duration of arthritis, presence of erosions or hemorrhagic lesions at the initial endoscopic examination, abdominal pain at base line, his-

Table 1. Base-Line Characteristics of 285 Patients with Arthritis Receiving Long-Term NSAID Therapy and Randomly Assigned to Receive Famotidine or Placebo (Intention-to-Treat Analysis).*

CHARACTERISTIC	STUDY GROUP		
	PLACEBO (N = 93)	LOW-DOSE FAMOTIDINE (N = 95)	HIGH-DOSE FAMOTIDINE (N = 97)
Age (yr)			
Mean	53.4	57.2	55
Range	22–78	18–88	22–83
Duration of arthritis (yr)			
Mean	9.6	12.2	10.1
Range	0–50	0–44	0–47
Health Assessment Questionnaire score†			
Mean	1.3	1.5	1.4
Range	0–2.9	0–2.9	0–2.9
		no. of patients (%)	
Female sex	71 (76)	69 (73)	68 (70)
Current smoker	32 (34)	28 (29)	42 (43)
Rheumatoid arthritis	76 (82)	80 (84)	79 (81)
H. pylori infection‡	46 (49)	48 (51)	48 (49)
Previous ulcer	9 (10)	15 (16)	13 (13)
Moderate or severe joint pain	60 (65)	74 (78)	71 (73)
Abdominal pain§	33 (35)	25 (26)	29 (30)
Heartburn	28 (30)	22 (23)	26 (27)
Nausea	13 (14)	13 (14)	11 (11)
Vomiting	5 (5)	2 (2)	2 (2)
Gastric lesion	29 (31)	40 (42)	32 (33)
Duodenal lesion	8 (9)	9 (9)	13 (13)
NSAID			
Diclofenac	24 (26)	26 (27)	22 (23)
Indomethacin	19 (20)	15 (16)	19 (20)
Naproxen	19 (20)	13 (14)	18 (19)
Ibuprofen	9 (10)	10 (11)	11 (11)
Ketoprofen	5 (5)	5 (5)	5 (5)
Fenbufen	4 (4)	6 (6)	6 (6)
Other¶	14 (15)	23 (24)	20 (21)
Disease-modifying drug			
Sulfasalazine	30 (32)	23 (24)	23 (24)
Gold	6 (6)	14 (15)	18 (19)
Penicillamine	6 (6)	13 (14)	6 (6)
Prednisolone	8 (9)	10 (11)	8 (8)
Hydroxychloroquine	5 (5)	6 (6)	4 (4)

*Patients in the low-dose group received 20 mg of famotidine twice daily, and those in the high-dose group received 40 mg twice daily. There were no statistically significant differences ($P<0.05$) in any of the characteristics among the groups.

†The score is the average of individual scores, on a scale of 0 to 3, for the ability to dress, rise, eat, walk, reach, grip, shop, vacuum, and garden (0 to 1, some or no difficulty; 1.1 to 2, much difficulty; and 2.1 to 3, in need of several devices or unable to perform the activity).

‡Data were not recorded for three patients in the low-dose group and two in the high-dose group.

§Among the patients with abdominal pain, the pain scores were similar in the three groups.

¶Other NSAIDs, used by fewer than 5 patients in a group, were nabumetone (12 patients), apazone (12), piroxicam (9), flurbiprofen (8), tiaprofenic acid (5), etodolac (4), acemetacin (3), benorilate (2), tenoxicam (1), and sulindac (1).

tory of peptic ulcer, score on the Health Assessment Questionnaire, second-line treatment with antirheumatoid drugs, prednisolone therapy, peripheral-blood cell counts, and *H. pylori* infection. The results are presented as hazard ratios, which express the increase in the risk that an ulcer will develop.

An overall comparison of the three groups of patients was performed, in addition to three pairwise tests. No formal adjustment was made for multiple tests. All tests were two-tailed.

RESULTS

A total of 570 patients were invited to undergo endoscopic screening for enrollment in the trial: 181 patients were unwilling to undergo multiple endoscopic examinations, and 389 accepted the invitation. Of these 389 patients, 104 had gastric or duodenal ulcers at the initial endoscopy and were therefore excluded from the study. The characteristics of the remaining 285 patients are shown in Table 1. A total of 165 patients (58 percent) were from Glasgow, 119 (42 percent) were from Nottingham, and 1 (0.4 percent) was from Leeds. The three treatment groups were well-matched for age, sex, smoking status, use of alcohol, underlying arthritis, and frequency of *H. pylori* infection, as well as for previous ulcer, frequency of joint pain, score on the Health Assessment Questionnaire, and use of individual NSAIDs or disease-modifying drugs.

The per-protocol analysis included 81 patients in the placebo group, 84 in the group receiving 20 mg of famotidine twice daily, and 83 in the group receiving 40 mg twice daily. For this analysis, 12 patients assigned to the placebo group, 11 assigned to the low-dose group, and 14 assigned to the high-dose group were excluded because of a subsequent change to low-dose NSAID therapy or poor compliance with the study drugs.

Cumulative Incidence of Ulcer

Estimates of the cumulative incidence of gastric or duodenal ulceration during the 24-week study period are shown in Table 2 and Figure 1. The cumulative incidence of ulceration, regardless of the site, was lower in both famotidine groups than in the placebo group. However, whereas the higher dose of famotidine was associated with a lower incidence of both gastric and duodenal ulcers, the lower dose was associated with a reduction only in the incidence of duodenal ulcers. The results of the per-protocol analysis were similar (data not shown).

Prognostic Factors

The risk of ulceration was increased by an increase in the peripheral white-cell count (hazard ratio, 1.2 per 1000 cells per cubic millimeter; 95 percent confidence interval, 1.0 to 1.4) and by duodenal erosions and submucosal hemorrhages (hazard ratio, 2.9; 95 percent confidence interval, 1.2 to 6.9). In the placebo group, ulcers developed in 5 of the 8 patients (62 percent) with duodenal lesions at base line, as compared with 19 of the 85 (22 percent) without duodenal lesions. In the low- and high-dose famotidine groups combined, ulcers developed in 23 percent of the patients with duodenal lesions at base line and in 11 percent of those without such lesions. There were also trends toward an increased risk of ulceration among patients with *H. pylori* infection (hazard ratio, 1.7; 95 percent confidence interval, 0.8 to 3.5) and a reduced risk among those receiving diclofenac, as compared with all other NSAIDs (hazard ratio, 0.5; 95 percent confidence interval, 0.2 to 1.3).

Table 2. Cumulative Number and Incidence of Gastric and Duodenal Ulcers at the Completion of the Study (Intention-to-Treat Analysis).

ULCERS*	STUDY GROUP		
	PLACEBO (N = 93)	LOW-DOSE FAMOTIDINE (N = 95)	HIGH-DOSE FAMOTIDINE (N = 97)
Gastric and duodenal			
Cumulative number	24	14	9
Cumulative incidence — % (95% CI)	28 (19–38)	16 (9–24)	11 (4–17)
P value	—	0.05	0.003
Gastric			
Cumulative number	16	11	7
Cumulative incidence — % (95% CI)	20 (11–28)	13 (6–20)	8 (2–14)
P value	—	0.24	0.03
Duodenal			
Cumulative number	10	3	2
Cumulative incidence — % (95% CI)	13 (5–20)	4 (0–8)	2 (0–6)
P value	—	0.04	0.01

*CI denotes confidence interval. P values are for the comparison with the placebo group.

Analyses of Secondary End Points

At four weeks, 25 patients in the placebo group had gastric Lanza scores of 1 to 4 for gastric lesions, as compared with 18 in the low-dose famotidine group ($P = 0.03$) and 12 in the high-dose group ($P = 0.01$). The scores for duodenal lesions in the three groups were similar. The results at the 12- and 24-week visits could not be analyzed directly, because they were confounded by the withdrawal of patients with ulcers (Fig. 1).

About 30 percent of the patients had abdominal pain at base line (Table 1). At the end of the study, 29 percent of the patients in the placebo group had abdominal pain, as compared with 19 percent of the patients in the low-dose famotidine group and 17 percent of those in the high-dose group. Among the patients with pain, the abdominal-pain scores and mean daily use of antacids during the study were similar in the three groups.

Safety Profile and Dropout

Both doses of famotidine were well tolerated. Patients dropped out of the study because of the development of ulcers (withdrawal per protocol, Fig. 1), the occurrence of adverse events, or other reasons, as shown in Table 3. In the high-dose famotidine group, there was a small but statistically significant reduction in the mean platelet count at the completion of the study, from 321,000 to 309,000 per cubic millimeter ($P = 0.02$).

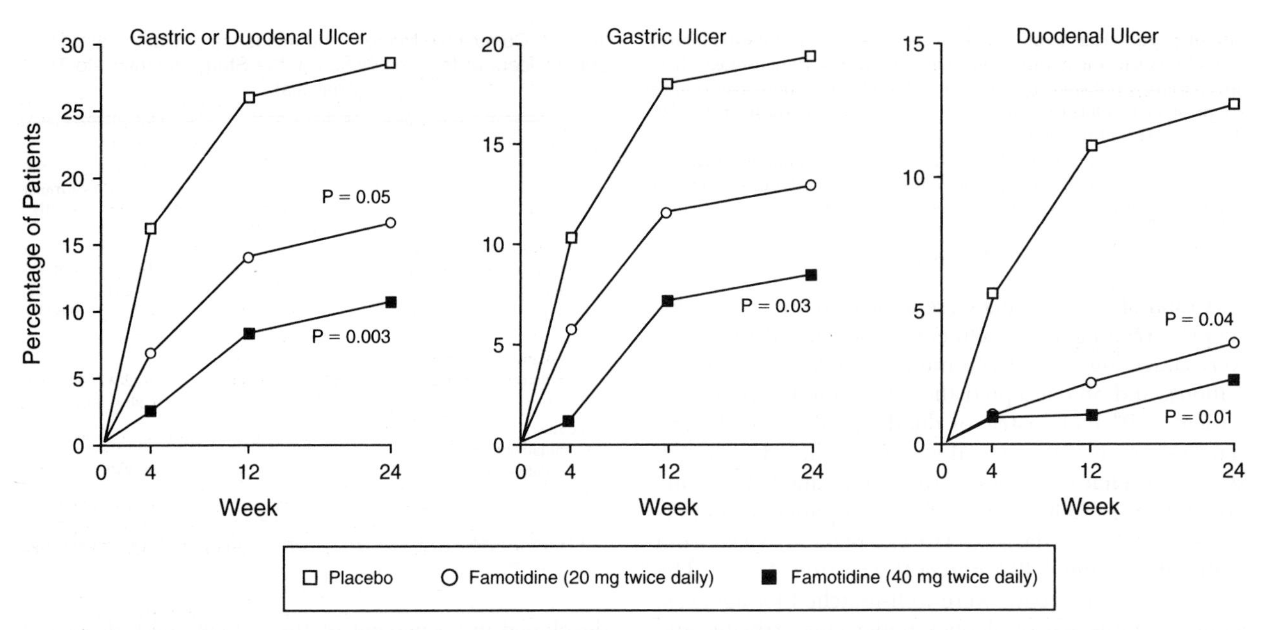

Figure 1. Cumulative Incidence of Gastric and Duodenal Ulcers at 4, 12, and 24 Weeks in Patients with Arthritis Receiving Long-Term NSAID Therapy, According to the Group Assignment.

Data are from the intention-to-treat analysis. P values are for comparisons with the placebo group.

There were no other important changes in the results of laboratory tests in any group.

Discussion

The results of this study show that treatment with a high dose of famotidine significantly reduces the cumulative incidence of both gastric and duodenal ulcers in patients with arthritis receiving long-term NSAID therapy. As in previous studies of patients with NSAID-induced ulcers,[14] many of our patients did not have abdominal pain or dyspepsia. Among those who did, however, there was a trend toward a reduction in dyspepsia among the patients taking famotidine. A strength of the study was that since only two physicians performed the endoscopic examinations, the likelihood of differences in the endoscopic evaluations was minimized. The design of previous studies of the efficacy of ranitidine in preventing NSAID-induced lesions may have militated against the detection of a protective effect against gastric ulcers, because the studies were relatively small and of short duration, with low event rates.[15] Some of these factors may also explain the lack of a protective effect of famotidine in another study.[16]

One might speculate that NSAID-related duodenal ulcers are more likely to be dependent on acid than gastric ulcers — hence, the greater ability of histamine-receptor antagonists to prevent duodenal ulcers. Although much of the gastroduodenal damage associated with NSAIDs is due to the inhibition of prostaglandin synthesis, acid plays an important part,[17] and in studies in humans, high doses of acid-inhibiting drugs were needed to achieve substantial protection against acute gastric damage.[10,18]

At a standard dose of 20 to 40 mg daily, which is approved for the healing of ulcers, famotidine is well tolerated,[19,20] although there are fewer data on the higher dose we used (40 mg twice daily). We found the higher dose to be well tolerated. Of the adverse events listed in Table 3, only three might have been related to famotidine: abdominal pain, rash, and diarrhea.

One of the prognostic factors that influenced the development of ulcers was the leukocyte count. We included the leukocyte count as a prognostic factor because studies in animals have suggested that neutrophils have a role in NSAID-associated gastric damage.[21] Our results are consistent with this hypothesis. In addition, base-line lesions in the duodenum were predictive of both duodenal and gastric ulceration. One possible explanation for this association is that duodenal lesions were a marker for *H. pylori* infection, although this infection appeared to be a separate risk factor in the multivariate analysis. Although the influence of *H. pylori* infection was not statistically significant, it may have been weakened by the exclusion of patients with ulcers at the base-line assessment, the majority of whom had *H. pylori* infection.[22]

In a recent six-month study of misoprostol,[6] there was a reduction in ulcer complications in patients being treated with NSAIDs, which is consistent with the reduced incidence of endoscopic lesions found in previous studies of misoprostol.[3-5] Since in our study the cumulative incidence of ulcers in the placebo group at 4, 12, and 24 weeks was similar to that reported in the placebo groups in endoscopic studies of misoprostol[3-5] and the reductions in gastric and duodenal ulcers in both famotidine groups were also similar to the reductions associated with misoprostol[3-5] it is likely that famotidine would have a similar effect on ulcer complications.

In conclusion, high doses of famotidine were well tol-

© N Engl J Med 1996; 334: 1435–1439

Table 3. Adverse Events and Other Reasons for Withdrawal from the Study (Intention-to-Treat Analysis).

REASON	STUDY GROUP		
	PLACEBO (N = 93)	LOW-DOSE FAMOTIDINE (N = 95)	HIGH-DOSE FAMOTIDINE (N = 97)
Adverse event			
Severe knee pain	1	0	0
Myocardial infarct	1	0	0
Thrombocytopenia	1	0	0
Abdominal pain	0	1	0
Pneumonitis	0	1	0
Cerebrovascular accident	0	1	0
Pharyngitis	0	1	0
Rash	0	1	0
Esophageal ulcer	0	1	0
Angina	0	0	1
Diarrhea	0	0	1
Unwilling to continue	6	5	12
Discontinuation of NSAID therapy	1	0	0
Loss to follow-up	1	2	0
Other	2	1	2
Total	13	14	16

erated and effective in preventing both gastric and duodenal ulcers in patients with arthritis receiving long-term NSAID therapy.

We are indebted to Dr. A. Axon for recruiting the study patient in Leeds; to Professor F.D. Lee and Dr. David Jenkins for their help in the histologic assessment of *H. pylori;* to Dr. I. Nakshabendi, Mrs. Christine Morran, and Mrs. Sandra Everett for help in conducting the study; to Mrs. Rosemary Dainty, Mrs. Ruth Simpson, and Mrs. Jane Dickson for secretarial assistance; and to Mr. David Thompson of Applied Statistics for performing the statistical analyses.

REFERENCES

1. Barrier CH, Hirschowitz BI. Controversies in the detection and management of nonsteroidal antiinflammatory drug-induced side effects of the upper gastrointestinal tract. Arthritis Rheum 1989;32:926-32.
2. Hawkey CJ. Non-steroidal anti-inflammatory drugs and peptic ulcers: facts and figures multiply, but do they add up? BMJ 1990;300:278-84. [Erratum, BMJ 1990;300:764.]
3. Graham DY, Agrawal NM, Roth SH. Prevention of NSAID-induced gastric ulcer with misoprostol: multicentre, double-blind, placebo-controlled trial. Lancet 1988;2:1277-80.
4. Bardhan KD, Bjarnason I, Scott DL, et al. The prevention and healing of acute non-steroidal anti-inflammatory drug-associated gastroduodenal mucosal damage by misoprostol. Br J Rheumatol 1993;32:990-5.
5. Graham DY, White RH, Moreland LW, et al. Duodenal and gastric ulcer prevention with misoprostol in arthritis patients taking NSAIDs. Ann Intern Med 1993;119:257-62.
6. Silverstein FE, Graham DY, Senior JR, et al. Misoprostol reduces serious gastrointestinal complications in patients with rheumatoid arthritis receiving nonsteroidal anti-inflammatory drugs: a randomized, double-blind, placebo-controlled trial. Ann Intern Med 1995;123:241-9.
7. Walt RP. Misoprostol for the treatment of peptic ulcer and antiinflammatory-drug–induced gastroduodenal ulceration. N Engl J Med 1992;327:1575-80.
8. Ehsanullah RSB, Page MC, Tildesley G, Wood JR. Prevention of gastroduodenal damage induced by non-steroidal anti-inflammatory drugs: controlled trial of ranitidine. BMJ 1988;297:1017-21.
9. Robinson MG, Griffin JW Jr, Bowers J, et al. Effect of ranitidine on gastroduodenal mucosal damage induced by nonsteroidal antiinflammatory drugs. Dig Dis Sci 1989;34:424-8.
10. Daneshmend TK, Prichard PJ, Bhaskar NK, Millns PJ, Hawkey CJ. Use of microbleeding and an ultrathin endoscope to assess gastric mucosal protection by famotidine. Gastroenterology 1989;97:944-9.
11. Aabakken L, Bjornbeth BA, Weberg R, Viksmoen L, Larsen S, Osnes M. NSAID-associated gastroduodenal damage: does famotidine protection extend into the mid- and distal duodenum? Aliment Pharmacol Ther 1990;4:295-303.
12. Sherrer YS, Bloch DA, Mitchell DM, Young DY, Fries JF. The development of disability in rheumatoid arthritis. Arthritis Rheum 1986;29:494-500.
13. Kalbfleisch JD, Prentice RL. The statistical analysis of failure time data. New York: John Wiley, 1980.
14. Skander MP, Ryan FP. Non-steroidal anti-inflammatory drugs and pain free peptic ulceration in the elderly. BMJ 1988;297:833-4.
15. French PC, Darekar BS, Mills JG, Wood JR. Ranitidine in the prevention of non-steroidal anti-inflammatory drug-associated gastric and duodenal ulceration in arthritic patients. Eur J Gastroenterol Hepatol 1994;6:1141-7.
16. Simon TJ, Berger ML, Hoover ME, Stauffer LA, Berlin RG. A dose-ranging study of famotidine in prevention of gastroduodenal lesions associated with non-steroidal anti-inflammatory drugs (NSAIDs): results of a U.S. multicenter trial. Am J Gastroenterol 1994;89:A1644. abstract.
17. Rowe PH, Starlinger MJ, Kasdon E, Hollands MJ, Silen W. Parenteral aspirin and sodium salicylate are equally injurious to the rat gastric mucosa. Gastroenterology 1987;93:863-71.
18. Daneshmend TK, Stein AG, Bhaskar NK, Hawkey CJ. Abolition by omeprazole of aspirin induced gastric mucosal injury in man. Gut 1990;31:514-7.
19. Rohner HG, Gugler R. Treatment of active duodenal ulcers with famotidine: a double-blind comparison with ranitidine. Am J Med 1986;81(4B):13-6.
20. Savarino V, Mela GS, Scalabrini P, Di Timoteo E, Magnolia MR, Celle G. Continuous 24-hour intragastric pH monitoring in the evaluation of the effect of a nightly dose of famotidine, ranitidine and placebo on gastric acidity of patients with duodenal ulcer. Digestion 1987;37:103-9.
21. Wallace JL, Keenan CM, Granger DN. Gastric ulceration induced by nonsteroidal anti-inflammatory drugs is a neutrophil-dependent process. Am J Physiol 1990;259:G462-G467.
22. Hudson N, Taha AS, Sturrock RD, Russell RI, Hawkey CJ. The influence of Helicobacter pylori colonisation on gastroduodenal ulceration in patients on non-steroidal anti-inflammatory drugs. Gut 1992;33:Suppl:S42. abstract.

© Gut 1996; 39: 513–520

Relation between gastric acid output, *Helicobacter pylori*, and gastric metaplasia in the duodenal bulb

A W Harris, P A Gummett, M M Walker, J J Misiewicz, J H Baron

Abstract

***Background*—Factors that determine gastric metaplasia in the duodenal bulb are ill defined. It is more common and extensive in the presence of high acid output and possibly in the presence of *Helicobacter pylori*. However, no quantitative relation between acid output and the extent of gastric metaplasia has been demonstrated and its relation to *H pylori* is uncertain.**

***Aim*—To determine the relation between *H pylori* infection and acid output and the presence and extent of gastric metaplasia in the duodenal bulb.**

***Subjects*—*H pylori* positive and negative patients with duodenal ulcer and healthy controls were studied.**

***Methods*—Quadrantic duodenal bulb biopsy specimens were taken and the presence and extent of gastric metaplasia determined using a computer enhanced image intensifier. Basal and stimulated acid outputs were measured.**

***Results*—Gastric metaplasia was significantly ($p<0\cdot05$) more common and significantly ($p<0\cdot05$) greater in extent in patients with duodenal ulcer than in controls. Neither the prevalence or extent of gastric metaplasia was affected by *H pylori* status. There were significant ($p<0\cdot01$) direct correlations between acid output and extent of gastric metaplasia.**

***Conclusions*—Prevalence and extent of gastric metaplasia are not related to *H pylori* in controls, or in patients with duodenal ulcer. Rather, high acid response to gastrin may be more important.**

(*Gut* 1996; **39:** 513–520)

Keywords: gastric acid output, *Helicobacter pylori*, gastric metaplasia, duodenal bulb.

Parkside Helicobacter Study Group, Central Middlesex and St Mary's Hospitals, London
A W Harris
P A Gummett
M M Walker
J J Misiewicz
J H Baron

Correspondence to:
Dr A Harris,
Department of Gastroenterology and Nutrition,
Central Middlesex Hospital,
London NW10 7NS.

Accepted for publication
9 May 1996

Index